CHRONICLE OF THE FIRST WORLD WAR

VOLUME I: 1914 – 1916

CHRONICLE OF THE FIRST WORLD WAR

VOLUME 1: 1914 – 1916

Randal Gray
with Christopher Argyle

Facts On File

New York • Oxford • Sydney

CHRONICLE OF THE FIRST WORLD WAR 1914-1916

Facts On File Limited
Collins Street
Oxford OX4 1XJ
UK

or

Facts On File, Inc.
460 Park Avenue South
New York NY10016
USA

or

Facts On File Pty Ltd
Talavera & Kartoum Rds
North Ryde NSW 2113
Australia

A British CIP catalogue record for this book is available from the British Library

Library of Congress Cataloging-in-Publication Data

Gray, Randal
    Chronicle of the First World War: a chronology of the First World War/
    by Randal Gray with Christopher Argyle.
    p.   cm.
    Bibliography: p.
    Includes index
    ISBN 0-8160-2139-2 Vol I
    1. World War, 1914-1916—Chronology. I. Argyle, Christopher, 1943. II. Title.
D523, G634 1990
940.3'02'02—dc19   90-31333
                                                             CIP
ISBN 0-8160-2139-2

Australian CIP data available on request from Facts On File

Facts On File books are available at special discounts when purchased in bulk
quantities for businesses, associations, institutions or sales promotions. Please
contact the Special Sales Department of our Oxford office on 0865 728399 or our New
York office on 212/683-2244 (dial 800/322-8755 except in NY, Ak or HI).

Produced by Curtis Garratt Limited,
The Old Vicarage, Horton cum Studley, Oxford, OX9 1BT

Index by D F Harding

Maps by Neil Hyslop

Additional typesetting, text correction, and proof-reading by Patricia Walters, Anne
Wilcock, and Diana Currant.

Printed and bound in Great Britain by
Butler & Tanner Ltd, Frome and London

10 9 8 7 6 5 4 3 2 1

This book is printed on acid-free paper

CONTENTS

To Mary and Rowland,
sustainers of the chronicling.

INTRODUCTION

This reference work was conceived in January 1986 on it being discovered that no general English-language chronology of 1914-18 had appeared since the Committee of Imperial Defence's *Principal Events* was published in 1922, the immediate aftermath of the Great War. The very detailed but specialist and unindexed *Economic Chronicle of the Great War for Great Britain & Ireland 1914-19* (with Supplement on 1920-22) by N B Dearle appeared at the start of the Great Depression — 1929. In other languages the gap of years scarcely lessened, Major Amedeo Tosti's *Chronologia della guerra mondiale* was published in 1932, and Félix Debyser's 263-page *Chronologie de la guerre mondiale* came out in that ominous year 1938.

So far as the authors can discover, no more modern chronologies exist in any language. No new German-language coverage seems to have been attempted after the course of the war itself. The date of Debyser's diplomacy-emphasized effort perhaps partially explains why nothing more recent has been published. The Second World War was imminent and there was no desire or leisure to rechronicle the horrors of the First. Even in 1920 Major-General Lord Gleichen, a 1914 BEF brigade commander and Director of the British Ministry of Information's Intelligence Bureau, had to seek funds from His Majesty King George V and other patrons to complete the third and final volume of his authoritative *Chronology of the War* (Constable, London 1918-20). This was the case even though a commercial publishing house was involved.

Furthermore a similar time-lag followed for the chronicling of the Second World War. Between the Royal Institute of International Affairs' 1947 chronology and Christopher Argyle's *Chronology of World War II* (Marshall Cavendish, London 1980) nearly a third of a century elapsed without a new general English-language book devoted to day-by-day events.

Perhaps chronologies are off-putting to modern historians and publishers as well as to readers. Yet chronology is the backbone of history, and can be popular as the recent phenomenal success of the Longman *Chronicle* series attests. All too often today it is treated both in general and particular works of scholarship with infuriating vagueness. Even official histories and sources can disagree on the dates of the most crucial and recent events.

This book is an attempt to chronicle the day-by-day events and mood of the First World War from the perspective of the late 1980s, more than 70 years after the Armistice and as its living veterans dwindle to ever fewer thousands. It says much for the current revival of interest in the first, shorter yet more important global conflict that over 30 per cent of our principal sources have been published in that decade. All three of the main English-language official or *The Times* chronologies, published between 1918 and 1922, have been reprinted in facsimile since 1985, further testimony to the curiosity of those who research their ancestors' experiences of the trenches and home privations.

No chronology can be omniscient or, however many help write it, trawl all that has gone before. It is a humbling thought that a 1987 Belgian bibliography of 1914-18 contains over 12,000 works. This chronology and its supporting features has aimed to be as international and detailed as possible within the inevitable limits of space, selection and time.

HOW TO USE THIS BOOK: THE CHRONOLOGIES

The nine parallel columns facilitate a coherent thematic approach. References to other dates are almost always forward looking. It is important to note that linked events, not just military operations over several days, in the same month are often consolidated into a single day's entry. Portentous events such as revolutions, invasions and declarations of war are emphasized in capital letters. Lesser but still important events and appointments are in bold type.

The arrangement of the nine columns or strands is as follows, across a double page.

WESTERN FRONT
Subheadings: **Flanders, Somme, Verdun, Vosges,** etc.

EASTERN FRONT
Subheadings in North to South geographical order: E Prussia, Poland, Galicia, Bukovina, Rumania, etc excluding Caucasus. From April 1918 this strand becomes simply Russia which was no longer formally at war with Germany and in revolutionary turmoil.

SOUTHERN FRONTS
Subheadings include: Serbia, Italian Front, Isonzo, Trentino, Bulgaria, Albania and Salonika/Greece, Macedonia.

TURKISH FRONTS
Subheadings: Mesopotamia, Palestine, Egypt, Gallipoli, Persia, Aden, Arabia, Armenia and The Yemen; includes Allied Pacific and Far East operations against German colonies in 1914 and India NW Frontier fighting.

AFRICAN OPERATIONS
Subheadings include: German SW Africa, E Africa, S Africa (esp 1914-15 rebellion), Cameroons, Tripolitania and Cyrenaica and W Desert for the Senussi Revolt, Morocco, Somaliland.

SEA WAR
Subheadings: North Sea, Atlantic, Channel, Baltic/White Sea, Mediterranean, Black Sea, Indian Ocean, Red Sea, Caspian, Pacific and Far East, Aegean and Adriatic.

AIR WAR
Subheadings: relevant front, sea or country.

INTERNATIONAL EVENTS
Subheadings include: Occupied countries, Diplomacy,

Neutrals, Secret War; coverage includes the Americas, PoW events and declarations of war.

HOME FRONTS
Subheadings include domestic events of all combatant nations.

Subheadings are not used for single entries on a day where the location is clear.

The *Chronicle* does not cover the internal events of the contemporary Portuguese, Mexican and Chinese Revolutions, all well under way by 1914; deaths of people essentially uninvolved in the war are not mentioned, nor are births, polar exploration, cultural or sporting events unconnected with it. Events in neutral countries unattributable to 1914-18 are similarly ignored.

NOMENCLATURE

Some mostly common abbreviations have been used and are explained in the glossary. Imperial measurements have been used as they were by the English-speaking world at the time. An important distinction should be made here between 'capture', 'take' and 'occupy' which historians often use interchangeably for the act of possessing hostile territory. We have tried to use the first two verbs when significant fighting was involved for the objective, with 'capture' implying the heaviest form of struggle. 'Occupy' means little or no resistance. 'Seize' implies a degree of surprise and rapidity in the operation. 'Storm' means a sudden costly seizure. 'Enter' means just that, no total occupation of a point or town, the opposing side may still be present. An 'action' is obviously a smaller engagement than a battle. Place names are the ones used at the time, hence Lemberg not Lvov. Eastern European place names in particular have undergone many baffling changes since 1914-18, not to mention many variations in their spelling then and now.

The term 'British' has often been used to denote any forces of the British Empire especially when several of its nation-alities were involved. This was practice at the time and no disrespect is intended to what were then the Dominions and the Colonies. In the case of Dual Monarchy of Austria-Hungary, the term 'Austria' has been used for the whole Habsburg Empire and 'Hungary' only mentioned when specifically meant.

Russia did not adopt the New Style Gregorian calendar until 31 January 1918 but we have applied it before for uniformity. The reader therefore should be aware that the Old Style Julian Calendar meant Russia was 13 days behind the rest of Europe excluding Bulgaria (changed 1915); Turkey (1918); Rumania and Yugoslavia (1919); and Greece (1923). This discrepancy is inevitably a fertile source of confusion. However, the most common

variation is 24 hours either side of a given date even in the most impressive sources. An event may happen overnight or only become general news in the next day's newspapers. We have tried to be right but often the choice can be little more than guesswork.

We hope our chronology and its supporting features will be of assistance to all those wanting precise and accurate reference on the Great War of 1914-18 and its turbulent aftermath.

OTHER FEATURES

The *Chronicle* is not simply a chronology, though that is its main purpose. Succinct background narrative can be found in the annual focus on the fronts essays as well as for the causes and consequences of the war. The map section covers all the main campaigns. The make-up of Europe before and after hostilities is compared in map form.

Tables provide statistics for all the important military operations, forces engaged and losses incurred. Annual losses on the fronts are also recorded or at least estimated. The symbol + means that they were certainly higher but available figures only add up to the one given. Numbers of guns and prisoners lost are stressed as they are traditional yardsticks of military success and the Western Front, in particular, often offered little else.

Overall war statistics are also given, though the reader will do well to remember that apparently precise figures are not necessarily the truth, and in such an appallingly wasteful conflict can never be exactly known.

The glossary provides listing of wartime terminology and abbreviations with entries also giving the strengths of military formations and units, and some of the weaponry used.

Sources are arranged by chronological strand and are the actual ones used to compile this work. The index is by date not page and non-chronological features are named.

LOOKING UP AN EVENT

Taking the great naval Battle of Jutland as an example. The reader will find it under SEA WAR on 31 May 1916. Ship types engaged will be detailed under 1916 Sea War Tables. The opposing commanders Jellicoe, Beatty and Scheer are each profiled. A map of the North Sea will locate the fighting. The battle is set in context under Focus on the Fronts 1916. Naval terms such as battlecruiser and flotilla are explained in the glossary. Other references to Jutland can be found in the index and particular sources are given under 'Sea War, North Sea and Grand Fleet'. If this appara-tus is borne in mind, much more information can be ac-quired than just the original factual chronological entry.

ACKNOWLEDGEMENTS

The authors would like to record their debt to the London Library; the British Library; Westminster libraries notably Maida Vale's superb military and naval history reserve collection; Leicester University Library; the Royal United Services Institute for Defence Studies' Library; and the Library of RMA Sandhurst. Without Mary Gray's unflag-ging word processing skills, and the book production expertise of Curtis Garratt, this superdreadnought of a project might never have entered the water.

PRELUDE TO SARAJEVO
Causes & Significance of the Great War

If the Great War of 1914-18 had any single root cause it surely was the desire of the French Army and Nation to avenge the humiliations of the Franco-Prussian or Franco-German War of 1870-71. Aware that France would never acquiesce to the unification of Germany under a Prussian King (or the appalling prospect of a German prince on the vacant Spanish throne), the 'Iron Chancellor', Otto von Bismarck, manoeuvred the inscrutable (but weak and vacillating) French Emperor, Napoleon III, into declaring war (19 July 1870).

Contrary to all expectations the Imperial armies of France quickly proved inadequately prepared, equipped and led. Neither Austria nor the supposedly anti-Prussian states of South Germany showed the least inclination to form an anti-Prussian alliance. The German campaign was masterminded by Moltke. The Germans crossed the frontier on 4 August 1870 and won a series of victories over Marshal Bazaine's optimistically named 'Army of the Rhine', culminating in his encirclement with 173,000 men at Metz. Napoleon III and Marshal MacMahon attempted to raise the siege but were surrounded at Sedan on 1 September 1870 and obliged to surrender with 83,000 officers and men. The Empress Eugenie fled from Paris to begin half a century in exile and the Third Republic was founded. A Prussia-dominated German Empire was proclaimed at Versailles 18 January 1871.

When Paris was shortly afterwards besieged, fiery Republican minister of the interior, Léon Gambetta escaped by hydrogen balloon to organize a *levée en masse* in the still unoccupied provinces. The garrison and National Guard of Paris, faced heavy odds after the ignominious surrender of Metz (27 October 1870). General Trochu continued to defend the capital and even counterattacked until January when near-starvation and heavy bombardment made further resistance impossible. The armistice was succeeded by the draconian 'Peace of Frankfurt'.

Terms of the Treaty of Frankfurt
10 May 1871

1. Cession of provinces of Lorraine & Alsace (less Belfort)
2. German army of occupation to be stationed in 43 depts
3. Reparations of 5 billion francs (£200 million) to be paid by instalments
4. Trade: Germany to enjoy 'Most Favoured Nation' status vis-à-vis France

The last German garrison (at Verdun) quitted France in September 1873.

Less than two months after the fall of Paris, a provisional government of Socialist and far-left Republicans was elected by the 'Commune' of Paris in response to an attempt by the right-wing National Assembly to disarm the Paris National Guard. Civil war broke out. In 'Bloody Week' (May 1871), MacMahon stormed the capital and at least 20,000 Communards and innocent citizens were massacred: 'The last stage of the Commune was not a battle but a massacre ... The victors were embittered by the shame of having to fight a fresh war against their own countrymen under the disdainful eyes of the Prussians ... Despite ... orders from MacMahon that the lives of prisoners should be spared, the victors killed without mercy' (*The Development of Modern France* by Sir Denis Brogan, London 1967).

The trauma of these catastrophic events was so severe that in 1889 a shallow opportunist general and Minister of War (Boulanger) was nearly able to provoke a war with his anti-German speeches. Seven years later, an accusation that Captain Alfred Dreyfus, born of a Jewish family at Mulhouse (Alsace), had betrayed the specification of France's revolutionary *soixante-quinze* (75mm) quick-firing field-gun to Germany, sparked off a protracted series of crises. These more than once threatened to tear French society apart. Although the entirely innocent Dreyfus was brought back from the living hell of Devil's Island (near the modern Kourou space centre), declared innocent on appeal and reinstated in his military rank (1906); the venom spewed out during the *Affaire* should have been a warning that if, and when, the opportunity ever arose for a renewed Franco-German trial of strength it could easily escalate into a bestial struggle for national survival.

Moreover, this anticipated conflict would be made even more terrible and widespread by a whole series of so-called 'defensive' pacts and alliances concluded between 1878 and 1907. Germany — now an empire under William I — had allied herself with Austria. They were joined by Italy in 1882. This 'Triple Alliance' could also count on a large measure of support from the German-born rulers of Rumania, Bulgaria and Greece. In reply, France concluded military and political pacts with Russia (1892-4). Between 1902 and 1907 Britain concluded the so-called 'Triple Entente' with France and Russia and formed an alliance with Japan. Thanks in some degree to the influence of a Francophile English king, Edward VII, the *Entente Cordiale* was negotiated in 1904. A similar understanding between Britain and Imperial Russia was reached in 1907. The Kaiser's ministers and generals responded by forging a close understanding with the 'Young Turks', the largely German-trained radical officers who seized power at Constantinople in 1908. A Turco-German treaty of alliance was signed in early August 1914.

Both Russia and Austria were eager to dominate the Balkans, where the once-omnipotent Ottoman armies of occupation had been pushed back almost to the gates of Constantinople in 1912-13. Germany, too, aimed at securing a trans-Balkan corridor as a key element of a grandiose Berlin-Baghdad rail link for which she had received a concession in 1899.

All the European Powers (except moribund Russia) had colonial ambitions. They had partitioned Africa from the 1880s and exercised an almost complete stranglehold over the trade and economic life of China, whose ancient, but defunct, empire had collapsed in 1911. Japan, too, would soon demand a rich slice of the 'Chinese cake' as a reward for her continued adherence of the Allied cause, after the occupation of Germany's Asiatic and Pacific possessions by Japanese/British Empire forces in August-November 1914.

Imperial Germany nursed the conviction that she had been cheated of a fair share of the spoils in the 19th-century 'Scramble for Africa' proper. Between 1884 and 1890 she had established protectorates over Togoland, the Cameroons, South-West Africa and Tanganyika. But compared with France's richly endowed and populous territories, stretching from Morocco to the lower Congo and east to the 'Great Red Island' of Madagascar, German Africa was of little account. Even so, Berlin felt impelled to initiate Tirpitz's naval expansion programme from 1897, to safeguard her developing overseas trade routes. This soon escalated into a deadly 'Naval Race' with Britain.

From 1904 to 1914 a series of crises increasingly threatened the long-established European balance of power — Algeciras (1906); Bosnia-Herzegovina (1908); Agadir (1911); Italo-Turkish War (1911-12); First and Second Balkan Wars (1912-13); Sarajevo (1914). On 28 June 1914 the Archduke Francis Ferdinand, heir to the venerable Austrian Emperor Francis Joseph, was assassinated by Serb-armed nationalists during an official visit to the town of Sarajevo. Austria declared war on Serbia, 28 July 1914, with the aim of achieving a rapid, local conquest of a perceived South Slav nuisance. When Russia mobilized in that Balkan kingdom's support, Germany declared war on Russia and France and invaded neutral Belgium, a country whose perpetual neutrality had been guaranteed by all the Great Powers since the 1839 Treaty of London. Britain declared war on Germany (4 August) and Austria (12 August 1914).

Although not legally bound to do so, the self-governing former British dominions, Canada, Australia and New Zealand joined forces with the Motherland in the hour of supreme trial. So did the Princes of the vast Indian Empire. Only South Africa hesitated. However, a pro-German Boer rebellion war was suppressed by Smuts and Botha and South Africa entered the war. Italy, invariably treated with condescending patronage by Germany and Austria (and not consulted by the latter after Sarajevo), saw no good reason to rush to the support of her Triple Alliance partners. Accordingly, she remained neutral until May 1915.

The Great War was the apocalyptic climax of the Age of European (& American) Imperialism. But what had begun as a relatively straightforward struggle for territorial and economic gain, and (in the cases of Austria and France) for revenge on perennial neighbouring foes, inexorably developed into what the German strategist Ludendorff called *Der Totalkrieg* ('Total War'). In other words, not merely a contest between the armies, navies and embryonic air forces, but a life-or-death struggle between peoples in which all the human, material and moral resources of the nation were utilized to the utmost.

Three dynastic mighty empires — Germany, Austria and Russia — were swept into the dustbin of history. And a far-flung but decrepit oriental despotism — Ottoman Turkey — also fell to be transformed into a compact westernized secular republic; her outer provinces ultimately becoming the new Middle East states of Arabia, Iraq (Mesopotamia), Syria and Jewish-settled Palestine.

Out of the European melting-pot there soon emerged Communist Russia, a restored independent Poland, the new states of Yugoslavia and Czechoslovakia, and later Fascist Italy followed by Nazi Germany.

SARAJEVO TO THE OUTBREAK OF WAR

JUNE 1914

Sun 28
Austria — MURDER AT SARAJEVO OF ARCHDUKE FRANCIS FERDINAND, AUSTRIAN HEIR, and his wife, Sophie, the Duchess of Hohenberg, on visit to Bosnian capital. Both shot by Gavrilo Princip, 19-year-old Bosnian Serb student belonging to the Serbian Black Hand terrorist organization (weapons obtained in Belgrade). **Germany** — Kaiser told news while racing his yacht *Meteor* in Kiel Bay. **Turkey** — Anglo-German-owned Turk petroleum company gains exclusive exploitation rights in Mesopotamia. **USA** — 'Suffragettes march on Capitol'.

Mon 29
Diplomacy — Sec of Austrian Legation in Belgrade suggests Serb complicity in Sarajevo murders. **Austria** — Anti-Serb riots in Vienna, Brünn, Sarajevo & throughout Bosnia.

Tue 30
Diplomacy — German Vienna Ambassador informs Berlin that Austrian Foreign Minister Count Berchtold holds Belgrade responsible. **Austria** — Francis Joseph receives Hungarian Govt's condolences, but its PM Count Tisza urges passive policy. **Britain** — Addresses in Parlt on murdered Archduke.

JULY 1914

Wed 1
Austria — Austrian battleship *Viribus Unitis* arrives at Trieste with Sarajevo victims' bodies. **S Africa** — Indian Relief Act (*see* 20). **China** — German Tsingtao colony gets railway extension. **USA** — Navy Prohibition begins, & in W Virginia.

Thu 2
Diplomacy — German Ambassador assures Count Berchtold & Emperor Francis Joseph ('I see a very dark future') of Berlin's support. **Austria** — Francis Joseph asks Col Bardolff 'And how did the Archduke bear himself?' 'Like a soldier, Your Majesty.' 'That was to be expected from His Imperial Highness.' **Germany** — Announced that Kaiser not attending Archduke's funeral; he annotates Count Tschirschky's 30 June dispatch 'As for the Serbs, it is necessary to finish with them as quickly as possible'.

Fri 3
Austria — Hungarian PM Count Tisza demands in letter to Count Berchtold that Council of Ministers meet (*see* 7). **Turkey** — Announced that Berlin-Baghdad Railway will terminate at Basra. **Diplomacy** — Anglo-Russian-Chinese Convention in Tibet.

Sat 4
Austria — Archduke's funeral at Artstetten family schloss, 50 miles W of Vienna, after Hofburg Vienna lying-in-state.

Sun 5
Diplomacy — Austrian Special Envoy Count Hoyos arrives in Berlin to find out German intentions after Sarajevo; **Germany** — Austrian Ambassador lunches at Potsdam New Palace with Kaiser who receives Francis Joseph letter about punishing 'this gang of criminal agitators in Belgrade'. After lunch Chancellor Bethmann endorses Kaiser's support for 'immediate action' by Austria v Serbia (Bethmann repeats pledge to Austrian Ambassador 6). Chancellor urges Kaiser not to give up usual summer cruise. **Austria** — Imperial rescript to the two Prime Ministers calls Sarajevo the outcome of 'the fanaticism of a small band of misguided men'. Emperor receives Army CoS Gen Conrad & refuses his martial law request.

Mon 6
Germany — Kaiser leaves Kiel in imperial yacht *Hohenzollern* for normal summer cruise in Norwegian waters (-26).

Tue 7
Austria — Council of Ministers & Chiefs of Staff meet for nearly 7 hrs; only Count Tisza disagrees on principle of unacceptable ultimatum to Serbia (*see* 14). **Germany** — Foreign Ministry instructs London Ambassador '... to avoid everything that could create the impression, that we incited the Austrians to go to war'. Chancellor tells adviser 'An action against Serbia can lead to world war' (*see* 8). **Switzerland** — King of the Belgians on visit.

Wed 8
Diplomacy — German Vienna Ambassador insists to Berchtold on necessity for an energetic attack on Serbia (ie before Russia can intervene). Austrian official to Rome Ambassador 'We are completely one with Berlin...they send complete backing against Russia'. Berchtold asks Conrad & War Minister Gen Krobatin to go on usual summer leave (-22) as a cover. **Germany** — Chancellor says 'If there is no war, if the Tsar does not want war or if France, frightened by the prospect, pleads for peace, we have at least the chance to divide the Entente by our action'.

Thu 9
Austria — Emperor receives Baron Wiesner initial report on (*see* 11) Sarajevo. Count Berchtold comments 'His Majesty seemed ready for action against Serbia'. **Britain** — *The Times* describes Austrian press campaign v Serbs ('pestilent rats'). Scheme for Prov Govt in Ireland drawn up in House of Lords (*see* 14). **Albania** — Epirot rebels capture Koritza, Klesura & Terpelen (*see* 19).

Fri 10
Serbia — Russian Minister dies suddenly at Austrian/Belgrade Legation. **Italy** — Gen Cadorna appointed CoS. **Ireland** — Ulster Prov Govt first meets at Belfast & reaffirms determination to resist Home Rule.

Sat 11
Austria — Baron Wiesner arrives from Vienna in Sarajevo to speed up inquiry & report (13); cables Vienna midday (13) that no evidence to implicate Serb Govt.

Sun 12
Diplomacy — French President Poincaré & PM Viviani embark at Dunkirk for long-arranged state visit to Russia; they sail in the newly completed battleship *France* (13, *see* 20). Austrian Berlin Ambassador urges Berchtold to take immediate & resolute action. **Serbia** — K Peter's birthday.

Mon 13
Serbia — Reports of projected attack on Austrian Legation at Belgrade. **Russia** — Woman stabs Rasputin at his Tobolsk home, Siberia. **France** — Senate revelations (-14) of Army deficiencies. **Britain** — *The Times* leader on 'Failure of Recruiting'.

Tue 14
Austria — **Council of Ministers finally decide on action v Serbia;** 48-hr ultimatum to be delivered 25 after French State visit to Russia & harvesting. Berchtold gives Berlin no details, only date (*see* 17). **Britain** — House of Lords passes Govt of Ireland Amending Bill.

Wed 15
Hungary — Count Tisza tells Budapest Chamber relations with Serbia 'must be cleared up'. **France** — Senate passes £56.3m military credits plus first general income tax (for 1916).

Thu 16
Diplomacy — Count Berchtold cables Minister in Sofia to seek Bulgaria's alliance v Serbia, but envoy fails to see Tsar Ferdinand by 31. Austrian official to Rome Ambassador 'we absolutely want to avoid the world war although Germany is completely ready to carry it out'. Krupp-Vickers shell fuse royalty agreement expires.

Fri 17
Austria — Report that Serbia has called up 70,000 reservists. Council of Ministers alter ultimatum delivery date to 23 (*see* 19). **Diplomacy** — Turk Berlin Embassy informs Constantinople war not avoidable.

Sat 18
Britain — **Spithead Naval Review** (-20): K George V reviews 260 RN ships off Portsmouth (*see* 27).

Sun 19
Austria — Council of Ministers meets secretly at Berchtold's house & approves ultimatum final text. It is to be delivered at 1800 on 23 when Pres Poincaré leaves Russia. Press scare over alleged 'Greater Serbia' conspiracy. **Britain** — King summons Buckingham Palace conference (21-24) on Irish Home Rule. **Albania** — Citizens of Valona meet & resolve to ask Great Powers for government by international commission.

Mon 20
Diplomacy — Tsar welcomes Pres Poincaré at Kronstadt naval base W of St Petersburg, evening banquet at Peterhof Palace. **France** — Mme Caillaux (wife of Finance Minister) tried & acquitted (-28) for murder of *Figaro* editor (16). **S Africa** — Gandhi leaves for India after farewell letter.

Tue 21
Austria — Conferences at Ischl & Budapest on Serbia; Francis Joseph tells Finance Minister 'Russia cannot swallow it. There's no mistake about it, it will be a big war'. **Diplomacy** — Russian Ambassador leaves Vienna for holiday after being assured Austrian demands will not cause crisis. **Germany** — Bethmann tells Allied Ambassadors that Austria's demand 'equitable and moderate'. French Ambassador informs Paris of German mobilization signs. **Russia** — Poincaré says France will fulfil

'all her obligations'. Great St Petersburg strikes incl barricaded streets v police (-25/26) in protest at troops' suppression of Baku oilfield strike. **Persia** — Ahmed Mirza crowned Shah at Tehran.

Wed 22
Diplomacy — Russian Foreign Minister Sazonov warns Vienna against drastic action v Serbia. Austrian Berlin Ambassador shows German Foreign Minister Jagow the ultimatum, which he approves. British Foreign Minister Sir E Grey learns from HM Ambassador Vienna that any ultimatum will be made unacceptable for Serbia; he sees German Ambassador Prince Lichnowsky, warning Berlin not to back ultimatum.

Thu 23
Diplomacy — AUSTRIAN ULTIMATUM TO SERBIA presented at Belgrade by Austrian Minister Baron Giesl. Agreement to its 10 points demanded within 48 hrs. Serb PM Pasic away electioneering in provinces is recalled and Russia appealed to for help. German London Ambassador warns Berlin v dangers of political adventures. **Germany** — Chancellor circularizes German Ambassadors 'action and demands of Austro-Hungary fully justified'. Officers' leave stopped. **Russia** — Poincaré & Viviani sail home after banquet for Tsar who tells them war unlikely. **Turkey** — Enver Pasha asks German Ambassador if agreement can be reached with Berlin (*see* TURK FRONTS 2 Aug).

Fri 24
Diplomacy — **Prince Alexander of Serbia cables Tsar for help.** Russian & Serb Councils of Ministers meet. Latter receive Sazonov telegram pledging aid, but Tsar must decide & France must be consulted. Sir E Grey calls Austrian ultimatum 'the most formidable document that was ever addressed from one state to another'. He proposes 4-Power mediation (Britain, Germany, France & Italy). German note to Britain & France approves Austrian ultimatum but she urges Austria to declare war on & attack Serbia at once if reply unsatisfactory & not wait for 16-day mobilization. Belgium says she will uphold neutrality 'whatever the consequences'. **Russia** — Council of Ministers decides in principle to mobilize 13 army corps that are 'eventually' destined to operate v Austria. **Germany** — Kaiser sees ultimatum in Norwegian

newspaper & orders Fleet home. **Britain** — Irish Home Rule Conference failure announced. Asquith writes on European crisis 'We are within measurable ... distance of a real Armageddon. Happily there seems no reason why we should be more than spectators'.

Sat 25
Diplomacy — Austria refuses to extend ultimatum 48 hrs for Russia who says she 'cannot remain indifferent'. **Serb Crown Prince signs mobilization order** at 1500. **PM Pasic hands in most conciliatory and almost humiliating answer to ultimatum** at 1758; only 1 point rejected (article 6, Austrian officials to investigate in Serbia). **Austrian Minister leaves Belgrade** for Vienna at 1830 after finding it unsatisfactory thus breaking relations. **Serb Govt leaves Belgrade** for Nis & requests Greek treaty support v Bulgaria, PM Venizelos assures her of same. Serb CoS Gen Putnik arrested on leave nr Budapest (released

26 on Francis Joseph's orders with apologies). **Austria** — Francis Joseph signs mobilization order. Council of Ministers' decree transfers some jurisdiction to military courts. Army artillery report reveals only c500 shells per gun. **Russia** — Tsar & Grand Duke Nicholas confer, premobilization measures for 1st & 2nd category reservists (26-28). **Germany** — CoS Moltke & Prussian War Minister Falkenhayn return to Berlin from leave. First warship passes through newly widened Kiel Canal. **Britain** — Asquith to Lady Ottoline Morrell on Austrian ultimatum 'This will take away from Ulster, which is a good thing'. **Canada** — Anglo-American-Canadian Battle of Lundy's Lane (Niagara) 1814 centenary commemoration.

Sun 26
Austria begins to mobilize 8 corps on Russian frontier. Count Berchtold adopts German idea of immediate war declaration despite Conrad saying no full invasion of

Serbia possible for several weeks (*see* 27). Germany threatens mobilization as Russia continues preparations, asks Britain & France to quieten her. Sazonov sees Austro-German Ambassadors to try direct talks with Vienna. Sir E Grey suggests London conference of uninvolved Great Power ambassadors. Russia says she will mobilize v Austria if latter invades Serbia. **Montenegro orders mobilization. Britain** — **At 1600 First Sea Lord countermands British Fleets' dispersal** after naval review (*see* 28). K George V sees Prince Henry of Prussia, latter convinced that Britain will remain neutral. **Ireland** — 'Bachelor's Walk Massacre': Gun-running riot at Howth nr Dublin (4 civilians killed & 38 wounded) when mob stones troops returning from capturing arms at Howth. **France** — German Ambassador Schoen visits Quai d'Orsay to try to moderate French position. **Germany** — Kaiser & German Fleet return from Norway. **Moltke drafts German**

ultimatum to Belgium, sent to Brussels Ambassador (29) to be delivered when instructed.

Mon 27
Diplomacy — Austria decides to declare war on Serbia next day. Tsar cables Belgrade that Russia not indifferent to Serbia's fate, proposes discussions with Vienna. Berchtold refuses to take Serb ultimatum reply as basis. Germany says she has taken mediatory steps (not recorded). France & Italy accept British proposal (of 24) but Germany refuses. After seeing German Ambassador Grey outlines 4-Power mediation to Commons. **Austria** — Emperor tells Baron Giesl 'We are not at war yet, and if I can, I shall prevent it'. Berchtold reports Serb attack on Austrian troops & shipping at Temes-Kubin, but found to be false rumour. Vienna Stock Exchange closed. **Germany** — Kaiser returns to Potsdam by train, **not told of Germany's rejection of mediation. Morocco** — Gen Lyautey telephoned by Paris to evacuate Protectorate except

coast & to send all troops (*see* AFRICAN OPS 31). Lyautey says 'A war among Europeans is a civil war. It is the most monumental folly the world has ever committed'.

Tue 28
AUSTRIA DECLARES WAR ON SERBIA at noon (Francis Joseph signs with tears in his eyes); manifesto declares no quarrel with Russia (telegram sent in French via Bucharest to Belgrade). Kaiser finally reads Serb ultimatum reply & calls it 'A great moral victory for Vienna, all grounds for war disappear'. William cables Tsar that he will use his influence with Austria, but also says 'England alone carries the responsibility for peace or war, no longer us'. His telegram of 22/25 to Vienna suggests mediation only after Belgrade falls. Russia says southern corps will be mobilized tomorrow (partial & general mobilization orders prepared) but no hostility to Germany. **Britain** — Fleets ordered to war bases.

JULY 1914	WESTERN FRONT 1	EASTERN FRONT 2	SOUTHERN FRONTS 3	TURKISH FRONTS 4
Tue 28				
Wed 29	*See* INT'L EVENTS. **Belgium** — Gen Leman allowed to start 3 lines of trenches at Liège.	PARTIAL RUSSIAN MOBILI-ZATION V AUSTRIA. War Minister Gen Sukhomlinov decides on general mobilization without Tsar's knowledge, who tries to stop it.	**Serbia** — FIRST SHOTS OF THE WAR: **2 Austrian river monitors bombard Belgrade** (pm); Serb guns reply from Topcider heights. Serbs demolish R Sava trestle bridge at Zemun. **Italy** — New Italian CoS Cadorna envisages Triple Alliance war v France incl removing fortress arty facing Austria, King approves 2 Aug despite 31 July diplomatic Cabinet policy of neutrality (*see* 5 Aug; INT'L EVENTS 3 Aug).	500 Turkish sailors arrive on the Tyne to fetch ***Sultan Osman I***; British Admiralty discuss takeover.
Thu 30	Sir J French C-in-C designate BEF.	Tsar signs general mobilization order (1st day actually 4 Aug).		
Fri 31	Germany declares 'state of danger of war' (*Kriegsgefahr*) & demands assurances of French neutrality within 18 hrs. France reserves her position.	Moltke cables Conrad with Germany's decision to mobilize (*see* 3 Aug).		Turkey orders mobilization for 3 Aug (all men 20-45).

AFRICAN OPERATIONS 5	SEA WAR 6	AIR WAR 7	INTERNATIONAL EVENTS 8	HOME FRONTS 9
	N Sea/Atlantic — At 1700 BRITISH FLEETS ORDERED TO SCAPA FLOW & OTHER WAR STNS.	Austria's embryo military & naval air arms *Kuk Luftfahrtruppen* (Army Air Service) 13 flying companies with 48 1st line & 27 training planes; 1 airship & 10 kite balloons. *Kuk Kriegsmarine* (Navy) 5 1st-line & 17 training flying boats (Lohners) & floatplanes. **Serbia** — A few Blériots & Farmans + a cadre of French-trained pilots. **Britain** — Sqdn Cdr Longmore RNAS makes **1st practice drop of air torpedo** from Short floatplane. **Russia** — Only 72 military pilots.		
Colonial Office cables Gov Belfield of British E Africa to take precautionary measures; Gov-Gen Merlin of French Equatorial Africa sanctions defence measures.	**N Sea/Baltic** — GERMAN FLEET MOBILIZING. **Med** — German battlecruiser *Goeben* leaves Pola for Trieste (some coal). British First Fleet sails from Portland for Scapa Flow at 0700, incl Beatty's 4 battlecruisers which arrive (31).		British Cabinet again presses Germany for mediation, but warns it cannot stay out in all circumstances. **Germany informs Russia that latter's partial mobilization must trigger war**; Bethmann also makes 'infamous offer' to Britain, stay neutral and Germany will not annex mainland French territory (see 30). **France** — Pres Poincaré & PM Viviani reach Paris from Russia. **Secret War : Britain** — Admiralty sends warning telegram. War Office sends out 'precautionary period' telegrams. CID War Book opened. Churchill sees Kitchener on military measures. **Bulgaria declares neutrality.**	
	Baltic/Black Seas — Russian fleets mobilize.	Norwegian Tryggve Gran in Blériot monoplane first to fly across North Sea.	Russian 0200 offer to Germany to stop mobilizing if Austria removes clauses v Serb sovereignty in her ultimatum. Last chance of peace not forwarded to Vienna, where cabinet learns of Russian mobilization when considering British proposals of 29 & *Berliner Lokal Anzeiger* newspaper falsely announces German mobilization and Russian Ambassador allowed to notify St Petersburg so. Prince Henry of Prussia wires to King George V, asking him to secure Franco-Russian neutrality. Latter replies he is trying, if Austria will not go beyond Belgrade, hopes Kaiser will influence Vienna. Kaiser instructs Chancellor to inflame Muslim world v Britain: 'If we are to bleed to death, England shall at the very least lose India'. **Britain** — Sir E Grey rejects 'infamous offer' but holds out olive branch. PM Asquith moves postponement Ireland Bill 2nd reading due to European situation. Churchill dines with Asquith. **Canada** — Militia Council discusses raising 25,000 men. **New Zealand** — Preliminary arrangments for NZEF. **Holland declares neutrality. Italy** — Fleet mobilizes off Gaeta (see 3 Aug).	**Russia** — **Zemstvos** Union of rural councils formed (*see* 1 & 8 Aug).
British Gold Coast mobilization complete. **Morocco** — Lyautey cables Paris from Rabat, he will send 20 bns & 24 guns at once but hold interior garrisons (in fact sends 37 bns, or 40,000 men, keeping 26 bns; 16 territorial bns arrive from	**Baltic** — Russians begin mine-laying in Gulf of Finland. **E Africa** — German cruiser *Königsberg* (Loof) leaves Dar-es-Salaam to raid Allied commerce (*see* 6 Aug); is shadowed by 3 RN cruisers but escapes.		GERMANY DECLARES IMMINENT DANGER OF WAR ALERT AT MIDNIGHT, ISSUES ULTIMATUMS TO RUSSIA AND FRANCE. Former must end all military steps in 12hrs (by noon 1 Aug), latter must declare intentions in	**Germany** — *Reichsbank* discontinues redemption of notes in gold. Kaiser attends 5th and youngest son Oscar's morganatic wedding. **Austria** — Army given control of Bukovina, Galicia & other areas outside Hungary.

AUGUST 1914	WESTERN FRONT 1	EASTERN FRONT 2	SOUTHERN FRONTS 3	TURKISH FRONTS 4
Fri 31 contd				
Sat 1 August 1914	French Govt orders general mobilization. German 69th Inf Regt coy (l6th Div) invades Luxembourg prematurely at 1700 to take rail/telegraph jctn as Kaiser cables for no frontier crossing. Moltke countermands order at midnight.	GERMANY DECLARES WAR ON RUSSIA AT 1910 HAVING ORDERED GENERAL MOBILIZATION AT 1700.	Conrad writes to Cadorna asking when Italian troops will be ready for Galicia (*see* 5; INT'L EVENTS 3).	Britain commandeers battleships *Sultan Osman I* & *Reshadieh* in the Tyne (£3m paid by Turk public subscription — £600,000 to pay), renamed *Agincourt* & *Erin* . *Sultan Osman* would have sailed to join German High Seas Fleet.
Sun 2	GERMAN ULTIMATUM TO BELGIUM demanding passage through her territory. German Fourth Army invades Luxembourg. Moltke appointed CoS German Field Armies, army cdrs named. Alsace — 11 violations of French frontier by German patrols (**first French soldier k**, Cp André Peugeot nr Belfort, but also kills German Lt leading patrol). French GHQ suspects diversionary ruse & transfers forces to Franco-Belgian border but an advance by VII Corps (Bonneau) into Alsace is ordered with aim of seizing Mulhouse & Huningen & destroying Rhine bridges.	**Poland** — HOSTILITIES BEGIN. **E Prussia** — Russian raiders invade nr Schwidden.	SERB MOBILIZATION COMPLETE of 489,500 men (after 6 days). Serb Uzice Army raiders capture Uvats, Rudo & Ustivar (-4) on Austrian Bosnian border.	Grand Vizier Said Halim Pasha signs SECRET MILITARY ALLIANCE WITH GERMANY, arranged by War Minister Enver Pasha as defence v Russia (*see* 4, 5 & 6).

AFRICAN OPERATIONS 5	SEA WAR 6	AIR WAR 7	INTERNATIONAL EVENTS 8	HOME FRONTS 9
France by 21, *see* 4 Aug). (Aug) Moroccan Div (Humbert) assembles at Bordeaux before fighting on the Marne.			Russo-German conflict within 18hrs. Kaiser says 'Frivolity and weakness are going to plunge the world into the most frightful war.'; cables Tsar a third time but gets evasive reply, invites K Constantine of Greece to join war (*see* 2 Aug). **Sir E Grey** does utmost to seek German help in settling Austro-Serb dispute, **asks France & Germany if they will respect Belgian neutrality**; France replies 'Certainly', Germany refuses to answer. **Britain** — Stock Exchange closed in financial crisis (*see* 2 Aug). **Belgian mobilization ordered for 1 Aug. Secret War** — Churchill sends Asquith RN reports on seizing bases in Frisian Islands & Baltic Approaches, Asquith agrees on War Office joining in. **France** — Socialist leader Jaurès shot & murdered in Paris café by royalist-instigated student. **USA** — New York Stock Exchange closes for first time since 1873, reopens 12 Dec.	
	N Sea — 2 U-boat flotillas (20 boats) assemble off Heligoland (*see* 6). German High Seas Fleet concentrated in Jade anchorage; 2nd & 3rd Battle Sqns join Fleet from Kiel. Mobilization order at 2000. **Med** — British Med Fleet concentrated at Malta. German battlecruiser *Goeben* & cruiser *Breslau* rendezvous at Brindisi. **Germany** — British ships being detained at Hamburg.	**France** — *Aeronautique Militaire* requisitions 50 MS 2-seat 'Parasol' monoplanes ordered by Turkey.	Russia ignores German ultimatum. GERMANY DECLARES WAR ON RUSSIA HAVING ORDERED MOBILIZATION of men aged 20-45 (to begin 2). Kaiser signs declaration, Bethmann says 'If the iron dice roll, God help us'. Tsar wires K George V that Russia had to mobilize for Serbia, but Germany had declared war although he had promised Kaiser not to move troops during talks. Austria appears conciliatory towards Britain. Grey protests v British ships' detention at Hamburg, but Cabinet does not agree to BEF dispatch. Grey asks Germany not to attack France if France remains neutral. Kaiser jubilant at chance to avoid 2-front war but K George V replies Russia included. BELGIUM DECLARES SHE WILL UPHOLD HER NEU-TRALITY. K Albert appeals to kinsman Kaiser. FRANCE MOBILIZES. **Denmark declares neutrality** & mobilizes emergency army. **Norway declares neutrality** (mobilizes navy 2 Aug). **Holland (-4) & Switzerland mobilize.**	**Serbia** — Parlt backs Govt actions. **Britain** — Bank rate raised to 10%, highest in Bank of England's history. **Germany** — SDP majority back war rather than general strike. **Prussian Law of Siege puts Empire under 24 army corps districts.** Kaiser discovers mobilization cannot be confined to E Front. **Italy** — War profits tax; cereal, sugar & cattle exports banned.
	British Admiralty orders mobilization at 1325. **Med** — 3 British battlecruisers & 8-ship 1st Cruiser Sqn (Troubridge) ordered to shadow *Goeben* & *Breslau* (which obtain 2000t German coal at Messina), sail at 0100 (3). **Baltic** — German cruisers *Magdeburg* & *Augsburg* shell Libau & lay mines (*see* 26).		GERMAN 12-HR ULTIMATUM TO BELGIUM at 1900 for troops' free passage to 'anticipate' French attack. Britain assures France that RN will stop German Fleet attacking French Channel shipping. **Britain** — Asquith writes to Venetia Stanley that strong Cabinet party '... against any kind of intervention in any event' (unless Belgium totally invaded). Remaining Reserves mobilized. **Canada** — offers to send troops overseas (*see* 6). **Greece** — Constantine replies to Kaiser that absolute neutrality needed (& 7, *see* 31).	**Germany** — Union-employer Truce *Burgfrieden* ('fortress truce') **for duration. France** — **'State of siege' declared** (law confirms 5), **military law & railway control. Britain** — Remaining RN & medical reserves mobilized. *London Gazette* announces 1-month postponement of payment on bills of exchange other than cheques (*see* 23 Sept).

AUGUST 1914	WESTERN FRONT 1	EASTERN FRONT 2	SOUTHERN FRONTS 3	TURKISH FRONTS 4
Mon 3	BELGIUM REJECTS GERMAN ULTIMATUM: BRITISH GOVT PLEDGES ARMED SUPPORT IN THE EVENT OF A GERMAN INVASION. GERMANY DECLARES WAR ON FRANCE. BRITAIN ORDERS GENERAL MOBILIZATION. French military attaché at Brussels, with authority of his Govt, offers Belgium the aid of 5 French corps; Belgian Govt declines. **German cav cross frontier at Gemmenich**. Joffre meets his 5 army cdrs in Paris.	**Grand Duke Nicholas Russian C-in-C**. Moltke tells Conrad German E Prussia defence only (*see* 9). **Poland** — Germans invade & occupy Kalish, Chenstokhov & Bendzin.	**Italy** — Cadorna urges immediate mobilization to forestall Austrian attack, but not allowed.	TURK MOBILIZATION BEGINS. **Enver Pasha becomes Deputy C-in-C** to Sultan. **Turkey declares armed neutrality**.
Tue 4	BRITISH ULTIMATUM TO GERMANY. BRITAIN DECLARES WAR ON GERMANY AT 2300. GERMANY DECLARES WAR ON BELGIUM. GERMANS INVADE BELGIUM ON 15-MILE FRONT & ATTACK LIÈGE (fortress on R Meuse). German cav take Visé 8 miles N of city & ford R Meuse N & S of city. Moltke peremptorily rejects offer by German Admiralty Staff to intercept BEF's cross-Channel transportation: '... this is not necessary, and it will even be of advantage if the Armies of the West can settle with the 160,000 English (ie est strength of BEF) at the same time as the French and Belgians .' Belgian field army concentrates (-6) behind R Gete, 36 miles W of Liège. Germans deploy opposite (10,*see* 11).		Serb Crown Prince proclamation to Army refers to 'our brethren' (Slavs under Austrian rule).	Enver implies Dardanelles open to German warships, Grand Vizier disagrees.
Wed 5	**Belgium** — Belgians reject German demand for free passage through Liège since it blocks strategic rail routes. Surprise night attack by 6 German composite bdes (25,000 inf) fails to capture any of Liège's 12 forts (garrison 35,000). German cav patrols reach Namur (& 7). Special Order of the Day issued to German First Army only at Aachen, in which Kaiser calls upon it to destroy the ' contemptible little English Army'. French *GQG* opens at Vitry-le-François on the Marne (-1 Sept). **Britain** — British Army Intelligence Corps formed (55 officers become 3000 by Armistice).	AUSTRIA DECLARES WAR ON RUSSIA AT 1200. Austrian Lt Pokorny solves first Russian cryptogram of war. **E Prussia** — Russo-German cav skirmish at Soldau.	MONTENEGRO DECLARES WAR ON AUSTRIA: her 50,000 militia & a few guns tie down 3 Austrian mtn bdes (*see* 7). Moltke letter to Conrad: 'Italy's felony will be revenged in history. May God grant you victory now , so that you will be able to settle accounts later with these knaves' (*see* 27).	Enver offers Russian Ambassador an alliance for Balkan concessions, latter told to gain time only (6). Enver also forms Special Organization to promote guerrilla risings in Libya, Macedonia, Persia & the Caucasus. Catholicos of Etchmiadzin writes to Russian Caucasus Gov-Gen Vorontsov offering loyalty of Armenians in Turkey (Vorontsov replies 2 Sept hoping they will obey his instructions).
Thu 6	BATTLES OF THE FRONTIERS (ie French frontiers) BEGIN (-24). **Belgium** — Maj Gen Ludendorff, QMG of Second Army, stops a panic in 14th Bde humiliated at Liège & himself leads 1500 men who penetrate between the forts & enter city. **France** — Germans invest Longwy fortress on	Two new Russian armies (Ninth & Tenth) to form nr Warsaw & Second Army E Prussia invasion widened. **Poland** — 400 of Col Pilsudski's Polish Legion invade, he follows (8), reaches Kielce 70 miles NE of Cracow (12, *see* 27).	Austrian attack on Obrenovats in R Sava loop W of Belgrade repulsed with loss of guns.	German Ambassador gives Turkey letter of guarantee incl war compensation, Aegean Is if Greece enters war, expanded E borders with Muslim Russia, & no peace before foes cleared from Turk land. **Pacific** — HMG asks Australia & New Zealand to seize German radio stns in Pacific.

AFRICAN OPERATIONS 5	SEA WAR 6	AIR WAR 7	INTERNATIONAL EVENTS 8	HOME FRONTS 9
	N Sea — First merchant ship lost: British *SS San Wilfrido* (6458t) sunk by German mine off Cuxhaven. **Med** — French Med Fleet sails from Toulon for Algeria to convoy transports (2 divs). **France** — Augagneur replaces Gauthier as Minister of Marine.		BELGIUM REJECTS GERMAN ULTIMATUM at 0700, K Albert appeals to K George V for diplomatic help but refuses 5 French corps. GERMANY DECLARES WAR ON FRANCE, falsely claims French aircraft have bombed Karlsruhe & Nuremberg. **Britain** — Sir E Grey tells Commons '... we cannot issue a declaration of unconditional neutrality'. Lord Morley resigns from Cabinet v war. BRITISH GENERAL MOBILIZATION. Asquith approves Anglo-French naval co-operation & Admiralty Shipping requisition authorized (*see* 14). **Australia** — offers HMG RAN & 20,000 troops. **Italy — declares neutrality** (*see* 26). **Rumania** — Crown Council rejects K Carol's demand to join Central Powers, instead **armed neutrality** (Central Powers welcome 5).	**Britain** — Keir Hardie & George Lansbury speak in Trafalgar Sq v war. **Austria** — Trotsky leaves Vienna for Switzerland. **France** — French Army deserter and *Telefunken* electrical engineer Paul Pichon hands over in Paris latest radio audion valve (US de Forest design): 100,000 supplied to French forces by end.
Morocco — 2 French bns evacuating besieged Ft Khenifra lose 66 cas to Zaians of Middle Atlas (*see* 9 & 20).	**N Sea** — **Jellicoe** succeeds Callaghan i/c reinforced British Home or First Fleet, **designated C-in-C Grand Fleet**; hoists flag in *Iron Duke*. Fleet leaves Scapa on first sweep at 0830 to prevent German raiders breaking out. **Med** — *Goeben* & *Breslau* bombard Bône barracks & port & Philippeville (Algeria) for 10 mins from 0608, then at 24 kts evade battlecruisers *Indomitable* & *Indefatigable* before war declared to recoal at Messina (5). **Pacific** — German E Asiatic Sqdn (Spee) leaves Tsingtao for S America (*see* 13).		BRITAIN PROTESTS V GERMAN INVASION OF BELGIUM. GERMANY DECLARES WAR ON BELGIUM. Sir E Goschen's 'scrap of paper' interview with Bethmann. BRITISH ULTIMATUM TO GERMANY, DECLARES WAR ON GERMANY at 2200 GMT. US DECLARES NEUTRALITY: **Japan** — Cabinet decides on strict neutrality (*see* 7). **Switzerland & Brazil declare neutrality. Sweden mobilizes.**	Bethmann tells Reichstag 'Necessity knows no law'; RM5bn war spending authorized; *Bundesrat* empowered to legislate without *Reichstag* 's consent. Kaiser receives *Reichstag* 'Henceforth I know no parties, only Germans'. **France** — *Union Sacrée*: Parlt passes national defence bills before adjourning (*see* 3 Sept). French Academy of Sciences puts itself at Govt's disposal. **Britain** — Army Reserves & Territorials mobilized. Govt exec ctee i/c railways. HG Wells press article identifies enemy as German imperialism & militarism (*see* 14).
German E Africa learns war has broken out from Kamina radio, Togo. British form E Africa Mtd Rifles (-May 1917) and CID sub-ctee for operations outside Europe.	**N Sea** — German auxiliary minelayer *Königin Luise* sunk by 2 British destroyers of Harwich Force (*see* 11), 50 miles off Suffolk coast. British cruiser *Amphion* (151 men lost) sunk (6) by 2 of the 180 mines. Heligoland Patrol of British submarines instituted. Five German overseas submarine cables (incl Emden-Vigo-Azores) cut by British cableship T*elconia*. **Germany** — 2 light cruisers building for Russia at Danzig requisitioned (*Elbing* completed 14 Dec, *Pillau* launched 21 Nov).		AUSTRIA DECLARES WAR ON RUSSIA AND MONTENEGRO v AUSTRIA. Zanzibar declares war on Germany (on Austria 13). **Cuba, Uruguay, Mexico, Argentina & Chile declare neutrality. Neutrals: USA** — Pres Wilson offers mediation. Neutrality censor put in all radio stns. US-Nicaragua (Bryan-Chamorro) Treaty gives former Pacific & Atlantic naval bases + right to build canal for $3m (*see* 14, Senate ratify 18 Feb 1916).	**France** — Milk export prohibited. Bill gives Alsace-Lorrainers enlisting French nationality & press censorship and separation benefits continued laws. **Britain** — **MI5 & police arrest all 21 known German spies** (7 in London) & 200 suspects (first of 32,000 wartime internees). KITCHENER MADE WAR MINISTER as about to leave Dover for Egypt. Ships' Cargoes War Risks Insurance Scheme and Aliens Restriction Act in force (est 70,000 over 14). **Ireland** — Irish Nationalist Party leader Redmond backs war in Commons, troops can be withdrawn. **Germany** — **Iron Cross reinstituted.**
German Togo — Capt Barker summons to surrender, rejected (7) but Lomé & coast evacuated. **SE Cameroons** — 158 French occupy Bonga (*see* 31) & Singa on border before Germans know of war (*see* 12 & 20). **Cyrenaica** — First of 6 rebel attacks on Italians (-30, caravan wiped out 26); 4 more	**N Sea** — **Kaiser orders German Fleet to stay on defensive U-boats & torpedo boats to carry out limited offensive** ops; 14 U-boats begin 9-day 350-mile scouting cruise (*see* 8 & 9). **Atlantic** — German *SS Schlesien* captured by cruiser *HMS Vindictive* off C Ortegal, 3 other German	At special tripartite conference (military/*Reichstag*/industry), manufacturers promise 200 airframes & 170 aero engines pm from mid-Aug. **W Front** — Army Zeppelin *L6* (4 arty shells) makes abortive bombing raid on Liège, holed by Belgian fire, crashes nr Bonn.	SERBIA DECLARES WAR ON GERMANY. Anglo-French Naval Convention signed in London. Britain asks Japan for naval help (*see* 7). **China declares neutrality. Neutrals** — US Sec of State, Bryan, asks belligerents to accept London Declaration (*see* 20). Cruiser *Tennessee* sails for	**France** — PM Viviani appeals to women to bring in harvest (already begun). **Britain** — Asquith outlines 'infamous proposal' & war aims to Commons which votes £100m war credit, 500,000-man Army and RN 67,000 more men. Postal orders legal tender. War Emergency Workers National

AUGUST 1914	WESTERN FRONT 1	EASTERN FRONT 2	SOUTHERN FRONTS 3	TURKISH FRONTS 4
Thu 6 contd	Luxembourg border (-28). French Sordet Cav Corps crosses into Belgium with King's permission, gets to within 9 miles of Liège.			
Fri 7	**Belgium** — Liège city occupied by Germans; Ludendorff forces old citadel's surrender. **Advance Party of BEF lands in France** (completed 16). BATTLE OF ALSACE BEGINS with French invasion by VII Corps which captures Thann & Altkirch after advance guard actions. Gen Lanrezac warns of grave danger of German sweep through central Belgium.	**E Prussia** — Rennenkampf's First Army sends car patrols over (*see* 12).	(c) Serb concentration complete after 11 days. Montenegrin forces raid Artovatz & Klobuchi (-11) but 3rd Austrian Mtn Bde & 47th Div repel them (*see* 15). Serbs check Austrian advance from Visegrad (in Bosnia) (*see* 16).	
Sat 8	**Alsace** — French take Mulhouse for 8 hrs, but after 15-mile advance and sharp engagement at Cernay (9) with superior German XIV & XV Corps, Bonneau retreats to avoid encirclement. **Belgium** — Belgian Army retreats towards R Dyle. First Liège fort (Barchon) surrenders. Main French concentration towards frontiers begins (-14) using 2500 trains.			
Sun 9	LANDING OF THE BEF (-17): British I & II Corps land at Le Havre & Boulogne. French cav enters Belgium.	Moltke tells Conrad no German units can be spared (*see* 14).		Turk inner cabinet decides to gain time until war's outcome clear & negotiate with France & Russia; Enver, Talaat & Finance Minister form Supply Commission for Army & People.
Mon 10	**Lorraine** — Gen Cordonnier destroys German bde at Mangiennes. **Alsace** — Joffre forms Pau's Army of Alsace to renew ops (-26,*see* 14), Bonneau sacked (11).	**E Prussia** — Grand Duke Nicholas' 1st directive orders NW Front to support France by invading E Prussia as soon as possible. Russian cav reach Tilsit. **Poland** — Dankl's Austrian First Army invades from Galicia and aims for Lublin and Kielce (*see* 19).		*Goeben & Breslau* anchor in **Dardanelles**. Enver tells Col Kress forts will protect them (*see* 15).

AFRICAN OPERATIONS 5	SEA WAR 6	AIR WAR 7	INTERNATIONAL EVENTS 8	HOME FRONTS 9
in Sept as Fezzan region rebels (*see* 27 Nov).	steamers taken similarly, another (10). **Indian Ocean —** *Königsberg* captures & scuttles 6601t British *SS City of Winchester* 280 miles E of Aden. **Atlantic —** RN cruisers capture 4 German merchantmen, others (10 & 11). British 10th Cruiser Sqdn (de Chair) or 'Northern Patrol' formed to patrol latitude of Shetland Is. (18 AMCs from Nov.) Grand Fleet remains W of Orkneys or N of Cromarty (-15) due to U-boat threat. **Caribbean —** Cruiser *Karlsruhe* escapes Cradock's cruisers *Suffolk*, *Berwick* & *Bristol* after moonlight action (no hits) with latter (*see* 31). **Med —** Allied Convention assigns supreme command to French Adm Boué de Lapeyrère (*see* 11). *Goeben* & *Breslau* leave Messina for Constantinople; cruiser *Gloucester* (Kelly) shadows them. **S Atlantic —** German cruiser *Dresden* captures but releases 3 British merchant ships, sinks first one (15) 180 miles NE of Pernambuco, Brazil, blows up another (26).		Europe with $6m for US citizens stranded there (*see* 19).	Ctee formed. Prince of Wales opens National Relief Fund (£2m by 3 Sept). *Evening News* calls Kaiser 'Mad Dog of Europe'.
Togo — Anglo-French invasion: 2 British coys occupy Lomé (9) from Gold Coast (*see* 12); 478 French & 2 guns cross E border from Dahomey.	British Channel (ex-Second) Fleet (Burney) constituted at Portland, 15 pre-dreadnoughts & 5 cruisers. **Med —** *Gloucester* briefly engages *Breslau* then receives Troubridge's order to abandon chase at Cape Matapan. **Adriatic —** Austrian Fleet (6 battleships, 2 cruisers, 19 destroyers & TBs) sails from Pola to cover *Goeben* in Austrian territorial waters; returns to port (8) while 2 cruisers shell Antivari, Montenegro (*see* 15).	**Britain —** Temp Lt-Col Trenchard appointed OC RFC at Farnborough i/c all home activity (*see* 11).	**Japan decides to take part in war** (*see* 9). **Spain & Haiti declare neutrality. Neutrals —** Norwegian steamer *Tysla* mined & sunk at Scheldt entrance (3 die). **Portugal proclaims loyalty to British alliance** (*see* 12).	Kaiser proclamation 'In the midst of perfect peace, enemies surprise us....we shall resist to the last breath of man & horse'. Call up of 900,000 *Ersatz* reserves begins. **Austria —** Lenin arrested nr Cracow, released 19 (*see* INT'L EVENTS 5 Sept). **Britain —** Banks reopen after closure (3-6), & 10s notes first issued. Police take & close German banks, military given requisitioning powers. First 'Your King & Country Need You' appeals.
German Cameroons — Chief Rudolf Manga Bell hanged at Duala. **E Africa —** German Gov Schnee leaves Dar-es-Salaam by train for Morogoro 140 miles inland (*see* SEA WAR).	**Aegean —** *Goeben* & *Breslau* coal E of Naxos. **Home Waters —** 96 British hired trawler minesweepers at work (100 more requisitioned by 22). **N Sea —** *U15* (Pohle) misses battleship *Monarch* with torpedo. 4 U-boats sent to attack Channel warships (-11), but heavy seas force 2 back & others sight only destroyer patrols. **E Africa —** Old British cruiser *Astraea* shells Dar-es-Salaam radio stn, boarding party disables 2 German ships. Brief local truce (*see* 13).	**W Front —** First French cas during recon mission; observer w by AA fire. **Britain —** 3 AA guns ready to defend London.	**Montenegro breaks relations with Germany**, latter in state of war with former. **All 3 Scandinavian countries & Venezuela declare neutrality.**	**Russia —** Tsar addresses Duma Municipalities. **Britain — Kitchener appeals for 100,000 volunteers** aged 19-30 (*see* 25). **1st Defence of the Realm Act**, 2nd 28.
Morocco — French incl Foreign Legion 1st Regt repulse tribal attack on Taza (E of Fez) & then sortie (*see* 20).	**N Sea — First decisive surface ship/submarine action on high seas**: surfaced for engine repair, *U15* (no survivors) rammed & sunk by cruiser *Birmingham*: **Channel** — Up to 79 Anglo-French warships (incl submarines) cover BEF crossing (*see* 14).	**Germany —** French Army airship *Fleurus* flies recon mission over Trier.	AUSTRIA DECLARES WAR ON MONTENEGRO. German peace terms to Belgium via Holland rejected. Belgium proposes African free trade zone, Germany agrees via Spain on (22, *see* 20 Nov). German Ambassador abuses Japanese Foreign Minister Baron Kato (*see* 11 & 15).	**Germany —** Falkenhayn agrees to War Ministry Raw Materials Section headed by Jewish civilian Rathenau, begins work (28).
Germans raid Cape Colony from SW Africa but give up Swakopmund & Lüderitz Bay radio stns (*see* 15 & 21). PM Gen Botha agrees to HMG's requests (of 6 & 9) to occupy them (*see* 9 Sept).	**Med —** *Goeben* & *Breslau* enter Dardanelles at 0830. 2 British battlecruisers belatedly reach Aegean. Turk blank shots warn off cruiser *Weymouth* (11). **Indian Ocean —** RN cruiser *Fox* captures 2 German merchant ships off Colombo (-11, *see* 13).		FRANCE DECLARES WAR ON AUSTRIA. French Military Mission arrives in London. Liberia neutral. **Neutrals : USA** — German-American weekly *The Fatherland* launched in New York (100,000+ circ by Oct, *see* 3 Mar 1915).	**Austria —** Fourth Army: 'Patriotic feeling was everywhere in evidence'. **Germany** — Kaiser swears to Prussian Guard leaving Berlin that he will not sheath his sword until peace can be dictated. **France** — Decree applies courts-martial procedure to whole country (& 8 Sept). **Australia**

AUGUST 1914	WESTERN FRONT 1	EASTERN FRONT 2	SOUTHERN FRONTS 3	TURKISH FRONTS 4
Mon 10 contd				
Tue 11	**Alsace** — Germans retake Mulhouse. **Belgium** — Belgians fight nr Tirlemont, St Trond & Diest.		**Serbia** — Austrian Second, Fifth & Sixth Armies, screened by heavy shelling, cross R Sava & Drina rivers (night 11/12); small Austrian det fails to take Ada Ciganlija Is nr Belgrade.	
Wed 12	**Belgium** — 10,000 Germans take Huy. 2 16.5-in (420mm) **Krupp howitzers pound Liège forts** from 1740. Kitchener reluctantly agrees to forward BEF concentration around Maubeuge. Belgian dismtd cav repel German cav attack on Haelen (Gete line) (*see* 18). **France** — French concentrate 37 Territorial & reserve divs (-18) using 4500 trains (*see* 19). **Germany** — Kluck's First Army begins marching from around Jülich and Krefeld.	**E Prussia** — Gourko's 1st Cav Div crosses frontier & takes soon evacuated Marggrabowa. **Poland** — Samsonov reaches Second Army HQ at Warsaw (*see* 19).	AUSTRIAN INVASION OF SERBIA: Austrian 44th Inf Regt (31st Div) capture Sabac (I Serb coy) across R Sava after 0315, kill male population, massacre children & rape women; repel 2 bns & 2 cav sqns at noon (*see* 14). Austrian 29th Div captures 3 villages nr Mitrovica to W. On Austrian Fifth Army Drina front, in dawn attack, VIII Corps (25,000 men & 96 guns) takes island N of Janja by noon but XIII Corps repulsed by 2 Serb coys from island to W of Krupanj though its 42nd Honved Div crosses & bridges Drina.	**C Pacific** — RN destroys German radio stn on Yap (*see* 7 Oct).
Thu 13	**Belgium** — 3 Liège forts surrender to Germans (one blows up) as Austrian 12in Skoda howitzers join in. **Alsace** — French Belfort garrison (57th Div) stops *Landwehr* pursuit at border.		Austrian slowness allows Serb C-in-C Putnik to switch Third & Second Armies by forced marching closer to the strategic R Jadar, Cav Div to Sabac and First Army to take over N sector W of Belgrade.	
Fri 14	BATTLE OF LORRAINE (-20): incl Battles of Morhange (14-20) & Sarrebourg (14-20). Dubail & Castelnau defeated. Sir J French lands at Boulogne (*see* 16). **Alsace** — Despite a reverse at St Marie aux Mines, Pau reoccupies Thann & takes Gebwieler (*see* 16). **Belgium** — Lanrezac, ordered to move his French Fifth Army to Charleroi, sees & appeals to Joffre for measures to protect his left (W) flank but told that 'the Germans have nothing ready on that side'. 2 Liège forts surrender.	Conrad requests (& 15) German Eighth Army offensive on Syedlets (50 miles E of Warsaw). **Galicia** — Ruzski's Third Army beats Austrians at Sokal on R Bug inside latter's frontier (*see* 18).	**Austrian Second Army withdrawing to E Front as Serb Military Intelligence learns** (*see* 16). Serb 1st Sumadija Div vainly attacks Sabac. Austrian VIII Corps drives back 2000 Serbs & 2 guns, taking Cer Ridge but too muddy to get guns on it. Austrian XIII Corps captures Loznica & advances to its S. Putnik orders Serb Second Army to counter-attack (night 14/15).	RN Mission (Rear-Adm Limpus) asked not to visit Turk ships. Admiralty buys stock in Anglo-Persian Oil Co.

AFRICAN OPERATIONS 5	SEA WAR 6	AIR WAR 7	INTERNATIONAL EVENTS 8	HOME FRONTS 9
				— AIF recruiting begins. **Britain** — Govt empowered to act v food hoarding. **First BEF special train reaches Southampton** (670 move 118,000 troops, -31). Queen Mary's Needlework Guild for unemployed women starts, sends 15.5m garments worldwide (-Feb 1919) from St James's Palace (1,078,839 British members).
	Secret War — RAN boarding party seizes German HVB naval code (used by Navy Zeppelins & outpost vessels until Mar 1916) from steamer unaware of war. It reaches Admiralty end Oct. **Med** — French Fleet ordered to concentrate on Malta (-13,*see* 15). **N Sea** — Harwich Force (Tyrwhitt) formed with 2 cruisers & 40 destroyers. *Arethusa* completed at Chatham first of 8 light cruisers, by Mar 1915. **Channel** — Admiralty requisitions 3 cross-Channel steamers to be seaplane carriers (*Engadine* & *Riviera* commission at Chatham 13, *Empress* 25, *see* 25 Dec). **Pacific** — German cruiser *Leipzig* at San Francisco (-17, *see* 12 Oct).	**W Front** — First RFC échelon cross Channel by sea.	German Chancellor proposes Ukraine buffer state to his Vienna Ambassador. Churchill modifies Grey's Tokyo cable to back wider Japanese Pacific intervention (*see* 15).	**Britain** — 'Business as usual' motto coined in WH Smith letter to *Daily Chronicle* (Harrods so advertises 13). **Press Bureau formed**, issues first communiqué. FM Lord Roberts inspects the Irish Guards. **France** — 1st contraband list issued.
Togo — Future RSM Alhaji Grunshi (Gold Coast Regt) **fires first British shot of campaign & probably of whole land war** nr Togblekove (*see* 14). **SE Cameroons** — 600 French occupy German Ft Mbaiki (*see* 20). **Tripolitania** — Col Giannini's Italians occupy Ghat, oasis town 600 miles from coast.	**E Africa** — British cruisers	**W Front** — **First German pilot killed on active service**: Oblt Jahnow (1912 Balkan War pilot for Turks) k in crash nr Malmédy. French recon units suffer first fatal cas, Sgt Bridou crashes on return to base. **Britain** — **First British airmen die on active service**: 2/Lt Skene & Mech Barlow No 3 Sqn RFC k in Blériot 2-seater crash nr Dover en route for France.	BRITAIN DECLARES WAR ON AUSTRIA. Kaiser attempts to buy off Japan (*see* 15). Anglo-Portugese Commercial Treaty. **Guatemala neutral**. Austro-German discussion of Polish question begins, Germans intend to put own Governor into Warsaw (18).	**Britain** — *Punch* magazine's 'Brave Little Belgium' cartoon. Lady Hamilton's diary 'Lord K is playing hell with its lid off at the War Office'.
L Nyasa — British steamer *Gwendolen* (3 guns) secures lake by disabling gunboat *Hermann von Wissman* on stocks at Spinxhaven (5 crew captured, *see* 19).	*Astraea* & *Pegasus* shell Dar-es-Salaam. **Pacific** — Spee detaches *Emden* & collier to raid Indian Ocean (*see* 21, 10 Sept). **Channel** — Record 44	**France** — Nos 2, 3, 4 & 5 Sqns RFC (Brig-Gen Sir D Henderson) begin crossing Channel (-15), first plane (of 44 Blériots, Farmans, BEs & Avros) to land is Lt Harvey-Kelly's BE2a of No 2 Sqn. RFC moves from Amiens to Maubeuge by 17.	Anglo-French Commission created in London for buying munitions. Churchill arranges for 200 Austrians to leave with Ambassador who is told by K George V 'I don't believe William wanted war...his son and his party made the war'. Egypt (state of war proclaimed 6) severs relations with Germany. Colombia declares neutral ports.	**France** — War Minister forms Press Commission. **Britain** — Mrs Pankhurst letter suspends WSPU activities (11 suffragettes already freed).
Togo — Capt Bryant's 582 troops, 2000 porters & 3 guns advance from Lomé on capital Kamina. **L Tanganyika** — German gunboat *Hedwig von Wissman* raids Uvira in Belgian Congo & disables Belgian ship (22). **L Victoria** — British tug *Percy Anderson* captures German dhow. **Cameroons** — Col Carter allowed to recce from Nigeria where 4 cols assemble nr border (13-19). Anglo-French London Conference agrees on joint attack (15, *see* 20).	transports convey BEF to France (30 pd-18). Germans finally realize	**W Front** — French Voisin (Cesari & Pindhommeau) attempts to bomb Zeppelin shed at Metz (*see* 26 Dec).	500 US Marines land at Bluefields, Nicaragua, with Govt's consent.	**Belgium** — **Bread rationing**. **Austria** — Labour Exchange Labour supply organization formed. **France** — Rent moratorium agreed. **Britain** — HG Wells calls conflict '**The War to End War**'. Admiralty Transport Board for Ship Requisitioning. **Russia** — Grand Duke Nicholas promises Polish kingdoms' reconstruction & autonomy (*see* 25 Nov).

AUGUST 1914	WESTERN FRONT 1	EASTERN FRONT 2	SOUTHERN FRONTS 3	TURKISH FRONTS 4
Sat 15	**Belgium** — Belgian staff at Namur warn that German forces are crossing R Meuse *en masse* , but Allies disregard. **Belgium** — FALL OF LIÈGE (-16): garrison cdr Gen Leman taken PoW in ruins of Ft Loncin: ' Put in your dispatches that I was unconscious ', he implores captors, who allow him to keep his sword. Last 2 forts surrender (16). d'Esperey's I Corps (1000 cas) with Pétain's 4th Bde repulses Richthofen's I Cav Corps R Meuse crossing attempt S of Dinant. See HOME FRONTS 23. **Lorraine** — French First Army drives I Bav Corps from 2 villages inside French frontier (*see* 18).	Austrian cav (10 divs) rides over Russian frontier on 250-mile front but only on far flanks pierces Russian screen (*see* 21).	**Herzegovina** — Montenegrins begin blockade of Bilek (-25/26). **Serbia** — Austrian VIII Corps continues Cer Ridge advance; XIII Corps reaches Krupanj 15 miles E of Drina as Serb Second Army forced marches but its 1st Combined Div begins night attack on Cer Ridge (-16), driving off Austrian 21st Div.	Germans mine Dardanelles from a merchant ship (& 19). **SW Pacific** — NZ Samoa force (2 transports) sails from Wellington (*see* 30).
Sun 16	Landing of original BEF completed. **Belgium** — Indecisive action at Wavre. Joffre & Sir J French first meet at *GQG*. **Alsace** — Main French advance resumed after *Chasseurs Alpins* cross Vosges passes (*see* 19).	STAVKA set up at Baranovichi (80 miles SW of Minsk) rail jctn.	**Serbia** — **Battle of the Jadar** (-24): Serb Second Army C-in-C Gen Stepanovic rallies 1st Combined Div v Austrian 9th Div until 1st Morava Div averts crisis at 1400. Serb Cav Div prevents Austrian link up with Sabac garrison. Austrian XIII Corps captures Krupanj forcing back whole Serb left wing. Conrad allows only IV Corps of Second Army to stay in response to Potiorek's pleas. **Bosnia** — Serb Uzice Army attack on Visegrad (& 20-21) repelled; Austrian Sixth Army counter-attacks forcing R Lim, retaking Uvats (20-22,*see* 22).	**Turkey announces formal purchase** for RM80m & renaming **of German ships** (actually done 11). *Breslau* anchors off Constantinople. Rear Adm Souchon asks for 548 extra German sailors (Adm Usedom leaves Berlin 22,*see* 21). **Diplomacy** — Russia offers defensive military alliance, rejected.
Mon 17	**Belgium** — Govt transferred from Brussels to Antwerp. Kluck put under Bülow. **France** — †Lt-Gen Sir J Grierson (heart attack in train), GOC II Corps BEF: Sir J French asks for Sir H Plumer to replace him but Kitchener appoints Sir H Smith-Dorrien.	**E Prussia** — **Rennenkampf invades** on 35-mile front. François (German I Corps) forces Battle of Stallupönen v orders & 5 miles inside frontier, takes 3000 Russian PoWs before retiring on Gumbinnen. **Poland** — Austrian First Army recce on Krasnik fails (*see* 23).	Serb 1st Sumadija Div stopped 3 miles from Sabac by entrenched Austrians, but 1st Combined Div captures 2 villages on Cer Ridge. Austrian 42nd Honved Div (XIII Corps) threatens Valjevo to S.	Allies guarantee Turkey's integrity in Churchill cable to Enver Pasha if she observes strict neutrality. Enver does not reply to Adm Limpus' (RN Mission) conciliatory visit for Churchill (*see* 16 Sept).
Tue 18	**Belgium** — Battle of the Gettes (-19): actions of Grimde & Hautem St Marguerite. Germans capture Tirlemont as Belgian Army retreats (1630 cas) to Antwerp (-20). **Lorraine** — French II Cav Corps enters Saarbourg after skirmish, VIII Corps follows pushing to N & E of town but attacks blocked (19-20), suffers 50+% cas by evening 23. French XV Corps occupies Dieuze.	63 Russian infantry divs operational (35 v Austrians). **Galicia** — Brusilov's Eighth Army invades v token resistance (-19).	**Serbia** — Austrian IV Corps fails to break out of Sabac bridgehead being massacred at R Dobrava. Serb Second Army attacks all day taking 3 Austrian 9th Div positions & repelling counter-attacks; night attack eventually gains Kosanin Grad (0500,19). Austrian XIII Corps attacks v Serb Third Army gain little.	
Wed 19	**Belgium** — RETREAT OF BELGIAN ARMY from R Gette on Antwerp after defeat at Aerschot by Kluck. Germans enter Louvain & destroy Aerschot (150 civilians shot). Siege of Namur (-25), 27,000 garrison with 9 forts face Gallwitz's 5 divs. **Alsace** — French again take Mulhouse (-25). Pau captures 1000 PoWs & 24 guns at Dornach, but simultaneous French reverses at Morhange & Saarbourg (Belgium) necessitate abandonment of entire op. **Lorraine** — Joffre forms Maunoury's Lorraine Army of res divs (-25 qv).	**E Prussia** — **Samsonov's Second Army invades** from S. On Rennenkampf's N flank 3rd Sqn Russian Horse Guards charge & take 2 German guns at Kauschen. **Poland** — Dankl's advance checked nr Kielce, but Russians evacuate (22).	**Serbia** — **Battle of the Cer: Decisive day.** Serb Second Army captures whole ridge as 1st Sumadija Div engages Austrian IV Div all day. Serbs pursue Austrian Fifth Army towards R Drina, its 36th Div losing 500 PoWs. Austrian XIII Corps takes 3 villages from Serb I wing. Austrians shoot 150 peasants at Lesnica (*Times History*), one of many invasion atrocities. **Italy** — Cadorna learns politicians want Trentino & Trièste by peace (*see* 22 & 27).	**Greece offers to attack Gallipoli Peninsula under British command, HMG reject** as it might precipitate Turkey's entry into war (*see* 9 Sept). Churchill telegram offers compensation if *Goeben* & *Breslau* crews leave at once. **SW Pacific** — Australian New Guinea Expedition sails from Sydney, arrives Pt Moresby on 4 Sept.
Thu 20	French suffer 140,000+ cas in Battles of the Frontiers (-24).	**E Prussia** — **Battle of Gumbinnen**: Rennenkampf	FIRST MAJOR ALLIED VICTORY OF WAR: Battle of	

AFRICAN OPERATIONS 5	SEA WAR 6	AIR WAR 7	INTERNATIONAL EVENTS 8	HOME FRONTS 9
300 Germans invade British E Africa, capture Taveta on border at SE foot of Mt Kilimanjaro; Uganda Railway threatened. **Togo** — British (45 cas) win action at Agbeluvoe stn (-16; 158 French join 18, *see* 22). **S Africa** — Gen de la Rey addresses 800 disaffected Boers at Trellerfontein (W Transvaal, *see* 15 Sept).	Austrians not going to reinforce *Goeben* with any ships. **Adriatic** — Anglo-French main fleet & Troubridge's sqn rendezvous off Straits of Otranto for 10-day sweep (-24) into Adriatic: Cattaro bombarded (24), Austrian lighthouses destroyed, small cruiser *Zenta* sunk by French battleships (16, nr Antivari, Montenegro). **Secret War** — (c) RN DNI Rear-Adm Sir H Oliver recruits Dir Naval Education Sir A Ewing to look at intercepted German signals (*see* Sept). **Med** — *Goeben* (renamed	**W Front** — Garaix, pioneer French aviator & de Taizieuz his observer shot down & k by AA. **Germany** — Boelcke gains Pilot's Certificate at Halberstadt Flying School (posted to *Feldfliegerabteilung* No 13, Sept). FM French visits RFC at Maubeuge (10 base changes 16 Aug to 4 Sept).	**Japan's ultimatum to Germany for evacuation of Tsingtao in China** (*see* 18 & 23); Berlin ignores. **Neutrals: Panama** — **Canal officially open** (*see* 10 Oct). **USA** — Sec of State Bryan declares loans to belligerents inconsistent with neutrality.	**Britain** — Bertrand Russell protests v war in *The Nation*. **Germany** — *Landsturm* called up. **France** — **2,887,000 reservists mobilized since 1**. **Austria** — Polish Parties' manifesto supports state duties.
Uganda — First 1000 porters leave for front (*see* 5 Sept).	*Yavuz Sultan Selim*) & *Breslau* (*Midilli*) hoist Turk war flag & (nominally) pass under Turk control (*see* 22). **Rear Adm Souchon i/c Turk Fleet from 23 Sept** (*see* TURK FRONTS). **N Sea** — Grand Fleet sweeps southward to Horn Reef to divert German attention from ferry service taking BEF to France (15-17,*see* W FRONT 4). **E Africa** — British cruiser	**W Front** — French troops shoot down Army Zeppelin *L7*.		**Germany** — Kaiser leaves Berlin for W Front. Hitler volunteers for 2nd Bav Inf Regt (to 16th 1 Sept). **Britain** — RND formed (announced 6 Sept).
	Pegasus raids Tanga, disables German ship *Markgraf*. **Japan** — IJN's first seaplane carrier *Wakamiya* converted from British-built freighter (Russo-Japanese war prize) (*see* AIR WAR 16 Sept). **N Sea** — RN cruiser *Fearless* chases German cruisers *Strassburg* & *Stralsund*, ending their tentative probe. **Pacific** — French cruiser		**Ecuador declares neutrality.** PM Count Okuma says 'Japan's object is to eliminate from continental China the root of German influence' .	**Belgium** — **Govt & Queen leave Brussels for Antwerp** (*see* 7 Oct). **Britain** — Special Constable recruiting begins. Flour prices fixed. **France** — CGT soup kitchens open in Paris, 6000 meals pd. **Russia** — Tsar at Moscow. **Canada** — Parlt in special war session (-22) votes $50m War Measures Act, Canadian Patriotic Fund.
India — IEF 'C's first unit, 29th Punjabis, sails for E Africa; **first Indian Army unit to go overseas** (*see* 1 Sept). **L Nyasa** — 3 British steamers land 400 KAR at Vua (-20).		**W Front** — **First RFC visual recon mission to cross German lines**: Capt (later ACM Sir P) Joubert de la Ferté in Blériot & Lt Mapplebeck in BE2a.	Morocco breaks with Germany. **Neutrals : USA** — Wilson Senate speech appeals to Americans to be 'neutral in fact as well as in name'.	**France** — Miners' day extended to 11 hrs. **Belgium** — **First mass shooting of civilians (150 at Aerschot) by Germans.**
c400 BRITISH INVADE CAMEROONS from Nigeria		DCNS Rear Adm Behncke urges Imperial HQ to sanction	Russian Foreign Minister Sazonov tells French	**Belgium** — Gen Bülow sanctions shooting of 311

AUGUST 1914	WESTERN FRONT 1	EASTERN FRONT 2	SOUTHERN FRONTS 3	TURKISH FRONTS 4
Thu 20 contd	**Belgium** — FALL OF BRUSSELS: German IV Corps (Arnim) 'Victory parade'. BELGIAN ARMY WITHDRAWS INTO ANTWERP FORTRESS; Kluck decides to send 2 corps to invest it. **Lorraine** — French XXI Corps defeats German XIV Corps attack, but VIII Corps forced from Saarburg as 6 German Seventh Army divs attack (*see* 23). French Second Army`s XV & XVI Corps routed by German XXI & I Bav Res Corps but Foch's XX Corps holds firm and then night retreats 12 miles to R Meurthe (*see* 25). BEF concentration S of Maubeuge nears completion.	(19,000 cas) just repels Germans (13,000 cas) up to 25 miles from border; occupies Goldap but no pursuit till 22. Prittwitz orders retreat to R Vistula, but then approves Lt-Col Hoffmann's idea of switch v Samsonov.	the Jadar — Serb guns shell Austrians fleeing in valleys below & pursuit reaches R Drina in evening. Potiorek orders Austrian Second Army to recross the Sava (*see* 23).	
Fri 21	**Belgium** — BATTLE OF CHARLEROI (-23) along R Sambre, Bülow forces river & smash 6 French div counter-attacks (22) driving them 8 miles S of it (-23) but Fifth Army (Lanrezac) escapes from German Sedan-style 1870 envelopment; Kluck, Bülow & Hausen thwarted by the quick manoeuvring of Lanrezac & Sir J French. Nevertheless, former severely criticized in France. German heavy bombardment of Namur begins at 1000. BATTLE OF THE ARDENNES (-23) begins with 10-15 mile multi-columned French advance into hilly forested region despite afternoon rain.	**E Prussia — Moltke replaces Prittwitz with Hindenburg & Ludendorff** after he requests reinforcements and considers switch 'too daring'. Germans request Austrian offensive. Conrad complies 'with a heavy heart'. **Galicia** — Austro-Russian cav battle at Jaroslawice (2500 horsemen in 4 charges) which Russian 10th Div win (during eclipse of sun).	Serb 2nd Morava Div reoccupies Krupanj.	Churchill 'violently anti-Turk' in Cabinet meeting (*see* 31). Turk battleship crews from Tyne reach Constantinople. Another 28 German officers arrive (23, *see* 8 Sept).
Sat 22	**Belgium — British first in action:** c80 Dragoon Guards scatter German sqn of 4th Cuirassiers 5 miles N of Mons, mtd & dismtd cav actions to NE. BEF aligned along Condé-Mons canal W of Mons — Kluck's intelligence erroneously places them at Tournai. Battle of the Ardennes involves 361,000 French v 380,000 Germans in piecemeal actions between Neufchâteau & Longwy (Rommel's baptism of fire), 2 French corps mauled incl 3rd Colonial Div (11,000 cas). **Alsace** — French near Colmar but 44th Div withdrawn to First Army; VII Corps entrained (25) to be new Sixth Army nucleus at Amiens (*see* 25). **Belgium** — Namur: 3 major forts ruined by Big Bertha-led bombardment; garrison & 4th Div (12,000 reach Antwerp 30) escape S to French lines. **Ardennes** — Foch's cadet son Germain (131st Inf) k aged 25, father learns 12 Sept. **Lorraine** — Germans occupy Luneville (-12 Sept).	**E Prussia** — Samsonov captures Soldau & Neidenburg. Hindenburg & Ludendorff first meet at Hanover stn.	Serbs back on whole line of R Drina. Austrian Sixth Army retires into Bosnia (-24). **Italy** — Only able to mobilize 380,000 troops without untrained militia & inadequate arty, also 200,000 uniforms short (*see* 27).	
Sun 23	**Belgium — Battle of Mons** (-24): 6 of Kluck's inf divs, advancing in textbook formations, blunder one after the other into British II Corps (36,000 men & 152 guns) to be decimated by rapid, accurate small arms fire. British suffer 1638 cas & 2 guns to 4000 German. Shortly before 2400, Germans appear to front & right (Hausen crosses Meuse at Dinant) of Lanrezac's army.	**E Prussia** — Hindenburg & Ludendorff arrive at Mari-enburg, then Tannenberg. Rennenkampf renews advance but W on Königsberg, his 1st Cav Div takes Angerburg at N end of Masurian Lakes. **Poland — First Battle of Krasnik** (-25) SW of Lublin: Austrian First Army v Russian Fourth, latter driven back 3 miles (24). **Galicia** — Austrian Fourth Army at last massed. 1st	Austrian IV Corps counter-attacks to cover retreat over Sava.	

AFRICAN OPERATIONS 5	SEA WAR 6	AIR WAR 7	INTERNATIONAL EVENTS 8	HOME FRONTS 9
(see 23 & 24). **Morocco** — French kill over 200 tribesmen to get convoy into Ft Khenifra (see 13 Nov).		Zeppelin raids on London ('to cause panic in the population'), major British ports, and 4 naval bases.	Ambassador Paléologue '... we must destroy German imperialism'. **First British Order-in-Council modifies London Declaration** (1910 blockade rules). **Neutrals : Italy** — †Pope Pius X (aged 79, see 3 Sept).	civilians (for alleged sniping) in Andenne on the Meuse (-21). **Britain** — Royal Commission on Women's Employment. Sugar Supplies Central Ctee formed. Postal censorship begins. **France** — National Unemployment Fund.
German patrol enters S Africa across R Orange.	*Dupleix* captures 2 of Spee's allocated supply ships. 2 Japanese cruisers sail to join RN sqn at Singapore (see 27 & 31). **N Sea** — German cruiser/		**Peru declares neutrality.**	**Britain** — 6 New Army Divs authorized (see 11 Sept).
Togo — 450 Allies lose 75 cas at Khra v 460 Germans with 3 MGs (5k) (see 26). **W Africa** — Sierre Leone troops embark for Togo & Cameroons.	destroyer sqn sinks 8 British fishing boats. **Med** — Adm Usedom's 522 German naval officers/technicians leave Berlin for Constantinople. **Britain** — Admiralty War Staff	**W Front** — RFC warn BEF II Corps that Kluck's First Army marching W on Brussels-Ninove Rd with Bülow's Second Army advancing through Charleroi. **First RFC aircraft shot down**: No 5 Sqn Avro 504 (Lt Waterfall) by German rifle fire in Belgium, first evidence of BEF. Observer Sgt-Maj Jillings, No 2 Sqn, w (on one of 18 recons 20-22). RFC Farman of No 5 Sqn with first Lewis gun mounting fails to intercept German aircraft over Maubeuge. **E Front** — Army Zeppelin *LZ5* pinpoints Russian Second Army troops in Tannenberg sector (repeated 25). Army airship *SL2* begins 24-hr recon mission for Austrian armies.	AUSTRIA DECLARES WAR ON BELGIUM (formally received 28).	**Russia** — **Imperial decree prohibits liquor sales for duration. Belgium** — Germans shoot 384 civilians in Tamines main square and levy £8m on Brussels.
Cameroons — Brig-Gen Dobell made Allied C-in-C land forces, sails from Liverpool (31, see 17 Sept).	(created 1912) forms Trade Div. **Atlantic** — Armed merchant	**W Front** — German troops by mistake shoot down Zeppelin *L8* at Badonvillers.	JAPAN DECLARES WAR ON GERMANY, latter severs relations. Germany tries vainly through US Berlin Ambassador to get Allies to recognize African colonies' neutrality (Berlin Act 1885). **Occupied Belgium** — FM Goltz made Gov-Gen with Sandt as Civil Administrator. **Neutrals : Rumania** — SDP & Trade Unions Special Congress oppose war.	**Belgium** — Gen Hausen's Saxons massacre 612 Dinant civilians and pillage town; 4000 flee from Visé into Holland from German shootings (700 deported to Germany for harvest labour) -24.

AUGUST 1914	WESTERN FRONT 1	EASTERN FRONT 2	SOUTHERN FRONTS 3	TURKISH FRONTS 4
Sun 23 contd	At 2400 a message from him reaches BEF that he has ordered a retirement to begin at 0300. Sir J French decides to follow suit. Verbal orders issued at 0900. Germans enter Namur (25 civilians shot -25). **Lorraine** — French First Army resumes offensive, driving Germans NE until stopped (28-31).	Kuban Cossacks charge & take Chertkov rail stn + 4 Austrian 1st Cav Div guns at R Sereth crossing.		
Mon 24	**Belgium** — BEF RETREAT FROM MONS BEGINS at c0400. Marching inf are ably covered on left (W) by Allenby's Cav Div. Only a few fierce rear-guard actions involve British 5th Div: BEF cas c2752 & 2 guns. Battles of Charleroi & the Ardennes end with French Fourth Army ordered to retreat behind R Meuse. Joffre orders that all inf attacks must have arty preparation. **Belgium** — 3 Namur forts fall. **Alsace** — Battle of Alsace ends. **France** — Lille declared open city, garrison evacuated. **Lorraine** — French Second Army's XX Corps (Foch) advances 2 miles in Battle of the Mortagne (-28) & blocks Germans E of Nancy (see 31). War Minister backs Joffre's policy of removing inadequate generals (140 by 6 Sept): 'eliminate the old fossils without pity'.	Grand Duke Nicholas accepts 'in principle' Churchill's offer (19) to send fleet to Baltic & land a Russian army in Germany. **E Prussia** — Samsonov takes Frankenau, forces Scholtz's XX corps back 10 miles (see AIR WAR).	Serbs recapture Sabac; by 1500 **all Austrian invaders out of Serbia**. Austrian Gen Krauss' diary (29th Div) 'One hoped to knock Serbia out quickly and then turn all forces against Russia — only this can explain the peculiar conduct of the High Command' (see 3 Sept).	
Tue 25	JOFFRE ORDERS GENERAL ALLIED RETREAT & secretly transfers troops from Alsace-Lorraine (Mulhouse evacuated, Army of Alsace disbanded 26) to bolster Maunoury's Sixth Army around Amiens (see 27). Moltke believes victory imminent so details 6 corps for threatened E Front (1 from each army; only 2 actually sent, see 26). **Alsace** — Germans retake Mulhouse. **France** — Gen Fournier ordered to hold Maubeuge fortress; he has 30,000 French troops (mainly Territorials) & 10,000 Allied stragglers. German VII Res Corps initiate siege works. **Lorraine** — German Sixth & Seventh Armies reach R Meurthe after very slow pursuit. Germans take Sedan. Since withdrawal of main French forces Dubail has been holding Vosges passes. His centre is now penetrated by German Seventh Army (Heeringen). Violent fighting continues into Sept but much of Heeringen's army is redeployed to the Aisne & Flanders (see 6 Sept) and the German offensive peters out leaving the French holding 3 important passes. Germans bump into BEF I Corps at Landrecies (night 25/26), 905 British cas. **Belgium** — Belgian 4-div night sortie from Antwerp (25/26) recaptures 3 villages S of Malines, but ended by news of Mons & Namur (see 9 Sept). **Last 3 Namur forts succumb** to German heavy arty.	**E Prussia** — **Germans intercept Russian radio orders in clear** for 25-26. At 2030 Hindenburg & Ludendorff order double envelopment of Samsonov for next day. **Poland** — First Battle of Krasnik won by Dankl's Austrians who take 6000 PoWs & 28 guns and advance on Lublin. Russian Fourth Army (Evert replaces Salza) retreats 4 miles. **Galicia** — Austrian Second Army arriving from Serbia (-28).	**Herzegovina** — Austrian Bilek garrison sortie & 3rd Mtn Bde raises Montenegrin blockade (-26).	Berlin tells its Constantinople Ambassador Wangenheim to organize a Turk raid on the Suez Canal.
Wed 26	TWO GERMAN CORPS TRANSFERRED FROM W TO	**E Prussia** — BATTLE OF TANNENBERG (-31): Russians	Putnik orders Serb Army regrouping for limited offensive	Adm Limpus suggests British landing between Smyrna &

AFRICAN OPERATIONS 5	SEA WAR 6	AIR WAR 7	INTERNATIONAL EVENTS 8	HOME FRONTS 9
Cameroons — c200 British capture Nsanakang on Nigerian border (*see* 6 Sept); in N, German Kuseri post repels 250 French (23 cas, from Ft Lamy -25) but falls 20 Sept. **E Africa** — Germans raid Portugese Maziwa post (*see* 19 Oct).		**W Front** — RFC HQ & ground staffs begin withdrawals across Belgium & N France. French Army airship *Dupuy-de-Lôme* shot down in error by own ground forces (*Montgolfier* from Maubeuge likewise 21 but *see* 26 Dec). **E Front** — Samsonov sends his CoS *by air* in vain bid to warn Jilinski of Russian Second Army's over-extension.		**India** — First IEF 'A' units sail for France. **Britain** — TUC-Labour industrial truce declared. War Refugees Central Ctee formed. First BEF wounded land at Southampton (27 ambulance trains follow).
Cameroons — 600 Nigerians capture Tepe on border (*see* 29).		**W Front** — **RFC achieves first combat victory**: 3 No.2 Sqn BE2s force down Aviatik B-type, pursuing crew into woods.	JAPAN DECLARES 'STATE OF WAR' WITH AUSTRIA having severed relations (24). Anglo-French loan of £20 million to Belgium agreed.	**Britain** — Kitchener's first speech as Minister: 100,000 volunteers almost secured; 69 TF bns volunteer for overseas service; New Army may be 30 divs in 6-7 months. **Belgium** — BURNING OF LOUVAIN (-30): town 1/8 destroyed by Germans as deterrent. **Germany** — XXII-XXVII Res Corps formed.
Togo — ALLIED CONQUEST COMPLETE OF FIRST	raider *Kaiser Wilhelm der Grosse*, having sunk 2 British	**E Front** — Russia's premier aerobatic pilot & first air hero	Austria accepts Italy's Triple Alliance reading, ie not obliged	**Britain** — Churchill vainly raises conscription in Cabinet.

AUGUST 1914	WESTERN FRONT 1	EASTERN FRONT 2	SOUTHERN FRONTS 3	TURKISH FRONTS 4
Wed 26 contd	E FRONT: Prussian Guard Res & XI Corps. **Belgium** — Fall of last 2 Namur forts & Longwy, 6700 Belgian PoWs in all. French First Army falling back across the R Meuse. BATTLE OF LE CATEAU: British II Corps (Smith-Dorrien), 55,000 men & 226 guns, fights day-long delaying action v Kluck's 140,000 & 340 guns for 7812 cas (2600 PoWs) & 38 guns. Sir J French, Joffre & Lanrezac confer at St Quentin but decide nothing. Kluck resumes indep command of First Army. Gallieni appointed Governor of Paris. French withdrawing in Alsace-Lorraine.	evacuate newly captured Allenstein (centre), 6-mile gap in their line. **Poland** — **Battle of Zamosc-Komarow** (-31, 2 Sept): Austrian Fourth Army v Russian Fifth. **Galicia** — FIRST BATTLE OF LEMBERG. Austrian Third Army v Russian Third & Eighth, 2 Austrian divs flee 25 miles back to Lemberg (27, see 28).	into Sava-Danube Srem region as prelude to invading Bosnia (see 5 Sept).	Dardanelles.
Thu 27	**French abandon Lille** & Charleville-Mézières on R Meuse. Newly formed French Sixth Army (Maunoury) takes over from d'Amade on Allied left in Somme valley. BEF (1180 cas) reaches St Quentin (2 bns prevented from surrendering there). Moltke radios orders (French intercept) for general advance, Kluck towards lower Seine. **Flanders** — British RM bde lands at Ostend but re-embark 31 (see 20 Sept). **Meuse** — French Fourth Army blocks German Fourth Army crossings (-28). **Vosges** — Germans enter St Die (see 11 Sept).	Conrad 'The German victories are achieved at our cost': **E Prussia** — François smashes Russian I Corps & turns Samsonov's left taking Soldau. Rennenkampf ordered to help, his 1st Cav Div captures Korschen rail jctn. **Poland** — Austrian Fourth Army takes Zamosc, but Don Cossacks rout 2 Austrian cav divs 6-10 miles. **Galicia** — Russians capture Tarnopol & Halicz (on Dniester).	Austrian Gen Rohr, put i/c Italian Front (SW Front). **Italy** — Foreign Minister Di San Giuliano disagrees with Cadorna's argument (& 23, 28) that early Italian mobilization & military intervention could decide the war. (c) War Minister vetoes scheme to add 7500 officers to Army (see 1 Sept).	German Gen Liman made C-in-C Turk First Army in Thrace. **Tsingtao** — IJN Second Fleet begins blockade & seizes 3 offshore islands, typhoon sinks destroyer (28). **Secret War** — Berlin cables Wangenheim (Constantinople) that 15 Germans ready to leave for Baghdad on Afghan Mission (see 16 Sept).
Fri 28	Kaiser orders advance on Paris. Germans capture Ft Manonviller (Avricourt) and Montmédy. Sir J French at Compiègne. German Third Army advances on Rethel (-29) as French Fourth Army withdraws to Aisne. **Lorraine** — Foch recalled to command 7 divs on Aisne as new Ninth Army on left flank of Fourth Army (29). BEF crosses Somme, withdrawing on Noyon & La Fère (BEF cav cause 300 German cas). Joffre redeploys Fifth Army for counter-attack. **Alsace** — French Belfort garrison advances into Alsace, 11 miles by 10 Sept (see 18 Sept). **Meuse** — Signy-l'Abbaye changes hands 3 times as Dubois' IX Corps stems Hausen's advance on Rethel (Aisne).	**E Prussia** — François drives E for Neidenburg to envelop Samsonov who joins troops & orders general retreat. Rennenkampf occupies Rastenburg. Hindenburg & Ludendorff move HQ to Tannenberg and Goltz's 1st *Landwehr* Div arrives by rail from Schleswig-Holstein. **Poland** — Komarow: Russian V Corps destroys Austrian 15th Div (4000 PoWs & 20 guns) but Austrian XIV Corps (Archduke Joseph Ferdinand) routs Russian 61st Div, taking 40 guns.	Italy reinforces troops covering Friuli in NE (more covering troops deployed from 1 Sept).	
Sat 29	BEF base to be transferred from Le Havre to St Nazaire. Maunoury engages Kluck at Proyart & Rosières. Sir J French and Joffre confer. BEF withdraw from Noyon & La Fère. **Battle of Guise** (German Battle of St Quentin): French Fifth Army counter-attacks Bülow's pursuing Second Army defeats 3 corps (6040 cas). French retire behind R Aisne. Maubeuge comes under systematic bombardment from German heavy guns (-5 Sept qv). Moltke to his wife 'How few suspicions the All-Highest has of the seriousness of the situation'.	**E Prussia** — German pincers (François & Mackensen) meet at Willenburg, 7 miles from frontier (29).		

AFRICAN OPERATIONS 5	SEA WAR 6	AIR WAR 7	INTERNATIONAL EVENTS 8	HOME FRONTS 9
GERMAN COLONY with Maj Döring's surrender of 200 Germans; 800 Africans; 3 MGs & 1000+ rifles at Kamina; radio stn destroyed (25). Allied losses 120+. Togo partitioned (31).	ships (16) caught coaling & sunk by British cruiser *Highflyer* at Rio del Oro off W Africa. **N Sea** — 2 German minelayers carry out several night drops this week off Tyne & Humber (394 mines) (*see* Sept). **Baltic** — German cruiser *Magdeburg* runs aground (later scuttled) on Odensholm I (Gulf of Finland entrance), shelled by **Russian cruisers** *Pallada* & *Bogatyr* which take prisoners & **recover priceless SKM codebooks** & cipher tables (copy to Churchill, told by Russian naval attaché 6 Sept, at Admiralty via cruiser HMS *Theseus* 13 Oct 1914). Germans merely change key afterwards, do not learn of loss till 1918.	Staff Capt Pet-Kesterov k when his Morane Type monoplane deliberately rams & destroys one of 3 2-seater raiders over his Sholkiv, Galicia base; Austrian Lt Baron von Rosenthal & Nesterov both k, **first Austrian air cas. W Front** — BE2 (Pretyman & Boyd-Moss) of No 3 Sqn flies armed recon of Le Cateau, Valenciennes & Cambrai, drops single bomb on parked motor transport nr Blaugies village, but hit by small arms fire W of Cambrai crew land, burn plane & join French cav retreating towards Arras; eventually rejoin sqn.	to enter war.	**France** — Gallieni replaces Michel as Paris Military Governor.
	Pacific — Anglo-Japanese blockade of Kiaochow Bay (Tsingtao) begins (-7 Nov *see* TURK FRONTS). Japanese Second Fleet uses 4 dreadnoughts, 4 battlecruisers, 13 cruisers, 24 destroyers, 4 gunboats & 13 minesweepers. **N Sea — Battle of the**	**W Front** — RNAS Eastchurch Sqn (10 aircraft) lands at Ostend, Belgium under W/Cdr Samson (-30) moves to Dunkirk & ordered to stay (1 Sept) for anti-Zeppelin ops & recon for French.	British censorship of mails begins.	**France** — Viviani Cabinet reshuffle: Briand, Deputy PM, Millerand War Minister (replaces Messimy), Delcassé Foreign Minister. *The Times* Paris correspondent reports 'The Belgian Baby Without Hands' atrocity story. **Britain** — First of 6000 'Jellicoe Special' Grand Fleet coal trains run. Germany — Victory communiqué says 'the enemy, in full retreat, is unable to offer serious resistance'.
	Heligoland Bight: RN total 5 battlecruisers, 8 cruisers, 31 destroyers; British Battlecruiser Force (Beatty) gives effective support during sweep by Harwich Force (flagship *Arethusa* damaged). German cruisers *Mainz*, *Köln* & *Ariadne* & a destroyer *V187* sunk, 3 more cruisers damaged (1162 cas to RN's 75). Adm Tirpitz's son among 381 PoWs (*see* 10 Sept). German battlecruisers leave port too late to help. Adm Milne (ignominiously			**Germany** — 1st Pan-German Exec Ctee lays down *Mittel-Europa* victory plans (*see* 9 Sept).
Cameroons — 600 Nigerians, 5 MGs & 2 guns (63 cas) beaten at Garua by 2 German coys, retreat to Tepe (-30). British Calabar col occupies Archibong on coast. Belgians agree to help French (28).	recalled from Med after *Goeben /Breslau* affair) takes up Thames sinecure command at the Nore. **Atlantic** — German cruiser	**Germany** — Philipp appointed Chief of German Naval Flying Units. **W Front** — German aircraft drops 3 bombs on RFC Compiègne airfield (no damage, *see* 1 Sept).		**Canada** — Princess Patricia's Canadian Light Infantry sails for England. **Britain** — TUC says war for 'Freedom and unfettered democracy'.

AUGUST 1914	WESTERN FRONT 1	EASTERN FRONT 2	SOUTHERN FRONTS 3	TURKISH FRONTS 4
Sun 30	BEF III Corps (Pulteney) formed. Mangin & Pétain promoted div cdrs in Fifth Army (*see* I Sept). Joffre replaces Ruffey (Third Army) with Sarrail and orders further retreat towards R Seine. Kluck starts wheeling from Amiens towards R Oise in support of Bülow who allows 36 hrs rest. Germans reach Noyon, La Fère & Laon and cross the R Meuse. German GHQ transferred from Koblenz to Luxembourg. **Lorraine** — French Second Army makes some gains around Luneville (-31,*see* 2 Sept).	**E Prussia** — Samsonov shoots himself. German 'Day of Harvesting' prisoners. Russian Gen Sirelius retakes Neidenburg. **Poland** — Dankl takes Krasnostav 40 miles inside Poland. Austrian Third Army takes many PoWs & 60 guns, threatens to encircle Russian Fifth Army but retreat ordered. **Galicia** — 14 Austrian divs & 828 guns on R Gnila Lipa lose 20,000 men & 70 guns in 18-mile rout by 22 Russian divs & 1304 guns (-1 Sept).	**Herzegovina** — Austrians drive Montenegrins back into their own country (-2 Sept).	**Armenia** — Zeitum rebels v Turk conscription (60 captured). **SW Pacific** — NZ force (1363) occupies German Samoa Is, landing at Apia.
Mon 31	French stand on line R Aisne-Reims-Verdun. Germans take Givet. **Kluck**, under orders to protect German right (W) flank & Bülow's exposed flank (on his left), **begins to move SE across Paris front** to aid Bülow against d'Esperey. Germans discount the BEF crossing Aisne as a 'spent force' despite 2 cav actions. German Naval Corps (Adm Schröder) formed to garrison Liège (& later Flanders coast). Austrian Skoda howitzers bombard Givet. **Lorraine** — **Battle of the Grande Couronne of Nancy** (-11 Sept).	**E Prussia** — Germans retake Neidenburg. Russian 1st Cav Div just disengages from raid on Allenstein (- 1 Sept). **Poland** — Russian Fifth Army evades trap but loses 40% incl 8 generals. **Galicia** — Austrian line broken nr Halicz. Austrian Aug deaths 15% of 1914 losses. Grand Duke Nicholas orders Ivanov to destroy Austrians.	**Italy** — (Aug) Garibaldi's son and grandson, between them veterans of the Franco-Prussian War, 2 Greco-Turk wars & Boer War, raised 14,000-strong Italian Legion to fight for France (*see* W FRONT 26 Dec).	**Egypt** — Egyptian Camel Corps ordered to Suez Canal. **Secret War** — Churchill & Kitchener agree on joint planning v Turkey.
Tue 1 September 1914	**France** — **Germans take Soissons & Craonne**. Pétain takes over 6th Inf Div (Gen Bloch removed). Kitchener and Sir J French confer at Paris; Maunoury put under Gallieni. Action at Néry: British take 8 guns & PoWs after surprised 'L' Bty RHA (3 VCs) fights to last, 2 other BEF actions.	**Poland** — Russian retreat to-wards R Bug. **Galicia** — Austri-ans beaten before Lemberg, but Conrad orders Second & Fourth Armies to attack Russian flanks. Cossacks stampede Austrian 11th Cav Div 12 miles.	**Italy** — Cadorna has decided on Isonzo offensive strategy, not dealing with Trentino be-forehand (*see* 16).	British Admiralty & War Office discuss Gallipoli landing (-5).
Wed 2	**France** — **Germans reach the Marne and occupy Laon**. Moltke orders Kluck to echelon his troops behind Bülow's. Both Kluck & Bülow disobey & continue divergent advances which French Fifth Army patrol captures maps of. Gallieni (Military Governor of Paris) detects this vital development (3). Foch gains touch with Fifth Army. First German occupation of Lille (-6). **Lorraine** — Castelnau sends 3 divs to W on Joffre's orders following a cav div & chasseur bde (1).	**Poland** — Austrian Fourth Army (13 divs & 558 guns) checked before Lublin by Russian Fourth & Ninth Armies (14 divs & 900 guns). **Galicia** — Routed Austrians evacuate Lemberg with loss of 130,000 men.		British Cabinet decides 'to sink Turkish ships if they issue from the Dardanelles' (*see* 27). **Ts-ingtao** — First of 23,980 Japanese troops (18th Div+) & 154 guns (Lt-Gen Kamio) land 150 miles NE on Shantung Peninsula at Lungkow Bay (*see* 13).
Thu 3	**France** — German cav at Ecouen **8 miles from Paris** (*see* AIR WAR). Battle of the Mortagne ends. **Lanrezac sacked, Franchet d'Esperey replaces him.** BEF crosses R Marne. Bülow occupies Reims. French composer Alberic Magnard k aged 49 in his burning house nr Senlis having	**Galicia** — RUZSKI OCCUPIES LEMBERG, capital of province, captures much booty, organizes govt (4).	**Hungary** — Gen Krauss of Austrian 29th Div warned of imminent Serb Sava crossing below Mitrovica (*see* 6).	

AFRICAN OPERATIONS 5	SEA WAR 6	AIR WAR 7	INTERNATIONAL EVENTS 8	HOME FRONTS 9
E Africa — British evacuate Vangel on coastal border.		FIRST CAPITAL CITY BOMBED: Paris bombed by German Taube monoplane (Hiddessen): four 4.4lb bombs & unopened bag of leaflets dropped between Gare du Nord & Gare de l'Est. Civ cas: 3 (1 woman k) (*see* 1 Sept).	Germany makes Belgian Govt responsible for Louvain's sacking. Belgian Mission leaves for US (*see* 16 Sept).	**France** — Seine-et-Marne Prefect says German atrocity stories demoralizing people, War Minister tells editors not to detail them. **Britain** — Alarming *Times* BEF retreat report. Govt publishes anonymous rebuttal (by Churchill) 5 Sept.
SE Cameroons — 375 French in 3 steamers from Bonga occupy Wesso on border, others hold line of R Lobaye. **S Africa** — 2500 SA troops (Lukin) land at Port Nolloth to cover Cape Province N border v SW Africa (*see* 9 Sept).	*Karlsruhe* sinks British *SS Strathroy* 100 miles off Brazil. 3 AMCs commissioned to reinforce Northern Patrol (Aug). **Far East** — Rear-Adm Jerram (China Sqn) arrives Singapore, sends his 3 cruisers to search Dutch E Indies for 22 German merchant ships (-13 Sept). **Red Sea** — (Aug) 2 RN cruisers capture 2 German merchantmen.	**W Front** — RFC recon reports warn BEF German First Army wheeling towards SE on line Compiègne-Noyon.	**Greece formally declares neutrality. Britain** — Cabinet meets & decides to send Kitchener to France.	**Germany** — Falkenhayn makes Wandel Deputy War Minister. Unemployment 22.4%. **Britain** — Intoxicating Liquor (Temporary Restriction) makes 5-6am opening 8-9am (*see* 4 Sept). All-Party Recruiting Ctee formed on day **record 30,000 enlist. France** — 43% **record unemployment**. Under 50% industry open eg Renault closed.
E Africa — First 780 Indian troops reach Mombasa, 29th Punjabis (*see* 6).	**Secret War** (Sept) — Sir A Ewing gets permission for first of 14 RN home signal intercept stns (at Hunstanton Coastguard Stn, Norfolk). Overseas stns later at Otranto, Malta & Ancona. Ewing has 6 cryptanalysts by mid-Oct (*see* 8 Nov). **N Sea** — Rear-Adm Charlton put i/c minesweeping on E coast (main base Lowestoft). U-boat false alarm drives Grand Fleet to L Ewe anchorage W of Scotland, recalled 7 (*see* 17). **Adriatic** — French battleships shell Austrian Cattaro forts (*see* 18).	**France** — A Taube bombs Paris (4 civ cas). **W Front** — RFC pilot drops 2 bombs stampeding German cav at a crossroads N of Villers-Cotterêts.	**Colombia neutral.**	**Russia** — **St Petersburg renamed Petrograd** to avoid sounding German. **Germany** — (Sept) 40% unemployment in Nuremburg (pencil export industry collapse). (Sept) Ernst Lissauer's 'Hymn of Hate' v England published. **Britain** — (Sept) Women's Hospital Corps leaves to take over Claridge's Hotel, Paris.
Nigeria — Gov-Gen Lugard returns from England, confines troops to frontier.	**Pacific** — Japanese landing at Shantung.	**E Front** — Russian air recon reports many Austrian trains leaving Lemberg to W.	**Neutrals : USA** — Treasury Bureau of War Risk Shipping Insurance formed.	**France** — **Govt leaves Paris for Bordeaux** at Joffre's request (*see* 18 Nov). **Germany** — Berlin: First captured French & Russian guns paraded. Catholic Centre Party leader Erzberger's memo to Govt, Germany to control Europe for 'all time' (*see* 9). **Britain** — Masterman (Chancellor of Duchy of Lancaster) confers with literary figures & 6 newspaper editors (7) to discuss propaganda organization; set up Wellington House, London. Kipling's first war poem 'For All We Have and Are' published in *The Times*.
	N Sea — Torpedo gunboat HMS *Speedy* sunk by mine off Humber.	**W Front** — RFC recon warns that Kluck's First Army again wheeling to left, closely monitors Kluck as he marches into a Marne salient between French Fifth & Sixth Armies. French pilots Bellinger (*Esc 313*) & Watteau (Paris Entrenched Camp) independently discover that Germans	France informs US she will observe London Declaration with modifications. **Neutrals : Italy** — Pope Benedict XV elected. Fleet sails to Taranto.	**France** — Paris Bourse closes. **Britain** — Q Mary starts Work for Women Fund (-24 Feb 1915).

SEPTEMBER 1914	WESTERN FRONT 1	EASTERN FRONT 2	SOUTHERN FRONTS 3	TURKISH FRONTS 4
Thu 3 contd	shot 2 Uhlans.			
Fri 4	**France** — Gallieni begins to reinforce Maunoury NE of Paris. Joffre, convinced by Gallieni telephone call, issues orders at 2200 for counter-offensive on 6 'to profit by the adventurous position of the First German Army'. BEF receives 20,000 replacements (-5). Foch orders civilian refugees off roads till 1500. Kluck's nearest railhead, St Quentin, 85 miles from front line, Hausen's same distance, and Bülow's 105 miles. Kluck & Hausen report units close to physical collapse. BATTLE OF THE GRANDE COURONNE (Nancy) rages with record German shelling (-11) in Kaiser`s presence: Castelnau & Dubail repulse furious German assaults (-7) on GC by Rupprecht (co-ordinator of Sixth & Seventh Armies (*see* 8).	**Poland** — Goltz's 2¹/2 German divs from E Prussia seize Mlawa.	**Bosnia** — Serb 2nd Sumaja Div storms Goles Height SE of Visegrad. **Albania** — Prince William leaves, Int'l Commission of Control takes over at Durazzo (*see* 13 & 27).	Turk Ambassador to France warns (& 28) 'Germany is isolated and doomed to defeat'.
Sat 5	FIRST BATTLE OF THE MARNE (-10) — Battle of the Ourcq: Maunoury (8 divs) surprise midday attack on Kluck's IV Res Corps (Gronau) nr Monthyon. 200-mile, 13-day BEF RETREAT FROM MONS ENDS. GERMANS REACH CLAYE, 10 MILES FROM PARIS. *GQG* reopens at Châtillon-sur-Seine, Joffre visits Sir J French at Melun & secures BEF participation. French nationalist poet & publisher Lt Charles-Pierre Peguy (276th Inf, Sixth Army) k aged 41. German inf storm 4 Maubeuge forts (-6,*see* 7).	Conrad agrees with Francis Joseph's military cabinet chief that Berlin has left them in the lurch. **E Prussia** — BATTLE OF MASURIAN LAKES (-15, *see* 7). **Poland** — Russian Fifth Army defeats Austrian II Corps (Fourth Army) at Tomashov.		
Sun 6	**Marne** — Kluck orders 2 of his 4 corps advancing SE of Paris to force march to aid IV Res Corps (Lt Juin, future marshal, w with opposing Moroccan Bde), later recalls the other 2 corps thus opening **30-mile gap between his army & Bülow's into which BEF & French Fifth Army advance. Germans reach Provins, 8 miles from Seine, southern-most point.** Foch battles to hold Marshes of St Gond v Bülow & Hausen (-7); Villeneuve changes hands 3 times. **Lorraine** — German Seventh Army disbanded, 1 corps sent W to R Ourcq, 2 put under Sixth Army. French 72nd Res Div from Verdun sorties to effect. **Alsace** — French Belfort Gap covering troops link with 58th Div at Thann, occupy 3 villages (9), but retreat to frontier after Gen Gäde's attack (11), return to occupy Dannemarie (18) for duration.	**Poland** — Dankl's centre broken at Krasnostav on R Vyeprj S of Lublin. **Battle of Grodek** SW of Lemberg (-12): Brusilov v Austrians whose Second Army panics after vain attacks from S. **Austrians dig trenches (esp 9-10).**	Serbs make 2 barge night crossings (from 0100) of the Sava E of Mitrovica & at Kupinovo loop into Serb-populated Syrmia. **Hungary** — Krauss' Austrians capture 5000 men of Serb 1st Timok Div trying to recross Sava (pontoon bridge never finished), but Serbs at Kupinovo make firm bridgehead v *Landsturm*, capturing 2 villages.	Zimmermann cables Constantinople Ambassador Wangenheim to '...incite unrest in Arabia, N Africa & Persian Gulf'. **Armenia** — Turk Third Army informed that Van Armenians contacting Russians (*see* 11 Oct). Govt sends coded circular to Armenian-populated provinces requiring leaders' supervision.
Mon 7	**Marne** — Maunoury in great peril; Gallieni embusses 6000 reserves (bde of 7th Div) & rushes them in 600 Paris motor taxicabs ('Taxis of the Marne') 18¹/2 miles to the Ourcq (night 7/8) with others by road/rail.	**E Prussia** — François (40 bns & 200 guns, -11) routs 16 bns & 30 guns (XXII Finnish Corps) from Biala area (*see* 9). **Galicia** — Battle of Tarnarka (-9), Dankl beaten, orders retreat to San (9). Reformed Russian	**Second Austrian offensive** (night 7/8) along R Drina with 4 corps, only gains N bridgehead at Parasbnitsa in Sava loop for 4000 cas (Fifth Army). **Hungary** — Serb Cav Div up to 13 miles N of Kupinovo	

AFRICAN OPERATIONS 5	SEA WAR 6	AIR WAR 7	INTERNATIONAL EVENTS 8	HOME FRONTS 9
		have wheeled SE **away** from Paris defences & towards the Marne. **Britain** — Admiralty to handle home air defence.		
Cameroons — Cruiser HMS *Cumberland* lands party at Victoria (-5). Nigerian flotilla (8 ships) joins (6).			Germany agrees to London Declaration if other belligerents do; issues contraband list. Asquith Guildhall banquet speech justifies Britain's entry into war (German Chancellor replies 13).	**Britain** — London pub closing 11pm instead of 1230 (*see* 19 Oct).
N Rhodesia — c116 Germans repulsed from Abercorn & retreat (9). Belgian bn arrives (22-25). Over 4800 British troops in E Africa with 5000-strong carrier corps by 11 (begun 13 Aug). **L Nyasa** — Armed steamer *Gwendolen* captures German port of Old Langenburg.	**N Sea** — British cruiser *Pathfinder* (259 lives lost) sunk off Firth of Forth by *U21* (Hersing), **first warship victim of a submarine in open sea** (*see* 22).	**Britain** — First night patrol over London by British plane: Lts Grahame-White & Gates, in RNAS Farman (*see* 22). **W Front** — (c) BEF Corps cdrs assigned RFC sqn each with radio plane in each. **E Front** — Lemberg: Russian gunfire brings down Zeppelin *L5* & crew of 30 captured (6).	LONDON AGREEMENT PLEDGES ALLIES TO NO SEPARATE PEACE. **Neutrals : Switzerland** — Lenin & family arrive in Berne. **Austria** — Foreign Ministry official '... afraid of the humiliating necessity of the Germans having to save us' (*see* 8).	**'Your Country Needs You' recruiting poster first published** in *London Opinion* weekly magazine; 174,901 enlist during week. Thomas Hardy poem '*Men Who March Away*' composed.
Cameroons — 220 British (62 escape) beaten by 500 Germans (126 cas) who take 2 guns & 5 MGs at Nsanakang. French from Gabon beaten at Mibang. **E Africa** — 200 Germans beaten nr Tsavo; **Indian troops first engaged.**			Kaiser's proclamation to French people drafted ready for Joffre's anticipated armistice request.	**Belgium** — Lt-Gen Deguise made Gov of Antwerp. Tilbury-Antwerp refugee boat service begins (8).
	Pacific — Spee arrives at Christmas I: his detached cruiser *Nürnberg* cuts Pacific cable between Banfield & Fanning I.			**Japan** — Diet votes $26.5m war credit. **Canada** — Shell Ctee first meets; 32,449 troops parade at Valcartier Camp (8, *see* 23).

SEPTEMBER 1914	WESTERN FRONT 1	EASTERN FRONT 2	SOUTHERN FRONTS 3	TURKISH FRONTS 4
Mon 7 contd	BEF's advance, delayed by Kluck's armed car screen & picked detachments, now reaches R Petit Morin in the 'gap'. D'Esperey pushes back Bülow's right wing 6 miles. Moltke to his wife 'This day is the decisive day'. **France — Fall of Maubeuge** with 40,000 PoWs and 377 guns (l4 forts) just as German shells almost exhausted (*see* 13).	Fifth Army resumes advance. Russian cav reaches Carpathians.	bridgehead.	
Tue 8	**Marne** — Struggle continues on the Ourcq; each side strives to outflank the other. As German corps begin to arrive from Maubeuge, Maunoury's N flank guard wavers. Gallieni again rushes up reinforcements to save day. BEF crosses R Petit Morin, attacks La Ferté-sous-Jouarre; British guns pound bridges crowded with Kluck's troops. D'Esperey also crosses R Petit Morin, captures Montmirail & threatens to roll up Bülow's whole front. Foch yields 3-4 miles to furious counterattcks by Bülow & Hausen. **Meuse** — Germans shell small Ft Troyon (-12) SE of Verdun on river but cav div relieves it (10). **Lorraine** — French 59th Res Div retakes Ste Genevieve village N of Nancy, count 2000 German k. **Belgium** — Lt-Gen Deguise becomes Cdt of Fortress of Antwerp.	Francis Joseph urges C-in-C Archduke Frederick not to punish defeated generals heavily 'because today's unlucky commander may well be victorious tomorrow'. **Poland** — Woyrsch's Silesian *Landwehr* Corps loses 8000 men & forced over R Vistula. **E Prussia** — Russian II Corps holds Lötzen Gap. **Galicia** — **Second Battle of Lemberg** (-11). Fierce fighting around Ravarusska 32 miles NW of Lemberg, Austrian Fourth Army (Auffenberg) being beaten; Brusilov's XXIV Corps takes Mikolajow.	**Serbia** — Austrian Sixth Army forces Drina at 2 points incl Zvornik (night 8/9) driving Serbs back gradually to Guchevo & its adjoining ridges, gaining 8 miles by 11 (*see* 12).	**Egypt** — Lt-Gen Sir John Maxwell GOC British forces. **Turkey** — About 800 Germans have arrived since *Goeben* .
Wed 9	**Marne** — GERMAN RETREAT BEGINS in high winds & drenching rain: Col Hentsch, Head of Foreign Armies (Intelligence) Dept at GHQ — Moltke's peripatetic 'trou-bleshooter' — arrives by car at Bülow's HQ, Bülow learns BEF have crossed R Marne. Kluck continues determined efforts to crush Maunoury, retaking Nanteuil. Shortly before 1200 Hentsch reaches Kluck's HQ & tells Kluck that, since Bülow now being forced back towards R Vesle & Kluck's own army at risk of double envelopment, a coordinated retreat to the Aisne is necessary. Kluck issues retreat order at 1100. BEF pushes 4 miles N of the Marne, d'Esperey gives Foch X Corps & issues inspirational Order of the Day to Fifth Army. Sir J French orders BEF to continue pursuit at 0500. Joffre orders a combined attack; the BEF moving NE with its left on Soissons; d'Esperey, on its right, to reach R Marne & establish bridgehead at Château-Thierry, Maunoury, on left, is to push N & envelop German right. Though these orders issued at 0145, Maunoury only starts 1400-1600 as air scouts detect German columns in retreat. Kluck, trying to pass NE across Allied front to regain touch with Bülow has running fights with BEF advance guard & has to reroute his forces. **Belgium** — Kaiser orders capture of Antwerp; Gen Beseler put i/c siege ops (*see* 17). RN	**E Prussia** — François cuts off Russians before Lötzen, taking 60 guns & 5000 PoWs, having marched 77 miles in 4 days (*see* 13). **Galicia** — Both sides attack in widest fighting yet. Conrad drives to Grodek.	**Hungary** — Serbs capture 2 villages W of Belgrade (-10) after heavy fighting. Belgrade garrison occupies Semlin opposite (10). **Bosnia** — Montenegrins again invade, capturing Visegrad (14, see 23). **Serbia** — Hungarian composer (Bartok contempo-rary) Aladár Radó kia at Boljevci, R Sava, aged 32.	**Egypt** — Turk Govt abolishes 'The Capitulations' (from 1 Oct) allowing self-governing nations within Empire eg Egypt in theory, & foreigners immunity from control. IEF'A' begins arriving at Suez (*see* 19). **Secret War** — Adm Mark Kerr (C-in-C Greek Navy) reports to Churchill (who asked on 4), Greeks can take Gallipoli if *Bulgaria* joins in attack. **C Pacific** — Cruiser HMAS *Melbourne* occupies Nauru I, destroys German radio stn.

AFRICAN OPERATIONS 5	SEA WAR 6	AIR WAR 7	INTERNATIONAL EVENTS 8	HOME FRONTS 9
S Africa — Lord Buxton made Gov-Gen.	**N Sea** — AMC *Oceanic* wrecked & lost off Shetlands. Battlecruiser Sqn & Harwich Force sweep an empty Heligoland Bight. **Indian Ocean** — *Emden* begins spectacular raiding cruise (23 merchant ships sunk or captured) with prize neutral Greek collier *Pontoporos*, sinks 11 British merchantmen (10-27), ties down 14 Allied warships in her pursuit.	**W Front** — Roeckel & Châtelain on arty observation over Vaubecourt sector (Marne) enable French guns to silence half the German XVI Corps arty.	Belgian protests v German occupation atrocities. Count Berchtold instructs Austrian Berlin Ambassador to hint at separate peace if German help not forthcoming.	**Britain** — Chancellor Lloyd George 'silver bullet' speech on need for economies. War costing est £5m pd (12). *The Times* reports pigeon spy mania. Christabel Pankhurst tells London suffragettes women should be used to the full. Bankers Cox & Co open Enquiry Office in London for w BEF officers' relatives (-1 Feb 1919). **France** — Civil Food Supply Service formed.
Morocco — Neighbouring German consulates carry Kaiser's pledge that French Muslim PoWs will be sent to Caliph (Sultan) at Constantinople. **S Africa** — PM Botha announces SW Africa expedition to Parlt (sails 15, *see* 18).			**German Chancellor's secret 'Sept Programme' lists massive war aims. Kaiser's pro-Muslim proclamation**, Muslim PoWs will be sent to Caliph (Sultan at Con-stantinople). In Commons Pres of Local Govt Board, H Samuel, offers British hospitality to Belgium, Local Govt dept formed.	**Germany — 1st War Loan opens**; thereafter 6-monthly.

SEPTEMBER 1914	WESTERN FRONT 1	EASTERN FRONT 2	SOUTHERN FRONTS 3	TURKISH FRONTS 4
Wed 9 contd	armoured train (6 x 4.7-in guns) joins Belgians as they make 2nd sortie (-13) with 6 divs advancing up to 15 miles (forcing German IX Res Corps to halt march S), but incurring 8000 cas (*see* 22). **Lorraine** — French night attack fails but VIII Corps advances back to R Meurthe (12).			
Thu 10	FIRST BATTLE OF THE MARNE ENDS: Joffre orders hot pursuit ('victory is now in the legs of the infantry') of Kluck; Maunoury links with BEF. French X Corps marches 12 miles. **First British general k**, Brig-Gen N Findlay lst Div CRA by shellfire. Formal op orders issued by German GHQ at 1630 confirm retirement from the Marne: Second Army sent behind R Vaste; Kluck demoted & placed under Bülow`s orders, which are to fall back behind R Aisne; Third, Fourth & Fifth Armies to continue to hold 'quiet' line Reims-Verdun.	**E Prussia** — Rennenkampf covers retreat (95 miles in 50 hrs) by counter-attack, evacuates Insterburg. **Poland — Second Battle of Krasnik**, Dankl beaten, also Archduke Joseph at Opole (40,000/ 50,000 men lost). **Galicia** — Dragomirov's Cav Corps & Plehve's Fifth Army turn Auffenberg's left. Charge by 7 sqns of Kaledin's 12th Cav Div checks Austrian Second Army attack after it outflanks Kornilov's 48th Div (26 guns lost) on Brusilov's S flank.		**Egypt** — Central Powers representatives expelled.
Fri 11	ALLIED PURSUIT CONTIN-UES TO THE R AISNE (-12). Foch reaches Châlons-sur-Marne & Maunoury Com-piègne. Joffre cables Govt in Bordeaux 'The Battle of the Marne is an incontestable victory for us'; **Vosges** — French XIV Corps reoccupies St Dié. **Secret War** — French present BEF Intelligence with first 15 homing pigeons.	**Galicia** — Brusilov closes in on Grodek. **Conrad orders general Austrian retreat** in pouring rain at 1730 behind R San after Auffenberg extricates Fourth Army thanks to radio intercepts. He also moves a bde by motor vehicles (12-13), but is soon replaced by Archduke Joseph Ferdinand.	**Hungary** — Austrians entrenched behind Roman Canal in Syrmia, Serbs have penetrated 20 miles. **Bosnia** — Montenegrins break through at Foca to make deep raids (*see* 23).	**German New Guinea** — c600 Australians land unopposed but skirmishes inland.
Sat 12	FIRST BATTLE OF THE AISNE (-28) begins: by 0300 British 11th Bde after 30-mile march scrambles across river at Venizel (3 miles E of Soissons) by damaged bridge & finds Germans on heights above as do French 45th Div. **French I Corps retakes Reims.** Bülow to command German right wing (First, Second & Seventh Armies), Einem replaces ill Hausen i/c Third Army. BATTLE OF THE GRANDE COURONNE ENDS, French 74th Res Div 5140+ cas since 24 Aug.	**E Prussia** — Russians evacuate Tilsit. Germans reach Wirballen and Suvalki across Russian frontier. **Poland/ Galicia** — Grodek falls as Austrians retreat over R San (6 bridges) under heavy fire (*see* 14).	**Hungary** — Serb First Army storm Jarak by the Sava but news from Drina halts advance in evening & leads to methodical unimpeded retreat back to Serbia (14, *see* 18). **Serbia** — Austrian XIII Corps crosses Drina at Kuriachista (night 12/13) threatening Jadar Valley from N & beginning complex struggle for wooded, mountainous summits.	**German New Guinea** — Australians occupy Rabaul & Herbertshohe, formal takeover (13, *see* 21).
Sun 13	**Aisne** — Main body of BEF & parts of French Sixth & Fifth armies cross the river & up to 7 miles beyond. **Germans escape disaster by an hour:** 10-mile gap between Kluck & Bülow's armies N of the river, just closed by arrival at 1430 of XV Corps from Alsace & VII Res Corps (after 40-mile march in 24 hrs) from Maubeuge. Only Conneau's Cav Corps succeeds in entering gap, but quickly retires. Falkenhayn (new German CoS) can now discard his worst case plan to withdraw 40 miles further N to line of R Oise. French reoccupy Soissons & Amiens.	**E Prussia** — Russian rearguard delays German pursuit at Vilkoviski, moves back over border, but destroyed there (15).	**Albania** — Italian troops land at Valona (Adriatic port) (*see* 27).	**Tsingtao** — Japanese seize Kiaochao railway stn; China protests. **SW Pacific** — Australians occupy Bougain-ville in Solomons.
Mon 14	**Aisne** — Despite major efforts (BEF I Corps capture 12 guns), Allies unable to enlarge much their shallow bridgeheads across the river v GERMAN TRENCHES. MOLTKE	STAVKA orders all radio messages in cipher, but Austrian Capt Pokorny cracks it by 19 (*see* 25). **Poland/ Galicia** — Russians hold Drohobycz oilfields & cross R		Enver authorizes Adm Souchon to act v Russia in Black Sea, but colleagues force compromise (20); can sail but no Turk responsibility.

AFRICAN OPERATIONS 5	SEA WAR 6	AIR WAR 7	INTERNATIONAL EVENTS 8	HOME FRONTS 9
E Africa — 300 Germans occupy Karungu nr L Victoria, theaten Kisii, but 300 British force German retreat (13), retiring as well.			Kaiser cables US Pres Wilson 'my heart bleeds' for Belgium, but Belgians to blame. He also condemns Allied use of 'dum dum' bullets.	**Britain** — Commons votes Army a 2nd 500,000 men: **439,000 recruits since 4 Aug** (physical standards raised 11); 12 more New Army divs authorized (11 & 13). **Germany** — 12 *Jäger* bns activated.
				Britain — Churchill speaks at all-Party 'Call to Arms' (London) but Tory Irish Home Rule row stops him speaking at Birmingham (14). Home Office forms Neutral Press Ctee (absorbed into Foreign Office News Dept Feb 1916).
	N Sea — First British submarine success *E9* (Horton), sinks small German cruiser *Hela*, 6 miles SSW of Heligoland (*see* 17 Oct). *E9* returns flying 'skull-and-cross-bones' flag, beginning RN submarine patrol tradition.	**W Front** — Storms wreck 4 aircraft of No 5 Sqn RFC at Saponay. Sqn of French 16th Dragoons captures German aviation park nr Villers-Cotterêts.		**Russia** — STAVKA cables War Ministry for more munitions (*see* 28). Grand Duke Nicholas notifies Tsar (21).
L Victoria — Tug *Kavirondo* sinks 2 German dhows.				**France** — Treasury to issue National Defence Bonds.
	S Atlantic — 90-minute AMC action: HMS *Carmania* (damaged) sinks German *Cap Trafalgar* coaling off Trinidada (Brazilian I). **Pacific** — Spee arrives at Samoa but finds		*The Times* Washington correspondent '... American correspondents are doing all the special pleading that can be wanted'.	**Britain** — King and Queen visit wounded officers at Princess Henry of Battenberg's Hospital, London.

SEPTEMBER 1914	WESTERN FRONT 1	EASTERN FRONT 2	SOUTHERN FRONTS 3	TURKISH FRONTS 4
Mon 14 contd	RESIGNS AS GERMAN COS; SUCCEEDED BY FALKEN-HAYN but not made public till 3 Nov. Foch's Ninth Army unable to cross Reims-St Menehould road (-15) & lacks arty to capture Moronvillers heights (16-17). **Lorraine** — Lt de Lattre (12th Dragoons, 2nd Cav Div) kills 2 Bav Uhlans with his sword, but suffers lance wound W of Pont-à-Mousson (Moselle), awarded Legion of Honour aged 25.	San at mouth in pursuit. Lechitski's Ninth Army retakes Sandomir on Vistula.		
Tue 15	**First Battle of the Aisne**: At 0115 Joffre cables army cdrs: 'It seems...the enemy is...going to accept battle, in prepared positions N of the Aisne . ....it is no longer a question of pursuit, but of methodical attack'. Stalemate continues, Maunoury unable to outflank the German right (W), reinforced by IX Res Corps (from Antwerp) with a corps & Conneau`s cav as instructed, but maintains pressure on German flank nr Noyon (-16). First German orders to conserve ammo due to low shell stocks; 26,000 railway troops working on captured line, but only 300-400 miles working in Belgium (*see* 22).	**E Prussia** — Battle of Masurian Lakes ends (*see* 18). Russians prepare to resist on Niemen. **Bukovina** — Russians occupy capital Czernowitz (*see* 22 Oct).	Serb First Army begins to reinforce Drina sector defenders. Serb Uzice Army crosses Upper Drina at 2 points into Bosnia with aim of taking Vlasenica (*see* 28).	
Wed 16	**Aisne** — Sir J French orders BEF to entrench; 6th Div arrives on Aisne. Haig Diary '... our gunners cannot "take on" the enemy's heavy batteries'. British armoured cars (Cdr Samson RNAS) rout Uhlans nr Doullens. French Fifth Army reaches Craonne Plateau.	**New German Ninth Army formed** to cover Silesia between R Oder & Polish frontier (*see* 22). **Galicia** — Russians advance on Przemysl.	Serb counter-attack recaptures some heights around Krupani (-18) before long trench stalemate ensues. Austrians & Krauss Corps gain 2 bridge-heads S of Sava before similar stalemate (*see* 31 Oct). **Italy** — PM Salandra discovers Army's full shortages in arty, officers, winter clothing & horses, it confirms his neutrality policy (*see* 25).	**British Naval Mission leaves Turkey: Turk Army mobilization** (13 corps with 36 divs or c400,000 men, 1000 guns) **virtually complete** in 4 armies. Berlin Conference (-19) on 15-man German mission to Afghanistan, 3 Indians present. Wassmuss leads most of mission to Aleppo by 30 (1st party reaches Constantinople 21,*see* 16 Oct).
Thu 17	**Belgium** — Battle of Malines-Aerschot ends. BELGIAN ARMY RETIRES ON ANTWERP. Gen Beseler's 'Antwerp Army Group' formed. **Somme** — Gen Bridoux new CO French I Cav Corps k in raid on German supply lines E of Péronne (de Mitry takes over 30). **Aisne** — French Sixth Army gains 4 miles between Soissons & Compiègne. British repel Germans W of Chemin-des-Dames. French Fifth Army evacuates Craonne & driven W of Aisne Canal. **Secret War** — Cryptographers attached to each French army HQ (*see* I Oct).	Falkenhayn orders Hindenburg to help Austrians (*see* 22). NW Front C-in-C Jilinski sacked, Ruzski replaces (Radko-Dmitriev takes over Russian Third Army).		
Fri 18	**Aisne** — Joffre orders Maunoury to halt at Soissons-Bailly, pending formation of new Second Army (Castelnau) NW of Noyon. ALLIED ADVANCE STALLS. BEF under heavy pressure at Troyon and French Fifth Army at Reims. GERMAN BOM-BARDMENT OF REIMS (-28): Cathedral 'intensive practice hate' shoots (-Oct 1918).	**Hindenburg C-in-C German armies**. Ludendorff sees Conrad (*see* 22).	**Hungary** — Austrians deport first 516 Serb subjects from recently Serb-invaded Srjem region.	Gen Liman abandons scheme for landing 4 Turk corps at Odessa in Russian rear after Adm Souchon considers it navally untenable. **Tsingtao** — Japanese land unopposed (-19) at Laoshan Bay 30 miles E of port (*see* 23).
Sat 19	**Champagne** — French Fifth Army engaged around Reims (-21).			**Egypt** — 3rd (Lahore) Div of IEF'A' sails for Marseilles (lands there 26).

AFRICAN OPERATIONS 5	SEA WAR 6	AIR WAR 7	INTERNATIONAL EVENTS 8	HOME FRONTS 9
	harbour empty (*see* 22).			
S Africa — REBELLION BEGINS. Rebels meet at Potchestroom; Gen de la Rey accidentally shot dead en route. Cmndt-Gen Beyers resigns, Defence Minister Gen Smuts succeeds. Lt-Col Maritz i/c v German SW Africa refuses Smuts' summons to Pretoria, resigns 25. 1st Rhodesia Regt recruiting begins (*see* 25 Dec). **L Victoria** — SS *Winifred* repulsed from Karungu Bay by German *Mwanza* (7pdr & 2 MGs), finds Germans sailed from Mwanza (16).		**W Front** — Lt Pretyman RFC flys first photorecon mission (5 exposures obtained) over Occupied Belgium.	Zimmermann note to US Berlin Ambassador tries to obtain white truce in Africa. US Advancement of Peace Treaties with France, Britain, Spain & China.	**France** — *Echo de Paris* 'The Wing-beat of victory shall carry our armies to the Rhine'. Paris' 18 car factories, led by Renault, produce 10,000 shells (63,000 pd Jan 1915). **Britain** — Churchill holds Admiralty aircraft conference, 3 firms to build seaplanes. **Germany** — *Kölnische Volkszeitung* tells of Belgian priest machine-gunning Germans in church.
Cameroons — HM Gunboat *Dwarf*, though rammed, sinks armed vessel *Nachtigal* on R Bimbia.		**China** — **First attack on warship by sea-based aircraft**: Japanese Farman launched from seaplane tender *Wakamiya Maru* bombs & damages German minelayer at Tsingtao. **Canada** — Aviation Corps (fore-runner of RCAF) established.	Pres Wilson receives Belgian Mission.	Govt denies rumour that Russians in Britain en route to W Front & announces railway takeover compensation terms.
S Africa — German border raid nr Nakob. **Cameroons** — 57 Nigerian police repel Germans at Takum. Allied force reaches Lagos (*see* 23).	**Home Waters** — Churchill in Grand Fleet conference at L Ewe; Baltic or Heligoland attack ruled out, but Keyes suggests sending 2 submarines into Baltic (*see* 15 Oct). Fleet returns to Scapa (24).			**Australia** — New Labour PM Fisher says Australia will back Britain 'to the last man & to the last shilling'.
SW Africa — 1824 S Africans (Col Beves) occupy evacuated Lüderitz Bay port (*see* 4 Oct).	**Adriatic** — French Naval (Grellier) Mission lands c140 men & 6 guns at Antivari, Montenegro (*see* S FRONTS 19 Oct).			**Britain** — Parlt prorogued after postwar Irish Home Rule bill receives royal assent. Asquith recruiting speech in Edinburgh (Dublin 25). **France** — Education Minister asks all teachers to keep local war records.
	N Sea — Royal Marine Bde lands at Dunkirk (250 already landed 8 with armoured cars).	**Flanders** — RNAS from Dunkirk establish inland airfield at Morbecque 3 miles N of	**Anglo-French guarantee to Belgian colonies.**	**Britain** — Lloyd George 'Ramshackle Empire' recruiting **speech** to London

SEPTEMBER 1914	WESTERN FRONT 1	EASTERN FRONT 2	SOUTHERN FRONTS 3	TURKISH FRONTS 4
Sat 19 contd				
Sun 20	**Meuse** — Crown Prince William launches 3 corps from W of Metz in drive (-25) towards St Mihiel, takes 3 villages & gains on 12-mile front, but repulsed from Ft Troyon. British RM Bde & Oxfordshire Hussars disembark at Dunkirk. **Aisne** — French Second Army reformed NW of Noyon. German VII Res Corps drives Moroccan Div from 3 positions. BEF repulses 3 attacks.	**E Prussia Frontier** — Russians abandon Augustovo; Germans besiege Osovyets fortress (*see* 26). **Poland** — Pouring rain as Gen Novikov's 25,000-strong Cav Corps begins raid N of Vistula, but diverted N from crossing (& his report deciphered 25) by German advance (-6 Oct).		
Mon 21	French reoccupy Noyon & dispute Lassigny (-22). Bavarian III Corps advance on St Mihiel, thus creating salient till Sept 1918 but Sarrail blocks its advance W of Meuse on Bar-le-Duc (-24).	**E Prussia Frontier** — German Eighth Army reaches R Niemen frontier & drives Russians across (24, *see* 26). **Galicia** — Plehve's Fifth Army takes Jaroslav on R San (*see* 11 Oct).		Adm Souchon holds naval review off Constantinople. **German New Guinea** — **German troops surrender**, Australians 10 cas, Germans 42 (*see* 24).
Tue 22	FIRST BATTLE OF PICARDY (-26) begins as French Second Army reach Roye & Montdidier only to be blocked (23). French novelist Lt Alain-Fournier k, aged 27, leading platoon charge at Vaux-les-Palaneix. French bde reoccupies Douai (-1 Oct). **Belgium** — 7 dets (total 700) of Belgian vol cyclists ride out from Antwerp and cut German rail communications in 3 provinces.	**Poland** — New German Ninth Army (250,000) **arriving N of Cracow** (*see* 28); only 2 corps left in E Prussia. Grand Duke Nicholas holds war council at Kholm, regroup on Vistula to entrap Ludendorff and then invade Germany. **Galicia** — Russians approach Przemysl (first shelled 18).		
Wed 23	Rupprecht's Sixth Army completes transfer from Lorraine to Artois (begun 16). **Aisne** — Battlefront extending N along R Oise, fighting nr Lassigny (& 29).		**Bosnia** — **Montenegrins & Serbs briefly threaten Sarajevo** but 2 Austrian mtn bdes sortie vigorously (*see* 27 & 30).	**Secret War: Britain** — Cabinet debate Turk policy. **Tsingtao** — First of 1369 British troops & 250 mules from Tientsin (N China) land at Laoshan to support Japanese (*see* 27).
Thu 24	Germans retake & then lose Péronne on R Somme. **Joffre orders shell economies**, reduces daily issue to 3rpg (27). **Aisne** — BEF's first 6-in howitzers (4 btys) come into action. **Argonne** — Lt Rommel w nr Varennes (*see* 29 Jan 1915), **Belgium** — Joffre requests 3rd Belgian Army sortie but *see* 26.	**Galicia** — **First Siege of Przemysl begins** (- 9 Oct). Ivanov begins secretly withdrawing 3 armies (30 divs) from W of San to E of Vistula for offensive from Poland (-11 Oct).	**Serbia** — Nearly 30,000 Austrian cas since 8 (l Serb div has 6000).	Kitchener orders secret messenger to Sherif of Mecca's son Abdulla. **German New Guinea** — c200 Australians occupy Friedrich Wilhelm (Madang) on mainland.
Fri 25	**Meuse** — Bavarians enter St Mihiel; after storming French Camp-des-Romains. Dubail soon drives them back to outskirts (*see* 29). **Aisne** — German II Corps recaptures Noyon. **Somme** — Battle of Albert begins: Castelnau driven out of Lassigny-Noyon.		**Italy** — Cadorna recognizes no offensive possible before March 1915.	
Sat 26	**Somme** — First Battle of Picardy ends: Castelnau halted at Ribecourt-Roye-Chaulnes-Bray-sur-Somme to await formation of new Tenth Army on his left (*see* 30). German XIV Corps takes Bapaume. British Indian Expeditionary Force begins landing at Marseilles (*see* 23 Oct). **Belgium** — GERMAN SIEGE OF ANTWERP BEGINS (-10 Oct). Malines shelled by German guns. Belgians halt German push 2 miles SW of	**E Prussia Frontier** — Battle of the Niemen (-28), vain German crossing attempts v Russian Tenth Army & vain German assaults on Osovyets till both broken off (29). **Galicia** — Russians occupy Rzeszov on R Wistock but Austrians re-form front E of R Dunajec, 50 miles from Cracow (*see* 7 Oct).		

AFRICAN OPERATIONS 5	SEA WAR 6	AIR WAR 7	INTERNATIONAL EVENTS 8	HOME FRONTS 9
	Adriatic — French sqn shells Cattaro. **E Africa** — British cruiser *Pegasus* surprised & sunk (95 cas) by *Königsberg* at Zanzibar. **Turkey** — Souchon reports Turk Fleet seaworthy but gunnery non-existent. Dardanelles secure now that German experts there (*see* TURK FRONTS 21 & 27).	Hazebrouck.		Welsh. **France** — War Minister asks industrialists at Bordeaux to boost shell production. **Britain** — Women's Imperial Service Hospital (27 staff) leaves for Antwerp to work for Belgian Red Cross.
BSA & Rhodesia police occupy German Caprivi Strip capital (Schuckmannsburg). **Cameroons** — French gunboat *Surprise* lands 600 troops to take Ukoko.	**Atlantic** — Cruiser *Karlsruhe* sinks neutral Dutch SS *Maria* with wheat for Belfast & British SS *Cornish City*.			**Britain** — Churchill recruiting speech to 15,000 at Liverpool, German Navy to be dug out 'like rats in a hole'.
S Africa — Botha C-in-C. **E Africa** — Coast Ft Majoreni repels 300 Germans, but British evacuate to Gazi, 25 miles S of Mombasa (26). German aim is to capture & wreck port from 29 but cruiser *Königsberg* fails to appear (*see* 7 Oct).	**N Sea** — **3 old British cruisers** *Aboukir*, *Cressy* & *Hogue* torpedoed & **sunk within an hr by *U9*** (Weddigen); 1459 dead, 837 rescued by trawlers & Harwich Force. **Indian/Pacific Oceans** — *Emden* (125 shells) bombards Burmah Oil Co facilities, Madras: 50,000t oil set on fire. Spee bombards Papeete (Tahiti); old French gunboat *Zélée* torpedoed.	**Germany** — FIRST BRITISH AIR RAID ON GERMANY: 4 RNAS Tabloids from Antwerp attack Zeppelin sheds at Cologne & Düsseldorf. Flt Lt Collet drops 3 20lb bombs (UXB) at Düsseldorf (*see* 8 Oct). **W Front** — RFC BE2 attempting to bomb kite-balloon intercepted by Albatros 2-seater; pilot w. **Britain** — RNAS airship *Beta* patrols over fog-shrouded London to test visibility of potential Zeppelin targets.		**Britain** — Extra 50 MGs pw ordered from Vickers for French Army.
Cameroons — Cruiser HMS *Challenger* arrives in estuary + 6 transports; 4962 Allied troops & 16 guns + 4356 carriers assemble (-24).				**Britain** — Record gold reserves of £51.6bn. Churchill memo asks for trench-spanning car research, designed within 2 months, but War Office tests reject (*see* 5 Jan). **Canada** — **CEF embarkation begins.**
E Africa : L Kivu — 50 Germans in canoes seize Belgian island. **S Africa** — 2500 S Africans reach Raman's Drift (*see* 26).				
SW Africa — **SA defeat at Sandfontein**: 330 S Africans & 2 guns surrender to 2000 Germans & 10 guns 24 miles inside German colony.	**Aegean** — RN turn back Turk destroyer (Germans on board) to Dardanelles (*see* TURK FRONTS 27).		US State Dept protest v blockade withheld at Col House's suggestion (*see* 28). **Neutrals: Norway** — 11 ships sunk on Archangel route (-4 Oct). **Occupied Belgium** — Germans arrest Brussels Mayor (in Silesian fortress 12 Oct). **France** — **Indian troops land at Marseilles.**	**Britain** — King, Queen & Kitchener inspect 140,000 recruits at Aldershot.

SEPTEMBER 1914	WESTERN FRONT 1	EASTERN FRONT 2	SOUTHERN FRONTS 3	TURKISH FRONTS 4
Sat 26 contd	Dendermonde & Scheldt (-27). **Aisne** — Churchill visits Sir J French. BEF 1st Div action at Chivy. **Meuse** — French repulse attempted German crossing of Meuse at St Mihiel (*see* 29).			
Sun 27	FIRST BATTLE OF ARTOIS (-12 Oct) begins. **Antwerp** — Beseler deploys 125,000 troops incl siege train of 173 guns & technical troops from Maubeuge. Germans re-enter Malines. **Aisne** — Pétain's 6th Div repels furious attacks. **France** — Sir J French asks Joffre to let BEF move N to Flanders (*see* 1 Oct) as Allied I wing for outflanking Germans.		**Albania** — Senate proclaims Prince Burham-ed-Din (son of deposed Turk Sultan Abdul Hamid) Head of Govt (*see* 4 Oct). **Bosnia** — Austrians drive Serb col back to Drina, capturing order revealing threat to Sixth Army rear.	Liman orders Dardanelles closure, German sailors to man batteries (*see* 1 Oct). **Egypt** — 42nd (E Lancs) Territorial Div lands (*see* 30). **Dardanelles** — Turk torpedo boat with German sailors turned back by RN (*see* 1 Oct). **Tsingtao** — Japanese (192 cas) storm key Prince Heinrich Hill in outer defences; 3 German gunboats scuttled (28).
Mon 28	**Belgium** — Germans take Malines. German superheavy howitzers bombard Fts Waelhem & Wavre-Ste Catherine, outer ring of Antwerp, both suffer magazine explosions (29).	**Poland** — New German Ninth Army (Hindenburg) attacks from nr Cracow to aid Austrians. **Carpathians** — Russians seize Dukla & Uzsok Passes & Krosno; cav raid Hungary (*see* 7 Oct).	**Bosnia** — Serbs occupy Vlasenica 40 miles from Sarajevo, but driven back to railway by 4 Oct.	**Mesopotamia** — Lt-Gen Barrett commander-designate of IEF'D' (*see* 14 Nov).
Tue 29	**St Mihiel** — Salient solidifies. **France** — French repulsed nr Roye, Lassigny & Chaulny, French XXI Corps checked before Thiepval (Somme). **Antwerp** — Bombardment intensifies: Fts Koningshoycht, Lierre & Kessel also heavily shelled. Governor Lt-Gen Deguise completes evacuation plans; hold Termonde & W bank of the Scheldte to keep open line of retreat for Belgian field army (100,000 men) (*see* 4 Oct). The evacuation towards Ghent proceeds almost without incident by rail at night (-7 Oct).	Hoffmann diary 'Everything is fine here except for the Austrians! If only the brutes would move.'		**Mesopotamia** — HM sloop *Espiègle* enters Shatt-al-Arab (head of Persian Gulf); AMC *Dalhousie* follows (*see* 7 Oct). **Tsingtao** — Germans repulsed from Prince Heinrich Hill, abandon 5 Kaiser outer forts (30, *see* 8 Oct).
Wed 30	Belgians appeal to Allies for help at Antwerp. **Artois** — French re-enter Arras. Gen Maud'huy given 4 divs & I Cav Corps of Second Army to operate to N (Tenth Army from 4 Oct).	**Poland** — New German Ninth Army advances 10 miles pd v Novikov's cav & entrenches S of Kielce.	**Bosnia** — Indecisive fighting at Vlasenica (- 1 Oct) involves Serb 2nd Sumadija Div (*see* 2, 21 & 30 Oct).	**Egypt** — British regular garrison (4 bns, 1 cav regt, 12 guns) sails for France from Alexandria.
Thu 1 October 1914	TRANSFER OF BEF FROM THE AISNE TO FLANDERS BEGINS (-20) with cav. Bav Res Corps enters Douai driving out 2500 French & RNAS armoured cars. BEF will occupy positions from Bethune to Hazebrouck S of Ypres. **Artois** — Rupprecht reinforced by Prussian Guard Corps. **Somme** — Actions around Roye SW of Péronne. Germans fail to break French line. **Meuse-Argonne** — French destroy German assault bridge over the river. **Antwerp** — Germans capture Ft Waelhem & a redoubt, but Belgian Ist Div counter-attack halts them (noon 2) but fails to retake fort. **Secret War— French break German Army Ubchi radio key;** *GQG* orders no careless talk (3), break new key (21) then Nov ones by 10 Dec.	**E Prussian Frontier** — **Battle of Augustovo** (-9), Russian Tenth Army recovers town & attacks retreating Germans (*see* 20 Sept). **Transylvania** — Austrian Army Corps Pflanzer-Baltin formed, soon transferred to Bukovina (*see* 22).	**Herzovgovina** — (Oct) Irregular fighting around Artovats.	Turkey closes Dardanelles, Col Weber Pasha i/c forts on own initiative later approved; 120 ships (347,880t) locked in Black Sea. **Egypt** — Enemy subjects ordered to register, those of military age deported to Malta.

AFRICAN OPERATIONS 5	SEA WAR 6	AIR WAR 7	INTERNATIONAL EVENTS 8	HOME FRONTS 9
Cameroons — **Allies occupy Duala** (-30, fine harbour with valuable booty). German C-in-C Col Zimmerman leaves by train (26) for Edea, 40 miles inland.		**France** — French night bomber group (*le Groupe de Bombardement/GB1*) formed: 3 sqns of Voisin pushers ('Chicken Coops') & Breguets. **W Front** — Gen Sir H Smith-Dorrien, GOC II Corps, praises RFC on the Aisne: 'Today I watched...an aeroplane observing for the 6-in howitzers. It was at times smothered with hostile anti-aircraft guns but nothing daunted it continued for hours through a wireless installation to observe the fire...'.		
	S America — Cradock searches Magellan Straits for Spee.		Pres Wilson's note to Britain stresses blockade's evil effects on US public opinion.	**Russia** — Shell production 35,000 pm, expenditure 45,000 pd; 2m shell order reduced to 800,000 (Sept).
			Neutrals : USA — Ex-German Colonial Minister Dr Dernburg in Los Angeles warns v Britain dominating world if she wins.	
		Germany — **Army Air Service adopts black 'Iron Cross'** insignia for its planes, airships & kite-balloons. **W Front** — First British single-seat fighter plane with fixed armament appears: Bristol Scout 'B' of No 3 Sqn RFC armed with 2 rifles mounted at 45° either side of cockpit.		**Germany** — Unemployment falls to 15.7%. Decree forbids money payments to British Empire.
Cameroons — c300 British in flotillas from Duala take Tiko & occupy Misselele Plantation. N Railway ops begin, c400 British take Bapele Bridge then Maka (2).	*U20* (Droescher) first submarine to circumnavigate British Isles, in 18 days. **N Sea** — RN start minelaying in open sea, 1264 mines by 7 old cruisers (Goodwin Sands — 10 miles N of Ostend); 2000 mines by end 1914 (*see* 21), 7154 mines by 16 Feb 1915 but mainly defective, c4000 sunk or drift away. Neutral shipping has to pass through Downs. British RN Div (Marine Bde) advance party lands at Antwerp. **Atlantic** — First CEF units sail for England in 31 ships, 4 cruisers escort, land at Plymouth (*see* HOME FRONTS).		Italy protests v Austrian mine-laying. Anglo-US agreement that American goods may go to Holland if not re-exported to Germany. **Secret Russo-Rumanian** (Sazonov-Diamanda) **Agreement**, promises territory for latter's benevolent neutrality.	**Britain** — (Oct) First of 30 ambulance trains sent to France (19 more built for US 1917-18). Armed Forces Family Separation Allowances increased. Free medical treatment for dependents (10). (Oct) Camps Library founded, sends 16m publications to fighting men. **Germany** — (Oct) K- bread (war bread) with *ersatz* content introduced; many 4-gun btys formed (standard 1915). **France** — Industrial life making good recovery.

OCTOBER 1914	WESTERN FRONT 1	EASTERN FRONT 2	SOUTHERN FRONTS 3	TURKISH FRONTS 4
Thu 1 contd				
Fri 2	Nr Arras Maud'huy under heavy pressure from 3 German corps (-6, *see* 5). **Antwerp** — Fts Koningshoyckt & Lierre abandoned. Germans take Termonde. Sir J French reports to K George ' .. the spade will be as great a necessity as the rifle...the heaviest...arty'.	**E Prussian Frontier** — Russians recover Mariampol.	**Bosnia** — Serb-Montenegrin threat to Sarajevo revived till 4.	**India** — 16th Bde (Brig-Gen Delamain) of 6th Poona Division ordered to embark at Bombay (*see* 16).
Sat 3	**Flanders** — Germans briefly occupy Ypres. *Landwehr* enter Tournai. **Belgium** — Antwerp outer defences now in German hands. Foreign legations leave. Churchill arrives from London with promise of 'possibility of Franco-British relieving army' if Antwerp inner defences can hold out 3 days. British 7th Div will be dispatched immediately to Ghent, 3 naval bdes with 10 heavy guns to Antwerp.	**Carpathians** — Russians take Maramaros-Sziget in N Hungary, retaken by Austrians (7).		
Sun 4	Germans advance towards Flanders coast taking Lens, Comines, Poperinghe & Bailleul, bombarding Lille. **Antwerp** — 2082 British Marines (Gen Paris) arrive by by rail from Dunkirk. German 37th *Landwehr* Bde attacks Scheldt at 2 points but Belgian 4th Div holds (& 5, *see* 7).	Tsar arrives at STAVKA, visits Osovyets (8). **Poland** — AUSTRO-GERMAN OFFENSIVE TOWARDS WARSAW BEGINS (*see* 11). Austrian First Army takes Opatow, but Guard Cav Bde (Mannerheim) covers Russian inf recrossing of Vistula at Sandomir.	**Albania** — Essad Pasha & army enters capital, Senate elect him President (5, *see* 26).	
Mon 5	**Antwerp** — 4 German bns cross R Nethe at Duffel, 6000 troops of British RND (partially equipped) arrive a day late. **Decisive day of siege**, Gen Pau on mission to Belgians halts 6670 French marines at Ghent. **Artois** — Bavarians force Maistre's XXI Corps from Souchez, Givenchy & Vimy Ridge N of Arras, but Foch's arrival inspires 77th Res Div counter-attacks (-7) that stabilize line N & S of city. **France** — Pres Poincaré first visits Joffre at *GQG*, Romilly-sur-Seine.			**Kaiser agrees to send Turkey T2m in gold** by 2 trains across Rumania (arrives 16 & 21, Enver requested T5m).
Tue 6	**Antwerp** — Germans take Lierre; **Belgian Army begins to evacuate city** (night 6-7). Rawlinson's **British** 7th Div & 3rd Cav Div (21,942 men, 9580 horses, 69 guns) **disembark too late at Ostend & Zeebrugge** (-8, *see* 10). **Artois** — Arras comes under heavy German bombardment. Foch tells Maud'huy '... hang on like lice'; Germans repulsed (-8). **Flanders** — French Territorials drive Marwitz's II Cav Corps back to line Lens-Lille.	**Poland and Galicia** — General Russian retreat, having lost 8000 men & 9 guns to Germans since 28 Sept.		
Wed 7	**Belgium** — Evacuation of Allied forces begins. 4 German bdes cross R Scheldt & threaten their line of retreat but Belgians hold vital Lokeren rail jctn (-8); 200,000 civilians try to leave city. **Flanders** — French XXI Corps (detrained at Bethune) attacks German cav (-8) who are saved by XIV Corps (by rail from Metz). German IV Cav Corps reaches Ypres outskirts.	**Galicia** — Russians back on R San. **Carpathians** — Russian raiders leave N Hungary but raid again (10).		**Mesopotamia** — Turk protests v RN in Shatt-al-Arab but ultimatum expires without action (21, *see* 26 & 31). **C Pacific** — Japanese marines occupy Yap I (*see* 14).
Thu 8	**Flanders** — **Foch takes supreme command** as Joffre's	**E Prussia** — Russians retake Lyck but Germans recover (13).	**Bosnia** — Serb Uzice Army driven back (-10, *see* 14).	**Tsingtao** — German fire slackening after week's

AFRICAN OPERATIONS 5	SEA WAR 6	AIR WAR 7	INTERNATIONAL EVENTS 8	HOME FRONTS 9
			Britain — Asquith's Cardiff speech reveals German 1912 proposals. Rest of Cabinet decide to send Churchill to Antwerp.	**Ireland** — **1st German wartime spy Karl Lody arrested**. Trial begins 30 (*see* 6 Nov). **Britain** — Adm Lord Beresford in Aberdeen recruiting speech says 'All alien enemies should be locked up!' Kitchener recalls Sir A Keogh as DG Army Medical Services.
			Neutrals : USA — Turk Ambassador Rustem Bey leaves after criticizing Filipino & negro treatment.	**Canada** — 1st CEF (31 ships) sails for Britain (*see* 14).
SW Africa — Col Mackenzie's Mtd Bde reinforces Lüderitz Bay landing. **E Africa** — Germans defeat Belgian attack on Kisenyi, Rwanda.			German Professors' manifesto issued (British reply 21).	
		W Front — First air combat victory by an MG-armed Allied plane: Sgt Frantz & Cp Quenault (French) in Voisin III of *Escadrille VB24* destroy Aviatik with 47 rnds at Jonchery-sur-Vesle (Reims), German crew Schlienting & Zangen k (*see* 22 Nov).		Asquith rejects Churchill's offer to resign if given Antwerp command.
Cameroons — 50 French from Duala capture Yapoma Bridge. **SW Africa** — Lt-Col Maritz confers with Germans (*see* 9).	**Atlantic** — Cruiser *Karlsruhe* sinks 8 British merchant ships (-26). **Secret War** — Admiralty ctee analyses German gunnery (-16). **N Sea** — HM Submarine *E9* sinks German destroyer *S116* (10 lost, 55 survivors) at mouth of Ems (*see* 17).			**Belgium** — Govt moves from Antwerp to Ostend.
E Africa — 480 Germans and 6 MGs (31 cas) attack Gazi, beaten by 850 British (18 cas) & 6 MGs.		**W Front** — No 6 Sqn RFC arrives in France.		**Britain** — Govt scheme to train women for market gardening & poultry farming. **Austria** — Subjects abroad suspected of working v monarchy to lose citizenship; families deported (further decree 13). Kronen has fallen 9% v RM; Germany sends RM100,000 pm in exchange credit for duration.
Cameroons — Lt-Col Haywood's 500 Nigerians		**Germany** — 2 RNAS Tabloids from Antwerp bomb Düsseldorf		

OCTOBER 1914	WESTERN FRONT 1	EASTERN FRONT 2	SOUTHERN FRONTS 3	TURKISH FRONTS 4
Thu 8 contd	assistant **of Allied armies between Lille & the coast**; Sir J French opens GHQ at Abbeville after meeting him at Doullens. German IV Cav Corps passes through Ypres but stopped 10 miles from Hazebrouck by Mitry's cav corps. German Fourth Army formed (-10). **Somme** — Renewed fighting at Roye. **Antwerp** — City centre under heavy bombardment, over 200 houses destroyed; Germans capture 2 inner line forts. Belgian 2nd Div & British retreat to join rest behind Terneuzen Canal N of Ostend.	François replaces Schubert i/c Eighth Army (*see* 7 Nov).		bombardment (*see* 15).
Fri 9	**Antwerp** — 1560 men of British 1st Naval Bde cut off & interned in Holland. Germans occupy inner defences & force 936 British to surrender. Burgomaster signs ceasefire Treaty of Contich at Beseler's HQ. **Flanders** — 400 French buses (French Army uses nearly 800 Paris buses for duration) take 10,000 British II Corps troops 22 miles E from Abbeville to St Pol (*see* 31). **France** — BEF III Corps entrains at Compiègne for St Omer. BEF Cav Corps (Allenby) formed.	**Poland** — Austro-Germans approach Ivangorod fortress (Schwarz) on R Vistula. **Galicia** — **Austrians relieve Przemysl** (*see* 28).		
Sat 10	FORMAL CAPITULATION OF ANTWERP TO GERMANS: Deguise offers his sword at Ft Ste Marie (Belgian garrison having decamped). Belgians stem German pursuit nr Ghent. **Flanders** — Germans bombard Lille. Battle of La Bassée (-2 Nov). Falkenhayn orders German Fourth Army (Württemberg) ' to cut off the fortresses of Dunkirk and Calais'. BEF guns rationed to 20rpd, IV Corps (Rawlinson) formed.	**Poland** — Frommel's Cav Corps occupies Lodz. Mackensen's XVII Corps defeats Russians at Grojec S of Warsaw, captures Army order belatedly revealing Grand Duke's plan.		
Sun 11	BATTLE OF FLANDERS (-22 Nov) 1914 begins: 6-week struggle for control of Channel ports, Belgian Army reforms around Bruges. BEF cav force German cav back to R Lys.	**Poland** — Germans take Sochaczew on R Bzura 30 miles W of Warsaw (*see* 12). Russian Fourth, Ninth & Fifth Armies begin bloody attempts to cross R Vistula (-15). Austrians recover Jaroslav (*see* 23).	**Italy** — New War Minister Maj Gen Zupelli gives PM 5½-month Army improvement programme, is given 940m lire by May 1915 (*see* 20, 1 Dec).	2nd Turco-German Treaty. **Armenia** — Turk Third Army HQ reports increasing Armenian desertions, Russians arming c800 (more similar reports).
Mon 12	**Artois** — First Battle of Artois ends though Germans counter-attack (21-23, *see* 16). Bülow given new German Second Army. German XIX Corps reoccupy Lille. **Flanders** — Allies evacuate Ostend & Zeebrugge (*see* 15). BEF comes into line as IV Corps & (with Belgians) reaches Roulers. Battle of Messines (-2 Nov) involves BEF Cav Corps. British II Corps (300 cas) attacks on 8-mile front, reaches Givenchy. **Champagne** — Fruitless French Fifth Army offensive (-15, *see* 26). **France** — Indian Secunderabad Cav Bde lands (in action at Ypres by 1 Nov).	**Poland** — Mackensen within 12 miles of Warsaw as Ludendorff orders him to dig in (*see* 14), Hindenburg says 'God be with us, I can do no more!'		
Tue 13	**Battle of Armentières** (-2 Nov); Allied offensive: Lt B	**E Prussia** — Germans recover Lyck. **Galicia** — Battle of		

AFRICAN OPERATIONS 5	SEA WAR 6	AIR WAR 7	INTERNATIONAL EVENTS 8	HOME FRONTS 9
occupy Susa & Kake (*see* 19). Col Gorges' cl000 men & 4 guns in 29 vessels repulsed from Yabasi inland on R Wuri, retire in heavy rain, but take it (14), total 79 cas.		& Cologne: Flt Lt Marix destroys newly delivered Army Zeppelin *Z9* in shed at Düsseldorf from 600 ft with 4 x 20lb bombs; AA damage plane, fuel runs out & he crash-lands 20 miles from Antwerp (pilot safe). Sqn Cdr Grey bombs Cologne rail stn, returns to join in Allied evacuation.		
S Africa — Maritz's l600 men rebel 25 miles W of Upington and hand over 60 loyal troops to Germans at Van Rooisvlei.	**E Indies** — Cruiser *HMS Yarmouth* sinks or retakes 2 *Emden* supply ships at Pulo Tapah, W Sumatra.	**Britain** — Part-time vol RNVR AA Corps formed to aid defence of London.	**Neutrals : Italy** — Cabinet crisis, War Minister resigns. Foreign Minister dies (16) (*see* 30). **Sweden** — Defence tax & govt control of goods. **Portugal declares neutrality**, calls up naval reserves (27), has military mission in London (Oct).	
S Africa — Maritz declares S Africa's independence and war v Britain.			**Neutrals : Rumania** — †K **Carol I, nephew Ferdinand succeeds** (*see* 23). Norwegian ship *Benesloet* leaves Brest with 2500t nickel delivery for Krupp.	
	Baltic — Russian cruiser *Pallada* sunk by *U26* (Berckheim) off Gulf of Finland; no survivors. **Channel** — Rear-Adm Hood i/c new Dover Straits command (becomes Dover Patrol 1915), *see* 18.	**France** — 2 *Tauben* drop 20 bombs on Paris (8 civ cas); Notre Dame Cathedral slightly damaged. Gen Bernard, incompetent *Directeur de l'Aeronautique,* replaced by Gen Hirschauer who immediately rescinds orders to close Pau & Avord flying schools & half aircraft production.	Grey wires Paris re Antwerp fiasco 'HMG must have the right to send troops for · separate operations'.	
S Africa — Martial law proclaimed.	**S Pacific** — Cruisers *Dresden* & *Leipzig* join Spee at Easter I.	**France** — Aerial bombs cause slight damage to Gare du Nord, Paris. **W Front** — RFC take up permanent HQ at St Omer.		**Austria** — 'Trial of Gavrilo Princip & his associates for high treason' at Sarajevo (*see* 26), 25 accused.
	N Sea — First U-boat scare on Southampton-Havre troop		**Belgian Govt moves from Ostend to Le Havre**.	**Britain** — *Morning Post* editorial 'The Antwerp Blunder'

OCTOBER 1914	WESTERN FRONT 1	EASTERN FRONT 2	SOUTHERN FRONTS 3	TURKISH FRONTS 4
Tue 13 contd	Montgomery (1st R Warwicks, 4th Div) twice w capturing Meteren village in III Corps 5-mile wide advance NW of Armentières (promoted Capt & awarded DSO, back in France Feb 1915); II Corps few gains for 700 cas (Givenchy lost). **Flanders — British occupy Ypres**. Germans take Ghent & Lille. Heavy fighting Bethune-La Bassée. BEF GHQ moves to St Omer. French 87th & 89th Territorial Divs (sailed from Le Havre to Dunkirk) moving inland since 9 to res positions W of Ypres.	Chyrow begins (-2 Nov) in heavy rain, involves Austrian cholera-stricken Second & Third Armies, Brusilov's Third and Eighth Armies S of Przemysl.		
Wed 14	**Flanders** — Germans occupy Bruges. Allenby's cav reach Kemmel & Messines, link with IV Corps; British III Corps occupies Bailleul. British 65th Howitzer Bty supports French XXI Corps (Maistre) at Vermelles NW of Loos with **first likely creeping barrage of war**. H Hamilton, GOC BEF 3rd Div, k by stray bullet from German dismtd cav.	**E Prussia** — Germans take Mlava just over border. **Poland** — Germans claim total occupation up to R Vistula (see I5).	**Bosnia** — Austrians reach Bajinabasta on R Drina frontier in surprise thrust despite bad weather.	**C Pacific** — **Japanese occupy German Mariana & Marshall Is.**
Thu 15	**Flanders** — Germans (III Res Corps) **occupy Ostend & Zee-brugge. With Belgian Army along R Yser,** Allied line now extends to sea & occupies Poperinghe. BEF cav finds Lys crossings, German-held but capture 2 villages on Ypres canal; British II Corps (2000 cas since 12) makes progress but meets German VII Corps (16) which relieves German cav corps.	**Poland** — FIRST BATTLE OF WARSAW (-23) all along Vistula; 4 German corps v 4 Russian armies, Germans within 7 miles of Warsaw whose evacuation is prepared.		**Tsingtao** — No running water; US Consul brings out several hundred women & children (see 29).
Fri 16	**Flanders** — BATTLE OF THE YSER BEGINS (-31): Germans attack Dixmude. Belgians retire from Houthulst Forest NE of Ypres. Foch visits K Albert. Allies occupy Aubers, Neuve Chapelle & Warneton, Givenchy. BEF across Lys in general advance up to 3 miles, its 7th Div digs in 5 miles E of Ypres. **Artois** — Pétain tells corps cdr 'One must...employ ...siege warfare', promoted i/c XXXIII Corps (20).			**India** — IEF'D' (4721 troops, 8 guns, 460 followers, 1290 mules & horses) sails from Bombay in 5 transports for Mesopotamia (see 23). **Secret War** — 3 Germans leave Constantinople with £60,000 in gold for Afghanistan mission (see 5 Dec).
Sat 17	**Flanders** — ALLIED OFFEN-SIVE ENDS with capture of Herlies & BEF 4th Div entry into Armentières. New German Fourth Army (Württemberg), incl 8 newly raised 'schoolboy' divs with III Res Corps (from Antwerp) & a Marine div begin to advance W from line Courtrai-Ostend towards Yser & Ypres. British II Corps occupies Aubers Ridge, reaches Givenchy-Festubert-N of Aubers (18), nearest to La Bassée for 4 yrs.	**Poland** — Crisis of battle, Russian reinforcements save city.		**Tsingtao** — German *S90* torpedoes and sinks Japanese cruiser *Takashiko* (271 dead) but scuttles herself.
Sun 18	**Flanders** — Germans take Roulers & thwart BEF Cav Corps attack. German III Res Corps captures 2 of 3 Belgian outpost villages E of Yser (see SEA WAR).	**Poland** — Ludendorff **decides to order retreat, secretly**. Galicia — Austrians begin vain attempts to recross San v Brusilov.		**Egypt** — Legislative Assembly prorogued, never meets again.

AFRICAN OPERATIONS 5	SEA WAR 6	AIR WAR 7	INTERNATIONAL EVENTS 8	HOME FRONTS 9
	transport route (destroyer escort provided from 6 Nov). **3 RN submarines** (-17) **sail** from Harwich (*see* 17) **to join Russians in Baltic**.		Germans levy £20m on Antwerp. **Occupied France** — Gen Heinrich Military Gov of Lille.	blames Churchill, press debate (-19).
		W Front — RNAS armoured car shoots down *Taube* with MG & rifle fire. **Germany** — HQ Naval Airship Div opens at Nordholz on coast (-25 July 1917).		**Britain** — **1st Canadian troops land at Plymouth**, Lt-Gen Alderson GOC 33,000 men; 7000 horses; 144 guns. FM Lord Roberts inspects on Salisbury Plain (23).
S Africa — Col Brits routs Maritz (70 PoWs) at Ratedraai (*see* 22) S of R Orange.	**N Sea** — Patrolling old British cruiser *Hawke* torpedoed & sunk off Peterhead by *U9* ; 525 dead, only 21 survivors.		**Neutrals** — USA: State Dept circular affirms US citizens' right to 'sell to any belligerent government or its agent any article of commerce ...'.	Lord Bryce to HAL Fisher 'People in London are depressed. Both Russia and France's capacities are obscure'; 4144 Belgian refugees arrive at Dover & Folkestone.
Maj-Gen Aitken's 8000-strong IEF'B' (14 transports) sails from Bombay for Mombasa (*see* 31).	**Indian/Pacific Oceans** — NZEF sails for France. First AIF units sail for France 17. *Emden* sinks 3 British merchant ships (2 more 18 & 19, *see* 28). **Adriatic** — Allied fleets bombard Cattaro. **N Sea** — Another U-boat scare (false) forces Grand Fleet to sea (*see* 18).	**Britain** — Admiralty/War Office conference decides areas of responsibility of home-based air formations: RNAS to protect major cities & intercept aircraft crossing coast.		NZEF (8574 men, 3818 horses, 12 guns) sails from Wellington having waited stronger escort since 25 Sept. **Austria** — 1st trading with enemy decree, 3 more (-28).
	N Sea — 4 German destroyers (abortive minelaying sortie) sunk (31 survivors, 200 cas) off Dutch coast (Texel) in chase by cruiser *Undaunted* & 4 destroyers (5 cas). Abortive U-boat op against Scapa. **Baltic** — *E1* (Laurence) & *E9* (Horton), former vainly attacks German cruiser *Victoria Luise* (18) first British submarines to enter this sea (-19), go on to Libau (21 & 22) and Helsinki. *E11* (Nasmith) forced to return to Harwich (24). **Pacific** — Japanese cruiser *Takachiho* torpedoed and sunk (271 dead) by German *TB S90* off Tsingtao.		**Neutrals : USA** — 25,000 visit 2-day German festival at St Louis, $20,000 war relief raised.	**Australia** — 1st AIF (20,226) embarks for France. **Russia** — Council of Ministers pass order for 30 large US locomotives.
	N Sea/Flanders — Hood's RN Flotilla (2 cruisers, 3 monitors, 4 destroyers joined by French ships pm) begins shelling (-31) Germans E of R Yser, invaluable contribution to crucial W Front battle (*see* 21,			**Britain** — Churchill meets RND survivors from Antwerp (PoWs in Doberitz Camp nr Berlin since 15).

OCTOBER 1914	WESTERN FRONT 1	EASTERN FRONT 2	SOUTHERN FRONTS 3	TURKISH FRONTS 4
Mon 19	FIRST BATTLE OF YPRES begins (-22 Nov). British & French join British 7th Div as German pressure is maintained. Battle rages from the Channel to Ypres & Armentières (4 divs attack to S). Indian Expeditionary Corps (IEF'A') (Willcocks) reaches the front (*see* 24).	**Poland** — Germans cross Vistula at Josefor. **First Russian armoured car unit formed**, assigned to SW Front.	**Montenegro** — 6 French naval guns, landed to support Montenegrins, begin shelling Austrian Cattaro, naval base defences (garrison 10,000) from Mt Lov'cen; Ft Verma'c damaged (*see* SEA WAR 21; S FRONTS 25 Nov).	
Tue 20	**Flanders** — General German Fourth & Sixth Army attack on whole allied front between La Bassée Canal & the sea, Fourth Army is to break through between Ypres & Nieuport & envelop N flank of Allied armies in France & roll them up. III Res Corps storms Lombartzgde village E of Nieuport (*see* 22). Kaiser arrives at Courtrai, anticipating triumphal entry into Ypres. BEF repulses Sixth Army's attacks at La Bassée, Armentières & Messines. British I Corps (Haig) arrives from the Aisne via Poperinghe-St Omer & enters the line (-21) just before Ypres, as Germans occupy Passchendaele Ridge. French Eighth Army (d'Urbal, HQ Roesbrugge) formed between Belgians & BEF.	**Poland** — GERMANS BEGIN PLANNED RETREAT FROM BEFORE WARSAW & abandon siege of Ivangorod.	Italy reinforces her border forts (-10 Nov).	(c) Wangenheim pledges the Young Turk triumvirate £30m loan (immediate initial payment) & Central Powers pledge to crush Serbs & open Balkan land supply route (*see* 22 & 24).
Wed 21	**Flanders** — German attack on Dixmude fails (& 23); now 7 divs v Belgian sector. Battle of Langemarck (-24): Haig's I Corps of BEF stands firm on line Zonnebeke-St Julien-Langemarck- Bixschoote. Joffre visits Sir J French & K Albert, forbids former's Boulogne entrenched camp idea. FM French orders line held to be 'strongly entrenched' **Argonne** — French recover some lost ground. Similar minor ops continue for 5 weeks. **Artois** — German shelling destroys Arras town hall's 16th-century belfry tower.	**Poland** — Battle of Kasimiryev: Ruzski annihilates German Vistula bridgehead.		
Thu 22	**Flanders** — Belgian 2nd Div re-enters Lombaertzyde but at night German III Res Corps bridges Yser nr Tervaete, capturing village & expanding bridgehead (23). Germans storm British trenches N of Pilkem. Smith-Dorrien retires on Givenchy-Neuve Chapelle-Fauquissart. 2 Indian bns rushed up by bus stiffen BEF dismtd cav before Messines, 129th Baluchis' MG det win first of 5 Indian VCs in France (31).	**Bukovina** — Austrians re-occupy Czernowitz but Russians retake (28). **Poland** — Austrian Battle of Ivangorod (-27) as Russian XXV Corps night crosses Vistula (-23).		**Enver Pasha sends war intervention plan to German General Staff in Berlin who approve** (23,*see* 24).
Fri 23	**Flanders** — French 42nd Div of 7000 Marne veterans enters line at Nieuport. British recapture Pilkem trenches. Heavy fighting round Langemarck. French IX Corps begins detraining at Ypres, relieves British I Corps (-24) after latter inflicts 1281 cas on German 45th Res Div. **Indian Corps' 3rd (Lahore) Div assists** British II Corps to repulse night attack on Givenchy-Aubers position (night 23/24, *see* 30).	**Poland** — Russians (incl Guard Corps) advance everywhere. **Galicia** — Russians retake Jaroslav.	**Bosnia** — Austrian river monitor flagship *Temes* mined (laid by 70-man Russian Navy contingent) & sunk in R Sava nr Sabac; other monitors have to fit mine detectors (*see* 5 Nov) in month of much shelling of Belgrade & waterlogged Serb trenches along Sava.	**Mesopotamia** — IEF'D' anchors off Bahrein (*see* 3 Nov). **Diplomacy** — Churchill to Grey: 'I am very unhappy about our getting into war with Turkey without .. Greece as an ally'. British Egypt High Commissioner Sir H McMahon (for Kitchener) reaches secret agreement with Sherif Hussein of Mecca 'to recognize and support the independence of the Arabs ....' (*see* 14 July 1915).

AFRICAN OPERATIONS 5	SEA WAR 6	AIR WAR 7	INTERNATIONAL EVENTS 8	HOME FRONTS 9
	24, 26).			
Cameroons — Nigerians at Kake (29 cas) repel 350 Germans (50 cas). **S Africa** — 150 troops rebel at Lichten-berg, Beyers leaves Pretoria (met De Wet there 14). **Portugese Angola** — 3 Germans killed at Naulila in misunderstanding (*see* 18 Dec).		**Germany** — Maj W Siegert, well-known prewar balloonist, appointed to advise *OHL* on military aviation. He quickly organizes an elite HQ flying corps (*Fliegerkorps der Obersten Heeresleitung*) of 36 aircraft at Ghistelles 11 miles SW of Bruges.	US Marines land in Haiti (*see* 17 Dec).	**Britain** — New naval decoration DSM founded. Churchill urges Kitchener to study invasion threat in detail, in Cabinet defends RN measures v invasion (21 & 23). London pub closing now 10pm (*see* 24).
	N Sea — British *SS Glitra* (866t), FIRST MERCHANT SHIP SUNK BY SUBMARINE; captured, boarded & scuttled by *U17* (Feldkirchner) 14 miles off Norway, she tows boats some miles towards coast (*see* 26, & 23 Nov). **E Med** — 22 suspect ships seized by Egypt in Suez Canal, 14 handed over to RN at Alexandria.		**Neutrals : USA** — Broadway musical 'Chin Chin' opens (295 perfs) incl song *It's a Long Way to Tipperary*.	Germany claims 149,000 French; 107,000 Russian; 32,000 Belgian & 9000 British PoWs.
	N Sea — French lay first mines off Ostend (Allies bombard 23) to deter U-boats. **Secret War** — DNC proposes anti-torpedo bulge protection for warships, Churchill endorses (23 *see* Apr 1915). **Adriatic** — Modern Austrian battleship *Radetzky* sent to Cattaro where she disables 2 French naval guns on Mt Lovcen (*see* S FRONTS 25 Nov).			British Contraband Ctee first meets.
S Africa — Col Brits routs 600 rebels at Keimoes & Kakamas (26, Maritz w, driven into SW Africa, *see* 30). Rebel leaders meet at Kopjes in Transvaal.			US & Spanish London & Brussels Ambassadors organize **Ctee for Belgian Relief** (1st US food shipment 30). **US withdraws insistence on London Declaration, but wants international law observed by combatants.** $100m War Revenue Act passed to offset declining import duties.	
S Africa — **Gen De Wet rebels in Orange Free State**, seizes Heilbron (*see* 29).			**Rumania closes frontier to German supplies for Turkey.**	

OCTOBER 1914	WESTERN FRONT 1	EASTERN FRONT 2	SOUTHERN FRONTS 3	TURKISH FRONTS 4
Sat 24	**Flanders** — British 7th Div expels Germans from Polygon Wood. French marines in Dixmude repel 15 attacks. Germans bombard Furnes, Belgian HQ 6 miles behind Yser sector (-27), Belgians have suffered 25+% losses & only 180 guns left serviceable. **Ypres** — French counter-offensive NE of town soon peters out but IX Corps recaptures Zonnebeke despite 6-div German attack.	**Poland** — Russian Second Army takes 11 guns from Frommel's Cav Corps and only XI Corps arrival (25) saves latter.		**Secret War** — **Enver orders Adm Souchon to enter Black Sea & attack Russians in his own time** (*see* 27).
Sun 25	**Flanders** — At 1600 **Belgians open Nieuport sluices** to flood area E of Nieuport-Dixmude railway, but water rises slowly (*see* 30). **Ypres** — 2000+ BEF replacements arrive, Haig's Intelligence chief blesses German corps cdr's plain language radio signals. Germans attack all around Salient (-31).		Serb-Montenegrin units back out of Bosnia behind Drina after evacuating Vlasenica. (c) Snows begin.	
Mon 26	**Flanders** — Fierce fighting on the Yser. K Albert rejects idea of 6-mile retreat to Furnes canal line. **Aisne** — Germans vainly attack French Fifth Army between Craonne & Berry-au-Bac (-27).	**Poland** — Russian Fourth & Ninth Army victory along Petrokov-Radom line v Austrian First Army (40,000 men lost) which retreats. Germans have retreated 60 miles in 6 days behind planned road/rail demolitions.	**Albania** — Italian marines land at Valona (*see* 31).	British Constantinople Military Attaché reports train has left Aleppo for Basra with mines for Shatt-al-Arab.
Tue 27	**Flanders** — Belgian Army comes under severe pressure from German III Res Corps & Marine Div. Haig's I Corps re-enters line E of Ypres. Falkenhayn visits Sixth Army HQ forms Army Gp Fabeck (6 divs S of Ypres). **Aisne** — Arty Col Nivelle promoted general. **Secret War** — Unknown to Allies until after Armistice, Germans fire c3000 shrapnel shells with non-lethal tear gas around Neuve Chapelle.			
Wed 28	8 German bns (14th Div) enter Neuve Chapelle, capture Kruseik S of Ypres-Menin road. Indian Corps relieves battered II Corps (*see* 31). French Eighth Army attack N of Ypres-Roulers railway gains little for 2000 cas.	**Poland** — Russians recover Lodz & Radom (Cossacks). **Galicia** — Austrians beaten at Sambor. **Re-supply of Przemysl** (- 4 Nov) with 128 trainloads.		
Thu 29	British II Corps reoccupies Neuve Chapelle for a few hours. Bav 6th Res Div repulsed E of Gheluvelt astride Menin Road. Germans 4th Res Div makes last big attack S of Armentières.			TURKEY ENTERS WAR. **Egypt** — 2000 Bedouin reported to be raiding Sinai frontier (*see* 1 Nov). **Tsingtao** — Japanese siege guns open fire; German gunboat *Tiger* scuttled.
Fri 30	**Ypres** — 2 British bns repel	**Poland** — Russians defeat		Allied Ambassadors present

AFRICAN OPERATIONS 5	SEA WAR 6	AIR WAR 7	INTERNATIONAL EVENTS 8	HOME FRONTS 9
S Africa — Beyers rebels in Transvaal, stops trains removing men and weapons. Govt tries to negotiate.	**N Sea/Flanders** — Allied sqn now 2 cruisers, 2 monitors, 1 gunboat, 2 sloops & 13 destroyers (fire directed by balloon since 21).		Christabel Pankhurst speaks in Carnegie Hall, NY.	**France** — Teachers' Federation Journal suspended at Marseilles for opposing war. **Austria** — Czech Union declares it has never been v the state, only v govts (*see* 15 Nov). **Britain — Kitchener appeals to public not to treat soldiers to drink.**
S Africa — Rebels routed at Calvinia.		**Britain** — 2 *Tauben* of *Feldfl Abt 9* attempt to bomb Dover; 1 crew returns early but Caspar & Roos claim success (no confirmation in British reports or records).		**Britain** — †CIGS Gen Sir C Douglas, Gen Sir J Wolfe Murray succeeds (26). Pensions of up to 10s pw for dependents of men killed.
Cameroons — Col Mayer's 1190 Anglo-French & 6 armed craft capture Edea on E Railway via R Nyong (*see* 29). **S Africa** — Govt promises no action v those who refuse active service but stay at home.	**Channel** — *U24* (Schneider) torpedoes French *SS Amiral Ganteaume* (carrying 250 Belgian refugees, mistaken for troops) without warning, 40 lives lost in panic off Cap Gris Nez. **N Sea/Flanders** — Pre-dreadnought *Venerable* joins Hood's sqn, her 12-in guns wreak havoc on German troops (12-28).	**W Front** — BE2 of No 4 Sqn RFC marked with Union Jack is shot down in error by BEF. HQ RFC in the Field proposes (30) **adoption of French-style roundels** with blue 'bull' & red 'outer' reversed (*see* 11 Dec).		**Austria — Sarajevo Trial defendants found guilty** (all plead so except Princip), verdict & sentences (29), up to 20 yrs prison for those under 20 incl Princip (5 death sentences later commuted, 10 acquitted).
E Africa — Anglo-Belgian Conference at Kibati. **S Africa** — Botha defeats Beyers at Commissie Drift nr Rustenburg, he flees SW (*see* 5 Nov).	**Atlantic** — FIRST DREAD-NOUGHT LOST: British battleship *Audacious* sunk by mines laid off 26 miles NW of Irish L Swilly (Tory I) by German auxiliary *Berlin* (200 laid on 26, not cleared till July 1915). Liner *Olympic* vainly tries to tow *Audacious*. Admiralty attempt to conceal loss, negated by her passengers' photographs. **Black Sea** — Turco-German Fleet sails from Bosphorus, ostensibly on exercise.		US protests to Britain re SS *Kroonland* detention at Gibraltar (copper cargo seized), also Standard Oil tanker *Platuria* seizure (23). **France — First 6 (of 450) FANYs land** to drive for BEF.	British Foreign Office warns press of harm its articles doing in neutral countries.
	Indian Ocean — *Emden* raids Penang roadstead (Malaya), torpedoes and sinks old Russian cruiser *Zhemchug* & French destroyer *Mousquet* (28 survivors).			**Britain** — Cabinet agrees to keep *Audacious* sinking secret, photo in US paper (14 Nov). **France** — Central Office for Unemployed & Refugees. **Canada** — Alien enemies to register.
SE Cameroons — 900 French from Wesso in S capture Dzimu on R Sanga at 3rd attempt. **S Africa** — De Wet denounces 'the miserable, pestilential English' while his 120 men loot Vrede.	**Black Sea** — *Goeben*, *Breslau* & Turk ships (cruiser *Hamidie*, 1 minelayer & 2 torpedo boats) make **surprise pre-emptive raid on Russian Black Sea Fleet** in its bases. Odessa (Russian gunboat *Donec* sunk), Sevastopol (59 *Goeben* shells fired in 25 mins), Novorossisk (*Breslau* sinks c6 steamers & hits 40 oil tanks) & Feodosia are shelled & mines laid, except at Novorossisk. *Goeben* damaged (14 men k by 2 Russian 12-in shells) but sinks Russian minelayer *Prut*. Souchon writes to his wife, 'I have thrown the Turks into the powder keg'. 4 new Russian destroyers commissioned at Nikolayev.		**British Order-in-Council extends contraband (3rd list) & revives doctrine of the continuous voyage** (*see* 23 Dec).	**Britain** — Home Office recognizes women police patrols.
S Africa — Maritz's 600 rebels	**First Sea Lord Lord Fisher re-**	**W Front** — Lt Madon of *Esc*	**Neutrals : Italy** — Cabinet	**Germany** — War Ministry

OCTOBER 1914	WESTERN FRONT 1	EASTERN FRONT 2	SOUTHERN FRONTS 3	TURKISH FRONTS 4
Fri 30 contd	German 40th Div (700k) N of Armentières, but Germans capture Zandvoorde & Hollebeke. **Champagne** — French Fourth Army vainly attacks E of Reims (-31). **Aisne** — French 69th Res Div suffers 3878 cas by German attacks being pushed to just before Soupir-Vailly (-2 Nov) on river & lost ground cannot be regained (6-12 Nov). **Yser** — Germans assault Belgian line at 0630 capturing 2 villages, break Belgian 2nd Div but 4 Allied bns penetrate back into Ramscapelle. **Germans retreat** (31), due to 2000-3000yd wide **waist-high waters behind them, yielding Ramscapelle** (*see* 2 Nov).	Germans at Bakalaryevo. **Galicia** — Brusilov takes Stanislau.		ultimatum at Constantinople, demobilize within 12 hrs, dismiss all Germans, or face war with France and Britain as well as Russia.
Sat 31	BATTLE OF YPRES, Phase 2: **Gheluvelt** begins. German 0900 attack on smaller scale than initial assault made between Messines & N of Gheluvelt; 7 fresh divs (Gen Fabeck) with 700 guns '3-hr 'earthquake' shelling are to break through at Ypres & roll up the enemy`s line on both sides'. Haig's I Corps sorely tried (4 bns destroyed & 2 div cdrs w), **Haig rides to fighting,** and **decisive German breakthrough** at Gheluvelt **seems imminent** when decisively repulsed by 10 scratch bns incl 2nd Worcs (350 charge & rout 1200 Germans from Gheluvelt château). But 9 German bns infiltrate onto Messines Ridge. French XVI Corps (Taverna) troops are driven off some ground N of the ridge. Foch promises Sir J French help, French IX Corps begins to arrive & join de Mitry's cav N of Ypres. By order of Foch, Gen d`Urbal i/c all forces around Ypres. 7th Indian (Meerut) Div enters line (night 30/31), having landed at Marseilles (11). (Oct) BEF receives 300 London General Omnibus Company B-type buses (over 900 used by Armistice).	Ludendorff sees Falkenhayn in Berlin. **Poland** — Battle of the Opatowka (-2 Nov) involves Austrian First Army. Snow-storms.	**Serbia** — Austrian VIII Corps attack links up the 2 bridge-heads S of Sava after trench warfare since 24. **Albania** — Italians occupy Saseno I off coast. Greeks retaliate & occupy Argyrocastro, S Quaranta and Premedi in S (*see* 25 Dec).	Turk Grand Vizier persuaded not to retire after Russia refuses compromise enquiry, but 4 moderate ministers resign. **Mesopotamia** — HM Sloop *Espiègle* escapes to Abadan & silences Turk rifle fire. IEF'D' advance elements reach Muhammera (30). **Tsingtao** — Final Japanese bombardment begins on Emperor's birthday, oil tanks hit.
Sun 1 November 1914	**Flanders** — Messines & Wytschaete taken by Germans, but held a mile W by French 32nd Div. End of gallant 48-hr stand by British cav at Messines. Kitchener meets Joffre & Foch at Dunkirk, former says a million men in France within 18 months (*see* 5). Hitler promoted *Gefreiter* (lance-corporal). **Artois** (Nov) — **Germans begin to use grenades** in Vimy sector.	**Hindenburg made C-in-C German E Front** (HQ Posen) (Nov). All Russian 8-gun btys reduced to 6 (divs have 36 not 48 guns) **Poland** — German retreat ending behind ravaged country, 40,000 cas since 28 Sept.	Serbs abandon Macva plain in NW for foothills of Cerrange.	BRITAIN BEGINS HOSTILI-TIES (*see* 5). TURKEY DECLARES WAR ON ALLIES. HM Ambassador leaves Constantinople. **Syria** — Turk Fourth Army formed at Damas-cus to act v Suez Canal.
Mon 2	**Flanders — Battles of Messines & Armentières** end. Germans withdraw from all but 2 villages W of Yser which repel French attacks (4) to concentrate on Ypres. They recapture Neuve Chapelle.	**E Prussia re-invaded by Russians:** (Sivers' Tenth Army, 20 divs). **Galicia** — Battle of Chyrow ends S of Przemysl in Brusilov success with Austrian retreat (night 2/3).	**Serbia** — Austrians reoccupy Sabac.	RUSSIA & SERBIA DECLARE WAR ON TURKEY. Allies announce Holy Places' immunity from attack. Britain publishes account of Turk provocations. **Armenia — Russian I Caucasus Corps**

AFRICAN OPERATIONS 5	SEA WAR 6	AIR WAR 7	INTERNATIONAL EVENTS 8	HOME FRONTS 9
routed at Schuit Drift on SW Africa border.	**appointed** (aged 74) replacing Prince Louis of Battenberg whose successful career is prematurely terminated by scurrilous public whispers & press campaign v his German ancestry & supposed disloyalty to the crown.	*MF 218* in Farman recon plane has engine shot away by AA over Chemin des Dames but keeps control & makes safe crash-landing.	resigns, Salandra stays PM. Finance Minister resigns over Army funds (*see* 5 Nov).	munition demands cut due to explosives' shortage. Unemployment down, 10.9% (Oct).
E Africa — IEF'B' reaches **Mombasa**, Maj-Gen Aitken C-in-C.	**N Sea** — British seaplane carrier *Hermes* (44 lost, 400 survivors) sunk by *U27* after ferrying aircraft to France, 8 miles WNW of Calais. **E Africa** — *Königsberg* located in Rufiji Delta hideout by cruiser *Chatham* (*see* 24 Nov).	**France** — **RNAS establishes seaplane base in Dunkirk shipyards.** British Aviation Supplies Dept founded at Paris to buy French equipment for RFC. RNAS separately represented from Dec. Serious inter-service disputes & delays compel Lt-Col Trenchard from Farnborough to bypass system & visit French firms in person.	HMG order hostilities v Turkey.	
	(Nov) RN reintroduces mines for harbour defence with special RM submarine miner corps to operate them. **Aegean** — 2 RN destroyers sink Turk minelayer gunboat *Berika / Zafer* in Smyrna harbour. **Pacific** — **Battle of Coronel**: Cradock's outgunned cruiser sqn defeated by Spee's sqn (3w from 6 minor hits) off Chile but at a cost of nearly half their ammunition. First major British naval defeat since US L Champlain victory (1814). Flagship *Good Hope* & *Monmouth* sunk (1400 dead), *Glasgow* (5 hits) & AMC *Otranto* escape.	**Germany** — (c) Grand Adm Tirpitz advocates mass firebomb raids on London. (Nov) German long-range bomber sqn formed at Metz, code-named *Brieftauben-Abteilung Metz* or *BAM* ('Metz Carrier Pigeon Flight'). **France** — (Nov) Paris air defence or-ganization created at Bourget with 13 aircraft & 2 75mm AA guns (34 in Mar 1915).	**Persia declares neutrality. Neutrals: Switzerland** — Lenin writes 'The epoch of the bayonet has begun', civil war must emerge. **India** — Viceroy declares 200,000 troops overseas in 5 theatres of war.	**Britain** — RFP 12¼%; 956 schools in military use. (Nov) Army Cyclist Corps formed, grows to 30,839 (May 1916). French Wounded Emergency Fund raises £228,000, helps military hospitals in 1200 towns by Mar 1918. **Australia** — Anzacs (38 ships & 5 escorts) sail from Albany (arrive Colombo 15, *see* TURK FRONTS 26). **Austria** — 1st War loan.
E Africa — **Battle of Tanga** (-5): Aitken's IEF'B' (7972) lands at Tanga from 2200 (-3), 80 miles S of Mombasa as Lettow arrives by train. **Uganda:Turkana** — (Nov) 300-strong Police Service Bn	**British Admiralty declares whole N Sea a 'military zone',** lays mines to strengthen blockade.			**Russia** — Bolshevik Ozerkov Conference (-4) ends in arrests incl 5 Duma deputies (Petrograd 1-day protest strike 12, *see* 25).

NOVEMBER 1914	WESTERN FRONT 1	EASTERN FRONT 2	SOUTHERN FRONTS 3	TURKISH FRONTS 4
Mon 2 contd	BEF now holds 9 miles to French 18. Poincaré visits K Albert.			**crosses frontier** at 5 points, occupies Bayazid (SW of Mount Ararat, 3). **India** — IEF'F' sails for Egypt (see 10). **Egypt** — Martial law. **Tsingtao** — Austrian cruiser *Kaiserin Elizabeth* dynamited in floating dock.
Tue 3	Falkenhayn confirmed as German CoS. **Flanders** — Allies occupy abandoned German positions on Yser.	Hindenburg decides to strike at Warsaw again, from NW; Ninth Army (4 corps) transferred N (by 9) in 800 trains. German Army Det Woyrsch formed (-15 Dec 1917). **Poland** — Russian Fourth Army defeats Austro-Germans at Kielce & recover it.		HMG recognizes Kuwait's independence. **Mesopotamia** — IEF'D' arrives off Shatt-al-Arab sandbar (see 6). **Tsingtao** — Radio & electricity stns destroyed; German attack repulsed.
Wed 4	**Flanders** — Allies temporarily recover Lombartzyde. BEF 1st Div now has only 3583 inf. Capt A O'Neill MP k with BEF, first MP (of 22) to be killed.	**Galicia** — Austrians beaten at Jaroslav; 19,000 PoWs & 40 guns lost in 12 days.	**Serbia** — Austrians attack from Sabac & also cross Savaat Mishar (night 4/5).	**Persia refuses to join Turkey v Allies. Armenia** — Russians occupy Diyadin & up to 17 miles over frontier.
Thu 5	**Somme** — German attack at Le Quesnoy-en-Santerre fails. **Flanders** — BEF 7th Div withdrawn from line only 2380 strong. Foch tells Sir J French that Kitchener had offered (1) to replace him with Hamilton; PM & Churchill have to send placatory letters.	**Poland** — German HQ retreats to Szestochowa (see 9). Dankl to Conrad: 'If the First Army is to be kept in existence...we must fall back'. It retreats, losing heavily, towards Cracow (6-10).	**Serbia** — Austrians shell along whole front (night 5/6) especially on Guchevo ridge.	BRITAIN & FRANCE DECLARE WAR ON TURKEY: BRITAIN ANNEXES CYPRUS.
Fri 6	**Ypres** — British repulse attack at Klein Zillebeke & recover ground there (-7). BEF 8th Div lands, one bde in action (11). Kaiser at Menin.	**E Prussia** — Battle of Goritten (-8). **Galicia** — Russians regain San line.	**Third Austrian offensive begins**: Potiorek masses 119 bns v 72 Serb in Loznica-Ljubovija sector of Drina front, promising 'annihilation of exhausted' enemy.	**Mesopotamia** — 600 British troops land at Fao after HM Sloop *Odin* silences 4-gun fort (see 8).
Sat 7	**Flanders** — Fierce attack on British positions at Givenchy. Germans regain Lombartzyde. First Territorials (London Scottish) reinforce BEF, 22 bns + 6 Yeomanry regts by mid-Dec. **Artois** — Heavy fighting at Arras.	**E Prussia** — Otto Below replaces François as C-in-C Eighth Army.	Austrian Sixth Army drives Serb Third Army off Guchevo ridge & forces Serb First & Uzice Armies back up to 4 miles in S.	**Armenia** — Battles of Köprüköy (-12) & Azap (-20): Russian advance on Erzerum blocked (see 11). **Tsingtao** — Ceasefire after Japanese storm redoubts before Fts Bismarck & Moltke.
Sun 8	**Flanders/Artois** — Fighting from Dixmude to Arras. Surgeon-Capt Martin-Leake VC (Boer War), RAMC, wins second VC for heroism nr Zonnebeke since 29 Oct. **Aisne** — French re-enter Vregny.	Conrad moves his HQ from Nowy Sacz to Teschen (-4), W of Cracow. **E Prussia** — Russians re-enter Eydtkihnen & Stallupönen, advance into imperial Romintern Forest (-16). **Poland** — Tsar visits Kholm, inspects Red Cross hospital. **Galicia** — Austrian Fourth Army back at R Dunajec, sends help to Dankl N	Austrian Fifth Army advances to within mile of Serb Second Army aided by heavy arty & river monitor fire. Other Serb armies fall back under pressure; 2 newly arrived French naval 5.5-in guns first fire from Belgrade into Hungary (see 21 & 29), also inhibit Austrian monitors.	**Mesopotamia** — 4500 British troops land & entrench at Sanniyeh (-9) 3 miles beyond Abadan; outposts repel 400 Turks (11), first 10 British cas.

AFRICAN OPERATIONS 5	SEA WAR 6	AIR WAR 7	INTERNATIONAL EVENTS 8	HOME FRONTS 9
raised for internal security ops (*see* Jan 1915).				
E Africa — Brig-Gen Stewart's 1500 British, 4 guns & 6 MGs first cross N frontier but are repulsed (53 cas) from Longido by Maj Kraut's 669 Germans (50 cas) who evacuate (6, *see* 17). Imperial Service Bde (300 cas) repulsed from Tanga. **Upper Senegal: Niger** — French capture Tuareg rebel leader Firhoun (jailed with 5 others 15 Jan 1915, *see* 13 Feb 1916).	**N Sea** — 3 German battlecruisers (Hipper) briefly shell Yarmouth to cover cruiser *Kölberg* laying 130 mines 15 miles off coast. Returning cruiser *Yorck* hits 2 German mines off the Jade & sinks (4). **Fisher orders Admiralty to build record 600 warships. Aegean** — 2 British battlecruisers & 2 French battleships bombard (76 shells) outer Dardanelles forts, Sedd-el-Bahr magazine explosion (150k, *see* 9). **E Atlantic** — Grand Fleet returns to Scapa from L Swilly. **Pacific** — Spee at Valparaiso (-4), he replies to German colony flowers 'They will do for my funeral'.		**Neutrals: Italy** — Baron Sonnino Foreign Minister. Salandra Cabinet reshuffle (5).	**Austria** — †War Poet Lt George Trakl from cocaine, Cracow Garrison Hospital.
E Africa — IE 'B' (517 cas) repulsed by Lettow's 1000 (148 cas) flank counter-attack after Lettow's bicycle recce (bees halt fighting). **Cameroons** — 120 French repulsed from Mora in N (-5).	**N Sea** — British Admiralty orders Rear-Adm Sturdee with battlecruisers *Invincible* & *Inflexible* to proceed secretly to S Atlantic to intercept von Spee (sail from Devonport 11). **Channel** — Old turret ship *Hood* scuttled to fill gap in Portland harbour's defences. **Caribbean** — *Karlsruhe*, having sunk 15 British ships, sunk by internal explosion (unstable cordite), 200 miles NE of Trinidad. RN do not know until Jan 1915.	Kitchener cables Sir J French on dire shortage of arty observation planes equipped with radio.	US National City Bank loans $10m short-term credit to France.	**Britain** — Gold reserves nearly £69bn. King & Queen + Kitchener inspect CEF. **Austria** — Military courts preside in war areas (*see* 26). **Russia** — Tsar inspects 2 hospitals in Minsk. **France — First voluntary and free canteen for BEF opens at Boulogne (**'coffee shop' at Rouen stn Dec).
E Africa — IEF'B' re-embarks (reaches Mombasa 8); Tanga fiasco not revealed in Britain (*see* 17). **S Africa** — De Wet's rebels blow up Kroonstad-Natal railway at 3 points, Beyers' 1000 men trek through loyal troops at Kingswood *en route* to join de Wet.	**Adriatic** — Austrian *U5* misses French cruiser *Victor Hugo* (*see* 8 & 21 Dec).		ZANZIBAR DECLARES WAR ON TURKEY. Belgium rejects Papal mediation (*see* 30 July 1915).	**Serbia** — Cabinet resigns, reformed 13. **France** — Paris Central Employment Agency formed, only places 14,850 by 5 Jan 1915.
L Victoria — Armed steamer *Sybil* wrecked (flotilla part of RN from 9).	**Black Sea** — Russian sqn bombards Turk Zonguldak coal port, sinks 3 troopships. **N Sea** — Damaged *U16* enters Esbjerg, Denmark, but later released. New battlecruiser *Tiger* joins Grand Fleet.			**Britain** — **German spy Lody shot at the Tower. Germany** — Britons of military age interned.
S Africa — Smuts reviews motor bde at Johannesburg. Loyal troops take Beyers' Gruis Drift camp & 350 men (*see* 7 Dec). Rebel Maj Kemp's 700 men beaten from Kuriman, Bechuanaland (*see* 16). **Cameroons** — German coy takes British frontier post at Danare & ambushes patrol nr Abunorok (12).	**Pacific** — Fall of Tsingtao: 4 German gunboats & sloop *Cormoran* found sunk.		TURKEY DECLARES WAR ON BELGIUM. **Britain refuses US demand to restrict right of search to high seas** (*see* 29 Dec).	**Hungary** — Different nationalities may wear colours & emblems.
S Africa — De Wet defeats Union Gen Cronje at Doornberg (but his son killed); enters Winburg (9).	**British Admiralty decoding unit Room 40 formed, centre of signals Intelligence assessment for duration,** strongly backed by new DNI Capt William 'Blinker' Hall who appoints Cdr HWW Hope to analyse intercepts (16, *see* 30).	**W Front** — French Army airship *Conte* bombs Tergnier rail stn by R Oise.		**Canada** — 30,000 more troops to mobilize for overseas.

NOVEMBER 1914	WESTERN FRONT 1	EASTERN FRONT 2	SOUTHERN FRONTS 3	TURKISH FRONTS 4
		of Vistula (10).		
Mon 9	British positions at Ypres come under fierce attack. Falkenhayn forms Army Group Linsingen for final effort. Indian Garhwal Rifles make successful night raid (Neuve Chapelle sector).	**Poland** — Woyrsch evacuates Kalish & Chenstokhov. **Russian 14th Cav Div raids Silesia**, cuts railway at Pleschen, penetrates 20 miles (-10).	**Serbia** — Austrian regt crosses Sava at Semendria E of Belgrade but is blocked by Serbs.	
Tue 10	**Flanders — Battle of the Yser ends**. German 43rd Res Div storms Dixmude (but French demolish bridge) & St Eloi. Over 20 German divs attack around Ypres (-11).	Col Hentsch, Falkenhayn's envoy, arrives at Conrad's HQ, promises 4 German corps from W by c22; Conrad switching 5 divs of Second Army from Carpathians to cover Silesia (-23) as he suggested (7). **E Prussia** — Russians re-enter Goldap. **Galicia — Siege of Przemysl** (120,000 Austrians) **resumed** by Russian Eleventh Army (*see* 25).	**Serbia** — Putnik decides to retreat to line covering Valjevo, but stand there prevented by 500,000 refugees, desertions (especially from the 2 Drina divs), ammo shortages & Austrian arty mobility.	**Arabia** — 29th Indian Bde (20 cas) storms Sheikh Said & blows up Ft Turba (5 guns) just outside Aden Protectorate. **Tsingtao — Formal surrender** (Japanese triumphal entry parade 16).
Wed 11	FIRST BATTLE OF YPRES Phase 3: **Battle of Nonne Boschen** (Nuns' Wood). Third German attack: fresh corps of 17,500 (composite Prussian Guard Div & 4th Div from Arras) pushes down Menin Rd (Gheluvelt-Ypres) in thick mist v Haig's I Corps (7850) now stiffened by 5 rear strongpoints & most of Smith-Dorrien's II Corps sent N from La Bassée. Again the Germans come within an ace of victory. They break through N of Menin Rd & British guns face being overrun, but are unaware of this & hesitate. **British scratch force** (306 2nd Ox & Bucks Lt Inf with engineers, cooks & batmen) counter-attacks repeatedly & pushes **back Prussian Guard.**	SECOND GERMAN OFFENSIVE ON WARSAW ASTRIDE VISTULA (-25): Mackensen's 3 corps smash V Siberian Corps (First Army) around Wloclawek, take 15 guns & 12,000 PoWs by 14, helped by Russian cipher signal with Army boundary (12).	Serb GHQ evacuates Valjevo, moves to Kragujevac (national arsenal).	SULTAN PROCLAIMS JIHAD (HOLY WAR) V ALLIES at Fatih Mosque, Constantinople. **Armenia** — 4 Turk divs counter-attack Russian flanks, force retreat (12).
Thu 12	TFlanders — German official communiqué for 11 claims: 'In the neighbourhood east of Ypres our troops advanced further'. A total of more than 700 French were taken...'(& Hill 60). No mention made of supreme effort hurled against BEF, nor of any Prussian Guard attack. Brig-Gen FitzClarence, VC, k leading night counter-attack against Prussian Guard, E of Nonne Boschen & Glencorse Wood, nicknamed 'GOC Menin Road' by his men.	Grand Duke Nicholas orders invasion for 14. **E Prussia** — Russians enter Johannisburg S of Masurian Lakes. **Poland** — Lechitski's Ninth Army occupies Miechow nr Cracow. Tsar inspects Ivangorod fortress.	**Serbia** — Putnik orders retreat to R Kolubara line (entrenched since early Aug). **Herzegovina** — Austrians beat Montenegrins at Grahovo on border.	
Fri 13	**Ypres** — German pressure begins to slacken. Aisne — French re-enter Tracy-le-Val, S of R Oise, repulse counter-attack (19).	**E Prussia** — Russians threaten fortress Thorn, are checked (14) but levy taxes (15). **Galicia** — Russians occupy Dunayetz & threaten Cracow.		

AFRICAN OPERATIONS 5	SEA WAR 6	AIR WAR 7	INTERNATIONAL EVENTS 8	HOME FRONTS 9
	Indian Ocean — *Emden driven ashore & destroyed* (206 dead, but 50 crew ashore escape, see TURK FRONTS 9 Jan 1915) on Direction Island, Keeling, Cocos I by cruiser HMAS *Sydney* (Glossop), 16 cas, hit 10 times. **First action ever fought by an Australian warship. Pacific** — German gunboat *Geier* interned at Honolulu, becomes USS *Carl Schurz*, 1917 (lost in collision 21 June 1918); AMC *Komoran* interned at Guam (14). **Dardanelles** — Adm Guépratte forms French Sqn. **N Sea** — **First U-boat** (*U12*) **enters Zeebrugge** base (*see* 11 & 23). **E Africa** — RN sinks blockship in Rufiji Delta v *Königsberg* & shell her (*see* 24).		Asquith's Guildhall speech on Allied war aims 'We shall never sheath the sword'. Anglo-French convention on naval prizes.	
	Channel — Anchored gunboat *Niger* (no cas) sunk by *U12* (Forstmann) at Deal pier.			**Britain** — Parlt re-sits (-27). Bonar Law demands Antwerp & Coronel explanations.
S Africa — Botha's 6000 men surprise & rout De Wet's 3500 (600 cas incl 22k) in Mushroom Valley 60 miles NE of Bloemfontein & 18 miles SE of Winburg (*see* 16).			**Grey informs Russia that Straits & Constantinople will be hers**. All 3 Scandinavian neutrals agree on protest notes v Allied blockade. Holland protests v London Declaration changes (13).	
Cameroons — French cruiser *Bruix* covers RM seizure of Victoria, Buea's port & German admin centre. British occupy 3 places on N Railway. **Morocco — Worst French defeat**: 3000 Zaians massacre 733 French, take 8 guns & 10 MGs outside Ft Khenifra which is blockaded for duration (*see* 13 Mar 1915).				

NOVEMBER 1914	WESTERN FRONT 1	EASTERN FRONT 2	SOUTHERN FRONTS 3	TURKISH FRONTS 4
Sat 14	**France** — †FM Lord Roberts VC, last C-in-C of British Army (1901-4) from pneumonia at St Omer after inspecting Indian Corps (12), aged 82. **Germans down to 4 days' shell supply.** BEF IV Corps enters line between II & Indian Corps opposite Aubers (night 14/15, see 18 Dec).	**Poland** — Battle of Kutno (-16): Mackensen marches 25 miles and drives wedge between Russian First and Second Armies.	**Serbia** — Serb Obrenovac Det & Second Army behind R Kolubara.	**Mesopotamia** — Lt-Gen Barrett GOC IEF'D' brings 18th Bde (18 transports) 7046 troops & 24 guns ashore by 16.
Sun 15	French Gen Staff issues studies & plans on resumption of offensive, assuming a German retreat after their setbacks at Ypres & on the E Front (see 6 Dec). **Ypres** — Relief of BEF I Corps by French (Foch) begins (-22). The French retain responsibility for Salient until early 1915. Sir J French tells Lord Stamfordham '... we can hold on here...but are not strong enough...to take a vigorous offensive'.	**Poland** — Russian Second & Fifth Armies retreat to line Gumbin-Lodz & switch corps to latter. Russian Guards Corps cas to date 14,000. **Carpathians** — **Second Russian invasion** (Brusilov) of N Hungary (-12 Dec, see 29, recover passes 17-28).	**Serbia** — Austrians occupy Valjevo. Vienna rejoices & Potiorek decorated, but rain turning roads into quagmires. Serbs abandon 20 guns by now (chronic shell shortage).	**Mesopotamia** — British beat 2000 Turks at Sahain. **Armenia** — c5000 Turkish irregulars wipe out 1 Russian bn at copper mine S of Batumi.
Mon 16	**Flanders** — Heavy rain & floods swamp Yser battlefield. Prince of Wales joins BEF. **Aisne** — German attempt to cross at Vailly.	**Poland** — Russian rearguards beaten at Vlotslavek & Kutno. Russian I Corps marches 70 miles along bad roads (-17) to cover Lodz. **Galicia/S Poland** — Austrian offensive (-25) from Cracow (12 divs of First & Fourth Armies) v Lechitski makes only local gains.	Serbs all on Kolubara line.	**Armenia** — Russian II Turkestan Corps reinforcements save I Caucasus Corps & stabilize front (-17).
Tue 17	Falkenhayn begins transferring 9 divs to E Front, 'low fighting strength...and bad autumn weather' ends German Fourth Army attacks.	**Poland** — Fighting round Plotsk N of R Vistula.	**Battle of Kolubara** (-22) mainly in rain & snow with thick morning fogs: Austrian XVI Corps mtn troops reach Pt 1000 in Maljen Mts; both sides suffer frostbite, Austrian XV Corps 3000 cas & 5000 sick.	**Mesopotamia** — **Battle of Ft Sahil** (Kut-az-Zain): British (489 cas) rout 4500 Turks, taking 2 guns & 150 PoWs. Turks fail to seal Shatt-al-Arab with 4 blockships.
Wed 18	Patrol skirmishes at various points.	**E Prussia** — Russians beaten at Soldau. **Poland** — Russians retreat on Lowicz, 150,000 nr Lodz encircled on 3 sides by 250,000 Germans; Grand Duke Nicholas countermands retreat order. Indecisive fighting N of Cracow on 16-mile front.	Austrian Sixth Army attacks Serb Second Army at Choka.	**Sinai** — 1st skirmish, 20 Bikanir Camel Corps men escape 200 Bedouin at Katia, 20 miles E of Kantara (Canal). **Secret War** — Capt Shakespear leaves IEF'D', reaches Kuwait on mission to Ibn Saud (joins him 31 Dec).
Thu 19	**Flanders** — Arty duels & skirmishes. Indian Corps fire their first 2 homemade mortars (see 26), gaining 1 or 2 direct hits.	**S Poland** — Austrian Second Army storms Mykanow & Klɛkoty but blocked by Russian Fourth Army. Conrad complains 'We...have been holding the door against half Asia'. Plehve's Fifth Army rescues wing of Second Army after forced marches.	Austrian centre captures W slopes of Vrace Brdo (521ft), Milovac hill & drive back Serb First Army.	
Fri 20	**Flanders** — Haig promoted general for Ypres defence. **Champagne** — French Fourth Army staff begin planning possible offensive ops. Harassing ops & on Aisne (21).	Captured documents tell Russians Germans reading their cipher so key changed, but Austrian Capt Pokorny solves again (22). **Poland** — Mackensen attacks Russian line, Lowicz-Skiernievitse, SW of Warsaw (-21). At Lodz 134 Russian bns & 380 guns v 70 German bns & 480 guns.	Putnik orders offensive at both Austrian flanks but Serb generals report unable to launch it.	
Sat 21			Austrian XI Corps breaks Serb Gukoshi-Maljen line. At Belgrade French naval guns fire 78 shells, scoring 2 hits that ground a monitor (see 29).	**Mesopotamia** — **British occupy Basra** (formal entry 23, 6 Germans arrested) & ally with Sheikh of Mohammera (22).

AFRICAN OPERATIONS 5	SEA WAR 6	AIR WAR 7	INTERNATIONAL EVENTS 8	HOME FRONTS 9
S Africa — Beyer's rebels routed at Bulfontein. **Rhodesia** — 1st Regt leaves Salisbury for Bloemfontein (*see* 25 Dec).			**Japan decides v sending troops or warships to Europe** (*see* 3 Dec). **Neutrals: Italy** — Mussolini launches and edits *Popolo d'Italia* newspaper (*see* 13 Dec). US 'Christmas ship' *Jason* sails from NY with $3m of gifts for war victims.	
Cameroons — 1247 Allies occupy Buea in Mt district (1200 Germans now captive, *see* 26).				**Austria** — Czech Parties' patriotic manifesto.
S Africa — De Wet breaks through Kroonstad-Natal railway at Virginia (*see* 22). Kemp forces pursuers to retire at Klein Witzand (*see* 25).				**Britain** — **First 9 VCs** (all BEF) **gazetted**. Interned enemy aliens total 14,500. Commons votes £225m war credit.
E Africa — EA Mtd Rifles occupy Longido. **Kitchener orders British on to the defensive, War Office assumes operational control** (22, *see* 20).	**Baltic** — German sqn shells Libau. Cruiser *Friedrich Karl* sunk by Russian mines off Memel. First Russian dreadnought *Sevastopol* completed at Baltic Yard, Petrograd. **Black Sea** — Russian sqn bombards Trebizond (repeated 20).			**Britain** — **Lloyd George introduces 1st War Budget**: income tax doubled; £350m 1st War Loan issued. **Germany** — Wheat Purchase Corp formed.
	Black Sea — 14-min action in fog between returning Russian bombardment sqn and *Goeben* & *Breslau*, 20 miles off the Crimea. *Goeben* (1 hit, 12k) & Russian flagship *Evstafi* damaged (4 hits, 28 cas). **Norway** — German auxiliary minelayer *Berlin* interned at Trondheim for duration.	**W Front** — 1st Wing, RFC, formed at St Omer from Nos 2 & 3 Sqns under Lt-Col H M Trenchard, to operate with Indian Corps & IV Corps, BEF (*see* 29).		**France** — **Govt returns from Bordeaux to Paris** (-10 Dec).
British Somaliland — Dismtd Camel Corps repulsed 3 times from 3 Dervish forts S of Shimberberris but muzzle-loading 7pdr aids their capture (22, *see* 3 Feb 1915).		**Britain** — All airworthy home-based RFC & RNAS aircraft scrambled at Admiralty's urgent request to oppose anticipated sortie by German fleet (*see* 21).		
E Africa — 400 Germans capture Ft Kyaka on Uganda border (*see* 6 Dec).			Trotsky arrives in Paris. Allies retract African free trade zone proposal (*see* 9 Aug).	**Britain** — Commons votes Army 2nd million men. Drink sales to women before 1130 prohibited. **France** — Belgian Flag Day (-25).
	Germany — Tirpitz tells American journalist 'England wants to starve us ... We are superior ... in U-boats'.	**Germany** — **First British long-range bombing raid**: 3 Avro 504s of RNAS (Sqn Cdr Featherstone-Briggs, Flt Cdr Babington & Flt Lt Sippe) attack Zeppelin works at Fried-richshafen, L Constance from temporary base at Belfort,		

NOVEMBER 1914	WESTERN FRONT 1	EASTERN FRONT 2	SOUTHERN FRONTS 3	TURKISH FRONTS 4
Sat 21 contd				
Sun 22	**Flanders** — FIRST BATTLE OF YPRES ENDS: Since suffering a decisive check (11), Germans manage only desultory local attacks. By 2400 BEF is re-established on 21-mile front Givenchy-Kemmel. BEF suffers first 'trench foot' cases. **Secret War** — Allies form tri-national espionage bureau at Folkestone (S Coast, England) for agents` reports from behind W Front.	**Poland** — Mackensen approaches Lodz but ammo running short and resistance stiffening; 6th Siberian Div takes Brzeziny to NE, 60,000 Germans surrounded, ordered to retreat at 1900. Ivanov defeats Austrians (6000 PoWs) on Cracow-Chenstokhov front.	Austrian Fifth Army attacks Kolubara line, takes Chopka & Konatitsa by 25 with 8000 PoWs & 42 guns.	**Armenia** — Russians re-occupy Köprüköy after Turks withdraw 5-6 miles, latter's losses to date 7100.
Mon 23	**Ypres** — German arty carries out heavy 'hate shoot': Cathedral & Cloth Hall damaged.	**Poland** — Isolated Germans launch breakout v Russian line Rzgov-Koliuszki SE of Lodz. Night temperature 10°F. Lechitski's Ninth Army (14 divs) 93,000-strong instead of 196,000.	Serbs evacuate Maljen line. First Army split from Uzice Army, but Austrians slow advance to let supply convoys come up (*see* 30).	**Mesopotamia** — RN sloops *Espiègle* & *Odin* recon Qurna, Turk position 45 miles from Basra at Tigris/Euphrates jctn.
Tue 24	**Flanders** — Indians recapture trenches with 100 PoWs between Armentières & La Bassée (lost 15).	**Poland** — Litzmann's 3rd Guard Div retakes Brzeziny, 6th Siberian Div destroyed.		
Wed 25	**Ypres** — 'Snipers' nests' — Gerfeld Farms nr Ypres blown up by British. **Artois** — German bombardment of Arras.	**Poland** — Gen Schäffer's **3 German divs** & 140 guns (XXV Res Corps) **escape** encircle-ment at Lodz, break out NW through 4-mile gap with 16,000 Russian PoWs & 64 captured guns (1500k, 2800w). **Galicia** — Artillery duels begin at Przemysl. Austrian First and Fourth Armies cease offensive, 26,000 PoWs taken but 55,000 cas (since 16). **Carpathians** — Russian 2nd Composite Cossack Div raids Hungary.	French Naval Mission ordered to withdraw from Montenegro, handing over its 4 guns to her.	Turco-German Treaty of 1890 extended.
Thu 26	**Flanders** — German attack on	**Bukovina** — Austrians again evacuate Czernowitz.	Austrians force cross Sava nr	Anzac troop convoy leaves

AFRICAN OPERATIONS 5	SEA WAR 6	AIR WAR 7	INTERNATIONAL EVENTS 8	HOME FRONTS 9
		Alsace (each carries 4 20lb bombs) Zeppelin *Z7* seriously damaged; a hydrogen gasworks destroyed & workshops damaged (*see* 27 June 1915). Heavy AA fire cripples Featherstone-Briggs' aircraft, he makes forced landing & is badly injured by civilians but military treat him well. Sippe returns safely to Belfort carrying a fused bomb, hung up on a crude rack. **France** — Future ace Guynemer accepted as pupil mechanic at Pau airfield. **N Sea** — All RNAS floatplanes & hangars at Scapa Flow seaplane stn wrecked in gale.		
S Africa — De Wet cut off to W, flees E again.		**W Front** — Lts L A Strange & F G Small of No 5 Sqn return from a recon in an Avro 504 (Lewis gun on jury-rigged rope tackle above observer's seat) encounter an Albatros 2-seater at 7000 ft. After 2 ammo drums are fired into the Albatros its pilot side-slips away & makes forced landing nr Neuve-Eglise (SW of Messines), behind British lines. Strange & Small land close by to take PoWs & see the German observer, a commissioned officer, drag the NCO pilot from the cockpit, knock him down & kick him. The RFC officers count 20 bullet holes in the downed Albatros. RFC GOC Maj-Gen Sir D Henderson temporarily commands 1st Div (-20 Dec qv), Col F H Sykes assumes command.	Allies vainly offer Greece S Albania if she aids Serbia (*see* 6 Dec).	
	Occupied Belgium — 2 British Channel Fleet battleships shell Zeebrugge. **N Sea** — *U18* (Hennig) enters Scapa Flow (Grand Fleet at sea), is rammed leaving by minesweeper close to Hoxa entrance, then by destroyer *Garry*, has to surrender (26/27 crew saved). **Channel** — *U21* (Hersing) sinks (with deck gun) 2 small British steamers off Havre (& 26 qv).	**France** — *le Group de Bombardement* (1st Bombing Group) formed of 18 Voisins under Cdt de Goys (*see* 4 Dec).	**Portugese Congress allows Govt to join Allies when it deems fit** (*see* AFRICAN OPS 4 Dec). **Mexico** — Last US troops evacuate Vera Cruz. Swiss complain that Friedrichshafen raiders overflew their land & killed citizen; HMG regrets 3 Dec. **Holland** — Netherlands Overseas Trust formed.	**Austria: Bukovina** — 30,000 Rumanian peasants' manifesto supports Emperor.
	E Africa — RNAS Curtiss seaplane confirms *Königsberg* 12 miles up Rufiji Delta (*see* 6 Dec). **N Sea** — 3 Harwich Force cruisers provoke Heligoland I fortress guns to fire for only time during war, after seaplane raid on Cuxhaven called off (*see* 6 Dec).	**E Africa** — Flt Sub-Lt Cutter, RNAS piloting delapidated Curtiss flying boat, spots German cruiser *Königsberg* at secret anchorage (*see* SEA WAR 6 Dec).		**Britain** — Army officers' pay increase, 7s 6d pd for subalterns.
S Africa — Kemp disappears W into Kalahari Desert; 580 men reach Nakob & Mantz nr SW Africa border (28, *see* 1 Dec).			**Santo Domingo declares neutrality. Britain** — 1st War Council on general war policy with proceedings minuted, 'invasion assessed as unlikely'.	**Russia** — Polish National Council forms in Warsaw, issues manifesto, Germany must be defeated (*see* 3 Apr 1915). Minsk Gendarmerie report Bolshevik cells in several units esp railway bns (*see* 12 Dec).
Cameroons — Germans force	**N Sea** — Battleship *Bulwark*			**Austria** — Conrad note to PM

NOVEMBER 1914	WESTERN FRONT 1	EASTERN FRONT 2	SOUTHERN FRONTS 3	TURKISH FRONTS 4
Thu 26 contd	Yser canal fails. **BEF forms Trench Mortar Service** ('The Suicide Club' -9 May 1915) nr Bethune, 11 men with 2 Crimean War 6-in mortars, but 100 copies of German *Minenwerfer* supplied by Christmas (*see* 18 Dec; 10 Mar 1915)		Kolubara jctn with 3 river monitors in support, but half landing force wiped out.	Aden for Suez (arrives 30).
Fri 27	**Champagne** — Germans bombard Reims Cathedral.	**Hindenburg promoted field marshal** (*see* 1 Nov). (c) Litvinov replaces Rennenkampf (Russian First Army) due to Lodz fiasco.	Serbs retake Covka.	**Mesopotamia** — 17th Bde completes 6th Indian Div.
Sat 28	**Artois** — German attacks round Arras. French poet Jean de La Ville de Mirmont killed by landmine explosion at Verreiul, aged 27.	**Carpathians** — Russians again secure Passes. **Galicia** — Austrian XI Corps retreats to Wieliczka c8 miles E of Cracow after fighting Russian Third Army since 22. Conrad returns Austrian Fourth Army S of the Vistula. Grand Duke Nicholas meets his 2 Front commanders at Siedlce (-30), Cracow offensive agreed. **Carpathians** — Austrian Third Army forced back to R Toplya & Bartfeld in N Hungary.	Putnik orders Belgrade's evacuation after Austrian Sixth Army's alarming gains. Front extends nearly 70 miles.	German FM Goltz ordered to Constantinople as Sultan's 'Adjt Gen' (*see* 10 Dec). Turks announce drive (fictitious) towards Suez Canal. **NW Frontier : India** — Skirmish at Miranshah (-29).
Sun 29	**Somme** — French advance between the R Chaulnes. **Argonne** — French recapture Bagatelle. **Vosges** — French repulse attacks at Ban-de-Sapt. Bavarians form first ski bn. **Artois** — Gen Fayolle (70th Res Div) writes 'I wonder whether those great leaders who push themselves forward...are not those who take no account...of the human lives entrusted to them'.		**Serbs evacuate Belgrade** (night 29/30), blowing up French naval guns after 240 rnds fired off. The garrison's 17 bns join Obrenovac Det (6 bns) to the S. Serb First Army retreats 12 miles. Serb I wing to S now astride W Morava Valley.	
Mon 30	**Flanders** — Arty duels. K George V first visits BEF, now 200,000 strong. **Artois** — Arty duels.	**Poland** — Battle of Lowicz-Sanniki (-17 Dec) involves German Ninth Army reinforced by 9 divs v Russian First Army (Litvinov) whose VI Corps & II Caucasus (Gourko) Corps hold firm until retreat behind shorter R Bzura line ordered (6 Dec).	Potiorek orders 4-day Austrian pause (-3 Dec) to bring up supplies.	**Armenia** — Tsar inspects front & tells Armenian Catholicos '... a most brilliant future awaits the Armenians' (*see* 12 Dec).
Tue 1 December 1914	**Flanders** - K George visits Indian Corps & field hospitals, confers GCBs on Joffre & Foch (2). French recapture Vermelles Château, SE of Bethune. **Aisne** — German attack fails at Berry-au-Bac.	(Dec) Russian troops receive first barbed wire. **Poland** — Fierce fighting in Lodz suburbs. **Galicia** — **Battle of Lima-nowa-Lapanow** (-17): Austrian Fourth Army saves Cracow (*see* 2). **N Hungary** — Brusilov occupies Bartfeld in Carpathians but Boroevic's Austrian Third Army retakes it from Russian XII Corps (8, *see* 8 & 12).	Austrian Fifth Army (Frank) occupies Belgrade. (c) Misi´c replaces Boyovic i/c Serb First Army. **Italy** — War Minister Zupelli expects to mobilize 1,404,000 troops in spring (*see* 15).	**Armenia** — Russians take Sarai & Bashkal, & repulse Turks S of Batumi (7). **Egypt**— First Anzac units arrive at Suez. NZEF lands at Alexandria (3, *see* 21 & 23).
Wed 2	**Flanders** — Allied guns smash German troop-carrying rafts on the Yser nr Dixmude (& 7). **Lorraine** — French advance W of Metz; they capture Xon & Lesmesnils. **Alsace** — French capture Aspach, occupy Burnhaupt and advance on Altkirch (3).	Tsar visits STAVKA, dines with Allied attachés (*see* TURK FRONTS 14). **Galicia** — Roth's (XIV Corps) 24,500 men in 4 divs incl German 47th Res Div, Polish Legion (+3 cav) flank & stop Radko's Third Army drive on Cracow (-6).	Having received small Allied ammo stocks via Bulgaria, Putnik orders general Serb counter-offensive for 3 'to restore the morale of our soldiers'. **K Peter enters trenches with rifle** & 50 rnds, inspiring patriotic feeling.	British Military Attaché leaves Constantinople.

AFRICAN OPERATIONS 5	SEA WAR 6	AIR WAR 7	INTERNATIONAL EVENTS 8	HOME FRONTS 9
150 French (50 cas) back on Edea (*see* 2 Dec).	destroyed by internal explosion while loading ammunition at Sheerness, 793k, 12 survivors. (Enquiry rules out sabotage, 15 Dec.) **Channel** — Churchill cables C-in-C Portsmouth 'It is desired to trap the German submarine which sinks vessels by gunfire off Havre. A small or moderate-sized steamer should be taken up....' First Q-ship is coaster *Victoria* but unserviceable & paid off by 9 Dec (*see* 4 Feb 1915). First of 7 French Q-ships, *Marguerite*, also introduced (Nov).			v Pan-Slavic anti-Austrian tendencies in Bohemia, Moravia & Silesia, but Emperor rejects suggestion of military jurisdiction. **France** — Poincaré decorates Joffre with *Médaille Militaire*, latter opens *GQG* at Chantilly (29).
Tripolitania: Fezzan — Revolt forces 191 Italians & 2 guns from Sebha to Brach where 2 coys join (8 Dec, *see* 25 Dec).		**Egypt** — RFC (5 Farmans, 3 arrived Alexandria 17) flies 1st recon over Suez Canal (*see* 23 Jan 1915). 7 French Nieuport seaplanes assist from ships in the Canal.	Pres Wilson condemns bombardment of unfortified towns.	**Britain** — Army & Admiralty able to take over private arms factories.
Adm King-Hall informed that **S Africa ready to resume SW Africa campaign.**	**E Africa** — Battleship *Goliath* (after disabling 2 German ships Cdr Ritchie w 8 times wins first naval VC) & cruiser *Fox* bombard Dar-es-Salaam for 15 mins (& 30): Governor's palace destroyed. **Germany** — Austria sells Germany 5 U-boats building for her at Kiel (launched as *U66-U70* 22 Apr-24 June 1915).		**Occupied Belgium** — Gen Bissing replaces Goltz as Gov-Gen (*see* TURK FRONTS 10 Dec).	**Britain** — **All moving into hotels must register with police.** Professional football continues before large male crowds, despite protests.
		W Front — RFC reorganized: 2 & 3 Sqns already form 1st Wing; 5 & 6 Sqns form 2nd Wing (Lt-Col C J Burke. 4 Sqn, a communications unit & the depot (Aircraft Park) remain with RFC HQ at St Omer. **Germany** — Despite makers' promise to deliver 200 aircraft pm from mid-Aug, Military Air Service has received only 462 aircraft since 3 Aug.		**Britain** — **King leaves to visit W Front** (-5 Dec).
	Secret War: N Sea — British fishing trawler off the Texel recovers German VB naval code from sunken German destroyer; in Admiralty hands by 3 Dec.		France publishes Yellow Book on war's origins.	**Germany** — Unemployment down to 8.2% **Britain** — Custodian of Enemy Property appointed. **France/Britain** — (Nov) Sculptor Rodin presents 20 works to V & A Museum as thank you to BEF.
S Africa — **De Wet surrenders** with c50 followers to Col Brits' motor col (left Vryburg 27 Nov) 110 miles W of Mafeking. Kemp & Maritz proclaim independent S Africa.	**Britain** — 4 dedicated monitors (*Abercrombie* class) laid down (1-17); main armament 8 14-in guns from US Bethlehem Steel after Churchill met its Pres (3 Nov). **Hong Kong** — (Dec) 10 RN river gunboats paid off to provide crews for more needed warships.	**W Front** — (c) First German aircraft with radio equipment on arty spotting duties. (c) French aviators Garros & Saulnier make first airborne firing tests of device for firing MG through arc of rotating tractor airscrew. Pioneer aviator Capt Saconney's French manlifting kite-section flies successful 5-hr arty observation mission. Saconney manlifting kite known as *Le Cerf Volant* ('The Flying Stag').	**Neutrals** — **USA** — †Rear Adm Mahan, influential historian of seapower, Quogul NY (aged 74). National Security League formed in NY. (Dec) Freight cost of US grain to England & cotton to Rotterdam has quadrupled.	**Germany** — (Dec) Imperial Govt subsidizes local unemployment relief. **Britain** — RFP c16%. (Dec) Soldiers and Sailors Dental Aid Fund formed. (Dec) First of 5 K Albert Belgian military hospitals opens at Highgate, N London.
Cameroons — French occupy Kribi; minor German attacks fail (5 & 9). **E Africa** — Germans defeat Belgian attack on Rwanda.	**S Atlantic** — E of the Horn cruiser *Leipzig* captures Scottish 3-masted barque *Drummuir*, takes her 2800t coal (1-6), Spee decides to raid Falkland Is (*see* 8).	**W Front** — Lt Marc Pourpe, celebrated French prewar stunt pilot, k with *Esc N23*.		**Germany** — Leibknecht alone votes v *Reichstag* 2nd war credits bill (RM 5bn).

DECEMBER 1914	WESTERN FRONT 1	EASTERN FRONT 2	SOUTHERN FRONTS 3	TURKISH FRONTS 4
Thu 3			**General Serb counter-offensive** or Battle of the Ridges catches Austrian Sixth Army off guard (heavy arty in rear). Misic's First Army advances several miles taking 1512 PoWs, 5 guns & 4 MGs; Second & Third Armies recapture important heights with 503 PoWs & 2 MGs.	
Fri 4	**Flanders** — French recapture Langemarck. K George visits Belgian HQ & decorates K Albert. Sir J French writes to Kitchener '.. Krupp is our most formidable enemy'; receives HM St Petersburg ambassador's message that Russians expecting W Front help.	**Poland** — Russian front broken at Ilov, 2 res divs reduced to 4 or 5 coys.	Serb First Army continues success taking Height 802, but Uzice & Second Armies held up till Austrians abandon Lipet with 2000 PoWs after Serb night attack.	**Mesopotamia** — **First Battle of Qurna** (-9): 1000 British & 2 guns land from 4 steamers + 5 RN ships (2 hit since 3) before Qurna but blocked at Tigris & retire to camp (*see* 7).
Sat 5			Potiorek orders Austrian Fifth Army to attack S of Belgrade, but Putnik extends Serb Second Army to meet threat. Uzice Army fought to a standstill, but Austrian Sixth Army retreating towards Kolubara after losing 15,000 PoWs & I9 guns since 3.	German Afghanistan Mission leaves Constantinople, reaches Aleppo (13) en route for Mosul (*see* 28).
Sun 6	**Dunkirk bombarded** (& Furnes 8) by German 15-in naval guns emplaced 20 miles E in Flanders. *GQG* note states that a German retreat not anticipated for time being, but an offensive is to be launched (on 13) to try encourage one & to help the Russians.	**Poland** — Russians evacuate Lodz & retreat to Bzura-Ravka river line.	Austrian centre & right in full retreat downhill to the Kolubara. Krauss and VIII Corps strike S from Belgrade but Serb Second Army holds until forced back (7, *see* 8). Serb Third Army reaches R Lig & First Army pursues.	**Armenia** — Enver Pasha arrives in Trebizond en route for Erzerum (*see* 14).
Mon 7	**Flanders** — French recapture Vermelles, Le Rutoire & trenches nr Carency. Joffre instructs Foch to start (in liaison with British) limited offensives in Yser sector of Ypres Salient.	**E Prussia** — Russian attacks. **Poland** — **Second Battle of Warsaw** (-30): German offensive. **Galicia** — Russians bombard N Cracow forts.	Serb Third Army outflanks Kremenika hill defences aiding Second Army drive on Lazarevac, they take 6501 PoWs & 28 guns.	**Mesopotamia** — 3700 British & 16 guns renew attack v 3000 Turks & 10 guns, another RN launch disabled, but they hold Tigris bank (*see* 8).
Tue 8	Joffre instructs 4 armies to plan for limited offensives towards NE, with follow-up ops against German communications; 2 main attacks to be by Tenth Army in Artois & Fourth Army in Champagne. Aim is to tie down as many Germans as possible.	**Galicia** — Brusilov sends 2 corps to aid Third Army. Roth regains some ground (-25).	Austrian Fifth Army captures, loses & then retakes Serb Kosmaj line S of Belgrade (-9) but Serb reinforcements arriving from S. Serb First Army retakes Valjevo (3000 Austrian w) by flanking move through hills, Third Army reaches Kolubara.	**Mesopotamia** — Qurna outflanked by RN & 2 Indian bns crossing via flying bridge & boats upstream.
Wed 9	Joffre rejects British proposal that BEF be transferred to extreme left of Allied line to permit combined ops along Belgian coast, as a '*mouvement eccentrique*'.	**Poland** — Heavy fighting around Mlava & Petrokov. **Galicia** — First Przemysl sortie (-10, *see* 15).	Serb Second Army reoccupies Lazarevac, while other pursuers retake Uzice. **Potiorek orders general Austrian retreat** in evening, Putnik orders continuation of offensive.	**Mesopotamia** — Subhi Bey surrenders Qurna (1242 PoWs & 9 guns taken since 4); British 331cas. **Secret War**— Col Newcombe, TE Lawrence, L Woolley & G Lloyd sail for Egypt from Marseilles to join Cairo GHQ Intelligence.

AFRICAN OPERATIONS 5	SEA WAR 6	AIR WAR 7	INTERNATIONAL EVENTS 8	HOME FRONTS 9
Cameroons — Brig-Gen Gorges begins N Railway advance, fighting daily, reaches terminus (10, *see* 11).			**Britain concedes to Japan that Australia occupies no German islands N of the Equator** (Japan will not yield them, 16). Japanese Peking Minister receives 21 Demands' text (*see* 18 Jan 1915). Austro-Italian talks resume. **Neutrals : Italy** — PM Salandra defines war policy. **Occupied Belgium** — Provincial govt powers go to German military governors. Germans impose 40m Fr pm war contribution (10, *see* 25).	**Germany** — Adolf Grober (Catholic Centre Party) 'We must enter upon a new Germany...we must set a good example to the whole world'. Kaiser returns to Berlin.
Portuguese EF leaves Lisbon for Angola (*see* 18). **E Africa** — Maj-Gen Wapshare C-in-C (Aitken recalled, leaves 7). **S Africa** — Botha beats rebels nr Reitz. **SE Cameroons** — 730 Franco-Belgians repulsed from Molundu, but force German evacuation (19).		**Germany** — French Voisin bombers of *GB I* raid Freiburg airfield (repeated 6).	**Britain** — Lends Russia £20m. Lord Bryce begins inquiry into German Belgian atrocities.	
S Africa — Rebels offer to talk, Botha demands unconditional surrender.			Nicaragua neutral.	**France** — 12 Scottish women doctors & nurses arrive in Calais to combat Belgian Army typhoid (-Feb 1915); 32 Scots women hospital arrives in Paris to tend French at Abbaye de Royaumont (-Feb 1919). **Britain** — 1000 German PoWs landed at Southend, Essex.
E Africa — c500 British retake 2 posts on Uganda border.	**E Africa** — Flt Sub-Lt Cutler RNAS taken PoW by *Königsberg* but RN tug *Helmuth* & her boat rescue his crash-landed seaplane.	**W Front** — French air-dropped *flechettes* mortally wound German Gen Meyer on horseback.	**Pope tries to arrange Christmas truce**. Rumania refuses Greece help v any Turco-German attack.	
S Africa — Rebel Gen Beyers defeated, drowned fleeing (with c25 followers) in R Vaal.			**Neutrals : USA** — Congress' private arms embargo bills brought (but shelved Jan).	Paris Bourse reopens. **Britain** — Compulsory registration of Belgian refugees. **Japan** — Diet opens with Emperor's speech.
Tripolitania — Sultan's rep in Tripoli declares holy war (see 25). **S Africa** — REBELLION COLLAPSES, 1200 surrender.	**Battle of the Falkland Islands**: Sturdee with battlecruisers *Invincible* (hit 22 times, no cas) & *Inflexible* (3 hits, 3 cas), old battleship *Canopus* & 5 cruisers incl *Glasgow* (hit twice), *Cornwall* hit 22 times, *Kent* hit 38 times (fired 646 rnds), surprises Spee as he prepares to raid Port Stanley; he retires SE, detaches light cruisers (only *Dresden* escapes, to Chile). Flagship *Scharnhorst*, *Gneisenau*, *Nürnberg* & *Leipzig* and 2 colliers sunk in 9-hr chase. German cas: 2100k, 215 survivors. British cas: 10k, 15w but battlecruisers down to 52 12-in shells, 1174 fired in first director control long-range gunnery.	**W Front** — RFC 'wireless unit', re-designated No 9 Sqn, detaches radio-equipped aircraft as required by the various army corps.	Anglo-Swedish contraband agreement.	**Britain** — Sir G Gibb to supervise Army contracts. **Germany** — Stresemann (industry rep) sees Chancellor about war aims.
SE Cameroons — 610 French force Germans to evacuate Baturi (*see* 29).		**E Front — Warsaw bombed by German aircraft**; US Consulate damaged. **Sea** — Commissioning of first purpose-built (from keel up) seaplane carrier HMS *Ark Royal II* (launched 5 Sept). First carrier with hangars below deck, but unable to fly off or land her 5 floatplanes & 2 land planes which are lowered & raised over ship's sides by pair of		**Britain** — Ahlers (ex-German consul Sunderland) sentenced to death but reprieved (18). **Russia** — Tsar arrives in Tiflis to wonderful reception, stays (-12).

DECEMBER 1914	WESTERN FRONT 1	EASTERN FRONT 2	SOUTHERN FRONTS 3	TURKISH FRONTS 4
Thu 10	Unsuccessful German attacks in Ypres Salient (& 11). **Champagne** — French gain ground nr Perthes.	**Galicia** — Austrian 3rd Div, nr Lapanow, loses 4000 PoWs to Brusilov's attacks, but new line holds.	Austrians begin steady retreat in N as Serb Third Army wheel around Ub slowed by mud. Uzice Army regains Drina line. Stepanovic put i/c Serbs S of Belgrade, storms Ralja railhead (11).	FM Goltz (aged 7l) leaves Germany to command Turk Army (arrives 14, boards *Goeben* for voyage 21).
Fri 11		**Poland** — Russians repel Germans N of Lovich, but evacuate town (15).		
Sat 12	**Artois** - Launch of Tenth Army offensive towards Vimy & Arras delayed till 17. **Argonne** - Dubail's First Army minor & subsidiary ops cost 9173 cas (-31).	**Carpathians** — Austrians retake Dukla Pass & Nowy Sacz.	Austrian Sixth Army recrosses Sava at Sabac (-13). **Bosnia** — Montenegrins retake Visegrad.	
Sun 13	**Flanders** — Germans pull back from Yser Canal.		Frank informs Potiorek Belgrade cannot be held. Serb Third Army retakes Obrenovac. Serb First Army reoccupies Loznica-Sabac line. Fighting in W almost over.	
Mon 14	**Flanders** — French 32nd & 16th Divs attack nr Klein Zillebeke. British 3rd Div advance in Petit Bois S of Wytschaete.	Russians change cipher alphabets, later adopt Caesar cipher, to no avail.	Austrians recross Sava at Belgrade (-15) covered by monitors as Serbs storm heights to S.	**Armenia** — **Enver Pasha** arrives at Köprüköy, **takes Third Army** from Hasan Izzet Pasha **to launch offensive** (*see* 19). Tsar decorates 1200 men from Front.
Tue 15	**Flanders** — Allied Nieuport Gp forces cross the Yser towards Lombaertzyde. Sir J French visits II Corps 'trenches... ground only a quagmire'.	**Poland** — Heavy fighting round Sokhachev on R Bzura. **Galicia** — 17 Austrian bns break out from Przemysl but driven back (17). Radko's Third Army back on R Dunajec, Brusilov reduced 70% back in Carpathian foothills.	**Serb patrols reoccupy Belgrade** at 1000 & gunners hit Austrian pontoon bridge. END OF THIRD AUSTRIAN INVASION with loss of 41,000 PoWs & 133 guns. K Peter proceeds to Belgrade Cathedral for Te Deum; Crown Prince follows with Lt-Col APB Harrison (Br Mil Attaché). American Hospital has 3000 Austrian & Serb military patients. Austrians leave 5 guns, 1000 horses, 448 wagons & 10,150 PoWs. Over 700 buildings damaged by shelling since 29 July incl University, Royal Palace; 180 civilian cas. **Italy** — Cadorna & Zupelli tell PM & Sonnino that Army will not be ready until April 1915 (*see* 21).	
Wed 16		**Poland — Russians end retreat & stand on Bzura-Ravka-R Pilitzu line 30 miles SW of Warsaw.**		

AFRICAN OPERATIONS 5	SEA WAR 6	AIR WAR 7	INTERNATIONAL EVENTS 8	HOME FRONTS 9
		cranes.		
	Black Sea — *Goeben* (15 shells) bombards Batumi (*see* 20).	**E Front** — **World's first heavy bomber unit formed** at Yablonna, nr Warsaw (Russian Poland). The EVK ('Flying Ship Squadron') flies RBVZ IM 4-engined biplanes designed by Sikorsky & Gakkel; CO is Maj Gen Shidlovski ex-Cdr, Imperial Russian Navy (Ret), RBVZ chairman. Special pilot conversion training, technical assistance & maintenance come from RBVZ engineers, inspectors & 1 test pilot (Sikorsky himself) seconded from company's Riga HQ.	US proposal for disabled PoW exchange, accepted by Germany (31). **Neutrals : USA** — Irving Berlin's first musical 'Watch Your Step' opens on Broadway.	
Cameroons — Gorges occupies Bare, booty incl 2 aircraft in crates.		**W Front** — **RFC & RNAS adopt roundel national marking** following example set by French *Aviation Militaire*. This supersedes Union Jack marking carried since war's early days and frequently mistaken for Iron Cross by Allied troops.		
	Baltic — 2 Russian destroyers lost in minelaying op off Gotland.		Chile protests v AMC *Eitel Friedrich* neutral waters violation. **Japan** — Brig-Gen Barnardiston (British Tsingtao GOC) arrives in Tokyo, decorated by Emperor (15).	**Russia** — Yaroslavl Gendarmerie reports Bolshevik factory propaganda. Dvina Military District orders stamping out of 'signs of socialist propaganda' (21). **Germany** — All Catholic Irish removed from Döberitz PoW camp.
	Dardanelles — **First battleship sunk by submarine**: old Turk battleship *Messudieh* sunk at anchor in shoal water N of Kephez Point by RN submarine *B11* (Holbrook) after passing 5 rows of mines & returning without compass. **Holbrook awarded first naval VC of war** (21).		**Neutrals: Italy** — Mussolini speaks in Parma 'Neutrals never dominate events. They always sink. Blood alone moves the wheels of history'.	
	Baltic — 4 Russian cruisers and a minelayer lay 424 mines at entrance to Gulf of Danzig (-15). **Secret War** — Thanks to Room 40, Admiralty warns Jellicoe of imminent German High Seas Fleet sortie (*see* 16).			**Turkey** — Sultan opens Parliament, ex-Khedive of Egypt present.
	E Med — British cruiser *Doris* shells Alexandretta, landing party cuts & sabotages railway nearby (18-20). Russian cruiser *Askold* sinks Turk sloop off Beirut (16). **Baltic** — Russian submarine drives off German cruiser sqn reconnoitring Aaland Is.	**Britain** — RNAS personnel now total 4245. **N Sea** - German Navy Zeppelins fly recon for battlecruiser force that bombards British E Coast targets & also help save battlecruisers from trap laid by British Grand Fleet.	**Neutrals : USA** — *NY Times* reports great European demand for film comedies.	**France** — 1915 conscript class incorporated (-18).
	N Sea — *Scarborough* (100 mines laid off by cruiser *Kolberg* ; 20 swept (19) but 21 vessels sunk before field cleared Apr 1915); ***Whitby & Hartlepool*** (2 fishing boats			

DECEMBER 1914	WESTERN FRONT 1	EASTERN FRONT 2	SOUTHERN FRONTS 3	TURKISH FRONTS 4
Wed 16 contd				
Thu 17	**Artois** — **First Battle of Artois** (-28): series of French Tenth Army attacks on 1¼-mile front nr Arras; minimal results (-24) hampered by fog & inadequate arty preparation cost 7771 cas (*see* 26). **Flanders** — Germans bombard Armentières. **Picardy** — French Second Army in secondary attack with 3 divs around La Boisselle (NE of Albert) fails by 20.	**Poland** — Austrian 27th Div occupies Petrokov. Battles of Lowicz-Sanniki & Limanowa-Laponow end, latter saves Cracow.		
Fri 18	**First German trench mortar unit formed** (6 lt mortars per pioneer coy Jan 1915). **Flanders** - British 7th & 8th Divs attack around Neuve Chapelle, Indian Corps at Givenchy (-23). Indian Cav Corps formed (-12 Mar 1916).	**Poland** — Battle of Rawka-Bzura begins. **Carpathians** — Austrians recover Lupka Pass (*see* 20).		**British Protectorate established over Egypt:** Hussein Kamal Pasha I, uncle of deposed Khedive Abbas Hilmi, proclaimed Sultan (19).
Sat 19	**Flanders** — Indian Corps (1672 cas) heavily engaged by German counter-attack with mining nr Cuinchy & Givenchy (-20). **Somme** — French repulse attack nr Lihons. **Argonne** — Sarrail's Third Army attacks astride Meuse, miniscule gains for nearly 12,216 cas (*see* 8 Jan).			**Armenia** — **First big fall of snow** (-20). Enver issues orders for complex enveloping offensive.
Sun 20	**Champagne** — FIRST BATTLE OF CHAMPAGNE ('Winter Battle in French Champagne') begins: Fourth Army (12 divs) attacks (-25) gains as much as 400 yds of trenches (24) v German Fifth Army (c9 divs). Joffre plans protracted battle of attrition designed to relieve pressure on Russians. It continues with c4wks pause in Jan-Feb, to 17 Mar 1915. **Secret War** — 21/28 carrier pigeons sent from BEF GHQ to Belgium since 2 Nov have returned.			**Armenia** — Russians defeat Turks nr L Van.
Mon 21	**Flanders** — British 1st Div bolsters Indian Corps defending Givenchy sector. **Aisne** — French XXV Corps (Sixth Army) attacks vainly (& 25), facing German grenade attacks (*see* 8 Jan 1915).	**Poland** — Vain German Bzura crossing attempts but cross at 2 points (23). **Secret War** — Col Knox tells London of Russian ammo shortages, 800,000 recruits without rifles.	**Italy** — Cadorna has prepared campaign plan v Austria, 2 battles & 60 days will bring Italians to Laibach plain for march on Vienna.	**Armenia** — **Turk winter offensive** (c95,000, 10 divs) **begins**, recovers Köprüköy & forces 64,000 (3 divs eqvt) Russians back. **Egypt**— Lt-Gen Birdwood GOC Anzac Corps.
Tue 22	**Flanders** — British I Corps relieves Indian Corps & German pressure eases at Givenchy, lost trenches regained (23). **Champagne** — French I Corps gains ground nr Beauséjour Farm.			
Wed 23	**Flanders** — Belgians cross the Yser S of Dixmude.		**Potiorek is sacked; Archduke Eugene becomes Balkans C-in-C,** Baron Sarkotic-Lovcen	**Armenia** — Istomin's bde (8000) forced by 3 Turk divs (X Corps) to abandon Olta in

AFRICAN OPERATIONS 5	SEA WAR 6	AIR WAR 7	INTERNATIONAL EVENTS 8	HOME FRONTS 9
	sunk) **bombarded** (694 civilians & 35 servicemen cas) for 30 mins by Hipper's 5 battlecruisers, who escape RN countermoves by 1545 thanks to signalling error & poor visibility. Adm Ingenohl covering Hipper with battle-fleet loses chance to destroy Beatty & Vice-Adm Warrender's 6 battleships. **Occupied Belgium** — RN bombards Westeinde.			
		N Sea — Sqdn Cdr Seddon & Ldg Mech Hartley RNAS forced down when their Short floatplane has engine failure; crew rescued & plane salvaged by Norwegian SS *Orn* ; repatriated (from Holland) 20 Dec. **W Front** — French Army airship *Conte* drops 15 shells on Sarrebourg railway stn; 10 shells & 1 case aerodarts on other rail targets.	**Neutrals : Italy** — Prince Bülow visits for Central Powers. **USA** — US Marines seize bankrupt Haiti's last $500,000 at Port-au-Prince.	**Britain** — Coast property war insurance rates raised after Hartlepool raid.
SW Africa/Angola — After 500-mile march 640 **Germans defeat Portuguese** (182 cas incl 37 PoWs) at Naulila. They hang 6 PoWs on return.	**N Sea** — *U5* mined & lost close to Flanders coast (*U11* mined & lost 9 in Dover Strs).		**Scandinavian kings meet at Malmö**, Sweden. Masaryk leaves Prague for exile (Rome).	**Britain** — Kitchener's resignation threat wins PM's veto on Churchill's visits to FM French, latter sees PM & Kitchener (20).
	Britain — Fisher proposes fast lightly-armoured 15-in-gun battlecruiser class to DNC (model by 24, builders chosen 29, keel laid 25 Jan 1915, ships become *Renown* & *Repulse*.	**Occupied Belgium** — Allied aircraft bomb Zeppelin sheds at Brussels (RNAS repeat 24).		
S Africa — Rebel Cmndt Fourie (captured 16 after killing 12 loyal troops), shot on Smut's orders, becomes Afrikaaner martyr (brother reprieved). **E Africa** — 1800 British re-occupy coast to R Umba (*see* 25).	**Black Sea** — *Goeben* & *Breslau* escort Turk troop transports toTrebizond. As *Goeben* returns to Con-stantinople she is badly damaged (23) by 2 Russian mines newly laid in Bosphorus approaches. Kept in port for 3 months (*see* 3 Apr 1915). Abortive Russian attempt to close Zonguldak coal port with 4 blockships (1 captured by *Breslau*). **Adriatic** — French submarine *Curie* reaches Austrian Pola naval base, but trapped in outer net barrage, captured & renamed *U14*.	**W Front** — Henderson resumes command of RFC on Kitchener's insistence.		
SA-Rhodesian force (6 transports) leaves Cape Town for Walvis Bay (SW Africa), lands (25).	**Adriatic** — **First Austrian U-boat success**: Austrian *U12* (Lerch) damages battleship flagship *Jean Bart* on 10th French sweep into Adriatic. Wine store destroyed 'Crew in despair!'. She limps back to Malta. French continue Otranto Straits blockade with destroy-ers.	**Britain** — **First German air raid**: FF29 floatplane from Zeebrugge drops 2 bombs in Dover Harbour, another drops 22lb bomb nr Dover Castle (24). Kitchener doubles RFC expansion plan for 35 sqns.		**Australia** — **War Pensions Act.**
S Africa — Maritz's rebels raid & defeat loyal Boers.				**France** — PM Viviani statement on war, Chamber votes new credits (26). **Britain** — War costing £14.5m pw.
			Neutrals : Italy — Britain accepts guarantees v re-export.	**Germany** — SMS *Yorck* capt gets 2 years detention for losing ship (*see* SEA WAR

DECEMBER 1914	WESTERN FRONT 1	EASTERN FRONT 2	SOUTHERN FRONTS 3	TURKISH FRONTS 4
Wed 23 contd			succeeds Potiorek as Austrian Governor of Bosnia-Herzegovina (1915).	frontier salient, loses 750 PoWs & 6 guns, retreats 12 miles NE to Avcali salt mines, snow blizzard (24), Istomin's 5000 survivors retreat 8 miles E of Merdenik (25).
Thu 24	**Champagne** — French 33rd Inf Div clears Bois des Moutons with bayonet. **Flanders** — 'CHRISTMAS TRUCE' (unofficial). Sniffily dismissed by British War Office as the 'Fraternization episode'. **Meuse** — French gains at Consenvoye.	Reported Rumanian rising in Transylvania.		**Armenia** — Myshlayeyski & Yudenich from Tiflis reach Bergmann's HQ on frontier. **Enver reaches Bardiz inside Russian frontier** with 29th Div; 17th Div 40% stragglers.
Fri 25	**Flanders** — CHRISTMAS TRUCE. Sir J French orders formation of first two British field armies: First (Haig); I, IV Indian Corps; Second (Smith-Dorrien); II, III & V Corps. **Alsace** — New French Army of the Vosges attacks with 2 divs & makes progress in mts, incl nr Cernay (26, *see* 31). **Champagne** — German counter-attack on 1200 yd-front fails (*see* 30).	**Christmas truce in many sectors**, incl Przemysl. **Poland** — Germans driven back over Bzura. **Galicia** — **Austro-German offensive ends with Austrians stopped at Tarnow.** **Carpathians** — Russians recover Lupkow & Dukla Passes.	**Albania** — Italians occupy Durazzo on coast due to revolt v Essad Pasha, check Muslim rebels by 3 Jan 1915.	**Armenia** — Russian retreat begins (-26); c8000 Turks (3rd Div) capture Ardahan (*see* 3 Jan). Yudenich takes over Turkestan Corps.
Sat 26	**Artois** — Pétain (XXXIII Corps) reports on deep mud delaying advance, Tenth Army attack postponed (*see* 28). **Argonne** — Italian Legion, 4th Regt of the Legion, first in action (-9 Jan 1915). Lt Bruno Garibaldi (grandson of Liberator) k, unit withdrawn Mar 1915 & disbanded on Italy's entry into the war.	Russian Chief of Staff tells British Mission no offensive till end July if no Allied shells supplied.		**Armenia** — **Battle of Sarikamish** (-4 Jan): Enver's 4000 men of 29th Div lose 3/8 guns v 3500 Russian & 2 guns. Turk X Corps loses 7000/20,000 men in 19-hr/25-mile horror march to join Enver.
Sun 27	**Artois** — 10 *Chasseurs Alpins* bns capture 800 yds of Bav trenches at La Targette after 2-hr arty preparation. **France** — Joffre & FM French confer at Chantilly. **Flanders** — Belgians take German trenches nr Lombaertzyde. **Vosges** — Germans bombard St Dié.	Conrad cables Falkenhayn 'Complete success in the Eastern theatre is... extremely urgent'. Tsar at STAVKA (26-29), inspects new 53rd Don Cossack Regt (28). **Poland** — Germans beaten on R Ravka.		**Armenia** — Turks repulsed from Sarikamish; 28th Div reaches but driven off Kars road.
Mon 28	Sir J French proposes amalgamation of BEF & Belgian Army (*see* 2 Jan 1915). **Flanders** — Allies recapture St Georges (Yser) & repel recovery attempts (29). **Artois** — Non-stop rain stops all but local ops.	Germans retreat & retrench W of R Bzura.	(Late Dec) Austrian Fifth & Sixth Armies dissolved, combined into Balkan Force. **Herzegovina** — Montenegrins repulse Austrians at Grahovo, & Albanians to S (29).	**Armenia** — Sarikamish: Turk 30th Div occupies Alisofu S of road & railway (-29) isolating Russians. **Secret War** — Lt Niedermayer & Wassmuss reach Baghdad, but Turks not very helpful.
Tue 29	**Argonne** — French advance at Apremont.	**Galicia** — Hard-pressed Austrians retreat. **Secret War** — Churchill letter to Asquith urges RN Baltic attack to land Russians for march on Berlin.		**Armenia** — **Sarikamish: Decisive day**, 18,000 Turks & c20 guns v Gen Przevalski's 14,000 Russians, 34 guns & many MGs. Turk 30th & 31st Divs repulsed & lose Alisofu; 17th Div night attack penetrates town but is annihilated (c800 PoWs). Turk IX Corps now only 3000.
Wed 30	Allies consolidate positions at Ypres. **Champagne** — French	**Poland** — German rearguard actions at Bolimow & Inovlodz;		**Armenia** — Sarikamish: 15th Turkestan Regt gets within

AFRICAN OPERATIONS 5	SEA WAR 6	AIR WAR 7	INTERNATIONAL EVENTS 8	HOME FRONTS 9
				4 Nov). **Britain** — Revised contraband list (4th).
			Britain recognizes French Morocco Protectorate.	**Russia** — 1915 conscripts called up. **Germany** — XXXIX-XLI Res Corps formed.
E Africa — 300 British surprise & storm German Yasini post 2 miles inside border. **Cameroons** — Gorges' troops 14 miles from N Railhead. Resume advance (26), with delays due to elephant-damaged telephone lines. **SW Africa** — 1st Rhodesia Regt lands at Walvis Bay (*see* 14 Jan 1915). **Tripolitania** — 1120 Italians reach Misurata on coast after repelling attack; Fezzan evacuated.	**N Sea** — **The Cuxhaven Raid**: British seaplane carriers *Empress*, *Engadine* & *Riviera* launch 7 Short floatplanes (4FTR) against Nordholz Zeppelin sheds (not hit). Alternative targets bombed despite fog. Short 135 (Kilner & Erskine Childers) visually scouts warships in Schillig Roads where battlecruiser *Von der Tann* badly damaged in hurried move. 2 Zepplins & seaplanes make **first air attack on warships underway at sea**; *L6* damaged by Harwich Force (no damage).	**N Sea** — **The Cuxhaven Raid**: *Engadine* & *Riviera* launch 7 RNAS floatplanes (4 FTR) for planned bombing raid on naval base (*see* SEA WAR). Mission fails due to adverse weather; 6 ditched aircrew picked up by HM Submarine *E11*. Retaliatory bombing attacks on *Empress* & Harwich Force by airship *L6* (over 600 AA holes) & 2 floatplanes. **Britain** — FF29 (Prondynski & Frankenburg) penetrate Thames Estuary to Erith but intercepted & damaged by prototype Vickers Gunbus (Chidson & Martin) — then the only MG-armed British operational aircraft. **France** — Zeppelin drops 14 bombs on Nancy.	Austrian Bucharest Ambassador warns Conrad Italy and Rumania will join Allies '... unless the Central Empires ... achieve a far-reaching victory by the Spring'. (*see* E FRONT 5 Jan 1915). **Occupied Belgium** — Cardinal Mercier writes pastoral letter v German excesses, to be read in all churches 3 Jan 1915.	**Germany** — Maj-Gen Gröner (Gen Staff Railways Section) rejects civilian appeal for food rationing & price ceilings (*see* 10 Jan).
	British Admiralty memo to French suggests switch of ops from Adriatic to E Med v Turkey, latter reply (28) only limited force can be spared (*see* 26 Jan 1915).	**W Front** — French Army airship *Montgolfier* damaged by AA fire crashes at Saizeraie (Toul). French airmen bomb Zeppelin sheds at Frescaty, nr Metz.	US protests to Britain over trade interference.	
Cameroons — Lt J P Butler wins **African land war's first VC** (awarded 23 Aug 1915) swimming R Nkam under fire.				
		W Front — Violent storm wrecks 30 RFC aircraft (16 DBR).		**Australia** — 2nd Anzac contingent sails from Albany for Egypt. **Britain** — Londoners warned to use basements if air attacks.
SE Cameroons — 360 French occupy Bertua after 3-day fight.			Churchill to Asquith: 'Are there not other alternatives than sending our armies to chew barbed wire in Flanders?' (Churchill & Lloyd George present non-W Front options 31. Serb PM vainly asks K Nicholas of Montenegro to make truce with Austria. **Neutrals : Holland** — Ex-MP & conman Trebitsch Lincoln sees German officer at The Hague, supplies code to British Intelligence.	
		France — German bombing raid (by *BAO*) on Dunkirk; 47		**Britain** — New Armies to be organized into 6 of 3 corps

JANUARY 1915	WESTERN FRONT 1	EASTERN FRONT 2	SOUTHERN FRONTS 3	TURKISH FRONTS 4
Wed 30 contd	33rd Div captures 300yds of trenches, but 34th Div pinned by German arty, weather worsening.	100,000 cas since 7, guns down to 10 rpd.		1000 yds of Bardiz Pass (-31) & Col Dovgirt (17th & 18th Turkestani Regts) captures Yayla Bardiz 3 miles from Turk base village. Bergmann agrees to halt 39th Div at frontier for Yudenich who sees chance of surrounding Turks. **Secret War— Grand Duke Nicholas suggests to British Military Mission expedition v Turks to ease Russia's situation in Armenia** (*see* 2 Jan 1915).
Thu 31	Arty duels from the Yser to Verdun. **Alsace** — French reoccupy part of Steinbach. Kitchener breakfasts with FM French, he & Joffre must 'break the German line' in next 5 wks or else New Armies may not come to W Front.	Russians again raid Hungary across Carpathian Passes. 37 German divs in this theatre incl 8 from W Ffront.		**Egypt** — 70,000 troops ready to meet Turk attack. **Secret War**— Churchill letter to Asquith, 'I wanted Gallipoli attacked on the Turkish declaration of war'. **Armenia**— Sarikamish: Col Voronov's col from Kars links with defenders; Turk IX Corps reduced to 2500 effectives, 14 guns & 14 MGs. Abdul Kerim Pasha's XI Corps (35,000, 30 bns & c100 guns) attacks Yudenich's 19 bns & 48 guns on border (-6 Jan).
Fri 1 January 1915	BEF orders assign 3 corps apiece to new W Front Armies. **Flanders** — Arty duels at Nieuport & Zonnebeke. **Champagne** — French capture wood nr Menil-les-Hurlus.	Falkenhayn, Conrad & Luden-dorff meet in Berlin (later at Breslau 8). Russian field army 3,850,000. Russians advance at Uzsok Pass (-2) and in Bukovina.	Austrians redesignate Combined Corps Krauss XIX. Both sides stricken by typhus epidemic (-May). British women take out 108t of hospital material to Valjevo. **France** — Poincaré & PM Viviani discuss possible Balkans offensive (Franchet d'Esperey plan given to Pres 1 Dec 1914). *See* INT'L EVENTS 4 Jan.	**Armenia** — Turk X Corps begins retreat, evades pursuit by 4. **Mesopotamia** — British recce finds Tigris blocked and Turk defences on Ruta Creek 8 miles N of Qurna (Ruta bombarded 21).
Sat 2	**Flanders** — Heavy rain hampers ops. K Albert vetoes BEF-Belgian Army amalgamation idea. **Somme** — French gains nr Verrelles. **France** — Joffre asks for 80,000 shells pd (production not achieved till after Jan 1916).	**Poland** — Russian successes on Bzura & Ravka. **Galicia** — Fighting nr Gorlice.		Kitchener tells Churchill no troops available for Dardanelles. **Armenia** — Enver narrowly escapes capture in ride for Erzerum (-3, leaves for Constantinople 7). **Persia** — Russians evacuate Urmia.
Sun 3	Memo from Sir J French advocates offensive to recapture Ostend & Zeebrugge (under development as U-boat bases) but plan rejected by 28 (*see* 9 & 19) despite FM's London visit (12-13). **Alsace** — French gains nr Cernay & at Steinbach. **Artois** — French gains nr Arras. **Argonne** — German attack on Boureuilles.	**Bukovina** — Russians occupy Suczawa, Kimpolung & reach Hungarian frontier (6).	Austrians occupy Ada Tsiganlia I nr Belgrade.	Fisher to Churchill: 'I consider the attack on Turkey holds the field, but only if it's immediate'. **Armenia** — Siberian Cossack Bde retakes Ardahan with 1300 PoWs & 4 guns. Turk XI Corps takes & loses Height 808, 4 guns & 300 PoWs to Yudenich. Dense fog stops ops at Sarikamish.
Mon 4	**Flanders** — French advance nr Nieuport. **Alsace** — Whole of Steinbach now in French hands.			**Armenia** — **Battle of Sarikamish ends:** Turk IX Corps destroyed, 1200 PoWs incl Ihsan Pasha, 30 guns & 20 MGs
Tue 5	Foch made C-in-C Allied N Army Gp (*see* 26). Dubail heads French E Army Gp. **Argonne** — French attack nr Courtechasse after mining 600 yds of German trench. **Alsace** — French advancing N of Altkirch capturing woods (-6).	Archduke Frederick to Francis Joseph: 'an attack by Italy or Rumania would place the Monarchy in a militarily untenable position ... makes ... imperative ... the earliest possible ... victory over Russia'.		**Persia** — Chernozubov evacuates Tabriz. Turks occupy (8, *see* 30).

AFRICAN OPERATIONS 5	SEA WAR 6	AIR WAR 7	INTERNATIONAL EVENTS 8	HOME FRONTS 9
		civ cas.		each. **France** — Tax on all incomes over 3000 Fr raised 10-90%.
S Africa — Defence Act permits conscription.	Churchill tells Asquith RN has transported 809,000 men (incl w & PoWs); 203,000 horses; 20,000 vehicles & 250,000t stores since 4 Aug, all without loss.	**France** — Prod figs last quarter: Oct — 100 aircraft & 157 aero engines; Nov — 137 aircraft & 209 aero engines; Dec — 192 aircraft & 304 aero engines. **W Front** — RFC sent 84 replacement aircraft so far.		**India** — NE Frontier ops in Kachin Hills (-28 Feb 1915). **France** — 42m Fr on refugees and unemployment spent so far, 70% of industrial plants working normally. **Russia** — Prices up 40% since Aug.
Cameroons — Lt-Col Mair's 400 Nigerians (Cross River Col) occupy Ossindinge. **E Africa** — Kenya Police Service Bn leaves Nairobi for Turkana Province in N (ops from 4).	**Channel** — Unescorted battleship *Formidable* sunk at 0230 in bad weather by *U24* (Schneider) (547k, 201 survivors). **Germany** — (Jan) First of 25 A1-type small torpedo boats commissioned for Flanders coastal ops, 16 assembled at Antwerp (*see* 1 May), 4 lost in 1915.	**W Front** — (c) French increase Voisin bomber units from 5 to 8. W/Cdr Maitland RNAS inspects Belgian 'Drachen'-type kite-balloon at Alveringheim; he seconds Flt Cdr Mackworth to Chalain-Meudon, HQ of the French balloon sections. **Russia** — First Russian 2-seat fighter, Sikorsky S16, under test, its imperfectly synchronized MG frequently damages the airscrew. **S Africa** — S African Aviation Corps formed.	**Fiji** — Lloyd George memo urges 'bringing Germany down by knocking the props under her'. Volunteers leave for Britain.	**Russia** — (Jan) Duma re-called for 3 sessions; 13-14m shells on order from British & US firms for delivery by 1 Sept. **Britain** — RFP 18% up 2%. (Jan) 1st attempt to release skilled workers from Army. MC announced. (Jan) Stokes begins designing his trench mortar (*see* 14 Apr). Govt helps maintain an av of 6500 refugees (-May 1919) after est £2m privately given.
Cameroons — Brig-Gen Gorges takes Chang (4525 ft), demolishes fort and retires (-6).	**E Africa** — Cruiser *Fox* & battleship *Goliath* again shell Dar-es-Salaam.		Kitchener telegram to Petrograd '... steps will be taken to make a demonstration against the Turks' (*see* 26).	
			Occupied Belgium — Cardinal Mercier arrested for pastoral letter v German cruelty.	**France** — Revised contraband list issued. **Britain** — Day of Intercession for victory.
	Adriatic — Austrian Adm Haus proposes using new lt cruiser *Novara* (completed 10) to run 300t munitions to Smyrna (for Dardanelles), but scheme abortive (-12 Apr). **N Sea** — British submarines *C31* & *E10* lost (4 & 18, cause unknown). **Black Sea** — Russian cruiser *Pamiat Merkurya* damages Turk cruiser *Hamidieh* W of Sinope.		Austrian Rome military attaché reports Italian Army will be ready for war end March.	**Britain** — Fisher withdraws resignation over Zeppelin threat. London Stock Exchange reopens.
Cameroons — Col Mayer's French at Edea & Kopongo repulse 500 Germans. **SW Africa** — S Africans occupy Schuit Drift on R Orange & Raman's Drift (12).	Italian Navy CNS Revel war appreciation study argues reliance on torpedoes & mines v Austrians before Fleet action (*see* 18 Apr).			Churchill begs PM to approve prototype armoured steam tractor (Kitchener starts some work, *see* 20 Feb).

JANUARY 1915	WESTERN FRONT 1	EASTERN FRONT 2	SOUTHERN FRONTS 3	TURKISH FRONTS 4
Wed 6				**Armenia** — Yudenich replaces Bergmann as field C-in-C.
Thu 7	**Meuse-Argonne** — German reverses in Argonne & nr Verdun. **Alsace** — French take Burnhaupt-le-Haut, but lose it (8).	Russian Christmas Day. **Poland** — Heavy German attacks on lower Ravka repulsed.	**Serbia** — RN 28-man mine & torpedo det (from Malta) joins Cdr H Cardale at Belgrade, they complete blocking of Sava & add to river defences of Belgrade (*see* 22 Feb).	**Armenia** — Battle of Kara Urgan (-15) v Turk XI Corps, Yudenich outflanks it from N (10-15). **India : NW Frontier** — Capt Jothan of N Waziristan Militia ambushed by 1500 Khostwals, wins posthumous VC.
Fri 8	**Aisne** — **Battle of Soissons** (-14): after 110-gun 90-min shelling Maunoury storms Hills 132 & 138 by 10 (*see* 11-14). **Champagne** — Second Battle of Perthes: French 34th Div captures village, repulses counter-attack (9) & advances N (10).	Kaiser overrides Falkenhayn, orders forming of *Südarmee* (Linsingen's 3 German divs + Austrians = 48,000) to support Austrians (*see* 26).		Kitchener backs Dardanelles attack but offers no troops (*see* 13).
Sat 9	British War Council memo to FM French to consider possibility of stalemate & eventuality of seeking decision in fresh theatre. **Aisne** — Germans shell Soissons Cathedral & counter-attack unsuccessfully nr city.			**Yemen** — SS *Choising* (50 *Emden* survivors) calls at Hodeida to ask GOC Turk 40th Div best way home. They reach Constantinople 1 June.
Sun 10				British War Council agrees to Russia's Constantinople/Straits claim provided Anglo-French get share of Turkey (*see* 12 Mar). **Armenia** — Yudenich sends force to outflank Turk XI Corps from N (-15). **Arabia** — 2 Indian bns (1000) in Muscat repel 3000 Omani Arabs (c500 cas, -11 *see* 24).
Mon 11	**Aisne** — German reinforcements counter-attack N of Soissons; river bursts its banks carrying away French-held bridges. **Champagne** — Heavy fighting round Beauséjour Farm.			
Tue 12	**Aisne** — French Sixth Army withdrawing under pressure from Hills I30 & 159. Venizel bridge retained; all others lost.	**E Prussia** — Russians take several villages nr Rosog (*see* 25).		
Wed 13	**Aisne** — Germans storm Hills 132 & 159 with Vregny heights; French retreating across river (-14).	**Poland** — Russians advance on Lower Vistula (-16), occupy Serpets N of Plotsk.		British War Council (incl FM French) decide to prepare Feb naval attack v Dardanelles, ask for French support 18.
Thu 14	**Aisne** — **Battle of Soissons ends**: Germans claim 5200 PoWs & 14 guns; French loss 12,411.			25,000 Turks (25th Div +), 10,000 camels & 56 guns begin 8 night marches from Beersheba towards Suez Canal (*see* 26; AIR WAR 23).
Fri 15	**Artois** — Germans recover some trenches on Notre Dame de Lorette ridge & at Carency, held for month by French. Foch writes to Joffre 'My formula is: work for the staff, rest for the troops'. **Champagne** — Since 15 Nov, French have advanced 1000 yds nr Perthes after c12 attacks & 20 counter-attacks.			**Armenia** — Battle of Kara Urgan ends.
Sat 16	**Flanders** — Germans retire	**Poland** — Russians repulse		**Armenia** — 3000 Turk X Corps

AFRICAN OPERATIONS 5	SEA WAR 6	AIR WAR 7	INTERNATIONAL EVENTS 8	HOME FRONTS 9
	Adm Souchon believes Allies cannot achieve much v Dardanelles, Marmara or Constantinople without troops.		Austrian Rome Ambassador begins talks on ceding Trentino to Italy.	Kitchener reviews war in House of Lords.
		Italy — *Corpo Aeronautico Militare* (Military Air Service) established with a few Blériots & Nieuports.		France — Absinthe sale prohibited or new liquor stores (*see* 31 Mar). Russia — Bolshevik Petrograd 'Military Group' issues leaflet to soldiers, workers & peasants urging non-payment of rents by end of month.
L Victoria — British occupy Shirati & organise flotilla.			*The Times* publishes preliminary report on German atrocities in France. French report on Bavarian Vosges atrocities (9).	Britain — Tea export ban lifted.
			British reply to US note of 29 Dec 1914 published (sent 7). Copper reaching Germany via neutrals. Limited rubber exports to USA granted. Berchtold diary after audience 'Emperor [Francis Joseph] again complains greatly about the Germans ...'.	Falkenhayn attends gas shell tests SE of Cologne (*see* E FRONT 31). Britain — King & Queen visit Indian wounded at Brighton (1st Indian VC bestowed 26).
E Africa — 500 British occupy Mafia Island (52 Germans, 22 miles from mainland) (-12). Gov Belfield speech in Nairobi '...this colony has no interest in the present war except ...its unfortunate position places it...close ...to German E Africa'.		W Front — Second French aerial victory: Sgt Gilbert (pilot) & Lt de Puechredon (observer) in a Morane 'Parasol' shoot down German biplane nr Amiens. France —16 German *BAO* aircraft surprise raid Dunkirk after a feint towards Kent coast (British home defences on alert) (*see* 22).	German Foreign Ministry invites Russian Jewish Socialist Dr Helphand to Berlin (*see* 11 Mar). Count Tisza blocks Austrian Foreign Ministry peace territorial settlement memo.	Germany — Moltke (interior CoS) appeals to Bethmann for food measures (*see* 25).
S Africa — Last Transvaal rebels' capture announced.	Med — Adm Carden assesses step-by-step naval attack on Dardanelles practicable (see TURK FRONTS 13).		Count Tisza refuses German Ambassador's request to buy off Italy with territory, proposes Berchtold's dismissal to Emperor. Britain loans Rumania £5m (*see* 25). Grey offers Venizelos Asia Minor territory for aiding Serbia but Greece declines, repeated (23) but refused (29).	
E Africa — German surprise attack on Yasini repulsed (*see* 18).	Baltic — Russian cruisers *Bogatyr* & *Oleg* lay 100 mines E of Bornholm I (E point of Denmark, *see* 25).			Britain — Letter to *The Times* starts Armenian Red Cross and Refugee Fund.
		Britain — Abortive German Navy airship raid on E Coast; adverse weather/mechanical problems (night 13/14).	Austrian Foreign Minister Count Berchtold resigns, Hungarian Baron Burian replaces him. Churchill New Year telegram to Russian people.	Britain — BEF VC & DSO Buckingham Palace investiture.
Cameroon — 900 Allies, 4 guns & 5 MGs join up v Garua (577 Germans, 4 guns & 10 MGs). SW Africa — Col Skinner's S Africans occupy Swakopmund (*see* 23)			Grey assures Russian Foreign Minister Sazonov on Constantinople & Straits.	
	Dardanelles — French submarine *Saphir* sunk (*see* 17 Apr) after hitting mine.		Italian-Rumanian mutual support agreement announced. Greek London Ambassador says Greece absolutely devoted to England's cause.	
E Africa — Brig-Gen Malleson				

JANUARY 1915	WESTERN FRONT 1	EASTERN FRONT 2	SOUTHERN FRONTS 3	TURKISH FRONTS 4
Sat 16 contd	from coast dunes nr Nieuport under French gunfire. BEF officer cas (-23) 29, lowest wk of war. **Artois** — Seesaw battle for Blangy; finally recaptured by French. **Champagne**- French advance nr Perthes. **Alsace** — French 47th Alpine Div formed in N Vosges from 10 bns (*see* 19) sent from Artois (6).	attacks nr Bolimow and nr Lipno in NW (30, *see* 31). **Bukovina** — Russians occupy Kirlibaba Pass, repulse Austrian attacks (20-21), but Pflanzer-Baltin's 50,000 retake it (22)		survivors reach Hasankale; Turk XI Corps (15,000) retreats on Erzerum (-18). (c) German staff estimate Turk Third Army at 12,400 effectives having suffered 86% losses in 4 wks.
Sun 17	**Somme** — Limited French advance at La Boiselle N of the river. **Aisne** — Unsuccessful German attacks nr Autreches, NW of Soissons. **Lorraine** — French occupy Bois-le-Prêtre (Pont-à-Mousson) & advance (20).			
Mon 18	**Champagne** — French seize positions nr Bois-le-Prêtre, only to lose them in counter-attacks. Rain & exhaustion halts ops until 20.	**Poland** — German plane bombs Russian Fifth Army HQ at Mogilnitsa (4 cas, 2 horses). Russians take Skempe (20).		**Armenia** — Lyakhov's 10,000 regulars & 24 guns with 4 destroyers drive c10,000 Turks W over R Coruh towards Russian frontier. **Egypt** — NZ & Australian Div formed.
Tue 19	Joffre admonishes BEF C-in-C that priority is massing of reserves rather than offensive towards Ostend-Zeebrugge. **Flanders** — Snowstorms impede ops. **Alsace** — German attack on Hartmannsweiler Kopf pre-empts French offensive (fighting continues-22).			
Wed 20				
Thu 21	**Champagne** — French seize woods at Beauséjour, but are forced back in Bois-le-Prêtre.			Fisher to Jellicoe: 'I just abominate the Dardanelles operation, unless...it is ...200,000 men with the Fleet'.
Fri 22	**Argonne** — Heavy fighting at Fontaine Madame & St Hubert.			**Syria** — Cruiser HMS *Doris* gives food to Ruad Islanders, landing party cuts telegraph line at Alexandretta (25).
Sat 23	**Flanders** — Slight Allied advance nr Nieuport. **Aisne** — Germans bombard Berry-au-Bac. **Argonne & Alsace** — Skirmishing.	Falkenhayn finally gives Hindenburg 4 reserve corps (*see* 26). **Carpathians** — **Austrian Third Army Winter Offensive** (175,000 men in 20 divs) to relieve Przemysl. Temperatures 0° to -20° F.		
Sun 24				**Arabia** — Pro-Turk Ibn Rashid defeats pro-British Ibn Saud's 6000 & 1 gun at Jarrab; Capt Shakespear killed, aged 36. Austrian orientalist Musil joins Rashid (26) & tries to make pro-Turk recce (*see* 5 June).

AFRICAN OPERATIONS 5	SEA WAR 6	AIR WAR 7	INTERNATIONAL EVENTS 8	HOME FRONTS 9
sent to liaise with Belgians (see 14 Feb).				
			Neutrals: Greece — Venizelos offers Britain military help if Allies land at Salonika (memos to his King on Bulgar relations 24 & Allies 30).	**Britain** — Woolwich Arsenal makes good TNT (3t pw by June, 30 factories making 1000t pw by end war).
E Africa — Lettow (w) attacks Yasini with 9 coys after quelling Arab coy mutiny. Yasini surrenders (19), garrison's (296 inc 35 k&w) ammo finished. Lettow loses 274 & 200,000 rnds; 3rd KAR relief col 1hr too late.	**Neutrals: Argentina** — First of 3 German merchantmen interned (-26 Feb) for violating neutrality.		**Japan presents 21 Demands to China**, denies doing so (27).	
	Germany — First UB-class coastal U-boat *U1* launched at Kiel, completed in 75 days (see 29 Mar), class of 17 launched by 23 Apr. **N Sea** — German aircraft sights Beatty's force on recon sweep W of Heligoland Bight.	**Britain** — FIRST ZEPPELIN RAID ON BRITAIN: German Navy airships *L3* & *L4* ineffectually bomb E Anglia (night 19/20, 20 civ cas incl 2 children w, £7740 worth of damage); 2 RFC FB5s (No 7 Sqn) fly first-ever night sorties but engine failures entail forced landings.	Germany protests to US v seaplane sales to Allies; Bryan replies (29) that not warships.	
		W Front — Capt Happe & Sgt Labouchere in Voisin destroy kite balloon at Neider Morschweiler with air-to-air bomb & 250 aerodarts.		Talaat Bey puts Kemal Bey i/c Constantinople food supply, poor mostly maize. Official war bread sold at inflated prices (- Feb 1916).
	N Sea — *U7* (Konig) torpedoed (1 survivor) & sunk in error by *U22* (Hoppe) off Dutch coast (signals failure).		British Washington Ambassador announces that SS *Dacia*, if captured, will be placed in a prize court. H Samuel reports to British Cabinet on possible Jewish Palestine.	**Germany** — Lt-Gen Hohenborn replaces Falkenhayn as War Minister. Adm Müller's diary: 'Kaiser obviously terrified by the thought of a long war'. **Britain** — Interned vessels to be used in coastal trade.
E Africa — **Kitchener forbids offensive ops**, coast area evacuation begins (29).		**Occupied Belgium** — RNAS drops 27 bombs on Zeebrugge U-boat base. **France** — 12 German *BAO* aircraft bomb Dunkirk, but RFC 4 Sqn shoot down 1 Albatros B-type with rifle.		Heavy snow in London. **Germany** — *Kölnische Zeitung* publishes Russian atrocity story.
Gen Botha sails for SW Africa (see 11 Feb). **E Africa** — Recruiting appeal for 500 more European volunteers fails. Nyasaland Rising (-3 Feb): US-educated John Chilembwe kills 3 whites on Dr Livingstone's grandson's estate; 140 British quell, 20 hanged, 400 imprisoned.		**France** — *BAO* again raid Dunkirk (1 aircraft FTR), drop 123 bombs (night 28/29). **Turk Fronts** — British recon aircraft (1 of 6 for Suez Canal defence) locates main Turk column advancing on Suez Canal (see TURK FRONTS 3 Feb).		**Britain** — **Mills submits grenade proposal**, in production June, perfects Mk II by Aug.
	N Sea — FIRST DREADNOUGHT ACTION **Battle of the Dogger Bank**: Thanks to signals intelligence 5 battlecruisers from Rosyth intercept & pursue Hipper's 3 & cruiser *Blücher* on sweep in 3-hr action begun at record 22,000 yds. Latter sunk (792k, 236 PoWs), 260 survivors, but RN errors (Beatty not told U-boats actually hrs away) allow rest to escape: Flagship HMS *Lion* has 21 of RN 95 cas & hit	**N Sea** — German Navy airship *L5* gives recon support & early warning for battlecruiser force during Dogger Bank Battle (see SEA WAR).	US Sec of State Bryan's letter published refuting partiality to Allies.	

JANUARY 1915	WESTERN FRONT 1	EASTERN FRONT 2	SOUTHERN FRONTS 3	TURKISH FRONTS 4
Sat 24 contd				
Mon 25	**Flanders** — First Action of Givenchy: British 1st Div repulse an attack. French stand firm nr Ypres. **Aisne** — German advance on Craonne plateau. **Champagne** — Germans attack at 4 points around Hill 200 nr Perthes (*see* 2 & 3 Feb). Joffre agrees (26) to postpone attack until drier weather (*see* 12 Feb). **Alsace** — Fog impedes ops.	By now Russian Twelfth Army forming to invade E Prussia from S (NE advances in Pillkallen area & on Tilsit 29).		
Tue 26	**Flanders** — Wilson (promoted Lt-Gen 18 Feb) becomes BEF Chief Liaison Officer to Foch (-21 Dec). **Aisne** — French XVIII Corps recover lost ground at Craonne. Front static to 16 Apr 1917.	**E Prussia** — New German Tenth Army (4 corps) formed under Eichhorn for Masurian offensive (plans ready 28). **Carpathians** — Brusilov success nr Dukla Pass. Extra corps on its way from NW Front. Austrian ammunition exhausted. *Südarmee* attacks, gains 100 yds pd. Brusilov strikes back 27, but repulsed nr Beskid Pass (28).	**Italy** — War Minister Gen Zupelli tells cabinet Army not ready until mid-April (*see* 31).	**Egypt** — Turk feint attacks at Kantara also Kubri (7 miles N of Suez) (-27). **Persia** — Chernozubov's 7000 & 16 guns defeats c5000 Turks at Safian (-28) & regains Tabriz 30.
Wed 27	**Argonne** — French repulse attacks. **Meuse** — French arty destroy German bridge at St Mihiel. **Vosges** — French advance nr Senones. **Alsace** — Half French Vosges Army makes some progress but snow stops other half (*see* 17 Feb).			
Thu 28	**Flanders** — Allies take Great Dune. **Artois** — German attack at Bellacourt. Argonne — French 58mm trench mortar first fired in action (*see* Apr).		Lloyd George proposes to British War Council that Allied army be sent to Salonika to lead Balkan powers v Austria (*see* 9 Feb).	Fisher resigns over PM's Dardanelles attack order, but Kitchener & Churchill dissuade him. Agreed any troops should be sent to Serbia via Salonika. Wassmuss, 'German Lawrence', leaves Baghdad for S Persia, but Turks stop 3 other Germans (c30, *see* 26 Feb).
Fri 29	**Flanders** — British repulse attack at Cuinchy nr La Bassée. BEF CoS Sir A Murray goes home, replaced by able QMG Robertson rather than French choice Wilson. **Aisne** — German attempt to cross river nr Soissons. **Argonne** — Lt Rommel wins Iron Cross 1st Class by capturing 4 block-houses with his platoon & beating French bn counter-attack (*see* 30 June).	**Carpathians** — Heavy fighting between Dukla & Wyszkow Passes; Russians giving way to *Südarmee*.		
Sat 30	**Argonne** — French setback (700 PoWs) nr Fontaine Madam.			Churchill sends Adm Carden Russian plan of Dardanelles defences.
Sun 31	**Flanders** — BEF 347,384 strong.	**Poland — First use of poison gas** (18,000 shells from 600 guns) by German Ninth Army at Bolimow in diversionary attack (-6 Feb). Gas nullified by intense cold & E wind, so Russians fail to inform	By now 30 regular Austrian bns sent to Italian Front (*see* 1 Mar, 6 & 26 Apr).	**Arabia** — Idrisi's Arabs occupy Farasan Is in Red Sea (*see* 28 Apr).

AFRICAN OPERATIONS 5	SEA WAR 6	AIR WAR 7	INTERNATIONAL EVENTS 8	HOME FRONTS 9
	17 times; German flagship *Seydlitz* hit 3 times (192k) badly damaged by fire. Former towed back to Rosyth by *Indomitable*. RN score 73 hits from 958 shells, Germans 25 from 1276.			
	Baltic — Russian submarine torpedoes German cruiser *Gazelle* off Rügen, but towed to harbour. Russian submarine sinks German torpedo boat off Cap Moen, Denmark (29).	**Baltic** — German Navy airship *PL19* shot down by Russian AA fire during bombing raid on Libau.	Rumania refuses to join Greece supporting Serbia. **Occupied Belgium** — Germans seize metal stocks (*see* 2 Feb). **Neutrals: USA** — Bell makes 1st transcontinental telephone call.	**Germany** — Govt decree seizes all grain & flour stocks from 1 Feb.
	Churchill & Minister of Marine Augagneur agree to French participation under British command in Dardanelles attack (*see* TURK FRONTS 28 & 30).		Grand Duke Nicholas replies Dardanelles action imperative but Russia cannot help. Allies extend 5 Sept 1914 London agreement to Turkey. Franco-Swiss petrol agreement.	
Cameroons — 450 WAFF troops reach Duala.				
	US Coast Guard founded (grows to 8835 men during hostilities with 48 vessels). **S Atlantic** — US vessel *William P Frye* (wheat for Britain) sunk by German AMC *Prinz Eitel Friedrich* (see INT'L EVENTS 15 Mar). **Black Sea** — Russian torpedo boats shell Trebizond & Rize.			
	Irish Sea — *U21* (Hersing) shells Barrow-in-Furness, sinks 4 (3 British) merchantmen (30).		Lloyd George to Churchill: 'Are we really bound to hand over the ordering of our troops to France as if we were her vassal?'	
SE Cameroons — French occupy Yukaduma.	British Admiralty advise British merchant ships to fly neutral ensign (or none) in home waters. *Lusitania* arrives Liverpool 6 Feb flying US flag. **Channel** — **First merchant ships torpedoed without warning**: British steamers *Tokamaru* & *Ikaria* sunk off Le Havre by *U20* (Schwieger) (*see* 7 May).		'Col' House sails in *Lusitania* for Europe as Wilson's special peace envoy (*see* 7 Feb). K Albert receives Japanese sword of honour.	**Canada** — Cavalry Bde formed.
				Germany — Dr Helfferich Finance Minister.

FEBRUARY 1915	WESTERN FRONT 1	EASTERN FRONT 2	SOUTHERN FRONTS 3	TURKISH FRONTS 4
Sun 31 contd		Allies of it.		
Mon 1 February 1915	**Flanders** — (early Feb) French arty has first sound-ranging sets (BEF experiments with them in Ypres sector Oct). **Flanders** — British 2nd Div storms trenches nr Cuinchy. **Champagne** — Third Battle of Perthes: German attack repulsed (3).	**Poland** — Mackensen's 100,000-strong Ninth Army attacks at Bolimow, takes 3 villages in 6-mile advance but Siberian and other reserves (3 divs) retake them & stabilize front (-6). German losses 20,000, Russian 40,000. **Carpathians** — Brusilov advances from Dukla Pass to Upper San; Russians evacuate Tucholka & Beskid Passes, advance nr Uzsok Pass (3).		
Tue 2	**Champagne** — Gen Brulard of 2nd Div reports 'First line units...stand knee-deep in water'; offensive postponed until reliefs arrive (*see* 12).	**Carpathians** — Austrian Croat Regt loses 1828 men to overnight frostbite.	**Herzegovina** — Montenegrins repulse Austrians.	Lt-Col Kemal reorganizes new 19th Div at Dardanelles (-25). Turk patrols invade Aden Protectorate.
Wed 3	**Somme** — Germans attempt to use incendiary-filled boats on R Ancre. **Champagne** — Germans take part of French front line in Noton Wood-Hill 191 with 600+ PoWs, 9 guns & 9 MGs (*see* 10).			**Egypt** — 12,000 **Turks try to cross Suez Canal** (-4) at 3 points; only 3 pontoons (c60 men) cross. Repulsed by Indian troops (163 cas) and Allied warships losing 1490 men (716 PoWs) & 3 MGs.
Thu 4	**Artois** — Slight French advance at Ecuries (Arras-La Bassée).			**Mesopotamia** — **Viceroy of India Lord Hardinge visits Basra** and Abadan oil refinery (-8). **Persia** — 700 Turks reported advancing on Ahwaz oilfields (24 miles NW by 10, *see* 3 Mar).
Fri 5	**Flanders** — Decreased shelling of British centre & left (seaward) flank.	**E Prussia** — Blizzards (-6). Russians capture (but ignore) documents from dead officer indicating German build-up. Hindenburg opens his HQ at Insterburg. **Carpathians** — Austrian attacks repulsed, furthest progress made. Brusilov retakes Mezolaborcz rail jctn. By 6 Austrian Third Army losses 89,000.		
Sat 6	**Flanders** — British counter-mine 2 German sap-heads S of La Bassée Canal. **Somme** — Germans detonate 3 mines in La Boisselle.	**Bukovina** — Austrian Seventh Army (6 divs) retakes Kimpolung, forces Russians beyond R Suczava (-9) & reaches R Sereth (11).		

AFRICAN OPERATIONS 5	SEA WAR 6	AIR WAR 7	INTERNATIONAL EVENTS 8	HOME FRONTS 9
Anglo-Belgian agreement on Uganda/Congo border. Brig-Gen Malleson opens military talks at Ruchuru (14). **Cyrenaica** — (Feb) Nuri Pasha (Enver's half-brother) smuggled in from Syria to aid Senussi (*see* 14 Nov).	British Admiralty bans neutral fishing boats from ports, due to erroneous Grand Fleet fear that they are minelaying. (Feb) Scapa Flow now has boom defences. **Germany** — Chancellor agrees to unrestricted U-boat war advocated by CNS Pohl. **Arctic** — (Feb) Old RN pre-dreadnought *Jupiter* arrives at Archangel at record early date to serve as icebreaker (-May).	**W Front** — (Feb) Future top French & Allied ace Fonck posted to Saint-Cyr for aviation training (*see* June). French introduce Dorand bombsight (*see* Apr). German military mission sent to Constantinople to reorganize Turk Army air corps. **E Front** — Russian heavy bombers first equipped with defensive armament (progressively increased, *see* 14).	**Bulgaria** — Duc de Guise in Sofia to persuade Tsar Ferdinand to join Allies. **Neutrals: USA** — By now US Army using films for training.	**Germany** — **Bread & flour rationing in Berlin,** 4.14lb pw (nationally June) where War Board for metal industry set up. **Austria** — (Feb) 'Metal Central Ltd' formed to requisition scrap (*see* 2 Mar). **Britain** — End of industrial truce (47 strikes 209,000 days in Feb). 15.6% of workforce now enlisted. 126,000t pd seaborne coal now by rail. Admiralty bans neutral fishing boats from British ports. Le Queux's best-selling *German Spies in England: An Exposure* published (Feb). First all-women-run military hospital opens (Endell St, London).
			Allies deplore Greek, Serb & Montenegrin intervention in Albania. Spain reaffirms neutrality. Sino-Japanese Conference on 21 Demands (-18). **Occupied Belgium** — Underground weekly *La Libre Belge* appears weekly for duration. German provincial governors given unlimited powers (5). **Neutrals: USA** — German Werner Horn fails to blow up Canadian Pacific railbridge at Vanceboro, Maine and is arrested.	
Cameroons — 750 British lose 120 at Mbureku (& checked again 27) & Harmann's Farm. **British Somaliland** — Camel Corps again defeats dervishes at Shimber Berris (-4, *see* 16 May 1916). **S Africa** — Kemp & last 500 rebels surrender at Upington. Germans repulsed from Kakamas on R Orange (4).			***Neutrals: Bulgaria*** — German £3m loan.	
	UNRESTRICTED U-BOAT WAR. **Germany declares 'War Zone' around British Is as from 18.** All vessels incl neutrals liable to be sunk by U-boats (only 30 available at start). Pohl replaces Ingenohl as C-in-C High Seas Fleet, Bachmann new CNS. **Channel** — Second RN Q-ship *Lyons* prepared for service. She patrols without success (*see* 12 Mar).		**Germany announces U-boat blockade of Britain from 18.**	**Britain** — King & Kitchener inspect 1st Cdn Div on Salisbury Plain. Northcliffe letter to Bonar Law why French allow journalists at front, but not British (ban lifted May). **France** — Reconstruction Commission appointed. **Canada** — Parlt (-15 Apr) votes $100m war credit & authorizes $50m war bonds.
		W Front — French pilot Pégoud in Morane 'L' scores 3 victories in single action: 2 German aircraft shot down, 3rd forced to land. Lts Wadham & Borton RFC in Morane 'L' force down Aviatik with rifle fire nr Lille airfield. Some first Vickers FB 5 'Gun Bus' 2-seat pusher-engined fighters reach No 5 Sqn RFC.		**Britain** — Commons votes Army 3m men, Navy voted another 32,000 (8). **Austria** — Körber (PM 1900-4) returns as Finance Minister and Bosnia administrator.
			Lloyd George returns from Paris conference with Franco-Russian finance ministers (since 5) having agreed to share resources. **Neutrals:** Rumania & Italy renew 23 Sept 1914 agreement. Bethmann writes to German Vienna Ambassador urging concessions to Italy (*see* 26). **Secret War: Germany** — Crown	**Britain** — Highest wheat prices for 40 yrs. Commons demand for Govt control rejected (11).

FEBRUARY 1915	WESTERN FRONT 1	EASTERN FRONT 2	SOUTHERN FRONTS 3	TURKISH FRONTS 4
Sat 6 contd				
Sun 7	**Argonne** — German attack at Bagatelle (-8).	**E Prussia** — **Winter Battle of Masuria** (-22): Hindenburg offensive in Kaiser's presence, takes Johannisburg (8) but snow hampers. **Carpathians** — 22 German attacks repulsed at Kosziowa NE of Tucholka Pass (again 10-11 & 20).		
Mon 8	**Flanders** — K Albert visits British front. FM French tells army cdrs offensive likely, Joffre suggests v Aubers Ridge (16).	**Carpathians** — Austrian VIII Corps from Serbia arrives.		
Tue 9	**Meuse** — French capture St Rémy (Woëvre). **Vosges** — Heavy snow (-10) delays ops (*see* 17).	**E Prussia** — Eichhorn takes Biala & turns Russian right. **Poland** — Army Det Gallwitz formed, takes Serpets in NW (11). **Galicia** — Russian shelling begins Siege of Przemysl proper (Austrian sortie repulsed 19).	Kitchener agrees to send 29th Div to Salonika (*see* INT'L EVENTS) but Greece rejects, wanting Rumania to threaten Bulgaria from N.	**Dardanelles/Aegean** — 2000 RMs occupy Greek Lemnos I (Mudros Bay) after Venizelos agrees loan. **Sinai** — Dust storms hamper pursuit of Turks, who return to Jaffa (Mar).
Wed 10	Germans attack Marie Thérèse Work in La Grurie Wood (Argonne) & Ban-de-Sapt (Alsace), repulsed at both (11). **Champagne** — French 60th Res Div mistakenly attacks Sabot Wood & loses 500 PoWs to German counter-attack.	**E Prussia** — Eichhorn takes 10,000 PoWs, cuts Russian Kovno line of retreat.		**Mesopotamia** — Half 12th Indian Bde arrives at Qurna, half to Ahwaz.
Thu 11				
Fri 12	French 60th Res Div advance nr Souain, captures part of Sabot Wood (later lost) but heavy snowstorm prevents arty observation & postpones major attack to 16 (qv) **France** — Ist Cdn Div lands at St Nazaire (-15,*see* 20).	**E Prussia** — c1500 Russian cav vainly raid across border Khorzel as Hindenburg occupies Mariampol etc. **Carpathians** — Austrians cross Jablonitsa Pass in E.		
Sat 13	**Flanders** — Franco-British advance E of Givenchy. **Vosges** — Germans capture Xon-Norroy. **Alsace** — German attack in Lauch Valley.			**Sinai** — 500+ Gurkhas & Egyptians surprise Turks (162 cas) at Tor (G of Suez) thanks to Lt-Col Parker's Arab spy network.
Sun 14	**Flanders/Artois** — German arty active. British recapture trenches lost at St Eloi. **Vosges** — French regain lost ground nr Zon-Norroy. **Alsace** — Sengern & Remsbach captured by Germans.	**E Prussia** — Clear of Russians, Litzmann's XL Res Corps takes Lyck (5000 PoWs). Gov of Königsberg (Pappritz) drives Russians N of Tilsit & takes Tauroggen (18). **Galicia** — Austrians retake Nadworna & Kolomea (16).		Capt Richmond RN's 'Remarks on Present Strategy' urges Army for Dardanelles; Fisher agrees (16), French Govt urges delay for troops (18) & decides to send div (19). **Secret War** — (c) Wasmuss enters Persia with Dr K Linders & 2 Indian revolutionaries, leaves for Shiraz (22), incites local tribesmen to attack British oil pipelines (damaged 4½ miles NE of Ahwaz, supply resumed 13 June); 4 more German

AFRICAN OPERATIONS 5	SEA WAR 6	AIR WAR 7	INTERNATIONAL EVENTS 8	HOME FRONTS 9
			Prince William writes to Grand Duke Ernest of Hesse (Tsarina's brother) urging separate peace with Russia. British Foreign Office statement justifies use of neutral flag at sea after *Lusitania* arrives at Liverpool (6) under US flag.	
Libya — Italians attack Dunedjen. **E Africa** — British evacuation of coastal area complete.	**E Med** — British cruiser *Philomel* raids Bab Yunis nr Alexandretta. **Black Sea** — *Breslau* shells Yalta (Crimea) & Russian cruisers bombard Trebizond. **N Sea** — Jellicoe back with Grand Fleet after Feb op for piles, Beatty made Vice-Adm of Battlecruiser Fleet (King first visits at Rosyth 26-28).		K George V receives French Foreign Minister Delcassé at Buckingham Palace. **Neutrals: USA** — DW Griffith's *Birth of a Nation* film epic opens in Los Angeles.	**France** — First BEF concert party at Harfleur (25 parties give 14,000 concerts pa later). Church Army recreation hut opens at Rouen (Feb).
		Germany — Maj Thomsen made *Feldflugchef*.	British War Council meets, mainly on Serbia, 29th Div to be offered to Greece (for Salonika). Rejected (15). K George V receives Russian Finance Minister Bark. Russian Orange Book on Armenia.	**Russia** — Duma reopens, passes $1.5bn budget (11), customs tariffs raised (28).
			British reply to US note of 29 Dec 1914 on neutral shipping interference. US notes to Britain on US flag use and to Germany (replies 16, suggests US mediation) on U-boat blockade; latter to be held to 'strict accountability' if lives lost.	
SW Africa — Gen Botha arrives at Swakopmund (*see* 22).		**Occupied Belgium** — 3 RNAS aircraft bomb Zeebrugge & Ostend U-boat bases & coast btys (at least 7k): 30 sorties (-16) by aircraft & seaplanes (4 FTR); 8 French aircraft fly diversionary raid on Ghistelles airfield (16).		**Britain** — King inspects 53rd Welsh Div at Cambridge.
		Germany — Imperial Order from Kaiser expresses 'Great hopes that the air war against England will be carried out with the greatest energy'. Target list: dumps, military bases, barracks, oil & petrol stores & London docks. Attacks on London's royal residences & residential areas specifically forbidden.	**Neutrals: Holland** — Protest v U-boat blockade (Sweden also 15). **Italy** — notifies Austria that further action in Balkans unfriendly act. **Neutrals** — China agrees to 12 of 21 Demands, publishes their full text (17).	
Col Kitchener arrives in Nairobi to investigate raising irregular corps. **Cameroons** — 250 French in skirmish nr Garua.	**Baltic** — Russian cruiser flagship *Rurik* grounded off Gotland after minelaying; she limps into Reval (*see* 2 July). **Channel** — Dover Patrol has 30 drifters barring straits with steel wire nets (*see* 8 Mar).			**Britain** — Railwaymen get 1st war bonus.
		E Front — IM heavy bomber *Kievsky* of the EVK drops 600 bombs on Polish Plotsk rail stn (*see* 25), 1st of 100 daylight raids & armed recon missions (-Dec) v German-held stns & jctns & trains in/nr Weidenburg, Soldau, Willenberg (all E Prussia border), Plotsk & Mlava: small formations employed by mid-summer. Total 20,000lb bombs dropped. The EVK occupies 5 different bases during 1915 retreat. 191		**Turkey** — Ctee of Union & Progress (3-man ctee under Talaat Bey) decides to exterminate the Armenians; soldiers made labourers from 19. **France** — *Le Miroir* fakes photo 'The Crime of The German Hordes in Poland' actually 1905 pogrom. '75' Flag Day for front-line soldiers. **NZ** — 3rd reinforcement (2480) sails.

FEBRUARY 1915	WESTERN FRONT 1	EASTERN FRONT 2	SOUTHERN FRONTS 3	TURKISH FRONTS 4
Sun 14 contd				agents leave Baghdad (26, see 9 Mar).
Mon 15		**Poland** — Gallwitz occupies Plotsk on Vistula, beats Russians & attacks Przasnysz fortress (17). German XXI Corps marches 22 miles to envelop 70,000 Russians in Augustow Forest (trapped 17). **Carpathians** — Böhm-Ermolli takes over enlarged Austrian Second Army (60,700 rifles).	Albanian irregular advance into S Serbia reported but driven back across frontier (16).	
Tue 16	**Champagne** — Fourth Battle of Perthes (-17 Mar): French attack on 5-mile front captures 3000 yds of trench with 400 PoWs, but German night counter-attacks now the pattern.	Russians retreating on R Niemen but maul XXI Corps in counter-attack from Grodno.		British War Council emergency meeting agrees to assemble shipping for 50,000 troops. Kitchener tells Churchill 'You get through! I will find the men'; 29th Div to sail for Lemnos, but held back (19, *see* SEA WAR) when Kitchener argues Anzacs enough (*see* 24)..
Wed 17	**Flanders** — Indian Corps repulses attack nr La Bassée. **Artois** — Slight gains by French nr Arras. **Champagne** — French gains NW of Perthes incl PoWs from 6 German corps, but face 2 night counter-attacks (17/18). **Meuse** — French gains NW of Verdun. French attack W flank of St Mihiel Salient. **Vosges** — French capture Ferme Sudel.	**Bukovina** — Austrians retake Czernowitz.		
Thu 18	**Champagne** — French repel 5 night counter-attacks & capture 2 redoubts (-19). **Vosges** — French recapture Xon-Norroy.	**Galicia** — Austrian R Dunajec attack nr Tarnow checked 19.		
Fri 19	**Meuse** — French capture most of Les Eparges after exploding 4 mines (17). **Vosges** — German pre-emptive attack captures Reichsackerkopf peak & enters N Metzeral-Sonder-nach but is pushed back from Lusse Wissenbach. **Champagne** — Gen Langle throws in 8th Div & 5th Bde (21) but gains minute nr Perthes (*see* 25), only 850 yds (16-20).	**Galicia** — Austrians retake Stanislau but Russians win to SE (21-24 March).		
Sat 20	**Flanders** — German capture small section of forward trench nr Ypres. Sniper's bullet kills talented Brig-Gen JE Gough VC, looking at Aubers Ridge. Sir J French inspects 1st Cdn Div (*see* 3 Mar). **Alsace** — German advance SE of Sulzern. **Paris** — A Terrier to Lyautey (Morocco) 'There is a campaign...against the temporisations of Joffre'.	**Poland** — Russian Twelfth Army (incl Gd Corps) counter-attacks fail nr Lomja & Plotsk.		**Egypt** — Anzacs earmarked for Dardanelles.
Sun 21	**Champagne** — French progress nr Perthes. **Vosges** — Huchrod & Strossweiler taken by Germans, but French 47th Div partially retakes latter with Reichskerkopf (night 21/22).	Russian XX Corps in Augustow Forest surrenders after vain breakout efforts (19-20). **Carpathians** — Russians storm heights nr Lupkow & Wyzskow Passes.		**Armenia** — Turks driven across R Ichkalen. Turk Gov of Bitlis reports local revolt.
Mon 22	**Marne** — Heavy bombardment of Reims Cathedral.	**Winter Battle of Masuria ends**: Germans claim 100,000 PoWs (+300 guns, 23). First Battle of Przasnysz (-22): Gallwitz after check takes town	**Serbia** — Rear-Adm Troubridge reaches Belgrade to command RN det, wears Serb general's uniform to avoid confusing sentries & soon	

AFRICAN OPERATIONS 5	SEA WAR 6	AIR WAR 7	INTERNATIONAL EVENTS 8	HOME FRONTS 9
Tripolitania — Italians arrive at Beni Ulid having abandoned Bu Ngeim SW of Sirte. They reoccupy Gadames Oasis on Tunisian border after fighting advance since 13 Jan (16, *see* 31 Mar).	Churchill to Commons '... we expect the [Dardanelles] losses will be confined within manageable limits ...'.		HMG answer to German blockade. Anglo-French Agreement supplements 9 Nov 1914 Prize Convention. Rockefeller Foundation's War Relief Ctee report published (*see* 17). German-British disabled PoW exchange.	**Singapore** — 5th Indian Lt Inf mutiny (-18); 39 Europeans killed, 37 mutineers executed (*see* AFRICAN OPS 11 Aug).
S Cameroons — French occupy Oyem. **E Africa** — British Mule Corps ordered.		**W Front** — British airmen highly praised for their 'fine services' to BEF in Sir J French dispatch.	US note to Britain on SS *Wilhelmina* wheat cargo seizure (11). Britain replies (19). HMG extends trading with enemy prohibition to territories in Allied or enemy occupation.	**Britain** — Disabled Soldiers & Sailors Employment Ctee formed, Merchant Sailors War Injuries Compensation (18). **Russia** — Enemy citizens' property confiscated.
		N Sea — 2 Zeppelins (*L3* & *L4*) wrecked in crash-landings on neutral Danish coast. **Dardanelles** — HMS *Ark Royal* (8 aircraft) arrives at Tenedos; her 2 Wright Navy planes attempt 4 recon sorties (1 successful) over Turk forts at Dardanelles (repeated 19, 20 & 26). **W Front** — French arty observation locate 21 German btys.	**Occupied Belgium** — All Allied nationals' industries & businesses sequestrated.	
E Africa — British Voi-Taveta Railway line ordered (*see* 23 June).	Germans postpone U-boat offensive start to 22.		**Neutrals: Italy** — Anti-Austrian demonstrations at reopening of Parliament.	**Britain** — King & Queen visit exchanged PoWs from Germany.
	N Sea — Norwegian tanker *Belridge* torpedoed without warning (by *U16*) but towed into Folkestone. **Aegean** — **Anglo-French bombardment of Dardanelles outer forts** (72 Turk guns under Col Djevad Bey), 2 aircraft observing, begun by flagship *Inflexible* & 7 battleships, fading light ends. Weather stops renewal till 25. Carden has 1 battlecruiser, 12 battleships; 4 cruisers; 1 aircraft carrier (see AIR WAR 17); 16 destroyers; 6 subma-rines; 2 hospital ships & 21 trawlers for minesweeping.		**Neutrals: USA** — SS *Evelyn* (cotton for Bremen) mined & sunk off Borkum I, *Carib* also (23).	
	Baltic — Russian seaplane carrier *Orlitsa* (5 aircraft) commissioned.		Iagow to Bülow, 'We have no means of compulsion against Austria' (*see* 26). US Sec of State Bryan sends mediation proposal to London & Berlin, U-boat attacks to stop for food supply of German civilians under US supervision. (Germany accepts with reservations 28.) German-Americans form American Independence Union for strict neutrality.	**Britain** — **1st formal Admiralty Conference on 'land ships'** in Churchill's bedroom ('flu). Land Ship Ctee meets 24, 2 working models to be built (*see* 20 Mar).
				Britain — Cabinet Munitions Production Ctee formed.
SW Africa — Botha begins recce towards Windhoek, occupies Nonidas & Goanikas (23, *see* 18 Mar) & declines Churchill's 23 Feb armoured	Only 3 U-boats at sea on first day of offensive (7.3 av — Sept). **Irish Sea** — British net barrage begun across N Channel, 7 lines of drifters	**Britain** — FF29 seaplane bombs Coggeshall & Colch-ester barracks; plane ditches at sea, crew taken PoW (night 21/ 22). **France** — German Army		**France** — Sarah Bernhardt has right leg amputated (stage injury), continues to act.

FEBRUARY 1915	WESTERN FRONT 1	EASTERN FRONT 2	SOUTHERN FRONTS 3	TURKISH FRONTS 4
Mon 22 contd		with 10,000 PoWs (24), loses it with 5400 PoWs (27). **Galicia** — Big battle begins S of Dolina-Stanislau; Russians claim 4000 PoWs (27).	establishes harmony with Russian & French contingents; 27 RN gunners follow with 8 4.7-in naval guns to complete Belgrade's river defences (*see* 30 Mar).	
Tue 23	**Flanders** — FM French refuses to relieve 2 French corps N of Ypres due to 29th Div's going to Salonika, Joffre replies French attack alongside British postponed (7 Mar), Haig already discovers this (28).			
Wed 24	**Meuse** — French arty in successful counter-battery ops. Fighting at Les Eparges.	Germans cross Niemen nr Sventsiansk.		Lloyd George suggests Mesopotamia 'Merely a side issue', whole force should go to Dardanelles. Churchill disagrees. Kitchener again v sending land forces incl 29th Div.
Thu 25	**Flanders** — British make slight advance N of La Bassée. **Champagne** — French advance nr Les Mesnil (& 26) but Germans reinforced. Gens Gerard & Dumas each now i/c 2 corps in Fourth Army sector.	**Poland** — Below bombards Osovyets fortress (-27). **Galicia** — Only half Russian 167th Res Inf Regt de-trains at Lemberg.		Enver Pasha orders no Armenians to be employed in Army, commanders can declare martial law. Yet Enver thanks Armenian soldiers & nation for support (26).
Fri 26	**Meuse — First use of flamethrowers:** 12 of *Abteilung Reddemann* support attacking inf in Bois de Malancourt NE of Verdun, first of 653 German flame attacks (*see* 26 Mar, 30 July).			War Council keeps 29th Div in England to Churchill's anger & written protest (27, *see* 10 Mar). **Dardanelles** — Turks have laid 5 minefields (184 mines) to protect the Narrows since 5 Nov 1914 (191 mines in 5 fields then).
Sat 27	**Champagne** — Beauséjour captured by French but only 1000 PoWs since 16. **Flanders — First Territorial div joins BEF**, 46th (North Midland). FM French writes to his mistress 'I have more trouble with the War Office than I do with the Germans'. **Vosges** — French 66th Div vainly attacks Hartmann-sweilerkopf despite help of 53 guns (*see* 19 Mar).	**Carpathians** — Renewed Austrian offensive (Second Army joins) soon loses impetus in early thaw, gains only 10 miles (-5 Mar).		Grand Duke Nicholas telegram answers Churchill's (of 26): Black Sea Fleet & over 47,000 men will attack Constantinople when Allies enter Sea of Marmara.
Sun 28	**Marne** — Bombardment of Reims (-3 Mar). **Aisne** — Soissons under German bombardment (Mar). **Champagne** — French Colonial Corps storms fort E of Oblique Wood & 3rd Div captures Hill 196 driving defenders 200 yds N. French 51st Inf Regt (II Corps) has suffered 1016 cas since 21 in gaining 540 yds. **Argonne** — French gain on Hill 263.	**Galicia** — Lechitski counter-attacks Austrians with 4 corps.		Churchill sends Grey suggested Turk surrender conditions.
Mon 1 March 1915	A rare Indian desertion (15 men) to Germans who return them & others to NW Frontier. (Mar) German 70-man storm det with armoured shields suffers 50% losses (*see* 29). **French first issue grenades to troops** (improvised ones earlier made at front). **Champagne** — French establish new line, since 16 Feb they have advanced 2000 yds in Perthes-Beauséjour sector. French capture trenches to 1000 yds on 3½-mile front. Unsuccessful attacks by 2 Prussian Guard regts NE of Mesnil (-4).	**Poland** — Heavy fighting nr Grodno & Osovyets (-2) as Russian Tenth Army counter-attacks. **Carpathians** — Austrian attacks repulsed (-9) but Hungarian Gen Szurmay holds Uzsok Pass, 3 times refusing orders to evacuate (Mar).	**Serbia** — British Serbian Relief Fund & Red Cross Society open typhus isolation colony; 16 workers incl organizer Lady Paget stricken (6-24) leaving 1 sister i/c 300 patients for a wk until 2nd Serbian Relief Fund surgical unit supplies 4 nurses. **Austria** — (Mar) Maj Primavesi of Austrian Intelligence organizes censors' gp for Italy (*see* May).	*Corps Expéditionnaire d 'Orient* formed for Dardanelles (sailed 3). By now 5 Turk divs in theatre (3 added in Feb). **Persia** — Gen Nazarbekov re-occupies Dilman, Azerbaijan. **Palestine** — Djemal told by Constantinople to seek Jewish co-operation.

AFRICAN OPERATIONS 5	SEA WAR 6	AIR WAR 7	INTERNATIONAL EVENTS 8	HOME FRONTS 9
car offer (but *see* 26 Apr). SA Central Force occupies Garub, 65 miles E of Luderitz.	eventually.	airship *LZ29* drops 2000lb bombs on Calais (night 21/22).		
	Channel — *U8* (Stoss) sinks 5 British steamers off Beachy Head (-24), total of 15,049t. **Red Sea** — French cruiser *Desaix* lands marines at Aqaba.			
	Adriatic — First French warship lost, destroyer *Dague* mined off Antivari, Montenegro (*see* 1 Mar).		HMG reject Russian London Ambassador's forwarded request to supply Zeitun Armenians with arms.	**Austria** — **Govt takes over all grain/flour stocks. Britain** — Second Territorial Div (N Midland, later 48th) leaves for France.
	Dardanelles — **Superdreadnought *Queen Elizabeth*** (8 x 15-in guns) **in first action** joins 7 Anglo-French battleships in silencing outer forts. *Agamemnon* (hit 7 times) fires 123 shells (12 cas).	**Britain** — French aircraft drop 60 bombs on German rail stns & concentrations in Champagne; 3 bombs on Metz barracks. **E Front** — IM *Kievsky* bombs 2 munition trains nr Willenberg.		**Britain** — King & Churchill inspect RND (9000) at Blandford prior to 1 Mar sailing for Dardanelles.
SW Africa — Deventer's SAS Force (9200) advances (*see* 6 Mar).	**Dardanelles** — 125 British sailors & marines (4 cas) land both sides, destroy 8 guns (2AA) & bridge. 80 land at Sedd-el-Bahr (27), blow up 6 mortars. Minesweepers sweep up 4-mile channel.	**Britain** — German Navy airship *L8* fails to reach London.	Conrad urges Germany must pay for concessions to Italy, 'Either you agree, or you fall into the water with us'. Germans consider giving up part of Silesia.	**Britain** — Welsh Guards formed, fully recruited 22 Apr.
	E Africa — Admiralty formally declare blockade.		Wyldbore-Smith (Chm Int'l Supply Commission) comments on Russian secrecy and lack of co-ordination in making orders. **Neutrals: USA** — French seize US ex-German SS *Dacia* (Bremen-bound from US 11) and take her into Brest (Prize Court validates 22 Mar). **Occupied France** — (Feb) Nord Dept Prefect Trépont taken hostage to Germany.	**Germany** — 2nd War Loan (-19 Mar). **France** — Paris: Moulin Rouge burnt down.
	Channel — **First ramming of submarine by merchant ship:** *SS Thordis* rams U-boat off Beachy Head. **Britain** — (Feb) 4 pre-dreadnought battleships lose main guns to arm 8 new monitors. (Feb) U-boats sink 8 ships of total 21,787t.	**Britain** — Adm Fisher demands small non-rigid airships with 'good turn of speed' for A/S duties. Within 21 days prototype SS (Sea Scouts) class airship ready for service: envelope/gas bag from Willows airship; crew car is made from BE 2 aircraft fuselages (150 built 1915-18, *see* 1 Mar).		Lloyd George Bangor speech on munitions urgency, 'an engineer's war'.
E Africa — RN blockade formally begins, of a 600-mile coast line (*see* 14 Apr).	HMG declare it 'WOULD PREVENT COMMODITIES OF ANY KIND ENTERING OR LEAVING GERMANY'. But, owing to fear of alienating USA & other neutrals, large cargoes continue to reach Germany via Dutch & Scandinavian ports, till 1917. **Dardanelles** — 50 RMs & sailors destroy 15 guns, 4 MGs & 2 searchlights at entrance. 3 British battleships engage Fort 8 & French ships shell Bulair (2). **Secret War** — (Mar) French physicist Paul Langevin begins echo-ranging research in Paris (Seine underwater end 1915, Toulon 1916). **Adriatic** — Austrian Navy raids Montenegrin port	(Mar) French Navy decides to introduce small non-rigid airships for A/S & minesweeping duties. **Turk Fronts** — (Mar) German crews to ferry 6 aircraft from S Hungary to Bulgaria & thence rail them to Constantinople: 3 arrive safely, 3 other impounded by Bulgaria. Henceforth until 11 Oct 1915 aircraft for Turkey flown direct from Hungary to Adrianople. **W Front** — Cdt Baron de Tricornet, Marquis de Rose, forms **world's first specialized fighter aircraft unit** (*Esc MS12*), equipped with MS type 'L' 'Parasol' 2-seaters based at Rosnay nr Reims. RFC 3rd Wing formed at St Omer. RFC	**Anglo-French Declaration to prevent trade with or by Germany** in all ships sailing after 11 (US protests 5).	**Britain** — RFP 24%.

MARCH 1915	WESTERN FRONT 1	EASTERN FRONT 2	SOUTHERN FRONTS 3	TURKISH FRONTS 4
Mon 1 contd				
Tue 2	**Champagne** — Germans counter-attacking nr Perthes.	**Poland** — Russian Twelfth Army night attacks W of R Bobr (-4) fail — 21,000 cas (2 armoured cars no help). **Bukovina** — Russians bombard Czernowitz. Reinforced Austrians fail to cross R Pruth (17) & raiders over R Dniester repelled (23). **Galicia** — Mannerheim GOC Russian 12th Cav Div, succeeds Kaledin.		**Mesopotamia** — 14,400 British troops + 40 guns; 500 Indian cav disengage from 1500-2000 Turks nr Shaiba.
Wed 3	**Flanders** — **1st Cdn Div enters line**, takes over Fleurbaix sector S of Armentières, aids Neuve Chapelle attack (10, *see* 7 Apr). **Artois** — German div counter-attack retakes Lorette ridge crest & drives French into Buvigny Wood, but French recover most ground (-5, *see* 20).	**Galicia** — Russians retake Krasna; Stanislau (4), claim 19,000 PoWs since 21 Feb.		**Persia** — c800 British + 4 guns lose 189 cas & 1 gun to Turco-Arab force (c800-900 cas) in vain attack nr Ahwaz.
Thu 4				
Fri 5	**Argonne** — 3 unsuccessful German counter-attacks at Hill 263. **Flanders** — In private letter Sir J French laments 'Silent Army' of dead.	**Poland** — Germans mass between Thorn & Mlava in N. **Carpathians** — Russians cross R Bistritza in E & threaten Austrian flank. Austrian Second Army vainly attacks (-10).		
Sat 6		German Tenth Army withdraws from Augustow Forest to just E of border, Russians pursue (-9).		
Sun 7	**Champagne** — French 64th Bde secures small part of Sabot Wood , fighting (-l5).			
Mon 8	**Flanders** — German attack nr Dixmude.			
Tue 9	**Argonne** — Fighting between Fou de Paris & Bolante (14, 18).	German Eleventh Army (Fabeck) formed. **Poland** — New Gallwitz offensive nr Przasnysz (-14) checked.		**Persia** — British arrest 2 Germans at Bushire consulate (Gulf); telegrams prove sabotage intent, but only Wassmuss diplomatic code

AFRICAN OPERATIONS 5	SEA WAR 6	AIR WAR 7	INTERNATIONAL EVENTS 8	HOME FRONTS 9
	Antivari.	flies 141 bombing missions (-20 June) but only 3 definite successes (see 24 July). **W Front** — RFC (No 3 Sqn) first uses new box-type 'A' camera to photo German trenches (see 10).		**Austria** — Metal Collection Week. **S Africa** — White Book on rebellion issued, Parliament debates (3).
	Dardanelles — RN landing party destroys 6 field-guns at Sedd-el-Bahr while 4 British battleships shell Fort Dardanus (S shore).	**Germany** — French bomber unit *MF29* (Happe) bombs Rottweil gunpowder factory (repeated 12). **Neutrals : USA** — National Advisory Cttee for Aeronautics (NACA) founded.	British War Council discuss Constantinople's future, Churchill even suggests hiring Turk Army as mercenaries v Austria after its capture. HM Ambassador in Petrograd cables that Russia 'could not consent to Greek participation in operations at the Dardan-elles' (see 14). **Neutrals : USA** — *Fatherland* advertises souvenir Iron Crosses (1500 already sold to fund widows & orphans).	**Britain** — Royal Family at horse show.
Cameroons — 2nd Action at Harmann's Farm: both sides retire, 550 British dig in at Ft Bare after some panic.	Anglo-French bombardment of Dardanelles forts continues. 5 troop transports arrive at Mudros. 300 RMs (48 cas) repulsed on both shores, only 4 MGs destroyed. Admiralty sends instructions on reducing Bosphorus forts. Enver Pasha request made in Vienna to buy 3 Austrian U-boats at Pola for Dardanelles defence, but only 2 operational & not feasible (5, see 15).	**Dardanelles** — RNAS & French floatplanes spot fall of shot for Allied bombardment of Turk forts (see SEA WAR). **W Front** — German Navy airship *L8* shot down by Belgian troops en route to London.	Italian Ambassador Imperiali tells Grey territorial conditions for joining Allies (see 20).	**Britain** — Admiralty decides *U8*'s 29 PoWs cannot receive 'honourable treatment'. Germany theatens reprisals (2 Apr). Shells & Fuses Agree-ment allows use of unskilled labour & women.
Anglo-Portuguese protocol defines Angola-Rhodesia border. **SW Africa** — 43,000 S Africans massed in 4 forces v 9000 Germans.	**Dardanelles: Aegean** — *Queen Elizabeth* fires 21,000 yds over Gallipoli Peninsula at Narrows' forts (-6). **Aegean** — 2 RN battleships & cruiser *Euryalus* shell Smyrna (& 7, 28, see 11). Turks sink 5 blockships making Smyrna Port unusable to U-boats (Allied fear).	**W Front** — German Army airship *L233* shot down by AA fire; crashes nr Ostend.	Germany replies to US protest on war zone (see 15).	
SW Africa — Deventer's S Force (9000) invades at Schuit Drift, R Orange; Berrange's E Force (2500 mtd inf & 2 guns) starts across Kalahari Desert (reaches Rietfontein on border 31).			**Neutrals: Greece** — **Venizelos resigns at King's refusal to send troops to Dardanelles** (Col Metaxas of Gen Staff so advises King) after PM offers 3 divs. Gounaris PM (9). King dissolves Parliament (11).	
	Dardanelles — 6 Anglo-French battleships (2 hit) engage Narrows' forts, apparently silence 2. **Black Sea** — Russian sqn shells Eregli and Zonguldak, sink 7 steamers & 1 sailing ship. Russian sub *Nerpa* off Bosphorus for first time (5-8).	**N Sea** — 6 RNAS aircraft bomb Ostend.	Greece protests v British Lemnos occupation, HMG pleads military necessity (9) & guarantees return (20).	**Britain** — Asquith calls Churchill 'far the most disliked man in the Cabinet by his colleagues'. King lends York House to Kitchener. 'Flu epidemic in London.
SW Africa — Namib Desert temperature 132°F.	**Dardanelles** — 2 RNAS seaplanes lost, only 2 serviceable.		At Council of Ministers Francis Joseph in principle accepts frontier changes for Italy, Conrad bitterly complains better to go to ruin.	**Britain** — Amatol explosive first tested, Kitchener authorizes immediate use (c400t pw by mid-1917, see Sept 1917).
Cyrenaica — Gen Moccagatta defeats 1500 rebels (& 11) but inland garrisons evacuated (-Oct). **E Africa** — Rhodesian 2nd Regt leaves for SW Africa.			HM Ambassador in Sofia meets Bulgar PM (v impressed with Dardanelles ops by 17).	**Britain** — Lloyd George Commons speech on mobilizing industry for war. Officers in uniform forbidden to visit nightclubs.

MARCH 1915	WESTERN FRONT 1	EASTERN FRONT 2	SOUTHERN FRONTS 3	TURKISH FRONTS 4
Tue 9 contd				captured. HM minister at Tehran protests at Persian pro-German attitude (16, *see* 3 Apr).
Wed 10	**Flanders — Battle of Neuve Chapelle** (-13): although Joffre has abandoned his planned Mar combined offensive, Sir J French persists with BEF contribution. After a 35-min bombardment by 342 guns (5 burst due to dud fuses) 4 divs (Lahore, Meerut, 7th & 8th) attack at 0805 on 4000-yd front. Neuve Chapelle village captured with 4 lines of trenches by 1200, but advance quickly bogs down after 1200 yds. Germans launch counter-attacks, ammunition runs short; by dusk German 2nd line trenches taken with 750 PoWs.			**Dardanelles** — Kitchener tells Hamilton (GOC Central Force England) he will command MEF; 29th Div ordered to embark.
Thu 11	**Flanders** — Neuve Chapelle: 2 German counter-attacks repulsed (c500k by 2nd Rifle Bde), but 6th Bav Res Div now present.	**Carpathians** — Brusilov's VIII Corps strikes at Austrian Second Army left flank, breaks XIX Corps (13). Second Army cas 51,086 from 148,848 (1-14).		**Mesopotamia** — British Euphrates Blockade Force (5-6 vessels) begins ops. Maj Leachman arrives from India to work among Euphrates tribes.
Fri 12	**Flanders** — Neuve Chapelle: 16,000-strong German counter-attacks from 0500, easily repulsed by IV & Indian Corps; III Corps takes L'Epinette. Fighting until nightfall when Haig orders entrenching on line won, but only a slight salient 2000 yds wide & 1200 yds deep has been pushed into German line. Total British cas: 11,652 men (4200 Indian Corps). German cas incl 1700 PoWs. Germans bombard Ypres. **Champagne** — Reinforced French Fourth Army offensive storms part of Grey Trenches, but no gains on 13.			**Dardanelles** — RND reaches Lemnos (*see* 27). French 1st Div arrives (15).
Sat 13	**Flanders** — Battle of Neuve Chapelle ends. British 7th Div makes ground towards Aubers Ridge; 612 PoWs taken.	**Galicia** — Selivanov storms hill in Przemysl perimeter.		**Dardanelles** — Hamilton + 14 officers leave London after Kitchener tells him 'If the Fleet gets through Constantinople will fall of itself' and vetoes land ops till 29th Div ready.
Sun 14	**Meuse-Argonne** — Joffre announces his intention of launching offensive. He proposes to attack in Woëvre, reducing St Mihiel salient by simultaneous surprise attack on both active faces of triangular-shaped salient by 3 corps, with subsidiary attacks on either flank. **Flanders** — Germans capture part of St Eloi after exploding mine; Belgian success nr Dixmude. **Champagne** — French secure most of Sabot Wood & make			

AFRICAN OPERATIONS 5	SEA WAR 6	AIR WAR 7	INTERNATIONAL EVENTS 8	HOME FRONTS 9
At Mwaika (E of L Victoria) c450 KAR beat 222 Germans. **Cameroons** — Dobell refused Indian troops, but 192 WAFF arrive Duala (31).				
	Dardanelles — Minesweepers try to work at night, 1 sunk, only 4 kts possible across current. **N Sea** — Destroyer HMS *Ariel* rams & sinks *U12* off Aberdeen.	**W Front** — **RFC simultaneously introduces 5 innovations** in Neuve Chapelle battle, uses 7 sqns with 85 aircraft. 1) 'Clock System' whereby the observer plots the fall of shot on a segmented celluloid disc; 2) photo-mosaic mapping of German trench system, by end Feb; 3) systematic medium & long-range patrolling of approaches to battlefield; 4) synchronization & co-ordination of bombing plan (mainly rail targets) with main battle plan (3 aircraft bomb German div HQ at Fournes); 5) 'contact patrols' intended to disclose precise locations of advancing inf. **E Front** — Warsaw bombed by German Army airships *LZ30* & *LZ34* .	**British War Council discusses postwar territorial claims and for 1st time war aims. Churchill urges German Fleet's surrender. Tory leaders Bonar Law & Lord Lansdowne attend for 1st and only time.** Chinese Revolutionary Party denounces Japan's 21 Demands, calls for President's overthrow. Shanghai rally resolves to boycott Japanese goods (18) but prohibited 25 (*see* 17 Apr). **Secret War** — German war aims ctee envisages controlling French coast to mouth of R Somme.	
L Victoria — HMS *Winifred* (4-in gun) drives German *Mwanza* ashore nr Rujenge but latter refloated 17 as transport. **L Nyasa** — Lt-Cdr Denniston RN takes command of flotilla (Mar).	**Churchill cables Carden, urging more decisive attack.** **Aegean** — German-commanded Turk torpedo boat *Demirhisar* torpedoes RN seaplane carrier *Anne* off Smyrna (op again Aug).		German treasury approves RM 2m to support Russian revolutionary propaganda. Britain extends absolute contraband list, France likewise (13).	**Britain** — Canadian Training Div estab at Shorncliffe, Kent. Liverpool Dockers Work Bn organized.
Cameroons — French Mission at Duala (-18) to arrange mid-Oct Allied advance on Yaunde after rainy season.	**Channel** — First Q-ship/U-boat encounter is bloodless: *U29* ignores *Vienna* S of Scilly Is, latter rescues crew of scuttled *Andalusian* (*see* 23 June). **Palestine** — French cruiser *St Louis* shells Gaza.		**HMG formally accepts Russian claim of 4 to Constantinople** (*see* 10 Apr). **Secret War** — British agent 'Frey' enters Germany from Switzerland but proves fraud by end 1915 (*see* 1 June).	
Morocco — Abd-el-Malek (Abd-el-Kader's grandson) leaves Tangier with 50,000 pesetas & German adviser for Taza to raise revolt with German Foreign Legion deserters but kept tribal captive till summer (*see* 15 Oct 1916). **Tripolitania** — Italian relief cols for Tarkuna stopped (& 20, 30) but 15th Eritrean Bn gets through (16).	**N Sea** — **Swedish SS *Hanna* first neutral merchant ship sunk without warning by U-boat** (*see* 25). **Dardanelles** — 7 trawler minesweepers & 5 picket boats with cruiser *Amethyst* (60 cas) repulsed from night-sweeping attempt (also nights 15/16 & 16/17).			
	Pacific — German cruiser *Dresden* (24 cas) blows herself up under white flag off Juan Fernandez after being trapped at anchor by RN cruisers *Kent*, *Glasgow* & *Orama* thanks to collier signal intercepted (13). Crew interned in Chile (Lt Canaris, 1934-44 *Abwehr* Chief, one of the escapees reaches Berlin 4 Oct, *see* 1 Oct 1916).		Churchill vainly cables Grand Duke Nicholas to allow Greek help in Dardanelles. HM Ambassador Buchanan tells Tsar 'After the war Britain and Russia will be the two most powerful empires in the world'. **Neutrals: Italy** — Chamber passes defence bill.	

MARCH 1915	WESTERN FRONT 1	EASTERN FRONT 2	SOUTHERN FRONTS 3	TURKISH FRONTS 4
Sun 14 contd	breaches around Hill 196, repulse several counter-attacks (15).			
Mon 15	**Flanders** — British 27th Div regain lost ground at St Eloi, repulse fresh German attack (17). **Aisne** — Gen **Maunoury** of Sixth Army **severely w** (partially blinded), aged 67, out of war except as military governor of Paris (*see* 28 and 2 Nov).		Italian Army reservists assemble.	Enver Pasha: 'I shall go down in history as the man who demonstrated the vulnerability of the British Fleet. Unless they bring a large army with them they will be caught in a trap.'
Tue 16	**Champagne** — French storm crest N of Mesnil & repulse counter-attacks all along Fourth Army front, 48th Div gains Yellow Wood & in Sabot Wood (-17).	Russian NW Front standfast ordered.		Kitchener memo to Cabinet urges annexation of Alexandretta, Aleppo & Mesopotamia.
Wed 17	**First Battle of Champagne ends** as Langle gets Joffre to halt offensive. By 23,2000 PoWs taken since 20 Dec 1914 but advances minute for 100,000 cas (incl 2450 PoWs).	**E Prussia** — 4000 Russians capture and burn Memel but Pappritz retakes (21), 3000 freed (PoWs & civilians).		**Dardanelles — Hamilton assumes command of MEF at Tenedos. Mesopotamia —** 33rd Indian Inf Bde lands at Basra (-25). Nixon made GOC. His orders (24) include plan for advance on Baghdad.
Thu 18	**Champagne** — Fighting for Jaune Brule Wood (*see* 23).			
Fri 19	**Vosges** — Fighting on Reichackerkopf & Hartmannsweilerkopf (*see* 23).	**Galicia** — Austrian sortie from Przemysl. Selivanov attacks on 3 sides (20-21).		**Dardanelles** — Hamilton cables Kitchener: 'It must be a deliberate and progressive military operation'. Adm Robeck agrees (26).
Sat 20	**Artois** — Germans storm trenches nr Notre Dame de Lorette, but French recover (21). Foch sends Joffre spring offensive plan.	**E Prussia** — 16,000 Russians take Laugszargen and attack Tilsit but Esebeck's German Bde retake latter (23). **Carpathians** — Brusilov takes 2400 PoWs nr Smolnik. *Südarmee* attacks nr Kosziowa (-27).		
Sun 21	**Argonne** — Fighting at Bagatelle.		Falkenhayn suggests to Conrad quick strike v Serbia to open way for supplies to Turks, but Conrad says no forces due to impending Galician offensive; Falkenhayn rekindles interest by hoping for Bulgar	

AFRICAN OPERATIONS 5	SEA WAR 6	AIR WAR 7	INTERNATIONAL EVENTS 8	HOME FRONTS 9
	Germans decide to send coastal *UB7* & *UB8* in sections by rail to Austrian Pola naval base (assembled by c10 Apr, *see* 6 May), & a large U-boat by sea to Dardanelles, *U21* selected (17), Kaiser approves 30 (*see* 25 Apr, *UB3* transferred by rail 15 Apr). **Britain** — Admiralty orders 15 Z Whaler type patrol craft, finished by Nov, based at Peterhead, Shetlands & Stornoway.	**N Sea** — First German air attack (bomb misses) on British merchant ship (SS *Blonde*) in home waters (3 miles off N Foreland).	British reply to U-boat blockade issued, Dedeagach in Bulgaria declared enemy base. Germany compensates USA for *William P Frye*.	**Britain** — Kitchener Lords speech urges increased output, offers workers profit sharing & war medals.
			Neutrals — Rumania refuses Russian request for eventual passage of troops, calls up 1909-15 conscription classes (18).	**Belgium** — Industrial base set up at Le Havre. **Britain** — Govt arms factory powers extended to all potential munition plants; War Depts can requisition (23).
	Secret War — British negotiators leave Bulgar Aegean port of Dedeagach after DNI's vain effort to bribe open Dardanelles with £4m is countermanded. **Dardanelles** — Carden goes sick, Robeck succeeds.	**France** — Calais bombed by German Army airship *LZ12* (night 17/18). **W Front** — French bombers attack 7 rail stns: Bazancourt (NE of Reims), Altkirch, Cernay (Alsace), Anizy, Chauny, Tergnier & Coucy le Château.	France claims Syria & Cilicia in secret message to HMG.	**Britain** — **Women's War Service Register opened** but only 8500/40,000 registered employed to end 1915. Treasury Agreement: 34 trade unions accept arbitration in industrial disputes (-19). **France** — Land bought for new Citroën shell factory, 2000 rnds pd 16 Aug, 10,000 29 Sept (50,000 pd end 1917).
SW Africa — Botha leaves Swakopmund to lead 21,000 men (13,000 mtd) in 3 cols, captures Jakalswater & Riet Water holes with 284 PoWs & 2 guns (20) after night march.	FINAL ANGLO-FRENCH NAVAL ATTACK ON DARDANELLES NARROWS BY 16 BATTLESHIPS FAILS, 3 sunk, 3 severely damaged: *Irresistible*, *Ocean* & French *Bouvet* (620 lost, 45 survivors) sunk by parallel mines to shore (laid undetected night 8 by Turk minelayer *Nusret*) in Narrows; battlecruiser *Inflexible* severely damaged. *Suffren* severely damaged for 6 wks. Damaged *Gaulois* runs aground on Rabbit I. **Allied seaborne breakthrough attempt now abandoned** for overland advance on Constantinople. Turk heavy shells almost exhausted (main 48 guns over 6-in have 46-230 rpg on 28). **N Sea** — HMS *Dreadnought* rams & sinks homeward-bound *U29* (sank Dutch SS *Medea* off Beachy Head). First U-boat 'ace' Weddigen k.	**Germany** — French raids on Freiberg rail stn. **E Front** — Russian pilot A A Kazakov, having failed to entangle an Albatros with tracking cable, rams it over Guzov village.	HMG gets US cotton interests to accept cotton as contraband, likewise rubber (29).	
			Holland protests v Allied blockade (*see* 22 Apr).	**India** — Defence Act passed.
		France — Paris outskirts bombed (52 bombs, 9 cas) by German Army airships *LZ29*, *LZ35* ; *SL2* bombs Compiègne instead. *LZ29* shot down by AA fire nr Saint Quentin (night 20/ 21). **W Front** — Belgian *Aviation Militaire* formed. **E Front** — Senior Austrian cdr escapes in waiting Albatros BII shortly before fall of Przemysl (*see* E FRONT).	Allies in principle accept Italy's conditions. Italian military attaché leaves Vienna (21). Would-be Danish mediator Hans Niels Andersen sees Kaiser at Charleville after visit to Petrograd (1-7).	**Germany** — *Reichstag* votes 3rd War Credit; Liebknecht + 1 other oppose, 30 abstain. **Secret War** — Churchill approves 18 'landship' prototypes, orders all haste (26, *see* 12 Aug).

MARCH 1915	WESTERN FRONT 1	EASTERN FRONT 2	SOUTHERN FRONTS 3	TURKISH FRONTS 4
Sun 21 contd			intervention (29, *see* 26 Apr).	
Mon 22	**Aisne** — Germans bombard Soissons Cathedral (- 23).	**Galicia** — **Przemysl surrenders**: 9 generals among 119,602 PoWs & 700 guns, 20% scurvy, 3 days rations left.		**Dardanelles** — Hamilton says troops cannot be ready till 14 Apr.
Tue 23	**Flanders** — Belgian landing on E bank of R Yser. **Alsace** — French 1st Chasseur Bde reaches German 2nd line on Hartmannsweilerkopf, taking 200 PoWs (-24). **Champagne** — French attacks finally slacken (*see* 8 Apr).			**Sinai** — 2000 British inflict 50 cas on Turk raiders 10 miles E of Canal.
Wed 24				**Dardanelles** — **Liman given command of Turk Fifth Army** (arrives Gallipoli 26).
Thu 25	**Artois** — French re-control Notre Dame de Lorette Ridge & repulse counter-attack.	**Galicia** — Only 1/3 of 4th Siberian Res Rifle Regt de-train at Lemberg. **Carpathians** — **Brusilov advances** (-4 Apr), retakes Lupkow Pass (26) & 8200 PoWs.		Hamilton arrives at Alexandria. **India: NW Frontier** — Action of Dardoni by Gen Fane v 10,000 Tochi threatening Miranshah (- 27). Colonial Sec Harcourt's Cabinet memo urges Mesopotamia's annexation for Indian immigration & US Palestine mandate.
Fri 26	**Alsace** — Despite German use of flamethrowers, French storm fortified summit of Hartmannsweilerkopf & exploit 160 yds along 2 ridges to E (*see* 30).	Gen Alexeiev replaces Ruzki as C-in-C NW Front.		
Sat 27	**Meuse** — French advance at Les Eparges & repulse counter-attacks (28).			**Egypt** — RND, French Div & 29th Div landing to re-stow equipment (-29). **Armenia** — Russians recapture Artvin on Upper Chorok. Turks evacuate Batumi (29). (Mar) Mahmud Kamil Pasha replaces Hasan Izzet Pasha as C-in-C but keeps same German CoS, Maj Guse (for duration). His Third Army reinforced to 35,000.
Sun 28	**Aisne** — Gen **Kluck** severely **w** in leg by French shell, visiting trenches nr Vailly, aged 68; Fabeck replaces i/c First Army (*see* 17 Sept).	**Carpathians** — German *Beskidenkorps* formed to bolster Austrians.		
Mon 29	1st German Gas Regt formed, 2 bns of 3 coys each (*see* 22 Apr). Allied conference at Chantilly (*GQG*), Kitchener, Joffre & FM French; latter agrees to release 2 French corps for spring offensive.	**E Prussia** — Esebeck's Bde retakes Tauroggen NE of Tilsit. **Carpathians** — Brusilov takes 11,140 PoWs, 9 guns & 35 MGs in Lupkow Pass sector (-30).		**Egypt** — Hamilton inspects 20,000 Anzacs (2480 NZ reinforcements arrived 26).
Tue 30	**Flanders** — Intelligence officers of XV Corps, French Tenth Army, learn from PoWs that extensive German preparations nr Zillebeke E of Ypres to employ 'asphyxiating	Austrian GHQ morale 'below zero. The Chief [Conrad] never stops grumbling'.	**Serbia** — Austrian river steamer *Belgrad* tries to break Allied Danube blockade (night 30/31), hits Russian mine & is sunk by Serb 75mm field guns (*see* 23 Apr).	

AFRICAN OPERATIONS 5	SEA WAR 6	AIR WAR 7	INTERNATIONAL EVENTS 8	HOME FRONTS 9
	Adm Robeck decides naval attack renewal not possible, troops needed (*see* TURK FRONTS 19 & 22), his CoS Keyes considers Dardanelles forceable with destroyer-minesweepers after 4 Apr.		Secret Sino-Japanese Agreement (4 demands) on S Manchuria.	
Tripolitania — 2 Italian cols restore Misurata's links (cut 18) with its ports.	**N Sea** — Fog fails Harwich Force seaplane attack on German *Nordreich* radio stn (also thwarted 3, 6 & 11 May); cruiser *Undaunted* & destroyer *Landrail* collide (7 cas) but get home (-26).	**Occupied Belgium** — 2 RNAS aircraft bomb coastal U-boat assembly yards at Hoboken, Antwerp (repeated 1 Apr).	**Secret War** — Churchill memo on capturing Borkum I after 15 May. **Neutrals** — Chile protests v RN violation of territorial waters (14-15).	
	Baltic — German warships shell Courland & Libau (28).		**Neutrals** — Allied military intelligence in Petrograd reports German weapons for Turkey being allowed through Rumania & Bulgaria. Grey vainly protests to envoys.	**Secret War: Germany** — Toxic gas trench mortar bombs tested at Wahn nr Cologne. **Japan** — Govt wins elections with 80 majority.
		Germany — 6 French aircraft bomb Metz Zeppelin sheds & rail stn. **Dardanelles** — Cdr Samson's No 3 Sqn RNAS (from Dunkirk) begins landing at Tenedos with 18 aircraft & 118 men, vineyard cleared to make airfield, 1st flight 28.	**Neutrals** — Dutch troops ordered to German frontier, invasion seems imminent; Churchill & Kitchener look at contingency plans (-28) but false alarm.	**Germany** — Local authorities authorized to ban alcohol sale; production cut (31) of 40% malt in breweries.
	Atlantic — Last German surface raider sinkings of British ships until 11 Jan 1916 (*see* 8 Apr).	**Sea War** — No 1 Kite-Balloon Section RNAS ordered to Dardanelles aboard ex-dredger *Manica* (arrives Mudros 9 Apr, *see* 19 Apr).	Austria makes Trentino territorial concession to Italy (*see* 8 Apr).	**Britain** — **Press campaign starts on munitions shortage** with FM French's statement to *The Times*. **Germany** — Tirpitz contacts Kaiser's doctor to explore his Crown Prince Regency idea. **Turkey** — Law for Encouraging Industry.
	Irish Sea — British liner *Falaba* sunk by *U28* in 8 mins (104 lost incl Americans, *see* INT'L EVENTS). **Black Sea** — 5 Russian battleships, 2 cruisers & 10 destroyers shell Bosphorus forts but fog (29) thwarts renewal (*see* 25 Apr). **N Sea** — Capt Fryatt of British ferry *Brussels* rams *U33*; he receives Admiralty thanks (*see* 23 June 1916). **Palestine** — French cruiser *D'Entrecasteaux* bombards Gaza (*see* 16 Apr).		**First US citizen killed** in British SS *Falaba* sinking by U-boat (*see* SEA WAR).	
E Africa — 300 British with 16 lorries (1st of campaign) beaten by Germans at Salaita Hill E of Taveta.	**Flanders U-boat Flotilla activated** with 127t coastal UB boats (6 op late Apr) & 168t UC minelayers assembled at Antwerp & towed to Bruges-Zeebrugge via canals (16 boats by Oct).			Lloyd George: 'Drink is a more dangerous enemy than Germany or Austria'. Shipbuilders urge prohibition. St Dunstan's War Blind Hostel opens.
SW Africa — McKenzie's SA Central Force (11,000) occupies Aus 80 miles inland from Lüderitz (Botha visits 26).				**Britain** — King offers total alcohol abstinence in Royal Household for duration (from 5 Apr, Kitchener 1 Apr).

MARCH1915	WESTERN FRONT 1	EASTERN FRONT 2	SOUTHERN FRONTS 3	TURKISH FRONTS 4
Tue 30 contd	gases' (ie chlorine cylinders) (*see* 2, 8 & 14 Apr). **Champagne** — Reims Cathedral under bombardment. **Vosges** — German counter-attack in Fecht valley reaches Herrenberg (*see* 25 Apr).			
Wed 31	German Army ration strength 5,029,672.			
Thu 1 April 1915	(Apr) **First French trench mortar**, a 58mm (2.1in) weapon **enters service** (*see* 4 May). **Flanders** — Cloister Hoek, nr Dixmude, occupied by Germans.	**Poland** — Russian advance checked in W, but cavalry defeat German cav in N (2).	**Serbia** — (Apr) 48,000 Serb troops still in hospital with typhus. British 3rd Serbian Relief Fund surgical unit (all women) lands & soon treats 12,000 civilians. Bulgar *Komitadjis* (irregulars) attack Serbs at Valandovo (*see* INT'L EVENTS 6).	**Armenia** — Russians occupy Tsria, defeat Turks at Oltu (4). **Mesopotamia** — II Indian Corps formed, **Nixon replaces Barrett (sick) as C-in-C** (9).
Fri 2	First full-scale German gas trial behind lines, mildly gases the scientists responsible (*see* 8). **Argonne** — German attack at Bagatelle.	**Bukovina** — No Austrian troops in Russia after raiding 1 mile inside. More fighting (4), Russians evacuate Bojan (-14).		
Sat 3	**Flanders** — British mine buries 100yds of German trench nr Cuinchy. **Meuse** — French capture Regnieville. **Artois** — D'Urbal replaces Maud'huy (to Vosges Army) i/c Tenth Army.	Hoffmann diary: 'Every day Russian airmen throw down proclamations on us: "Surrender, lay down your arms, your wives & children are starving!"'.		**Persia** — Niedermayer's Mission enters with Austro-German Ambassadors at Kasr-i-Shirin which Raouf Bey's 3000 Turco-Kurd irregulars occupy (12) but Germans halt them at Karind due to brutality. By end May Niedermayer reckons hopeless to draw Persia in (*see* 20 May).
Sun 4	**Flanders** — Gen Putz takes over *Détachement de Belgique* (aka *Groupement d'Elverdinghe*). Gen Bülow of German Second Army put on retired list after suffering a stroke, F Below succeeds (-19 July 1916).	Conrad requests German attack in Gorlice sector (*see* 9). **Carpathians** — After snowstorms (2-3) Brusilov reaches Sztropko, 15 miles inside Hungary, W & E of Lupkow Pass.		
Mon 5	**Meuse-Argonne** — French First and Third Armies attack in very bad weather, aiming to flatten out St Mihiel salient. Little progress v MG fire, barbed wire & mud (-14). **Flanders** — Belgians repulsed at Driegrachten.	Conrad meets Falkenhayn, proposes peace with Russia to contain Italy.		
Tue 6		**E Prussia** — Russians advance in Niemen border area and progress nr Suvalki (9). **Carpathians** — Marwitz's *Beskidenkorps* counter-	Conrad tells Falkenhayn war with Italy inevitable, but not allowed to transfer 7 divs from Galicia (*see* 26). **Serbia** — Serb guns silence Austrian	

AFRICAN OPERATIONS 5	SEA WAR 6	AIR WAR 7	INTERNATIONAL EVENTS 8	HOME FRONTS 9
	U-boats sink 29 ships (161 British lives lost) worth 89,517t, more than in whole war to date. Adm Haus defends Austria's defensive naval strategy in long memo to ex-PM Baron Beck,'in many cases not to do anything is the only correct thing', recognizes U-boats as 'masters of the sea'. Francis Joseph approves (7 Apr).			**Britain** — Armaments Output Ctee to organize skilled labour. **Russia** — Transport Ministry created. **France** — Absinthe Prohibition law.
E Africa — German forces: 2275 Europeans; 7647 askaris; 1858 others; 32 guns; 78 MGs (*see* 31 Dec). British withdraw from Longido (-11) for rainy season. **SW Africa** — SA E Force occupies Hasuur and Kalkfontein & Ukamas (5), S Force occupies Warmbad (3). They meet 14.	**Secret War** — (Apr) Duddell D/F aerial installed in 5 Grand Fleet battleships, able to detect German signals in Heligoland Bight. First 2 bulge-protected warships (*Edgar*-class cruisers) on trials. **Britain** — (Apr) First 50 motor launches (MLs) ordered from Elco, Bayonne, NY; 551 built.	**Dardanelles** — (Apr) German airmen in action (*see* 18 & July). **W Front** — Lt R Garros of *Esc MS 23* in Morane 'N' shoots down Albatros 2-seater nr Dixmude, 2nd victory (15), 3rd (17, *see* 19). Jean Navarre & Robert in Morane 'L' (*Esc MS 12)* shoot down Aviatik 2-seater nr Soissons with rifle fire (Pelletier-Doisy & Chambe from same sqn likewise shoot down one, 2, *see* 28). French aircraft bomb rail stns & bivouacs at Vignuelles (Champagne) & nr Soissons (night 1/2). (Apr) French introduce Lafay bombsight.		**Germany** — Bismarck's birth centenary celebrations. Rosa Luxemburg imprisoned in Berlin for attacking Army. State nitrogen plant (175,000t pa capacity) laid down at Piesteritz (Elbe). **Britain** — Union unemployment lowest for 25 yrs.
	N Sea — *U10* sinks 3 British minesweeping trawlers (226 minesweepers in home waters incl 12 new & effective converted paddle steamers). German surface minelayer lays 360 mines off Humber (4) sinking 9 steamers & minesweepers, but 127 mines swept in May & cleared by mid-July.		US note to Britain on blockade treatment of neutrals. **Austria offers Italy Trentino concessions** (*see* 8).	**Egypt** — Anzacs & British riot in Cairo brothel area.
Cameroons — War Office takes control of ops.	**Channel** — A/S barrage completed across Dover Straits (*see* 10). **Black Sea** — Turco-German raids on Odessa (cruiser *Medjidieh* mined & sunk, *see* 29 Oct), Sevastopol & Nikolayev. Russian Fleet pursues smoke-screening *Goeben* & *Breslau* back to the Bosphorus but they sink 2 steamers & 2 Russian destroyers en route (*see* 25; 9 May).	**W Front** — French pilot Adolphe Pégoud scores 3rd victory (*see* 31 Aug).	Asquith telegraphs France & Russia 'The attack...on the Dardanelles will be pressed to a decision', asks for another approach to Greece where Venizelos publishes Jan memos to K Constantine (-4) & retires from public life (9).	
		Aegean — Wright Navy plane from HMS *Ark Royal* drops six 20lb bombs on Turk torpedo boats at Smyrna (*see* SEA WAR 6).		
W Tripolitania — Italians break out from Jebel Nefusa into French Tunisia. Col Gianinazzi's col returns to Mizda in S minus baggage, food, & ammo (7, *see* 28).				**Britain** — 2 German officer PoWs escape from Denbigh (Wales), recaptured 11 (*see* 13 Aug).
	Aegean — Allied battleships shell Smyrna (& 22).		Greek note to Bulgaria and latter's note to Serbia on *Komitadji* irregular outrages.	

APRIL 1915	WESTERN FRONT 1	EASTERN FRONT 2	SOUTHERN FRONTS 3	TURKISH FRONTS 4
Tue 6 contd		offensive (2 divs) (-8) claims 6000 PoWs, storms Hill 992 (SW of Kosziowa 9); all captors win Iron Cross.	bombardment of Belgrade, but monitor repeats (10, *see* 19).	
Wed 7	**Flanders** — 1st Cdn Div transferred to Second Army, takes over vulnerable N Ypres salient from French (17,*see* 22).			**Egypt** — First units sail for Dardanelles (Anzacs 10), Hamilton sails for Lemnos (8). Skirmish NE of Kantara.
Thu 8	**Champagne** — Germans repulsed at Beauséjour (*see* 16 May). **Ypres** — German poison gas cylinders ready but weather postpones attack. **Lorraine** — French anti-militarist animal story writer Louis Pergaud k aged 33 at Marcheville by own arty when w in German lines.			
Fri 9	**Meuse-Argonne** — French offensive renewed. French storm Les Eparges crest. Unsuccessful German counter-attacks (11). **Flanders** — French sink rafts laden with German assault troops attacking St Jacques Capelle, S of Dixmude.	**Falkenhayn decides to attack in E**; Kaiser sanctions (13); 8 W Front divs ordered to move (15). Mackensen to lead new Eleventh Army (16) (*see* 21). **Carpathians** — Russian advance resumes, gains mtn crest for 70 miles from Dukla to Uzsok Pass (fighting -14).		
Sat 10	**Meuse** — French advance in Bois de Montmare (Woëvre), but repulsed nr Maizeray (13).	**Ivanov halts Carpathian offensive in spring thaw** but continues SW of Rostoki Pass (-16) where counter-attacks repulsed (18-19). Russians take Height 1002 (21). Conrad to Emperor's military cabinet head: 'I cannot at all express how distasteful is the infiltration with German troops, but the heart has to follow the head'.	Albanian rebels shell Italian-held Durazzo (& 16).	Hamilton decides on maximum Gallipoli landings. Main troop convoy assembly (15-22).
Sun 11	**Somme** — French engaged in heavy fighting nr Albert.	CoS Yanushkevich vainly warns NW Front C-in-C Alexeiev of threat to W Galicia. **Carpathians** — Brusilov claims 70,000 PoWs, 30+ guns & 200 MGs since 19 Mar (12).		**Mesopotamia** — Turks bombard Qurna & Ahwaz (-12).
Mon 12	**Flanders** — Unsuccessful German attack nr Dixmude. **Alsace** — French rebuffed SE of Hartmannsweilerkopf.			Hankey memo warns Asquith Gallipoli: '...a gamble upon the supposed shortage of supplies and inferior fighting qualities of the Turkish armies'. **Mesopotamia** — **Battle of Shaiba** (-14) SW of Basra: 6156 British (1265 cas) rout 12,000 Turks (3177 cas, 2 guns lost); Maj Wheeler (7th Hariana Lancers) wins 1st VC (13, posthumous) of campaign.
Tue 13	**Aisne** — French success nr Berry-au-Bac.			
Wed 14	**Flanders** — French Gen Putz obtains details of planned gas attack from Pte Jäger, PoW of 234th Res Inf Regt, XXVI Corps taken nr Langemarck. But he & BEF cdrs are mistakenly suspicious that such detailed info is a German 'plant'. **Meuse-Argonne** — Germans claim that French are using mines emitting asphyxiating gases NW of Verdun.			**Secret War** — 2nd German (Hentig) Afghan Mission leaves Berlin

AFRICAN OPERATIONS 5	SEA WAR 6	AIR WAR 7	INTERNATIONAL EVENTS 8	HOME FRONTS 9
		N Sea — **First successful attempt to direct naval gunfire by radio from an aircraft out of sight**, RNAS from Eastchurch directs battleship HMS *Revenge* to score hits on Maplin Sands range (-8).		**Germany** — Minority Socialist manifesto v war. **Britain** — War Office begins machinery census for munitions work.
	Atlantic — German raiders *Prinz Eitel Friedrich* (sank 5 British ships) & *Kronprinz Wilhelm* (sank 9 British ships) interned at Newport News, Va (8 & 26).	**W Front** — Future French ace Nungesser joins Voisin recon/ bombing unit *VB106* , is shot down (26, *see* Nov). No 7 Sqn joins RFC.	**Italy demands Trentino, Dalmatian Is, Gorizia & Gardisca + primacy in Albania as Austria's price for her neutrality**, presses for reply (13, *see* 16). Asquith establishes ctee on British aims for Turkey in Asia. Germany protests to USA over sending absolute contraband to Allies.	ARMENIAN MASSACRES BEGIN. Up to 1m die (-Sept) for alleged co-operation with Russia. Men shot, women, old men & children deported to Cilicia & Syria; c200,000 forcibly Islamized. **Egypt** — Attempt on Sultan's life. **France** — Croix de Guerre instituted. 1916 class called up (-12).
Cameroons — 1600 Allies in preliminary advance on Yaunde, take R Kele bridges (14, *see* 1 May).	High Seas Fleet U-boats ordered not to force Dover Straits due to nets & minefields (-Dec 1916).		France recognizes Russian claims to Constantinople.	
		Germany — Zeppelin VGO I (Staaken R I) giant trimotor bomber first flies.		
Cameroons — 80 Germans cut telegraph line in Nigeria.		**W Front** — French Army airships *Adjt Vincent* & *Conté* fly 4 night missions in Apr (incl 29/30), bomb rail targets at Bussigny, Antoiny, Strasbourg, Aulchin, Marley & Aulnoye. *Adjt Vincent* bombs Douai rail stn & jctn (night 11/12 May, *see* 15 June).	Greece refuses Serb troops railway use. Pope (prayers for peace 9) sends peace note to Pres Wilson. **Allies offer Greece Smyrna & hinterland for war v Turkey, Greece rejects 14.**	
	Battleship *Agamemnon* at Bulgar port of Dedeagach on diplomatic visit (-14). **Channel** — Rear-Adm Bacon replaces Hood i/c Dover Patrol.	**W Front** — German Army airship *L235* damaged by AA fire while bombing Poperinghe & wrecked in forced landing nr Ypres.		**Britain** — Lloyd George chairs new Cabinet munitions ctee.
E Africa — Cruiser HMS *Hyacinth* cripples German blockade-runner *Kronborg* in Manza Bay, but 1800 rifles, 6 MGs, & 2 guns salvaged to reach Lettow as British learn 23 June.		**Britain** — German Navy Zeppelin *L9* (Mathy) drops 31 IBs at Wallsend, NW England (2 civ cas).	Colonial Secretary says Dominions will be consulted on peace terms. Japan informs HMG of German peace overtures.	**Occupied Belgium** — Belgium Red Cross suppressed. **Russia** — Moscow MD has sent 500,000 men to front so far. **Britain** — Stokes mortar trial successful, but turned down (*see* 30 June).

APRIL 1915	WESTERN FRONT 1	EASTERN FRONT 2	SOUTHERN FRONTS 3	TURKISH FRONTS 4
Thu 15	**Alsace** — French progress nr Lauch. German tactical withdrawal (19).	**E Prussia Frontier** — (c) Russian 1st Cav Div withdrawn to Grodno and Vilna for rest after 8 months campaigning for 2/3 cas.	Italian forces of Advanced Occupation facing Austrian frontier now 142,000 in 5 zones (*see* 21 & 23).	
Fri 16	**Artois** — Unsuccessful German attacks at Notre-Dame de Lorette.			**Persia** — Kalil Bey (Enver's uncle) reaches Urmia in NW with 36th Div & 6 guns, retakes Dilman 29 (*see* 1 May).
Sat 17	**Flanders** — British 5th Div take Hill 60 nr St Eloi after detonating mines, repulse attacks (& 19, 20 & 29).	Archduke Frederick dissolves Czech-Austrian 28th Inf Regt (fd 1698) for Dukla Pass surrender (3). Only 256 of 2000 men reassembled.		
Sun 18				**India : NW Frontier** — 1st Action at Hafiz Kor v Mohmands.
Mon 19	Sir J French rebuffs German accusations that British have used poison gas. **Flanders** — Fighting at Hill 60 (-29).		**Serbia** — Austrians monitor shells Sep nr Iron Gates (Rumanian frontier).	

AFRICAN OPERATIONS 5	SEA WAR 6	AIR WAR 7	INTERNATIONAL EVENTS 8	HOME FRONTS 9
E Africa — Maj-Gen Tighe replaces Wapshare as GOC.	**Black Sea** — 3 Russian destroyers sink 4 Turk steamers (*see 25*).	**W Front** — Vaughan & Lascelles RFC in BE2 shoot down Aviatik 2-seater with 24 rifle shots. First all-BE2 Sqn (No 8) flies to France. **Britain** — Airships *L5* & *L6* bomb Lowestoft & Maldon: *L6* damaged by rifle fire (night 15/16).	**Austria** — Conrad asks Foreign Minister to keep Italy out at least 4 weeks.	
	Aegean — Turk torpedo boat *Demirhisar* intercepts but fails to torpedo British transport *Manitou* S of Skyros (51 lost in panic); cruiser HMS *Minerva* & 3 destroyers force Turk craft aground on Chios (17). *Manitou* reaches Mudros.	**Neutrals : USA** — AB-2 flying boat (Bellinger) catapulted from a barge in US trials. **Britain** — First German Army aircraft over England: Albatros BII of *Fl Abt 41* drops 8 bombs (without effect) at Sittingbourne & Faversham, Kent; 14 defence sorties. **Germany** — French bombers attack Rottweil gunpowder factory, Leo-poldshoehe rail workshops, Mézières-les-Metz power stn; 3 Aviatiks forced to land. **Turk Fronts** — 2 Farmans & a BE2 of RFC Ismailia Flt bomb El Marra, Sinai.	Austria finds Italy's proposals mainly unacceptable.	**Canada** — $100m voted for war. 101,000 under arms (11).
Rhodesians take German stockade 35 miles E of Fife.	**Atlantic** — British SS *La Rosarina* beats off attacking U-boat S of Ireland using her single fo'c'sle gun. **Palestine** — French cruiser *St Louis* shells Turk camp S of Gaza (El Arish 16). **Dardanelles** — British submarine *E15* lost aground (24 PoWs) nr Kephez Point, destroyed by *Majestic's* picket boat (18), but *E14* gets through, first 1915 Allied submarine to do so (*see 27*).		**Neutrals : USA** — Ex-German Minister Dernberg's peace campaign includes unofficial terms (25). Sino-Japanese talks break down at 24th session but Japan revises demands (26).	**NZ** — 4th Reinforcement (1761) sails.
SW Africa — SA S Force occupies Seeheim rail jctn; Germans evacuate Keetman-shoop (19).	Italian Naval C-in-C receives Adriatic war plan (*see INT'L EVENTS 26 & 27*).	**Gallipoli** — RNAS aircraft bomb (6 x 100lb) & destroy hangar at Chanak with German aircraft inside.	**Neutrals : Holland** — International Women's Peace Congress opens in Hague (1136 delegates from 12 countries). Admiralty suspen-sion of ferries (22 Apr-1 May) stops 25 from Britain.	
	Japan completes 2 battlecruis-ers, now has 4 (*see 18 Nov*).	**W Front** — Morane 'L' fighter (Lt Roland Garros), damaged by German rifleman Schlenst-edt in Courtrai rail stn, makes forced landing behind German lines, nr Ingelmunster. Attempts to burn plane fail to prevent SECRET MG BULLET DEFLECTOR DEVICE (designed Feb 1915) FALLING INTO GERMAN HANDS. Garros tells captors he has shot down 5 aircraft since 1 Apr. **Germany** — The armoured airscrew is sent post haste to Doberitz, Berlin. *Feldflugchef* Thomsen orders it to be copied, but a 1st attempt (by Brunnhuber) fails. Anthony Fokker is sent for. Within 6 days, at his Schwerin works, Fokker's engineers, Luebbe, Heber & Leimberger, devise a MECHANICAL INTERRUPTER GEAR to fire the MG only when propeller blades are clear of its line of sight. This Fokker device (for which AF claims sole credit) differs entirely from the captured device & is actually based on a system patented by German engineer Franz Schneider (15 June 1913). At Doberitz, a Fokker M 5K (EI/15) monoplane is fitted with the Parabellum gun, Fokker interrupter gear & adjustable		**Turkey** — Djevdet Bey orders Armenian extermination in Van Province, 55,000 murdered (-20). **Britain — Record day at London central recruiting office.**

APRIL 1915	WESTERN FRONT 1	EASTERN FRONT 2	SOUTHERN FRONTS 3	TURKISH FRONTS 4
Mon 19 contd				
Tue 20	**Flanders** — Gas shells test-fired at Hill 60 by German Fourth Army. 'Hate shoot' on Ypres kills & expels civilians. BEF now 18 inf (1 Cdn, 2 Indian) & 5 cav divs (2 Indian) holding 36 miles (*see* 25 Sept). **Lorraine** — Germans recapture Emberménil.	Austrian High Command estimate 1,001,000 Austro-Germans (11 armies) fighting 1,540,000 Russians on 720-mile front.		**Armenia** — Kazim Bey besieges Van (1300 armed Armenians defend 30,000, *see* 8 May).
Wed 21	**Meuse** — 'The Cow's Head', 2 lines of trenches nr St Mihiel, taken by French, more gains (22).	8 German divs begin rail move (60 trains pd) to S of Cracow. Russians discover from 25. Austrians repulsed nr Gorlice (20) which sector Eleventh Army takes over 28.	**Italian Front** — Conrad orders 'the passages across the Isonzo...be closed, and the defences along the western edge of the Carso organised' (*see* 26). Italian War Minister announces that million men can be sent to front.	**Dardanelles** — Hamilton issues landing orders. **Mesopotamia** — Gorringe (GOC 12th Indian Div) takes 12,556 men & 17 guns from Basra to secure Ahwaz (*see* 14 May).
Thu 22	SECOND BATTLE OF YPRES (-13 May): Battle of Graven-stafel (Ridge) (-23). Big Berthas shell Ypres. FIRST W FRONT POISON GAS ATTACK begun by German Fourth Army at 1700 nr Langemarck: 3¾ mile front lined with 4000 chlorine cylinders. 168t of chlorine released within 5 mins. 2 German divs attack French 45th Algerian Div supported on right by Cdn 1st Div, nr St Julien. Germans wearing respirators cautiously 'mop up' on Pilkem Ridge, taking c2000 PoWs & 51 guns. French Colonials flee across canal causing 800 yd gap in Allied line. Fierce fighting for Canadian wood W of St Julien; finally secured by Germans.		**Serbia** — RN steam picket -boat launches 2 torpedoes at Austrian Danube Flotilla anchorage (night 22/23); British believe monitor *Koros* sunk, actually a dummy vessel.	**Mesopotamia** — Townshend, new GOC 6th Indian Div, arrives Basra.
Fri 23	**Ypres** — 2nd German gas attack: they take Langemarck, Steenstraate bridge & positions S of Lizerne as Allied counter-attack collapses. **First Canadian VC of the war**: L/Cp F Fisher (13th Bn).		Italian Advanced Occupation region raised to 8 corps, a *Bersaglieri* div & 2 *Alpini* gps (-5 May, *see* 24 May).	**Dardanelles** — †**Sub-Lt Rupert Brooke, war poet**, of blood-poisoning aboard hospital ship at Skyros, aged 27.
Sat 24	**Ypres** — Battle of St Julien begins: with 0400 gas cloud aid Germans capture St Julien. Franco-Belgians hold W of			

AFRICAN OPERATIONS 5	SEA WAR 6	AIR WAR 7	INTERNATIONAL EVENTS 8	HOME FRONTS 9
		head-rest & successfully demonstrated. **EI single-seat fighters**, armed with 7.92mm LMG 08 MGs are **ordered from Fokker** (*see* 20 May). **Occupied Belgium** — Lt L G Hawker in a BE2, bombs Zeppelin sheds at Gontrode. **Dardanelles** — Sqn Cdr Mackworth of No 1 Kite-Balloon Section, RNAS, directs battleship shelling with remarkable success; Turk camp destroyed; battleship *Turgud Reis* forced to retire (25); ammo dump explodes (26); troopship/supply ferry *Scutari* sunk (27, *see* SEA WAR).		
14 Germans blow up bridge on Uganda Railway (line again cut 27).			Pres Wilson declares US hopes of restoring peace.	**Britain** — Asquith Newcastle speech denies shell shortage.(Lloyd George also 21, *see* 14 May).
Cameroons — Dobell estimates 12,970 Allies & 41 guns v 3980 Germans. Capt Crailsheim's 300 sortie from Garua through Allies (-22), vainly attack Ft Gurin (Nigeria) 47 miles S (29) and return (8 May). Formal Allied naval blockade declared (midnight 23).	**N Sea** — High Seas Fleet sorties to prevent feared Harwich Force seaplane attack (7 abortive attempts 3-12 May) on Tondern Zeppelin sheds but Germans return (22) in belief attack called off. Room 40 warns Grand Fleet which steams to Skaggerak, but dense fog forces it home.			**Russia** — Trade & Industry Minister refuses full powers. Kronstadt Police HQ makes secret report on revolutionary propaganda in Petrograd factories.
			Anglo-Norwegian Oil Agreement.	**Britain** — Adm Lord Beresford criticizes Dardanelles ops in Lords.
	E Atlantic — British blockade of the Cameroons formally begins (raised 29 Feb 1916). **Home Waters** — Fisher tells Churchill U-boats able to radio 300nm day or night (*see* May). **Aegean** — Allied Gallipoli landing force (200 ships) belatedly arrives off beach-head. After the naval failure the transports (not loaded to permit rapid disembarkation under fire) have had to be withdrawn to Egypt for reloading. **Baltic** — *U26* (Berckheim) stops and sinks Russian SS *Frack*. RN submarine *E1* towed to sea (27, *see* 8 May) by icebreaker.			**Turkey** — Constantinople police arrest 235 leading Armenians (-24) for internal exile. **Britain** — Pensions for dependants of civilians killed on War Depts' work. **Austria** — Vienna: bread of poor quality, flour hardly available (*see* 1 June).
			Catholicos Kevork cables Pres Wilson over Armenian massacres. Russian Washington Ambassador also	**Turkey** — Armenian Day of Mourning (still kept). **Russia** — 2nd War Loan (1bn roubles). **Britain** — *Oxford Times*

APRIL 1915	WESTERN FRONT 1	EASTERN FRONT 2	SOUTHERN FRONTS 3	TURKISH FRONTS 4
Sat 24 contd	Lizerne. Successful Canadian counter-attacks at Lizerne. British extend GHQ line S of Ypres. **Meuse** — Unsuccessful German counter-attacks at Les Eparges.			
Sun 25	**Ypres** — Lizerne again in German hands. British 10th Bde loses 2419 cas in vain bid to recapture St Julien.			BRITISH LANDINGS ON GALLIPOLI PENINSULA: 33,000 Allies land round C Helles, at Anzac Cove (mistakenly) and Kum Kale in Asia (3000 French in feint (-26). Losses: Allies c4178, Turk c4730.
Mon 26	Kitchener declares that 'Germany has stooped to acts which vie with those of the Dervishes' (see HOME FRONTS). **Ypres** — 15,000 British counter-attack; Lahore Div relieves Canadians (5200 cas). Germans reply with gas. 149th Northumberland Bde vainly secures temporary hold on S end of St Julien for 1964 cas inc GOC Brig-Gen Riddell k. Total British loss 4000. Gas attack on Franco-Belgians S of Dixmude. **Alsace** — See-saw battle for Hartmannsweilerkopf; French finally secure crest after losing it & 4 coys (25).		Allied-Italian Treaty of London soon triggers move of 3 Austrian corps (XV & XVI with c282 guns from Serb Front, VII with 162 guns from E Front) to Italian Front (see 11 &14 May). (c) Forces already there formed into 5 divs (90th-94th), total c81,400 & 324 guns excl fortress troops & guns.	**Gallipoli** — Hill 141 stormed and V Beach secured. Turk attacks on Anzac & Y Beaches repulsed but latter abandoned in panic.
Tues 27	**Ypres** — Allies advance, French recapture Lizerne. **FM French replaces Smith-Dorrien by Plumer** i/c Second Army because of former's 'pessimism' (see 6 May).	**Galicia — Army Group Mackensen formed** to include Austrian armies. **Poland** — Diversionary Ninth Army (new C-in-C Prince Leopold of Bavaria, aged 69) attack in NW. **Baltic Provinces** — Lauenstein's strategic diversion (3 cav + 3 inf divs formed 22) towards Shavli on Libau-Dvinsk railway, takes 2 stns (30). **Carpathians** — Russian cav beat Austrian Seventh Army at Gorodenko (-28).	**Italian Front** — Austrians begin improvised defence line.	**Gallipoli** — Allies dug in across Helles peninsula, but only 28 guns ashore. **Armenia** — First Battle of Tortum (-12 May).
Wed 28	**Flanders** — German guns nr Dixmude shelling Dunkirk. **Champagne** — Germans storm French position at Les Mesnils.			**Gallipoli — First Battle of Krithia**: 14,000 Allies advance 2 miles (3000 cas). Anzac: 2 RM bns reinforce. **Yemen** — British treaty with Chief Idrisi v Turks.

AFRICAN OPERATIONS 5	SEA WAR 6	AIR WAR 7	INTERNATIONAL EVENTS 8	HOME FRONTS 9
			requests US intervention (27). **Occupied Belgium** — Germans requisition all coal production for Army & railways (also oil 3 June).	predicts 893 students for summer term (3000 prewar).
SW Africa — Smuts (arrived Kalkfontein 10 to command in S) mauls German rearguard at Gibeon (-26), C Railway.	**Aegean/Dardanelles** — Allied landings on Gallipoli Peninsula supported by 18 battleships, 2 cruisers, 29 destroyers & 8 submarines which fire 8010 shells. *River Clyde* , converted collier landing ship at V Beach, fails to work as planned but her crew win 5 VCs. Australian submarine *AE2* sinks Turk gunboat in Narrows & is first Allied boat into Sea of Marmora (*see* 27). **E Africa** — RNAS Short 'folder' seaplane photographs *Königsberg* but unable to bomb (*see* 3 June). **N Sea** — First sea-going U-boat *U21* (Hersing) sails for Med from Wilhelmshaven (refuels with wrong fuel oil off NW Spain 2 May, *see* 13). **Black Sea** — Russian sqn bombards Bosphorus forts (repeated 2, 3, 4 May).			
SW Africa — Botha repels Germans at Trekopjes aided by new RNAS armoured cars (German planes mistake for field kitchens). **E Africa** — Cdr Spicer-Simson put i/c Naval Africa Expedition for L Tanganyika (Game hunter J Lee persuades Admiralty 21). **Senegal** — Black enlistment authorized (*see 19 Oct*).	**Germany** — First UC-class coastal minelayer launched at Hamburg (10 by 15 July, all war losses, *see* 10 & 29 May).	**W Front** — First air VC: Lt Rhodes-Moorhouse, RFC, flying a BE2, attacks (1 100lb bomb) Courtrai rail stn. Severely wounded by intense AA & small arms fire, he flies 35 miles to his Merville base over German lines, receiving further wounds (awarded posthumous VC 22 May). 7 BE2s & 2 RE5s bomb trains in Ghent area as RFC attempts to disrupt troop movements from there to Ypres Salient. 11 BE2cs & 2 REs despatched to 7 stns & trains on Staden-Cortemarck-Roulers line.	LONDON PACT: ITALY SECRETLY JOINS ALLIES after talks since 23.	**Turkey** — German Gen Posseldt (Erzerum) to Embassy 'The Armenians would have stayed perfectly quiet, if they had not been harrassed and provoked...' **Britain** — Kitchener & Asquith address Parlt on German war crimes.
	Adriatic — Austrian *U5* (Georg, Baron Trapp) sinks French cruiser *Leon Gambetta* (Adm Senes) in Straits of Otranto (night 26/27). Senes & all officers among 684 drowned, only 137 survivors. All French cruisers now withdrawn from Otranto blockade & submarines from Navarino base (Greece). **Dardanelles** — RN submarine *E14* sinks Turk gunboat in Sea of Marmora & transport (29,*see* 10 May). Australian submarine *AE2* (32 PoWs) scuttled in Marmora Strait after damaged by Turk torpedo boat *Sultanhisar* (30). Many Turk troops for Gallipoli rerouted to land (*see* 1 May). **Adriatic** — Austrian Fleet warned of likely war with Italy (& 9 May). **Dardanelles** — *Queen Elizabeth* sinks Turk transport in Narrows with 4 shots at 7 miles range.		Bethmann says no to Burian's idea that if Belgium concessions satisfied England, forces would be freed to face Italy.	**Germany** — Pan-Germans' Chairman tells Crown Prince that if unsatisfying peace made '... revolution would be only a question of time'. **Britain** — Gallipoli news released. Kitchener gets Cabinet permission to retaliate with gas (*see* W FRONT 25 Sept).
SW Africa — Botha resumes advance (see AIR WAR 30). **S Tripolitania** — Senussi rout Col Miani's 3750 troops, gaining 5000 rifles,8 guns & MGs nr Sidra.		**W Front** — Capt de Bernis (pilot) & Sub-Lt Jacottet (observer) in *Esc MS 12* Morane 'Parasol' shoot down an Aviatik with rifle fire, S of Reims. **Germany** — French *MF29* bomber unit raids Friedrichshafen.		

APRIL 1915	WESTERN FRONT 1	EASTERN FRONT 2	SOUTHERN FRONTS 3	TURKISH FRONTS 4
Thu 29	**Flanders** — Foch asks Sir J French to await result of imminent French attack before withdrawing to new British line. Belgian guns smash 3 German boatbridges across the Yser.			**Sinai** — 100 Bikanir Camel Corps inflict 42 cas on c250 Turks & Bedouin E of Canal.
Fri 30	**Ypres** — Foch launches inconclusive attack. **Alsace** — French Vosges Army 1915 losses to date 20,300. **Lorraine** — French war poet Antoine Dujardin (b1887) dies of wounds at Toul, his *Dans Les Tranchées 1914-15* published 1915.	Austrian Gorlice deserters reveal 2 May attack date.		Enver Pasha orders Liman to 'drive the invaders into the sea'; 2 divs from Asia Minor transferred to Gallipoli (29). Allied losses now total c11,000. (War Office est for all ops c5000).
Sat 1 May 1915	(May) German Army has 171 divs (fig 172 or 173 - June 1916) with 106 in W. French Army combatant strength 1,525,000 inf; 102,000 cav; 395,000 gunners; 104,000 engineers; 8000 air service. (May) **British Mills Bomb grenade first issued** as 'Grenade Hand, No 5'. **Meuse-Argonne** — Small-scale but almost continuous trench warfare in the Woëvre woods (-20 June). **Ypres** — Gas attack on Hill 60 fails. British begin withdrawal to new line after French counter-attack fails (-4). **Champagne** — (May) African explorer Gen Marchand put i/c elite 10th Colonial Div which he commands for duration being w twice (*see* 25 Sept).	**Baltic Provinces** — Lauen-stein occupies Shavli and nears Libau (taken 7 despite check S of Mitau (5). **Galicia** — AUSTRO-GERMAN OFFENSIVE: BATTLE OF GORLICE-TARNOW (-5) starts with 610-gun bombardment incl gas shell. **Carpathians** — Austro-German attack towards Uzsok Pass.	**Serbia** — (May) Maj Primavesi of Austrian Intelligence begins finding whole Serb Army by means of questions inserted in Red Cross letters to PoWs in Austria (-Sept). Austrians reduce forces in theatre by 5 divs (partially replaced by 3 newly forming German ones (*see* 22 & 27). **Germany** — Italian military attaché in Berlin deliberately allowed to see 2 Hindenburg letters, one saying he will command v Italy, other contemptuous of her (*see* INT'L EVENTS 3).	**Gallipoli : Helles** — 29th Indian Bde landing, vain Turk night attack (-2). **Persia** — Nazarbekov forces 10,000 Turks N of Dilman over frontier.
Sun 2	**Flanders** — Ypres: Gas attacks nr St Julien-Fortuin. These & similar (3) are repulsed.	**Galicia** — After 4-hr bombardment (700,000 shells) Austro-Germans capture Gorlice & Ciezkowica, cross R Biala.		**Gallipoli** — Allied counter-attack fails (c4800 cas).
Mon 3	**Artois** — French preliminary bombardment begins. Germans expect offensive (4).	**Galicia** — 12-mile gap in Russian line, Sakharov's 3 divs (X Corps) destroyed in 8-mile advance since 2.		**Gallipoli : Helles** — French repulse Turk night attacks (-4). Gen Gouraud replaces d'Amade (4). Kitchener assures Cabinet 'no doubt that we shall break through'.
Tue 4	German GHQ moves to Pless, Silesia (*see* E FRONT 9). **Artois** — French bombardment by 1073 guns (690,000 shells) & 92 mortars begins (-9,*see* E FRONT 2). **Flanders** — Ypres: Battle of St Julien ends. Sir J French advises War Office that German High Command has definitely decided to use poison gases as normal weapon. British withdrawal completed to line, Mouse-trap Farm-Frezenberg Ridge-Huuge Zillebeke Ridge-Hill 60. French advance between Lizerne & Het Sas. 1st Cdn Div withdrawn to GHQ Reserve, joined by 1500 dismtd cav (8).	**Galicia** — Radko resists briefly on R Wisloka (-5).	Italian troop trains running, but mobilization takes 48 days not 23 as planned.	**Gallipoli : Anzac** — 2 RM Bns repel Turk breakthrough. Latter's losses reach 14,000.
Wed 5	**Flanders** — Ypres: Hill 60 falls after German heavy gas attack.	**W Russia** — Germans bombard Grodno.	Cadorna learns that Italy committed to war by 26. Conrad changes his mind, now accepts that 'war with Italy must be unconditionally avoided' (*see* INT'L EVENTS 16).	**Gallipoli : Helles** — 42nd Div arrives from Egypt (-7).
Thu 6	**Flanders** — Gen Smith-Dorrien told ''Orace — you're for 'ome''	**Galicia** — Austrian Fourth Army occupies Tarnow, takes		**Gallipoli : Helles** — **Second Battle of Krithia** (-8): 25,000

AFRICAN OPERATIONS 5	SEA WAR 6	AIR WAR 7	INTERNATIONAL EVENTS 8	HOME FRONTS 9
		Britain — First raid by German Army Zeppelin: *LZ38* (Linnarz) drops IBs at Ipswich & Bury St Edmunds, Suffolk (opportunity targets); some damage incl 3 cas (night 29/30, *see* 10 May).		**Britain** — Lloyd George sets limits on alcohol sale and increased duties (*see* 7 May).
	Dardanelles — Battleship *Lord Nelson* sets Chanak alight night 30 Apr-1 May (*see* 25 June).	**SW Africa** — First British aircraft — 3 Farman, 2 BEs — land at Walvis Bay to give valuable cover for Union Expeditionary Force v German colonists. **N Sea** — Patrolling German airship *L9* (Mathy) attacks 3 RN submarines; *D4* damaged.		**Britain** — King & Kitchener visit Royal Small Arms Factory, Enfield Middx. **Occupied France** — (Apr) Bread ration cards in Lille.
Cameroons — Allied advance on Yaunde begins in heavy rain. **SW Africa** — SA troops occupy Kubas, take Otimbingwe (2).	First US merchant ship torpedoed without warning: by *U30* SS *Gulflight* off Scilly Is, 3 die (*see* INT'L EVENTS). **N Sea** — 4 Harwich Force destroyers sink 2 German torpedo boats (42 survivors). *U16* sinks destroyer *Recruit* off Galloper lightship. **Germany** — (May) 10 new UE-type ocean-going minelaying U-boats with 5.9-in gun ordered (launched from 16 June,*see* 31 Mar 1916). (May) By now RN able to track U-boats to within c20nm either beam. **Dardanelles** — British submarine *E14* sinks Turk gunboat in Sea of Marmara (*E11* too, 23) & 5000t transport *Guj Djemal* (10) with 6000 troops & arty bty N of Kalolimno I (*E14* returns 18, CO Boyle awarded VC,*see* 23). French submarine *Joule* mined & lost with all hands. **Britain** — (May) 11 monitors launched, 9 completed in June.	**France** — (May) De Goys & Happe activate first French & Allied strategic (*sic*) bomber group (*GB1*). **Britain** — (May) 500 on waiting list for RFC commissions.	China requests Tsingtao's return by Japan (*see* 7). **Neutrals** — U-boat torpedoes US tanker *Gulflight* off Scilly Is, 3 die. Germany apologizes 1 June. **France** - Nationalist *Czech Nation* first appears (smuggled to Prague).	**Austria** — 2nd War Loan. **Britain** — Northcliffe writes to FM French urging him to air his grievances (*see* 14).
			Neutrals: USA — German notices in NY press warn that ships flying Allied flags targets in war zone.	
Cameroons — 1st Action at Wumbiagas (-4): c600 Nigerians cross R Mbila.			ITALY DENOUNCES TRIPLE ALLIANCE.	
			Catholicos of Armenians appeals to K George V to get neutrals' intervention (*see* 23).	**Britain** — 2nd War Budget, only duties increased.
E Africa — Brig-Gen Malleson & car escape capture nr Mbuyuni.		**Germany** — Kaiser allows *OHL* to attack docks & 'war factories' in E London. *OHL* orders sustained Zeppelin raids (11).	**Neutrals: Italy** — Poet D'Annunzio's pro-war entry speech to 150,000 in Genoa, repeated at Rome (12).	
SW Africa — Botha occupies Karibib rail jctn after 40-mile	**Ionian Sea** — Austrian cruiser *Novara* escapes French		Churchill in Paris for secret Anglo-Italian naval talks	

MAY 1915	WESTERN FRONT 1	EASTERN FRONT 2	SOUTHERN FRONTS 3	TURKISH FRONTS 4
Thu 6 contd	by BEF CoS Robertson. British regain some trenches on Hill 60. **Aisne** — Slight French advance E of Fôret de l'Aigle.	30,000 PoWs (8). **Carpathians** — Kornilov & 48th Div cut off, surrender to Austrians (*see* 5 Sept 1916).		Allies + 105 guns gain only 600 yds for 6500 cas. **Mesopotamia** — RN sending 12 river gunboats.
Fri 7	**Artois** — French begin demolition fire (-8) but hampered by no high ground for observation.	Russians retreat to R Wistok & blow up Lupkow Pass tunnel.		
Sat 8	**Ypres** — Battle of Frezenberg Ridge (-13): Germans take ridge after heavy bombardment from 0530 of British V Corps front which has only 18 heavy guns. Gallant stand by PP's, British 84th Bde almost wiped out, but line gives only 1000 yds (-13). **Artois** — French blow 5 mines in prelim op (night 8/9) but lose objective to counter-attack.	Russian XXIV Corps reduced to 1000 men in counter-attack nr Dukla Pass. Prussian Guard breaks through to N.		
Sun 9	ALLIED SPRING OFFENSIVE begins: French estimate only 4^1/$_2$ German W Front res divs (actually 7^1/$_2$ but only 2 in N), pit 15 divs v 4 German on 8-mile front. **Britain** — First New Army div leaves for France, 9th (Scottish) Div, 12th (Eastern) Div follows (29). **Flanders** — **Battle of Aubers Ridge**: British inf attack at 0530, after 40-min poor shelling by 637 guns (shell shortage) costs 4000 cas (watched by C-in-C) to box-protected V-shaped MG emplacements every 20 yds. British recapture Wieltje E of Ypres. **Artois** — Second Battle of Artois: After 4 hrs final shelling, from 1000, Pétain's corps with Moroccan (incl 2nd Regt of Legion) & 77th Divs storms through up to 3^1/2 miles in 90 mins on 4-mile front onto Vimy Ridge but pushed back losing Souchez before 18th Div can reinforce; 70th Div cuts off Carency, XX Corps storms La Targette. French X Corps has 3000 cas in 10 mins NE of Arras.	Kaiser arrives at Pless *OHL* (*see* 3 June). **Baltic Provinces** — Lauenstein beaten at Krakinow, retreats 10, evacuates Shavli 11.	Ex-Italian PM Giolitti writes 'the generals are worth little ...'	**Gallipoli** — Jack Churchill to Winston: 'It has become siege warfare again as in France'. Hamilton asks Kitchener for 2 more divs (52nd granted 10), requests 4 more (17,*see* 9 June).
Mon 10	**Flanders** — FM French reluctantly sends 22,000 shells to Marseilles for Gallipoli (*see* 27; HOME FRONTS 14). Another British attack on Aubers Ridge fails bloodily raising cas to 11,619. **Artois** —	Radko reports his Third Army 'bled to death' at Battle of Sanok's close, allowed to retreat to R San (-11). Losses nearly 210,000 & 200 guns. **Bukovina** — Vain diversionary Russian Ninth Army offensive		

AFRICAN OPERATIONS 5	SEA WAR 6	AIR WAR 7	INTERNATIONAL EVENTS 8	HOME FRONTS 9
desert march. Colonial Minister statement to British Parlt on German well poisoning. **E Africa** — 25th Royal Fusiliers (1166 vols) land at Mombasa.	warships off Cephalonia, having successfully towed & released German *UB8* (Austrian destroyer *Triglar* tows *UB7* through Otranto Straits night 15/16, *see* 17); *UB3* towed from Pola (23) but lost without trace.		(convention 10, *see* SEA WAR).	
	Irish Sea — Unescorted unarmed British Cunard liner *LUSITANIA* (32,000t) **SUNK** in 20 mins, torpedoed from 765 yds without warning off Old Head of Kinsale (SW Ireland) by *U20* (Schwieger) (*see* 5 June), 1198 (incl 124 Americans) dead. **N Sea** — British destroyer *Maori* mined & sunk. **Baltic** — Russian cruisers engage German cruiser *München* off Libau which Russians evacuate (see E FRONT 1). New German destroyer *V107* crippled by mine entering the port (8). New RN submarine base is Dago I off Gulf of Riga. German land advance has forced move from Libau. *E9* attacks & wrongly claims German transport off there (10, *see* 2 July) after firing 5 torpedoes at 3 transports & cruiser *Roon* escort (see 14).		LUSITANIA SUNK, 1198 lives lost incl 124 US. Japanese ultimatum to China accepted by deadline (9, *see* 25).	**Britain** — Compulsory 3-yr bonding replaces increased liquor duties (*see* 26).
		Britain — British airship *SS1* snares telegraph wires & crashes in flames. First coastal stn for A/S patrol airships opened at Capel (Folkestone).		**Canada** — War Purchasing Commission formed.
	Dardanelles — Naval attack resumption discussed and rejected (-13). **Turkey** — Adm Souchon warns Enver Pasha of Fleet's coal shortage.	**W Front** — RFC (9 sqns with 103 aircraft) attempts to refine contact patrol tactics at Aubers Ridge. British inf optimistically given 7 ft x 2 ft strips of white cloth to drape on parapets of captured trenches for report by 3 radio-equipped BE2s (42 signals) cruising at 4000 ft.	**Neutrals: USA** — 'Col' House urges Pres Wilson to declare war. **Italy** — Partial mobilization ordered.	
	Med — Secret Anglo-French Italian Naval Convention: a First Allied Fleet to be formed (base Brindisi) under Italian C-in-C incl 4 British battleships (*see* 27) & 4 cruisers; 12 French destroyers & 6	**Britain** — German Army airship *LZ38* bombs Southend (night 10/11, 3 cas); causes 6 civ cas (night 26/27).	**Neutrals: USA** — Pres Wilson *Lusitania* speech: 'There is such a thing as a man being too proud to fight'. Germany assures US that neutral shipping will not be attacked, but issues no such order.	*Lusitania* sinking sparks **anti-German riots in London & Liverpool** (-12): British Industries Fair (London -12): 620 firms exhibit goods formerly enemy imports.

MAY 1915	WESTERN FRONT 1	EASTERN FRONT 2	SOUTHERN FRONTS 3	TURKISH FRONTS 4
Mon 10 contd	Neuville-St-Vaast cemetery & part of Carency (Arras) taken by Pétain's corps & XX Corps but Moroccan Div crippled (Legion 1939 cas), Gen Barbot of 77th Div k by shell.	across Dniester (-14), takes Nadworna & c20,000 PoWs.		
Tue 11	**Flanders** — Germans bombard Ypres-Menin Rd but own 2 bns gassed. **Artois** — French XXI Corps finally captures fort & chapel of Notre-Dame de Lorette, but XXXIII Corps fails v ridge heights 119-140; Pétain dissuades further frontal attacks (*see* 16).		**Serbia** — British Military Attaché at Nis Lt-Col APB Harrison tells London that Sava floods & lack of forage have postponed projected Serb offensive; no plans to co-operate with Italy (*see* 16 May & 7 July). **Italian Front** — Francis Joseph orders frontier fort arming & 5th Div to Isonzo line; *Standschützen* & volunteers mobilize (12). Austrian div from Serbia sent to Isonzo.	**Mesopotamia** — Nixon orders Tigris offensive (Viceroy of India outlines plan to London, 23).
Wed 12	**Artois** — French 70th Div takes Carency with 1000 PoWs. **Ypres** — British 1st and 3rd Cav Divs relieve 28th Div (15,533 cas in the battle) (night 12/13).	Woyrsch occupies Kielce (Poland) in general Austro-German advance.		**Armenia** — First Battle of Tortum ends in Turk success. **Gallipoli: Helles** — Gurkhas capture Cape Tekeh (Gurkha Bluff). 2900 Anzac mtd troops arrive as infantry.
Thu 13	**Ypres** — Battle of Frezenberg Ridge ends. Heavy German bombardment. BEF MG crews get first primitive flannel-bag gas masks. French complete capture of Bois le Prêtre.	Russian SW Front shell reserve only 100,000. Cossacks occupy Sniatyn nr R Pruth.		
Fri 14	**Ypres** — Franco-Belgian advance nr Het Sas & Steenstraate. British relieve French of 3 miles S of La Bassée canal (night 14/15) as 400 guns prepare Haig's next blow.	German Guard Corps capture Jaroslav (-16, 93 miles from Gorlice). English novelist Hugh Walpole becomes Russian officer in Otriad (Red Cross mobile hospital), reaches Lemberg (24).	**Italian Front** — Advanced dets of 3 Austrian divs from Poland detrain on Isonzo line, main VII Corps body reach Agram (21, *see* 22 & 27).	**Mesopotamia** — Gorringe captures Arab fort (-16) in Persian Arabistan, but Turks withdraw to Amara; 2 British aircraft reach Basra, first fly 27.
Sat 15	**Battle of Festubert** (-25) begins at 2330: first British major night attack with 3 divs takes 3 miles of trenches to ½ mile depth; CSM Barter wins VC, with 8 bombers captures 500 yds of trench (105 PoWs). French retake Het Sas & regain E bank of canal.	Russians change cipher to no avail. **Poland** — Austrians beaten between Kielce & Ostrovyets (7000 cas), retreat 12+ miles (-17).	**Serbia** — Russian 6-in naval gun in Belgrade fortress sinks Austrian patrol boat.	**Gallipoli** — Gens Birdwood (14) & Bridges (GOC 1st Australian Div) wounded by snipers, latter dies 18.
Sun 16	**Festubert** — British advance to La Quinque Rue-Béthune road to consolidate gains continues. **Artois** — D'Urbal orders Tenth Army to clear flanks only (*see* 21). **Champagne** — French Colonial Corps recover trenches after 2 German regts attack in wake of 3 mine explosions.	**Battle of the San** (-23): Austro-Germans cross river by 15 bridges, take Sieniawa (18).	Italian-Russian military agreement pledges Italy to try and reach Serbs with Isonzo offensive.	
Mon 17	Festubert: 450 Germans surrender during BEF shelling after which 'Quadrilateral' strongpoint captured, but rain &			**Armenia** — Russians occupy Ardjiche, L Van, Turks leave town. Oganovski occupies Malazgirt (*see* 10 July).

AFRICAN OPERATIONS 5	SEA WAR 6	AIR WAR 7	INTERNATIONAL EVENTS 8	HOME FRONTS 9
	submarines. Potential Second Allied Fleet to have French C-in-C. **Italy** — New dreadnought *Duilio* completed. **Black Sea** — *Goeben* (hit twice) cut off from Bosphorus & damaged in hr's action with 6 Russian (2 damaged) battleships & 11 other ships off Bosphorus but outmanoeuvres them at 30 kts to reach Stenia Creek base (*see* 17 & 22). **Germany** — Tirpitz decides to send *UB1* & *UB15* to Austrians at Pola, *UC14* & *UC15*, first minelaying boats, also to be sent (*see* 4 June). Enver Pasha appeals for more (23), Tirpitz replies 8 now allocated.			
Cameroons — 600 French capture Eseka rail terminus.	**Dardanelles** — 17 Allied troop transports withdrawn to Imbros (U-boat threat warning by Room 40 to RN Adm Robeck).		Russia receives Rumania's demands, talks suspended (30).	Russian Red Cross Flag Day in London. **Germany** — Caricaturist Georg Grosz released as unfit for Army before ever going to front (likewise 27 Apr 1917).
SW Africa — Botha occupies capital Windhoek (pop c8000); Gov-Gen Seitz asks for meeting (13, *see* 20).	**Dardanelles** — Superdreadnought *Queen Elizabeth* withdrawn for Grand Fleet.		Bryce Ctee reports on German atrocities in Belgium.	
E Africa — 200 Rhodesians repel 200 Germans on R Tsavo; British donkey transport experiment fails.	**Dardanelles** — British battleship *Goliath* (570 lost) sunk by Turk torpedo boat *Muavenet-i-Millet* (German Lt Firle) at 0116 in thick mist. *U21* (Hersing) reaches Cattaro with ½t fuel left having survived 3 Allied warship attacks, sails for Dardanelles (20, *see* 25).		**Neutrals:** 1st US *Lusitania* protest (*see* 28). **Italy** — PM Salandra resigns, but King refuses to accept (16).	**Britain — Govt decides to intern all enemy aliens of military age**. Enemy Emperors & Princes lose KGs etc. Leeds National Shell Factory approved.
	Baltic — Russian submarine *Drakon* twice vainly attacks German cruiser *Thetis* (initially towing U4).		British War Council meets, Kitchener accuses Admiralty, fears invasion. Churchill stiffens Gallipoli resolve. **Neutrals: Portugal** — Navy & Democrats overthrow Gen Castro 'dictatorship', 1150-1300 cas (-18); Castro deported to Azores, later flees to Germany.	*The Times* military correspondent highlights BEF shell shortage in dispatch prompted by FM French. Press blame Kitchener (esp Northcliffe *Daily Mail*) (19-21). Venetia Stanley tells shattered Asquith she is marrying E Montague & ceasing correspondence.
	Lord Fisher, First Sea Lord, **resigns over Dardanelles fiasco**. Succeeded by Adm Sir H Jackson (*see* 27).			
L Victoria — RN flotilla salvage HMS *Sybil* (*see* 5 Nov 1914).	**N Sea** — German minelayers lay 480 mines at E Dogger Banks.	**Britain** — *LZ38* bombs Ramsgate & Dover (night 16/17), but is 1st Zeppelin to be caught by searchlight & also seen by a defending pilot. **W Front** — French-style rudder stripes specified for RFC aircraft.	Austrian concessions to Italy (& 21). Rome patriotic demo before royal family in Quirinial Palace. Allies offer Kavalla to Bulgaria for continued neutrality (*see* 29).	**Britain** — King visits factories, shipyards and hospitals in N (-21).
	Black Sea — Russian destroyers launch blockade of Bosphorus, play havoc with coast-hugging Turk colliers	**W Front** — 9 RNAS aircraft from Dunkirk climb to intercept *LZ38* but instead find *LZ39*, Grey, Warneford & Meddis		**Russia** — Bolshevik meeting in quarry nr Odessa arrested. **Britain** — Lloyd George persuades Asquith to form

MAY 1915	WESTERN FRONT 1	EASTERN FRONT 2	SOUTHERN FRONTS 3	TURKISH FRONTS 4
Mon 17 contd	mist hamper exploitation. German reserves from N block British penetration. **Artois** — Fayolle on Pétain '... the best general I have met so far in the war'.			
Tue 18		Austrians re-occupy Galician oilfields NE of Uzsok.		**Gallipoli** — Hamilton gets pessimistic Kitchener telegram, interprets as instruction not to encourage evacuation.
Wed 19	**Flanders** — Virtual stalemate at Festubert as 1st Cdn Div re-enters line to replace 1st & 7th Divs (*see* 23).	**Galicia** — Mackensen crushes Radymno salient W of San, shells Przemysl (20) while 3 new Russian corps counter-attack Austrian Fourth Army.		**Gallipoli** — 17,356 Anzacs repel 40,000 Turks (*see* 24). **Armenia** — Nikolayev enters Van, relieving Armenians who received Tsar's thanks (18).
Thu 20	**Flanders** — First British (RN) kite balloon ascends nr Poperinghe.			
Fri 21	**Artois** — French take 'White Road' nr Souchez (Vimy).	**Galicia** — Russian counter-attack (-24) to cover Przemysl's evacuation. Austrian VII Corps entrains for Italian Front (*see* 3 June).	German *Alpenkorps* formed for Tyrol. Conrad to Emperor's ADC '... an Italian offensive will have for its chief objective the valley of the Isonzo. All defensive measures have ....been taken'.	**Persia** — Small Russian force lands at Enzeli on Caspian after Isfahan vice-consul murdered (18).
Sat 22	**Flanders** — British advance S of Quinque Rue.		Austrian Archduke Eugene made C-in-C SW Front, HQ Laibach (v Italy) with able Gen Krauss as CoS (*see* 27). Gen Tersztyanski left i/c v Serbia.	**Mesopotamia** — Nureddin Pasha arrives at Baghdad with reinforcements.
Sun 23	**Flanders** — Unsuccessful German counter-attack at Festubert.		ITALY ENTERS WAR. Austrian guns in Carnic Alps fire first shots shortly before midnight.	
Mon 24	**Ypres** — Battle of Bellewaarde Ridge (-25): 4 German divs attack, capture Mouse-trap Farm, but lose other gains despite 0245 4½-mile wide gas cloud v British 28th, 4th & 1st Cav Divs (*see* 16 June).	**Galicia** — Mackensen resumes offensive, destroys V Caucasus Corps reaching 11 miles E of San (-25), takes 21,000 PoWs, 39 guns and 49 MGs. *Südarmee's* Battle of Stryj (-11 June) successful by 31 v Russian Eleventh Army.	Italian Carnic Gp capture Plöchen Pass & frontier peaks but does not exploit v Austrian VII Corps.	**Gallipoli** — 10-hr Anzac armistice to bury 3000 Turk dead. **Helles** : 3 British divs form Corps (numbered VIII 5 June).
Tue 25	Flanders — **Second Battle of Ypres ends**. Battle of Festubert ends with 16,648 BEF cas for 5800 German (800 PoWs) & 1000-yd advance on 3000 yd front.		Italian 6th Inf Div attacks in Chiese valley W of L Garda but is easily held. 4 Austrian forts at Lavarone (SE of Trento) shelled (*see* 28). Italian advance guard arrives on Isonzo.	**Persia** — Russians retake Urmia, occupy Miandab. **Gallipoli** — 1st improved Anzac periscope rifle (L/Cp Beech) used at Quinn's Post.
Wed 26	**Flanders** — 'Two Years' position warfare [ie completely stalemated, trench warfare] on Yser begun (*The Times Diary and Index of the War*). †Capt Julian Grenfell, British war poet	**Baltic Provinces** — German *Niemenarmee* formed from Lauenstein's force.	**Isonzo** — Italians occupy Brado.	**Gallipoli** — Churchill urges Kitchener to use gas, cables brother Jack '... afraid of troops moving in so slowly that you will have to fight whole Turkish Army in relays'.

AFRICAN OPERATIONS 5	SEA WAR 6	AIR WAR 7	INTERNATIONAL EVENTS 8	HOME FRONTS 9
	(see 31 July). **Aegean** — *UB8* arrives at Smyrna, sinks British *SS Merion* (dummy of battlecruiser *Tiger*) off Mudros (30, see 25).	attack, Meddis scores hits with 2 0.45-in incendiary bullets. Bigsworth's Avro 504 air-to-air bomb attack damages *LZ39* over Ostend (1k, several w). **Gallipoli** — Marix RNAS observes Turk reinforcements landing & making camp at Ak Bashi Liman. Later Samson & Marix in Breguet-Michelin bomb the camp (57 cas), panicking work parties unloading boats.		Coalition Govt. 7000 London tramway men lose strike for extra war bonus (-4 June). Kitchener asks for another 300,000 men.
	N Sea — German torpedo boats capture 3 British fishing boats off NW corner of Dogger Bank. **E Med** — RN ship captures 1000t Greek *SS Proton* (hired by Germans as U-boat supply ship) & interns her at Alexandria.			**Turkey** — Interior Ministry orders deportation of Erzerum Armenians to Urfa & Mosul.
	Adriatic — 4 Austrian U-boats with cruisers & destroyers at sea to prevent Italian surprise attack (see 24).	**Gallipoli** — Forewarned by RNAS recon, Anzacs repel fanatical Turk counter-attacks (-24, see TURK FRONTS).		**Britain** — Asquith announces impending Coalition Govt. Recruiting age raised to 40, height reduced to 5ft 2in.
SW Africa — Botha meets Seitz at Giftkop (c30 miles N of Karibib) during 48-hr ceasefire. Seitz proposes armistice and neutral zone until general peace. Botha insists on unconditional surrender. 4000 Germans still at large to N (see 14 June).	†Adm Essen, C-in-C Russian Baltic Fleet, aged 55. Succeeded by Vice Adm Kanin.	**E Front** — Airship *LZ30* accidentally burned in Posen shed. **W Front** — First FE2b flown to France; RFC No 6 Sqn has 4 by Sept, 32 in service by Dec. 2 German MG-armed **Fokker Els with interrupter gear arrive.**	**Neutrals: Italy** — Govt given extraordinary war powers, publishes Green Book on negotiations. Mobilization ordered (22).	**Britain** — Jockey Club suspends racing for duration except at Newmarket.
			Italo-German treaty on mutual safety of citizens & property.	Churchill accepts dismissal after final vain appeal to Asquith: 'Let me stand or fall by the Dardanelles'. Accepts Chancellorship of the Duchy of Lancaster, stays on War Council.
	Black Sea — Russian battleship *Pantelimon* torpedoed but not sunk.			**Worst disaster in British railway history**, 3-train collision in Scotland, 226 die incl 214 men of 52nd Div en route to Gallipoli.
	RN submarine *E11* (Nasmith) torpedoes Turk torpedo gunboat *Pelengi Deria* (salvaged) off Seraglio Point, Constantinople then torpedoes Turk transport *Stamboul* in Constantinople harbour (25), one of 8 victims on cruise.	Italy has 6 sqns Blériots, 4 sqns Nieuports, 4 sqns Farmans (total 79 op aircraft); also 3 floatplanes.	ITALY DECLARES WAR ON AUSTRIA. Allies warn Turkey on Armenian massacres (see 31).	**France** — Flag Day for the 9 occupied depts.
Morocco — Lyautey given Arabic letter containing German appeal for revolt on 29. Rebel chief Abt el-Selam submits to him at Casablanca (June).	**Austrian Fleet** from Pola **bombards Ancona, Porto Corsini, Rimini, Senigallia** & railways & bridges on Italian coast; flying boats raid Venice & Chiaravalle airship sheds; Italian destroyer *Turbine* sunk off Pelagosa I by cruiser *Heligoland* & 3 Austrian destroyers (see 5 June).			
Cameroons — 1290 Allies begin advance from Wumbi-agas, fight 3 main actions, gain 12 miles in 19 days till blocked (-13 June); Germans cut supply route (28), 60 British sick evacuated by 31.	**Dardanelles** — *U21* (Hersing), sinks British battleships *Triumph* (73 lost) off Gaba Tepe & *Majestic* (27, 43 lost), capsizes in 7 mins off W Beach; *U21* proceeds on to Constantinople after 4000-mile voyage (see 4 July).		Sino-Japanese treaties grant Japan new treaty ports and 99-yr Port Arthur lease. U-boat torpedoes US SS *Nebraskan* but she reaches Liverpool.	BRITISH COALITION GOVT: 12 Liberals & 8 Tories, **Lloyd George Munitions Minister**. 2nd Cdn Div formed.
	Adriatic — **Italy announces blockade of Austria. E Med** — Allies shell Alexandretta, Haifa, Bodrum & Makri.			**Turkey** — Enver writes to Talaat on Armenian deportation details already 'orally decided'. **Britain** — Liquor Control Board formed.

MAY 1915	WESTERN FRONT 1	EASTERN FRONT 2	SOUTHERN FRONTS 3	TURKISH FRONTS 4
Wed 26 contd	(poem *Into Battle*, Apr), aged 27, at Boulogne from w on Railway Hill, Ypres.			
Thu 27	**Artois** — Nr Souchez French capture Les Quatre Bou-quetaux & Ablains-St Nazaire. **Meuse** — Fighting in Bois-le-Prêtre. **Flanders** — FM French cables London, no more attacks until arty ammo replenished, German Fourth Army reports the same.	**Baltic Provinces** — Russians retake Kindowary nr Shavli & Bubie (28). **Galicia** — III Caucasus Corps reduced to 4000 retaking Sieniawa.	**Italian Front** — Gen **Boroevic** (from Third Army outside Przemysl, E Front) **takes over new Austrian Fifth Army**, orders that 'the troops should construct positions, place obstacles in front of them and remain there'. K of Italy's Order of the Day warns of tough Austrian resistance. Cadorna orders further Italian advance. **Isonzo** — Italian Second Army attack Mt Sabotino 5 times & attempt to seize Gorizia (-28). **Trentino** — Italians occupy Ala & Grado in front of Austrian defences.	
Fri 28	**Artois** — French 53rd Div advance in savage hand-to-hand fighting in the 'Labyrinth' N of Arras (-1 June, *see* 8 June).		**Italian Front** — Austrian Ft Lusern (Trento) nearly surrenders but fire from neighbours stiffens it. Italians vainly attack Sleme & Mrzli massifs S of Mt Nero (-4 June); *Modena* Bde loses 1237 cas (*see* 2 June).	
Sat 29			**Albania** — Italians reinforce Valona.	**Gallipoli** — Turks take but then lose Quinn's Post after firing mine.
Sun 30	**Flanders** — German attack at Hooge. **Artois** — French gains nr Souchez.	Austro-Germans shell Przemysl forts (American cameraman John A Everets films).		
Mon 31	Despite Allied attacks, Germans send 2 divs (May) to E Front. BEF May loss of 65,730 worst until July 1916. Souchez sugar refinery stormed by French.	**Poland** — German Ninth Army gas attack N of Bolimow (-1 June) causes 1000 Siberian VI Corps cas but 56 Germans gassed (*see* 12 June). **Galicia** — Mackensen storms 3 forts N of Przemysl; *Südarmee* takes Stryj. Russian SW Front losses 412,000 (153,000 PoWs) & 300 guns.	**Trentino** — By now elite Bavarian *Alpenkorps* (13 bns, 11 MG coys, 36 guns) reinforces Austrian First Army (Dankl) in this sector.	**Gallipoli** — GHQ lands at Imbros I; 38,000 Allied cas to date. **Mesopotamia** — **Second Battle of Qurna**: 'Townshend's Regatta' with 372 local bellum boats (2560 inf, 17 guns) & 7 RN vessels beats Halim Bey's Turks, taking 4 hills, 3 guns and 271 PoWs for 24 cas.
Tue 1 June 1915	**Artois** — French gain trenches at Souchez. **France** — (June) Gen Dumézil designs his trench mortar (35lb-99lb stick bombs), used by French (standard), Italian, Russian & US Armies (*see* 25 Sept).		**Italian Front** — Italians hold slopes of Mt Nero (Isonzo), make further gains there by 20 & advance in Adige valley.	**Gallipoli** — Kemal promoted Col, also given Iron Cross & St Alexander (Bulgar) decoration (-6). **Mesopotamia** — 3 RN sloops lead Tigris pursuit, capture Turk gunboat *Marmaris* & steamer *Mosul* (2). **India : Baluchistan** —Kalat ops (-10 July).

AFRICAN OPERATIONS 5	SEA WAR 6	AIR WAR 7	INTERNATIONAL EVENTS 8	HOME FRONTS 9
	First Lord of the Admiralty CHURCHILL RESIGNS, **Balfour succeeds. N Sea** — Minelayer *Princess Irene* destroyed by internal explosion at Sheerness, Thames estuary. *Adriatic* — RN battle sqn (4 ships) joins Italian Fleet, Allied admirals meet at Taranto.	**Germany** — **First major French bombing raid**: 18 Voisins attack poison gas works at Ludwigshaven, 90 bombs start fires.		
			Bethmann denounces Italy in *Reichstag*. German reply puts all *Lusitania* responsibility on Britain.	**Ceylon** — Riots (-5 June). **Germany** — 1st *Reichstag* annexation debate.
	Channel — **First UC-type minelaying boat patrol** from Zeebrugge *UC11* (Schmidt) lays 12 mines off S Foreland, Downs, first of 420 mines in 46 fields (-Sept), 648 mines (150 in Dover area, 180 off Thames, 306 off Lowestoft, 12 off Grimsby) by 31 Dec. RN find first field off S Foreland (2 June).		Allies offer Bulgaria much territory if she intervenes v Turkey (Austria offers Serb Macedonia for neutrality, 24). Serbia informed 27 but protests with Greece (*see* 15 June).	
SE Cameroons — 400 Franco- Belgians take R Monjo position (-1 June). **L Nyasa — Sphinxhaven Raid**: 2 RN steamers land 180 KAR on E side of lake. They storm fort and blow stern off gunboat *Hermann von Wissman* (*see* 18 Mar 1918).		**Adriatic** — Italians first bomb Pola.		**Russia** — Opera season begins. **Ireland** — Casting vote vetoes Irish volunteers' immediate revolt proposal.
N Cameroons — 1834 Allies, 7 guns & 12 MGs surprise, bombard Garua (-10 June).		**Britain** — RFC cas to date 134, strength 5147 (23 sqns). So far 530 aircraft brought into service, c300 lost or worn out, 2260 on order from 31 stns. 234 RFC pilots & observers training at 11 stns. Army Zeppelin *LZ38* drops 120 small bombs on E London (42 cas, £18,596 damage) & at 10,000 ft evades 15 defence sorties (1 Vickers Gunbus crashes, night 31 May/1 June).	US dissatisfied with German *Lusitania* reply. HM Ambassador says *Lusitania* never carried guns (untrue). Baron Wangenheim cables Berlin on need to *'mitigate'* not hinder measures v Armenians (*see* 17 June).	
	Arctic — U-boats also minelay off Archangel; 6 RN trawlers sent to help Russians destroy 150 mines by Oct for AMC, *Arlanza* damaged, 1 trawler & 9 steamers (1 Russian) sunk. **Atlantic** — **First transatlantic crossing by submarines**: Canadian-built (at Montreal) 'H' class of RN, 10 boats delivered but rest delayed by US till entry into war. US Bethlehem Steel used.	**France** — (June) Fonck joins *Escadrille C47*. **Britain** — RNAS causes confusion by redesignating sqns 'wings' & flts 'sqns' (rescinded Dec). **Italy** — (June) French floatplane sqn (Conneau) arrives at Venice. Austrians bomb Bari & Brindisi. **E Front** — (June) Cav Lt Richthofen posted as air observer, lands safely after German inf MG brings his Albatros B1 down. **Britain** — First flight of Airco (De Havilland) DH2 single-seat pusher-engined fighters. Govt D-Notice orders Press to publish only official statements on air raids. **Neutrals : USA** — First USN airship ordered (first	**Secret War** — (June) British agent in Switzerland receiving regular reports from 5 German cities (*see* 19 Aug). Tsar's telegram to K of Denmark refuses to receive German peace mediator at Petrograd (*see* 3 Aug).	**Britain** — RFP 32%. Asquith returns from 4-day W Front visit. (June) **First women skilled workers in private munitions factory** (Glasgow). Cotton industry accepts female substitution (9), NUR accept women members (24). **Austria** — (June) 2000 wagons of flour from Berlin saves Vienna food position. **France** — (June) 100,000 conscripts diverted to munitions factories.

JUNE 1915	WESTERN FRONT 1	EASTERN FRONT 2	SOUTHERN FRONTS 3	TURKISH FRONTS 4
Tue 1 contd				
Wed 2		**Galicia** — Only 3-mile corridor links Przemysl after Austro-Germans break in from N & SW. Germans check Russian blow at Austrian Fourth Army (-4).	**Isonzo** — Italians fail to break through at Krn (-4); Austrian XV Corps counter-attack between Tolmin & Karfreit (-4) called off after heavy losses. Cividale *Alpini* Bn climbs Sleme massif only to be repulsed by Austrian avalanche of stones.	Allied blockade of Turkey formally declared.
Thu 3	**Flanders** — British capture trenches at Givenchy but abandon them. Germans shell Ypres.	**Austro-Germans retake Przemysl**. High Commands incl Kaiser meet at Pless; Mackensen to get 4½ more divs & control 2 Austrian Armies. 3 Austrian divs + Third Army HQ (Boroevic, Puhallo succeeds) leave for Italian Front.		**Mesopotamia** — 5 RN launches (Townshend & Capt Nunn) occupy Amara, take 1000 Turk PoWs (Turk officer cables wife 'safely captured').
Fri 4		**Galicia** — Russians cease costly attacks (since 27 May) on Austrian Fourth Army. Austrians restrict Russian 2nd Rifle Div bridgehead S of Prut.	Falling Isonzo (after sudden floods) finally lets Italian Third Army (Duke of Aosta) cross in strength (*see* 11).	**Gallipoli : Helles** — **Third Battle of Krithia**: 30,000 Allies (6500 cas) win only 250-500 yds on a mile front. NZ & Australian Div 4332 cas/8543 since landing.
Sat 5	**Artois** — Attack & counter-attack N of Arras & E of Lorette Ridge, in which French sculptor Henri Gaudier-Brzeska k, aged 24.		**Isonzo** — 4 Italian corps vainly attack Doberdo plateau, Gorizia & Monte Kuk (-8) with poor arty support. **Secret War** — **Austrians solve first 4 Italian cryptograms**; 16 more (-30) by Marburg intercept stn (*see* 5 July).	**Syria** — Austrian envoy Musil returns to Damascus after 3000-mile trip in Arabia since mid-Nov.
Sun 6	**Aisne** — 4 French bdes launch attack in salient S of Quennevières, between the Oise & Aisne. Small advances achieved for 7913 cas (-16).	**Galicia** — British Liaison Officer Maj Neilson: 'This [Russian Third] Army is now a harmless mob'. Lesh has replaced Radko as C-in-C. Austrian Seventh Army regains touch with *Südarmee* which takes Zurawno on N bank Dniester (5) but is ejected (9). Retakes it (11) but is stopped to N (13).		**Gallipoli : Helles** — British 52nd Div begins landing.
Mon 7	**Somme** — Part of French XI Corps attack & capture German salient at Touvent farm between Hébuterne & Serre on 2-mile front, German counter-attack fails.	**Galicia** — Lechitski evacuates Kalusz & Nadworna in E (& all Bukovina 12). Austrians retake Stanislau (8) & Kolomea (12).		British Dardanelles Ctee (Cabinet) first meets. Hamilton rules out general attack for present. Anzac: 4th NZ reinforcement (1761) arrives.

AFRICAN OPERATIONS 5	SEA WAR 6	AIR WAR 7	INTERNATIONAL EVENTS 8	HOME FRONTS 9
		flt Apr 1917).		
	Britain announces blockade of Asia Minor. **N Sea** — Harwich Force cruisers (seaplane each) on anti-Zeppelin patrol without success (-4 & 9) though twice bombed vainly by German seaplanes (*see* 3 July).			**Turkey** — Armenian town Shabin Karahisar fights to death (-30). Deportation & massacre of 65,000 Erzerum province Armenians begins (-30 July), also Erzinjan (7-10).
	E Africa — Monitors *Severn* & *Mersey* (4ft 9in draught) reach Mafia I off Rufiji (*see* 6 July).	**W Front** — French air raid (178 bombs) on field HQ of German Crown Prince.	**San Marino declares war on Austria**. Allied Economic War Conference first meets in Paris.	**Italy** — Prefects authorized to requisition farm machinery, labour & animals.
	Adriatic — First German coastal U-boats *UB1* & *UB15* (rail-transported) join Austrian Navy as *U10* & *U11* at Pola (*see* 10). **Constantinople** — *UB8* arrives (*UB7* 21). **Baltic** — RN submarine *E9* (Horton) severely damages German destroyer *S148* & collier (2 crew lost,*see* 28 & 2 July).	**Britain** — Attempted raids on London by German Navy airship *L10* & on Hull by *SL3*; *L10* bombs Gravesend (night 4/5, 8 civ cas).		**Germany** — 1914 Bar to 1870 Iron Cross instituted.
W Tripolitania — Italians retake Chicla but evacuate Mizda (15-21).	**N Sea** — *U14* rammed & sunk by trawler *Hawk*. **Adriatic** — Italian cruisers etc shell Dalmatian Is lighthouses & stns & Ragusa-Cattaro rail line. **Med** — French sending 10 armed trawlers for patrol work. Anglo-Italian battle sqns rehearse in Gulf of Taranto (& 11), latter using much US coal, but U-boat threat ends exercises after 13-14 Aug.	**E Front** — IM heavy bomber (Buschko) destroys Austrian munitions train in Prjevorsk Stn.	**First Anglo-French War Conference held at Calais.**	**Britain** — Churchill speech at Dundee (his seat) defends record: 'We are the grand reserve of the Allied cause'.
	Berlin orders U-boat cdrs to spare large passenger ships (not strictly observed). **Adriatic** — French cruiser minelayer *Casabianca* sinks on one of her own mines.	**Britain** — *L9* drops 52 bombs on Hull for 20 mins around midnight (62 civ & 2 military cas), 3 German Army airships (target London) all return early (night 6/7); *LZ38* docks at Brussels-Evère only to be destroyed by 2 RNAS Farmans' bombs (Wilson & Mills). Flt Sub-Lt R Warneford of No 1 Sqn RNAS in Morane type 'L' pursues *LZ37* (Haegen) from Ostend to Ghent (despite heavy defensive gunfire) & destroys her by air-to-air bombing with 6 x 20lb bombs dropped from 150 ft above (9 of 10 crew k); Helmsman Muhter survives 8000-ft freefall crashing through convent roof (4 nuns k). Damaged by the huge blast, Warneford lands for 35 mins behind German lines to repair fractured petrol feed (night 6/7); awarded first VC for RNAS (8); dies (17) when his Farman pusher-tail collapses. Surviving *LZ39* withdrawn to E Front, Army Airship Service abandons forward bases. **E Front** — Russian IM heavy bomber severely damaged (cdr w) by German fighters (1 shot down).		
Cameroons — Dobell decides to abandon advance on Yaunde, still 40 miles away.				War Propaganda Bureau's first report to Cabinet estimates 2.5m publications circulated in 17 languages since Sept 1914. **Russia** — Special Council for Armament set up under Tsar. War Industries Ctee formed (9).

JUNE 1915	WESTERN FRONT 1	EASTERN FRONT 2	SOUTHERN FRONTS 3	TURKISH FRONTS 4
Tue 8	**Artois** — Further French progress in the 'Labyrinth'. French now hold all Neuville St Vaast, advancing at Hebuterne (S of Arras).			**Persia** — German Hentig mission enters bound for Afghanistan & India, reaches Tehran c15; 3 other German-led parties reported in June.
Wed 9		**Baltic Provinces** — German attacks repulsed in Shavli district (more attacks 12). Gen Plehve arrives at Riga to lead new Fifth Army (10).	**Italian Front** — Italian attack on 6178-ft Tonale Pass fails (Adamello Range, W Trentino). Italian Second Army attacks on Gorizia bridgehead (Isonzo) fail with heavy losses (-10), although it crosses the Isonzo (9-11), but Third Army occupies Monfalcone close to sea E of Isonzo.	**Gallipoli** — British Cabinet approves sending 3 new divs; 2 cruisers; 14 monitors; 6 submarines & 4 sloops.
Thu 10				**Armenia** — Turks win Second Battle of Tortum (-12). **Gallipoli** — Hospitals in Lemnos, Malta & Egypt swamped. First Anzac bread issue (11).
Fri 11	**Artois** — French advance 1100 yds on 1¼-mile front & repulse counter-attack S of Hébuterne, more progress (13).		**Isonzo** — Italians heroically attack Hill 383 nr Plava (-17) N of Gorizia without significant gains v Austrian 1st Mtn Bde (2300 cas). Italians destroy Austrian dam nr Sagrado lowering flooded area below Carso plateau (see 27).	
Sat 12		**Poland** — Gas aids Germans advance almost 4 miles on R Bzura despite 350 own gas cas (see 6 July).	In Carnic Alps Italians occupy 2 passes & repel Austrian attacks (25, see 11 July). **Isonzo** — Italians attack Hill 383 seven times (see 17).	**Mesopotamia** — Nixon asks for more aircraft (2 RFC Egypt flights allotted by 30), also more medical personnel (18). Townshend reaches Bombay for sick leave (11 July) after falling victim like 1100 of his men at Amara.
Sun 13	**Artois** — French checked at Souchez. Pétain & Fayolle vainly oppose mass offensive renewal (see 16). **Flanders** — Canadians discard unreliable Ross rifle for standard SMLE, enter Messines sector (28).	**Galicia** — Mackensen resumes attack on 31-mile front, forcing Russians towards Grodek line, claims 40,000 PoWs (-16).		**Aden** — Turks shell Perim I, but 23rd Sikh Pioneers repel dhow landing attempt (14).
Mon 14	**Artois** — French novelist Jules Leroux disappears in action, aged 34, at Neuville St Vaast.	**Galicia** — English novelist Hugh Walpole helps tend 800w in 12 hrs, develops dysentery by 30.		
Tue 15	**Flanders** — 2nd Action of Givenchy (-16): British 7th & new 51st Highland Div attack at 0558 NE of Festubert without surprise element after 2 days of shelling and with inadequate grenades, repeat failures (16 & 18).		**Isonzo** — Italian Second Army attacks Austrian Podgora position W of Gorizia. 3 *Alpini* coys capture 2 peaks & Monte Nero (Upper Isonzo) with bn of Hungarians.	**Gallipoli** — Hamilton vainly asks Kitchener for Byng or Rawlinson as new corps cdr.
Wed 16	**Flanders** — Well-prepared British local 3rd Div advance N of Hooge (3500 cas incl Maj Wavell who loses eye) after 1¾ hr shelling makes some ground towards Bellewaarde Farm but causes only 457 cas (157 PoWs) leaving ridge with defenders. **Artois** — Major French 20-div attack against reinforced defenders (307 heavy guns); **only Moroccan Div reaches Vimy Ridge crest for 2nd time** (2nd Regt of 1st	**Galicia** — **Third Battle of Lemberg** (-22), 41 divs on each side.	**Isonzo** — *Alpini* capture Krn peak (c8000 ft) from Bosnians then evacuate it without realising its importance.	

AFRICAN OPERATIONS 5	SEA WAR 6	AIR WAR 7	INTERNATIONAL EVENTS 8	HOME FRONTS 9
	Dardanelles — *Humber* first RN monitor to arrive, these shallow-draught heavy-gunned vessels reduce need for more vulnerable battleships.	**Italian Front** — Italian airship *M2* (Felice di Pisa) shot down by Austrian 2-seater (Kissing & Gronenwald).	**Neutrals : USA** — Bryan resigns as Sec of State, unwilling to sign 2nd Lusitania protest note. Lansing succeeds (permanently 23), condemns German accusations (9, *see* 8 July).	London 86°F in shade.
L Tanganyika — 800t gunboat *Graf von Götzen* launched.	**Adriatic** — Austrian *U4* torpedoes RN cruiser *Dublin*, she returns to Brindisi at up to 17 kts.	**W Front** — Cp Guynemer joins *Esc MS3* at Vauciennes, wrecks 3 aircraft in faulty landings (10-22, *see* 19 July).	**Secret War** — 74-yr-old Baron Schluga (Agent 17) reports from Paris (Berlin receives 11): 'English complaining over lack of munitions ... ... regret ... promised support of the French attack north of Arras is not possible ...'.	**Britain** — Ministry of Munitions Act passed.
N Cameroons — **German Ft Garua surrenders** (-11): river flood bars mutinous garrison's escape; 249 PoWs, 4 guns & 10 MGs (*see* 28).	**Adriatic** — Austrian *U11* alias German *UB15* (Heimburg) surprises & sinks Italian submarine *Medusa* (*see* 7 July).			**Russia** — **Anti-German riots in Moscow** (-12). Interior Minister Maklakov replaced by Prince Shcherbatov. **Britain** — Commons votes £250m war credit, war costing £2.66m pd since 1 Apr.
	Black Sea — *Breslau* disables Russian destroyer *Gnevny* but sister *Derzkoi* tows her to safety (*see* 18 July).	**N Sea** — **First-ever use of recon seaplanes with battlefleet at sea**: Sopwith Baby seaplanes from HMS *Campania* observe movements of 'hostile' sqn in British Grand Fleet exercises.		
Cameroons — 200 Germans capture Allied food convoy. Dobell cables War Office that sickness & rainy season will preclude large ops till Nov, suggests starving out Germans. War Office agrees (15). Allies withdraw 12 miles to Wumbiagas, repel Germans from there and So Dibanga (14-15).			Britain informs Germany via US Ambassador U-boat PoWs now treated as ordinary ones. **Neutrals : USA** — By now film *Guarding Old Glory* released.	
			Neutrals : Greece — Venizelists win Gen Election.	
SW Africa — Botha's final advance N begins, occupies Omaruru (20, detaches 2 mtd bdes to cut off Germans 27, *see* 1 July).				
		Germany — Karlsruhe factories bombed by 23 Voisins of *GB1* (130 bombs, 84 civ cas). **W Front** — French airships *Adjt Vincenot* & *Cmndt Coutelle* fly 3 night missions v rail targets (15/16, 18/19 & 19/20). **Britain** — *L10* drops 59 bombs on Tyneside (night 15/16, record 90 civ cas to date).	Evasive Bulgar reply to Allied 29 May offer. **Secret War** — French decrypts of German Navy radio signals help arrest of 7 agents in British ports in 2 weeks.	**Germany** — The 24 military region COs sent guidelines on worker exemptions & dispute mediation.
Cameroons — Harrassed Allies withdraw to R Ngwe (-18) but clear main road of Germans by 26 (301 Allied cas & 600+ sick since 25 May).			**Occupied Belgium** — Tax & property seizure imposed on all Belgians not returning by 1 Mar (*see* 26 July).	**Britain** — **Lloyd George takes oath as Munitions Minister**. **Russia** — Odessa gendarmerie chief reports 200 Latvian Bolsheviks have infiltrated Army as volunteers.

JUNE 1915	WESTERN FRONT 1	EASTERN FRONT 2	SOUTHERN FRONTS 3	TURKISH FRONTS 4
Wed 16 contd	Legion has 645 cas), but cannot be supported (-17) as flanking corps fail v fierce resistance. **Vosges** — Limited French advance in Fecht Valley.			
Thu 17	**Artois** — Fond De Buval (N of Arras) captured by French. **Alsace** — Germans burn & evacuate Metzeral (*see* 19).	STAVKA Conference at Kholm, armies 500,000 under strength, sanctions fighting retreat. Russians announce 120,000 enemy losses on Dniester in last month, claim 40,000 PoWs (18).	Italian 3rd Div captures Hill 383 on R Isonzo after attacks since 10, but 2093 cas.	
Fri 18	**Artois — Second Battle of Artois ends** at Foch's bidding, 25 sq miles 'liberated' (official date but heavy clashes continue, French XXI Corps losses 18,000 by 20 June).			
Sat 19	**Artois** — French gains nr Souchez (& 28). **Alsace** — French enter Metzeral & bombard Munster (*see* 21).	**Galicia** — Mackensen attacks Brusilov's Grodek line along 40 miles and forces retreat. Mackensen takes Zolkiew & Rawaruska (20).		
Sun 20	**Meuse-Argonne** — German Crown Prince launches attack which leads to costly actions until 14 July. French First Army cas since 1 May: 16,200. **Paris** — Terrier to Lyautey (Morocco) 'People are blaming the Generalissimo [Joffre] for waiting too long, and for remaining himself too far from the Front'. Pétain made C-in-C Second Army (*see* 29), Fayolle takes over XXXIII Corps.			Armenians & Cossacks take Sevan on L Van & Sorp (25): 4000 cav reach N side of lake (26).
Mon 21	**Artois** — Unsuccessful German counter-attacks N of Arras. **Alsace** — French advance on Sondernach, take it (22) & repulse several counter-attacks (27).			**Gallipoli : Helles** — Third French Battle of Kereves Dere/ Turk Battle of Hill 83: French (77 guns fire 31,400 shells) secure Haricot Redoubt for 2500 cas causing 6000+ Turk loss.
Tue 22	**Meuse** — French recover recently lost positions on Meuse heights, repel German counter-attacks (24-27). **Vosges** — Hill 627 nr Ban de Sapt falls to Germans.	AUSTRIAN SECOND ARMY RETAKES LEMBERG: Mackensen made FM.	**Trentino** — Italians repel Austrians at Freikofel.	
Wed 23		Col Knox cables London that lack of rifles makes Russian offensive impossible for 8 months.	FIRST MAIN BATTLE OF THE ISONZO (CASTELNUOVO) (-5 July) begins with a week's Italian arty bombardment (*see* 30): 75 Italian bns & 530 guns v 40 Austrian bns & 242 guns. Attacks on Podgora, Oslavice & Peuma fail (-26), as does assault on the Sabotino (29-30).	
Thu 24	Joffre & FM French agree at Chantilly on W Front primacy, reject passive defence as unfair to Allies, & plan major offensive for Aug (*see* 6 July).			
Fri 25				

AFRICAN OPERATIONS 5	SEA WAR 6	AIR WAR 7	INTERNATIONAL EVENTS 8	HOME FRONTS 9
			Neutrals : USA — League to Enforce Peace organized.	**Turkey** — Djevdet Bey massacres Armenian Nestorian & Jacobite Christians at Sirt, S of Bitlis, whose 15,000 Armenians he murders (-25). **Britain** — Food Home Production Ctees established. Royal Society makes Nov 1914 advisory science council into War Ctee (150 staff), gas and trench warfare emphasis.
E Tripolitania — Tarhuna's 3 Italian bns wiped out in breakout attempt 40 miles S of Tripoli; 2 relief cols foiled (*see* 5 July).	**Adriatic** — Austrian sqn shells Fano.			**Britain** — 2 Glasgow iron ore merchants jailed for trading with Krupps.
RN Naval Africa Expedition sails for Cape Town (*see* 2 July).			Boulogne Conference of Lloyd George and A Thomas, French junior War Minister. German Socialist manifesto calls war no longer defensive, cannot be supported (*see* 20 Dec).	
	N Sea — *U39* torpedoes cruiser *Roxburgh* (in dock till Apr 1916,*see* 12 Feb 1918).			
				S Africa — De Wet found guilty of treason (6 yrs prison + £2000 fine).
SE Cameroons — 400 Franco-Belgians occupy Assobam & Lomie (24). **L Victoria** — Brig-Gen Stewart's 1600 British in 7 steamers (240-mile voyage) raid, capture & loot port Bukoba, destroy radio stn (only Berlin link) & fort, take 1 gun (-23).			Russia asks Rumania price of intervention (evasive reply 30). Turkey cedes Thracian border strip to Bulgaria. *La Liberté* papal interview causes Allied fury when Pope allegedly equates *Lusitania* sinking with blockade suffering. **Neutrals : USA** — Broadway musical *The Ziegfeld Follies* opens.	Swinton's memo 'The Necessity for Machine Gun Destroyers' sent to War Office who send spec to Landships Ctee (1 July).
E Africa — **British Voi-Maktau railway completed** (& water pipeline) despite German sabotage (14).	**N Sea** — **First Q-ship success:** *U40* torpedoed & sunk off Aberdeen by British submarine *C26*, towed in action by decoy trawler Q-ship *Taranaki* (*see* 20 July).			**Britain** — German spy Karl Muller shot at the Tower. Prince of Wales' 18th birthday.
			Conciliatory British memo to US on neutral trade. **Neutrals : USA** — 70,000 at National German-American rally, Madison Sq Gdns, NY.	**Britain** — War Munition Volunteer Scheme begins, 6-month posting in any firm chosen by Ministry.
	Dardanelles — With balloon spotting, battleship *Lord Nelson* (55 shells) again sets Chanak	**W Front** — French aircraft bomb Douai rail stn.		Kitchener asks Lloyd George's Parlt Sec Dr Addison to run Trench Warfare Dept.

JUNE 1915	WESTERN FRONT 1	EASTERN FRONT 2	SOUTHERN FRONTS 3	TURKISH FRONTS 4
Fri 25 contd				
Sat 26	Asquith discusses desirability of replacing FM French with Haig (*see* 14 July).	**Galicia** — Lechitski repulses German attacks on Bukaczowce-Halicz front in E but retreats to R Gnila Lipa while *Südarmee* occupies Halicz and Mackensen advances to R Bug (-27).		
Sun 27			**Serbia** — Serbs capture Danube island of Michaiska (*see* 4 July). **Isonzo** — Italian Third Army has pushed Austrians up slopes S of Mt San Michele (900 ft) & gained bridgehead for assault on Carso Plateau.	**Mesopotamia** — Gorringe's c3000 men and 4 RN gunboats anchor in Euphrates 45 miles W of Qurna for advance on Nasiriya as ordered by India (21) but vetoed by Whitehall (14).
Mon 28				**Gallipoli** — British gain half a mile on Gully Spur for 3800 cas and repel Turk counter-attacks (16,000 cas -5 July). **Mesopotamia** — Nixon put i/c Bushire, Persia.
Tue 29	Pétain memo to GQG : 'The present war...of attrition ...will belong...to the side which possesses the last man', urges only decentralised attacks & ample reserves (*see* 1 Nov).	Mackensen advances between Vistula and Bug, reaches Tomaszow (Poland, 30).		**Anzac** — Last serious Turk attack fails.
Wed 30	**Argonne** — German attacks at Bagatelle: Lt Rommel's coy of 124th Inf Regt to the fore with heavy mortar support. **Aisne** — (June) 2 French 8th Inf Regt soldiers first to be killed by German elecrified wire defences in Bois de la Mine nr Berry-au-Bac, both sides use on limited sectors.	**Galicia** — *Südarmee* crosses Gnila-Lipa. Germans claim 150,650 PoWs in June.	**Isonzo** — **Main Italian inf assault begins** along 21-mile front but only gains, for fearful losses, a small bridgehead E of the river at Sagrado (*see* 5 July).	**Gallipoli : Helles** — Gen Bailloud replaces Gen Gouraud (wound costs arm).
Thu 1 July 1915	**French Army peak mobilized strength** 4,978,000 plus 152,000 released to industry & agriculture but recallable. (July) First 180,000 French steel helmets delivered (prod reaches 55,000 pd in Aug). **Flanders** — Prussian Guard Cav Div in transit to Poland.	Russian losses now 3.8m (*see* 1 Nov). (July) German cavalry sword officially withdrawn, lance becomes sole shock weapon (most units in E). **Poland** — Mackensen occupies Zamosc fortress in S. Austrian Fourth Army loses Second Battle of Krasnik (-9). Russians by now forming Thirteenth Army (HQ Kovel). **Galicia** — *Südarmee* crosses Gnila Lipa, reaches Zlota Lipa (4) but repulsed there (9-11, trench warfare -27 Aug). Bavarian Count Bothmer replaces Linsingen as C-in-C (6, latter goes to new *Bugarmee*).	(July) 58 yr-old Socialist deputy Leonida Bissolati joins 4th *Alpini* as vol sgt, twice w, serves till June 1916 appointment as minister. **Trentino** — 15 Italian attacks in the Dolomites repulsed (-20) despite 3:1 advantage.	**Gallipoli** — Birdwood suggests germ of Suvla Bay landing (*see* 11).
Fri 2	**Argonne** — Germans advance nr Four De Paris, but repulsed nr Blanleuil.	At Posen **Kaiser backs Falkenhayn v Hindenburg & Ludendorff for Polish salient limited encirclement** ie as far as Brest-Litovsk.	**Isonzo** — 2 Italian divs attack Carso Plateau taking 400 PoWs.	**Persia** — British begin E cordon to stop German parties reaching Aghanistan. 120 Cossacks enter from Meshed (16) and engage one German party (30).
Sat 3	**Flanders** — German raid on			

AFRICAN OPERATIONS 5	SEA WAR 6	AIR WAR 7	INTERNATIONAL EVENTS 8	HOME FRONTS 9
	alight.			**Russia** — War Minister Gen **Sukhomlinov resigns** (jailed for suspected corruption), Gen Polivanov succeeds. **Germany** — Socialist paper *Vorwärts* suppressed for publishing peace call.
Cameroons — British take German Ft Koncha.	**Baltic** — Battlecruiser *Izmail* launched at Petrograd, first of 4, never completed. **Aegean** — Destroyer HMS *Hussar* shells Asia Minor coast opposite Chios. **Adriatic** — *UC12* first German U-boat of Pola half-flotilla based at Cattaro (*see* 16 Sept).	**Germany** — French pilot Gilbert tries to bomb Zeppelin works at Friedrichshafen, but is interned on landing in Switzerland (escapes 1916).		**France** — Orphans Flag Day. **Russia** — Tsarina to Tsar: 'Be more autocratic, my very own sweetheart'.
N Cameroons — c200 Nigerians from Garua capture Ngaundere (-29), 140 miles S. **Rhodesia** — Anglo-Belgian Ft Saisi, a mile inside border, repels Germans (*see* 25 Jul).	**Baltic** — German landing attempt at Windau (Courland) covered by old battleships, 4 cruisers & torpedo vessels ended by Russian destroyers who drive off ships (*see* 2 July).			**Secret War** — Churchill & Lloyd George watch Killen-Strait barbed-wire cutter tractor, Wormwood Scrubs, London. They also see Stokes mortar demo there (30), Lloyd George agrees to urge prod of 1000 thanks to Lt FA Sutton (lost right arm at Gallipoli 22 May, *see* 12 Aug).
		Gallipoli — British give up Cape Helles airfield except for emergency landings.	Austria protests to US v munition exports to Allies, urges food embargo if Central Powers' legal trade not allowed (*see* 12 Aug).	**Britain** — PM & Bonar Law Guildhall speeches on need to economize. 10 VCs awarded. Exchanged wounded PoWs arrive home.
Cameroons — British main force totals 2747 + 723 sick. 9 Allied warships on blockade, in SE 470 French occupy Ngangela.	**Adriatic** — 4 Italian armoured cruisers transferred N to Venice to support Army (*see* 7 July). (June) U-boats sink new record of 29 British merchant ships (76,497t with 78 lives) & 58 fishing vessels (17 lives lost), **worst month of war for British fishing fleet** (36 more sunk in both July & Aug). Total U-boat score 114 ships worth 115,291t.		Canadian PM sails for England. US exports to Germany in year ended only $28m v $344m (1913/14). Exports to Britain $911m v $594m. British munitions credit deficit with US almost $1bn (*see* 28 Sept).	
SW Africa — Col Brits' mtd bde reaches Otavi rail jctn (SA infantry arr 4), Germans retreat 10 miles N.	First trials of British depth charges (*see* June 1916). **N Sea** — (July) Henderson stabilizing gun director fitted to battleship *Centurion* (the one ship so equipped at Jutland). **Med** — German U-boat Half-Flotilla, Pola, formed (*see* 4). **Channel** — British Leyland liner *Armenian* torpedoed off Cornwall (sister *Iberian* 30). (July) **Adriatic** — First (of 7) Italian Q-ship commissioned, *Gallinara* (*see* 22 Nov).	**W Front** — (July) 2/Lt Bishop transfers to RFC from Cdn Mtd Rifles, starts as No 21 Sqn observer (*see* 25 Mar 1917). **Gallipoli** — (July) Turco-German air activity becomes noticeable with av of 8 aircraft in use (only 4 before), all but 2 German pilots with Turk observers.		**Turkey** — Austrian Ambassador tells Talaat Bey mass deportations 'seemed hardly justified'. Talaat orders Islamized Armenians sent S as well (*see* 7, 10, 12). **France** — Under Secretaries of War for Supply & Health appointed.
RN L Tanganyika Flotilla arrives at Cape Town for rail move to Belgian Congo, reaches Elizabethville (26, *see* 5 Aug).	**Baltic** — In fogbound action 4 Russian cruisers (*Rurik* hit) drive German minelayer *Albatros* onto E coast of Gotland (Sweden) and damage cruisers *Roon* & *Augsburg* while RN submarine *E9* (Horton) torpedoes cruiser *Prinz Adalbert* in Gulf of Danzig (*see* 23 Oct). **N Sea** — *UC2* blows up on own mines off Yarmouth. **Aegean** — RN repair ship *Reliance* mutiny at Mudros soon suppressed.		**Neutrals : USA** — Bomb destroys Senate reception room, planted by German Cornell University tutor who also shoots & wounds banker and British ally W Pierpont Morgan (3), committing suicide in jail (6).	**Britain** — **Munitions of War Act passed** and £250m War Loan Act; 46,000 women munition workers enrolled in 1st week. Munitions Tribunals set up (12).
	N Sea — Another Harwich		**Neutrals : Haiti** — 2000 US	Armenian Ctee of National

JULY 1915	WESTERN FRONT 1	EASTERN FRONT 2	SOUTHERN FRONTS 3	TURKISH FRONTS 4
Sat 3 contd	advanced trenches on Verlorenhoek rd (Ypres). **Meuse** — German attacks on Calonne trench, Meuse heights.			
Sun 4	**Argonne** — Crown Prince's attack diminishing, but captures La Fille Morte mill (7, *see* 13).		**Albania** — Serb punitive expedition enters Durazzo, but evacuates at Italian request (17, *see* 7).	**Aden** — 6000 Turks & Yemenis storm Lahej (-5) 20 miles NNW of Aden; Sultan mortally wounded. 1000 British late, forced back to Aden (-7, *see* 21).
Mon 5	**Artois** — French poet & writer Jean-Marc Bernard k, aged 33, by shell taking rations up to front line at Souchez (*see* 7).	Russian counter-offensive halts Mackensen's advance on Lublin-Kholm.	**Isonzo** — Italian Second & Third Armies attack from 1800 on whole line from Podgora to Doberdo Plateau (Carso) with 6:1 superiority, but gain scarcely a mile although Austrian bns reduced to ⅓ strength on vital Carso sector. Austrian 4th & 5th Mtn Bdes eject *Re* & *Casale* Bdes from Heights 205 & 240 overlooking Gorizia where Italians lose 4000 men. Italian losses 14,947 (1500 PoWs); Austrian 9948. **Secret War** — Austrians first read Italian red cipher (acquired before war), but key changed (20, *see* 12 Aug).	**Gallipoli: Helles** — British repulse Turks. Dardanelles Ctee decides to send 2 more divs, Kitchener says war over as soon as Peninsula captured. **Mesopotamia** — Gorringe's 1719 men (later 4600, 26 guns, 1 plane) attack towards Nasiriya, resume ops 6 miles S (14), beats Turk 35th Div (24) inflicting 2000+ cas & taking 15 guns and occupies (25).
Tue 6	Entire BEF now equipped with sack-like 'Hypo Helmet', a crude counter-measure against tear gas (T-Stoff) shells. **Flanders** — Kitchener visits the front (-8). British storm trenches between Boesinghe & Ypres. **Meuse** — Slight German gains at Vaux Féry nr St Mihiel.	**Poland** — German Ninth Army gas attack (1450 cas) on R Bzura fails (*see* 6 Aug).	**Isonzo** — 8 Austrian divs & 350 guns face 18 Italian divs with 700 guns (*see* 18) but morale of former boosted by defensive success.	
Wed 7	Joffre tells Allied conference at Chantilly that simultaneous attack on all 4 fronts best strategy. **Artois** — French advance at Souchez, but Germans recover trenches there (8), and French fall back S of it (11).	**Poland** — Russian Guard Corps (40,000 men & 128 guns) detrains at Kholm after 11-day transfer from Lomja.	Allied Chantilly Military Conference vainly urges Serbia to attack in support of Italy.	
Thu 8	**Vosges** — French recapture Hill 627 also trenches between Fey-en-Haye & Bois-le-Prêtre.		**Trentino** — Italians take Monticello; then Malga Sarta & Costa Bella (9).	**Gallipoli** — Liman refuses to return to Constantinople, postpones Enver-suggested handover to Goltz (26).
Fri 9				**Gallipoli** — Turk Second Army C-in-C Wehib Pasha takes over Helles sector, is refused armistice to bury dead.
Sat 10				**Armenia** — **Battle of Malazgirt** (-26): Oganovski's advance (-16) reversed by Abdul Kerim's 5-div counter-attack (20-26) and Malazgirt evacuated.
Sun 11	**Joffre decides main autumn offensive will be in Champagne** with secondary one in Artois. **Meuse** — German attacks on Frenes nr St Mihiel.		Italians make gains in Carnic Alps & repulse Austrians (28).	**Gallipoli** — IX Corps GOC Stopford arrives at Mudros, told Suvla plan (22), but it is revised (26).

AFRICAN OPERATIONS 5	SEA WAR 6	AIR WAR 7	INTERNATIONAL EVENTS 8	HOME FRONTS 9
	Force abortive seaplane raid (7 Zeppelins shadow). **Dardanelles** — *E14* returns after 24 days in Sea of Marmora (*see* 17).		Marines begin landing to restore order (-4 Aug, *see* 16 Sept).	Defence (Alexandria) urge Gen Maxwell to invade Cilicia from Cyprus but Foreign Office objects. **Turkey** — 1st paper money issue (7 in all).
SW Africa — Col Myburgh's mtd bde surprises & takes Tsumeb (farthest N rail stn) & 600 PoWs. Armistice at Otavifontein.	**Dardanelles** — *U21* sinks French ammunition liner *Carthage* (6 die) off Cape Helles, but *U21* docked damaged at Constantinople (16); 2 more large U-boats (*U34* & *U35*,*see* 23 Aug) to be sent from Baltic (20). **E Atlantic** — HM Horse Transport *Anglo-Californian* (Capt F Parslow, posthumous VC, aged 60) saves herself from U-boat 90 miles SW of Queenstown by 3-hr refusal to stop & summoning 2 destroyers.	**Britain** — German naval pilot Sub-Lt Pluschow (the 'Tsingtao Pilot') escapes with comrade (swiftly recaptured) from Donington Hall, Derbyshire. Pluschow reaches Germany via Holland, only German PoW to do so.		
Tripolitania — **All Italian inland garrisons ordered to Homs & Tripoli on coast** (-5 Aug); Senussi have 30,000 rifles & 19 guns (*see* 12 & 15).			**Neutrals : USA** — American peace socialist Jane Addams tells Carnegie Hall meeting that troops in Europe doped with drink to fight.	**Britain** — Fisher made Chairman of Inventions Board. Vicar's letter to *The Times* urges 'compulsory closing of the picture palaces...more serious menace...now than even drink'.
Botha gives Gov Seitz draft surrender terms & 2am, 9th deadline.	**E Africa** — *Severn* & *Mersey* (hit twice, 3k) fire 635 rnds at *Königsberg* (hit 6 times) in 8-hr action (*see* 11).		Anglo-French Calais Conference (-7).	
	Adriatic — Italian cruiser *Amalfi* sunk off Venice by *UB14* (Heimburg) masquerading as Austrian *U26* (*see* 18).			**Turkey** — Trebizond's 1000 Armenian houses empty, only 100/17,000 survive massacres (-23) involving 15,000 troops. **Italy** — Any factory may be taken for munitions.
SW Africa — Col Brits takes Namutoni, 40 miles NW of Tsumeb, releases officer PoWs.			German reply to 2nd US *Lusitania* note fails to give pledges asked (*see* 21).	**Canada** — CEF expanded to 150,000; 140,000 recruits by 26.
GERMAN SW AFRICA SURRENDERS. Officers retain swords and paroled, NCOs & men interned. Paroled reservists allowed back to farms. S Africa annexes (15).			**Neutrals : USA** — German radio stn at Sayville, Long I taken over. Anglo-Portugese Commercial Treaty ratified at Lisbon.	Kitchener Guildhall appeal for more recruits. By July 2m volunteers, 260 hutted camps house 850,000 & 150,000 horses. **Egypt** — Bomb misses Sultan.
	Black Sea — Russian submarine *Kreb* lays mines at Bosphorus mouth.			Turks massacre Armenians from c100 villages nr Mush. **France** — Minimum Wage Act.
	E Africa — ***Königsberg* disabled** in Rufiji R after 90-min shelling by British monitors *Mersey* & *Severn* with Farman spotter plane assistance (crashed). *Königsberg* scuttled	**E Africa** — 2 RNAS floatplanes spot for 2 British monitors in elimination of raider *Königsberg*, Rufiji Delta (*see* SEA WAR). **Italy** — Austrians bomb Venice for 4th time.	**Neutrals : USA** — Sec of State Lansing memo, 'Germany must not be allowed to win this war, or to break even ....'.	

JULY 1915	WESTERN FRONT 1	EASTERN FRONT 2	SOUTHERN FRONTS 3	TURKISH FRONTS 4
Sun 11 contd				
Mon 12	**Artois** — Germans counter-attack in the 'Labyrinth'. FM French observes ground for BEF offensive around Loos, decides it is unfavourable (20) but bows to Joffre's view (28, *see* 23 Aug).			**Gallipoli : Helles** — 12,748 Allies take a few trenches & 600 prisoners (-13) for 3900 cas; British 155th Bde refuses to advance a 2nd time. Gen Masnou of French 1st Div mortally wounded.
Tue 13	**Argonne** — Germans (incl gas shell) make transient gains at Vienne-le-Château & La Fille Morte, but French Third Army cas since 20 June 32,395 incl 4000 PoWs (*see* 22). **Flanders** — **BEF Third Army** (HQ St Omer) **formed** under Gen Monro with 6 divs & Indian Cav Corps, relieves French Second Army of 15-mile sector from Somme to Hébuterne.	**Poland** — **Gallwitz's Twelfth Army** (150,000, 12 divs, 1000+ guns) **attacks towards Narew on 25-mile front**. By 17 has gained 5 miles, Przasnysz (14) and inflicted c70,000 cas. *Bugarmee* fights 5 local battles nr Sokal (-31). **Bukovina** — Austrians across Dniester but beaten (16).		
Wed 14	Haig discovers King has lost confidence in FM French (Monarch tells CoS Robertson that he should be replaced 1). **Flanders** — Belgians repulse attack along Yser Canal. **Artois** — French storm some trenches S of Souchez. (German attacks there repelled 18.)		**Montenegro** — Montenegrins repulse Austrian attack at Grahovo (*see* 16 Aug).	
Thu 15	(c) BEF has 7 coys of special gas troops. **Argonne** — French repulse German attack.	**Baltic Provinces** — *Niemen-narmee* strikes towards Riga, takes Windau (18) & Shavli (23) but repulsed at Shlok on G of Riga (26) until it crosses R Aa (31). **Poland** — Battles of Sokal and Krasnostav (-24): Mackensen attacks Russian Third Army.		
Fri 16	**Aisne** — German attack nr Fontenoy. **Lorraine** — German attack in Parroy Forest.	**Poland** — Austrian first Army crosses R Bug.		
Sat 17		Russian Corps report: 'Super-human efforts were required to keep the men in the trenches'.		**Gallipoli : Helles** — GOC VIII Corps Hunter-Weston invalided out with sunstroke (Davies succeeds).
Sun 18		**Poland** — **General Russian retreat** after Russian Guard fights Prussian Guard for 1st time, former's losses 9438 (-28 CO sacked), Mackensen takes Krasnostav & 15,000 PoWs. Woyrsch re-occupies Radom.	**Second Battle of the Isonzo** (-3 Aug): Italian Second & Third Armies (260 bns v 129 Austrian bns with 462 guns) again attack after shorter, better barrage, taking 4000 PoWs by 22, but same obstacles of insufficient heavy arty & shells against wired defences in depth. **Trentino** — Italian 18th Div attacks in Dolomites towards Fedajp Pass without success.	
Mon 19	Foch note to *GQG* urges 'precise and defined objectives' for future attacks (see 23 Aug). **Flanders** — British mine redoubt at Hooge & occupy it,	STAVKA tells Alexeiev: 'You can evacuate Warsaw, if you feel you must'. **Baltic Provinces** — Special commission arrives in Riga to remove		

AFRICAN OPERATIONS 5	SEA WAR 6	AIR WAR 7	INTERNATIONAL EVENTS 8	HOME FRONTS 9
	by crew; German divers salvage her 10 4.1-in guns later for use ashore. **Adriatic** — Italians occupy Pelagosa I (*see* 28) & install 90-man garrison & 2 3-in guns, as French scout nearby Lagosta I (12), but Italian Govt vetoes occupation (27).			
Tripolitania — Italian Ghadames garrison takes refuge in Algeria (*see* 11 Aug).	**Dardanelles** — Liner *Aquitania* brings troops to Mudros. New monitor *Abercrombie* (twin 14-in guns, 10-ft draught) arrives, 3 sisters follow. Soon firing at Turk Asia btys from Tenedos (*see* 6 Aug).			**Turkey** — Wangenheim vainly demands Reshid Bey's punishment for Diyarbekir's Bishop & Christians' murder.
	Adriatic — Austrian destroyer *Tatra* shells Pelagosa I radio stn but deterred by French submarine *Fresnel* (bombed by seaplane).	**W Front** — 35 French aircraft drop 171 bombs on Vigneulles rail jctn nr Metz, fires started.		
E Africa — Action at Mbuyuni Hill (l0 miles E of Taveta): Brig-Gen Malleson's 1223 British (211 cas) bungle attack on 714 Germans (35 cas) and retreat.				**Britain** — **National Registration Act for citizens 15-65** (*see* 15 Aug). Dominion PM (Borden of Canada) first attends Cabinet.
Gen Ameglio made Gov of Tripolitania as well as Cyrenaica (see 8 Aug 1918).		**W Front** — (c) About 12 Fokker EIs in use (*see* 1 Aug).		200,000 Welsh miners' illegal strike for pay (-20) settled by Lloyd George who deplores 'Business as usual' attitude (29). German spy Rosenthal hanged at Wandsworth Prison after MI5 gain info on methods. (2 German-Dutch spies shot at Tower 30.)
	3 US battleships transit Panama Canal.		Lloyd George & Delcassé agree on approach to Bulgaria, but Central Powers have already suggested intervention v Serbia (7).	**Italy** — Poet D'Annunzio made official war chronicler.
S & SE Cameroons — French occupy Bitam, capture Bertua (2), occupy Dume (25) and Abong Mabang (29).	**Sea of Marmara** — RN submarine *E7* shells Turk Berlin-Baghdad railway in Gulf of Ismid & blocks it (*see* 4 Aug).		**Central Powers' secret treaty with Bulgaria**, latter declares continued neutrality but receives 600 sq miles of frontier territory from Turkey (22). Bulgar PM says no intention of joining Central Powers or attacking Serbia (31).	Women's 'Right to Serve' march in London.
	Adriatic — Italian cruiser *Giuseppe Garibaldi* sunk off Gravosa by Austrian submarine *U4* while bombarding Ragusa-Cattaro coast railway. **Black Sea** — *Breslau* mined on Russian mine, out of action for several months.			
N Cameroons — Allies occupy Tingere, repel 154 Germans (23).	**Adriatic** — German *UC13* reaches Pola by rail & is assembled as cargo submarine.	**W Front** — Guynemev's 1st victory (of 54) with gunner Guerder (w), Aviatik nr Soissons. Promoted sgt & given *Médaille Militaire*.	Anglo-Netherlands Overseas Trust Agreement.	**Britain** — Govt insurance v air & naval bombardment begins. Kent training scheme for leisured ladies to do weekend munitions work.

JULY 1915	WESTERN FRONT 1	EASTERN FRONT 2	SOUTHERN FRONTS 3	TURKISH FRONTS 4
Mon 19 contd	but 2 more attacks fail (22, German attack fails 24, *see* 30). **Meuse** — German attack SE of Les Eparges.			
Tue 20	**Alsace** — French advance toward Munster in Fecht Valley. **Flanders** — Canadian PM visits his troops (-27).	industry. Kövess' Austrians occupy Radom. Russian delaying counter-attack on Narew Line.	**Isonzo** — Italians capture Mt San Michele but 15 Austrian bns retake soon after dawn 22. Cadorna informs British Military Mission Chief Brig-Gen Radcliffe that he will attack for as long as no risk run; he has already replaced 27 generals.	**Gallipoli** — Kemal letter 'Really, we are living in hell'.
Wed 21		Conrad urges Burian to keep separate peace with Russia in view (& 6 Aug) but no Russian interest. **Poland** — Woyrsch besieges Ivangorod (-5 Aug) and crosses Vistula to N (28). 192 Terek Cossacks rout German inf regt in moonlight charge.		**Gallipoli** — NZ Sgt Pilling diary 'We...will be satisfied if we do our work and get back home alive'. **Aden** — 28th Indian Bde (arr 18) retakes Sheikh Othman wells 7 miles NNW & fortifies; Maj-Gen Younghusband replaces sacked Political Resident (16).
Thu 22	**Argonne** — French advance nr Bagatelle. **Joffre sacks Sarrail from Third Army** (*see* S FRONTS 5 Aug); Humbert replaces him for duration. **Alsace** — German counter-attack nr Metzeral.			
Fri 23		**Poland** — Gallwitz storms Rozan & Pultusk fortress bridgeheads & crosses Narew (-25), takes Goworowo (27) after violent Russian counter-attacks (26-30).	In Julian Alps Italians advance along Luznica Ridge & repel Austrian attacks (-24).	
Sat 24	**Vosges** — La Fontenelle-Laanois position stormed by French.	**Baltic Provinces** — Charge by 1600 men of Russian 1st Cav Div checks Germans S of Mitau after Siberian inf regt gives way.		Dardanelles Ctee refuses Churchill's plea to plan for possible Suvla failure.
Sun 25		Russians evacuate Riga & Warsaw factories.	Italian Third Army general assault with last res corps (XIII from Verona area).	
Mon 26	**Argonne** — German setback. **Alsace** — 'Second Battle of Munster': French advance on Lingenkopf (-27).	Russian Govt allows Lett (Latvian) rifle div of 50,000 to be formed.	**Isonzo** — Italians capture most of Mt Sei Busi (Carso) but impetus faltering.	
Tue 27	Germans shell Reims & Soissons.	STAVKA secret circular describes Bolshevik propaganda being hidden in gifts for troops.		
Wed 28	French adopt first gas mask (gas shell prod begun 1)		Italians attack in Cordevole valley (Venetian Alps) (-29).	
Thu 29	FM French diary on Paris views 'They think that we should organise much better against bad recruiting & strikes...complain that we don't have conscription'.	**Poland** — Battle of Biskupice: Mackensen cuts Lublin-Kholm railway, Russians evacuate both (30, 31) after II Siberian Corps broken and unhelped by Guard.		**Gallipoli** — British cas announced as 49,238.
Fri 30	**Flanders** — 6 German trench **flamethrowers used v BEF**; 1/2-mile of British 41st Bde (New	War Minister Gen Poplivanov tells Ministers 'Demoralization,	Italians shell Austrian forts around Cadore valley (Carnic Alps).	**Mesopotamia** — 80-mile British Tigris recce from Amara to Ali Garbi.

AFRICAN OPERATIONS 5	SEA WAR 6	AIR WAR 7	INTERNATIONAL EVENTS 8	HOME FRONTS 9
	N Sea — British submarine *C27* towed by Q-ship *Princess Louise* torpedoes & sinks *U23* (Schulthess).			**France** — Decree for evaluating war damages.
			Neutrals : USA — 3rd Wilson *Lusitania* note almost an ultimatum.	**Turkey** — 4000 Armenians nr Antioch repulse Turk troops (*see* 12 Sept). **Britain** — 843,000 married recruits now drawing separation allowances.
			Neutrals : USA — Ex-Pres Roosevelt denounces Americans as accessories after the fact to Germany's crimes in Belgium.	
Cameroons — Dobell cables War Office that dry season ops must be v Yaunde.	**Adriatic** — Austrian cruisers & destroyers shell Ortona, Termoli & Tremliti Is, repeated with aircraft (28) between Ancona-Pesaro railway & Fano (28).	**Austria** — Italian Caproni bombers bomb Innsbruck.	Britain defends blockade by referring to US in American Civil War. **Neutrals : Rumania** — PM Bratianu maintains ultimate policy to join Allies.	**Britain** — BMA forms Central Medical War Ctee. 1/4 of 25,000 doctors in uniform (*see* 15 Oct).
	Atlantic — Q-ship *Prince Charles* sinks *U36*.	**W Front** — **RFC suspends all bombing missions** except on GHQ direct orders due to lack of reliable bombsight (*see* 23 Sept).	US Secret Service find briefcase of German propaganda director on NY subway train (*see* 15 & 30 Aug).	
Rhodesia — Maj Gen Wahle's 800 Germans & 2 guns besiege Ft Sasi (462 Anglo-Belgians, -2 Aug), 350 Belgians fail to relieve 28, surrender summons rejected (31).	U-boat torpedoes US SS *Leelanaw*. Q-ships to be commissioned as naval tenders so as not to be pirates under Hague Convention.	**W Front** — Capt Hawker of No 6 Sqn RFC in Bristol Scout armed with Lewis gun on own 45° mounting defeats 3 German 2-seaters E of Ypres; first VC award for aircraft v aircraft combat (24 Aug). RFC issues 1st communiqué (intended to be twice weekly hereon).	HMG guarantees Mytilene (Lesbos) cession to Greece (from Turkey).	**Serbia** — Govt established at Nish. **Britain** — *Daily Mirror* pictures 3 Prussian officers 'loaded with golden and silver loot', actually Army steeple-chase 9 July 1914.
Uganda Railway sabotaged at 5 different points (-31).	**Adriatic** — French destroy Austrian U-boat supply stn at Lagosta I.		Anglo-US Standard Oil Co Agreement (with US tin importers 29). **Occupied Belgium** — Germans take over gas, water & electricity (*see* 5 Aug).	American novelist Henry James takes oath of allegiance as British citizen.
	N Sea — U-boat torpedoes 3 Danish schooners. **Dardan-elles** — French submarine *Mariotte* lost in Turk net defences.			Asquith announces losses (-18): Army 330,995; RN 9106. MI5 report discounts 'Stop-the-War-Ctee' recently formed by ILP leader CH Norman.
	Adriatic — 2 Austrian cruisers, 6 destroyers & torpedo boats (sailed from Sebenico) shell Italian-held Pelagosa I & land 108 troops (12 cas) who are repulsed for 2w (*see* 5 Aug).	**France** — Germans bomb St Omer & Nancy (29).		Lloyd George says 20,000 volunteer munition workers found and 26 munition plants to be built.
		W Front — Capt John Liddell of No 7 Sqn RFC lands shell-torn RE5 recon aircraft despite bad leg wound; awarded VC 23 Aug (dow 31).		
	Baltic — RN submarine *E1* (Laurence) sinks German minesweeper *Aachen* off Libau.	**Germany** — 45 French aircraft bomb Freiburg (Aviatik aircraft	Papal peace appeal letter to all belligerents. US protest v German spies' false passports.	**S Africa** — Botha lands at Cape Town to hero's welcome. **Turkey** — Cholera among

JULY 1915	WESTERN FRONT 1	EASTERN FRONT 2	SOUTHERN FRONTS 3	TURKISH FRONTS 4
Fri 30 contd	Army 14th Div, arrived France 18 June) trenches stormed by 126th Inf Regt (53rd Res Div) on Menin Rd (Hooge), No Man's Land 15 yds at narrowest (see 9 Aug).	surrender & desertion are assuming huge proportions'.		
Sat 31				**Gallipoli** — 200 Australians storm Turk trenches opposite Tasmania Post (-1 Aug): so far 600 1st Div Australians evacuated with dental disease & 80,000 Turk sick evacuated.
Sun 1 August 1915	**Flanders** — British counter-attack at Hooge. **Artois** — French repulse several attacks with grenades, then occupy trenches in sunken road between Ablain & Angres N of Bethune-Arras road. Mortar fire & grenades exchanged nr Souchez. (Aug) French inf first issued with trench knives. **Champagne** — In Perthes-Beauséjour sector, mining & counter-mining. **Argonne** — Mortars & grenades prepare several vain German inf assaults at Marie-Thérèse & St Hubert. **Meuse** — Between Les Eparges & the Calonne trench, 3 German attacks on Bois Haut positions, all repulsed by French arty & MG fire. German incendiary shells fall on Pont-à-Mousson.	**Baltic Provinces** — *Nieme-narmee* occupies evacuated Mitau but repulsed SW of there (7, 12, 16, see 19). **Poland** — Germans held on Blonie line, 15 miles W of Warsaw (-4). Gallwitz takes Ostrolenka on R Narew (3).	(Aug) **Falkenhayn decides to eliminate Serbia** (see 2). Serb Army ration strength 572,171. **Carnic Alps** — Austrian counter-attacks on Mt Medetta repulsed.	**Syria** — (Aug) Djemal hangs 11 Arab leaders after summary trial.
Mon 2	**Argonne** — German advance at Hill 213. Berlin communiqué: '... by a surprise bayonet attack we occupied several enemy trenches, capturing four officers, 142 men and one machine gun'. **Alsace** — Germans repulse attacks at the Lingenkopf & Barrenkopf. They explode mines under French positions at several points. **Champagne** — Pétain arrives to prepare Second Army for offensive.		**Isonzo** — Italian advance near Mt Sei Busi, but driven back on Polazzo plateau. **Secret War** — British Ambassador at Sofia informs Foreign Office that Bulgar Col Gancev has left for Berlin (see INT'L EVENTS 6 Sept).	**Armenia** — Abdul Kerim occupies Karakilise, but Yudenich has assembled Baratov's 22,000 men & 36 guns for counter-stroke (30 July) that begins to outflank Turk advance (4). **Gallipoli : Anzac** — Br 13th Div begins landing.
Tue 3	**Argonne** — French repulse German night attacks; German setback at Hill 213 (7).	**S Poland** — Austrian First Army cav enter Vladimir Volinski.	Second Battle of the Isonzo ends with Italian cas 41,866 (see 15).	
Wed 4	Canadian Minister of Militia & Defence in France (-14).	Russians abandon Blonie line & evacuate Ivangorod.	**Trentino** — Austrians destroy Lizzan fortress nr Rovereto. Italians occupy Col di Lana (Cordevole, Venetian Alps). Joffre agrees to send French mission to Salonika to assess its harbour & rail facilities (see 22 Sept).	**E Persia** — 300 Indian troops reach Seistan nr Afghanistan (see 19).
Thu 5	French strip frontier fortresses, especially Verdun (300 guns & 128,000 shells), of 2300 heavy guns (-4 Sept) & 1.6m shells to support autumn offensive.	GERMANS ENTER WARSAW. German Tenth Army attacks Kovno (-17) but repulsed (8 & 9, see 15). Austrian Fourth Army wins Battle of Lubartow (-8) N of Lublin.	Gen **Sarrail made C-in-C French Army of the Orient** ostensibly for Gallipoli but **possibly for Salonika** (see 28 Sept).	**Sarrail replaces Gouraud as French C-in-C Near East.** **Armenia** — Turks re-occupy Van; Russians retreat towards Dilman in Persia.
Fri 6		**Poland** — German gas attack at Osovyets fails due to Russians lighting fires.		**Gallipoli** — BRITISH SUVLA BAY LANDINGS BEGIN at 2130 (11th Div) after 1420

AFRICAN OPERATIONS 5	SEA WAR 6	AIR WAR 7	INTERNATIONAL EVENTS 8	HOME FRONTS 9
			Neutrals: Holland — £7.5m naval programme voted for 2 cruisers, 4 submarines and 6 aircraft.	troops at Constantinople.
	Black Sea — Russians have now sunk c100 Turk colliers drastically reducing coal supplies to Constantinople & industry. (July) U-boats sink 86 ships worth 98,005t.	factory, & 31) & Pechelbronn. **Italian Front** — Italian seaplanes bomb Riva & Garda on L Garda.	French publication on German outrages at Roubaix.	**Russia** — (July) Shell production nearly 900,000, double early 1915 months but only 2 rifles for every 5 recruits. Cost of living up 50%.
E Africa — (Aug) Lettow promoted colonel. He has 2217 whites under arms incl c900 merchant & imperial Navy sailors.	British submarines blow up Galata bridge, Constantinople.	**W Front** — 'FOKKER SCOURGE' BEGINS: Immelmann scores first Fokker EI victory, over Douai, with his first MG burst in anger, wounds British BE2c pilot (1 of 9 raiding airfield) forcing him to land. Immelmann awarded Iron Cross 1st class. (Aug) Lt-Col Brooke-Popham (RFC GSO 1) calls for expansion in prescient memo 'If the enemy brings troops over from the Eastern Front and resumes his offensive...Then will commence the real struggle for air supremacy where numbers will be one of the essentials for success', on which advice War Office orders revolutionary light alloy Hispano-Suiza V8 aero engine from France. Adm Jellicoe demands 'aeroplane carriers' for British Grand Fleet.	Kaiser & Tsar each issue first anniversary war manifestos. **Secret War** — (Aug) Britain obtains c32,000 binoculars from Germany for rubber via Swiss intermediary (*see* 19).	**Britain** — RFP up 2% to 34%. (Aug) Manchester Univ release Zionist chemist Dr Weizmann to continue his cordite solvents research for Admiralty (-May 1918, patented 9 Feb 1916). **France** — Dept War Charities Flag Day. **Russia** — Re-sitting Duma votes 100% to win war, 35m roubles for refugees (5), and to investigate munition abuses (10).
E Africa — Germans raise Siege of Saisi (-3). Gen Tighe cables War Office with 20,000 estimate of German strength (*see* 14).	**Black Sea** — Russians sink 450 sailing vessels.		US receives German note on *William P Frye*, accepts compensation (10). Third French atrocities report.	**Canada** — £200,000 subscribed for MGs.
	Aegean — French battleships shell Smyrna plus Spelia & Scanlanova opp Samos (4) as diversion before Suvla Bay landings.		Allies reply to Bulgar 14 June note with undefined offer. Allied ultimatum to Greece offers Smyrna as compensation. Italy demands free Italian departure from Anatolia (consuls in Turkey prepare to leave 9). **Berlin learns of Tsar's 3rd and clinching refusal of its peace overtures.**	**Britain** — Treasury appeals for banknotes use, not gold. Army Council officially employ Women's Legion Cookery Section.
	N Sea — First Sea Lord visits Harwich Force (*see* 18). **Dardanelles** — *E7* caught in nets & mined (loss announced 17 Sept).		**Occupied Belgium** — German police arrest Nurse Edith Cavell in Brussels for helping 200+ Allied servicemen escape (*see* 12 Oct). Coalminers strike, are fired on (5). Penalties for refusing to work for Germans (14-15). **Neutrals: Rumania** — £4m military spending voted, 10 reservist classes mobilize (7), refuses to let German munitions pass to Turkey (10).	**Britain** — St Paul's Cathedral 1st war anniversary service. Losses: 381,982 (75,957 k).
RN L Tanganyika Flotilla reaches Funguvume railhead, Belgian Congo. Begins traction engine journey (15) but covers only 30 miles by 28 (*see* 28 Sept).	**Adriatic** — Austrian *U5* (Trapp) sinks Italian submarine *Nereide* off Pelagosa I. (Italians land 4 guns, 2 MGs & 30 more men 9, *see* 17.)	**Adriatic** — Italian airship captured at Pola.		
SW Africa — Rhodesians meet S Africans in Caprivi Strip (*see* 17 Sept).	**Dardanelles** — **Suvla Bay landings** supported by 6 cruisers, 10 monitors, 8	**E Front** — German airship *L5* damaged beyond repair by AA fire/forced landing. Zeppelin	Bulgaria secures new Central Powers 400m Fr loan	**Russia** — Council of the Empire opens. **Britain** — Munitions Ministry now i/c 345

AUGUST 1915	WESTERN FRONT 1	EASTERN FRONT 2	SOUTHERN FRONTS 3	TURKISH FRONTS 4
Fri 6 contd				Helles attack (-7) & Anzacs storm Lone Pine (1730). Battle of Sari Bair (-10): Anzac-Gurkha-Indian night advance halted 1000 yds from Chunuk Bair summit. **Armenia** — Turks hold Baratov at 'Gap of the Sword' Pass, but Mirgemir Pass night storming (7/8) forces Turk retreat after 16,000 cas (6000 PoWs) since 2. Cossacks re-occupy Karakilise.
Sat 7	**Alsace** — Germans repulsed at Lingenkopf Ridge.		**Trentino** — Italian guns reach Ercavallo Peak. Austrian night raid (8).	**Gallipoli : Suvla** — 20,000 British (10th Div joins 11th) ashore at wrong places in burning heat, short of water, no guns landed (-8). Chocolate & Green Hills taken at nightfall. 4 Anzac charges v The Nek fail.
Sun 8		**Poland** — Germans occupy Warsaw Praga suburb, Novo Georgievsk fortress cut off. Gallwitz fights Battle of Ostrov (-10), takes Lomja (9). Mackensen forces Russians E of R Veprj.		**Gallipoli : Suvla** — Stopford finally lands, Hamilton arrives 1800 to stir advance inland. **Anzac** — NZ Wellington Bn captures Chunuk Bair summit. **S Persia** — 300 British occupy Bushire on Gulf, take & demolish Dilbar fort & village (12-16), 26 miles away (*see* 9 Sept).
Mon 9	**Flanders** — 3rd Action of Hooge: 2 British 6th Div bdes (1800 cas) recapture trenches lost 30 July & make further gains N & W of Hooge. **Meuse** — German attack in Bois-le-Prêtre. Verdun fortified region created under Gen Herr (-26 Feb 1916).			**Gallipoli : Suvla** — Liman gives Kemal 12th Div: he stops British advance, overwhelming 32nd Bde. **Anzac** — 450 Gurkhas & British take Hill Q (2/Lt W Slim wounded) NE of Chunuk Bair where British relieve Kiwis. **Palestine** — Jerusalem-Beersheba railway opens.
Tue 10		**Poland** — Siege of Novo Georgievsk (Modlin) (-20) by Beseler, captor of Antwerp.	Italian Isonzo attacks & also advance in Ortler range (Upper Adige); 45th Inf Regt capture Cima Bois.	**Gallipoli : Anzac** — **Decisive Kemal counter-attack retakes Chunuk Bair**, the Farm & the Pinnacle, annihilating 2000 British. Gurkhas retire from Hill Q. **Suvla** — 54th Div lands joining 53rd (8-9).
Wed 11	**Argonne** — Unsuccessful German attacks at Marie-Thérèse & La Fontaine-aux-Charmes, more Argonne attacks fail (13).	**W Russia** — Dvinsk evacuated but Russians retake Kovarsk & Toviamy SSW (12).	Austrian *Neue Freie Presse* on Italian Front 'The enemy knows how to look death in the face...*Bersaglieri*... fought until the last man had fallen'.	
Thu 12		Alexeiev's NW Front evacuates Sokolov, Syedlets & Lukow in 15-mile retreat E of Warsaw.	Serbs shell Semlin & Panchevo in retaliation for Austrian bombardment of Belgrade. **Secret War: Italian Front — Austrians have solved 63 Italian messages since 5 July,** soon capture field radio instructions, 50-70 solutions pd.	**Gallipoli** — Lt Compton Mackenzie RND invalided out from GHQ with dysentery (12,968 Aug cases) to Athens (*see* INT'L EVENTS 1 Dec).

AFRICAN OPERATIONS 5	SEA WAR 6	AIR WAR 7	INTERNATIONAL EVENTS 8	HOME FRONTS 9
	destroyers (2 French), 2 kite-balloon vessels (-10): 10,000 troops land from 10 destroyers & 10 motor lighter landing craft (500 men each).	bombs Novi Minsk & Syedlets stns, causes cas to Russian NW Front HQ (night 6/7).		factories. War Women's League formed.
	N Sea — German minelayer *Meteor* lays 380 mines off Moray Firth, they sink British destroyer *Lynx* & blow bows off sloop *Lilac* (both 8), armed boarding steamer *Ramsey*. *Meteor* scuttles (9) when Harwich Force intercepts & rescues *Ramsey's* 43 survivors; 222 mines soon removed & 10-mile channel swept along shore. **Sea of Marmora** — *E14* on 2nd patrol sinks 5000t steamer (one of 22 vessels, returns from 23-day cruise 12) also, with *E11*, shells troops on Bulair-Karac road.		**Neutrals: USA** — Film *The Battle Cry of Peace* opens, shows 'enemy' in spiked helmets taking New York.	**Germany** — British PoW privileges removed due to British alleged treatment of German interned civilians. **France** — Dalbiez Law releases skilled workers back to industry & pursues shirkers.
S Cameroons — Action nr Njabesan: c300 British retreat down R Campo (-11), but reinforced resume ops (19-30).	**N Sea** — AMC HMS *India* torpedoed & sunk by *U22* off Norway. **Dardanelles** — Turk battleship *Heirredin Barbarossa* sunk by British submarine *E11* (Nasmith) S of Bulair which sinks 2 transports & 2 ammo ships (-15,*see* AIR WAR 12). *E14* torpedoes Turk steamer which beaches. **Baltic** — First German attempt (incl High Seas Fleet ships) attempt to penetrate Irben Straits (Riga) fails with 3 minesweepers & cruiser *Thetis* mined.	**Italian Front** — Italians bomb Monfalcone dockyard (d'Annunzio flies 1st op mission in 4-seaplane bombing raid on Trieste 7).	**German peace overtures to Russia via Denmark fail (see** 28), with Tsar's 3rd refusal (3).	**Britain** — Naval General Service medal instituted.
	Sea of Marmora — RN submarine *E2* shells Mudania rail stn (repeats with *E11* 28) & sinks steamer in Artaki Bay (21) on Asian shore.	**Britain** — 4 German Navy Zeppelins carry out scattered bombing on E Coast (night 9/10, 38 cas). *L12* damaged by Dover AA fire & forced to ditch off Zeebrugge; towed by torpedo boats into Ostend (despite RNAS bombing by 9 aircraft in succession, 1 lost) but destroyed by fire while being dismantled. **Germany** — Aviatiks shoot down 4 *GB4* aircraft (*see* 25) in Saarbrücken raid.	German Ambassador to Turkey protests v Armenian policy, Talaat Bey pleads 'excesses of subordinates' and (31) says question 'no long exists'. Bulgaria seeks Serb & Greek Macedonia plus Silistria.	**Britain** — *The Times* publishes Lawrence Binyon's poem 'For the Fallen'.
	Baltic — German fleet shells Riga but is driven off (as on 8,*see* 19). Russian battleship *Slava* engages German battleships *Nassau* and *Posen* (16).		Marquis Okuma, Japanese Foreign Minister, replaces PM Kato (resigned 9), Baron Ishii succeeds Okuma (12). **Neutrals: USA** — Plattsburg NY State military training camp for civilians opens.	**Turkey** — Armenian Anatolian College: 400 students deported, all male students murdered. **Germany** — Kaiser awards Tirpitz *Pour le Mérite* on 25th anniversary of Heligoland occupation.
Cameroons — 5th Indian Lt Inf (595) arrive at Duala. **S Tunisia** — French garrison again reinforced, totals 3000+, 13 guns & 6 MGs (*see* 13 Sept).	**Adriatic** — Austrian *U12* sunk (1 survivor) by mine off Venice. **Channel** — HM Special Service smack *GRE* sinks *UB4* off Sussex coast.			
	Palestine — French cruiser destroys munition factory nr Jaffa.	**Dardanelles** — **First ship torpedoed from air**: Short 184 floatplane (Edmonds) from carrier *Ben-my-chree* torpedoes beached 5000t Turk steamer in Sea of Marmara (2 other vessels torpedoed & 1 sunk, 17). **Britain** — 3-Zeppelin raid on E Suffolk & Essex (night 12/13, 30 civ cas).	US reply to Austria says munitions export not infringing neutrality.	**Secret War : Britain** — First tank begun: No 1 Lincoln or Tritton Machine called 'Little Willie', moves on tracks (8 Sept). Lloyd George orders 1000 Stokes mortars (first 20 delivered 6 Sept and sent to France 11 Sept, *see* 25 Sept).

AUGUST 1915	WESTERN FRONT 1	EASTERN FRONT 2	SOUTHERN FRONTS 3	TURKISH FRONTS 4
Fri 13		*Bugarmee* repulsed from Vlodava on Upper Bug after 3 days fighting but breaks through (19). Russian First Army has retreated 73 miles since 5.	Italians progress on the Carso and in Sexten Valley (Carnic Alps).	**Gallipoli** — 22,000 Allied sick & wounded evacuated to Egypt & Malta since 6.
Sat 14		**W Russia** — Russian sortie from Kovno repulsed (-15). **Bukovina** — Russians attack nr Czernowitz.		
Sun 15	**Flanders** — Shelling on Yser sector. **Champagne** — Gen Dittfurth warns his div to expect French offensive.	**Poland** — Germans take 3 towns W of Bug and 5000 PoWs. Col Knox passes 20 miles of refugees nr Bielsk.	**Italian Front** — Austrian Fifth Army losses since 15 July 46,640 (12,290 missing).	**Gallipoli : Suvla** — Turks repel British from Tekke Tepe foothills (also 12) in far N. De Lisle replaces Stopford as GOC IX Corps, Mahon GOC 10th Div resigns (-23).
Mon 16	Kitchener visits France to see Joffre, convinced Allied autumn offensive necessary due to Russian collapse (*see* 23). **Artois** — Falkenhayn warns German Sixth Army that Allied offensive imminent.	Russians retreat to Brest-Osovyets-Kovno line.	Montenegrin border success v Austrians (*see* 25).	
Tue 17		**Litzmann** (Tenth Army) **takes Kovno** with 1360 guns & 853,000 shells. Austro-Germans approach Brest-Litovsk as Russians being driven beyond Bug.	Italian advance on Bacher valley (Dolomites), Sta Maria & Lucia hills (Julian Alps).	**Gallipoli** — Hamilton asks Kitchener for 95,000 men, meanwhile 8500 more land at Suvla (-21).
Wed 18	**Vosges** — French storm trenches on Ablain-Angres road, but Germans retake (19). French storm trenches on Schratzmännele crest, take crest (22).		**Isonzo** — Italian progress towards Tolmino & in Upper Rienz (Julian Alps); attack on former (23).	
Thu 19		German G of Riga landing attempt at Pernau foiled (-21). **Poland** — Battle of Niemen (-8 Sept). Russian First Army absorbs Twelfth. Austro-German cav begin advance on Kovel.		Dardanelles Ctee meets (-20): Bonar Law says Hamilton 'was always nearly winning'. Churchill suggests separate peace with Turkey, Grey says Russians would never agree. **E Persia** — Niedermayer-Hentig party evade Russians & enter Afghanistan, reach Herat (24), leave for Kabul 7 Sept.

AFRICAN OPERATIONS 5	SEA WAR 6	AIR WAR 7	INTERNATIONAL EVENTS 8	HOME FRONTS 9
E Africa — Germans capture Indian OP at Kasigao.	**Aegean** — First British transport lost: *UB14* (Heimburg) (towed from Cattaro 16 July) sinks 11,117t *Royal Edward* nr Cos I, 865/1366 troops lost. **Adriatic** — French destroyer *Bisson* sinks Austrian *U3* NE of Brindisi.			**Britain** — 3 German naval officer PoWs escape from Dyffryn Aled Camp, N Wales, just fail to reach *U38* off Llandudno (14), recaptured.
E Africa — Tighe reports his non-African infantry as only 4000, situation serious (*see* SEA WAR 24).		**W Front** — 10 French aircraft bomb Spada valley, St Mihiel.		**NZ** — 6th Reinforcement sails.
	E Africa — Cruiser HMS *Hyacinth* shells Tanga. **Baltic** — Russian cruiser-minelayer *Ladoga* (ex-*Minin*) lost on *UC4* mine off Oro I. **N Sea** — RN submarines *E8* (Goodheart) & *E13* (Layton) sail for Baltic (*see* 18 & 4 Sept).	**Italy** — Austrian seaplane bombs Venice (Austrians bomb Brescia 25).	Allies offer conditional land gains to Serbia, talks at Nis (16-20). **Neutrals: USA** — *NY World* starts publishing German propaganda documents.	**Britain** — **National Register of all civilians aged 15-65.**
HMG accepts 1000 S Africans for defence of Rhodesia. **W Desert** — Pro-Senussi bedouin attack 2 RN submarine crews at Ras Lick anchorage.	**Irish Sea** — U-boat shells Cumberland coast at Whitehaven (no cas).		Greek Govt resigns after Chamber defeat, Venizelos again PM (*see* 21 Sept).	**Britain** — All-Party manifesto on National Service. Lloyd George tells War Policy Cabinet Ctee 'The longer you delay, the nearer ... disaster'. Kitchener defends voluntary service (24).
	Adriatic — 22 Austrian warships incl 2 cruisers, 4 destroyers & torpedo boat shell Pelagosa I destroying its fresh water cistern forcing Italian evacuation (18,*see* 11 Sept). Italian submarine *Jalea* sunk by Austrian mine in Gulf of Trieste. **N Sea** — Harwich Force minelaying N of Heligoland aborted (-18) by German destroyers torpedoing RN destroyer *Mentor* (reaches base).	**Britain** — 2 of 4 Zeppelins sent cause 58 cas in Kent, Essex & London (night 17/18).	Prince of Wales visits Argentina. Germany claims 2m PoWs (330,000 Anglo-French-Belgian). Actually 726,694 Russians (10); Austria has 699,254 (1 Sept).	**Russia** — Special Councils of Defence Fuel, Food & Transport set up.
	Baltic — 2 German destroyers shell & machine gun and cripple RN submarine *E13* (14k) stranded on Saltholm I in the Sound (international waters) despite 3 Danish torpedo boats (*see* INT'L EVENTS 24); *E8* gets through, meets *E9* & Russian destroyer (22).		Bulgar War & Foreign Ministers resign (19).	**Britain** — Police raid Labour Leader offices. Fri 20 **Germany** — In *Reichstag* Liebknecht demands immediate peace talks, alone votes v war credit. **Britain** — Munitions Inventions Dept of 20 scientists and engineers (482 by Jan 1918) first meets. Kitchener to Churchill; 'We have to make war as we must, and not as we should like to'.
	Irish Sea — White Star liner *Arabic* (Americans aboard, 44 lives lost incl 3 US) sunk by *U24* (Schneider) (*see* 30) & SS *Nicosian* sunk by *U27*; Q-ship *Baralong* (Lt-Cdr G Herbert) using US flag on approach (*see* 14 Sept) sinks *U27*. **'Baralong Incident'** becomes German atrocity accusation at British, demand trial of crew for 'murder' of 4 submariners in *Nicosian*, but British acceptance refused of int'l tribunal if 3 recent U-boat attacks included (4-14 Jan 1916). **Baltic** — Submarine *E1* torpedoes battlecruiser *Moltke* in Gulf of Riga, she returns to Kiel at 15 kts. Russian gunboat *Sivach* sunk. **German Baltic Fleet abandons attempt** since 17 **to penetrate Gulf of Riga** by Northern route (Moon Sound) when submarines sighted; 4 Russian & 2 British boats now present. German losses 2 destroyers, Russian 2 gunboats.	**Britain** — **Trenchard gazetted GOC RFC,** succeeds Henderson who returns to Whitehall to head Military Aeronautics Directorate.	Bethmann *Reichstag* speech blames Allies for war (Grey rebuts 26). **Neutrals** — 3 US lives lost in British SS *Arabic* (*see* 1 Sept). Swiss police accuse British Zurich Consul-Gen of spying, leaves & British network smashed (-27) but disguised Basle press bureau opens (27).	

AUGUST 1915	WESTERN FRONT 1	EASTERN FRONT 2	SOUTHERN FRONTS 3	TURKISH FRONTS 4
Fri 20		**Poland — Beseler captures Novo Georgievsk** with 90,000 PoWs (incl 30 generals) & 700 guns. Gallwitz fighting Battle of Bielsk (19-25), 60,000 cas since 13 July.	**Isonzo** — Italian writer Renato Serra k on Mt Podgora, aged 30.	Asquith to Kitchener, '... The Generals & Staff engaged in the Suvla part ... ought to be court-martialled & dismissed from the Army'.
Sat 21				**Gallipoli : Suvla — Battle of Scimitar Hill & W Hills**: 4 British divs fail to break through, lose 5300 cas, but Hamilton rejects proposed evacuation (22).
Sun 22	**Vosges** — French gains include trenches on Tingenkopf & Barrenkopf.	**Pripet** — Austrian Fourth Army occupies Kovel. **Poland** — Russians evacuate Osovyets, blow up defences.		
Mon 23	FM French bows to Joffre & Kitchener (19), BEF will attack fully alongside French armies. Joffre writes to War Minister 'a breakthrough is possible ... provided powerful attacks are made simultaneously in different areas and each on a very wide front'.			**Gallipoli** — Hamilton cables Kitchener, 'It is only possible for me to remain on the defensive'. Kitchener recalls Hammersley GOC 11th Div. Byng, Maude & Fanshawe arrive to take over IX Corps and divs (24).
Tue 24			**Italian Front** — Austrian counter-offensive.	
Wed 25		**Poland — Linsingen's Bugarmee occupies Brest-Litovsk** (-26) as Mackensen advances to N.	Austro-Montenegrin fighting at Cattaro, Austrians repulsed at Grahovo (27).	
Thu 26		**Poland** — Gallwitz occupies Bialystok (110 miles NE of Warsaw), Eichhorn occupies Ft Olita on Niemen. *Bugarmee* crosses Brest-Kovel road.	**Trentino** — Italian progress in Val Sugana, capture Monte Cisa (28).	**India: NW Frontier** — 2 British cols defeat Swats & Bunerwals (-31) after latter attack Rustam Camp (17).
Fri 27	**Alsace** — French storm trenches between Sondernach (foothold on crest since 17) & Lardersbach.	Falkenhayn orders div from Mackensen to Danube despite Hindenburg & Ludendorff's opposition; another 10 follow (*see* 19 Sept). **Galicia** — Austrian 'Black Yellow Offensive' (-12 Sept).	**Julian Alps** — Italians storm Mts Rombon & Maronia (30).	**Mesopotamia** — Townshend returns to Amara after sick leave in India, ordered to advance on Kut (23). *Firefly* gunboat assemblage begun at Abadan (24, *see* 1 Dec).
Sat 28		Ludendorff orders Tenth Army advance on Vilna (*see* 9 Sept).		
Sun 29	**Argonne** — Fierce arty duel.	**Baltic Provinces** — *Niemenarmee* storms Friedrichstadt bridgehead S of Dvina. **W Russia** — Germans storm Lipsk, 20 miles from Grodno.		**Gallipoli : Suvla** — 3000 Anzacs, British & Gurkhas finally cease attacks on Hill 60 (since 21). Kitchener to Dardanelles Ctee '...the Turks could not last much longer'.
Mon 30		New Russian N Front formed (Ruzski i/c 3 armies).		**Mesopotamia** — Nixon memo to India urges advance on Baghdad.
Tue 31	**British Guards Div consti-**	**Pripet** — Austrian First Army	**Albania** — Serb troops at	

AFRICAN OPERATIONS 5	SEA WAR 6	AIR WAR 7	INTERNATIONAL EVENTS 8	HOME FRONTS 9
		Italy begins sustained strategic bombing incl by night (31 Caproni Ca2s available 1915); 12 Capronis raid Austrian airfield at Asiovizza.	ITALY DECLARES WAR ON TURKEY	
	Allies declare blockade of Turk coasts from Samos I to Egypt. **Gallipoli** — 4 RN cruisers support Battle of Scimitar Hill & W Hills (Suvla).		Britain declares cotton absolute contraband (France 22). Anglo-Danish (23) and Norwegian cotton agreements (31).	
W Africa — Dahomey Rebellion v French (-15 Feb 1916).	**N Sea** — 2 French destroyers sink German *A15* coastal torpedo boat nr Ostend (night 22/23). Dover Patrol monitors shell Zeebrugge & Knocke. **Adriatic** — *U34* & *U35* reach Cattaro after leaving Heligoland (4), sail for Med (27 & 28) after Liman & Kaiser ask for more boats (*see* 3 Sept).			**Italy** — Munition disputes regulations & ctees formed. **Russia** — Progressive Bloc formed in Duma.
Cameroons — **Allied Conference at Duala (-26) to plan final advance on Yaunde after rainy season.** Brig-Gen Cunliffe recces Mora in N (*see* 1 Sept).	**E Africa** — RN C-in-C reports 2 planes & 2 guns landed at Mombasa, 150 men available, but fears U-boats' arrival!	**Germany** — French bomb Lorrach, S Baden, & Mülheim (27). **Germany** — 62 French bombers (2 lost to AA fire) attack Dillingen steelworks nr Trier using converted 155mm arty shells.	Germany regrets shelling British submarine *E13* in Danish waters (see SEA WAR 18) & signs trade agreement. Serb Athens Minister demands Greek help under 1913 Treaty. **Occupied Poland** — Gen Beseler made Gov-Gen. (Pilsudski arrives Warsaw 15.)	**Britain** — 12,000 S Wales miners win bonus strike (1 Sept); Aug days worked a 20-yr record. **Russia** — Duma Pres Rodzianko's letter begs Tsar not to become C-in-C (*see* 2 Sept).
		N Sea — Dunkirk RNAS Sqn Cdr Bigsworth's Farman bombs & damages U-boat 6 miles NW of Ostend (2 more such attacks 6 & 26 Sept, *see* SEA WAR 15 Sept). **Germany** — French *Esc MF29* raid Roessler poison gas works at Dronach (*see* 1 & 25 Sept). **Mesopotamia** — 4 Martinsyde Scouts reach Basra, 4 Maurice Farmans already in theatre with No 30 Sqn.	**Germany announces merchant ships will not be attacked without warning.** Neutrals: USA — House warns Wilson war with Germany will mean widespread city sabotage.	*Reichstag* deputy praises War Ministry's union relations compared with civil authorities. **France** — PM Viviani wins confidence vote. **Britain** — Clyde Shipbuilders strike (-4 Sept).
	Adriatic — Italian CNS Revel warns Abruzzi to conserve ships, war likely to be long.	**W Front: Argonne** — French bomb Chatel rail stn.		
		France — German air raid on Compiègne.	**Russian Foreign & War Ministers say no peace with Germany while single enemy soldier on Russian soil**, 2m more troops to be used.	Kaiser signs order creating Finn 27th *Jäger* Bn (2000 vols), formed 1 May 1916.
Cameroons — Dobell's British force 3607 (inc 338 sick but minus 743 on leave), 10 guns, 31 MGs; 1990 British in N.	**U-boats ordered not to sink liners without warning** (ie allow crews & passengers time to abandon ship (*see* INT'L EVENTS 1 Sept). No neutrals to be sunk unless taking cargo to Britain (*see* INT'L EVENTS 26).	**Gallipoli** — French aircraft bomb Chanak & Akbachi Sliman.	Grey declares Allies guarantee eventual freedom for Bosnia, Herzegovina, Slovenia, Croatia & S Dalmatia. Austrian Ambassador in US admits to munitions sabotage letter seized in England.	
	(Aug) U-boats sink record 42	**W Front** — Early French ace	Britain decides to allow	**France** — Consultative

AUGUST 1915	WESTERN FRONT 1	EASTERN FRONT 2	SOUTHERN FRONTS 3	TURKISH FRONTS 4
Tue 31 contd	**tuted.** 21,581 Cdn troops with BEF (46,195 in Britain, *see* 14 Sept). (Aug) French Capt André Laffargue writes his study *The Infantry in the Attack* (published May 1916) describing the infiltration tactics only employed by the Germans in 1917-18.	takes Lutsk with 7000 PoWs from Brusilov. **W Russia** — Germans reach Orani SW of Vilna.	Durazzo. **Italy** — Mussolini called up aged 32, joins 11th *Bersaglieri* training at Brescia, arrives at front 16 Sept (*see* 29 Feb 1916).	
Wed 1 September 1915		**W Russia** — Scholtz's Eighth Army attacks Grodno. **Pripet** — German war poet Capt August Stramm killed, aged 41, with *Bugarmee*. **Galicia** — Austrian Second Army re-occupies Brody, reaches R Sereth W bank (3).		**Syria** — French occupy Ruad I between Latakia & Tripoli. **Gallipoli** — French offer to land Sarrail's 6 divs in Asia Minor at Yukyeri Bay opposite Tenedos but only after W Front offensive (*see* S FRONTS 28). **Persia** — Russians capture German party nr Tabas in E. HM Isfahan Consul-Gen w, Shiraz Vice-Consul mortally (7), Allies leave (14).
Thu 2		**W Russia** — Battle of Vilna (-2 Oct). Germans take Grodno (-3) despite temporary Russian re-entry.	**Isonzo** — Italian attack on Tolmino bridgehead fails. (Sept) Capello promoted Maj-Gen & given VI Corps v Gorizia (*see* 6 Aug 1916).	**Gallipoli** — Hamilton's envoy to London Maj Dawnay calls former's telegram 'hopeless' (in London 10-30).
Fri 3				**Gallipoli** — Dardanelles Ctee: Churchill and Lloyd George press for priority over W Front offensive.
Sat 4	Arty duels round Arras & N of Châlons.	**Poland** — *Bugarmee*'s Battle of Drohiczyn-Chomst (-6).	Italian successes in Plezzo basin (Julian Alps) & Trentino. Austrians active (6).	
Sun 5		TSAR TAKES SUPREME COMMAND: Alexeiev his CoS, Grand Duke Nicholas & staff leave (7).		**Gallipoli** — Anzacs repulse Turk night attack. Churchill asks Balfour to plan for winter campaign (*see* 23). **India: NW Frontier** — 2nd Action at Hafiz Khor, Mohmands beaten.
Mon 6	French journalist notes '... rumour is confirmed of a great offensive...on the 25th'.	**Poland** — Gallwitz fights 3 battles (-17).	**Falkenhayn, Conrad & Col Gancev (Bulgaria) sign military convention for crushing of Serbia** (*see* 22).	
Tue 7	**Champagne** — German songwriter Fritz Jürgens k, aged 27.	**W Russia** — Germans take Volkovisk. **Galicia** — Battle of Tarnopol (-16). Russian Ninth & Eleventh Army counter-	**Serbia** — Serbs drive Austrians from positions on Drina & Danube in minor ops.	**E Persia** — 300 British get to Birjand, join Russians.

AFRICAN OPERATIONS 5	SEA WAR 6	AIR WAR 7	INTERNATIONAL EVENTS 8	HOME FRONTS 9
	British ships (not equalled till Nov 1916 or passed till Mar 1917) with 135,153t (record tonnage till Oct 1916) with 205 lives, total score 107 ships worth 182,772t. **Germany** — 6th (Battle) Sqn of 8 elderly coast defence ships (small battleships) abolished; crews reduced and ships used as accommodation vessels	Pégoud (6 victories) shot down & k nr Belfort, aged 26.	German goods made before 2 Mar to be exported to US.	economic ctees formed in each military district.
	N Sea — (Sept) Isle of Man passenger steamer *Vindex* converted to carry 7 aircraft (joins Harwich Force end Nov after Bristol Scout makes first take-off from RN carrier 3 Nov, *see* 4 Dec).	(Sept) **Heavy losses to Fokkers compel French to abandon long-range daylight bombing** from Nancy-Malzéville; shorter-range ops (Lens & Cambrai areas) continue from Humières (Pas de Calais) until Dec. (Sept) RFC flies a record 4740 hrs 50 mins. Fokker E-type fighters temporarily grounded while 3 serious crashes investigated (ban lifted later in Sept). **France** — (Sept) René Besnard made first Under-Sec of State for Aviation (-Feb 1916), aged 36.	Serbia replies to Allies, refuses concessions to Bulgaria. Count Bernstorff makes *Arabic* pledge to US but specific indemnity refused (7). **Occupied France — Allied Agent 'Ramble' begins using radio** from Lille Convent till arrest by 2 Nov (*see* 22). **Neutrals : USA** (Sept) — First Central Powers film propaganda shown in NY.	**Britain** — 16 National Shell Factories now established (Sept) Sir E Ward DG of Voluntary Organizations, War Office. **France** — Interior prefects & mayors regain police powers lost 5 Aug 1914. **Italy** — (Sept) First British Red Cross unit arrives on Isonzo front.
Ox-drawn RN L Tanganyika Flotilla covers 6 miles (*see* 28 Oct).	**Aegean** — British transport *Southland* sunk (24 troop cas in 1444 rescued) sunk 20 miles off Lemnos I by *UB14* which reaches Constantinople (4, *see* 5).			**Russia** — Council of Ministers vainly begs Tsar not to replace Grand Duke Nicholas or suspend Duma indefinitely (done 3). **Britain** — King & Kitchener inspect 2nd Cdn Div at Shorncliffe (crosses to France 14-17).
E Africa — Action nr Maktau: 67 British mtd inf lose heavily v German train raiders, (Australian Lt Dartnell wins posthumous VC) but score success 14. **Cameroons** — French occupy Akoafim.	German CNS Adm Bachmann (resigned) replaced by Adm Holtzendorff for advocating unrestricted U-boat warfare but both refuse to send more U-boats to Med (13 already sent, only 18 for home waters) or declare that sea a war zone. **Aegean** — British troop liners *Mauretania* (5000 troops) & *Empress of Britain* arrive at Mudros (Lemnos). *E11* returns from 2nd Sea of Marmora cruise (2 warships, 27 steamers & 57 sailing craft sunk).	**N Sea** — German airship *L10* crashes (19k, no survivors) in flames off Cuxhaven, struck by lightning while valving hydrogen to lose height.	**Neutrals: Switzerland** — Czech nationalists Masaryk & Dr Benes meet in Geneva, latter left Prague via Bavaria and is sent to Paris (*see* 14 Nov).	
	Black Sea — Russians destroy 300 Turk sailing vessels. **N Sea** — RN submarines *E18* (Halahan) & *E19* (Cromie) sail for Baltic, both get through (8-9) despite brushes with German cruiser *Amazone*, destroyers and a Zeppelin (*see* 28).		Lord Reading's Anglo-French financial mission leaves London for US, negotiates first £100m loan (28) but under 40% subscribed.	**Germany** — 3rd War Loan opens (-22), raises £601.5m.
	Dardanelles — RN submarine *E7* trapped in new Nagara nets & destroyed by explosive charge from *UB14*.		**Neutrals: Switzerland** — Zimmerwald International Socialist Conference (-8): 38 delegates from 11 European countries (Trotsky present) pass manifesto for immediate peace.	
	Black Sea — First tow coastal U-boats ops; *UB7* off Odessa, *UB8* off the Crimea. **E Atlantic** — British liner *Hesperian* (32 lives lost) sunk by *U20* (Schwieger) 80 miles SW of Fastnet (*see* 18).	**Germany** — 40 French aircraft bomb Saarbrücken (German Lorraine barracks bombed at Dieuze & Mörchingen 5).	**Secret Central Powers Military Convention with Bulgaria** signed at Pless. Turco-Bulgar Convention (20) & Dedeagach frontier protocol (22). **Neutrals: USA** — 'Archibald' docs compromise Austrian Ambassador, US demands recall (8), granted 28.	
N Cameroons — 2nd Allied attack on Mora (-9) fails, more efforts abandoned 15.	**N Sea** — Dover Patrol & French bombardment of Ostend with air-spotting, monitor *Lord Clive* damaged by	**Britain** — Airships *LZ74* (George) & *SL2* (Wobeser) bomb London (night 7/8, 46 civ cas).		British War Policy Ctee finds for conscription but 4 members dissent (*see* 17).

SEPTEMBER 1915	WESTERN FRONT 1	EASTERN FRONT 2	SOUTHERN FRONTS 3	TURKISH FRONTS 4
Tue 7 contd		offensive on R Sereth & at Trembovla as Austrian First Army enters Dubno. Former takes 17,383 PoWs and 33 guns.		
Wed 8	**Argonne** — Renewed German attacks.		Italians attack in Cadore (Dolomites) but are repulsed at Doberdo (Carso).	**Grand Duke Nicholas made Viceroy of Caucasus**, arrives Tiflis (24) & urges more Persian intervention. (Sept) First snow in Armenia. Turk Third Army now 58,000 with 20,000 training at Erzerum.
Thu 9	**Alsace** — Unsuccessful German attacks from Lingenkopf to Barrenkopf.	**W Russia** — **Ludendorff Vilna Offensive** (-26): Garnier's 6 German divs (3 cav) on raid to outflank Vilna to N and to threaten Minsk. **Battle of Dvinsk** (-1 Nov).		**Persia** — c1100 British & 4 guns (ex-Turk) defeat 2000 tribesman at Bushire. **Arabia** — Sherif Hussein asks British to state definite boundaries (see 12 & 24 Oct).
Fri 10	**Flanders** — Germans shell Ramscapelle & Skenstraate.		Greek officers summoned to Athens (see 23).	**Aden** — Indian 28th Bde leaves for Mesopotamia; Brig-Gen Price GOC, regains Waht (25).
Sat 11		III Siberian Corps retreats 50 miles (-12) to cover Dvinsk. **Galicia** — Austrian retreat towards R Strypa.		
Sun 12	Foch visits Haig re coming offensive.	German cav cut Vilna-Riga railway taking Sventsyani.	**Italian Front** — Active fighting. Both sides have small successes (14).	**Syria** — French battleship *Guichen* (+ 4 other warships) begin taking 4000 Musa Dagh Armenians to Port Said. **Mesopotamia** — Townshend's 11,080 men & 30 guns begin Tigris & land advance to Kut in 110-120° F (-26). **Secret War** — Gallipoli deserter Arab Lt Muhammed al Faruqi interrogated in Cairo and at own request made agent 'G' to mediate with Sherif.
Mon 13		**W Russia** — Prince Leopold & Woyrsch's Battle of Slonim (-18), their advance checked.	Bulgars & Macedonians called up.	
Tue 14	**Flanders** — 2nd Cdn Div moves to France (Folkestone-Boulogne 17), enters line before Kemmel (23).	**W Russia** — German 1st Cav Div occupies Smorgoni on Vilna-Minsk railway, but Russians retake (l9).		**Gallipoli** — Canterbury NZ Mtd Rifles' 40 survivors land in Lemnos (637 cas since 12 May) among 4000 Anzacs who start re-training 20.
Wed 15	Kitchener announces that 11 New Army divs have been sent to France & BEF now hold additional 17 miles of French front.	**W Russia** — German cav occupy Vileika & Krivichi on railway E of Vilna (inf arr 18, but Russians retake 26-27); 4 sqns raid to Borisov on R Beresina. **Baltic Provinces** — Russian Twelfth Army retreats to R Dvina covered by cav rearguard actions.		
Thu 16		Kaiser visits Kovno. **Pripet** — *Bugarmee* occupies Pinsk.		
Fri 17	German First Army dissolved (see 19 July 1916). French	Brusilov's 4 divs check Austrian Fourth Army W of Rovno (-22).		

AFRICAN OPERATIONS 5	SEA WAR 6	AIR WAR 7	INTERNATIONAL EVENTS 8	HOME FRONTS 9
	5 shells from new Tirpitz Bty (4 11-in guns); shelling repeated (19, along Belgian coast 25-27, 30).			
British settlers at Nairobi unanimously vote for compulsory service (1st in Empire), Central War Council formed.	**Aegean** — Southampton-Jersey ferry *Sarnia* with gun repels U-boat gun attack off Strati (*see* 19).	**Britain** — Zeppelin *L13* (Mathy) starts major fire in London's 'City' district (night 8/9, 109 cas).		
	Adriatic — Italians shell Monfalcone dockyard (Isonzo).	**Britain** — On Kitchener's orders Henderson bases 2 BE2s at Chelmsford & Joyce Green to intercept next new moon's Zeppelin raids. **E Africa** — 2 RNAS Caudron aircraft reach Maktau.		Lloyd George tells TUC at Bristol (6-11) 'This country is not doing its best'.
	N Sea — Harwich & Rosyth forces escort 3 minelayers laying 3 fields W & NW of Amrum Bank.		**Occupied Poland** — Germans suppress Polish law courts. **Neutrals: Sweden** — Disguised British Stockholm Telgrambyra Bureau set up.	Churchill asks Asquith if he can leave Govt and command bde on W Front, Kitchener prevents (-13).
	Italy — Rear Adm Millo removed from lower Adriatic Scouting Div to Naval Academy for opposing Pelagosa evacuation despite Abruzzi's support.	**Britain** — Abortive German airship raids (2 Army, 1 Navy) nights 11/12, 12/13 & 13/14. None reach primary target, London; trifling damage in Harwich area.	Allied Calais Conference: Joffre opposes E ops extension.	**Britain** — Association Ctee report on war work fatigue. Health of Munitions Workers Ctee appointed (17).
		Britain — RN gunnery expert Adm Sir Percy Scott put i/c London's AA defence asks for 104 more guns & 50+ searchlights, studies Paris example.		
S Tunisia — 500+ Tripolitanian rebels (total 5000 regulars, 9 guns, 13 Turk officers) 1st attack French forcing them over border (-15), then besiege Dehibat (18-24, *see* 25).		**Germany** — 19 French aircraft drop 100 bombs on Trier rail stn & lines. **Secret War : W Front** — RFC makes first effort to land an agent behind German line (nr Courtrai) but he & pilot injured & captured; successful missions (28, 3 Oct). **Britain** — Hit & run raid on Margate by German floatplane causes 8 civ cas.	Germany demands Rumanian passage for troops and £8m benzine.	
			Last Allied note to Bulgaria offers part Macedonia unconditionally.	
	Med — 3 RN 'S'-class small submarines (-26) transferred to Italian Navy. **Baltic** — (c) 3 more RN E-class submarines have reached Reval (*see* 11 Oct).	**Gallipoli** — (c) Kemal Pasha (Atatürk) in staff car E of Suvla narrowly escapes injury by RNAS Nieuport (Samson) bombing.		Munitions Ministry issues profit limitation rules. Commons 4th 1915 credit vote. **Turkey** — National Assembly first reopens.
E Africa — British officials' home leave ended except on medical grounds.	**Adriatic/Med** — Now 5 U-boats based at Cattaro, they sink 99 ships worth 346,786t by end 1915 (*see* 30).	**Mesopotamia** — Turk rifle fire shoots down British Caudron, but Maj Reilly in a Martynside maps Turk Kut defences (*see* TURK FRONTS 28) & 5 aircraft support Townshend (*see* 6 Oct).	**Neutrals: Haiti** — 10-year US protectorate proclaimed.	
SW Africa — BSA Police capture last 8 Germans after 8-			2 Bulgar ex-PMs & Stamboliski warn Tsar v entering war v	**Britain** — Commons National Service debate.

SEPTEMBER 1915	WESTERN FRONT 1	EASTERN FRONT 2	SOUTHERN FRONTS 3	TURKISH FRONTS 4
Fri 17 contd	Chemical Warfare Service formed (commission since 28 Apr).			
Sat 18	**Flanders** — French guns & RN shell German-held Belgian coast (*see* SEA WAR 6).	**German Tenth Army (Eichhorn) takes Vilna** & 22,000 PoWs.	Slight Italian successes along whole front.	
Sun 19		Falkenhayn forces Hindenburg to release 7+ divs, Kaiser backs him. **Galicia** — Army Group Böhm-Ermolli (Col-Gen) formed from Austrian Second Army & *Südarmee*.	**Serbia** — Danube arty exchanges nr Orsova & Tekia, as well as in Drina sector (20).	
Mon 20	**Aisne** — French consolidate hold on Aisne-Marne canal. **Alsace** — French advance at Hartmannsweilerkopf.		**Italian Front** — Heavy fighting on Plezzo & Carso sectors. **Serbia** — British Military Attaché reports more than usual troop & train movements beyond rivers & steady increase in Austro-German forces. **Hungary** — FM Mackensen secretly sets up his HQ at Timisoara (*see* 30).	Hamilton's 2nd Gallipoli dispatch (26 Aug, covering 5-30 May) published.
Tue 21	**Champagne — French preliminary bombardment begins** (-25) with 1300 heavy guns, 47 to a mile.			
Wed 22		**Tsar's stern order to restore discipline**. Fabeck replaces Gallwitz i/c Twelfth Army.	**Bulgar Army mobilization decree** issued by Tsar Ferdinand. Bulgar PM says not v Serbia (24). French Mission arrives at Salonika (*see* 25).	**Gallipoli** — Australian cas to date 19,183. **Syria** — Turk preparations for attack on Egypt reported.
Thu 23	Joffre Order of the Day to 'Soldiers of the Republic... ...Your élan will prove irresistible'.	Brusilov's 4th Div (Denikin) retakes Lutsk (12,000 PoWs); Conrad sacks Fourth Army CoS as he cannot remove Archduke.	Precautionary Greek Army mobilisation of 180,000 after Venizelos persuades King.	Dardanelles Ctee (-24) declines Lloyd George idea of sending Suvla troops to Salonika & decides on winter campaign (*see* 30).
Fri 24			**Serbia** — Austrian aircraft bomb Pozharevats. Drina crossing attempts foiled. **Salonika** — Kitchener suggests British 10th & 11th Divs be sent from Suvla (Gallipoli, *see* 26, also TURK FRONTS 23).	
Sat 25	**Champagne — FRENCH AUTUMN OFFENSIVE:** with 16 divs with flags flying & bands playing at 0915 in drenching rain (-29), 10th Colonial Div (Gen Marchand w) advances 2500yds in an hour, penetrates German 1st line 2 miles along 15-mile front taking 1800 PoWs & 17 guns. **First use of French 9.45-in Batignolles**	Austrian strength down from 480,000 to 230,000 (since 1). **W Russia** — Russians retake Drisviati, S of Dvinsk. **Pripet** — *Bugarmee* crosses R Styr (-26) but repulsed N of Pinsk.	Kitchener & Sir E Grey (26) dissuade Serbs (Lt-Col Pavlovic, sub-CoS to Putnik) from pre-emptive strike v Bulgaria, but Pavlovic urges that 100,000 Allied troops be sent to Veles (Greece) as deterrent. Gen Bailloud (at Gallipoli) ordered to spare 1 French div for Salonika. **Italian Front** — Cadorna replaces	

AFRICAN OPERATIONS 5	SEA WAR 6	AIR WAR 7	INTERNATIONAL EVENTS 8	HOME FRONTS 9
day 135-mile pursuit (*see* 30 Oct).			Allies, Stamboliski jailed (19, *see* 21).	
	Holtzendorff withdraws all U-boats from SW Approaches & Channel due to US diplomatic protests. Pohl recalls High Seas Fleet U-boats as he refuses to operate under Prize Regulations: **U-boat campaign virtually confined to Med** (*see* 30).	**W Front** — Immelmann & Boelcke share a victory, latter's 3rd.		
	Aegean — British transport *Ramazan* (312k, of 418 aboard, all but 1k Indian troops) sunk by U-boat gun-fire (*see* 23 Oct).		Germany promises not to sink ships carrying conditional contraband.	**Russia** — Col Knox reports 'If...ever a Govt richly deserves a revolution, it is the present one...'.
E Africa — Action of Longido W just across German border: 80 dug-in Germans repel 450 British; KAR carry flag in action for last time (probably last time for any British troops).			5 Swedish banks announce Kr 40m loan to Germany for coal. German-Danish trade agreement (24).	**Australia** — NSW Compulsory Service League formed.
			Partial Bulgar mobilization ordered, begins 23. Venizelos asks for 150,000 Allied troops at Salonika (Serb obligation v Bulgaria) as condition for Greek entry. Allies agree (24).	**Germany** — 1915 field service uniform introduced. Austria adopts field grey (Sept). **Britain** — **3rd War Budget**: income tax up 40%, 50% on excess profits tea & tobacco duties. War costing £4.5m pd. **Russia** — Moscow Zemstvos Conference (-23) demands Duma's recall.
Cameroons — Orders for 2nd Allied advance on Yaunde (*see* 6 Oct).	**N Sea** — Mined Dutch liner *Koningin Emma* towed up Thames (250 passengers saved). **Adriatic** — 60 British trawlers (almost all armed by 8 Nov) arrive at Taranto (-30) to begin Otranto Barrage after Italian request for 16 French (16) cannot be met (*see* Dec).	**W Front** — French airship *Cmdt Coutelle* shot down by German AA fire. **Germany** — French bomb Stuttgart.	**Occupied France** — 4 Lille citizens shot by Germans for aiding French soldiers to reach Allied lines, another shot for spying (8 Nov).	
	Dardanelles — Cmdre Keyes vainly submits new plan for naval forcing of Straits (& 18 Oct), C-in-C Robeck opposes.	**W Front** — **RFC & *Aeronau-tique Militaire* launch 5-day combined attack** (-28) on Lille-Douai-Valenciennes rail 'triangle' for Allied autumn offensive, despite poor weather. RFC (92 bombing sorties) drops 5^{1}/2t or 245 bombs hitting 5/6 trains, damaging lines in 16 places, setting Valenciennes sheds alight (2 aircraft FTR).	Greek Army precautionary mobilization. Franco-Russian Ambassadors ask Rumania's attitude re Bulgaria. Rumanian leaders Ionescu & Filipescu demand mobilization (24).	
SE Cameroons — Germans have forced French back to line Bertua-Dume-E of Abong Mbang-Lomie.	**Atlantic** — *U49* sunk by Q-ship *Baralong*. **Italy** — Navy Minister Adm Viale resigns, ostensibly for ill-health, but really due to criticism (*see* 30).			**Britain** — Liquor Control applied to Greater London. **NZ** — National Registration Bill passed (*see* 15 Oct). **Russia** — 500 reservists attack police at a Petrograd railway stn in protest v Duma suspension, other protests in Rostov & Astrakhan (see 29).
S Tunisia — French evacuate 2 frontier posts; Remsta repulses 27 hrs of attacks (-26, *see* 2 Oct).	**Baltic** — Russian Fleet shells German positions on Gulf of Riga.	**Germany** — RM25,000 price on French day bomber leader Capt Happe of *Esc MF29*; he evades Boelcke after raid on Rottweil in which the 2 other French aircraft lost. **W Front** — RFC has 12 sqns with 189 serviceable aircraft & 4 RNAS balloon sections. **Occupied Belgium** — 8 RNAS Dunkirk aircraft drop 28 bombs on	Serbia promises Greece Doiran & Gevgeli and not to claim Strumitsa.	**Austria** — Conrad memo to Emperor tries to get a new PM to improve home morale. **Britain** — Churchill tries to hasten Stokes trench mortar production (1000 ordered 12 Aug, only 50 made by 30 Sept but 800 by mid-1916).

SEPTEMBER 1915	WESTERN FRONT 1	EASTERN FRONT 2	SOUTHERN FRONTS 3	TURKISH FRONTS 4
Sat 25 contd	heavy mortar (192lb bomb; BEF adopt 1916). Falkenhayn orders 3½ divs to reinforce defenders. Artois — BATTLE OF LOOS (-8 OCT)/THIRD BATTLE OF ARTOIS: after 25 days bombardment by 951 guns, British attack with 6 divs at 0630 on 6½-mile front S of Le Bassée Canal to E of Grenay-Vermelles. They advance up to 4000 yds, capturing part of Hohenzollern Redoubt, Loos village & Hill 70 but German 2nd line holds & FM French releases the 2 res divs only at 1230 while Rupprecht orders up 22 bns. French Tenth Army (14 divs attack from 1225) only manages to capture remainder of 'Labyrinth'. Allied feints (diversionary attacks) on the Yser, nr Ypres-Comines Canal, Bois Grenier, nr Neuve Chapelle & nr Givenchy. FIRST BRITISH USE OF POISON GAS : 2400 chlorine cylinders blown off (70t gas) with Stokes mortar smokescreen; 2400 German cas (600 dead).		Gen Nava of Fourth Army with Gen di Robilant (see 18 Oct).	
Sun 26	Loos — 2 BEF res New Army divs (21st & 24th) attack too late & are shattered (8246 cas in 3½ hrs) before 19-ft-thick wire. American-born playwright Harold Chapin k as L/Cp in RAMC. Allies repel counter-attacks. 2 British div generals (Capper & Thesiger) k at front. FM French visits cas clearing stns for 2 hrs. French capture Souchez. Champagne — Germans drive French 39th Div from Maisons des Cham-pagnes and their 2nd line proves formidable. Army Gp German Crown Prince created for duration.	Ludendorff orders building of Dauerstellung line, 30,000 Russian PoWs taken since 9.		
Mon 27	Loos — British pushed back in cold & rain between Fosse 8 & Hohenzollern Redoubt but Guards Div storms Pit 14 & chalk pits, recaptures Hill 70. German reserves stabilize French sector. Champagne — French before German 2nd line on a 6-mile front, but resistance growing. Argonne — French repulse German attack.	Baltic Provinces — Niemen-narmee beaten at Eckau (Riga).		Mesopotamia — British Chief Political Officer Cox 'Baghdad is within our grasp … without reinforcing our troops'.
Tue 28	Loos — British Guards (2000 cas since 27) capture chalk pit nr Hill 70. French relieve hard-pressed British line at Double Crassier-Loos (30). OHL orders XI Corps from E Front. Champagne — French penetrate German 2nd line but on too narrow a front, V Cav Corps returns to St Remy as breakthrough not imminent.	Brusilov forced back (-30) & abandons Lutsk to Linsingen. Hoffmann diary: 'We want a good long rest for our tired divisions'.	Gen Sarrail told his destination will be Salonika (see 7 Oct).	Mesopotamia — Battle of Kut: after night flank march, Townshend (1233 cas) storms Turk defences (700 cas) at Es Sinn, taking 1153 PoWs & 14 guns. Nureddin makes orderly retreat towards Baghdad.
Wed 29	Flanders — Germans capture British trenches at Hooge, but BEF recaptures most (30). Artois — French briefly capture Vimy crest for third time. Champagne — Germans retake Tantes trench in their 2nd line.	Niemenarmee now Eighth Army, original disbanded.		Mesopotamia — Townshend's cav occupy Kut but ships stuck in falling river for 2 days.
Thu 30	Sir J French & Kitchener Order of the Day congratulates BEF. King sends message to Sir		Italian attacks continue in snow & ice. Serbia — Army Gp Mackensen & German	Gallipoli : Suvla — 10th Div leaves for Salonika (-2 Oct, see S FRONTS 4 Oct). Helles —

AFRICAN OPERATIONS 5	SEA WAR 6	AIR WAR 7	INTERNATIONAL EVENTS 8	HOME FRONTS 9
		Tirpitz Bty (only 1 hit).		
			Bulgar PM says no intention of attacking Greece. Rumania desires understanding with Bulgaria.	**France** — War Victims Flag Day. **Britain** — †Keir Hardie 1st Socialist MP & anti-war campaigner aged 59 (*see* 26 Nov). **Turkey** — Armenian property liquidated.
N Cameroons — Nigerians surprise German Gandua outpost. **Chad** — French administrator denounces Sultan Ali Dinar of Darfur (Sudan) for Senussi & Turco-German intrigues; Anglo-French collaboration from Nov (*see* 1 Mar 1916).	**Adriatic** — Italian battleship *Benedetto Brin* destroyed by Austrian saboteurs at Brindisi (595 cas incl 456 dead with Rear Adm Baron de Cervin).		Venizelos gets King's consent to Allied landings at Salonika.	
	Baltic — Russian submarine *Bars* with British boats *E8* and *E19* (first kill 3 Oct) sail from Reval to attack German merchant shipping (*see* 11 Oct).			
	N Sea — Harwich Force sweeps to Jutland Bank, sinks or captures 14 German fishing trawlers (-1 Oct) (another 15 by 7 Oct; 12 sent to Dardanelles & Suez).		Venizelos proposes simultaneous Greco-Bulgar demobilization.	**Russia** — Interior Minister Prince Shcherbatov (resigns 10 Nov) witnesses unprecedented disorderliness among 2500 convalescing wounded at Orsha.
2 SA staff officers to examine possible SA role in E Africa (*see* 1 Nov).	**Med** — 13 German U-boats (out of 44 total) present, 8 at sea, 5 at Constantinople plus		**Neutrals : Switzerland** — German Berne Minister reports to Chancellor on Lenin's peace	**Britain** — Special Branch head Thomson gets publishers Constable to withdraw

147

SEPTEMBER 1915	WESTERN FRONT 1	EASTERN FRONT 2	SOUTHERN FRONTS 3	TURKISH FRONTS 4
Thu 30 September contd	John. **Champagne** — Minor French gains. Joffre announces close of ops with haul of 25,000 PoWs & 150 guns.		Eleventh Army (Gallwitz) activated.	VIII Corps 15,212 fit, many sick.
Fri 1 October 1915	**Artois** — French advance at La Folie Heights (Vimy Ridge). German counter-attacks at Hohenzollern. **Champagne** — French advance N of Massiges. Unsuccessful German counter-attacks on Maisons de Champagne.	**W Russia** — German attacks on Dvinsk & Smorgoni. **Galicia** — Linsingen gains 25 miles E of Lutsk.	**Isonzo** — Italian attacks on Tolmino fail. Cadorna issues orders for third offensive (*see* 18). Preparations continue despite cholera epidemic caught in Austrian ex-E Front troops' trenches; whole units isolated to stamp it out. **Secret War** — (Oct) Austrians break Italian 'pocket cipher'. **Serbia** — Military dead 125,864 to date incl typhus deaths. **Salonika** — Brig-Gen AB Hamilton's British advanced party land (*see* 5).	**Gallipoli** (Oct) — c700 British evacuated pd, more mining & bombing ops. 2nd French Div leaves Helles for Salonika (3). **Armenia** — (Oct) Turk 5th & 6th Divs diverted S to protect Baghdad from British.
Sat 2		**Battle of Vilna ends.**		**Afghanistan** — German Hentig Mission reaches Kabul but kept virtual prisoners; Amir interviews 13.
Sun 3	**Loos** — Germans recapture part of Hohenzollern Redoubt from BEF 28th Div whom Guards relieve (5).	**W Russia** — Russian Postavi-Smogoni offensive collapses but they reopen Polotsk-Molodechno railway (Germans blew 7 bridges & damaged 66 miles 15-27 Sept).		**Mesopotamia** — Townshend diary: 'We are now some 380 miles from the sea and have only 2 weak divisions...line of communication should be secured before everything'; his flotilla reaches Aziziyeh, 102 river miles NW of Kut, only 50 from Baghdad & Whitehall orders Nixon to stop (5,*see* 24).
Mon 4		**W Russia** — Russian Tenth Army L Drisviati-Smogoni offensive fails (-7).		
Tue 5	**Artois** — Skirmishes. **Champagne** — Skirmishes.		**Serbia** — Austro-German arty bombardment begins incl c170 guns (nearly 40 305mm & 420mm superheavy mortars) for Belgrade crossing. **Salonika — 13,000 French & British troops land. Trentino** — Italian progress towards Rovereto.	
Wed 6	**Champagne** — Second push: French capture Tahure & the Butte (Hill 192).		AUSTRO-GERMAN INVASION OF SERBIA: Kövess' Austrian Third Army secure footholds S of Sava W of Sabac. Demonstration at Orsova close to Rumanian frontier. German X Res Corps (Kosch) forces Danube at Ram to enter strategic Morava valley (night 6/7) while IV Res Corps seizes Temes Sziget Island, but German III Corps foiled at all points (*see* 10).	
Thu 7	**Champagne** — French advance SE of Tahure, French war poet Auguste Compagnon k, aged 36 (*Poemes et Lettres*		**Serbia** — Austrian VIII Corps (Scheuchenstuel) & German XXII Res Corps (Falkenhayn's brother) cross 1000-yd wide	

AFRICAN OPERATIONS 5	SEA WAR 6	AIR WAR 7	INTERNATIONAL EVENTS 8	HOME FRONTS 9
	11 Austrian craft. **Italy** — Vice Adm Camillo Corsini new Navy Minister (*see* 11 Oct).		aims.	American book *The Socialists and the War*.
	U-boats begin first major campaign v Allied shipping in Med: *U33* & *U39* sink 18 steamers (62,000t) in Aegean. Kaiser approves (7) sending parts for 6 UB boats to be assembled by German workers at Pola. **Black Sea** — 3 Russian battleships, 2 cruisers, 7 destroyers (new dreadnought *Imperatriza Maria* & 5 destroyers covers) bombard Zonguldak & Kozlu (little damage). **N Sea** — British monitors shell Lombaertzyde & Middelkerke, Zeebrugge shelled (3, 17). **Britain** — (Oct) Cdr Burney RNVR gets Admiralty approval to develop his Feb **minesweeping paravane proposal.** Operational 1916, fitted to 180 HM ships by end 1916 (*see* 15 June 1916). **Adriatic** — All 12 French destroyers (& 5) withdrawn to cover troop ships going to Salonika, despite Italian objections (*see* 10 Dec).	(Oct) Bulgarian Army Aviation Corps reformed (moribund since 1913 Balkan War). **W Front** — (Oct) French air strength 800 aircraft in 93 sqns.	Anglo-Russian financial agreement. (Oct) US Naval Consulting Board formed under Edison for research.	**Britain** — RFP up 5% to 30%. Munitions Ministry now i/c 979 factories, recommends weekly wages (22). (Oct) 2 film cameramen allowed on W Front. **Austria** — 3rd War Loan. **France** — (Oct) Education Minister and mathematician Painlevé persuades President to form *Direction des Inventions Intéressant la Défense* in Paris.
S Tunisia — Up to 2000 Tripolitanians attack French post (-9) until 1650 troops relieve.		**W Front** — French airship *Alsace* shot down. First German 'Giant' heavy bomber ferried to E Front. 62 unescorted French bombers (2 lost) raid German HQ town of Vouziers on the Aisne but are intercepted by 2-seaters (*see* 12). **W Front** — British kite-balloons range successfully on 10 targets. French bomb Metz.	**Bulgaria agrees with Central Powers to enter war** (15). Russian ultimatum to Bulgaria.	
			Anglo-French ultimatum to Bulgaria. Allied Ambassadors leave Sofia (5). **Neutrals: Greece** — Venizelos resigns at King's request despite 46 majority for aiding Serbia (4), Zaimis new neutral PM (6). US Turkey Ambassador protests v Armenian massacres.	**France** — 1st War 'Loan of Deliverance' starts (*see* 25 Nov). **Britain** — Lord Derby made DG of recruiting, calls on all fit men (18-41) to volunteer by 12 Dec (11).
Cameroons — **2nd Allied advance on Yaunde begins**; British capture Wumbiagas (9).	**Black Sea** — Bulgaria's small coast defence fleet (1 gunboat; 8 torpedo boats; 3 patrol boats; 1 minelayer; 2 transports) joins Central Powers (*see* 16 & 21). 2 Russian destroyers sink 19 Turk supply vessels (7). **Italy** — Italian seaplane carrier *Europa* (8 aircraft) commissioned.	**Mesopotamia** — RFC Martinsyde flies first recon over Baghdad.	German White Book v Allied use of coloured troops in Europe.	**Britain** — House of Lords discuss Armenian massacres.
			Anglo-French London Conference on Salonika.	

OCTOBER 1915	WESTERN FRONT 1	EASTERN FRONT 2	SOUTHERN FRONTS 3	TURKISH FRONTS 4
Thu 7 contd	*des Tranchées* published 1916).		Danube & Sava by boat under searchlight & monitor cover on either side of Belgrade; 4 Anglo-French naval guns fight to end, damage 2 monitors, 6 remaining RN guns join Serb Army (after 8) but all eventually lost. Sarrail sails from Toulon for Salonika (*see* 12).	
Fri 8	**Loos** — BEF First Army repulse 4-div German counter-attack, battle officially ends. British capture trench nr Cité St Eloi. French setback nr Double Crassier (Loos). **Champagne** — Unsuccessful German attack on Navarin Farm-Butte de Tahure.	**Galicia** — Brusilov takes 1000 PoWs at Novo Alexinatz on border.	**Serbia** — Serb counter-attacks broken up by superior arty as Mackensen builds up bridgeheads.	**Gallipoli** — Hamilton's Suvla landings dispatch; storm damages Anzac & Suvla piers, more damage (27-31). **India** — Minister & Viceroy consider asking for 2 Japanese divs for Mesopotamia. **NW Frontier** — 3rd Action at Hafiz Kor: British maul 9000 Mohmands, armoured cars first used. Ops end 28.
Sat 9	**Loos** — Fighting. Haig tells Lord Haldane FM French's mishandling of reserves cost success.		AUSTRIANS ENTER BELGRADE after Serb evacuation follows bitter street fighting (city's fall cost 7000 Austrian cas). AUSTRIANS INVADE MONTENEGRO. **Isonzo** — Austrian attack repulsed.	
Sun 10	**Artois** — Slight French gains in Souchez valley; Givenchy-en-Gohelle Wood & nr La Folie. **Champagne**- Slight French gains (-12).	**W Russia** — Russians forced back NW of Dvinsk & SW of Pinsk, take Garbunovka (9 miles from Dvinsk, 19).	**Serbia** — German III Corps (Lochow) takes Semendria (10-11) on Danube after losing 45/53 boats (night 7/8) but securing bridgehead to E & unaffected by RN torpedo tubes (damaged by shelling).	**Gallipoli** — MEF strength 114,087; estab 200,540, v 17 Turk divs.
Mon 11	**British Machine Gun Corps formed**: MGs taken from bns overseas & formed into coys with each bde (Nov), Training Centre at Grantham, England.	**Galicia** — Ivanov captures 3000 PoWs on R Strypa, takes Visniovtchyk (12), driven back over Strypa but then checks Austrians (13-14).	**Bulgars attack Serbs** from Belogradchik in frontier incident, but driven off S of Zajecar (12). British Dardan-elles Ctee decides to send strong force to Egypt 'without prejudice to its ultimate destination'.	After telling Dardanelles Ctee 'that abandonment would be the most disastrous event in the history of the Empire' Kitchener cables Hamilton for cost of evacuation, replies impossible (12) then 50% losses. **Armenia** — Turks repulsed at Ichkau; Van Pass & at Arkhava on coast (12).
Tue 12			**Sarrail lands at Salonika**, orders French regt & arty up Vardar valley railway to Greek frontier. **Serbia** — Mackensen orders general advance as Kossova gale from SE springs up; Gallwitz sees him & says horses not across Danube yet, gets postponement till 18.	
Wed 13	**Loos** — British fresh 46th (N Midland) Div captures main trench of Hohenzollern Redoubt, but 2 other divs fail v the Quarries & Hulluch. War poet Capt Charles Sorley of Suffolk Regt k, aged 20.			**Gallipoli** — Walker GOC 1st Australian Div wounded.
Thu 14	**Loos** — Unsuccessful German counter-attack on Hohenzollern Redoubt.	**Baltic Provinces** — Germans cross R Eckau, SE of Mitau. **W Russia** — Violent fighting at Illukst (Dvina).	**Serbia** — MAIN BULGAR INVASION BEGINS with First Army (Boyadiev) attack along R Nisava. Germans storm Pozarevac E of Morava valley. **Salonika** — French 57th Div (18,000) begins landing (-23) as comrades of 176th Regt 15 miles across Greco-Serb border (*see* 21).	

AFRICAN OPERATIONS 5	SEA WAR 6	AIR WAR 7	INTERNATIONAL EVENTS 8	HOME FRONTS 9
E Africa — CIGS memo for Kitchener recommends 1 bde - 10,000 reinforcements (*see* 1 & 12 Nov).		**France** — German airship *LZ74* bombs rail targets. Returning to Darmstadt in dense fog she strikes a summit in the Eifel & is crippled.	Anglo-French Munitions Agreement. Chantilly Conference fixes Salonika Army at 150,000. **Bulgaria** — War Minister Gen Jekov named C-in-C.	
S Tunisia — Gen Boyer's 2000 French defeat Ben Asker at Wadi N Nekrif, but Senussi leader disowns attacks (13, *see* 23 June 1916).				**Bulgaria** — Cabinet reshuffle.
		W Front — 6 RFC crews encounter Fokker fighters (-16, *see* 26 & 31).	Greece refuses Serbia's appeal; 1913 Bucharest Treaty irrelevant (*see* 17).	**Germany** — Poet Rilke writes from Munich, 'Can no-one prevent it and stop it'? **Russia** — Lenin letter, 'News from Russia testifies to the growing revolutionary mood'.
	Baltic — 3 RN submarines sink 14 German iron-ore steamers coming from Sweden (-19) & German torpedo boat (14) forcing German patrol craft reinforcements from N Sea, but Baltic C-in-C Prince Henry rejects convoy. 6 Russian submarines in Gulf of Bothnia take 2 prizes from 24. **Italian CNS Adm Revel resigns** to become C-in-C Venice (-Feb 1917), not replaced instead a Sub-Chief appointed.			
	Austria orders 8 German UB11-type submarines to be built under licence at Pola (*see* 19 Oct 1916).	**W Front** — 19 French bombers with 3 Nieuport fighter escorts raid Bozancourt.	**Occupied Belgium** — NURSE CAVELL EXECUTED BY GERMAN COURT MARTIAL (began 7) at Brussels: 'Patriotism is not enough. I must have no hatred or bitterness towards anyone'.	Britain — Kitchener defends voluntary recruitment in Cabinet. **Germany** — Kaiser's quarters being redecorated for RM 70,000. **Bulgaria** — Ferdinand's war manifesto.
		Britain — **Most severe German airship raid** by 5 Zeppelins (189 bombs of total 13,672lb dropped): *L13* (Mathy), *L14* (Bocker) & *L15* (Breithaupt) bomb London (night 13/14, 149 cas, 50 cas elsewhere). **W Front** — RFC observers help silence German guns in 17 places on BEF First Army sector.	Britain breaks relations with Bulgaria. French Foreign Minister Delcassé resigns v Salonika expedition.	
Cameroons — Cunliffe's 500 Nigerians & 3 guns advance S from Koncha, occupy Banyo (24) having covered 445 miles from Mora in 35 days.			BULGARIA AND SERBIA DECLARE WAR ON EACH OTHER.	**Britain** — 2 Peers in Lords urge Gallipoli's evacuation (& 18 Nov). Revised contraband lists issued. English physicist JA Fleming in *Nature* '...this war is a war of engineers and chemists quite as much as of soldiers'.

OCTOBER 1915	WESTERN FRONT 1	EASTERN FRONT 2	SOUTHERN FRONTS 3	TURKISH FRONTS 4
Fri 15	**Alsace** — French gains on Hartmannsweilerkopf.		**Serbia** — Bulgar regt seizes Vranje in Morava valley after daring mountain march, cutting Nis-Salonika railway. Others bombard Valandova. **Trentino** — Italians occupy Pregasina (N of L Garda), offensive resumed (19).	**Gallipoli** — Gen Monro new **C-in-C MEF** (leaves London 22, *see* 28) after Dardanelles Ctee decides to recall Hamilton (cabled 16, leaves 17). Birdwood acting C-in-C (17-28).
Sat 16			**Serbia** — Bulgars storm frontier forts E of Zajecar (*see* 25). Gallwitz has advanced only 8 miles on 40-mile front for 5000 cas since 7. Serbs retreat about another 9 miles S of Belgrade to new line v Kövess.	
Sun 17		**Baltic Provinces** — German Eighth Army active about Jacobstadt & Mitau (19) captures Dvina bank E of Riga (20). **W Russia** — Russian attacks S of Dvinsk (& 23).	**Serbia** — Austrian Third Army takes Arda Ridge S of Belgrade.	
Mon 18		**Pripet** — Denikin's 4th Div takes Chartorysk & 4 guns on R Styr from German 14th Div in Brusilov 4-div counter-stroke, but Germans take Kolki to W (22). Fighting on Oginski Canal (23).	**Italian Front** — **Third Battle of the Isonzo** (-4 Nov): Cadorna deploys 19 divs (5 in reserve) & 1250 guns (1m shells collected for 3-day barrage) v 11 Austrian & 604 guns. Italian Second Army storms Mt Sabotino only to lose it to prompt counter-attack. Italian Third Army almost reaches Mt San Michele summit, but stubborn Austrian resistance with ample MGs restricts attackers to miniscule gains. **Dolomites** — Italian 2nd Div attacks in 3 sectors with minimal gains (-25). **Serbia** — Mackensen launches general attack & drives Serbs off R Ralya line (-19). Serbs evacuate Ovchepoyle frontier (-19) region after Bulgar advances to N & S take Kocam & Veles (cav).	
Tue 19	**Champagne** — German 10-mile wide gas cloud attack (500t chlorine/phosgene mix) on Ft Pompelle nr Reims. Total French gassed: 5096 (815 dead). **Loos** — Unsuccessful German counter-attacks at Quarries, Hulluch & Hohenzollern Redoubt. No penetrations of British line.			
Wed 20	**Champagne** — German gas attack E of Reims.	Hindenburg's HQ moves from Lötzen to Kovno. **Galicia** — Ivanov takes 7500 PoWs nr Tarnopol & about same 30.	**Dolomites** — Italian 17th Div captures Cima Layazuoi & secures Cima Falzarego.	**Gallipoli** — Churchill memo urges gas helmets be sent as large German gas stocks reported (falsely) to have reached Constantinople; also urges use of gas v Muslims.
Thu 21	K George V visit to BEF, stays at Château de la Jumelle at Aire nr St Omer.	**W Russia** — Fighting at Baranovichi, Russians take 3500 PoWs, but Germans storm Illukst (23) & advance beyond (26). **Galicia** — (border) Shcherbachev's Eleventh Army vainly attacks Austrian Second in Second Battle of Novo Alexinatz (-23).	**Serbia** — **Bulgars take Kumanovo & Uskub** (Skopje). **French first in action** holding Strumica rail stn v Bulgar 14th Regt (Second Army) (*see* 24). In N Bulgars occupy Negotin & contact Gallwitz's Orsova det.	
Fri 22		**Baltic Provinces** — Russian landing party repulses Germans nr Dömesnes (W	**Serbia** — Austrian 62nd Div cross R Drina from Bosnia, causing mass civilian exodus	

AFRICAN OPERATIONS 5	SEA WAR 6	AIR WAR 7	INTERNATIONAL EVENTS 8	HOME FRONTS 9
	Med — Adm Dartige du Fournet (from Dardanelles sqn) replaces Adm Lapeyrère (cabled for relief due to health, 10) as French & Allied C-in-C aboard battleship *Courbet* at Malta.		BRITAIN & MONTENEGRO DECLARE WAR ON BULGARIA. Rumania refuses to aid Serbia.	**NZ** — Discharged Soldiers' Settlement Act (National Registration ordered, 26). **Britain** — Lord Askwith Thorneycroft strike judgment says non-unionists should join unions for duration. Army demands 2500 doctors by Jan 1916, only 500 supplied due to civil need. **Ireland** —Food production campaign begins (-18).
	Allied blockade of Bulgarian Thrace begins (*see* 21).		FRANCE DECLARES WAR ON BULGARIA.	**France** — Food Supply Ministry organized.
Cameroons — Nigerian company takes Kentu close to border, but repulsed from hill to S (20).	**Italy** — First of 9 rail-transportable midget submarines launched at La Spezia for harbour defence (-25 Nov 1916) but not successful, struck off Navy List 1918-19.		Britian offers Greece Cyprus if she aids Serbia, but offer refused (20).	
Rhodesia — 300 BSA police relieve Belgians (last leave 3 Nov) but Ft Saisi evacuated & demolished (-30). German raiders engaged nr Fife (20). **E Cameroons** - Gen Aymerich arrives at Dume to lead 1450 French.				**Britain** — Attorney-General Carson resigns over Serbia.
British E Africa HQ empowered to deal direct with S Africa. Senegal — Natives liable to conscription (extended 29 Sept 1916).			RUSSIA & ITALY DECLARE WAR ON BULGARIA (as does Zanzibar, 18).	**Serbia** — Govt leaves Nis for Prisrend. **Britain** — John Buchan's *The Thirty-nine Steps* published.
			Britain abolishes London Declarations's Article 57 (ship's nationality denoted by flag).	**Italy** — New taxes & increases for duration. **Britain** — **Women bus & tram conductors permitted**. (1st 2 in Glasgow, Apr). Lord Cecil abolishes press censorship of foreign affairs, subject to DORA. **S Africa** — Botha wins general election.
	Aegean — Anglo-French sqn of 4 cruisers & 4 destroyers shells Bulgar port of Dedeagach for 3-hrs & Porto Lagos causing numerous fires (est 10k only as pop gone inland), Bulgar protest (25).		K George V visits France (-1 Dec); thrown from horse & injured (28, *see* W FRONT). US blockade protest note to Britain. US blockade protest note to Britain.	**Britain** — Dardanelles Ctee decide that Kitchener not fit to stay but absent Asquith dissents.
W Cameroons — c400 British take Bamenda & road jctn S of Chang (24). Half Bamenda	**Black Sea** — Russian Fleet bombards Varna (repeated 27).		**Austria** — Conrad memo to Emperor hopes Serbia's defeat may lead to peace.	

OCTOBER 1915	WESTERN FRONT 1	EASTERN FRONT 2	SOUTHERN FRONTS 3	TURKISH FRONTS 4
Fri 22 contd		headland Gulf of Riga).	towards Novipazar. **Salonika** — British troops authorized to leave & to help French (26, *see* 31).	
Sat 23	Allenby GOC British Third Army (Monro to Gallipoli).		Serbs retake Veles (-29), forcing Bulgars back on Stip & fight N of Pirot. Gallwitz has advanced 25 miles up the Morava since 19 although Austrians only up to 30 miles S of Sava-Danube.	
Sun 24	Haig diary ' .. it was not fair to the Empire to retain French in command', tells King so. **Champagne** — French capture 'La Courtine' SE of Tahure (Butte du Mesnil Salient), unsuccessful German counter-attacks (25 & 30).	**Baltic Provinces** — German Eighth Army repulsed on Lower Aa but takes Dahlen I (Dvina) within 10 miles of Riga, more fighting 25-28.	**Bulgars have cut off Serb main armies from French.**	Goltz relinquishes First Army (Thrace) for Sixth (Mesopotamia and Persia, *see* 10 Nov). **Mesopotamia** — London allows Nixon to continue advance, partly to influence Persia; Indian Corps to come from France. **Arabia** — McMahon's letter to Sherif Hussein concedes most boundaries but Hussein's 5 Nov reply wants Aleppo & Beirut (*see* 13 Dec).
Mon 25	K George writes to Lord Stamfordham, his private sec & confidante. 'The troops here are all right but... several of the most important Generals have entirely lost confidence in the C-in-C [FM French] and they assured me that it was universal and that he must go, otherwise we shall never win this war. This has been my opinion for some time'.		Serbs evacuate Zajecar.	
Tue 26			**Germans link with Bulgars S of Danube. Isonzo** — Italians capture Globna & Zagora but lose latter.	
Wed 27	K George visits French armies & issues Orders of the Day. Writes in his diary '...long serious talk with General Robertson [CoS to Sir J French] and he is strongly of the opinion that a change should be made here as soon as possible. He thinks Ditt [Sir D Haig] would be an excellent C-in-C and that he would work well with Joffre ...'. **Champagne** — Unsuccessful German attack. Castelnau`s report on offensive baffled at its failure (*see* 1 Nov).		Serbs evacuate Knjazevac on E border. Kosch's German X Corps takes record single haul of 1400 Serb PoWs.	
Thur 28	K GEORGE SERIOUSLY INJURED. He visits British First Army at Labuissière, SW of Charleroi, then goes on to Hesdigneul & inspects parade of 1st Wing RFC. As he rides past the men raise a sudden cheer, the King's mare rears in fright, slips on the wet ground & falls backwards. The King is partially pinned under her. His pelvis is fractured in 2 places. He is rushed back to Aire in his limousine: 'I suffered great agonies all the way' (Diary), returns to England (1 Nov). French Army M2 gas mask adopted (30m made - Feb 1918).	German Army Det Scholtz formed.	**Isonzo** — Italian Gen Montanari k in attempt to capture Hill 383. Heavy rains & mud. **Dolomites** — Gen Peppino Garibaldi's (a grandson) 3 bns attack Panettone (taken 30) & Capello di Napoleone (taken 28, *see* 7 Nov).	**Gallipoli** — **Monro assumes command** at Imbros, cables Kitchener for winter trenching materials & experienced company cdrs. Visits all 3 sectors (30) and urges evacuation (31). **Secret War** — Sykes' report to War Office urges 'a new political bureau in Cairo' for Muslim propaganda.
Fri 29	Joffre confers in London.		Stepanovic's Second Army	

AFRICAN OPERATIONS 5	SEA WAR 6	AIR WAR 7	INTERNATIONAL EVENTS 8	HOME FRONTS 9
captors beat 100 Germans nr Bagam (27).				
	Baltic — Cruiser *Prinz Adalbert* sunk (672 dead, 3 survivors) W of Libau by *E8* (Goodhart). **Aegean** — *U35* torpedoes & sinks Salonika-bound British transport *Marquette* (140k out of 646 troops), 3rd & last 1915 loss out of 242 ships conveying 330,000 troops, but one of *U35's* 12 victims (-Nov) worth 48,813t.		**Neutrals : USA** — 2 German agents arrested, charged with conspiracy to destroy munitions ships leaving NY.	**Turkey** — Urfa Armenians wiped out. **Britain** — King appeals for more men. †WG Grace, cricketer, aged 67.
Cameroons — 750 French occupy Sende after strenuous opposed advance.	**N Sea** — British destroyer *Velox* mined off Nab Lightship.		K Constantine says Greece only 'loosing her sword' (see S FRONTS 31). †German Constantinople Ambassador Wangenheim from heart attack, Count W Metternich succeeds (30).	**S Africa** — 1st Cape Corps begins recruiting coloureds.
		W Front — Observer Lt Hallam, hit in hand, lands a 10 Sqn BE2c after pilot unconscious from Fokker attack.		**Britain** — Asquith letter to Tory Lord Selborne predicts FM French's replacement by Haig.
			Serb PM Pasic cables Allies for help.	**Britain** — Food Home Production Ctee urges more intense farming, use of female labour & guaranteed prices.
L Tanganyika — RN Flotilla (2 motorboats) launched at Lukuga after 2800-mile trek from Cape (*see* 26 Dec).	**N Sea** — Cruiser *Argyll* wrecked off E Scotland (no lives lost).		**French PM Viviani resigns over Bulgar fiasco, Briand succeeds (29).**	
	Black Sea — Salvaged ex-		Allied no separate peace	**Britain** — Cas to 9 Oct given

OCTOBER 1915	WESTERN FRONT 1	EASTERN FRONT 2	SOUTHERN FRONTS 3	TURKISH FRONTS 4
Fri 29 contd			retreats from Pirot area before Bulgars who took town (28) but makes another lengthy stand at Bela Palanka to cover Nis. Bulgar Second Army retakes Veles.	
Sat 30	**Champagne** — Germans recapture Butte de Tahure.	**Galicia** — *Südarmee's* Battle of Siemikowce (-5 Nov).	Mackensen's armies within 13 miles of Kragujevac (*see* 1 Nov).	
Sun 31	**Official issue of steel helmets to British troops.**		**British join French**, relieve 2 bns NW of L Doiran. **Secret War: Greece** — With King's approval, Greek CoS Gen Doumanis & Col Metaxas question German Military Attaché Capt Falkenhausen at length (-1Nov) about aid from Central Powers if they intervene v retreating Allies. Falkenhausen urges continued neutrality for the moment.	
Mon 1 November 1915	Sir J French's 15 Oct 1915 Dispatch published: he attempts to cancel his responsibility for Loos failure by deliberately mistiming the hour he transferred the reserves into Haig's hands. **Champagne** — German bombardment on front of 5 miles followed by regular attack by troops from E Front. Pétain's report on failed offensive advocates attrition by arty attacks before 3:1 decisive blow.	(c) Col Knox estimates Russian strength at 650,000 inf, 4000 field-guns, 2590 MGs, only 14 heavier guns per corps (*see* 1 & 13 Jan 1916). Russian losses to date 4.36m (1.74m PoWs). **W Russia** — Battle of Dvinsk ends in stalemate.	Serbs evacuate Kragujevac, blowing up arsenal & evading Mackensen's trap. 5000 Serbs hold Babuna Pass SE of Uskub (Skopje) v Bulgars for a wk. **Salonika** — French 122nd Div (18,000) lands (-8). (Nov) British Army daily newspaper *The Balkan News* begins for duration.	(Nov) Turk Army at peak strength of 800,000 (52 divs). Grey to McMahon: 'What we want is Arab help now against the Turks'.
Tue 2	**Flanders** — Ypres again heavily bombarded. **France** — Maunoury succeeds Gallieni as Paris Military Governor.			**Gallipoli** — Monro estimates evacuation loss at 30-40%, visits Egypt (-8).
Wed 3	**Champagne** — Germans storm some trenches on Hill 199, but in spite of asphyxiating shells, they are repulsed with loss.	**Galicia** — Russian XVII & VI Corps victory at Siemeikowice, 5000 Austrian PoWs taken after Strypa boat crossing (1).	Serbs evacuate Yagodnya & Kraljevo (*see* 7) but counter-attack (4) halts Austrian Third Army & allows disengagement. French 57th Div at Krivolak repulse unblooded & not fully trained Bulgar 11th Div with 3000 cas. British flying bridge built there (2-9) while French 156th Div attack from NW of L Doiran, taking 2 villages but loses 1 (6, *see* 11).	
Thu 4	**Champagne** — Fighting between Hill 199 & the Maisons de Champagne and round Massiges (5).		**Italian Front** — Third Battle of the Isonzo ends: Italian losses 67,008 (10,733k, 11,985 missing); Austrian 42,000 (*see* 10).	**Gallipoli** — Turk attacks at Anzac repulsed. Kitchener appoints Monro to Salonika, Birdwood C-in-C MEF; latter suppresses news, begs Kitchener to reconsider, is told to plan evacuation as Kitchener leaves England for visit.
Fri 5		**W Russia** — Germans heavily repulsed at Platonovka, S of Sventen (Dvinsk).	**Serbia** — **Fall of Nis** after 3 days fighting to Bulgar First Army **gives Central Powers rail link with Turkey** (German munition convoys arrive	

AFRICAN OPERATIONS 5	SEA WAR 6	AIR WAR 7	INTERNATIONAL EVENTS 8	HOME FRONTS 9
	Turk cruiser *Medjidieh* incorporated in Russian Fleet at Nikolayev under the name *Prut*. **Adriatic** — Conrad writes to Adm Haus saying Serbia cut off from Salonika & attack needed on Montenegro/Albania supply routes (*see* 22 Nov).		agreement published.	as 493,294.
Cameroons — French occupy Eseka rail terminus (*see* 23 Nov). Railway in full Allied use by 13 Dec. **SW Africa** — SA Interior Sec E Gorges becomes Administrator (- Oct 1920), military gov Gen Beves leaves but martial law (-3 Jan 1921).	**Dardanelles** — French submarine *Turquoise* having been first French boat into Marmora, forced ashore by gunfire & captured by Turks with details of *E20* rendezvous (*see* 6 Nov).			**France** — Gen Gallieni War Minister (Millerand resigned 29). Now PM Briand soon streamlines propaganda with new *Maison de la Presse*. (Oct) 123,000w from Champagne pass through Troyes.
	Gallipoli — RN destroyer *Louis* wrecked at Suvla, later destroyed by Turk guns.	**W Front** — 55 Fokker Es on strength (*see* 31 Dec).		
S Africa offers inf bde, 2 bns & 2 mtd regts for E Africa (*see* 13).	**Med** — (Nov) U-boats sink 44 Allied & neutral ships (only 23 British in all seas) totalling 152,882t, especially off Crete & Malta. **Secret War** — (Nov) British Board of Invention & Research sends 3 scientists to Hawkcraig (Firth of Forth) to work on sound receivers, 1 listens to RN submarine with head in water (team moved to Harwich Nov 1916). **Baltic** — Disturbances over food & officers in Russian battleship *Gangut* & cruiser *Rurik* at Helsinki, order soon restored (50 arrests). Both ships in 10/11 Nov minelaying op nr Gotland I (*see* 28). **Arctic** — (Nov) RN 7th Cruiser Sqn begins escorting convoys to White Sea (Archangel).	(Nov) Lambe of RNAS obtains official authorization for two-wing bombing force in Dunkirk area. RFC 5th Wing established in Egypt (Nos 14 & 17 Sqns + 'X' Aircraft Park). **W Front** — (Nov) Nungesser joins *Esc N65* nr Nancy after 1st victory on unauthorized night sortie (*Croix de Guerre* & 8 days' detention); 2nd victory (28).		**France** — (Nov) R Benjamin's heroic war novel *Gaspard* published (150,000 copies), wins Prix Goncourt. 10,000 anonymous denunciations of supposed deserters from Front. **Britain** — Telegraph charges up 3d to 9d/12 words.
E Africa — Tighe orders planning for Kilimanjaro offensive. Prelim deployment approved (29).			Asquith declares Serb independence essential war aim and compulsory service possible. China rejects Japan's advice re royalist movement. Princes vote for monarchy (5).	**Britain** — Asquith pledges single men call up before married, conscription only by general consent.
Cameroons — c500 Allies & 2 guns occupy Tibati after bombardment.	**W Med** — *U38*, newly arrived from Heligoland, shells HM Transport *Mercian* (54 cas) nr Oran but is driven off.	**N Sea** — RNAS Bristol Scout (Towler) takes off from seaplane carrier HMS *Vindex* : **first carrier deck take off by wheeled aeroplane.**	New French PM Briand calls for closer Allied co-operation. British Cabinet War Ctee (ex-Dardanelles Ctee) first meets. **Neutrals : Greece** — PM Zaimis resigns; Skouloudis succeeds (7). Greece accepts Allied £1.6m loan.	British W Indies Regt recreated (eventually 11 bns or 15,601 all ranks, suffering 1963 cas).
	W Med — *U38* sinks French transport *Calvados* (Senegalese bn aboard) with heavy loss of life, Algeria-Marseilles traffic suspended for 36 hrs. **N Sea** — *UC8* runs aground off Dutch Terschelling I, interned.			**France** — Clemenceau elected chm Army & Foreign Affairs Senate Commission (-5).
W Desert — (c) 130 Turks + munitions, landed from *U35* at Bardia, reinforce Senussi (*see* 14 & SEA WAR).	**E Med** — *U35* sinks RN armed boarding steamer *Tara* & Egyptian coastguard vessel *Abbas* (6) at Sollum. *U35* has already landed 10 Turkish	**E Front** — German Army airship *LZ39* (hitherto bombing rail targets in Poland) destroyed in shed fire nr Grodno. **Neutrals : USA** —		**S Africa** — Gen De Wet declares for Britain in election campaign (released with 118 others 20 Dec).

NOVEMBER 1915	WESTERN FRONT 1	EASTERN FRONT 2	SOUTHERN FRONTS 3	TURKISH FRONTS 4
Fri 5 contd			Ruschuk (6). French 57th & 122nd Divs begin advance to 2¹/₂ miles W of Crna (-9). **Salonika** — British 22nd Div (from France) begins landing (all inf by 10).	
Sat 6	**Champagne** — Heavy-calibre shelling in entire region without infantry action.	**Baltic Provinces** — Russian counter-attack with Baltic Fleet support retakes Olai (Riga-Mitau railway), Kemmern (11), Germans retreat (13).		
Sun 7	**Champagne** — Grenade attacks repulsed.	Alexeiev estimates 90 Austro-German divs on front.	**Serbia** — Mackensen reaches Kragujevac & forces R Morava at Kraljevo. Bulgars capture Leskovac S of Nis. **Italian Front** — Gen Peppino Garibaldi's Italians storm Col di Lana (Venetian Alps), but lose it to Austrian shelling (night 8/9) till 17 Apr 1916 (qv).	**Persia** — Russian troops leave Kazvin for Tehran to pre-empt German coup (*see* 12).
Mon 8	**Champagne** — E of Tahure & N of Massiges arty duels continue.			
Tue 9	M Poincaré & Gen Joffre visit Front. House of Lords attacks v FM French & GHQ (& 16).	**Pripet** — Brusilov occupies German position nr Kolki on R Styr, 3500 PoWs taken (9), breaks German lines W of Chartorysk, 2050 PoWs taken, loses Chartorysk (15) but retakes (19).	**Serbia** — Putnik attacks Bulgars E of Pristina with 5 divs (*see* 11 & 15), his defence on Morava line ends having extricated Timok Army survivors from NE. Mackensen prepares XXII Res Corps for transfer (*Alpenkorps* replaces).	
Wed 10	'No special events in the Western theatre' (German communiqué). King's sec returns Loos documents to Lady Haig (*see* 15). **Flanders** — Indian Corps completely relieved by XI Corps from line (since 4) after 34,252 cas since 22 Oct 1914, prior to leaving France (*see* 22); first bde entrains for Marseilles (7)*see* TURK FRONTS 5 Dec and W FRONT 28 Dec.		**Italian Front** — **Fourth Battle of the Isonzo** (-3 Dec): Italian *Sassari* Bde prominent in Carso fighting (-12) after 4-hr bitter intensive barrage; 28 Italian divs v 15 Austrian. **Salonika** — French mainly hold 3 Bulgar regts (5877+ cas) from Crna-Vardar river loop (-14).	Goltz leaves for Baghdad and Sixth Army (i/c from 24). **Gallipoli** — **Kitchener arrives**, visits Anzac (13) & Suvla (14).
Thu 11	**Champagne** — Renewed attacks at Tahure reported. Germans twice repulsed. **France** — *Régiment de Marche de la Légion Étrangère* (3186) formed from 4 bns incl one of Italian Legion, becomes 2nd most highly decorated French regt of war (*see* 4 July 1916).		**Serbia** — Serbs recapture most of Kacanik Gorge N of Uskub (Skopje). French attack to outskirts of Kosturino *inside* Bulgar frontier (-12) but fatigue, supply problems & Bulgar reinforcement halt it there (*see* 6 Dec).	**Mesopotamia** — Townshend begins advance on Baghdad, surprises Turks at El Kutunie, occupies Zor (19, *see* AIR WAR 21), but getting only 3/4 of daily supply requirement.
Fri 12	'There is nothing new on the	Hindenburg meets Kaiser,	**Isonzo** — Italian *Ancona* &	**Persia** — Gen Baratov lands at

AFRICAN OPERATIONS 5	SEA WAR 6	AIR WAR 7	INTERNATIONAL EVENTS 8	HOME FRONTS 9
	officers, 120 men (in 2 towed schooners) & ammo at Bardia for Senussi in **first-ever submarine clandestine landing op** (*see* AFRICAN OPS 5 & 14).	**First steam catapult launch of aircraft from a ship**: Curtiss flying boat (Mustin) from bows of anchored battleship *North Carolina* in Pensacola Bay, Florida (repeated while underway 6).		
Cameroons — 250 British occupy Chang; Cunliffe's 450 Nigerians capture Banyo Mt in rain (since 4) for 60 cas, Germans lose 116/c223. Advance S resumed (8). **E Africa** — Churchill asks PM for post of C-in-C & Gov-Gen. Bonar Law backs idea (12, but *see* 22).	**Dardanelles** — British submarine *E20* torpedoed & sunk by *UB14* (Heimburg) thanks to Allied submarine rendezvous code capture, but *E11* returns (*see* 3 Dec).			**Britain** — *Globe* newspaper suspended (-20) for false rumour of Kitchener's resignation. (Asquith proposed Gallipoli visit 3.)
	W Med — **Ancona Affair:** *U38* (Valentiner) flying Austrian flag shells 8210t Italian New York-bound emigrant ship off Sardinia then torpedoes her as passengers & crew abandon ship, 208 dead (incl 25 Americans), also sinks Italian SS *Firenze* (9,*see* INT'L EVENTS). **Baltic** — Cruiser *Undine* sunk (24 lost) by British submarine *E19* (Cromie) NE of Rugen I.		US protests to Austria re sinking of Italian liner *Ancona* (25 Americans die) off Sardinia (see SEA WAR), Vienna's reply (18) unsatisfactory (*see* 6 Dec).	**Japan** — Emperor Yoshihito's enthronement at Kyoto (-10).
	Jellicoe to First Sea Lord 'I confess to being quite unable to recognize the necessity for sending further ships to the Med...'	**W Front** — 6 RFC 7 Sqn aircraft bomb (2 x 100lb each) Gits airfield, agents report wounding 30-40 men & destroying 5 cars (others try to bomb Bellenglise airfield NW of St Quentin 11). **Turkey** — 3 RNAS aircraft (2 x 112lb bombs each) from Imbros & Enos first attack Kuleli Burgas rail bridge & damage its installation, nr Bulgar border (R Maritsa, raids repeated on this Berlin-Constantinople line strategic point 10, 13, 16, 18 & 24). **Salonika** — Seaplane carrier HMS *Ark Royal* arrives.		**Britain** — Underground coalminers' enlistment stopped.
	W Med — German U-boat sinks Japanese steamer off Morocco.		Asquith Guildhall speech affirms 'Be the journey long or short we shall not pause or falter'. Grey proposes conditional military convention to Rumania, Bratianu refuses (12).	
			Austrian Foreign Minister in Berlin (-11), discusses Poland & *Mitteleuropa*; Vienna rejects Jagow's 'Germanic Eastern March' role, values non-German subjects (24). **Neutrals: USA** — Great fire at Bethlehem Steel Co munition works, German sabotage suspected, & in 2 other industrial accidents (11 & 30).	**Germany** — War Ministry compromises with Iron & Steel Industrialists Assoc over future use of Army-eligible manpower (600,000 workers). **Britain** — Ship Licensing & Requisition Ctees formed; statutory War Pensions Ctees organized. Commons votes £400m war credit.
			Neutrals: Greece — King dissolves Parliament, German Mission arrives.	**Britain** — **War Council of Five appointed**: Asquith, Bonar Law, Balfour, Lloyd George, McKenna. Churchill resigns from Cabinet (public 13), farewell speech (15), joins BEF (18). **Britain** — Lord Derby warns single men of compulsion if not enlisted before (30). Marriage after Registration Day (15 Aug) will not exempt.
Cameroons — c250 British				

NOVEMBER 1915	WESTERN FRONT 1	EASTERN FRONT 2	SOUTHERN FRONTS 3	TURKISH FRONTS 4
Fri 12 contd	front' (German communiqué) but Paris reports 'Particularly violent artillery duels in Artois' [ie at Lens etc].	threatens to resign if Riga & Dvinsk's capture ordered.	*Lombardia* Bdes reach but cannot hold Oslavia (*see* 17).	Enzeli on Caspian with first of 14,000 men & 28 guns (*see* 26).
Sat 13	German official communiqués of 13 & 14 Nov state nothing to report. **Flanders** — In Belgium effective bombardments silence German btys.		Serbs retreat on Kossovo Plain & their new temporary capital Mitrovica. They evacuate Babuna Pass E of Prilep (14).	
Sun 14	**Artois** — Determined but unsuccessful German attacks on 'The Labyrinth'. **Meuse** — Poincaré, accompanied by Gens Dubail & Rocques visits fortifications of Bois-le-Prêtre & Pont-à-Mousson 'which has just undergone its 178th bombardment' (*The Times* correspondent). **Champagne** — German grenade attacks on barriers around French Butte de Tahure.listening posts		**Isonzo** — *Sardinia* Bde captures Trincea dei Razzi for 1521 cas incl Gen Berardi (+ 1000 sick) on Carso.	
Mon 15	**Flanders** — Hard night frost after a week of heavy rain. Comparatively little activity for past week except for occasional sharp arty duels. BEF CoS Robertson tells Haig his main aim 'to get you in command'.		**Serbia** — Gen Ribarov's Bulgar gp in dire straits but rescued by part of First Army from Leskovac as Austro-German pursuit reaches R Ibar at Kossovo Plain N end. French estimate c213,000 Allies v 400,000 Central Powers' troops. **Salonika** — British Gen Mahon forms GHQ Salonika Army.	**Gallipoli** — Kitchener cables home evacuation might not be so costly. 52nd Div Helles mining success nr Krithia Vineyard. **Persia** — Central Powers' Ambassadors leave Tehran for Kum with 3000 Persian gendarmes, expecting Shah to follow, but he takes refuge in Russian Embassy.
Tue 16	Arty duels at different points. FM French to his mistress '... I am only thankful that the army I have commanded really saved the country from dire disaster'. **Argonne** — French explode 2 mine chambers destroying some trenches, spring 2 more at Bolante (20).		**Serbia** — Bulgars take Prilep. Serbs evacuate Monastir.	
Wed 17	British Cabinet's War Ctee in Paris. French Army Senate Ctee insist on use of asphyxiating gases.		**Salonika** — Sarrail sees Kitchener who tells him Joffre will not spare more troops (now 120,000 for this new theatre), British sending 3 more divs (*see* INT'L EVENTS 20). **Italian Front** — Italians attack & take Oslavia & Hill 188 (latter kept). **Serbia** — Weather breaks with deluges & sudden floods on chronically muddy roads.	**Gallipoli** — Storms smash Anzac & W Beach piers (-18). 2 more divs to go to Salonika (19).
Thu 18	**Flanders** — Canadian trench raid SW of Messines.		**Italian Front** — Italian guns begin levelling Gorizia after air-dropped leaflets warn civilians. **Serbia** — Sarrail makes vain last effort to reach Serbs (-20) despite Joffre's orders (14) to fall back to frontier.	
Fri 19	**Alsace** — Lively fighting with arty, trench mortars & grenades on Hartmannsweilerkopf & on Uffholz plateau.		**Serbia** — Bulgars reach Tetovo barring last route to Greece. **Battle of Kossovo** (-24): Last Serb effort to reach Allies but on half-rations, typhus-ridden & only 200 guns left (*see* 23).	

AFRICAN OPERATIONS 5	SEA WAR 6	AIR WAR 7	INTERNATIONAL EVENTS 8	HOME FRONTS 9
occupy Gorori, cross Mban & take Bumbo (24). **E Africa** — Whitehall recommends, 'conquest of this German colony with as little delay as possible'. Brig-Gen Northey made GOC Rhodesia-Nyasaland border (arrives Cape 24 Dec). S Africa announces raising of 6 inf bns, 5 arty btys, 5 mtd regts, all fully recruited by 1 Dec.	**Adriatic** — **Allies to supply Serbia via Brindisi**, Britain to provide supplies & Italian Navy to protect (*see* S FRONTS 24).	**Bulgaria** — 2-6 RNAS aircraft bomb & damage key Ferejik rail jctn (Salonika-Constantinople line, 16, 18, 19 qv & 1 Dec, total 41 bombs). **Mesopotamia** — Capt F Yeats-Brown (future novelist) & his pilot captured by Arabs when their Farman fails to take off after they cut telegraph line N of Baghdad (*see* 21).		
W Desert — **Senussi Revolt** (Turk-backed) **begins** with sniping at Egyptian post, Sollum, 300 Senussi occupy Zaura Monastery at Sidi Barrani (17, *see* 23).	**Black Sea** — *Goeben* missed off Bosphorus by 2 Russian submarine torpedoes but taken off coal convoy route (*see* 8 Jan 1916). **Dardanelles** — Cruiser *Chatham* brings Kitchener to Mudros (from Marseilles), only general not seasick visiting Suvla in destroyer *Laforey* (17).	**Italy** — Austrian aircraft bomb Verona (79 cas).	Czech leaders Masaryk & Durich issue revolutionary manifesto for independence & form Czech National Council.	
	Med — 452 Anglo-French ASW vessels deployed incl 85 destroyers (but 28 French broken down by 30) & 63 torpedo boats. Adm Dartigue est 140 destroyers needed (*see* 3 Dec).			**Austria** — PM writes 'The English war of starvation , ...3 bad harvests...has brought us into the most difficult situation'. **Italy** — Late Nov: class of 1896, the 19-yr-olds, called to colours.
	Channel — First British hospital ship sunk: *Anglia* (139k), sunk by U-boat mine off Dover.	**Germany** — Airship *L18* burned out in shed at Tondern. Navy airship *SL6* destroyed in mid-air explosion (18, 20k, no survivors).	British War Cabinet arrives in Paris to discuss Gallipoli & aid to Serbia, approves Allied War Council in principle (*see* 4 Dec).	**Britain** — 2nd 1915-16 Budget trebles beer duties.
	Med/Adriatic — Full German Cattaro U-boat Flotilla formed. **Pacific** — *Fuso*, Japan's first true dreadnought, completed, 3 more by 30 Apr 1918.			
		Turkey — Sqn Cdr R Davies wins VC rescuing fellow pilot Lt G Smylie (No 3 Sqn RNAS) after bombing Ferejik rail jctn on Gulf of Enos, Thrace.	Allied commercial blockade of Greece begins.	

NOVEMBER 1915	WESTERN FRONT 1	EASTERN FRONT 2	SOUTHERN FRONTS 3	TURKISH FRONTS 4
Sat 20	French arty active at different points. **Meuse** — German set of mines exploded in Bois des Chevaliers (Meuse Heights).		**Serbia** — Bulgars force French S of R Crna.	
Sun 21	Arty duels in Artois & Champagne.		Serbs driven from Novi Pazar. French retreat S of R Crna & prepare for retreat to Salonika (22, 23). Putnik gives order for retreat into Albania (Serb First Army down to 15,381 rifles, 20, but morale still good), other units worse off with sickness & desertions.	
Mon 22	**Flanders** — 'Major Winston Churchill has been attached to the Grenadier Guards and is now having his first spell of duty in the trenches' (*The Times,* London). Sir J French Farewell Order of the Day to Indian Corps. Prince of Wales conveys King-Emperor`s thanks (25, *see* 28 Dec).		Falkenhayn letter informs Conrad that 8 German divs being withdrawn. Conrad replies (25) by withdrawing Austrians from Mackensen's command, but quarrel patched up at meeting (27).	**Gallipoli** — **Kitchener advises Anzac & Suvla evacuations,** sails home (24). **Mesopotamia** — **Battle of Ctesiphon** (-24, 22 miles SE of Baghdad): Townshend's 13,756 men & 30 guns take 1300 PoWs & Turk 1st line from Nureddin's 18,000 (4 divs) & 52 guns, (6188-9500 cas incl deserters) but Turk counter-attacks (Khalil Pasha present) & 4593 cas force a halt. RN 4-strong flotilla held up in hairpin Tigris bend by Turk guns and unable to give close support.
Tue 23	Asquith has decided to relieve FM French & sends Lord Esher to tell him (*see* 29).	STAVKA orders Seventh Army from Black Sea coast to E Galicia for offensive (*see* 12 Dec).	**Serbia** — Fall of Mitrovica & Pristina drives Serbs W of Kossovo Plain. Germans claim 17,000 PoWs & 35 guns. **200,000 Serbs begin epic 100-mile retreat W & SW into Albania** across mountains in 4 cols having burnt last trucks & guns but kept 24,000 Austrian PoWs (-15 Dec); 20,000 Serb refugees die in I col. **Salonika** — British 26th Div begins landing (sailed Marseilles 13). **Italian Front** — Austrians evacuate Mori & Rovereto (Trentino).	
Wed 24	**Artois** — 50 German shells directed at Arras rail stn. **Meuse** — Germans fire a few gas shells at Bois Brûlé (Woëvre). **Argonne** — French mine destroys small German post in Boluntre sector.	**W Russia** — Russians retake Yarnopol, N of Illukst (Dvina) & turn German N-flank; Germans abandon salient. Another Russian success at Illukst (29).	Allied Serbian Relief Ctee first meets in Rome. **Albania** — British Adriatic Mission lands at Scutari without knowing French Mission also sent (*see* 28). RE party follows to help with roads & ferries.	**Gallipoli** — Russell GOC NZ & Australian Div orders 72-hr ceasefire at Anzac (-26) to accustom Turks to silence.
Thu 25	Grenade fighting during night on some sectors in Artois & Lorraine.		**Serbia** — Putnik issues last order on home soil 'Convince your troops that this retreat is a national necessity...our salvation will come when our allies carry all before them in the final victory'.	**Mesopotamia** — **Townshend begins retreat** after air recce reports Turks returning. **Gallipoli** — Monro C-in-C MEF, Birdwood GOC Dardanelles Army.
Fri 26	'The night was quiet all along the Front' (Friday afternoon official communiqué). Arty duels at many points. **Argonne** — French arty destroys German ammunition depot nr La Fille Morte. **Meuse** — German gas attack between Forges & Bethincourt.			**Gallipoli** — **Great Storm** (-30). **Persia** — Baratov occupies Karaj 20 miles NW of Tehran (*see* 4 Dec).
Sat 27	**Artois** — Unsuccessful German trench raid N of 'The Labyrinth', French capture a German-occupied crater to N of it (28).		Rumanians mine Danube.	**Gallipoli** — **Great Blizzard** (-29): 280 British die, 16,000 frostbite cases.
Sun 28		**Pripet** — 900 Terek Cossacks	**Isonzo** — Italian progress on	**Mesopotamia** — Townshend

AFRICAN OPERATIONS 5	SEA WAR 6	AIR WAR 7	INTERNATIONAL EVENTS 8	HOME FRONTS 9
			Canada declares war on Turkey & Bulgaria. Neutrals : Greece — K Constantine assures Kitchener that Greece will never attack Allies but will attack Bulgaria if Germany uninvolved. Germany offers Greece RM40m loan, accepted (22).	
Cameroons — 2 British cols (550 men) meet at Bagam in W, advance 12 miles E to R Nun (-23) & cross by raft (27-29), unite for advance on Fumban (30, *see* 2 Dec).		**Mesopotamia** — Maj Reilly RFC shot down by MG fire & captured nr Ctesiphon before he can report crucial Turk reinforcements (51st Div) (*see* TURK FRONTS 22 & 25); 4 surviving aircraft help cover Townshend's retreat to Kut (25-30).		
E Africa — **Gen Smith-Dorrien selected as C-in-C** in Kitchener's absence (formally appointed 18 Dec).	Holtzendorff (for Tirpitz) ready to supply mines to Greece as her naval chief requests. **Adriatic** — **Italian Navy begins supplying Serb Army (-May 1916,** *see* 1 & 12 Dec & S FRONTS). **Adriatic** — 2 Austrian cruisers & 6 destroyers sink 2 small Italian supply vessels & Q-ship en route to N Albania (night 22/23,*see* 4 Dec).		US rejects German offer of £1000 per American lost in *Lusitania*.	**Britain** — Restricted Occupations Ctee issues 1st list. **Canada** — War Loan issued.
Cameroons — **Allied advance on Yaunde resumes. W Desert** — **British begin ops v Senussi** (WFF of 2 composite bdes 20, *see* 11 Dec). Sollum & Sidi Barrani evacuated.			Preliminary British agreement with Netherlands Overseas Trust for Holland rationing.	**Turkey** — Military Censor restricts letters to 2 pages good handwriting.
			M Thomas announces permanent Allied munitions organization in London.	
	Aegean — 6 Allied battleships, 2 cruisers, c30 lt craft anchor at Melos I as act of gunboat diplomacy v Greece (the 3 British battleships sail for Dardanelles 12 Dec).		**Secret War** — Tentative German-Belgian talks in Zurich (*see* 5 Jan 1916).	**France** — **1st Victory Loan,** yields Fr 13.3bn (£580m) since 16. **Britain** — **Rent Restriction Act pegs rents at prewar levels** for duration + 6 mths. Munitions Ministry takes control of all military research.
Cameroons — British drive Germans from Matem & capture R Puge position (28). In S French again fail to cross R Campo (night 25/26). French E Force advances on Tabene & Lembe (28) but halts (29) to deal with counter-attacks.	RN Adm Robeck estimates 30% losses in Gallipoli evacuation.	**Britain** — Army Council & Admiralty agree that RN to deal with hostile aircraft approaching coast, Army to take over when they have crossed coastline.	Kitchener in Rome. **Neutrals: USA** — $50m credit to 8 London banks announced.	**Britain** — Merthyr Tydfil by-election, ILP wins.
		W Front — 21 RFC 1st Wing aircraft damage Don railway stn (10k, 12 repeat 2 Dec).		**Germany** — 2 British officer PoWs recaptured at Rostock boarding Danish ship.
	Baltic — Most successful	**N Sea** — RNAS FBA flying		

NOVEMBER 1915	WESTERN FRONT 1	EASTERN FRONT 2	SOUTHERN FRONTS 3	TURKISH FRONTS 4
Sun 28 contd		(54 cas) capture German 82nd Div staff (80+ cas, incl GOC, who later shoots himself) in swampland raid nr Pinsk having covered 24 miles from 25 in 14° of frost.	the Carso & towards Gorizia (30). **Albania** — Serbia GHQ reaches Scutari.	back at Aziziyeh after 22-mile night march, Tigris rearguard actions (30) after RN gunboat *Shaitan* sinks due to leak from much towing work (29).
Mon 29	Kitchener in Paris. Sir J French in London sees Asquith but does not take hint to resign, fears friction with King if he becomes C-in-C Home Forces (*see* 3 Dec).		Despite Misic's pleading for drive to Greece & Allies and news of Germany withdrawing 6 divs, Serb Army commanders in conferences at Pec (& l Dec) keep to Albanian retreat, preparations too advanced. **Italian Front** — Italian Second Army finally takes Oslavia ridge.	**Gallipoli : Anzac** — Turk shells cause 262 cas at Lone Pine.
Tue 30			Austrian 62nd Div occupies Plevlje in NW Montenegro (*see* l Dec) & secures bridgehead S of R Cehotina (-3, *see* 24 Dec) but too weak to interfere with Serb retreat.	**Gallipoli** — 53rd (Welsh) Div down to 2590 fit men among 134,728 Allies, 393 guns & 14,587 animals. **Secret War** — Gertrude Bell arrives in Cairo to work for British Intelligence on Arab tribes, met by TE Lawrence among others, sails for India 28 Jan 1916.
Wed 1 December 1915	Col Driant, Nancy deputy & CO *Chasseur* Regt nr Verdun, informs Chamber of Deputies that Verdun defences are unorganized & inadequate (*see* 16 & 20). **Flanders** — British explode a mine E of Bois Français; Germans reply with mine.			**Gallipoli** — Monro to London: 'If decision cannot be reached v shortly, it may be equivalent to deciding against evacuation' (*see* 7). **Mesopotamia** — Action of Umm-at-Tubul: Townshend's 6500 (536 cas) check 12,000 Turks (748 cas), gunboats *Firefly* & *Comet* run aground and captured by Turks.
Tue 2	German communiqué reports arty duels & mining at different points. French evening communiqué: 'Between the Somme and the Oise there was a violent bombardment of our positions of Dancourt, Marqui-Villiers and Le Cessier — region of Roye — to which our batteries successfully replied'.	**Galicia** — Austrians driven back to W Bank of R Styr, repulsed again (17), attacks at several points beaten (3).	German HQ reports invasion of NW Montenegro where Crown Prince of Serbia arrives (Cetinje). Army of the Orient (Sarrail) comes under Joffre. Italian writer & Trieste-born volunteer Scipio Slapater k, aged 27, on Mt Podgova.	
Fri 3	JOFFRE APPOINTED C-IN-C ALL FRENCH W FRONT ARMIES (*see* 9). FM French returns to France for last time, told he must resign (4), letter reaches PM (6) urging Robertson as successor (*see* 15, 18, 21). **Artois** — Arty duels. Fighting with aerial torpedoes NW of Hill 140.		**Italian Front** — **Fourth Battle of the Isonzo ends**, but some fighting on sector till 15; Italian losses 48,967, Austrian 30,000. **Serbia** — Bulgar 3rd Div pursuers defeat Serbs on White Drin river & take much booty. French begin retreat back down Vardar, Bulgars pursue in 4 cols & press from 6.	**Mesopotamia** — Townshend reaches Kut after 90-mile retreat. 'I mean to defend Kut as I did Chitral'. Sends all but 11 boats away (4).
Sat 4	'Heavy rain interfered with the fire of the artillery' (French official communiqué). 'In the Western theatre of war along the entire front actions are impeded by misty, stormy and rainy weather' (German official communiqué).		At Calais Asquith insists on Salonika's evacuation. French agree, but other Allies incl Tsar's telegram force policy change at Chantilly (6). **Serbia** — Gen Vassich evacuates Monastir just N of Greek border, Bulgar cav occupy. **Albania** — Gen Bertotti made C-in-C Italian troops to be increased to a div (28,000 by 12) & under War Ministry direct control; *Savona* Bde to Durazzo, rest at Valona (more	**Persia** — Baratov advances from Kazvin on Tehran, drives Turco-German mercenaries from Sultanbulak Pass (9), occupies Hamadan (14) as rebels retreat to Kermanshah.

AFRICAN OPERATIONS 5	SEA WAR 6	AIR WAR 7	INTERNATIONAL EVENTS 8	HOME FRONTS 9
	Russian submarine *Akula* mined & sunk off Windau.	boat routs 4 German seaplanes (1 shot down) off Ostend.		
	Black Sea — *UC13* runs aground & has to be abandoned.		**Neutrals: Sweden** — Belligerent submarines barred from territorial waters save in emergency on surface with flag (*see* 19 Jul 1916).	**Britain** — London area licensing hrs reduced to 5¹/2 daily.
Cameroons — Germans attack Semini.		**W Front** — 20 RFC 3rd Wing aircraft damage Miraumont quay & rail line despite very high wind.	K of Montenegro appeals for help to diplomatic corps. **Allies formally sign London Pact. Neutrals : USA** — Large postwar German order for copper. **Secret War** — MI1c Switzerland station chief claims to have detected 11 German divs moving from E to W Fronts (*see* 10 Jan 1916).	**Britain** — Kitchener returns to London, Asquith refuses his proffered resignation. Munitions Ministry-Union Negotiating Ctee appointed. **Austria** — 10 Cabinet changes. **France** — 1917 Class call-up.
Cameroons — French occupy Yoko. German Mora garrison has collected food to last to Mar 1916. British occupy Fumban (2), Kuti & Ngambe (4).	**E Med** — (Dec) *U38* & *UC12* (from Cattaro) land munitions nr Bardia (Cyrenaica) for Senussi. **Adriatic** — Now 92 RN drifters (based at Brindisi) trying to seal 45-mile Otranto Straits (*see* 13 May 1916).	**Germany** — (Dec) Maiden flight of Junkers J-1, world's first all-metal (steel) Cantilever wing monoplane. **E Front** — (Dec) First Russian single-seat fighter units created with a few Sikorskys having forward-firing MGs & interrupter gear, but unreliable. **Britain** — (Dec) RNAS adopts revised nomenclature: unit of 6 pilots designated a flight; 2 or 3 flights combine to form a sqn. RFC bases 3 BE2s at Cramlington to defend Tyneside v Zeppelins.	**Secret War: Greece** — (Dec) Novelist Compton Mackenzie heads British counter intelligence in Athens as 'Z'. **Diplomacy** — 'Transito' Syndicate formed to speed goods via Sweden to Russia.	**Britain** — RFP 44%. Bank closing time 3pm from 4pm. (Dec) Rail passengers ordered to pull down blinds (rescinded Mar 1917). Ian Hay's *The First Hundred Thousand* best-seller on original BEF published. **Germany** — (Dec) Butter scarce, copper roofs in Berlin removed. **Russia** — (Dec) Order of St George annual parade before Tsar incl reps of all Army Corps and the Fleets.
L Tanganyika — Lt Rosenthal (Capt of *Kingani*) discovers RN Flotilla at Lukuga but is captured (*see* 26).	**Aegean** — Battleship *Agamemnon* smashes Kavak Bridge at head of Gulf of Xeros (see 27). **Black Sea** — 50 landing craft (760-man capacity) ordered for Russian Black Sea Fleet, only 20 completed with engines (-1916).		**Occupied Poland** — US Dr Kellogg confers with Germans on food relief.	
	Anglo-French-Italian agreement divides Med into 18 national patrol zones (French 10, others 4 each). **Sea of Marmora** — British submarine *E11* (Nasmith) sinks Turk destroyer *Yarhisar* (42 survivors) during record 48-day patrol sinking 46 vessels. Also takes presumed first-ever submarine periscope photo of Constantinople defences (13). **N Sea** — New Grand Fleet battleships *Barham* & *Warspite* collide but repaired by 23.			**Serbia** — Govt arrives at Scutari. **Britain** — Asquith gives war losses to 9 Nov at 510,230. **Secret War** — Churchill circulates memo 'Variants of the Offensive' (*see* 25).
	Adriatic — Italian destroyer *Intrepido* sunk off Valona by mines from German *UC14*. **N Sea** — Harwich Force trial sortie with carrier *Vindex*, 2 aircraft wrecked in fog. Foul weather ruins sorties (13, 20-22). **E Med** — *U33* (Gansser) captures Lt-Col HD Napier (British Athens military attaché, formerly in Bulgaria) & King's Messenger Capt Seymour Wilson MP & some documents from Greek SS *Spetse*	**Mesopotamia** — Last 2 seaplanes leave Kut, last 2 aircraft (6) leaving 3 unserviceable machines.	**First Allied War Conference** at Calais, moves to Chantilly (6). US requests recall of German Naval & Military Attaches (done l0). Henry Ford's 'Peace Ship' *Oscar II* sails with peace women & journalists: 'Get the boys out of the trenches & back to their homes by Christmas' (*see* 19).	

DECEMBER 1915	WESTERN FRONT 1	EASTERN FRONT 2	SOUTHERN FRONTS 3	TURKISH FRONTS 4
Sat 4 contd			troops land 16).	
Sun 5	**Flanders** — French guns shell communication trenches nr Het Sas. **Artois** — Franco-German arty duel at double slagheap SW of Loos. A few German incendiary shells fired at Arras. **Somme** — Trench fighting N of Herbecourt & nr Tilloloy. **Meuse** — French mining ops at Les Eparges. **Argonne** — French mining ops.	**Baltic Provinces** — Germans report Russian attack's collapse nr L Babit, W of Riga (shelling & German gas attack 9). **W Russia** — Germans bombard Dvinsk sector.		**Mesopotamia** — **Siege of Kut begins**. 7th Indian Div arr Basra (6, *see* 10).
Mon 6	ALLIED WAR COUNCIL AT CHANTILLY (-8, *see* INT'L EVENTS) incl Joffre, Haig, Alexeiev & Cadorna.		**Bulgaria/Salonika** — Bulgar 2nd Div bombards & probes British 10th Div position S of Kosturino & in dense fog forces it back up to 2 miles (7) with loss of 4 guns. **Albania** — Essad Pasha declares for Allies & has already helped Serbs but authority limited. Arnauten tribesmen decimate Serb cols in revenge for 1912-13 bloodshed.	
Tue 7	**Flanders** — Germans abandon flooded trenches on the Yser. **Champagne** — French lose, then recapture advanced position nr St Souplet.		**Serbia** — Austrian Third Army captures Pec & then links with Bulgar 3rd Div, as fighting peters out. **Albania** — **Putnik** in sick litter arrives at Scutari & **resigns** because of ill-health (*see* 8)	**Gallipoli** — Cabinet agrees to Suvla & Anzac evacuations.
Wed 8			**Salonika** — Bulgars attack Anglo-French retreat NW of L Doiran & in Vardar valley but fog screens it (9). **Albania** — Serb GHQ reassumes command at Scutari with Gen Bogovic C-in-C, no meat & only 14oz bread ration pd.	**Gallipoli** — EVACUATION BEGINS (-20), 83,048 troops, 186 guns, 1718 vehicles, 4695 horses & mules. Half removed on last 2 nights.
Thu 9	ALLIED WAR COUNCIL IN PARIS. Gen Castelnau appointed French CoS. **Artois** — French arty actions (Loos & Givenchy sectors) and between the Somme & the Oise (nr Fouquescourt). **Champagne** — Arty duels. Grenade fighting E of Butte de Souain.			**Mesopotamia : Kut** — Townshend rejects surrender summons, blows pontoon bridge to S bank (night 9/10). Turks attack N Sector (-13), dig in 400-600 yds away, their shelling by 38 guns causes 202 cas (11).
Fri 10	**Flanders** — Germans fire 3000 shells on Ypres Salient.		**Italian Front** — Italians capture positions above Bezzecca basin (Carnic Alps). At Pless Conrad first proposes to Falkenhayn joint Trentino offensive to knock Italy out in spring 1916 with 16 divs (& 18, *see* 6 Feb 1916).	**Mesopotamia** — Gen Aylmer VC signals Townshend that relief force forming (*see* 28).
Sat 11	Arty duels at different points. Belgian national ammunition factory in France at Le Havre blows up with heavy cas. **Champagne** — Rifle-firing grenade & bomb fights despite persistent rain.		**Serbia/Salonika** — **Anglo-French retreat into Greece** begins in some confusion under pressure, 122 British k or captured (-12).	
Sun 12	**Flanders** — British trench raid at Neuve Chapelle.	**Galicia/Bukovina** — Ivanov orders offensive with new Seventh Army (Shcherbachev) & Ninth Army (*see* 27).	Allied troops begin arriving back in Salonika by train (-17). Bulgars do not cross frontier. **Serb Army evacuation begins** (*see* SEA WAR). 1st Drina Div loses 981 men (-14).	
Mon 13	**Meuse** — French destroy last German pontoon bridge at St		Bulgars occupy Doiran & Gevgel (*see* INT'L EVENTS	**Arabia** — McMahon letter to Sherif Hussein asks for more

AFRICAN OPERATIONS 5	SEA WAR 6	AIR WAR 7	INTERNATIONAL EVENTS 8	HOME FRONTS 9
	(Austrian PoWs till 1917).			
Uganda — 500 British bridge R Kagera, occupy 2 empty German border posts (-6). **L Victoria** — 3 British ships shell Kemondo Bay, land 100 troops at Lubembe Point who repulse 3 attacks, re-embark.	**Adriatic** — Austrian cruiser *Novara* & destroyers torpedo & sink stranded French submarine *Fresnel* off Durazzo, Albania, after sinking 3 steamers & several small craft. Austrian cruiser *Helgoland* & 6 destroyers raid Durazzo (6,*see* 29) sinking 5 schooners.	**W Desert** — 2 BE2cs fly first of many recon for WFF v Senussi from Matruh; 2 other RFC dets sent to Fayum (8) & El Hammam (18) to watch Sahara oases.	K Constantine *Times* interview pledges friendship with Allies.	
Cameroons — French have advanced only c8 miles from Eseka, fighting every day but 2 since 24 Nov (*see* 21). **E Africa** — 250 Germans retake Kasigao Hill. By 31, 650 Germans pin down 5000 British S of Uganda Railway.			**Chantilly Conference** (-10): Allies decide on general summer 1916 offensive, also to hold Salonika (10). **Neutrals: Greece** — Venizelos withdraws Party from election. **Diplomacy** — US note to Austria demands *Ancona* sinking disavowal & punishment, Austria replies (14). 2nd US note (19), Vienna complies (29).	**Britain** — Army officers disablement pension increased. Munitions Ministry now controls 2026 factories.
Cameroons — Gen Dobell orders British solo advance on Yaunde (*see* 15).			**Neutrals : USA** — Pres Wilson denounces disloyal foreign-born Americans in annual message to Congress.	
		W Front — 16 RFC 3rd Wing aircraft bomb Hervilly airfield despite est 60mph W wind (14 repeat 14, *see* 29).	Russian Munitions Delegation arrives Paris, asks Joffre for more rifle ammo (ll). K George V receives (18).	**Russia** — 1st performance Sibelius' Symphony No 5 at Helsinki. **Britain** — Hosiery trade agrees to take women at men's rates (-9), so does woodworking industry (14). *Punch* publishes 'In Flanders Fields'.
	Dardanelles — RN *E2* last Allied submarine to enter (*see* 2 Jan 1916).		**Germany** — Dr Scheidemann declares in *Reichstag* that Socialists refuse to discuss cession of Alsace-Lorraine. Bethmann secret memo doubts Germany can get all her terms or a domestic status quo. **Neutrals: Greece** — Gen Sarrail demands Greek troops' withdrawal from Salonika (refused ll). **USA** — Suspected incendiary fire burns down Du Pont Powder Co factory town, Hopewell, Va. 500,000 bushels of Canadian wheat for Allies burn at Erie, Pa (10).	**Secret War** — MI5 Aliens Registry notes Mata Hari's return to Paris. **Britain** — Triple Alliance of Mining, Rail & Transport Unions ratified (1.25m members).
	Adriatic — 6 French destroyers & 2 submarines arrive at Brindisi after Italian appeals for aid to Serbs. Adm Dartige meets Abruzzi at Taranto (13). **Black Sea** — Russian destroyers sink 2 Turk gunboats off Kirpen Is.		**Turkey** — **Direct rail link with Central Powers restored**, helps food supplies.	
W Desert — British drive 300 Senussi W of Mersa Matruh, defeat 1200 at Wadi Shaifa (13), 5000 at Jebel Medwa (26). (*See* SEA WAR Dec.)		**Germany** — Navy airship *SL4* wrecked in gale when shed doors blown open.		**Britain** — Recruiting rush last 2 days under age-group system.
	Aegean — Last 2 French battleships leave Mudros (Lemnos). **Adriatic — Allied Navies begin Serb Army's evacuation** (-5 Apr 1916).	**W Front** — RFC reports 11 Fokkers in actions (-15) & 3 together (19).		**France** — Artillery Col JE Estienne sees Joffre about land ships, released (31) to work with Schneider (*see* 25 Feb 1916).
	Adriatic — 4th & final Austrian *Tegetthoff*-class dreadnought,			

DECEMBER 1915	WESTERN FRONT 1	EASTERN FRONT 2	SOUTHERN FRONTS 3	TURKISH FRONTS 4
Mon 13 contd	Mihiel.		14).	time but sends £20,000 (see 17). British friendship treaty with Ibn Saud (26, *see* 1 Jan 1916).
Tue 14	Paris & Berlin communiqués agree that no important events had occurred (*The Times*, 15 Dec).		Allies decide on line of defence for Salonika up to 14 miles inland, work begins (16).	
Wed 15	FM **French resigns** as C-in-C BEF. Sir D **Haig to succeed** (*see* 18); warm personal letter received from K George.	German War Minister at Hindenburg HQ. **W Russia** — Russian penetration N of L Drisviati (S of Dvinsk) repulsed. Russians also repelled nr mouth of Beresina but German col broken up N of L Miadzol (19).	**Albania** — Most Serbs have reached plains around Scutari, Podgovica & Elbasan (*see* INT'L EVENTS). French supplies from Brindisi beginning to arrive. Serbs have saved 81 guns, 179 MGs & 55,000 rifles.	**Persia** — Turk div occupies Kasr-i-Shirin close to border, Baratov occupies Holy City of Kum (20), skirmishes with enemy at Asadabad, SW of Hamadan (25).
Thu 16	French War Minister Gallieni brings Verdun defences' defects to Joffre's attention. **Flanders** — British trench raid nr Armentières.			
Fri 17	Arty activity all along the front. **Artois** — German grenade attack about the quarries N of Loos.			Mark Sykes argues for Egypt offensive and Arab revolt before War Ctee, fears Sherif will be killed; approach to Paris agreed.
Sat 18	**Flanders** — Sir J French's farewell to BEF, leaves France (21); HAIG ASSUMES COMMAND OF BEF at noon. Joffre laments his departure.			
Sun 19	**Flanders** — **Germans introduce phosgene gas** (10 times toxicity of chlorine) against British at Pilkem-Wieltje N of Ypres; I069 gassed (120 dead), but no panic as hoped.			
Mon 20	**The Falkenhayn Memorandum**: German CoS proposes unprecedented battle of attrition at Verdun to enthusiastic Kaiser. On return journey from Potsdam to Mezières (German GHQ) Falkenhayn's train boarded at Montmedy by Gen Knobelsdorf, CoS Fifth Army, who receives a full briefing to pass on to his CO, the Crown Prince. The Prince is disquieted by Falkenhayn's reported insistence that French Army must be 'bled white' at Verdun (*see* 24). Ypres again shelled by Germans.	Gen Ruzski invalided from N Front command. Russians begin 13th wartime cipher, but no securer.	Bulgar-Greek collision at Koritisa, N Epirus.	**Gallipoli** — ANZAC & SUVLA EVACUATED BY 0510 (20,652 men & 38 guns since 19). Monro urges Helles evacuation (*see* 27), fierce storms (22-23).
Tue 21	Sir W **Robertson** succeeds Sir A Murray as **CIGS**; like Haig, Robertson believes in attrition tactics & concentration of every man, gun and horse on the W Front. Monro to succeed Haig i/c British First Army. Alsace — French 66th Div advances down far slope of Hart-mannsweilerkopf, takes 1300 PoWs but CO Gen Serret is killed.		'Salonika is clearly defined as a defensive operation' (British War Office).	
Wed 22	**Alsace** — **First use of storm troops**, Sturm Bn Rohrin (night 22/23) in successful German counter-attack on Hart-mannsweilerkopf: 82nd *Landwehr* Bde recaptures the ridge, taking 1553 PoWs but		120,000 Bulgars just N of Greek frontier.	**Egypt** — Sir A Murray replaces Maxwell as C-in-C.

AFRICAN OPERATIONS 5	SEA WAR 6	AIR WAR 7	INTERNATIONAL EVENTS 8	HOME FRONTS 9
	Szent Istvan completed at Pola.			
Strong Kitchener memo v E Africa offensive overruled. British troops reformed in 2 divs (16). **Cameroons — Gov Ebermaier & Col Zimmermann decide to evacuate Yaunde** secretly, retreats S of R Nyong, moving Govt to Ebolowa (-25).		**N Sea** — RNAS Nieuport & German seaplane (trying to bomb stranded British steamer) shoot each other down.	Bulgar & Greek Gen Staffs agree on temporary frontier neutral zone. K Peter of Serbia lands at Brindisi, Italy. **Secret War:** — (c)337 German agents in W.	Asquith refuses to reduce ministerial salaries.
Cameroons — British occupy Chang Mangas & halt there (-22) after 11-day advance.	*U24* (Schneider) sails from Heligoland to intercept troop transports entering Le Havre, sinks 5 ships worth 22,767t in SW Approaches but heavy weather forces return (-4 Jan).			**Britain** — Unlimited 5% Exchequer war bonds issued.
Cameroons — 1100 of French E Force slowly advances S of Lembe (-28). Cunliffe takes Ditam & Linte. French S Force (c1000) forces passage of R Campo (20), captures Ambam (31).	**Baltic** — Cruiser *Bremen* & destroyer *V191* sunk by Russian mines off Windau (Courland). **E Med** — 2 French cruisers arrive off Syria & cruiser *Foudre* at Dedegach to blockade Turk-Bulgar coasts (*see 27*). **Dardanelles** — Aided by 37 motor lighters or 'beetles' (8-20), RN sqn (Keyes) confounds prophets of doom by completing evacuation Sulva & Anzac in a single night (19/20) without fatalities (3 men w).	**Germany — First French night bombing raid** damages Metz rail stn. **W Front** — 48 Anglo-German air encounters.	Pres Wilson marries Mrs Edith B Galt in Washington. **Neutrals : Norway** — 'Peace Ship' *Oscar II* arrives, stays till 22, but Ford leaves (*see 28*).	
		W Front — 6 German aircraft bomb K of Belgians' HQ at La Panne.	Germany disavows her secret agents in USA. **Neutrals : Greece** — Gounaris Govt win election.	**Britain** — Lloyd George's 'too late' munitions speech, Britain behind Germany esp in MGs & howitzers.
Cameroons — French occupy Mangeles.	**Adriatic** — Italian destroyer sinks Austrian arms ship & rams U-boat.			*Reichstag* votes 5th war credit, 20 Independent Socialists oppose. **Britain** — Robertson CIGS (Murray resigns), forms new Military Intelligence Directorate (*see 3 Jan 1916*): Maurice replaces Callwell as DMO (29).
				Britain — Churchill home on leave (-27), discusses conscription crisis with Lloyd George.

DECEMBER 1915	WESTERN FRONT 1	EASTERN FRONT 2	SOUTHERN FRONTS 3	TURKISH FRONTS 4
Wed 22 contd	French success (23). **Flanders** — Lt-Gen H Wilson (ex-Chief Liaison Officer to Foch) takes over IV Corps (-1 Dec 1916).			
Thu 23	Nivelle promoted to command French III Corps (*see* 19 Apr 1916).			
Fri 24	Falkenhayn initiates preparations for the Verdun offensive codenamed *Gericht* (Tribunal, Judgement, place of execution): Fifth Army (Crown Prince) to be reinforced with 4 army corps & 2000 guns & to attack French centre between R Meuse & Woëvre.	**Galicia** — Heavy fighting on R Strypa.	Austrian 62nd Div finally crosses R Tara after heroic Montenegrin resistance.	**Gallipoli : Helles** — Fierce Turk shelling but British patrolling prevails. **Mesopotamia : Kut** — Turk 52nd Div twice repulsed from fort (-25 Dec) with 2000 cas for only 315 defenders (total 1625 since 5). 4-hr burial truce (26).
Sat 25	**Flanders** — Intermittent minor arty duels (with mining 26). King's Christmas message to BEF. **Vosges** — French bty claims hit on munitions train stopped in Hachimethe rail stn SE of Bonhomme.			**Gallipoli** — Evacuated troops mainly at sea between Lemnos & Egypt (-31). **Helles** — French inf gone (12-22) but Gen Brulard leaves guns to cover British who begin loading stores.
Sun 26				
Mon 27	**Meuse** — German VII Res Corps (Zwehl) completes secret move from Valenciennes to N of Verdun.	**Galicia/Bukovina** — **Ivanov Offensive** with 18 inf & 4 cav divs + 1000 guns (1000 shells each) along 90-mile front from R Prut to N of Dniester (-9 Jan 1916) v Austrian Seventh Army (8 inf & 5 cav divs) which repels 6 attacks on first day; Ivanov loses 50,000 men (6000 PoWs) for few gains.		**Gallipoli** — British Cabinet agrees to Helles evacuation.
Tue 28	Last of **Indian Corps leaves France**. Arty activity nr Armentières & Ypres.	**Baltic Provinces** — Letts rout Germans on R Aa.	**Salonika** — British 29th Bde sent by sea round Khalkidike Peninsula to complete defence line E of Gulf to Rendina, ie the sea (*see* 10 Jan 1916).	**Mesopotamia** — Turks begin fortifying line 3 miles E of Sheikh Sa'ad v Kut relief force.
Wed 29	**First conference between Joffre and Haig**: summer 1916 (Somme) offensive mooted. Joffre proposes great combined offensive by 65 divs on a 60-mile front Arras-W of Péronne-Lassigny. **Flanders** — German trenches raided by British nr Armentières.			
Thu 30	**Artois** — Germans explode 5 mines nr Loos. **Alsace** — French capture Reh-Felsen & Hirzstein in Hartmannsweil-		**Salonika** — First Zeppelin raid (*see* AIR WAR).	

AFRICAN OPERATIONS 5	SEA WAR 6	AIR WAR 7	INTERNATIONAL EVENTS 8	HOME FRONTS 9
Cameroons — Final British advance on Yaunde resumes in 4 cols. Smith-Dorrien sails for Cape (where Brig-Gen Northey arr) but catches pneumonia. **Somaliland** — Anglo-Italian Agreement on R Juba border.	**Med** — U-boat torpedoes & sinks French liner *Ville de Ciotat* (80 lives lost). **Britain** — First Lord of Admiralty Balfour in Commons refers to 'terrible level' of shipping freight charges.			**Secret War : Britain** — Word 'tank' is coined.
Uganda Railway: Germans repulsed from Ndi stn (-26), 17 British cause 24 German cas in cross-border raid. **Cameroons** — British reject Christmas Day ceasefire & force Ngoa (26).				Lloyd George Glasgow speech says 80,000 skilled munition workers needed, shouted down by 3000 shop stewards. **Secret War** — Haig notes on Churchill memo 'Is anything known about the caterpillar [tank]?' **France** — Soldiers' Day (-26). (Dec) 850,000 people in munitions work.
L Tanganyika — HM motorboat *Mimi* sinks German steamer *Kingani* which is raised & renamed HMS *Fifi* 15 Jan 1916.	**N Sea — Disguised raider *Möwe*** (Dohna-Schlodien) **leaves Bremen**, bluffs her way through Northern Patrol. On 16 Jan she captures British liner *Appam* (£2m cargo & governors of Sierra Leone & Nigeria) N of Madeira, puts prize crew aboard, arrives Norfolk, Va 1 Feb. *Möwe* returns to Bremen 4 Mar 1916 (*see* 29 Feb 1916) having sunk 14 ships (11 British) or 57,520t.		Berlin pays Dr Helphand 1m roubles for Petrograd propaganda, after its Copenhagen ambassador Brockdorff-Rantzau convinced (6) that only revolution can remove Russia from Allies.	
	Med — British Govt decides to evacuate Cape Helles (*see* 8/9 Jan 1916. **Gallipoli** — *Agamemnon* & 2 monitors bombard Kum Tepe. 2 French cruisers occupy Castellorizo I, E of Rhodes, despite Greek protests.			**Bulgaria** — Tsar Ferdinand's speech from the throne hails Serbia's defeat.
	Adriatic — French submarine *Archimède* torpedoes & sinks Austrian transport *Kupa* off Cape Planka.		US 'Col' House sails for Europe (*see* INT'L EVENTS 21 Jan 1916). British War Ctee agree main 1916 effort to be on W Front. **Neutrals: USA** — NY Federal Grand Jury indicts German Capt Rintelen & 7 Americans with conspiracy to restrain foreign trade. **Neutrals: Sweden** — 4000lb German-bound rubber seized in *Oscar II*.	**British Cabinet decides for conscription.**
	Adriatic — High-speed action chase off Cattaro, between Austrian sqn (2 of 5 destroyers sunk in Durazzo minefield after sinking 3 vessels there, cruiser *Helgoland* damaged) & Allied sqn of 4 cruisers incl *Dartmouth* & *Weymouth*, follows Austrian raid on Durazzo. French submarine *Monge* sunk before it by Austrian destroyer *Balaton*. Both sides dissatisfied with results.	**W Front** — 6 Fokkers shoot down 1 RFC 8 Sqn BE2c W of Cambrai, but Lt Sholto Douglas (future MRAF) in the other BE2c evades both Boelcke & Immelmann by coming down to 10 ft. 26 other RFC aircraft damage Comines rail stn & Hervilly airfield.	Grey circulates Cabinet with Russian Foreign Minister Sazanov's report from Armenia via Constantinople sources that Djemal Pasha willing to rebel v Sultan and Germany if recognised as Sultan of non-European Turkey minus capital & straits. French law gives Allies perpetual rights to soldiers' graves in France (*see* HOME FRONTS Jan 1916).	Leicester Square première of *Britain Prepared*, 3-hr documentary film. Balfour introduces, goes on worldwide distribution (*see* E FRONT 5 Apr 1916).
Cameroons — Ebermaier & rearguard leave Yaunde. **E Africa** — First S Africans land at Mombasa.	Falkenhayn advocates unlimited U-boat war as naval equivalent of Verdun v Britain; Adm Holtzendorff convinced,	**Salonika** — First German air raid (by Zeppelins), a Greek shepherd k on outskirts, but incident does not infuriate	Gen Sarrail arrests & deports Central Powers' Salonika consuls + their 54 staff.	

171

DECEMBER 1915	WESTERN FRONT 1	EASTERN FRONT 2	SOUTHERN FRONTS 3	TURKISH FRONTS 4
Thu 30 contd	erkopf sector.			
Fri 31	**Flanders** — Germans attack (& slight advance) nr Hulluch. **Alsace** — German counter-attack at Hirzstein. German Army now has 8000 MGs. French Army has 13,000 motor vehicles.	**Pripet** — Brusilov attack across R Styr at Chartorysk.		**Armenia** — Yudenich's top secret steps for 10 Jan pre-emptive surprise winter offensive almost complete, goes to Tiflis to inform Grand Duke.
Sat 1 January 1916	**Vosges** — German attacks at Rehbelsen recapture all ground lost 28 Dec and advance S (2). **Flanders** — 3rd Cdn Div formed.	Russian strength 1,693,000 (1,243,000 have rifles, *see* 20 Mar). **Baltic Provinces** — In-decisive fighting throughout month.	K Peter of Serbia reaches Salonika (*see* AIR WAR 7).	**Mesopotamia: Kut** — 1st Ger-man plane seen (4 arr Baghdad a few days later,*see* 13 Feb). **E Persia** — 1140 British troops on cordon duty, drive back a German party (18). **Arabia** — Sherif Hussein accepts British alliance (*see* 15 May). **Egypt** — Col Clayton forms Arab Bureau in Cairo (*see* Feb 16).
Sun 2	**Vosges** — Arty fire & clashes in Hirzstein sector (2-8) but no change in situation. Both sides suffer heavy losses.	**Bukovina** — Heavy fighting NE of Czernowitz (4 also 7, 11, 14).		
Mon 3	Brig-Gen J Charteris becomes BEF Intelligence Chief (-24 Jan 1918); his optimistic reports frequently mislead Haig.			
Tue 4	**Champagne** — German trench raids.			**Mesopotamia** — 1st attempt to relieve Kut: Gen Aylmer's 19,000-strong Tigris Corps begins advance astride river, probes Sheikh Saad defences (6), but facing overall 30,000 Turks & 83 guns.
Wed 5	**Champagne** — Violent German bombardment & attack between Hill 304 & Tahure.			
Thu 6	**Verdun** — Falkenhayn approves Fifth Army attack plan; it entails 10 light railways, concrete bunkers, & plank pathways. Arty plan (8,*see* 27).		**Albania** — (c) Rear-Adm Trou-bridge organizes feeding & care of Serb refugees at San Giovanni di Medua (Scutari's port), leaves in Italian destroyer	

AFRICAN OPERATIONS 5	SEA WAR 6	AIR WAR 7	INTERNATIONAL EVENTS 8	HOME FRONTS 9
	calculates only 650,000t new shipping built in 1916 & 70 U-boats can destroy 160,000t pm (*see* 15 Jan). **N Sea** — RN cruiser *Natal* (304k) destroyed by internal explosion in Cromarty Firth. **E Med** — *U38* (Valentiner) torpedoes & sinks P & O liner *Persia* (334 lives lost, 2 US incl Aden consul) without warning c70 miles off Crete.	Greece (*see* 7 Jan 1916).		
E Africa — Lettow writes to Kaiser listing Gov Schnee's interferences (Berlin receives Aug 1916 & reprimands). He now has 14,298 troops (2988 whites).	Northern Patrol (4 AMCs lost) intercepts 3098 vessels in 1915 of which 743 sent into Kirkwall (Shetlands, av 66 pw), 817 fishing boats & 408 Allied allowed to pass.	**W Front** — 86 Fokker Es on strength. RFC has lost 50 pilots & observers since 1 Nov.		**Britain** — 6000 pulmonary TB cases discharged from HM Forces to date. TU membership up 5% (to 4.3m), unemployment 1%, lowest since 1872; only 74 people claim employment relief (6055 in Dec 1914). Imports up 18% on 1914, exports down 11%. Net immigration 25,000 due to war. **Turkey** — Kemal on sick leave, Constantinople.
Cameroons — **British occupy Yaunde**; nearly 15,000 Allied troops & 34 guns in colony. **Morocco** — Lyautey holds New Year reception at Rabat (*see* 24).	**British introduce depth charges** but only 2 per ASW vessel, insufficient supply till June 1917 (*see* 22 Mar 1916; 1 June). RN now has 35 paddle-minesweepers (24 more being built) plus 14 specialized sloops with Grand Fleet. New 'Hunt' class soon ordered (12 allocated to Grand Fleet, join it 1917).	**Britain** — (Jan) Future top RNAS ace Canadian Collishaw joins RNAS (*see* 12 Oct).	Tsar appointed British FM. K Peter of Serbia reaches Salonika (leaves 15). **Occupied Serbia** — (Jan) Germans give their zone to Austrians & Bulgars (*see* 18). **Neutrals: USA** — Polish Aid Day.	**Austria** — 'The state of exhaustion here is already very great' (Freud). **France** — Income tax law takes effect. Britain Home Secretary Simon resigns v conscription, Samuel succeeds (10). (Jan) MO5 becomes MI5, Secret Service becomes MI61c. Brig-Gen Macdonogh becomes DMI (3). 1st series of W Front films released. (Jan) National Ctee for the Care of Soldiers' Graves formed (*see* INT'L EVENTS May). **Germany** — SPD repudiates *Vorwärts* for pacifism (*see* 12).
	Dardanelles — British submarine *E2* recalled; **end of Allied submarine campaign.** Half Turk merchant fleet now sunk & warships immobilized by coal shortage. **Secret War: E Indies** — Capt Müller's 8-man U-boat telegraph party leave Dutch Java (neutral) for Yemen (arrive Sana, Mar).			
Cameroons — French resume advance E from Mangeles, c600 British march S from Yaunde (5) where Gen Aymerich arrives (8).			Franco-British Ottoman Empire partition agreement. **Neutrals: Greece** — Govt protests v arrest of Central Powers' Salonika consuls.	**France** — General Press Relations Directorate formed. **Britain** — Clydeside Socialist newspaper *Forward* suppressed for 4 weeks.
			Britain answers Germany on Q-ship *Baralong* affair, offers impartial tribunal if 3 similar German cases included, Germany contests (14). **Secret War: Austria** — Conrad to Count Tisza: 'There can be no question of destroying the Russian war machine; England cannot be defeated; peace must be made in not too short a space, or we shall be fatally weakened , if not destroyed'.	**Britain** — Lord Derby's recruiting report published, 2,675,149 vols to date but over 2m of military age unattested justifies conscription. Fuller-phone (non-tappable) approved for prod & distribution to BEF (10,000 hand-made sets + c5000 for US Army 1917-18).
		W Front — Nieuport 11 fighter begins entering service with *Esc N3*. 25 RFC aircraft attack Douai airfields & Le Sars stores dump (16 repeat on 17).	**Secret War** — K Albert asks what are Berlin's guarantees for postwar Belgium if she renounces neutrality (*see* 25 Feb).	**Britain** — Asquith introduces Military Service Bill (conscription). TUC oppose (6). **Germany** — Dresden Industrial War Board formed (employers & unions, *see* 10 Feb).
	Atlantic — Battleship *King Edward VII* sunk W of Scapa off Cape Wrath on mine (1 of 252) laid by *Möwe*; 2 neutral steamers also destroyed but 71			

173

JANUARY 1916	WESTERN FRONT 1	EASTERN FRONT 2	SOUTHERN FRONTS 3	TURKISH FRONTS 4
Thu 6 contd			(19/20) having correctly insisted Serb main evacuation take place farther S (*see* 12).	
Fri 7		**Pripet** — Brusilov storms Chartorysk (50 miles E of Kovel).		**Gallipoli: Helles** — Garrison 19,000 men, 63 guns after all French gone (1-4), repulses half-hearted Turk attack at Gully Spur. **Mesopotamia** — **Battle of Sheikh Saad**: Aylmer only dents Turk defences for 4007 cas (but *see* 9). Euphrates: Gorringe's 1000 men occupy Butaniya 12 miles N of Nasiriya.
Sat 8	**Vosges** — German attack checked at Hart-mannsweillerkopf (8-9).	**Galicia** — Severe fighting as Ivanov offensive resumes.	**Montenegro — Austrian offensive**: Gen Webenau's 50,000 troops incl 5000 Bosnian Muslims & 3 *Kaiserjäger* bns from Italian Front begins at dawn with 500-gun barrage + naval shelling & aircraft. **Salonika** — Gen Milne lands with his British 27th Div to be i/c XVI Corps (*see* 5 May) on r flank.	**Gallipoli** — EVACUATION COMPLETE (-9) with last 16,918 men & 37 guns taken off in 3 batches in worsening weather; Maj-Gen Maude last to leave at W Beach (see AIR WAR 12). Total evacuated since 28 Dec 35,268 troops; 3689 horses & mules; 127 guns; 328 vehicles; 1600t of stores. 15 guns, 1590 vehicles wrecked & abandoned, 508 mules shot (*see* 20). No casualties during evacuation.
Sun 9	**Champagne** — German attacks E & W of Butte de Massiges. French line penetrated at number of points (incl Butte du Mesnil & Mt Têtu), ground partially regained (10-11).		**Montenegro** — Austrians storm 4850ft Mt Lovcen ('the Gibraltar of the Adriatic'); Montenegrins retreat 12 miles to capital Cetinje & begin talks for soon-agreed local truce (12 *see* 13).	**Mesopotamia** — Turks retreat to Wadi, British occupy Sheikh Saad. Goltz replaces Nureddin with Khalil Pasha. **Egypt** — Sir A Murray succeeds Monro (leaves 11) as C-in-C MEF.
Mon 10			**Salonika** — RN motorboat from Mudros launched on L Langaza, 2 more patrol L Beshik from 15. This sector of defences for the Allied Entrenched Camp well developed, 80-mile line but 45 miles covered by lakes & marshes.	**Armenia** — **Yudenich's winter offensive** Battle of Köprüköy (-19) during Russian Christmas. Turk Third Army driven back on Erzerum, losing 25,000 cas & 20-30 guns for 12,000 Russian (2000 frostbite cases in hospital).
Tue 11	**Somme** — Lt-Gen Earl of Cavan i/c new BEF XIV Corps of 3 divs (-10 Mar 1918).		French marines occupy Corfu, despite Greek protests, as base to refit Serb Army (*see* 15). **Montenegro** — Austrians take Cetinje, but 3-day battle at Mojkovac 50 miles to N before Gen Vesovic orders his troops home (*see* 17).	
Wed 12	**Argonne** — German gas attack in Forges sector between R Meuse & the Argonne.		**Serb Army evacuation to Corfu begins** (*see* SEA WAR). **Salonika** — Special Allied force blows Demi Hissar bridge on R Struma in presence of Greek troops (*see* 28).	

AFRICAN OPERATIONS 5	SEA WAR 6	AIR WAR 7	INTERNATIONAL EVENTS 8	HOME FRONTS 9
	mines cleared by May. **Flanders** — 5 Dover Patrol monitors shell German coast btys without reply (*see* 15).	**Salonika** — German air raid causes 18 cas.	Britain arranges to ration Holland. **Austria** — Count Tisza argues only war indemnity will ensure post-war development.	**France** — 1917 conscript class called up (-11).
	Adriatic — 5 old Austrian battleships give effective fire support to troops assaulting Mt Lovcen (Montenegro) (8-10,*see* S FRONTS) thus freeing Cattaro naval base from hostile observers & allowing cruiser force to be stationed there. **Aegean** — **Final Evacuation of Gallipoli** (-9): 2 battleships (*Cornwallis* fires 6500 shells), 1 cruiser, 6 destroyers & 15 motor lighters take part at Cape Helles. **Black Sea** — *Goeben* straddled at 1914-18 record naval sea range of 24,000 yds by new Russian battleship *Empress Catherine II* (*Imperatriza Ekaterina II*) but escapes after 1 of last 5 Turk colliers sunk.			**Turkey** — Govt officials get 15-20% cost of living bonus.
Cameroons — Main German force (2500) retreating on Ebolowa, aiming for Spanish Muni; Capt Stein returns 214 Allied PoWs to British on R Nyong. **E Africa : Coast** — Wavell's 80 Arabs defeated at Mkongani but British drive 3 German coys from Ngurungani (10).				
			Allies inform Greece of Serb Army's proposed transfer to Corfu where French troops land, Greece refuses consent (13) but Serbs land (15). **Neutrals: Switzerland** — Lenin moves to Zurich (or 11), soon lecturing to earn money. Police have by now arrested many British MI1c agents (*see* 15). **Mexico** — Gen Francisco Villa shoots 18 US mining engineers taken from train at Santa Isabel (US demands punishment 12).	**Italy** — 3rd War Loan opens; maximum cereal prices fixed (11).
	E Atlantic — Raider *Möwe* sinks 8 British ships (-20), incl 3 on 13, totalling 27,888t almost matching Jan U-boat sinkings (5 British ships).	**Occupied France** — Lille: German munitions dump explosion nr rail stn (night 11/12) hills 108 civilians (see 2 Apr).		**Russia** — 10,000 workers strike at Nikolayev, Black Sea naval base, 45,000 at Petrograd (22). **Germany** — *Reichstag* votes OAP age reduction from 70 to 65.
		W Front — Immelmann & Boelcke first German airmen (8 victories each) to receive *Pour le Mérite*. **Gallipoli** — Turco-German Fokkers (3 recently arrived) shoot down a second RNAS aircraft off Helles (first 11); last Allied air cas of campaign in which British dropped 1155 bombs weighing total 27t.	**Austro-Montenegrin armistice** (-20), broken off (*see* 23).	**Germany** — Liebknecht expelled from SPD in *Reichstag*. **Canada** — Parlt (-18 May) votes $250m war credit + 25% profits tax.

175

JANUARY 1916	WESTERN FRONT 1	EASTERN FRONT 2	SOUTHERN FRONTS 3	TURKISH FRONTS 4
Thu 13		Russian artillery 4894 guns (inc Armenian Front & only 210 6-in howitzers) with 4,915,000 shells (*see* 20 Mar). **W Russia** — Russian Fifth Army (Gourko) success at Garbonovka nr Dvinsk, more fighting (14).	K Nicholas of Montenegro cables Vienna for peace, but terms uncompromising (*see* 19) yet refuses to order army to follow Serbs (*see* 17).	**Persia** — Baratov defeats German Count Kaunitz & Turk bn at Kangavar, concentrates 8000-10,000 men & 22 guns at Hamadan (31,*see* 8 Feb). **Mesopotamia — Battle of Wadi** (-14): Aylmer (1613 cas) takes Turk position but fails to cut Turk retreat (2000 cas) on Um-el-Hanna. Heavy rains & wind (14-18) break British Tigris bridge.
Fri 14			**Italian Front** — Heavy fighting nr Gorizia, but Italians lose Hill 188 to Austrian counter-attack (24) & evacuate to a less unfavourable Peuma-Oslavia line.	
Sat 15		**Pripet** — Russian progress on R Styr S of Pinsk.		**'Balkan Express' rail link between Turkey & Germany opens** (*see* INT'L EVENTS 18 Jan 1916). **Mesopotamia : Kut** — Goltz inspects siege lines.
Sun 16			**Gen Sarrail takes formal joint Allied command** (incl 3000 Serb troops) at Salonika, but British retain veto over anything but defensive measures.	**Mesopotamia** — Townshend radios Aylmer that Kut has 17-21 days rations + tinned meat & cattle (*see* 21 & 25).
Mon 17			MONTENEGRO SURRENDERS: Gen Vesovic signs a general capitulation.	**Mesopotamia** — Nixon vetoes Aylmer's suggestion that Townshend break out and is invalided to India (18). Viceroy agrees to send 3 more bdes.
Tue 18				
Wed 19			K Nicholas of Montenegro flees to Scutari, thence sails to Brindisi (*see* INT'L EVENTS 23).	**Mesopotamia — Lt-Gen Sir P Lake succeeds Nixon as C-in-C.** Aylmer resumes advance. Kut: Turks repulsed from Woolpress village on S bank (night 19 /20).
Thu 20	**Verdun** — Castelnau, Joffre's deputy, inspects defences, puts improvements in hand (*see* 24 Feb).			**Gallipoli** — 36,000 Turks (2+ divs) leave for Mesopotamia.
Fri 21		Renewed Russian attack in E Poland.	**Albania** — Austrian patrols enter Scutari (*see* 28).	**Mesopotamia — Battle of Hanna**: Aylmer's 7600 (2741 cas) repulsed by 9000 Turks & 26 guns 23 miles from Kut; 2 Indian Army VCs won but only a few score men get into Turk trenches before torrential rain worsens awful cold & mud (-31). Kut: Tigris floods (-mid Feb) NW British defences & Turk front trenches, they fall back 2000 yds (27); garrison put on half rations.
Sat 22			**Montenegro** — Austrians occupy Antivari & Culcigno on	

AFRICAN OPERATIONS 5	SEA WAR 6	AIR WAR 7	INTERNATIONAL EVENTS 8	HOME FRONTS 9
Cameroons — 850 French march S from Yaunde, occupy Ebolowa (19); British join (22).	German Naval Staff declare their support for unrestricted submarine warfare, can force England to make peace in 6 months (*see* 15; 6 Mar).			**Germany** — Chancellor promises Prussian Diet post-war electoral reform. **Britain** Commons votes RN 50,000 more men (total 350,000).
		W Front — Due to heavy losses every RFC recon plane to have 3 fighter escorts.	**Neutrals: Portugal** — Lisbon warehouse fire perhaps due to German sabotage (*see* 24 Feb).	**Ireland** — Lord Lieutenant reports 146,000 enlistments to date, 100,000 more available (*see* 16 Oct). **France** — Col Estienne & Creusot engineer Brillié design tank with 75mm gun & 10mm armour, Joffre wants 400 (31, *see* 25 Feb).
	N Sea — Dover Patrol monitors shell Westeinde, Belgium (& 27). **Germany** — CNS Holtzendorff claims new U-boats can put Britain out of war in 6-7 months, pressing Kaiser (24).		**Neutrals: USA** — Papen papers published incl cheque book payments to German agents. **Neutrals: Switzerland** — 2 Swiss colonels charged with reporting to Austro-German military attachés (acquitted 29 Feb).	**Turkey** — Kemal rides in triumph into Adrianople.
		W Front — Allies bomb Lille.		**France** — French Soldiers Flag Day.
	Black Sea — Russian torpedo boats sink 163 sailing vessels, 40 more (22).		**Neutrals: Greece** — Govt newspaper reports on 'Anglo-French organization of secret police'.	**Britain** — War Pensions Ctee first meets. Churchill writes to his wife: 'Imbecile govt, and purblind Kitchener. Wait & see'.
	Aegean — Allied warships again shell Bulgar Dedeagach & Porto Lagos (19).		**Occupied Serbia** — Tsar Ferdinand arrives in Nis, greets Kaiser off new 'German Balkan Express'; town hall banquet, Ferdinand made German FM. **Neutrals: USA** — Lansing asks Allies not to arm merchant ships, or liners (28). **Diplomacy** — Baron Beyens succeeds Davignon as Belgian Foreign Minister. **Secret War** — German agent Steinwachs reports on Estonian revolutionary Keskula. Allied War Council in London.	
S Cameroons — French S Force takes Mansin, French Campo col captures Ngat (23), reaches Ekob (30).			Britain buys 800,000t of Rumanian wheat (Austro-German protest 26, *see* 7 Apr).	**Britain** — First Derby scheme recruits called up. Munitions Ministry invites schools & universities to help with inventions.
E Africa — c600 British reoccupy Longido, Mbuyuni (22), reach Serengeti (24); German mine blows up armoured train at Maktau (22).			US 'Col' House in Paris, at Berlin (26), returns Paris 2 Feb. **Neutrals: Switzerland** — Severely wounded Franco-German PoW exchange.	
	Montenegro — Allied evacuation at San Giovanni di	**Britain** — Hit-&-run single or dual German aircraft raids on	Rumania opens talks for Russian military help.	

JANUARY 1916	WESTERN FRONT 1	EASTERN FRONT 2	SOUTHERN FRONTS 3	TURKISH FRONTS 4
Sat 22 contd			coast (*see* 28). **Albania** — Austro-Bulgars take Berat.	
Sun 23	**Artois** — Violent German attack nr Neuville-St-Vaast, renewed 25 with mine explosions (& 26).			**Armenia** — Grand Duke authorizes attack on Erzerum. Yudenich has 20 aircraft (1st in theatre), motor convoys & 34 siege guns to help.
Mon 24	**Flanders** — German diversionary attack on Nieuport (Yser).			
Tue 25		Direct Vienna-Warsaw train service begins.		**Armenia** — Russian bn seizes key Kargapazar ('Crow Bazaar') Ridge (c9750 ft) 15 miles NE of Erzerum, whole 4th Caucasus Rifle Div concentrates there by 31. **Mesopotamia** — Aylmer encamps at El Owasa; Townshend radios that he has 84 days food due to Arab barley store discovery.
Wed 26			Falkenhayn orders Gallwitz to prepare attack across Greek frontier (*see* 28); despite Bulgar protests Germans stock shells at Veles, but single-line railway overstrained (*see* 27 Feb).	
Thu 27	**Flanders/Artois** — German attacks at Loos & Neuville-St Vaast. **Argonne** — Mining & counter-mining activity. **Verdun** — Falkenhayn's final orders for Op *Gericht*, 'an offensive in the Meuse area in the direction of Verdun'. Scheduled to begin 12 Feb but Crown Prince's Army Orders specify object as being 'to capture the fortress of Verdun by precipitate methods'. Falkenhayn deceives Crown Prince by promising him a 4-div reserve but ensures they remain on other sectors under his (Falkenhayn's) personal control.		**Isonzo** — Austrians repulsed on upper river.	
Fri 28		Prince Lvov & Mayor of Moscow visit Gen Alexeiev, Army morale much improved but hardly an able officer above regt CO, Tsar does not interfere.	**Albania** — Austrians occupy Alessio & San Giovanni di Medua (Scutari's port). **Salonika** — 3000 Allies occupy Karaburun coast defence btys (250 Greeks) on gulf 12 miles to S of city after talks during which battleship HMS *Albion* & Russian cruiser *Askold* to seaward with 3 aircraft above. Joffre orders Sarrail to prepare apparent offensive.	**Mesopotamia**: Kut garrison 8356 effectives (600 rifle rnds per man), 2157 sick, 2908 followers. Lake visits Aylmer's HQ (-29): Gorringe made Tigris Corps CoS.
Sat 29	**Somme** — German Second Army success NE of Dampierre (*see* 6 Feb).	Alexeiev to Adm Eberhardt (Black Sea Fleet) '... we have no right ... to disperse our troops ... to ... tasks ... secondary even if appreciable in themselves, in remote theatres of war'. **Pripet/ Bukovina** — Renewed fighting, Austrians claim success.	**Corfu** — 5400 Serbs die from retreat hardships (-30 Apr, *see* 10 Feb; 3 & 11 Apr).	
Sun 30		Another German gas regt arrives.		

AFRICAN OPERATIONS 5	SEA WAR 6	AIR WAR 7	INTERNATIONAL EVENTS 8	HOME FRONTS 9
	Medusa (8338 men) ends (see S FRONTS 6).	Dover & Folkestone airship sheds cause little damage (night 22/23 & 23, but 7 cas).		
W Desert — Maj-Gen Wallace (322 cas) beats 6000 Senussi (700 cas) at Halazin & captures their camp (25 miles SW of Matruh, see 11 & 26 Feb).		First RFC all-FE2b 2-seat pusher sqn (No 20) reaches France (No 25, 20 Feb; No 23, 16 Mar; No 22, 1 Apr, see 7 Feb).	King of Montenegro arrives at Rome; his son Prince Mirko accepts Austrian terms (25) which King disowns (24 May).	
Cameroons — 900+ Allies drive in German rearguard at Mafub, but advance only 4 miles, occupy Abang & beat rearguard again (25, last British action). **Spanish Morocco** — Decree organises admin, many tribes submit.	**N Sea** — Vice Adm Reinhard **Scheer becomes C-in-C German High Seas Fleet** in succession to Pohl (resigns 19, dies Feb of cancer, aged 60). Scheer advocates offensive & proposes battlecruiser raids on British coast to draw Grand Fleet into traps sprung by battlecruisers & torpedo craft (destroyers & U-boats) (see 10 Feb).			
			US protest v Allied neutral trade restraint (see 21 Feb).	**Britain** — Mile End (E London) by-election, Tory wins by 1991 votes. Press Bureau publishes blockade figures. Churchill writes to Lloyd George suggesting meeting, but no reply.
S Cameroons — Allies occupy Nkan; the 550+ British withdraw to Kribi (29-31).			**Neutrals: Greece** — War Ministry orders troops in Macedonia to withdraw from frontier if Germans or Bulgars appear (see 9 Mar).	**Britain** — Grey defends blockade in Commons.
E Africa — Gov Schnee's Kaiser's birthday speech at Dar-es-Salaam: 'The enemy cannot crush us economically . We get all we require from the country'.	**Adriatic** — Austrian cruiser *Novara* thwarted from raid on Durazzo by Italian cruiser *Puglia* & French destroyer *Bouchier* (see 6 Feb).		*The Times* publishes Enver Pasha admission that Turkey on verge of defeat in Mar 1915. **Neutrals: USA** — Pres Wilson speaking tour in W (-3 Feb).	**Britain** — 1st Military Service Act passed 383-36. **France** — Chamber adopts Parlt Ctee supervision of military zone. **Spartacus Communist group founded in Berlin.**
N Rhodesia — c80 Rhodesian & BSA police repulse German patrol nr Ikomba (70 miles SE of Abercorn).	**N Sea** — Harwich Force again (fog aborted attempt 18) abandons *Vindex* seaplane raid, 20 miles from Ems estuary, when German torpedoes fired & one brushes cruiser *Arethusa's* stern (-29).			
		France — Second & last Zeppelin raid on Paris causes 54 cas, last air raid until Jan 1918.	**France** — Anglo-French Munitions Conference.	**Secret War: Britain** — 'Mother' prototype tank begins successful trials (see 2 Feb). **Russia** — Première of Prokofiev's 'Scythian Suite', Petrograd.
Cameroons — French gunboat *Vauban* reports nearly 800 German Europeans at or over Spanish Muni frontier (see 4				**Britain** — War Savings Ctees begun. **France** — BEF arrest Attorney-Gen F E Smith for visiting Churchill's HQ without a

JANUARY 1916	WESTERN FRONT 1	EASTERN FRONT 2	SOUTHERN FRONTS 3	TURKISH FRONTS 4
Sun 30 contd				
Mon 31				
Tue 1 February 1916	**Verdun** — Maj-Gen Beeg, i/c German Fifth Army arty, informs Falkenhayn that all 1220 additional guns (incl 13 Big Berthas) for prelim 'hurricane' bombardment now in concealed emplacements in woods N & E of Verdun; 1300 trains have delivered 2.5m shells. Verdun fortified zone put under French Central Army Gp (Langle). (Feb) **BEF passes million men**, 1,037,600, 121 German divs in W. **Secret War** — (Feb) French produce field telephone cipher notebook at Gen Dubail's request.	**Baltic Provinces** — Violent shelling SE of Riga (& 7).	**Albania** — Serbs repulse Austrians nr R Ishmi, but latter occupy Kroja 25 miles N of Durazzo (4, *see* 27).	
Wed 2				
Thu 3		**Bukovina** — Renewed Russian attack, Lechitski reaches W bank of Dniester (8), has more success (20).		
Fri 4				**Mesopotamia** — New Kut relief plan approved.
Sat 5	**BEF Fourth Army** (Rawlinson) **formed** (*see* 2 Mar).			**Mesopotamia** — Turks begin redoubts E of Kut. **Armenia** — Black Sea sqn aids Gen Lyakhov to take Turk R Arhavi line (-6) & R Vice (15-16) (*see* SEA WAR 4).
Sun 6	**Somme** — French attacks on Vache Wood & Signal (Frise), recaptured (6-13). **Flanders** — Germans shell Loos (& 3).	**Conrad offers all German troops** S of Pripet **back to Falkenhayn** who insultingly refuses, **but only 2 divs remain by June** with German Army commanders.	**Italian Front** — Conrad gives first orders for spring offensive in Trentino: 14 divs & 240 heavy guns to be assembled for 6 Apr attack incl VIII Corps from Serbia & 3 divs & 60 heavy guns from E Front, troops begin arriving mid-Feb along single railway S of Trent (*see* 20). **Salonika** — British 7th Mtd Bde begins arriving, and temporarily an RND bde (21-early Mar) before Admiralty recall whole div from Mediterranean: French 17th Colonial Div arrives late Feb.	
Mon 7				**Mesopotamia** — CIGS orders British 13th Div & 7th Mtn Arty Bde to theatre (*see* 27). Euphrates: 2900 British evacuate Butaniya harrassed

AFRICAN OPERATIONS 5	SEA WAR 6	AIR WAR 7	INTERNATIONAL EVENTS 8	HOME FRONTS 9
Feb). Gen Aymerich takes over final ops from Dobell.				pass. He, Bonar Law & Lloyd George agree at St Omer that Asquith must go (31).
S Cameroons — Final French advance begins from Nkan with 600+ men & 2 guns. **E Africa** — Smith-Dorrien (ill) resigns as C-in-C (*see* 6 Feb). Sir H Byatt made Civil Administrator of Occupied German E Africa. British have lost 30 killed by wild animals to date.	**USA** — Pres Wilson says USN ready (*see* 11 Mar).	**Britain — First German airship raid on the Midlands** by 9 Zeppelins (night 31 Jan/1 Feb) sporadic & off course, Liverpool not reached but frequent false alarms (-5 Mar); Naval Airship Div CO Strasser aboard *L11* (183 cas from 389 bombs, material damage worth only £53,832). Returning *L19* lost in N Sea 2 Feb (16k, no survivors). 22 British fighters ascend, 8 damaged or wrecked on landing, 2 pilots dow.	**Neutrals: Holland** — SA Guest (War Propaganda Bureau) reports on trip to contact German socialist groups.	**Britain** — 8062 children exempted from school to date for farmwork.
Italian Somaliland — Buloburti garrison disperse Dervishes (*see* 27 Mar).	**First merchant ship sunk by air attack:** Zeppelin bombs 970t British *Franz Fischer* (13 lost) 2 miles S of Kentish Knock. Only 3 other British ships so lost (all 1917). **Britain** — (Feb) Shipping Control Ctee formed under Lord Curzon (*see* 15 Mar). Fisher writes to Asquith 'There is grave anxiety and serious misgivings in the Fleet ...'. (Feb) Russia establishes independent Arctic Flotilla.		**Neutrals: USA** — *Möwe* prize crew brings British liner *Appam* into Newport News, Va, denied asylum (2 Mar).	**Russia** — PM Goremikin resigns, pro-German Stürmer succeeds (*see* 22). (Feb) Tsarina at opening of 200-bed Anglo-Russian hospital, Petrograd. **Britain** — RFP up 3% to 47%. (Feb): War Office forms propaganda dept; War Propaganda Bureau reports 7m publications distributed. Novelist Sir H Rider Haggard sent to Dominions to arrange postwar settlement of ex-servicemen.
E Africa — N Jubaland tribe take Serenli border post (night 2/3) causing c95 cas (1 MG taken). Tribe dominates locally till post remanned Aug 1917 (*see* l Nov 1917).				**Britain: Secret War** — Kitchener calls 'Mother' tank 'a pretty mechanical toy' on seeing trials with Lloyd George, but reports to War Ctee (3) that 'impressed'. King has a ride (8). Scientists Ctee to promote war science formed.
		W Front — Guynemer destroys 2 LVGs (4th & 5th victories) above Roye, is commissioned 2/Lt (Mar).	**Neutrals: Rumania** — Cereal crop sold to Austro-German syndicate (170,000t exported Feb). Recalls reservists from Salonika (8); partial mobilization complete (14).	
S Cameroons — Germans begin crossing into neutral Spanish Muni (-15), after 125-mile retreat from Yaunde.	**Black Sea** — *Goeben* carries Turk troops to Trebizond (-7, *see* 14 Apr).		French PM Briand meets Masaryk and is persuaded to give Czechs official support.	**Britain** — Whole coastline prohibited to enemy resident aliens (all to register 14).
E Africa — Anglo-Belgian Conference at Lutobo. **Smuts selected to succeed Smith-Dorrien** (public 10, *see* 19).	**Adriatic** — 2 British cruisers, French destroyer *Bouchier* & Italian destroyer *Bronzetti* drive 6 Austrian torpedo boats (2 collide) & a destroyer back to Cattaro thus covering Serb Army evacuation to Corfu. Bad weather helps further (-26).	**W Front** — Immelmann flies 3-gun Fokker EIV in combat.		
		No 24 Sqn (Maj Hawker VC) **first RFC single-seater fighter sqn reaches France** (No 29, 25 Mar; No 32, 25 May) with DH2s. **W Front** — 3 RFC		**Britain** — 4 Glasgow shop stewards arrested for conduct prejudicial to war effort, sentenced 10 (*see* 19). 2 more arrested & deported (29 Mar).

FEBRUARY 1916	WESTERN FRONT 1	EASTERN FRONT 2	SOUTHERN FRONTS 3	TURKISH FRONTS 4
Mon 7 contd				by 5000 Arabs.
Tue 8	**Artois** — Germans attack W of La Folie — 700 yds of trenches taken. French partially recapture (9-10).			**Persia** — Baratov disperses 3000 gendarmes & Kurds at Nihavend, occupies Daulata-bad, is ordered to occupy Kermanshah at once (13).
Wed 9		**Pripet/Galicia** — Severe fighting (& 13-14).	**Serb evacuation (88,153 men) at Durazzo completed** (*see* SEA WAR, 19 & 24).	
Thu 10			75,000 Serb troops now recovering in Corfu although 450 pw die in hospital (*see* 16).	
Fri 11	**Verdun** — German offensive postponed to 21 (rain & snowstorms). French 14th & 51st Divs given vital time to get up. **Champagne** — French attack W of La Main-de-Massiges.	**W Russia** — Russians repulsed S of Dvinsk but retake Garbonovka, repulse German attacks (15).		**Mesopotamia** — British Tigris bridge completed upstream of Wadi. **Armenia** — **Yudenich attacks Erzerum** (-16).
Sat 12	**Champagne** — German diversionary attacks, S of Sainte-Marie-a-Py. **Flanders** — German diversionary attacks nr Steenstraate & Boesinghe E of Saint-Die, Germans attack Wissenbuch positions.			
Sun 13	**Champagne** — German success between Tahure & Somme-Py; French counter-attacks fail (14-16). **Vosges** — Between Seppois & French frontier, Germans penetrate & hold French positions (13-14).		**Albania** — Bulgar First Army takes Elbasan.	**Mesopotamia** — Kut first bombed from air (*see* 22). 140 Indian scurvy cases (14), c5 pd thereon (*see* 24).
Mon 14	**Flanders** — German attacks take 600 yds of trench N of Ypres canal, S of Ypres-Comines railway & nr Saint-Eloi. British 17th Div loses the Bluff (*see* 2 Mar). **Franco-British Conference at Chantilly determines final shape of Somme offensive**, Joffre writes to Haig (18) that date will be c1 July.			
Tue 15				**Persia** — Anglo-Bakhtiari agreement for oilfield protection.
Wed 16	**Champagne** — German gas attack in Reims sector (*see* 25). **Argonne** — Mine warfare.	Hoffmann diary: 'I have recently spoken to hundreds of men on the fronts of 3 armies'.	Montenegrin troops land in Corfu.	**Armenia** — **Yudenich captures Erzerum**, many Arabs desert Turks, who have lost 15,000 men incl 5000 PoWs & 327 guns v 9000 Russian losses (4000 frostbite).

AFRICAN OPERATIONS 5	SEA WAR 6	AIR WAR 7	INTERNATIONAL EVENTS 8	HOME FRONTS 9
		FE2bs of No 20 Sqn protect Second Army recon aircraft E of Ypres despite 14 German aircraft approaching.		
S Cameroons — French reach R Campo opp Ngoa (-10), cross & occupy (10-11), occupy Banyassa (15).	**E Med** — French cruiser *Admiral Charner* (374 drowned, only 1 survivor) sunk in 4 mins by *U21* (Hersing) off Beirut, but otherwise she sinks only 1 steamer on this cruise.		Britain gives France £18m credit in US and requests Japan's naval help.	
L Tanganyika — HM vessels *Fifi* & *Mimi* sink gunboat *Hedwig von Wissmann* , but Cdr Spicer-Simson declines to engage 800t *Graf von Götzen* (10). **E Africa** — 1st RFC flight by 26th SA Sqn (8 BE2cs).	**Serb evacuation at Durazzo completed,** 88,153 men (*see* 26). Jap Govt refuses British request for major naval assistance in European waters (*see* Apr 1917).	**Britain** — 2 German seaplanes from Zeebrugge drop 13 bombs on Broadstairs & Ramsgate (3w); 18 defending aircraft ascend (*see* 20).	Serb Govt established at Corfu. French PM Briand visits Italy (-14), agrees on Allied Paris Conference (12). Tsar Ferdinand at Austro-German GHQs (-14).	
	N Sea — German High Seas Fleet destroyer sortie to Dogger Bank sinks minesweeper sloop HMS *Arabis* of Humber Patrol (*see* 23; 5 Mar).	**Britain** — Air defence responsibilities reallocated: demarcation line fixed at the coast; Army/RFC supplant RN/ RNAS inland. Army to 'also provide the aeroplanes required to work with the home troops and to protect garrisons and vulnerable areas and flying stations'. **C-in-C Home Forces (FM French) assumes responsibility for London's defence** 1200 (16) & elsewhere 1200 (22).	Germany warns US that all armed merchant ships will be attacked without warning from 29. **Neutrals: USA** — War Secretary Garrison resigns (*see* 6 Mar).	Military Service Act in force, single men 19-30 called up for 3-17 March.
W Desert — RFC watch 1000 Senussi from Siwa occupy Baharia oasis, drop 8 x 2016 bombs (12) & scatter Senussi (*see* 27).	Kaiser order allows **U-boats to attack armed steamers as from 29, but passenger liners excluded** (24). Harwich Force flagship cruiser *Arethusa* mined (by Flanders U-boat) off Felixstowe returning from vain sortie to catch German ships.			**BEF GHQ orders 40 tanks,** Lt-Col Swinton increases order to 100 (appointed CO of MG Corps unit for crews 16). **Canada** — 240,000 enlisted to date.
E Africa — **Action at Salaita Hill** (8 miles from Taveta): Maj Kraut's 1320 Germans (43 cas) repulse Malleson's 6000 British (138+ cas).		**Italy** — Austrian air raid on coast (*see* 18).		
French W Africa — Tuareg chief Firhoun again rebels, attacking Menaka (13 & 28 Mar, *see* 7 May).			Allies notify Greece of Montenegrin Army's transfer to Corfu, arrives 16.	**Germany** — 2000 periodicals reported to have ceased due to paper shortage.
		Italy — Austrians bomb Milan, Treviglio, Bergamo & Monza (*see* 18).	**Allied Le Havre Declaration:** No peace without Belgium's restoration & indemnification. **Chantilly Conference fixes 1 July for Somme Offensive.** Novelist Hugh Walpole returns to Petrograd to run Allied Propaganda Bureau.	**Turkey** — Bill extends military age to 50, plus payments from those excused.
		W Front — Ball joins No 13 Sqn (BE2c arty spotters, *see* 22 May).	**Neutrals: USA** — Senator Root attacks foreign policy but Republicans promise support for anti-U-boat policy. Govt announces merchant ships' right to arm for self-defence. USNA cadet intake increased.	**Britain** — Asquith Commons speech, increased taxation necessary; Kitchener in Lords on Mesopotamia.
				Britain — Severe Commons criticism of Govt's anti-Zeppelin measures (Shipping debate 17).

FEBRUARY 1916	WESTERN FRONT 1	EASTERN FRONT 2	SOUTHERN FRONTS 3	TURKISH FRONTS 4
Wed 16 contd				**Mesopotamia** — War Office takes control of ops from India Office. **Persia** — Goltz reports gloomily on prospects. **Egypt** — Arab Bureau starts weekly *Arab Bulletin* (*see* 18, also 6 June).
Thu 17				**Mesopotamia** — K George V message of encouragement to Kut. **Armenia** — Siberian Cossacks & inf take 5000 PoWs & 42 guns in pursuit from Erzerum. **E Persia** — Brig-Gen Dyer made GOC, takes command Seistan 3 Mar.
Fri 18			Italian advance in Collo zone.	**Arabia** — Sherif letter to Cairo says time needed to prepare rebellion, requests £50,000 for food & rifles (British approve 10 Mar).
Sat 19			**Albania** — Italian *Savona* Bde outposts repel Austrian attacks on R Arzen & Pjesha heights, but (23) blow bridge, & retreat to Durazzo.	
Sun 20	**Flanders** — Germans make 3 attempts to cross Yser canal nr Boesinghe.		**Bulgaria** — Greeks of Xanthus deported. **Italian Front** — Italian First Army C-in-C Gen Brusato aware of Austrian Trentino build-up (*see* 22 Mar).	**Armenia** — Cossacks & 39th Div storm Abdalcik & Askale from Turk rearguard (-22). Gen Abatsiev reoccupies Tatvan SW L Van (*see* 3 Mar).
Mon 21	BATTLE OF VERDUN (-18 Dec) BEGINS: From 0715 violent 9 hr arty preparation by 1240 guns (incl 150 mortars) on 8-mile front incl gas shells (French field guns reply from 1300). Led by 6000 picked men (incl 96 flamethrowers), 140,000 Germans (600 cas) attack across 656-1203-yd No Man's Land. They enter Herbebois & Le Bois de Ville; seize Haumont Wood & part of Caures Wood; shelling heard 100 miles away in Vosges. (see AIR WAR). **Flanders** — Germans attack French positions in Givenchy woods nr Béthune & take PoWs; gas attack at Maucourt Rouvray.		Gen Sarrail sees K of Greece.	
Tue 22	**Verdun** — Despite French counter-attacks (2350 cas), Germans develop gains of 21 to win Brabant-sur-Meuse woods, all Caures wood (Col Driant k, only 118 of his 1300 *Chasseurs* escape) & Haumont village. French stand at Wavrille & counter-attack S of Caures wood (-23). **Creation of the *La Voie Sacrée* 'Sacred Road'**: since mid-Feb French have repaired & reserved for continuous military motor traffic the 21-ft wide 2nd class road from Bar-le-Duc to Verdun. **French introduce phosgene gas shell.**	Kuropatkin (aged 68) **made C-in-C N Front**, retired since 1905, replaces Ruzski (sick leave) and ill Plehve (Fifth Army, *see* 10 Apr) whom Gourko (aged 53) succeeds. Gen Novitski (73rd Div) comments: 'It is as if the French were to recall Bazaine from the grave, or the Austrians Benedek'. N Front has 500,000 rifles for 750,000 men.		**Mesopotamia** — Kut garrison hears relief guns as Gorringe (w 23) recces in force on S bank (-24). 3 Turk planes bomb Aylmer's Wadi relief camp. **Persia** — Baratov beats c2000 Turks at Sinna NW of Hamadan (*see* 26).
Wed 23	**Verdun** — French abandon Brabant-sur-Meuse; counter-attack without success S of Caures wood & at Wavrille. By end of day Germans also occupy Herbebuis & Wavrille,			**Armenia** — Russians take Ispir in slow fighting advance on Bayburt (*see* 1 Mar).

AFRICAN OPERATIONS 5	SEA WAR 6	AIR WAR 7	INTERNATIONAL EVENTS 8	HOME FRONTS 9
Cameroons — Gov Ebermaier reports to Berlin that his entire force (c975 Germans inc 400 civilians, 6000 askaris, 8000 natives) interned in Spanish Muni; 832 Germans later taken to Spain (13 escape in schooner from Vigo 8 Oct).				
N Cameroons — END OF CAMPAIGN: Mora surrenders (Capt Raben's 156 men + 4 MGs). **Uganda** — 30 police repulse 80 Germans (59 cas) at Kachumbe & take an MG without loss; 170 British surprise & burn German Dwakitiku post (22).		**Austria** — **First long-distance Italian bombing raid**: Capronis drop almost 4000lb bombs on Laibach in retaliation for Austrian raid on Milan (14, *see* 1 Aug).	RN cruiser removes 38 Central Powers' nationals from US SS*China* at Yangtze entrance; released 13 May.	**France** — Govt wins confidence vote.
E Africa — **Smuts reaches Mombasa & assumes command**, forms Lake Force & reaches Nairobi (23). Kitchener approves his offensive (25, *see* 5 Mar).			US protest to Turkey on Armenian massacres.	**Britain** — MI5 form Munitions Ministry intelligence dept. Fisher to *Observer* editor: 'We are at the very blackest period of the war.'
		W Front — 34 Anglo-German air combats (7 on 24). **Britain** — 4 German seaplanes drop 25 bombs on Walmer & Lowestoft, 2 cas; 26 defending aircraft ascend.		
		Germans begin 'barrage patrols' over Verdun offensive, 168 aircraft incl 21 Fokkers (Boelcke from own landing ground 7 miles behind front). French shoot down Zeppelin *L77*.	Anglo-French reply to US 25 Jan protest offers postwar international tribunal. Gen Sarrail in Athens.	**Britain** — Commons votes £120m (total £1420m for yr). Adjt-Gen Home Forces Sclater resigns, Macready succeeds (22). 2nd Industries Fair (London -3 Mar).
Cameroons — K George V telegram congratulates Gen Dobell. (Naval blockade lifted 29.)			House-Grey memo on US mediation appeals to Pres Wilson.	**Russia** — **Duma reopens**, Tsar greets them in person for first time at Rasputin's suggestion. **Britain** — War Savings Certificates on sale.
	British Minister of Blockade (Lord Robert Cecil) appointed (*see* INT'L EVENTS). **Germany** — Kaiser visits Wilhelmshaven and approves Scheer's new strategy.		Portugal seizes 76 German steamers (240,000t) interned in Tagus at British request. German note (29, *see* 3 Mar).	**Germany** — Kaiser visits Wilhelmshaven. **Britain** — **Blockade Ministry created**. Commons peace debate.

FEBRUARY 1916	WESTERN FRONT 1	EASTERN FRONT 2	SOUTHERN FRONTS 3	TURKISH FRONTS 4
Wed 23 contd	have advanced just over 2 miles & taken 3000 PoWs since 21 Feb.			
Thu 24	**Verdun** — French arty counter-bombard. Germans take Samogneux (fighting all day), Hill 344, Beaumont Fosses wood, & Chaume with 10,000 PoWs (now total incl among 16,224 cas to French 72nd & 51st Divs). They capture whole of French 2nd line between Samogneux & Bezonvaux in total advance so far of 3½ miles. French withdrawal from Woëvre Plain to Meuse Heights ordered (begins 25, *see* 27). **Verdun's one full-gauge rail link severed** by 2 German rail-mtd 15-in naval guns. Joffre's deputy Castelnau sent on fact-finding mission. Pétain i/c Second Army summoned to Chantilly.	STAVKA conference on offensive to help French; 1.5m men and 6585 guns v 940,000 Austro-Germans.	**Albania** — Essad Pasha's troops and 8500 Italians (after 800+ cas) with 16 guns evacuate Durazzo & he leaves for Italy. Italians slaughter 900 draught & pack animals & destroy stores (*see* SEA WAR).	**Mesopotamia: Kut** — Indian troops ration nearly halved to 14oz pd. **Armenia** — Beaten Turks cross upper Euphrates at Kotur.
Fri 25	**Verdun** — Castelnau arrives at 0700. Germans take Louvemont, but are stopped before Douaumont village (-26). **Fall of Ft Douaumont**, to Lt Brandis' patrol while garrison asleep after firing for 4 days, & Bezonvaux. W of battlefield French 37th African Div withdraw at Belleville & blow Meuse bridge at Bras. (At 2400 Pétain assumes command, HQ Souilly SW of Verdun, gets double pneumonia.) **Champagne** — French attack regains recently lost positions at Bonnet d'Evêque (345 PoWs).	Col Knox finds new 110th Div W of Riga has only 2 regular officers.		**Persia** — Baratov's 4400 men & 20 guns occupy Kermanshah, forcing Col Bopp's 2000 Turks to Pai Tak Pass.
Sat 26	**Verdun** — GQG admits loss of Ft Douaumont. Recapture attempt fails. Pétain orders '... retake immediately any piece of land taken by him', tells Castelnau *'On ne passe pas'* **(They shall not pass).** Germans enter Hardaumont work, gain a hold on Cote du Poivre. French cas now 25,000, but XX 'Iron' Corps (Balfourier) & I Corps (Guillaumat) arriving in strength. **Somme** — Fayolle promoted to command of Sixth Army (-22 Dec).	**Pripet** — Archduke Joseph Ferdinand (Fourth Army) promoted Col Gen but German Linsingen also, backdated to 20.		**Mesopotamia** — Aylmer informs Lake & Townshend new relief attempt in 8-9 days.
Sun 27	**Verdun** — Pétain reorganizes defences, halts withdrawal from Woëvre. French retake La Feuille wood (night 27/28), defend Soupple village & d'Eix-Abaucourt stn. On N Verdun front Germans attempt to enlarge gains E & W of Ft Douaumont. On bank of Meuse, Mort Homme ridge receives violent German shelling. *Voie Sacrée* conveys 190,000 men (incl 132 bns or 11 inf divs), 23,000t ammunition, 2500t equipment (-6 Mar). **Champagne** — Germans capture Navarin Ridge after 3 days shelling, & repel French counter-attacks (1000 cas) (-1 Mar).		**Albania** — **Austrians occupy Durazzo**, but Italians form Valona entrenched camp in S for what becomes XVI Corps (3 divs, *see* 12 Mar & 11 Dec).	**Mesopotamia** — British 13th Div (Gallipoli veterans) begins landing at Basra (-12 Mar).
Mon 28	**Verdun** — **Sudden thaw after long cold spell turns battlefield into a sea of mud** but *Voie Sacrée* kept open with			

AFRICAN OPERATIONS 5	SEA WAR 6	AIR WAR 7	INTERNATIONAL EVENTS 8	HOME FRONTS 9
		W Front — Germans attack RFC Bailleul airfields; 5 RFC aircraft bomb Lille airfield.	Essad Pasha's provisional Govt leaves Albania, arrives Naples (28).	
			Pres Wilson writes to Senator Stone that he will not abrogate Americans' rights in travelling by sea. **Secret War** — Berlin's terms of a naval base, strategic railway use and 60% control of Antwerp end peace-feeler talks with Belgium in Zurich.	**French Army orders 400 tanks** from Schneider by 25 Nov qv (*see* 8 Apr).
W Desert — Action at Agagiya (14 miles SW of Sidi Barrani): Brig-Gen Lukin's 2400 men (184 cas) & 4 guns defeat 1600+ Senussi (239 cas) & 4 guns; 184 Dorset Yeomanry (58 cas) charge & capture Turk leader Jaafar Pasha (w). Lukin reoccupies Sidi Barrani (28).	**E Med** — French transport *Provence II* (930 lost from 2000 Salonika-bound troops) sunk by *U35* off Cerigo. Italian Navy & 30 steamers evacuate Italian Durazzo garrison (8500 men & 16 guns, *see* S FRONTS 5 Apr) under fire, convoyed to Valona.	**W Front** — 21 RFC aircraft bomb Don rail stn with one 112lb bomb apiece. **Verdun** — Navarre shoots down 2 German aircraft within French lines (*see* 19 May).		**Germany** — War profits tax ordered.
W Desert — Senussi now occupy Farafra & Dakhia oases (*see* 14 Mar).				
		Mesopotamia — RFC & RNAS to be administered as one service under W/Cdr Gordon; 4 aircraft reinforce Tigris Corps (-	†Henry James, aged 72, American-born novelist at Rye, Sussex.	**Russia** — Dvinsk Secret Police chief reports widespread Army & civilian anger v Govt.

FEBRUARY 1916	WESTERN FRONT 1	EASTERN FRONT 2	SOUTHERN FRONTS 3	TURKISH FRONTS 4
Mon 28 contd	gravel by 3000 Territorials. Germans attack astride d'Eix stream; to N they regain ground lost (27), on S bank they take Champlon & Manheuller. Farther N Germans repulsed at Douaumont village & Haudromont wood. **Vosges** — Germans penetrate French positions nr Thionville.			
Tue 29	**Verdun** — Bloody struggle round Fresnes & salient. **Falkenhayn finally agrees to attack on W bank of Meuse**, releases 4 divs & 84 heavy guns (*see* 6 Mar). Feb losses: 30,000 French, 25,000 Germans.		**Salonika** — Malaria discoverer Sir R Ross writes to warn British Army Medical DG Keogh, urging regular quinine & anti-mosquito measures: 'You still have about 2 months grace before General Malaria comes in the field...' (*see* 12 Oct). **Italian Front** — Mussolini promoted corporal for steady service.	**Mesopotamia: Kut** — Battle cas to date 2927 + 443 deaths from disease.
Wed 1 March 1916	**Verdun** — Whole front under violent German bombardment 0900-1700. Both sides consolidate. Visit by Pres Poincaré.	(Mar) Dr Daniel Gardner in Petrograd arranges supply of British gas shells. (Mar) STAVKA issues first general trench warfare regulations.	**Serbia** — (Mar) Falkenhayn begins to withdraw 103rd Div and *Alpenkorps*, leaving only 101st Div (reducing to cadre) to bolster Bulgars v Salonika (*see* 9).	**Armenia** — 1st of 4 Turk Second Army (Ahmed Izzet Pasha) divs from Gallipoli arrive Diyarbekir (*see* 1 Apr). (Mar) Ferid Vehib Pasha replaces Mahmud Kamil Pasha i/c Turk Third Army (-June 1918). **Syria** — (Mar) Feisal watches Turk propaganda film with Djemal in Damacus. **Mesopotamia** — Kut: Shelling by 22 Turk guns cause 37 cas to garrison (*see* AIR WAR).
Thu 2	**Flanders** — British 17th Div retake positions lost 14 Feb N of Ypres-Comines Canal. BEF Fourth Army relieve French Tenth Army (15-mile Loos-Ransart sector). British 12th Div engaged at Hohenzollern Craters (-18). **Verdun** — German bombadment N of city. Street fighting in Douaumont. French repulse attack on Vaux (Capt de Gaulle w & captured).	Joffre requests Russian offensive to relieve pressure on Verdun (*see* 18).		
Fri 3	**Verdun** — French success at Douaumont (& 7, *see* 30).			**Armenia** — Gen Abatsiev's 10,000 men capture Bitlis after surprise night bayonet charge in blizzard, take 1000 PoWs & 20 guns; 2 Russian bns land at Atina to advance on Trebizond, 60 miles W, more land at Mapavri (night 6/7). Gen Lyakhov occupies Rize, port 30 miles from Trebizond (8), drives Turks beyond R Kalopotamus (9,*see* 20). **Mesopotamia** — Gertrude Bell arrives at Basra to be Arab Bureau rep (*see* 22).
Sat 4	**Verdun** — Franz Marc, German Expressionist painter k, aged 36, by French shell at Gussainville Castle. Wrote of German w coming back 'like a vision in hell' (3). Germans repulsed E of Poivre Ridge.			

AFRICAN OPERATIONS 5	SEA WAR 6	AIR WAR 7	INTERNATIONAL EVENTS 8	HOME FRONTS 9
		6 Mar) after 4 lost in accidents.		
	Chancellor Bethmann memo to Kaiser expresses fear that unrestricted U-boat warfare will precipitate US intervention. U-boat campaign to resume in War Zone, but only enemy vessels to be attacked inside or out (*see* 4 Mar). **N Sea** — 20-min action between German raider *Greif* (crew 306) & British AMC *Alcantara* NE of Shetlands, both sunk. *Möwe* gets home as RN radio D/F assumes she is sailing westward. (Feb) Record 14 British ships sunk (4 in Med) by mines, number equalled only in Apr & May 1917.	**Verdun** — Cmndt Peuty i/c French air force in sector orders offensive patrols in formation to destroy German aircraft.	Germany tells US she will not postpone 'unlimited' U-boat war from midnight (actually intensified till end May). Italy seizes German ships in her ports.	**France** — Maritime Transport Ctee formed. **Britain** — National Volunteer Force accepted for Home Defence. Prohibited list of enemy firms in neutral countries published. FM French takes seat in Lords as Viscount Ypres.
Sudan — Sultan of Darfur rebels v British (*see* 16). **Cyrenaica** — (Mar) Senussi leader Ahmed's brother Muhammed Hilal joins Italians at Tobruk and helps pacification for food.	Germany has 52 U-boats (20 in Flanders Flotilla, 12 in Med, 4 in Baltic). **Britain** — (Mar) **First submarine fitted with hydrophones**, probably *B3* fixed unit on each bow, able to get sound bearings within 2° in Firth of Forth trials. **Baltic** — Russia begins large-scale minelaying ops (German Fleet follows suit Apr). From 1 Mar all ships over 500t trading to & from Britain need licence. **Med** — *U68* sinks sloop HMS *Primula*. **N Sea** — (Mar) First of 5 R-class 15-in-gun battleships, *Revenge*, joins Grand Fleet, 2 in May, 1 in Dec, last Sept 1917.	**Britain** — 2 hit-&-run raids on E Kent coastal towns by German floatplanes (7 sorties, 3 FTR of which 2 shot down by British aircraft (41 cas to 55 bombs, 100 houses damaged 1 & 19, *see* 20). **France** — Only RFC Martinsyde G100 (nicknamed the Elephant) unit arrives, No 27 Sqn. **Mesopotamia** — 3 German aircraft drop 50 bombs on Kut, hitting hospital (26 cas).	**Secret War: Greece** — (Mar) MI5 report favourably on 'Z' (Compton Mackenzie), promoted Capt & monthly funds quadrupled.	**Britain** — RFP up 2% to 49%. War Savings Guildhall national meeting. **India** — Budget raises duties and income tax by half or more.
	Allied Malta Conference (-7) **reduces 18 patrol zones to 11.** Italian delegate admits their 4 zones need 76 patrol craft (50 available).		**Neutrals: Rumania** — †Dowager Q Elizabeth (writer 'Carmen Sylva'), aged 72.	**Britain** — **All single men of 18-41 liable for call up**; Lord Derby criticizes exemptions, women must replace men at home. Royal Commission on VD Final Report obtains free treatment for the 10% urban population infected.
	N Sea — First RN minelaying submarine *E24* lays minefield close to Elbe, but lost on next sortie (21).		Portuguese seize 4 German ships at Madeira. **Neutrals: USA** — Gore-Mclemore Senate Resolution v American sailing in belligerent ships & denying passports, but defeated (7).	
5th Indian Lt Inf (517) lands at Mombasa from Cameroons (*see* 16 June). Portuguese seize German ships at Lourenço Marques.	**Tirpitz & Adm Holtzendorff fail to get Kaiser's Crown Council to back unrestricted U-boat warfare** (*see* 12 & 15: postponed till 1 Apr). **E Atlantic** — *U32* (Spiegel) opens new offensive sinking British tanker		Anglo-Russian Military Demarcation Agreement on Persia expands latter's 1907 share to line Khanikin-Isfahan-Birdjan.	**Germany** — 4th War Loan (-24).

MARCH 1916	WESTERN FRONT 1	EASTERN FRONT 2	SOUTHERN FRONTS 3	TURKISH FRONTS 4
Sat 4 contd				
Sun 5				**Mesopotamia** — New large RN gunboat *Mantis* joins Tigris flotilla.
Mon 6	**Verdun** — After hurricane barrage **German** 4th Div **attack on W bank of Meuse**, on 4-mile front captures Regnéville & Hill 265 NW of city.			
Tue 7	**Verdun** — Germans take Fresnes SE of city; French success S of Forges, but 67th Div on W bank has lost 3000 PoWs.	**Baltic Provinces** — German artillery active SW of Dahlen I, R Dvina. German Dvina attack repulsed (9). Riga sector bombardments (14).		**Mesopotamia** — **2nd attempt to relieve Kut**: Aylmer's 23,335 men & 68 guns night march to turn Turk S wing.
Wed 8	**Verdun** — Germans repulsed at Vaux. Brilliant French regt's bayonet charge restores W bank line by retaking Bois des Corbeaux after 2½-mile German advance.			Enver Pasha returns to Constantinople from Syria/Palestine inspection. **Mesopotamia** — **Battle of Dujaila Redoubt** (-9): Aylmer surprises Turks but muddles belated attack, loses 3474 men (1285 Turk cas). **Persia** — Russians occupy Sennah (see INT'L EVENTS 4).
Thu 9	**Verdun** — **German attacks on both banks of the Meuse**: small gains at Vaux village & on the Mort Homme. Pétain demands uninterrupted supply of reinforcements, gets 7 fresh divs (10-31).	**Galicia** — German attack at Cebrow repulsed.	**Salonika** — Falkenhayn orders Gallwitz to drop offensive plans & hold defensive line around L Doiran & in Vardar valley.	
Fri 10	**Aisne** — After 10-hr barrage Germans attack between Troyon & Berry-au-Bac captures valuable ground from French 55th Div; fighting persists (-18, *see* 25 Apr). **Verdun** — Germans recapture Corbeaux Wood: secure foothold at Vaux in first attack on fort. Joffre first visits Pétain. **Meuse** — French recover German floating mines at St Mihiel (& 20).	**Poland** — German attacks repulsed E of Koslov.		**Mesopotamia: Kut** — Khalil Pasha letter to Townshend suggests surrender, rejected.
Sat 11			**Italian Front** — **Fifth Battle of the Isonzo** (-15/16) begun to help French at Verdun with 7 corps & 2 Alpini gps, but snow & rain a handicap that ends it prematurely.	**Mesopotamia** — **Gorringe replaces Aylmer as GOC Tigris Corps.**
Sun 12			Allied Chantilly conference decides on status quo for Salonika; Italians say offensive in Albania impossible. **Italian Front** — Italian arty action on Middle Isonzo.	**Persia** — Baratov occupies Karind, W of Kermanshah. **Afghanistan** — Amir tells Hentig Mission he will allow c20,000 Turco-Germans to attack Baluchistan, but Britain has given 40,000 rupees.

AFRICAN OPERATIONS 5	SEA WAR 6	AIR WAR 7	INTERNATIONAL EVENTS 8	HOME FRONTS 9
	Teutonion 36 miles SW of Fastnet, 13 boats sent to SW Approaches (-24 Apr). UC-boats lay 73 minefields (710 mines) sinking 30 ships (-Apr).			
Smuts' Kilimanjaro Offensive begins: Stewart's 1st Div (4000) advances from Longido. Smuts has 18,400 men (+ 9000 in garrisons); 57 guns (+ 9); 99 MGs (+ 25); 4 planes v est 6000 Germans, 18 guns, 37 MGs.	**N Sea** — Scheer sorties with High Seas Fleet (-6) to position off Texel (farthest S ever), nearly traps Harwich Force but Admiralty recalls it & weather thwarts Grand Fleet sortie (*see* 24).	**Britain** — Attempted raids on Forth area, Tyneside & Teesside by 3 German airships; 70 cas in Hull, Lincs, Leics & Kent (night 5/6). **Mesopotamia** — Turk MGs shoot down RFC Voisin at Es-Sinn.	**Secret War** — German Agent 17 Baron Schluga's last report from Paris, retires, †aged 76, 1917. New British DMI orders review of non-W Front Intelligence Corps.	
Cameroons — British half detached to Nigeria, troops begin leaving (16). **S Algeria** — 500 Senussi & 3 guns take Djanet border post, repulsing relief force (-25, *see* 12 May).		**Sinai** — RFC bomb El Hassana (& 14), destroy Turk base at Bir-el-Hassa (26). **W Front** — 31 RFC aircraft attack railheads & billets at Carvin (2t bombs dropped, PoWs report at least 37k).	**Neutrals: USA** — War Secretary Baker appointed.	**Britain** — Russian journalists' visit. **Women's National Land Service Corps formed.** Brewing constituents reduced 12½%.
E Africa — British 2nd Div (8500) starts from Mbuyani railhead & airfield, re-occupies Salaita (9).	**N Sea** — RN destroyer *Coquette* mined & sunk off E Coast.	**Palestine** — 2 RNAS seaplanes from carrier *Ben-my-Chree* photograph new German *Jasta 300* (14 Rumplers) airfield nr Beersheba, 1st German aircraft seen over Sinai mid-Apr.		**France** — Gallieni criticises Joffre in Cabinet (*see* 16). **Britain** — Australian PM Hughes arrives. Churchill attacks Admiralty slowness in Commons when Balfour introduces Navy Estimates but impact nullified when he asks for Fisher's recall; returns to France (12) after causing outcry.
			German Mexico Minister Eckhardt recommends Swedish diplomat for Crown Order 2nd Class for sending German Washington cables to Berlin. RN Room 40 intercept and realize significance May (*see* 12 Nov).	
			GERMANY DECLARES WAR ON PORTUGAL (AUSTRIA 15) when ships' release refused. **Neutrals: USA** — Pancho Villa night raids Columbus, New Mexico, with 500 men (100 cas) killing 17 Americans (*see* 15).	**Britain** — Lords air debate urges Air Board, more powerful planes & AA guns (*see* AIR WAR 21).
E Africa — 2nd SA Horse retake Taveta after skirmish, British Voi railway reaches it (23).				**Britain** — E Herts by-election: Airman Pemberton Billing (Ind) beats Tory. Maiden speech demands Air Board (21). **Occupied Belgium** — Kaiser at Charleville complains 'I might as well be living in Germany'; Falkenhayn telling him nothing.
E Africa — Tighe's British 2nd Div (270 cas) takes Latema Nek (Kilimanjaro) (-12) from Maj Kraut's 1000 men (123+ cas).	**Neutrals: USA** — 14-in-gun battleship *Nevada* completed, she & sister *Oklahoma* (finished 2 May) have heavy deck armour & centralized fire control. Larger *Pennsylvania* & *Arizona* follow (12 June & 17 Oct).		Scandinavian kings reaffirm neutrality at Copenhagen.	
	TIRPITZ RESIGNS. **Adriatic** — Adm Haus memo to Conrad prevents Austrian Fleet making a 'ruthless undertaking' with Army's planned Tyrol offensive, cites 25 or more narrow escapes by cruisers & below from Allied submarines.		Allied Chantilly Conference (-13) on summer offensives.	

MARCH 1916	WESTERN FRONT 1	EASTERN FRONT 2	SOUTHERN FRONTS 3	TURKISH FRONTS 4
Mon 13		STAVKA sends 504 telegrams (52,814 words).	**Salonika** — French 243rd Bde (122nd Div) begin skirmishing advance up Vardar to frontier, drives German patrol from Machukovo village (16). British 7th Mtd Bde add to line just S of L Doiran by 31. **Italian Front** — Italian 21st Div gains one hump of Mt San Michele (*see* 21).	
Tue 14	**Verdun** — French repulse heavy attack between Bethincourt & Cumières after German shelling since 12 but Germans gain foothold on Mort Homme lower ridge (Hill 295). French success there (15).			
Wed 15			**Isonzo** — Italian Third Army losses 1882, Austrian 1985.	**Mesopotamia** — Tigris rises 3 ft, floods Dujaila Redoubt, & damages British boat bridge (-23). **Secret War** — Maj Baron Stotzingen Mission (aim to contact E Africa via radio from Arabia) leaves Berlin, arrives Constantinople (17, leaves by rail 26, *see* 12 Apr).
Thu 16	**Verdun** — Renewed German assaults on Mort Homme & Vaux, latter repels five. German III (Brandenburg) Corps withdrawn to regain strength (1916 class conscripts joining from 7).			**Armenia** — Russians take Mamahatun, 800 PoWs & 5 guns (c47 miles W of Erzerum). **S Persia** — Brig-Gen Sykes' Mission lands at Bandar Abbas, recruits 180 police (-31, *see* 17 May). **Egypt** — Chauvel GOC new Anzac Mtd Div.
Fri 17		Spring thaw begins unexpectedly early, but Russian offensive not postponed.		
Sat 18		**W Russia** — **First Battle of L Naroch** (-14 Apr): Record 1271 Russian guns fire blind for 8 hrs before Ragoza's Second Army (20 divs - 350,000) of Evert's W Front attacks German Tenth Army (7 divs - 75,000 with 300 guns), gains only 1 mile on 2-mile front for 15,000 cas, switches to night attacks (19-21).		**Mesopotamia: Kut** — Townshend radios that food will last to 15 Apr; British troops' rations cut by 2oz. **Egypt** — Prince of Wales arrives as Staff Capt.
Sun 19		**Galicia** — Russian success NW of Uscieczko bridgehead on R Dniester (-21).		**Egypt** — **Murray succeeds Maxwell as C-in-C**: 2-day conference on Kut at Ismailia and Cairo. MEF & garrison renamed EEF (20). **S Persia** — Russians drive small German party from Isfahan.
Mon 20	**Verdun** — W bank: 11th Bav Div captures Avocourt Wood and 2825 French, with flame-throwers, but Germans are repulsed on Poivre Heights (E bank).	(c) Russian strength 1,670,928 inf (130 divs); 178,123 cav (39 divs); 6180 guns; 6224 MGs; 500 armoured cars v 86 Austrian and German divs.		**Armenia** — Yudenich meets Adm Eberhardt at Batumi to plan ops v Trebizond; Lyakhov reaches Humurgan (28-30) 20 miles E (*see* 8 Apr) v Maj Hunger's Turks.
Tue 21	**Verdun** — German shell Hill 304. (c) French now have 1294 guns (570 medium & heavy), the 155m heavy guns alone fire 278,000 rnds in Mar.	**Baltic Provinces** — Russian N Front offensive (-26): Fifth Army crosses Dvina nr Jakobstadt with 4 divs, takes 1000 yds of marshes for 28,000 cas. **W Russia** — Gen Baluyev takes 1000 German PoWs at L Naroch in fog as 2 German	**Isonzo** — Austrian gas shelling (*see* 28 June) forces Italian evacuation of gains in S.	

AFRICAN OPERATIONS 5	SEA WAR 6	AIR WAR 7	INTERNATIONAL EVENTS 8	HOME FRONTS 9
		Verdun — Guynemer w in one arm by Aviatik barely returns to base; out of action 3 months. Now 6 French fighter *escadrilles* ; 36 aircraft nominally in sector, as French gaining air superiority.		
E Africa — Deventer's SA Mtd Bde occupy Moshi and contact 1st Div which has advanced 60 miles. **W Desert** — Maj-Gen Peyton reoccupies Sollum: 10 armoured cars storm Senussi camp 20 miles to W, take 3 guns, 9 MGs & 40 PoWs incl Turk officers; 9 cars rescue 97 mainly RN PoWs, c115 miles E of Sollum (17).				
	Adm Capelle succeeds Tirpitz as German Minister of Marine. British notice diverts long-distance Far East or Australia-based ships to Cape route to avoid U-boats in Med.		**Occupied Belgium** — Germans order all Ghent Univ lectures in Flemish. **Neutrals: Mexico — US Army enters Mexico to pursue Villa**: Brig Gen Pershing's 6000 cav plus first US military use of armed aircraft, 7th Cavalry (370, 5w) disperse 380 Villalistas (91 cas) at San Geronimo (29, *see* 14 May); 6 smaller fights in Apr.	**Portugal** — Dr Almeida forms 'Sacred Union' national ministry. **Britain** — Board of Trade appeals for less meat consumption, and household fuel economy (29).
Sudan — 2000 Egyptians invade Darfur from Nahud (*see* 22). **E Africa** — After Pacific voyage German blockade-runner *Marie* reaches Sudi in S, lands 6 guns, *Königsberg* gun shells*; gunners, 12 MGs; 5m SAA rnds; clothing; tobacco & Iron Crosses (*see* 15 Apr).	**Ionian Sea** — Austrian *U24* (ex-German *UC12*) sinks on own mines off Taranto, raised & reconstructed as Italian XI (Mar 1917). **N Sea** — U-boat sinks Dutch liner *Tubantia, Palembang* likewise (18).		Germany loans £20m to Turkey. **Occupied Belgium** — Brussels court martial sentences 2 female agents & 4 other Belgians to life imprison-ment or forced labour.	**France** — Gen Roques succeeds Gallieni (sick) as War Minister.
E Africa — Smuts begins Usambara Railway advance to R Ruwu, halts there (23). Sheppard replaces Stewart (to India) as GOC 1st EA Div (19).	**Adriatic** — Austrian *U6* sinks French destroyer *Renaudin* off Durazzo.	**W Front** — **Ernst Udet scores 1st victory of 62**: Farman F 40 over Mulhausen while flying a Fokker EIII of an a*d hoc* fighter unit.		**Britain** — Munitions factories total 3078.
E Africa — RN occupy Yambe I & Ulenge I (22), shell Tanga (22).				
E Africa — 5 German moonlight charges v 1st Div (33 cas) fail.	4 RN minelayers at work on Thames & Dover Straits approaches. RN seaplane carriers *Riviera* & *Vindex* attack German seaplane base on Zeebrugge Mole (*see* AIR WAR), escorts (destroyer HMS *Lance* hit) beat off 3 German destroyers.	**Occupied Belgium** — 19 British, 19 French & 16 Belgian aircraft drop 4^1/$_2$t bombs on Zeebrugge floatplane base. **W Front** — 10 indecisive Anglo-German air combats.		
E Africa — SA Mtd Bde captures Kahe Hill but 1st Div attack (290 cas) held between crocodile-infested rivers to N (171 German cas).		**W Front** — *Escadrille Americaine* **(N 124) author-ized** ,volunteer fighter unit & forerunner of legendary *Escadrille Lafayette* (*see* 20 Apr). Little flying possible (-24, & 26). **Britain** — 'Fokker Fodder' scandal: Noel	Denmark agrees not to re-export French goods to Central Powers.	**Ireland** — Loyalist demo v Sinn Fein HQ at Tullamore; 3 police injured in firing from it. **Britain** — War Office to buy & import all Russian flax & tow.

MARCH 1916	WESTERN FRONT 1	EASTERN FRONT 2	SOUTHERN FRONTS 3	TURKISH FRONTS 4
Tue 21 contd		regts break.		
Wed 22	**Verdun** — Germans advance at Haucourt & Mort Homme but stopped short of Hill 304.		Italian *Comando Supremo* at Udine receive more reports of Austrian Trentino build-up & reinforce First Army defences (incl 4 extra bdes) (*see* 2 Apr).	Capt T E Lawrence leaves Cairo on secret mission to Mesopotamia, arrives Basra (c30, *see* 28 & 28 Apr). Kut endures 1300 shells.
Thu 23	**Somme** — British trench raid at Gommecourt.	**W Russia** — 300 men of Baluyev's V Corps freeze to death.		**Mesopotamia** — Kut's 2 5-in guns + air observers disable 2 Turk siege guns.
Fri 24				
Sat 25		**W Russia** — Baluyev's first vain attack on 'Ferdinand's Nose' salient (repeated 27, 31; 7 & 14 Apr).	**Trentino** — By now Austrian Eleventh (Dankl) & Third Armies (Kövess) assembled between Bozen (Bolzano) & Trent despite spring snowfalls & avalanches, but attack postponed 5 wks due to deep snow (*see* 10 April & 15 May).	**Mesopotamia** — Still only 45 steamers & 79 barges with 338t daily capacity v 490t required; most of Maude's 13th Div now at front, begins relieving 7th Div (31). **Armenia** — Przevalski's II Turkestan Corps now 20-30 miles SE of Bayburt.
Sun 26	**Flanders** — British success at Hohenzollern Redoubt.		**Carnia** — Austrians surprise capture Pal Piccolo, but Italians retake it after 4 attempts & 689 cas.	
Mon 27	**Flanders** — British 3rd Div attack at St Eloi craters S of Ypres, captures 1st & 2nd line trenches on 600-yd front, repels counter-attack (28, *see* 6 Apr).	**W Russia** — Front line totally waterlogged, Russian N wing ceases attacks (W Front losses 70,000).	At Paris Cadorna says Italy still has inadequate arty (-28).	
Tue 28	**Flanders** — Haig writes 'all reports agree as to the efficiency of the 3-in Stokes mortar'.	**Galicia** — Russian success N of Bojan.		**Egypt** — II Anzac Corps formed for W Front (Gen Birdwood & staff sail 30). Herbert and Storrs of Arab Bureau sail for Basra in cruiser *Euryalus* (arr 9 Apr).

AFRICAN OPERATIONS 5	SEA WAR 6	AIR WAR 7	INTERNATIONAL EVENTS 8	HOME FRONTS 9
		Pemberton Billing MP taunts Govt in Commons over officially approved obsolete aircraft produced for RFC by Royal Aircraft Factory: 'I would suggest that quite a number of our gallant officers... have been rather murdered than killed' (*see* 28).		
E Africa — Germans retreat 20 miles behind R Ruwu to Lembeni, leaving behind *Königsberg* gun.	**First depth charge submarine kill**: Q-ship *Farnborough* (Campbell) sinks *U68* off SW Ireland. Germans aware of new weapon after vain attacks (15 & 20 Apr). **Aegean** — RN minesweeper *Whitby Abbey* tows 6 caiques into Bay of Lebedos (S of Smyrna) & lands 36 Greek irregulars; they kill or capture 6 Turk soldiers & rustle 600 livestock (British convinced Turk cattle going to Germany, *see* 30 Apr). French submarine *Ampère* attacks Austrian hospital ship *Elektra* in error, forced to beach but with few cas.		**Occupied France** — Germans conscript 2000 workers from Roubaix; Lille Gov invites local unemployed to 'volunteer' (25).	
	Med — *U35* sinks 13,543t British Transport *Minneapolis* (12 lost) 195 miles E of Malta. First Pola-built U-boat in service *UB42*.		Lloyd George addresses Paris Economic Conference. K George V receives Gen Cadorna. Allies reject US 18 Jan Lansing note.	
	Channel — British Folkestone-Dieppe packet *Sussex* torpedoed by *U29* (Flanders Flotilla) as suspected troopship, 50 dead incl 3 Americans & Spanish composer Granados (*see* 24 Apr). **N Sea** — Harwich Force sorties with carrier *Vindex* (5 planes) to raid supposed Zeppelin base at Hoyer, Schleswig, but 2 planes (lost) find sheds at Tondern instead (25). Destroyers sink 2 German armed trawlers but *Medusa* lost after collision with *Laverack*.		3 Americans die aboard French SS *Sussex*; US Berlin Ambassador demands reason (27).	**Turkey** — Language law makes company use of Turkish compulsory after 10 July; also in schools & signs.
French N Africa — Gen Langle, retired from W Front due to Verdun, on mission (-1 Dec 1917).	**N Sea** — Harwich Force Flagship Cruiser *Cleopatra* rams & sinks German destroyer *G194* but cruiser *Undaunted* collides with flagship & is sent to Tyne for repairs. Remainder & Battlecruiser Fleet steam nr Horns Reef (26) but Scheer out in force declines action in SW gale, snowstorms & violent seas. British (incl Grand Fleet) return to bases (-27).	**W Front** — **First British aircraft** (Bristol Scout) **with MG interrupter gear arrives in France** (*see* 18 Apr, SEA WAR 24).		**Britain** — **Military Medal instituted for Army NCOs & privates.**
			Briand opens Allied Paris Conference (-28); 8 powers declare unity, form Permanent Ctee of International Economic Action.	
Italian Somaliland — Buloburti garrison repulses dervishes; 320 inf vainly pursue (-6 Apr, *see* 21 Oct).		**Salonika** — German aircraft raid detonates French ammo dump.		
	Black Sea — Russian torpedo boats sink 10 Turk vessels & destroy munition depot (*see* 30).	**Britain** — Under-Sec for War H J Tennant defends Royal Aircraft Factory: 'We do not produce quantities [of aircraft & aero engines] there, and it is not a manufacturing plant'. Critics demand to know why then Factory employs 3000 skilled workmen (*see* 12 May).	Russo-Chinese Agreement for former to build 460-mile Manchurian railway.	**Germany** — *Reichstag* Conservatives vote for immediate unrestricted U-boat warfare.

MARCH 1916	WESTERN FRONT 1	EASTERN FRONT 2	SOUTHERN FRONTS 3	TURKISH FRONTS 4
Wed 29	**Verdun** — W bank: 2 French regts recapture SE corner of Avocourt Wood & Avocourt Redoubt (lost 23) & repulse counter-attack, but Germans reach Malancourt.		**Isonzo** — Italian VII Corps gains some ground at Selz (Carso).	**Mesopotamia** — Gorringe postpones Hanna assault from I-4 Apr to get 3 extra planes.
Thu 30	German attacks at Ft Douaumont & Malancourt. **France** — British GHQ leaves St Omer for Montreuil.			
Fri 31	(Apr) German Army ration strength 6,767,144, c8000 MGs in service. **Verdun** — French evacuate Malancourt & also lose ground at Vaux. German setback at Mort Homme. German cas now 81,607 in 39 days, French 89,000. *LA VOIE SACRÉE* **('Sacred Way'): during March reaches 6000 trucks pd. Max 50,000t stores & 90,000 men transported pw** (-June). Name *La Voie Sacrée* coined by French political writer & ardent nationalist Maurice Barrès (1862-1923).			
Sat 1 April 1916	German Army forms 200 indep MG units (16 guns each), 83 get 18 guns by Oct 1916. First 10,000 British gas shells delivered, but French ones mainly used on Somme. **Verdun** — Germans repulsed between Douaumont & Vaux, front shifts under 1000 yds in month.	(Apr) Russians issue gas mask of own design modelled on French 'snout' pattern.	**Italian Front** — (Apr) Italian Army has formed 8 new divs, 18 *Alpini* bns, 71 militia bns; 75 garrison coys & 560 labour dets since entering war. MG sections have increased from 350 to 1000. Arty has increased by 506 btys + 38 of AA guns. **Salonika** — French Army of the Orient has 42,000 horses & mules with 7000 wagons.	**Armenia** — Kemal promoted Brig Gen & Pasha (aged 35). **India: NW Frontier** — (Apr) 17 Mahsud raids.
Sun 2	**Verdun** — German advance in Caillette Wood (Douaumont-Vaux) & approach Ft Souville.	Germans repulsed in Liakhovichi region.		
Mon 3	**Flanders** — British success at St Eloi. **Verdun** — Germans driven from N edge of Caillette Wood & W part of Vaux (Verdun) by Mangin's newly arrived 5th Div (*see* 22).	**Baltic Provinces** — Germans repulsed at Üxküll bridgehead (Dvina), repulsed nr Dvinsk (12).	Greece refuses Serb Army land route from Corfu to Salonika (*see* 11).	
Tue 4	**Verdun** — German attack on French centre fails; French advance in Caillette Wood. **Somme** — Micheler put i/c French Tenth Army. **Argonne/ Lorraine/Alsace** — D'Esperey replaces Dubail i/c E Army Gp,	**Brusilov replaces Ivanov as C-in-C SW Front** (HQ Berdichev), and hands over Eighth Army to Kaledin.		

AFRICAN OPERATIONS 5	SEA WAR 6	AIR WAR 7	INTERNATIONAL EVENTS 8	HOME FRONTS 9
		E Front — *LZ86* raids Minsk (& 2 Apr). **W Front** — 9 Anglo-German air combats (1 aircraft forced down on each side); 7 combats (30, 3 RFC aircraft lost) & 13 combats (31, 2 Fokkers hit).	Britain rescinds London Declaration art 19, ships sailing to non-blockaded ports no longer immune.	**Russia** — **Reforming War Minister Gen Polivanov resigns** after Tsarina & Rasputin's intrigues; Gen Shuvaev succeeds. **Japan** — War Minister Lt Gen Oka resigns, Lt Gen Oshima succeeds (30).
	Black Sea — *U33* sinks Russian hospital ship *Portugal* (115 lost) off Ofi nr Trebizond allegedly mistaking her for a troop transport. *U33* rammed by destroyer *Strogiy* 6 Apr & forced back to Bosphorus (*see* 5 Apr).			
	N Sea — First German UE ocean-going minelayer U-boat *U74* operational (20 completed), *see* 27 May.	**Britain** — Attempted airship raids by 9 Zeppelins (6 cross coast) on London (German Navy) & E Anglia (Army). 13 RFC aircraft go up, 1 hits a Zeppelin with Ranken darts; no bombs on target. 112 cas (incl 86 soldiers & sailors) in Lincs, Essex & Suffolk. *L13* & *L15* hit by AA fire. *L15* (Breithaupt) ditches in N Sea (1 dead, 16 taken PoWs, night 31 Mar/1 Apr).	Asquith arrives in Rome (sees Pope 2 Apr). Serb Crown Prince arrives in London.	**Britain** — Army Council takes over hay & straw supplies. Largest number of working days (327,000) lost since July 1915. 114,934 (mainly Belgian) refugees have passed through London to date.
Ethiopia (Apr) — Muslim pretender Lij Yasu acknowledges Sultan as Caliph by sending flag with crescent to Turk Consul at Harar (*see* 27 Sept).	**Med** — (Apr) French Battle Fleet shifts base from Malta to Argostoli (Cephalonia, Ionian Is) the better to watch Otranto Straits, trains at Corfu from July (*see* 12). Allied admirals aboard battleship *Provence* divide Med into national zones of responsibility & patrol fixed shipping routes, a great help to U-boats (*see* 27). **Black Sea** — U-boat located by hydrophone for first time. **Red Sea** — 6 RNAS seaplanes (from carrier *Raven II* arrived Aden 30 Mar) bomb 3 Turk camps & leaflet tribesmen (-4, *see* 7 June). **Japan** — (Apr) Naval air arm founded at Yokosuka. **Baltic** — Russian minelayer *Amur* begins 1916 ops in this sea. Germans lay almost 4000 mines (Apr, *see* AIR WAR 27).	**W Front** — RFC arty observers help engage 52 targets; 16 indecisive air combats. **Britain** — German airship *U1* bombs Sunderland; 152 cas (night 1/2).	(Apr) British Munitions Ministry and French first exchange liaison officers.	**Turkey** — Boys of 12-17+ must belong to boy scouts (German prompting). **Britain** — King gives £100,000 to war effort. (Apr) Film *Battlefield of Neuve Chapelle* released.
		Britain — *L14* & *L22* bomb Leith & Edinburgh (aiming for Rosyth naval base & Forth Bridge); 37 cas from 44 bombs (night 2/3). **W Front** — 20 Anglo-German air combats (3 German aircraft thought to have been hit).	**Occupied France/Belgium** — *OHL* notifies 5 Army HQs of **intention to raise 50,000 forced labourers**. Sixth Army orders Lille Governor (11), 1400 workers impressed pd from 22 (*see* 12 May). **Neutrals: Holland** — Raemakers' cartoon 'The Last Throw' (Kaiser & Crown Prince dicing with death) in Amsterdam *Telegraaf* (*see* 31 Dec).	**Britain** — Munitions factory explosion at Faversham, Kent kills 106.
E Africa — Deventer's SA Mtd Bde (1200 & 8 guns) begins 150-mile surprise advance from Arusha on Kondoa Irangi in heaviest rainy season for years.		**Britain** — German airships make 5 minor raids on provincial England: 11 Navy, 5 Army sorties. *LZ97* (Linnarz) bombs Ongar-Barkingside (nights 3/4, 5/6, 24/25, 25/26 & 26/27, total cas 12).	Bulgaria informs Greece that troops ordered to withdraw over frontier (closed save to mails, 9). Greece refuses Serb Army land route from Corfu to Salonika.	
E Africa — S Africans attack Lolkisale Hill (35 miles SW of Arusha), capture it (6) with 171 Germans and 2 MGs. Belgian Maj Rouling attacks Capt Wintgens' German position at Kissenji at N end of L Kivu as				**Britain** — **3rd War Budget** raises income tax to 5s in £. **Germany** — War Ministry asks military region COs to form industrial war boards, which some do (-Oct). **India** — 3rd Baron Chelmsford new Viceroy.

APRIL 1916	WESTERN FRONT 1	EASTERN FRONT 2	SOUTHERN FRONTS 3	TURKISH FRONTS 4
Tue 4 contd	Mazel takes over Fifth Army (*see* 25). **Ypres** — Cdn Corps moves to St Eloi-Menin Rd sector; 2nd Cdn Div has 2000 cas by 19 (*see* 6, 19).			
Wed 5	**Verdun** — Germans take Haucourt, but are repulsed at Bethincourt. **Meuse** — German floating mines detonated in river at St Mihiel.			**Mesopotamia** — **3rd Kut relief attempt**: Tigris Corps 30, 357 men, 127 guns, 11 planes, & 4 gunboats but lacking officers v 20,000 Turks & 88 guns. Battles of Hanna & Fallahiya: British 13th Div (1868 cas) takes 2 lightly held Turk forward positions.
Thu 6	Joffre circular abolishes special courts-martial at Front; he suspends Argonne attack to help Verdun, as too many troops needed. **Verdun** — German advance at Hill 304, but repulsed (7). **Flanders** — Germans retake crater at St Eloi, but British 2nd Div retake (10).		**Dolomites** — 59 Italian survivors (from 208) driven off Rauchoe 6493-ft summit, but another det briefly captures Punta Serauto (9715 ft) in Marmolada gp (-14), then Capt Menotti Garibaldi (a grandson) retakes it. **Trentino** — Cadorna has detached 9th & 10th Divs with more *Alpini* & 72 extra guns to First Army, after 24 sends another bde & 40 more guns. Cadorna visits First Army defences (end Apr, *see* 8 May).	**Mesopotamia** — **First Battle of Sannaiyat** (-8): 7th Indian Div charges into a 'torrent of death' 3 times, gains only 500 yds, 16 miles E of Kut. First few motor ambulances in use.
Fri 7	CIGS cables HMG's approval of Anglo-French summer offensive.	Reception at German GHQ (Kovno) to mark Hindenburg's 50 yrs military service. Tsar inspects Ninth Army at Kamenets-Podolsk, meeting Brusilov there (-10).		
Sat 8	**Verdun** — W bank: French evacuate Bethincourt salient.			**Armenia** — 5000 Russians (sailed from Novorossiysk in 22 ships, 5), land nr Humurgan.
Sun 9	**Verdun** — **Germans launch major costly & mainly repulsed assault**; Mort Homme forward trench line entered. Pétain issues famous Order of the Day (No 94) to Verdun Army: *'Courage, on les aura'* ('Take courage, we'll get them.`)			**Mesopotamia** — **Second Battle of Sannaiyat**: 13th Div (7354 inf) is bombed out of Turk 1st line with 1807 cas, 3 VCs won. Fly-ridden & very hot days follow.
Mon 10	**Champagne** — German *Alpenkorps* (ex-Macedonian Front) receives reinforcements. **Verdun** — German advance on Mort Homme, but 1 German div takes 2200 cas. Rain (-21) turns ground into thigh-deep morass.	Orthodox Easter: 4 Russian Eighth Army rifle regts fraternize with Austrians who capture 135 (*see* 18). †Gen Plehve ex-N Front C-in-C (aged 65).	**Salonika** — British cav troop (Sherwood Rangers) ambush 2 German cav troops SE of Doiran Stn in first real clash since 1915 (*see* 24). **Trentino** — Austrian Eleventh Army (8 divs) now concentrated.	**Mesopotamia: Kut** — Daily grain ration reduced to only 5oz from 8oz, the 9239 Indians finally accept horsemeat.

AFRICAN OPERATIONS 5	SEA WAR 6	AIR WAR 7	INTERNATIONAL EVENTS 8	HOME FRONTS 9
prelude to main offensive from Congo (*see* 19).				
	Allied Navies complete Serb Army's evacuation without losing a single soldier after 1159 escort voyages (*see* 12): 81 Allied (25 French, 45 Italian, 11 British) steamers made 322 voyages since 12 Dec to evacuate 260,895 men (145,957 to Corfu), 10,153 horses & 68 guns. LARGEST SEA EVACUATION IN HISTORY UNTIL DUNKIRK. 25 Austro-German air & 26 U-boat attacks sink 8 Italian & French steamers & 11 Allied warships (3 Italian incl cruiser, 5 British minesweepers, French destroyer & 2 submarines). **Black Sea** — *Breslau* active nr Trebizond as Russian battleship *Rotislav* , 4 destroyers & 2 gunboats assist coastal combined ops (-16, *see* TURK FRONTS 8, 14 & 18). **Channel** — *UB26* , caught in RN drifter net, scuttles off Le Havre but refloated & becomes French submarine *Roland Morillot* 30 Aug 1917.		**Occupied Belgium** — Bethmann *Reichstag* speech outlines Flemish protectorate policy.	**Italy** — War Minister Gen Zupelli resigns, Gen Morone succeeds. **Russia** — *Britain Prepared* film première in Moscow (*see* E FRONT 17 May).
E Africa — 400 Portugese occupy Kionga Triangle (-10) S of R Rovuma mouth.				
W Desert — British armoured cars raid Moraisa (18 miles NW of Sollum): 2 German radios, 287,000 cartridges & some rifles captured in Apr (*see* 18).		**Italian Front** — Future top Italian ace Baracca scores 1st victory, an Austrian Aviatik forced down nr Gorizia (Isonzo).	Bethmann replies to Asquith: German food prospects good; Allies refused to consider peace in Sept 1915; Central Powers will settle Polish question (*see* 14). Rumanian-German grain treaty.	**Britain** — Sheffield Exhibition of enemies former imports (-13).
	Adriatic — French submarine sinks Austrian transport.	**W Front** — **First Fokker makes forced landing behind BEF lines**; MG interrupter gear salvaged. Aircraft test-flown at CFS Upavon 30 May. **E Front** — Russian AA guns drive off German aircraft over Tsar's review of IX Corps.		**France** — 400 St Chamond tanks ordered by War Ministry (see June); (Apr) Col Estienne i/c first assault arty unit (Schneider) nr Marly-le-Roi (*see* INT'L EVENTS 20 June).
Sudan — Col Kelly occupies Abaid 90 miles W of Darfur capital El Fasher (*see* AIR WAR May 10).				
E Africa — S Africans occupy Madukani S of L Mangara.		**Ypres** — German AA downs RFC Morane Parasol from 8000 ft.	Asquith addresses French deputies visiting London. British report on Wittenberg PoW camp published (typhus among 15,000 in early 1915).	

APRIL 1916	WESTERN FRONT 1	EASTERN FRONT 2	SOUTHERN FRONTS 3	TURKISH FRONTS 4
Tue 11	**Somme** — British repel attack at La Boisselle (Albert). **Verdun** — Germans repulsed in Douamont-Vaux sector, & W bank of Meuse (12).		**Serb Army begins embarking at Corfu for 4-day voyage to Salonika** (-31 May) in Anglo-French transports without being attacked once (*see* 25).	
Wed 12	**Flanders** — German attack on British trenches on Ypres-Pilkem road.		**Trentino** — (W of L Garda) Italian 5th Div attacks towards Mt Fuma in Adamello Range at over 10,000ft in a blizzard, gains objective (17, *see* 21) after *Alpini* bn storms Alba-Poson di Genova ridge.	Stotzingen 8-man mission reaches Damascus (*see* 2 May). **Mesopotamia** — 3rd Div gains c1 mile on S bank for 400 cas, floods affect both sides on N bank. **E Persia** — Gen Dyer's 200 men defeat 2000 Sarhad tribesmen & secure submission (-30).
Thu 13				**Sinai** — 90 ALH break up Turk camp at Jifjaffa 52 miles from Canal (*see* 23).
Fri 14		**W Russia — First Battle of L Naroch ends**: Russian losses 122,000 (incl 12,000 frostbite deaths), German 20,000. STAVKA planning conference with Tsar at Mogilev: Brusilov offers to attack in summer with minimum reinforcements (*see* 20). Main offensive to be 15 June by Evert's W Front W of Minsk.		**Mesopotamia: Kut** — Townshend reports 29 Apr as extreme supply limit, civilians' grain finished. Arab Bureau confer with Lake in HQ ship at Hanna (*see* 19). **Armenia** — Lyakov's 20,000 men & 30 guns take Turk Kara-dere position, are 8 miles E of Trebizond (16).
Sat 15	**Verdun** — French reoccupy trenches at Douaumont, taking 200 PoWs.			**Mesopotamia: Kut — Air food supply drops start** (9 planes max) drop 16,800lb (-29) in 140 flights. 3rd Div takes Bait Aisa (S bank) in heavy thunderstorm.
Sun 16	**Flanders** — British trench raid S of Béthune-La Bassée road.	**Baltic Provinces** — Russian Twelfth Army CoS orders secret police, informers, patrols & officers to deal with anti-war leaflets in XIII Corps.		106 RMs & Greek irregulars occupy Long I in G of Smyrna entrance (-27 May, *see* SEA WAR 30). **Mesopotamia: Kut** — Flour ration cut to 4oz per man, Indian issued opium pills v hunger.
Mon 17	**Verdun** — Germans repulsed between Meuse & Douaumont.		**Dolomites** — Italian mine exploded (night 17/18), kills 100 & 160 PoWs made as Col di Lana taken, but later assaults on Mt Sief fail with loss of 2000 Italians.	**Mesopotamia** — **Battle of Bait Aisa** (-18): 3rd Indian Div (8362 inf) storms salient in Turk defences, Gurkhas take 2 guns but 10,000 Turks incl German officers (4000 cas) counter-attack 5 times to regain salient (British losses 1600 + 15 MGs).
Tue 18		Brusilov reprimands Easter fraternization: 'I declare once and for all that converse with the enemy is permitted only by gun and bayonet'; officers to be tried.		**Armenia** — **Lyakhov occupies Trebizond** (Turks evacuated night 15/16) & engages Turk rearguard 15 miles S (19).
Wed 19	**Flanders** — German advances at St Eloi & on Ypres-Langemarck road but British recapture ground (21). **Verdun** — 3 German attacks at Les Eparges (Woëvre) but repulsed (20). **Pétain promoted to command of Centre Army Gp** (Langle retires, aged almost 67); **Second Army & Army of Verdun under Nivelle** (*see* 1 May). *GQG* orders Ft Douaumont's recapture (28).			**Mesopotamia** — †FM Goltz (aged 73) from typhus, spotted fever or cholera, rumour that Turks poisoned him; buried in Constantinople. Enver's nephew Brig-Gen Khalil Pasha (aged 34) succeeds. Lawrence arrives at Tigris Corps HQ, catches fever.
Thu 20	**France** — First 8000 Russian	Brusilov orders his 4 Army		

				Britain — Last German spy to be shot at the Tower.
Germans blow up Uganda Railway nr Maungu.				
S Algeria — 500 French retake Djanet border post but Senussi escape (-16, see 21 July).	Med — Allied navies under Adm Gueydon (incl 6 French destroyers, 24 RN drifters) convoy 125,000 Serb troops from Corfu to Salonika (-31 May).	Britain — Lord Montagu warns in speech at Birmingham: 'There is no part of industrial England to which a Zeppelin cannot fly and rain destruction'. He demands end to 'inters-ervice and inter-departmental jealousies' & a Ministry of Aviation to galvanize aircraft production as Ministry of Munitions has transformed shell & gun deliveries.	German *Lusitania* medal published in Britain; photos sent to US, published 7 May, propaganda replica later sold for duration. Germany replies to US *Sussex* note, will submit case to mixed tribunal. Neutrals: Mexico — Carranza troops attack US cavalry entering Parral, 400 miles S of frontier. Carranza demands US pull-out (16, see 29).	
E Africa — 800 SA horse pursue c200 Germans for 20 miles in rain and occupy Salanga; 190 animals lost to tsetse fly (since 7).		E Front — Russian IM heavy bomber *Mourometz X* (Konstenchik w) returns on 1 engine after severe damage from AA fire over Dandsevas rail stn (see 26). W Front — Poor weather hampers flying (-15, 17-19 & rain 22).		Britain — Lloyd George tells confidant he might resign.
E Africa — Rainfall at Moshi (-30) 17.86 ins — sometimes 4 ins pd.	Black Sea — *Goeben* (4 88m AA guns since end 1915) first bombed from air: unsuccessful Russian raid on Stenia Creek (see 9 July).	Turk Fronts — 4 RNAS Short floatplanes from Mudros bomb Zoitunlik explosives factory & hangars at Constantinople & Adrianople rail stn.	Austro-German Berlin talks on Poland deadlocked (-15). Neutrals: USA — Cabinet approves Wilson's *Sussex* note to Germany (sent 18), demands U-boat CO's punishment & future guaran-tees.	Russia — Secret Police head reports revolutionary spirit among 2000 at Petrograd Military Drivers School. Turkey — Currency unification law.
N Rhodesia — Northey issues prelim orders to column cdrs (see SEA WAR).		N Sea — French 'battleplane' fires 16 cannon shells at German patrol craft from height of only 300 ft.		France — Public dispensary & anti-TB measures. Canada — 309,000 enlisted to date.
		W Front — 9 French aircraft bomb Conflans & Arnairlle rail stns & factories at Rombach (night 16/17).		Austria — War Profit Taxes imposed.
	E Atlantic — First UE minelayer *U73* lays 12 mines off Lisbon (Norwegian steamer sunk) (see 27).		Italy prohibits trading with Germany. US meat packers agree to British supervision of meat exports to European neutrals for duration.	Britain — London rumours of PM's resignation. Ireland — Gen Stafford letter from Cork gives Dublin GOC only warning of Rising (unheeded).
E Africa — 650 S Africans capture Kondoa Irangi (-19) from c400 Germans. W Desert — 1600 British reoccupy Kharga Oasis evacuated by Senussi, also Moghara Oasis (27, see 9 May).	Black Sea — Russians capture port of Trebizond. Black Sea Fleet transports 53,000 troops in 2 ops during this campaign.			Britain — Cabinet conscription crisis; Milner & Derby urge it in Lords.
E Africa — 3 Belgian bns (Olsen's S Bde) invade nr Shangugu, Belgian N Bde (Molitor) invades Ruanda (25). Belgians have 10,000 troops, 12 guns & 60 MGs. Smuts has 30,000 porters.				Britain — Nearly 200,000 women in weapon & chemical industries. Turkey — Provincial Governors empowered to seize transport & fix food prices (see 23 July).
	Irish Sea — German disguised	W Front — American volunteer	France — First 8000 Russian	Ireland — Casement lands

APRIL 1916	WESTERN FRONT 1	EASTERN FRONT 2	SOUTHERN FRONTS 3	TURKISH FRONTS 4
Thu 20 contd	troops land at Marseilles.	commanders to prepare for offensive by 11 May without reserves.		
Fri 21	**Verdun** — Gen Knobelsdorf moves doubting German E bank cdr Mudra back (Lochow replaces) to his Argonne corps & resists Crown Prince's doubts same day.		**Trentino** — (W of L Garda) *Alpini* capture Crozzon di Fargorida with Lares & Cavento Passes, but Austrians cling to Fargorida Pass (*see* 30).	
Sat 22	**Verdun** : E bank — Mangin's 5th Div reaches Ft Douaumont but MGs drive it off. **Somme** — BEF XV Corps (Horne) formed, takes over XIII Corps front (29).			**Mesopotamia** — **Third Battle of Sannaiyat**: 7th Div (2241 inf) repelled on flood-restricted narrow front. Armistice for 1283 cas removal.
Sun 23	**Verdun** : German gains at Caurettes Wood.			**Sinai** — 3655 Turks (Kress) destroy Yeomanry posts at Oghratina & Katia, 280 PoWs, but fail at Dueidar, 12 miles E of Kantara. British reoccupy Katia (25). **Mesopotamia: Kut** — Townshend suggests to Lake that surrender talks begin, latter says Townshend must negotiate (*see* 26).
Mon 24			**Salonika** — Gen Mahon authorized to move British troops right up to Greek frontier, French already pushing N & W (along Monastir railway, *see* 2 May).	**Mesopotamia** — 15-volunteer-crewed paddle steamer *Julnar* gets within 8½ river miles of Kut with 270t of food before being snared in Turk steel wires (2 VCs won). In Kut 15 dysentry deaths pd.
Tue 25	**Aisne** — After 8-hr barrage 3 French bns fail to regain ground lost 10 Mar (-26), Gen Mazel suspends op.		Joffre writes to CIGS Robertson suggesting Salonika offensive as soon as Serb Army arrives, argues Rumania will come in as a result, but British only acknowledge on 3 May (*see* 14 May).	
Wed 26				**Mesopotamia: Kut** — After Kitchener cable authorizes talks, Townshend letter asks for 6-day armistice & 10 days food while surrender agreed. Garrison starts destroying anything of value.
Thu 27	-**Artois** — German gas attacks (-29) S of Hulluch v British 15th & 16th Divs (First Army). British trench raid nr Double Crassier (Loos, 28).			**Mesopotamia: Kut** — Townshend (with Lawrence and Aubrey Herbert) meets Khalil Pasha aboard launch. Former suggests HMG £1m gold ransom, latter says 'Your gallant troops will be our most sincere & precious guests'.

AFRICAN OPERATIONS 5	SEA WAR 6	AIR WAR 7	INTERNATIONAL EVENTS 8	HOME FRONTS 9
	gun-runner *Aud* scuttles after capture by sloop *Bluebell*. Roger Casement (former British colonial civil diplomat) lands from *U19* in Tralee Bay.	fighter unit N124 *Escadrille Americaine* formally incorporated in French *Aéronautique Militaire*. Based at Luxeuil-les-Bains (Haute Saône) (*see* 13 & 17 May) 16 of its 42 pilots will die in action.	**troops land at Marseilles** (Austrians knew c9 Mar from PoW postcards). **Neutrals: Greece** — German RM40m loan.	from U-boat at Tralee, Co Kerry (arrested 21). Asquith tells Commons manpower proposals to be submitted to secret session (*see* 25). Gen Wilson to Lord Milner: 'If ever a man deserved to be tried & shot that man is the PM'. **France** — Food & coal prices fixed plus commodities (-22).
E Africa — Lettow decides to concentrate 20 coys (2 mtd) v SA advance (*see* 9 May) leaving Kraut to face Smuts and Wahle v NRFF & the Belgians.		**Occupied Belgium** — 8 RNAS aircraft first bomb German Mariakerke airfield W of Ostend (12 bombers repeat 24, *see* 5 May). **W Front** — Lt Ward & 2/Lt Champion (captured 29 Feb 1916) report to RFC HQ having escaped from Germany 18 Apr. **Sinai** — 8 RFC aircraft fly 4000 miles & for 68 hrs (-25), drop 96 bombs on Turks.		**Turkey** — Djemal Pasha's punishment of 200 Syrian notables announced.
	N Sea — After US protests **Germany decides to adhere to prize law in U-boat ops** (Scheer told during sortie & radio recalls all U-boats to base (25, *see* 23 May), but *U20* & *U45*, unaware, sink 8 ships of 26,751t (-8 May qv). **N Sea** — Dover Patrol begins laying 13-15-mile 'Belgian coast barrage' of moored nets with mines & 2 lines of deep mines (10 minelayers), 4862 in 16 fields (12 miles from shore). Despite attacks by seaplanes, 3 destroyers & shore guns (which hit destroyer *Melpomene* & 3 sisters) barrage completed by 7 May & destroys *UB13* (24).	**W Front** — French aircraft bomb rail stns at Longuyon, Stenay & Nautillois with bivouacs nr Dun & Monfaucon. 15 Anglo-German air combats (2 German aircraft lost).	**Neutrals: Switzerland** — 2nd Int'l Socialist conference (-30), Kienthal; 43 delegates (10 parties incl German & French). Lenin fails to convince majority. **Diplomacy** — Britain replies to US 21 Oct 1915 note.	**Ireland** — EASTER RISING (-30). **Russia** — Tsar approves tax on incomes over 850 roubles pa (from 1 Jan 1917).
E Africa — 1st British through train from Voi reaches Moshi thus joining the German Usambara or Tanga Railway.	**N Sea** — 4 battlecruisers (under Boedicker, Hipper ill) shell Gt Yarmouth & Lowestoft (20 civilian & 3 military cas, c200 houses destroyed) for 20 mins. Yarmouth's shelling shortened by Harwich Force intervention (flagship cruiser *Conquest* sustains 5 hits, 25k). Cruiser *Penelope* torpedoed by *UB29* on way home but towed into Chatham.	**W Front** — 16 Anglo-German air combats. RFC aircraft & balloons range 72 arty targets (65 on 28, 49 on 29).	Coal for Scandinavia not to sail in neutral ships unless with Allied return cargoes.	**Ireland** — Martial law in Dublin. **Britain** — Parlt secret session postpones call up of married men 27-35.
	Irish Sea — British gunboat *Helga* destroys Liberty Hall, Dublin during Easter Rising.	**E Front** — Zeppelin *SL7* raids Dünamunde (Wenden 28) & German planes Dvinsk (*LZ86* raids its railways 28 & Rieshiza 27).	**Sykes-Picot Agreements for Franco-Russian partition of Asia Minor** (*see* 9 & 23 May). Anglo-German PoW exchange via Switzerland signed in Berlin (signed London 13 May).	
Uganda — British frontier & L Victoria demonstrations to cover Belgian advance (29).	**Med** — British battleship *Russell* (124 lost) sunk by German new *U73* mine off Malta, field of 22 also sinks a sloop, armed yacht (28) & trawler. **N Sea** — *UC5* (Mohrbutter) captured by destroyer *Firedrake* while stranded on Shipwash Shoal,	**W Front** — 20 Anglo-German air combats. **Baltic** — 3 German floatplanes operating from tender *Santa Elena* drop 31 bombs (3 hits) on Russian battleship *Slava* in Gulf of Riga (*see* SEA WAR 12 Sept).	Turk War Minister announces Turkey replaces Italy in Triple Alliance. Allied Paris Commercial conference.	

APRIL 1916	WESTERN FRONT 1	EASTERN FRONT 2	SOUTHERN FRONTS 3	TURKISH FRONTS 4
Thu 27 contd				
Fri 28				**Mesopotamia: Kut** — Townshend offers £2m (increase prompted by TE Lawrence), his 50 guns & promise not to fight Turks for duration for his men's freedom. Khalil prepared to accept but Enver wants absolute surrender.
Sat 29	**Verdun** : W bank — French gain N of Mort Homme & Cumières.			**Mesopotamia** — FALL OF KUT: 13,309 surrender incl 3248 non-combatants after 146-day siege (3776 cas): 1136 badly wounded & 1450 sick exchanged as agreed with Arab Bureau negotiators. Tigris Corps relief attempt losses total 23,000. **Persia** — Baratov (5000 men) expels Sevket Bey from Karind after 9-day march (20) to aid Kut.
Sun 30	**Flanders** — British arty defeat German gas attack from Messines Ridge. **Verdun** — German Apr losses 39,000, French 44,000. (Apr-June) French tank pioneer Col Estienne i/c arty in key Vaux-Douaumont sector.		**Trentino** — (W of L Garda) *Alpini* cadets capture Crozzon di Fargorida. Crozzon & Passo del Diavolo taken later & Austrians forced to evacuate Fargorida & Topete Passes. This sector secure for Italy for duration.	**Mesopotamia** — Kut garrison begins march into captivity (4818 do not return). Turks kill 250 Kut civilians. CIGS cable orders defensive strategy.
Mon 1 May 1916	German reverses E of Ypres & N of Albert (Somme). British trench newspaper parodies 'How to Win the War' ideas. **Verdun** — Nivelle succeeds Pétain in command, boasts 'We have the formula'. Latter to head French Centre Army Group. French take trenches SE of Ft Douaumont. 40 French divs have fought since start v 26 German (no relief of formations, only replacements of men). (May) French Capt. André Laffargue publishes pamphlet on revolutionary infiltration tactics for inf (Germans apparently capture copy).		**Italian Front** — (May) French begin sending 250 MGs pm to Italy.	
Tue 2	**Somme** — French in planned offensive to be led by Micheler, Pétain obvious choice but jealous Joffre will not consider him.		**Macedonia** — French occupy Florina 23 miles S of Monastir.	**Mesopotamia** — King's message to Tigris Corps (new 14th Div formed 12), cholera outbreak (shade temp 115° F). **Secret War** — Stotzingen leaves Jerusalem for Arabia, heads for Wejh but only reaches Yanbo (late May) due to RN blockade (*see* 15).
Wed 3	**Verdun** — French storm positions NW of Mort Homme, but 500 German guns on a mile front shell Hill 304 (-5); one French bn reduced to 3 men.			**Persia** — Baratov occupies Kasr-i-Shirin on border (110 miles from Baghdad) & learns Kut's fate by radio, takes Khanikin (15,*see* 18).
Thu 4				**Mesopotamia** — Kut garrison's 420 officers taken away by paddle steamer to Baghdad.

AFRICAN OPERATIONS 5	SEA WAR 6	AIR WAR 7	INTERNATIONAL EVENTS 8	HOME FRONTS 9
	towed into Harwich. Italian Navy commissions its first of 10 wartime monitors (mainly converted captured Austrian barges or lighters).		**Neutrals: USA** — Scheele & other Germans indicted for conspiracy to destroy munition ships. British agreement with Chicago International Harvester Corp.	
	N Sea — RN 3rd Battle Sqn (7 ships) transferred from Grand Fleet to Thames (Sheerness) as stronger coast guard.		Allied Havre Declaration guarantees Belgian Congo's integrity. **Neutrals: Mexico** — US & Mexican generals agree withdrawal conditions (-3 May).	**Ireland** — IRB leader Pearse surrenders to Brig-Gen Lowe, tells others to do likewise.
E Africa — Belgian N Bde occupies Kasibu. 3rd SA Inf Bde (less 1000 sick) arrives Kondoa Irangi (-1 May). 2nd Rhodesian Regt 50/600 fit.	**Aegean** — 2 RN minesweepers tow 14 caiques to land opposite Samos (150 irregulars involved, 2k), capture 1870 cattle (night 30 Apr/1 May, *see* 12 May). (Apr) British merchant shipping losses, 43 ships worth 141,193t with 131 lives (total Allied & neutral loss 187,307t incl 56,000t or 20 ships in Med).	**Verdun** — Count Holck k over Verdun: his Fokker shot down by 10 Caudrons; Richthofen comments 'with a bullet through his head, he fell from an altitude of 9000 ft — a beautiful death'.		**Ireland** — 707 Dublin rebels surrender. **France** — Building reconstruction service set up for occupied territory.
Rhodesia — 1st Native Regt formed, leaves for E Africa 18 July.	**Channel** — Vice Adm Ronarc'h becomes French C-in-C for duration. **Adriatic** — (May) First Italian *MAS* motor launches (299 built) enter service (ordered Apr 1915). (47 Japanese fishing boats bought 1916 for escort role.) 4 Italian battleships now based at Valona, Albania. **Med** — (May) Adm Haus promoted Austria's first & only Grand Admiral (c28). U-boats sink 37 ships or 72,072t in Med out of grand total of 119,381t. **Germany** — First of 24 All-type coastal torpedo-boat/minesweepers commissioned for Flanders ops (6 finished at Antwerp).	(1 May) **First flight of French Spad S7 fighter** (140hp Hispano-Suiza V8 engine). Caquot (French) introduces the classic kite (observation) barrage balloon. MG synchronized to fire through the propeller arc introduced into RFC sqn service ('1½-Strutters' of No 70 Sqn).	(May) British Grave Registration units formed in Egypt, Salonika, Mesopotamia and E Africa. **Neutrals: Spain** (May) — French agent and war widow Marthe Richer begins work as German Madrid Naval Attaché's lover. **Holland** (May) — Mata Hari recruited as German agent, sails for Spain (24, *see* 16 June).	**Ireland** — REBELLION ENDS: British cas 521, rebels 58, civilian 736; 16 rebel leaders shot (-8), 79 jailed. **Britain** — RFP up 6% to 55%. (May) War Propaganda Bureau forms special pictorial section with painter Muirhead Bone 1st of 90 war artists. Sassoon's 1st war poetry (*The Old Huntsman*) published. **Germany** — Liebknecht arrested in 10,000 Berlin workers anti-war protest. (May) 1917 conscript class called up gradually (-Aug), 15 months early.
		Britain — 8 Zeppelins cause 39 cas in Yorks, Northumbria & Scotland (night 2/3); storm wrecks *L20* nr Stavanger, Norway on return (3).		
E Africa — Belgians occupy Shanzugu (L Kivu) & Kigali (6).	**N Sea** — Weather thwarts British carrier raid (*Vindex* & *Engadine*) on Tondern Zeppelin sheds (-4), but cruisers *Galatea* & *Phaeton* force Zeppelin *L7* down (submarine *E31* finishes it off & rescues 7 survivors, also survives 5.9in shell hit & ramming attempt by cruiser *Rostock*). Main rival fleets briefly sortie in support (4-5).	**E Front** — Zeppelin *ZX11* raids Luninetz & *LZ86* Minsk railways.		**Russia** — Ex-War Minister Gen Sukhomlinov arrested on treason charges. **Britain** — 10% lighting reduction requested to save coal.
	Rules of cruiser warfare to be observed by U-boat cdrs if ships do not try & escape or resist. **Adriatic** — French submarine *Bernouilli* blows stern off Austrian destroyer *Csepel* at Cattaro entrance.	**E Front** — IM heavy bomber *Ilia Mourmometz II* (Pankratiev) flies 1st of 5 May successful armed recon missions over Yazlovetch-Bugatch & Yazlovetch-Rusilov sectors & helps capture of Yazlovetch.	German *Sussex* 'pledge' reply to US 18 May note, will not sink vessels without warning, US accepts (8). **Neutrals: USA** — Congress doubles West Point cadets. US Marines land in Santo Domingo to restore order.	

MAY 1916	WESTERN FRONT 1	EASTERN FRONT 2	SOUTHERN FRONTS 3	TURKISH FRONTS 4
Fri 5	**Verdun** — German gain at Hill 304. French 135th Inf Regt sgt writes '... how could anyone cross the zone of extermination around us?'		**Salonika** — Milne told he will succeed Gen Mahon (to Egypt) as British C-in-C (*see* 10).	
Sat 6				**Mesopotamia** — **Death march from Kut begins**: 2592 British soldier PoWs (Kurd cav regt escort) start 1200-mile forced march to Anatolia; reach Ctesiphon (14). **Syria** — Djemal Pasha hangs 21 'Autonomous Syria' Arab leaders without trial incl Ottoman senator.
Sun 7	**Verdun** — Violent German attacks gain ground at Hill 304 (attacks fail 8) & Ft Douaumont.	(c) Austrian military intelligence discovers 4 Brusilov corps between Kolki & Rovno but warning disregarded (*see* 1 June).		**Mesopotamia** — Khalil Pasha orders 6000 Turks & 14 guns from Kut to Persian frontier.
Mon 8	**Verdun** — 650 Bavarians perish in Ft Douaumont magazine explosion (*see* 18). **France — Anzacs join BEF line**.		**Italian Front** — Cadorna sacks Gen Brusati of First Army for latter's over-aggressive dispositions (2nd & 3rd lines neglected), Gen Count Pecori-Giraldi replaces him. 67 bns & 80 guns reinforce First Army by 15.	
Tue 9				
Wed 10	**Verdun** — German assault on Hill 287. French counter-attack at Mort Homme.		**Milne i/c British Salonika Army** (for duration); Sarrail occupies Greek frontier Ft Dova Tepe between Vardar & Stuma (*see* 26).	
Thu 11	**Artois** — Germans seize 500 yds of British 15th Div trenches NE of Vermelles; part regained in counter-attack. **Verdun** — German attack W of Vaux pond.			
Fri 12	**Verdun** — German attacks on French centre.			**Mesopotamia** — Townshend leaves Baghdad, reaches Mosul (19).
Sat 13	**Artois** — British repulse attack on Ploegsteert Wood. Lt H Macmillan (Grenadier Gds) writes to his mother '... the most extraordinary thing about a modern battlefield is the desolation and emptiness ...'. **Verdun** — Vain German attacks W of Hill 304 & NE of Mort Homme. **Falkenhayn orders despairing Crown Prince to prepare 1 June offensive** (*see* 30).	Tsar & Brusilov inspect new 10,000-strong Serb Div (ex-Austrian PoWs) at Benderi and visit Odessa (-14), before imperial family leave for Sevastopol.		**Mesopotamia** — Col Rybalchenko takes Rowanduz E of Mosul (*see* 2 June).
Sun 14	**Artois** — German attacks on Hohenzollern Redoubt-Hulluch (Loos).	1000 British PoWs detrain at Zeren, SW of G of Riga for reprisal tree-felling, frequently refuse to work (-26).	Joffre forwards 1916 Macedonian offensive plan to British, asks for 2 more divs (*see* 17). **Isonzo** — Austrians recapture Adria shipyard with Hills 12 & 93 at Monfalcone (*see* 14 June).	**Mesopotamia** — Gorringe reports Turk air superiority (German Fokkers).

AFRICAN OPERATIONS 5	SEA WAR 6	AIR WAR 7	INTERNATIONAL EVENTS 8	HOME FRONTS 9
		Occupied Belgium — 19 RNAS aircraft (1 FTR) bomb Mariakerke airfield (night 5/6, repeated 21); Ghistelles airfield bombed (19). **W Front** — Unfavourable weather reduces flying (-10 & 25).	Tsar receives Serb PM Pasic. **Neutrals: USA** — Villalistas loot 2 Texas settlements (*see* 9).	
S Algeria — French defeat Tuareg revolt (-9). Leader Firhoun k (25) and submission by 1 Sept.			Serb Govt set up at Salonika.	**Germany** — Unpopular & ill Interior Minister Delbrück resigns (*see* 22).
E Africa — Portuguese repulse Germans from Nhika, but 400 repulsed by 45 Germans on R Ruovuma at Mwambo (27, *see* 27 June).	**E Atlantic** — *U20* sinks British US-bound liner *Cymric* (5 lost) 140 miles WNW of Fastnet, 37th unarmed liner sunk by U-boats since *Lusitania* and 4th in current offensive (despite orders).	**Egypt** — German air raids on Port Said from El Arish (& 21). 6 RFC retaliate v El Arish (18), also establish airfield & 2 aircraft at Port Said (*see* 1 June).		**Britain** — Churchill back from W Front in Commons speaks (9) v Ireland retaining voluntary enlistment, Irish Nationalist MP cries 'What about the Dardanelles?'.
E Africa — **Battle of Kondoa Irangi** (-10): Lettow's 4000 men's 4 night attacks repulsed by S Africans; others occupy Mbulu, SW of L Manyara (11). **W Desert** — Mahon becomes GOC WFF (*see* 25).	Enver Pasha appeals for Central Powers' naval help v Russian Black Sea advances, Falkenhayn backs it & Germans send *U38*, but she sinks only 4 small ships (-11 Aug).		K George V receives Russian Duma members (Briand also, 22). **Neutrals: USA** — Wilson orders 4000 more regulars to Mexico & border. Nationals advised to leave Mexico (10).	
		Sudan — 2 RFC planes & airfield at Abaid for ops v Sultan of Darfur (*see* 23).	**Neutrals: Greece** — Sarrail occupies frontier Ft Dovatepe (*see* 22).	**Ireland** — Royal Commission of Inquiry into Rebellion formed under Lord Hardinge (opens 18). Lord Wimborne resigns Lord Lieutenancy (Chief Sec Birrell resigned 3). **France** — 17 British conscientious objectors refuse Army orders outside Le Havre (*see* 6 June).
		W Front — Cmdt de Rose, creator & motivator of the French fighter units defending Verdun, killed when his Nieuport stalls at low altitude, aged 40.		
L Tanganyika — Cdr Spicer-Simpson returns to Lukuga (left 21 Feb), soon rows with Belgians.		**Britain** — Burbidge Ctee set up to inquire into alleged mismanagement of Royal Aircraft Factory, Farnborough; Chmn, Sir R Burbidge, MD of Harrods store.	**Occupied France** — German Lille deportation order grants 1½ hrs packing, 25,000 deported incl women & girls for farm work (-Sept).	**Ireland** — Asquith's surprise visit to Dublin (-18). **Britain** — Home Office letter to JPs on juvenile crime rise.
	Adriatic — RN Otranto Barrage drifter sinks Austrian *U6* & forces her to scuttle, **only definite Otranto Barrage U-boat kill of war** (*see* 31).	**W Front** — *Esc Americaine* flies its first patrol with Nieuport fighters (*see* 17 & 24).	**Kitchener receives Tsar's invitation to visit Russia**, visit widely rumoured (*see* 19 & 26).	**Britain** — Married men 36-41 call up for 13 June (*see* 25).
	Aegean — Turk shore guns sink British monitor *M30* in Gulf of Smyrna, British evacuate Long Island (27). **Med** — French Fleet divided into battle sqn, Orient, Syria & Adriatic divs.		**Neutrals: China** — Huimin Corporation signs **contract with France to provide 200,000 Chinese labourers** for war (*see* 20 Oct). **Mexico** — 2nd Lt Patton shoots Pancho Villa's bodyguard & is promoted (26, *see* 29).	**France** — Pres Poincaré speech at Nancy.

MAY 1916	WESTERN FRONT 1	EASTERN FRONT 2	SOUTHERN FRONTS 3	TURKISH FRONTS 4
Mon 15	**Artois** — British mine & storm 250 yds trenches on Vimy Ridge but Germans take crater (17, *see* 21).		AUSTRIAN TRENTINO OFFENSIVE begins on 21-mile front with 4 hr intensive barrage from 0600. Elite XX *Edelweiss* Corps (Archduke Charles) has 253 guns in direct support + 140 from III Corps, captures Costa d'Agra & Mt Coston (5745 ft) breaking Italian 1st line (-16), but VIII Corps to W fought to a standstill by *Roma* Bde & *Alpini* (*see* 18); as is XXI Corps though XVII Corps secures parts of Armentera Ridge (4954ft) in E diversion along Val Sugana that Pecori-Giraldi mistakes as main threat.	**Arabia** — Allied blockade of Hejaz coast begins (*see* 5 June).
Tue 16			**Italian Front** — Cadorna arrives at Thiene from Udine to conduct Trentino defence.	**Armenia** — 15,000 Russians (new 127th Div) sail from Mariupol (Azov Sea) for Trebizond in 28 ships & land (-21), 123rd Div follows (30). **Sinai** — Anzacs storm Turk camp at Bayud; NZ troops raid Bir Salmana (20 miles E of Katia (31). British railway reaches Romani (19).
Wed 17		By now 103,000 of Brusilov's men have seen *Britain Prepared* film (Tsar views at STAVKA).	Austrians claim 6300 PoWs. Tyrol *Kaiserjäger* capture Mts Maggio & Sima di Campulozzo. **Salonika** — British War Ctee rejects Macedonian offensive (*see* 26).	**Mesopotamia** — Kut garrison humiliated through Baghdad (US consul gives money & gets 500 hospitalized), entrained (19) just to Samarra, reach Tekrit (23) where stoned. **S Persia** — Sykes' 638 troops leave Bandar Abbas for Kerman (*see* 11 June).
Thu 18	**Verdun** — Unsuccessful German attack on Avocourt Wood & Hill 304 (repeated 19); 300 French guns (incl 4 14.5-in mortars) begin shelling Ft Douaumont sector (*see* 22).		Austrian VIII Corps finally has success capturing Zugna Toirta (4124 ft), E of R Adige, after annihilating *Roma* Bde. Austrian 10th Mtn Bde storms Mt Col Santo (6936 ft) farther E, *Ancona* Bde broken & Italian centre endangered.	**Mesopotamia** — 113 Kuban **Cossacks reach Tigris Corps** after 200-mile march, officers given MC for first Anglo-Russian allied military meeting since 1815.
Fri 19	**Verdun** — Germans capture position S of Hill 287. **Germans introduce diphosgene gas** shell at Chattancourt. Disphosgene is a liquid (phosgene is gaseous) & is easily handled by gunners.		Italians abandon Mt Toraro-Mt Melignone line, destroying their forts, but after 5-mile advance Austrian XX Corps waits for arty to come up for next phase as Italian First Army commits last reserves (6 *Alpini* bns); *Volturno* Bde saves Mt Pasubio (4055 ft).	**Mesopotamia** — Turks evacuate Es Sinn S bank position & retreat to Kut (-20). British follow up 10 miles for 10% heat-stroke cas. Enver reaches Baghdad to instigate Persia offensive (-25) despite German objections.
Sat 20	**Verdun** — Gallwitz's 5 German divs assault Mort Homme, **seize top summit** of Hill 295.	**Italy appeals to STAVKA for diversionary Russian offensive**, culminates in King's telegram (22) to Tsar.	**Cadorna orders First Army to fight to last man**, meets the 2 Isonzo army cdrs at Udine & agrees measures for evacuation if Austrians reach plains behind them. Trentino 2nd line to be abandoned in favour of stronger 3rd (*see* E FRONT). Austrian III Corps attacks Italian 34th Div, takes Cima di Leva. **Secret War** — Austrians intercept Italian radio signals about counterattack, by 0400 (21) deploy to check it.	**Armenia** — Cossacks capture dissident Kurd major (nr Kigi) with Turk Second Army plan.

AFRICAN OPERATIONS 5	SEA WAR 6	AIR WAR 7	INTERNATIONAL EVENTS 8	HOME FRONTS 9
	Red Sea — Allied blockade of Hejaz coast begins.		Grey states Allies fighting for a free Europe. Bethmann replies (23) that Germany will make peace on basis of security v attack. **Occupied Belgium** — Gov-Gen Bissing decrees unemployed will accept work for Germany.	**Ireland** — Casement charged with high treason (*see* 25 June).
British Somaliland — Dervish-surrounded Las Khorai relieved. **Chad** — 737 French defeat Sultan Bakhit (submits 23 June) but flees into Darfur; captured 16 July.	**N Sea** — Dover Patrol engages German destroyers off Belgian coast. **Med** — *U39* (Forst-mann) cruise (-6 June) sinks 21 ships (2 neutral) worth 52,812t for only 5 torpedoes & 5 HE charges but 365 88mm shells (incl 18-min shelling of Porto Ferraio, Elba). **Black Sea** — Russian Navy begins major amphibious ops (-30, *see* TURK FRONTS).	**W Front** — 27 Anglo-German air combats, RFC lose 2, Germans lose 2 (13 indecisive ones, 17). 2/Lt Ball in 11 Sqn Bristol Scout sees first action v Albatros over Givenchy (*see* 22).	Iceland agrees with Britain to divert all exports from Germany.	
Germans blow up Uganda Railway nr Mackinnon Road.	**Baltic** — Russian submarine *Volk* sinks 3 German steamers off Sweden, greatest such Russian success until 1945. 3 British & 2 Russian submarines begin patrols (25). RN *E18* blows bows off German destroyer *V100* (12k) 30 miles from Libau (26), but is lost (28 or later) either to mine or German decoy ship *K*. Tsar breaks Russian rules to award CO Halahan & crew posthu-mously.	**W Front** — German bombing raid on Luxeuil-les-Bains; 10 American cas (*see* 24). **Britain** — **Air Board established** under Lord Curzon to organize & co-ordinate supply of *materiel* (airframes, engines, compo-nents) to RFC & RNAS.	**Neutrals: USA** — Wilson Washington speech, US may be forced to intervene, in any case must have say at peace settlement (*see* 27).	
	E Med — 2 RN monitors shell El Arish, Sinai, for 50 mins.			**France** — Ministerial Ctee formed to restore devastated districts.
E Africa — Belgians occupy Nyanza, contact Molitor at Kigali (by 21) when Ruanda fully occupied.		**W Front** — Navarre of *Esc N67* scores his 12th & final victory (Verdun, *see* 17 June). RFC aircraft & balloon range 61 targets (88 on 20, 76 on 21 & 87 on 22), claim 4 German aircraft. **Britain** — 7 German floatplanes (1 lost to RNAS Nieuport from Dunkirk) fly moonlight raid on 4 E Kent coast towns; c59 bombs on land; 3 cas (night 19/20). **Flanders** — German day & night bombing of Dunkirk (-22, 2 aircraft destroyed by RNAS) causes 121 cas (372 bombs).	Asquith refuses to see Russian Gen Gourko re Kitchener's visit, plays 2 hrs 'bridge' at No 10 as usual (*see* 26). London conference with Danes on limiting food exports to Germany (agreement with Danish Coal Bureau 30 and phosphates 8 June, *see* 26).	**Britain** — 1916/17 Army fixed at 4m. Boys' welfare supervi-sors appointed to munition factories.
		W Front — 18 inconclusive Anglo-German air combats.		**Montenegro** — PM Miuskovic open letter accuses King of treason; PM resigns, Radovic succeeds.

MAY 1916	WESTERN FRONT 1	EASTERN FRONT 2	SOUTHERN FRONTS 3	TURKISH FRONTS 4
Sun 21	**Artois** — Aided by 320-gun 14-hr barrage German 18th Res Div captures 1500 yds of British 47th Div trenches at Vimy Ridge to counter Allied tunnelling, line driven 300 yds W (*see* 23). **Verdun** — French storm trenches between Avocourt Wood & Meuse; repel attacks on W slopes of Mort Homme.		Cadorna forms res Fifth Army (whose 5 Corps & 2 cav divs concentrate in Vicenza-Padua-Citadella triangle by 5 June, *see* 1 June); puts Lt Gen Lequio from Carnia i/c Sette Commune area N of Asiago. Austrian III Corps storms ridges S of Mt Vezena (6624 ft) forcing defenders (34th Div) to blow up 2 more forts.	**Afghanistan** — German mission leaves Kabul, Hentig to China (*see* INT'L EVENTS 1 Apr 1917).
Mon 22	**Verdun** — French 5th Div (Mangin) takes German trenches on 2000-yd front Thiaumont Farm-Ft Douaumont & enters fort after 11-min charge, captures most of it in 30 mins. **Artois** — BEF Res Army (Gough) formed, becomes Fifth Army (30 Oct).		**Trentino** — Austrian XVII Corps takes Borgo on R Brenta, completes advance as flank guard.	
Tue 23	**Verdun** — German counter-attack cuts off French in fort who cannot be reinforced. Germans take Cumières. **Artois** : Vimy — BEF IV Corps 2 bde counter-attack ruined by German counter-barrage; British losses 2500 to 1344 German.		Austrian XXI Corps E of R Adige attacks Buole Pass (4773 ft) (-28 qv) v Italian 37th Div.	
Wed 24	**Verdun** — Fighting on whole front: Germans regain Douaumont ruins & Caillette woods with 100 PoWs. Mangin temporarily disgraced. French recapture part of Cumières (W bank). One French div's arty relieved on E bank after firing 180,000 shells since 21 Apr, losing 17 guns to German fire & 19 exploded accidentally.	Brusilov cables Alexeiev that he can attack a week from when ordered or 1 June & so telegraphs Army cdrs. Postponed till 4 June to allow W Front more time. **Secret War** — Lt Slezkin & 20 men of Russian 10th Ingermanland Hussars swim R Prut to do night recce into Bukovina via Rumania; all awarded St George's Cross.	Heavy snow halts Austrian VIII Corps drive on Mt Pasubio, but it captures Mt Cimone (24) from 2 *Alpini* bns. Italian 27th Div replaces battered V Corps.	
Thu 25	**Verdun** — Great German attack between Hardaumont Wood & Thiaumont Farm, French counter-attack (27). **Somme** — German Second Army CoS vainly proposes pre-emptive attack.		Austrian III Corps occupies Corno di Campo Verde (6815 ft) & captures Portule line E of Val d'Assa.	
Fri 26	Joffre visits Haig & gets assurance of 1 July BEF Somme offensive (*see* 31). **Verdun** — Unsuccessful German attack on Avocourt Wood & Mort Homme (French regain trenches to SW, 27).		Archduke Eugene shifts main thrust E onto Asiago Plateau so as to reach Brenta valley towards Bassano & Venetian plains. Cadorna orders surplus heavy arty & stores from Isonzo to withdraw in case of Trentino collapse. **Salonika** — Joffre-Robertson deadlocked on future offensive (*see* 9 June).	**Mesopotamia** — Enver speaks only to Indian Muslims from Kut, N of Tekrit, sees Townshend in his private train (c30).
Sat 27		Linsingen tells Kaiser at Brest-Litovsk that, 'Our formidable positions' will 'automatically hold' any attack. **Galicia** — Russian 9th Lancers success-fully charge Austrian inf nr Vonchach.	**Salonika** — Bulgar div & Germans occupy evacuated Greet Ft Rupel & 3 villages S of frontier thus blocking Struma valley (*see* INT'L EVENTS 22, 3 June). **Trentino** — Austrians closing on Arsiero.	
Sun 28	**Verdun** — German *Alpenkorps* (from Champagne) again in action. **Flanders** — Haig warns Second Army (Plumer) to hasten preparations for		Austrian *Kaiserschütz* Div repeatedly but vainly attacks Buole Pass (*Taro* & *Sicilia* Bdes) & loses 629 cas. Three final attacks (30) fail; defenders	

AFRICAN OPERATIONS 5	SEA WAR 6	AIR WAR 7	INTERNATIONAL EVENTS 8	HOME FRONTS 9
		W Front — German aircraft lands by mistake in mist on No 27 Sqn airfield at Treziennes.		**Britain** — **Daylight saving in force**.
E Africa — **Smuts resumes advance** in 3 cols through Pare & Usambara Mts, covers 130 miles (-31). **Sudan** — Battle of Beringia: Col Kelly's 800+ Egyptians & Sudanese (26 cas), 8 guns & 14 MGs (advanced from Abaid 15) defeat Sultan of Darfur's 5000-strong attack (357+ cas) 12 miles N of El Fasher. Kelly occupies (23), takes 4 guns & 55,000 cartridges (*see* AIR WAR 23, *see* 6 Nov).		**Verdun** — French Nieuports of *Esc N65* destroy 6 kite-balloons using very short-range firework-type rocket projectiles devised by French Navy Lt Le Prieur. **W Front** — 2/Lt Ball forces down 2 German aircraft, his 1st successes (2 more combats 29).	Germany notifies Greece that troops must enter Ft Rupel, evacuated under protest (27), Allies protest to Greece (31).	**Germany** — Finance Minister Dr Helfferich takes Interior & Deputy Chancellor portfolios as well. War Food Office (Batocki) created, introduces food premiums for hard workers (*see* 5 June).
	N Sea — 10 U-boats (sailed from 17) begin to take up minelaying stns off Grand Fleet bases & in key areas (*see* 29) ready for Scheer's planned sortie.	**Sudan** — Future MRAF Lt Slessor RFC (w) bombs fleeing Sultan of Darfur.		**Britain** — Commons votes £300m war credit (11th); war cost est £4.8m pd since 1 Apr.
		W Front — Raoul Lufbery joins *Esc Americaine* (7 US pilots originally).		
E Africa — **Northey's** 2593-strong **NRFF**, 14 guns & 26 MGs **invades at 4 points** v c817 Germans (1 gun & 8 MGs), but fail to trap border garrisons (-3 June). **Cyrenaica** — 2 Italian bns land at Moraisa W of Sollum (*see* 31 Aug).				**Britain** — GENERAL CONSCRIPTION: King's message hails Military Service Act (passed 16 takes effect 24 June) covers all married men 18-41 plus relook at rejects; 5,031,000 volunteers to date.
		W Front — RFC aircraft & balloons range 62 targets (68 on 27).	British War Ctee decides Kitchener shall visit Russia to co-ordinate supply (Tsar's invitation accepted, 27). **Neutrals: Denmark** — MI5 claim heavy German use of Danish diplomatic bags.	
E Africa — Smuts narrowly escapes German patrol.	**N Sea** — *U74* minelayer caught on surface & sunk by 4 armed trawlers' guns off Peterhead. *UC3* mined off Zeebrugge.		Sazonov says Anglo-Russian alliance eternal; Russia has no aggressive aims v Sweden or any other European neighbour; Poland to be autonomous. **Neutrals: USA** — **Wilson's first League of Nations hint**, mentions a universal league to preserve peace & freedom of seas.	**France** — †Gen Gallieni (aged 67) at Versailles, made Marshal of France 1921.
		London-Paris airmail service begins.	**Neutrals: USA** — National German-American Chicago Conference (-29) on presidential candidates (*see* 10 June).	

MAY 1916	WESTERN FRONT 1	EASTERN FRONT 2	SOUTHERN FRONTS 3	TURKISH FRONTS 4
Sun 28 contd	offensive as it might be needed (ie before planned Somme offensive) due to French concentration at Verdun. Germans are already warned of it; Falkenhayn has reinforced Sixth Army with 3 divs, only 1 new div assigned to Second Army on Somme. Lt-Gen Sir J Byng put i/c Cdn Corps (*see* 2 June).		suffer 911 cas, but 'we have not given way an inch' (Col Gualtieri).	
Mon 29	**Verdun** — German attacks on Hill 304 (unsuccessful) & NW of Cumières (trenches carried).	Kaiser & Falkenhayn visit Hindenburg & Ludendorff at Kovno.	Italians lose Mt Aralta, Pria Fora (*Bisagno* Bde regains & loses several times), evacuate Asiago.	**Mesopotamia** — Kut PoWs split into British, Hindu & Muslim (*see* 3 June). **Armenia** — Vehip Pasha surprise attacks weak I Caucausus Corps; his 29th Div retakes Mamahatun & 2 guns (-31,*see* 4 June).
Tue 30	**Verdun** — French withdraw from Bethincourt-Cumières road & Caurettes Wood, withdraw towards Chattancourt. Later drive Germans back to Cumières. Gen Knobelsdorf decides to stick to E bank offensive only despite Gallwitz success on W bank. **France — Heavy arty prod programme begins**, 4690 guns ordered.		Austrian XX Corps secures Mt Pria Fora (5423 ft SW of Arsiero) after bloody fighting following Italians losing their way & failing to occupy it.	
Wed 31	**Verdun** — French guns destroy 500,000-shell dump at Spinville. Pres Poincaré tells Haig that Pétain, Nivelle & another general at Verdun fear '*Verdun sera prise!*' ('Verdun will fall') & that counter-offensive must be launched without delay (ie on the Somme). Foch reprimanded by PM Briand for asserting that Allies should avoid 1916 offensive.	Alexeiev orders 'A powerful auxiliary attack [Brusilov] on the Austrians...the main blow being delivered, later, by...the W Front'.	**Trentino** — Austrian div from Isonzo joins battle in which, via Astico valley, XX Corps' 59th Salzburg Regt gets below Mt Cegnio (4432 ft) in final effort (*see* June); 30,000 PoWs to date. **Salonika** — 112,000 Serb troops (6 divs) & 8000 horses now transported from Corfu to 6 camps 10 miles SE of Salonika; 25,000 sick, w, recruits & surplus officers left at Corfu or in N Africa. French occupy Poro. **Italy** — Cadorna requests MGs from France which supplies 250 pm from now on.	

AFRICAN OPERATIONS 5	SEA WAR 6	AIR WAR 7	INTERNATIONAL EVENTS 8	HOME FRONTS 9
E Africa — Sheppard's Pangani River col camps nr Mabirioni after marching 112 miles in week. NRFF occupies Neu Langenburg, German district HQ NW of L Nyasa. **Morocco** — Battle of Oued Khellal: French storm tribal positions.	**E Atlantic** — *U75* (Beitzen) lays 22 mines W coast of the Orkneys in special op resulting from radio intercept by *Lange* (Norwegian) at German Neumunster listening station (26) indicating sudden British Admiralty interest in minesweeping along this neglected westabout shipping route (*see* 5 June).		**Neutrals: Mexico** — US Col Dodd defeats Villa (*see* 11 June).	**Britain** — Civilian cas to date 550k, 1616w.
E Africa — 300 Rhodesians capture 'German bridge' W of Bwiko which Smuts occupies (31) & halts on half rations to ease supply (*see* 7 June).	**N Sea** — RN's Room 40 gives early warning of German Fleet sortie & that 16 U-boats out. Main body of Grand Fleet (Jellicoe) leaves Scapa & Invergordon at 2200. Battlecruiser Force (Beatty) leaves Rosyth. **Adriatic** — (end May) Rear-Adm Mark Kerr takes over British Adriatic Sqn.	**W Front** — Rain & low clouds.		**France** — Great arty production programme adopted for modernization and motorization.
	Ionian Sea — Abruzzi visits French Fleet (10 battleships, etc) at Argostoli (Cephalonia), 'personal' visit does not solve co-ordination & command problems. **Adriatic** — 5 Austrian destroyers & torpedo boats raid RN Otranto patrol line, sink (drifter *Beneficient*) (night 31/1 June). BATTLE OF JUTLAND (-1 June, German Battle of the Skaggerak): Scheer orders northward sweep to raid Allied shipping off Scandinavia & perhaps attack British 10th Cruiser Sqn. German Fleet leaves Jade anchorage at 0200 (Hipper's 5 battlecruisers in van). *U32* makes only torpedo attack (failed) at 0355 of planned mass ambush. At 1400 Beatty (55 ships) & Hipper (42 ships) are on converging courses W of Jutland. At 1420 Beatty turns SE hoping to cut off Hipper's line of retreat but instead Hipper turns NW. They sight each other at 1525, fire at 1548. Hipper now reverses course. British battlecruiser *Indefatigable* (1017 lost) & *Queen Mary* (1266 lost) blow up; flagship *Lion* & *Seydlitz* (torpedo hit & 22 shell hits) both damaged. Two main fleets engage each other (96 ships v 59) from 1800 until dark (only 20 mins in all). At 1833 Hipper's flagship battlecruiser *Lützow* disabled by 24 hits, but she sinks *Invincible* (only 6 survivors). At 1835 Scheer successfully carries out carefully rehearsed emergency retirement. Even so, Jellicoe gets between Scheer & his base but has no star shell & only poor searchlights while Admiralty withholds Harwich Force (5 cruisers, 18 destroy-	**W Front** — 2 of 5 FE2bs lost on recon over Cambrai to 3 Fokkers (1 lost). **N Sea** — Battle of Jutland: seaplane from HM carrier *Engadine* shadows German cruiser/destroyer force, but its radio reports not received.		**Britain** — School exemptions for farmwork 15,753. £ = c$4.76 for duration ($5 prewar).

MAY 1916	WESTERN FRONT 1	EASTERN FRONT 2	SOUTHERN FRONTS 3	TURKISH FRONTS 4
Wed 31 contd				
Thu 1 June 1916	**Verdun** — Gen Lochow's **c80,000 Germans** (5 divs) **attack** (Op 'May Cup') on 3½-mile front Thiaumont Farm-Vaux-Damloup. **Paris** — 'The campaign against Gen Joffre has started up again even more strongly'.	Conrad assures Francis Joseph no need to worry about Front. **W Russia** — German attacks repulsed E of Krevo (& 5), also in Vilna area (8, 11, 29) & W of Minsk (20, 22). Evert switches planned W Front offensive from Krevo area to Baronovichi, postponed from 14 to 17 (4) then end June (*see* 4 July).	**Trentino** — Austrian offensive faltering as arty support dwindles over distance as Italians reinforced. Reformed 35th Div back in line (*see* 14; 24 July & 11 Aug) and *Granatieri* bn holds Mt Cengio v 5 Austrian bns (-3) until survivors ordered to withdraw to lower slopes. **Secret War** — Austrian Penkalas radio-intercept stn detects Italian call-sign & cipher key changes, finds new call-sign (4) which is new Italian Fifth Army (*see* 8).	**Armenia** — Yudenich has c200,000 men (7 inf & 2 cav divs +) & 400 guns v 130,000 Turks (14 inf & 2 cav divs) & 220 guns. He checks Turks 35 miles W of Erzerum (2-5).
Fri 2	**Ypres** — **Battle of Mt Sorrel** (-13): Heavy German attack between Hooge & Ypres-Roulers railway drives bulge 700 yds deep & 3000 yds wide into British Second Army (Cdn Corps of 3 divs + 20th Div) trenches towards Zillebeke. Gen Mercer k & Gen Williams w & taken PoW (*see* 13). (June) British Tucker arty sound-ranging microphone comes into service (13,540 made — Dec 1918). **Verdun** — German gains in Caillette Wood, S of Vaux & at Damloup (captured by 50th Div) isolate Ft Vaux (under gas attack). French advance S of Caurettes Wood. Mangin now i/c XI Corps.		Cadorna writes to First Army cdr 'the general situation now enables us to resume the initiative', informs Third Army (Aosta) of resumption of Isonzo preparations (*see* 8 & 16). **Trentino** — Massed Austrian inf attacks on R Posina fail (-5).	**Mesopotamia** — Turks retreat after 3 days fighting v Russians W of Rowanduz.
Sat 3	**Ypres** — Cdn counter-attack recovers lost trenches. **Somme** — British repulse German attack N of Fricourt. **Verdun** — Unsuccessful German outflanking move at Vaux.	Brusilov resigns when Alexeiev suggests postponement so allowed to continue. Austrians intercept his attack message to troops.	**Allies proclaim state of siege in Salonika and oust Greek authorities** occupying all official buildings (*see* INT'L EVENTS 6, 21 & 27). 3500t of Allied forage burnt in supply depot.	Townshend arrives at Constantinople to lavish reception. Kut PoWs reach Mosul, get 1st stew since capture (*see* 20). **Persia** — Border action at Khanikin: 6000 Russians & 12 guns attack 7000 Turks (6th Div) before Baratov evacuates Kasr-i-Shirin (6) which Ali Ihsan Pasha retakes (8).
Sun 4	**Verdun** — Fresh German attack at Ft Vaux which sends back c100 men to save water & supplies and last carrier pigeon. **Vosges** — 3 lines of French Casspach trenches taken & retaken.	BRUSILOV OFFENSIVE (-17 Oct) begins on 200-mile front with 1938-gun shelling at 0400. Eleventh & Ninth Armies take 26,000 PoWs & 14+ guns.		
Mon 5	**Verdun** — German attacks repulsed between Vaux & Damloup.	**Pripet** — Kaledin's Eighth Army breaks through Austrian Fourth on 16-mile front,	**Trentino** — Austrians renew offensive (-15) but attacks S & SW of Asiago repulsed as	**Arabia** — ARAB REVOLT: Sherif Hussein of Mecca begins revolt outside Medina

AFRICAN OPERATIONS 5	SEA WAR 6	AIR WAR 7	INTERNATIONAL EVENTS 8	HOME FRONTS 9
	ers). During night Scheer breaks through & escapes despite RN destroyer attacks. RN losses 155,000t; 3 battleships; 3 cruisers; 8 destroyers — 6097k, 510w, 177 PoWs. German losses 61,000t; 1 battleship; 4 cruisers; 5 destroyers — 2551k, 507w.			
Belgians resume advance, invade Urundi, their S Bde beats German rearguard at Kokawani & occupies Usumbura (6). 5th KAR raised for border defence in N.	**N Sea** — German battleship *Pommern* sunk in last Jutland torpedo attack, another, *Ostfriesland*, mined 0720. 2 U-boat attacks on returning Grand Fleet battleships fail (*see* HOME FRONTS 2 & 5). **Britain** — (June) Standard Shipbuilding Co formed at Chepstow, R Wye; yards later taken over by Govt, but output disappointing. **Effective RN depth charge appears**, 1000 ordered (Aug), on general distribution, but av prod only 264 pm from Nov (*see* 17 Apr 1917). **Med** — Admiralty can spare only 10 drifters from home waters for Otranto Barrage (40-50 wanted Apr). **Neutrals: USA** — (June) Rear Adm Henry T Mayo becomes C-in-C US Atlantic Fleet (-1919).	**Italian Front** — Austrian flying boat ace Gottfried Banfield scores his 1st night victory over Italian bomber illuminated by searchlight at Trieste (night 1/2). **W Front** — RFC observers engage 100 targets. 2/Lt Ball in Nieuport of 11 Sqn engages 2 German aircraft over Douai; No 9 Kite-Balloon blown over to German lines, but both observers parachute safely. **Egypt** — A German aircraft's 8 bombs cause 30 cas & 45 horse cas to 1st ALH Bde.	Anglo-French coal agreement for British supply to France (*see* 30 Oct).	**Britain** — RFP up 4% to 59%. New Exchequer bond issue. (June) Munitions Invention Dept form nitrogen fixation ctee to examine Geman process (pilot plant by 27 Oct 1917, *see* 22 Feb 1918).
	N Sea — **Grand Fleet again ready for action**, High Seas Fleet repairs take longer (see 30; 18 Aug).		**Neutrals: Rumania** — PM Bratianu tells Russian Ambassador that intervention conditions not nearly ripe.	Kitchener informally briefs MPs who applaud after Tory hostile motion (31 May). **Belgium** — Belgians up to 40 called up. **Germany** — Despite Jutland news Kaiser spends weekend at Hohenzollern home farm, Cadinen, E Prussia.
British occupy Namena.	**Black Sea** — Russians shell Bourgas, Bulgaria, sink Turk steamers (29).	**W Front** — 20 RFC bombers (1 lost to AA fire) + 6 escorts raid 4 rail stns (4t bombs).	**Neutrals: USA** — National Defense Act increases regular Army by 5 annual stages to 175,000; National Guard to 450,000; officers reserve corps created.	
	Adriatic — Italian submarine *Atropo* sinks Austrian Lloyd *SS Albanien* (1122t) without warning. French flotilla pursuing 2 U-boats believed to be homeward bound for Cattaro stop at Otranto Barrage patrol boundary & leave 2 Italian destroyers to continue pursuit. **N Sea** — 3 German destroyers N of Zeebrugge briefly engage British ones (*see* 8).			
Skirmishing at Kondoa Irangi (5-8); Smuts inspects 2nd Div (1031 sick by 3) there (-7).	**Atlantic** — Russia-bound cruiser HMS *Hampshire* sunk by mine from *U75* (Beitzen)	**E Africa** — 2 RFC aircraft join S Africans at Kondoa Irangi (*see* 10; AFRICAN OPS 24).	KITCHENER DROWNED.	**Germany** — Kaiser tells flagship crew 'The spell of Trafalgar is broken'; cables

JUNE 1916	WESTERN FRONT 1	EASTERN FRONT 2	SOUTHERN FRONTS 3	TURKISH FRONTS 4
Mon 5 contd		crippling 3 Austrian divs.	*Sassari* Bde reinforces *Alpini* (-7).	with 50,000 Arabs (under 10,000 rifles) v 15,000 Turks. His son Feisal repulsed from Medina (6) as British Arab Bureau lands at Jeddah.
Tue 6	**Ypres** — German gains at Hooge. **Verdun** — Besieged Ft Vaux's heroic CO Maj Raynal (fort reduced to 12 gals water) appointed Cdr Legion of Honour. Stretcher-bearer Vanier escapes from fort to French lines.	**Galicia** — Shcherbachev's Seventh Army attacks, widens frontage taking Buczacz (8); by 10 has made 30-mile breach & taken 16,000 PoWs.	**Salonika** — Milne informs Sarrail that British ordered (3) not to take part in planned offensive (*see* 12), tries to moderate his actions v Greeks (& 8). British allotted own distinct sector along Struma, occupied by 27 often in 100°+F.	**Egypt** — T E Lawrence edits 1st weekly issue of *Arab Bulletin* (-Aug 1919).
Wed 7	**Verdun** — FALL OF FT VAUX for 2678 German cas to 50th Div after heroic 5-day defence by Maj Raynal's 600 men. Crown Prince congratulates Raynal & returns his sword. 2 French officers shot for cowardice.	**Pripet** — **Kaledin recaptures Lutsk** (Austrian Fourth Army HQ) thanks to Denikin's 4th ('Iron') Rifle Div; claims 50,000 PoWs & 77 guns; crosses R Styr in pursuit and retakes Dubno (9).		**Arabia** — Sherif proclaims Hejaz's independence.
Thu 8	**Verdun** — French 151st Div repulses I Bav Corps attacks E & W of Thiaumont but they take Thiaumont Farm & works from 52nd Div. Special bde vainly makes 6th attempt to relieve Ft Vaux (French cmnd unaware of its fall). Pétain orders Nivelle to desist from further attempts.	In Berlin **Falkenhayn forces Conrad to send 2 divs from Italian Front** (1½ more & 4 German to come, *see* 10 & 30).	Austrian Intelligence find Italian First Army cipher key changed, correctly predict attack on R Isonzo (*see* 16). **Trentino** — 2 Austrian divs withdraw to E Front (*see* E FRONT), but Italians forced back to Mt Spil-Monte Miele line, lose Mt Lemerle (4048 ft) though *Forli* Bde immediately regains it. Austrians force Italians off Mt Castelgomberto, only 3 miles from Valstagna in lower Brenta valley, but time has run out after 12-mile advance.	
Fri 9	**Verdun** — W bank: Unsuccessful German attacks E & SW of Hill 304. E bank: French XII Corps reoccupies Thiaumont works after Germans evacuate them (night 8/9) as untenable, then drives back German 0600 attack (*see* E FRONT 10).	**Bukovina** — Lechitski transfers 2 divs to S bank of Dniester, fierce struggle for Hill 458 (-10) before Pflanzer-Baltin orders retreat to R Prut .	Allied War Council defers decision on 1916 Balkan offensive (*see* 12).	Arabs attack Mecca & Jeddah garrisons, 4000 cut off latter's water supply (*see* SEA WAR 11).
Sat 10		Falkenhayn orders 5 **Hindenburg Ludendorff divs S + 4 divs from Verdun** (*see* 14).	**Greece** — French occupy Thasos I, N Aegean, as air base. **Trentino** — Eritrea veteran & volunteer Gen Prestinari k i/c militia bde.	
Sun 11	**Champagne** — German trench raid N of Bruges. **Verdun** — Unsuccessful German attacks W of Vaux & at Thiaumont. **Somme** — After Pétain's pleas to Joffre zero day for Allied offensive advanced from July to 29 June.	Col Knox lunches with Tsar 'in good spirits' at STAVKA. **Galicia** — *Südarmee's* Battle of the Strypa (-30). By now Gen Tersztyanszki replaces sacked Archduke Joseph Ferdinand i/c Fourth Army.		**Arabia** — Stotzingen Mission reaches Umm Lejj on coast, withdrawing to Damascus (early July). **S Persia** — Sykes enters Kerman after 270-mile march. **Sinai** — Skirmishes at Katia (*see* AIR WAR 11 & 18).
Mon 12	**Verdun** — Germans carry French forward positions on Hill 321, 4 miles from Vaux. Nivelle's reserves down to 2000 men. *Tranchée des baïonnettes* (Ravin de la Dame, c20 French infantry men of 137th Regt buried with bayonets fixed) caused but French 21st Div holds.	Brusilov reports 192,992 PoWs, 216 guns, 645 MGs & I96 mortars: Ist of 4 corps reinforces him (-24). **Bukovina** — Austrian XI Corps only has 3500/16,000 left.	**Salonika** — Sarrail ordered not to involve British in offensive & then to postpone it (14, *see* 25).	

AFRICAN OPERATIONS 5	SEA WAR 6	AIR WAR 7	INTERNATIONAL EVENTS 8	HOME FRONTS 9
	NW of Scapa. Careless minesweeping, stormy seas & inexplicable failure of Grand Fleet C-in-C Jellicoe & subordinates to expedite rescue efforts dooms War Minister Lord Kitchener & staff; 12 survivors. *Aegean* — Lt-Cdr JL Myres RNVR, 'Blackbeard of the Aegean', leads 25 Greek irregulars' raid on Karada (Anatolia), 15 Turk troops k & w.			Krupp from Wilhelmshaven to applaud Jutland guns/armour performance. Bethmann tours S German states to get food control policy accepted. **Russia** — Duma debates supply shortages. **Britain** — First police raid on Non-Conscription Fellowship; B Russell fined and sacked from Cambridge fellowship.
Smuts resumes main advance on Handeni (90 miles marched by 24).	**Med — Anglo-French 'pacific' blockade of Greece** (-22) v machinations of pro-German K Constantine. France orders detention of all Greek merchant vessels (8), special sqn earmarked for future action. *U35* (Arnauld) sinks 40 ships worth 56,818t (-3 July, se*e* July), despite French destroyer *Arquebuse* attack (15).		**Neutrals: Greece** — Allies resume 'pacific blockade' (-22) because Greeks (protest 7) allowed Bulgars over frontier. Secret police instigate anti-Allied riots (12). **China** — †Pres Yuan Shihkai (aged 56), Vice Pres Liyuanhang succeeds (7).	**France** — Chamber decides to hold secret Verdun inquiry (16-21); Govt win vote. 30 British conscientious objectors sentenced to be shot, then sent home (29) when PM pledges no repeat & gives alternative work, 4000 on it already, *see* 26 July).
	Adriatic — 2 Italian MAS boats torpedo Austrian SS *Locrum* in Durazzo harbour (night 7/8), SS *Sarajevo* likewise sunk (night 25/26).			**Germany** — Leipzig paper on Kitchener's death: 'It is as if our Hindenberg were taken from us, nay worse'.
L Tanganyika — c800 BSA & N Rhodesia police occupy Bismarckburg after Germans escape in canoes, RN Flotilla only arrives (9, see AIR WAR 10).	**Channel** — Dover Patrol engages 12 German destroy-ers (2nd Flotilla from High Seas Fleet) off Dunkirk, but they retire to Zeebrugge before Harwich Force arrives. **Adriatic** — U-boat sinks Italian transport *Principe Umberto* (9, many lives lost).			
L Victoria — 826 British occupy Ukerewe I (-15) from 6 ships. Action at Mkalamo: Sheppard's River Col holds Kraut's counter-attack & occupies intact bridge (10).			Allied War Council in London (-10).	**Britain** — Petrol sub-ctee appointed for priority distribu-tion, reveals civil use of 150m gal pa but only a month's supply in country (20).
		E Africa — 2 Belgian seaplanes vainly bomb gunboat *Graf von Götzen* at Kigoma, L Tanganyika.	**Neutrals: USA** — Republicans nominate Charles E Hughes as pres candidate.	**NZ — Compulsory Service Bill passed.**
	Red Sea — Cruisers *Fox* and *Hardinge* shell Turk positions N of Jeddah (*see* TURK FRONTS 16).	**Egypt** — German aircraft drops 8 bombs on Kantara (*see* 18), another strafes Romani garrison.	**Neutrals: USA** — Mexicans attack US troops at Laredo, also at San Ugnacio, Texas (15).	**Italy** — **Salandra Govt resign** over Trentino reverse & budget defeat, Socialist Boselli heads new coalition Govt (16).
British occupy Wilhelmstal (570 German civilians surrender). Belgian S Bde beats 700-strong German rearguard at Ngawiogi.	**Adriatic** — Italian destroyers raid Perenzo, Istria.	RFC has taken 2568 aircraft into service & struck off 1427 in past year or 47.7% wastage; 8403 aircraft on order (2970 delivered); 15 training stns with 193 all ranks under instruction.		

JUNE 1916	WESTERN FRONT 1	EASTERN FRONT 2	SOUTHERN FRONTS 3	TURKISH FRONTS 4
Tue 13	**Ypres** — Canadians recapture Zillebeke-Sanctuary Wood positions lost on 2.	**Galicia** — Lechitski retakes Sniatyn for 3rd time in war.		**Arabia** — 1000-strong Turk Mecca garrison surrenders after damaging Kiswa Mosque. **Egypt** — 7 Egyptians suspected of German espionage arrested from 2 Cairo hotels.
Wed 14		**Pripet — Marwitz's X Corps arriving at Kovel from Verdun.** Austrian cav (3 divs + 1 bde) plug 30-mile gap between Fourth and First Armies v Russian cav.	**Isonzo** — Italians retake Adria shipyard & hills at Monfalcone, repel Austrian counter-attacks (17). **Trentino** — Italian counter-offensive ordered (*see* 16). Last Archduke Charles inf assault on Mt Ciove. *Cagliari* Bde holds for ²/₃ losses despite its 35th Div HQ being hit (12). Conrad accuses Dankl (Eleventh Army) of co-ordination failures, latter relieved of command at own request.	
Thu 15	**Verdun** — Germans carry trench on Mort Homme S slope & contain French 65th Div attack on Caillette Wood.		**Trentino** — Last Austrian bid to break through after army orders says only 3 mtns block way to Milan, I Corps' 20 bns, around Mt Lemerle at narrowest point of Asiago forest, crumple under Italian fire (-16 & 18).	**Persia** — Heavy fighting at Saripul 100 miles W of Kermanshah, Turks repulsed by 19.
Fri 16	**Verdun** — Unsuccessful German attacks W of Hill 304.	**Pripet** — Austro-German counter-offensive (-24): Marwitz's 12¹/₂ divs gain only a few miles on R Stokhod v Kaledin (2000 PoWs & 4 guns) for 40,000 cas.	**Trentino — Italian counter-offensive** (-24 July) with 4 corps (177 bns & 800 guns v 168 bns & 680 guns) recaptures Mt Magari & Cima Isidora (18). Cadorna decides Isonzo attack will aim just to take Gorizia.	**Arabia** — 1505-strong Turk Jeddah garrison & 16 guns surrender after naval and seaplane bombardment (*see* 28).
Sat 17	**Verdun** — Germans repulsed at Mort Homme-Thiaumont-Hill 320. French gains on Hill 321, Germans repulsed there (18 & 19).	**Bukovina** — Lechitski's XII Corps reoccupies Czernowitz, crosses Prut to W as Austrians retreat to R Sereth and beyond (19).	**Conrad calls off Trentino offensive.**	
Sun 18				Turk papers announce Sherif Hussein's deposition.
Mon 19				
Tue 20	**Verdun** — Tremendous German barrage begins. New French standard-gauge railway ready.		**Trentino** — Slight but very cautious Italian advances on Asiago Plateau (-21). **France** — PM Briand defends French Balkans policy & wins 300+ majority in secret Chamber debate, but Delcassé wishes	**Mesopotamia** — Kut PoWs entrain at Ras-al-Ain in open trucks (*see* HOME FRONTS 21).

AFRICAN OPERATIONS 5	SEA WAR 6	AIR WAR 7	INTERNATIONAL EVENTS 8	HOME FRONTS 9
Pegasus gun slightly wounds Lettow at S Hill HQ v Kondoa Irangi (*see* 24). **L Nyasa** — British land & occupy Alt Langenburg.				
	N Sea — K George V visits Grand Fleet at Scapa (-15). Beatty letter (9) to Jellicoe offers 'deepest sympathy in being baulked of your Great Victory' (*see* 25). **Baltic** — Russian destroyers attack German convoy, sink auxiliary cruiser *Hermann*, 2 torpedo boats & also claim 2 steamers. RN submarine *E19* (Cromie) survives 34 German aircraft bombs (10 & 12).		Allied Paris Economic Conference (-21, 8 states), enemy to be denied favoured trade treatment for fixed postwar period. Britain approves (2 Aug). **Neutrals: USA** — Pres leads Preparedness Parade, Washington.	
3rd KAR seize Korogwe Bridge W of Tanga completing conquest of Usambara Mts region (*see* 13 July). Belgian N Bde crosses R Kagera nr Ukuswa.	(c) **RN first operates shore-controlled minefields** (hydrophone & magnetophone) mainly in Flanders & Shetlands (sink 2 U-boats; 2 possible, 2 damaged). Paravanes begun to be fitted to merchant ships (code name Otto), 274 by end of hostilities.	**Arabia** — 3 seaplanes from HMS *Ben-My-Chree* bomb Turks at Jeddah (*see* TURK FRONTS 16).	**Neutrals: USA** — Wilson renominated Democrat pres candidate (*see* 26).	
5th Indian Lt Inf (400) occupy Mwakijembe S of coastal border & Jasin (17). Belgians occupy Urundi capital Kitega (King submits 27).	**Channel** — Destroyer HMS *Eden* sunk by collision with SS *France*.			**Secret War** — Mata Hari books into Grand Hotel, Paris, takes many military lovers but falls in love with Russian Capt Maslov (Aug).
		W Front — First French ace Navarre shot down & severely w over the Argonne, never fights again. RFC observers engage 73 targets, 30 Anglo-German air combats (1 German crashes).		
Sheppard occupies Handeni, Kraut retreats on Central Railway.		**W Front** — Oblt Max **Immelmann** (15 victories) **k,** aged 25, in Fokker E III, shot down by Lt McCubbin & Cp Waller, No 25 Sqn RFC in FE2b or victim of interrupter gear malfunction causing structural failure. 3 other German aircraft definitely shot down & 3 RFC FE2bs lost. **Sinai** — 11 RFC BE2cs (3 fall to ground fire) bomb El Arish airfield, destroy 1 aircraft & fire 2 hangars. **Verdun** — Balsley 1st American volunteer fighter pilot shot down in action; no serious injuries (*see* 23). **Germany** — FRENCH LEAFLET RAID ON BERLIN: Lt Marchal, in special Nieuport monoplane op from Nancy drops hundreds of leaflets proclaiming war guilt of German & Austrian Imperial Houses & force lands at Kholm, Poland; taken PoW by Austrians he later escapes (19/ 20 June).	**Neutrals: USA** — 80,000 militia called up to police Mexican border (*see* 21).	**Germany** — †Col Gen Moltke the Younger (aged 68), Berlin. **Britain** — War costing £6m+ pd.
5th SA Inf lose heavily to Boedecker detachment 6 miles S of Pongwe. **S Tunisia** — 800-2000 Tripolitanians attack Dhibat garrison (2000), wipe out 100-man relief force but routed at Battle of Bir-el-Moghri	Vice-Adm Sir C Thursby takes over RN E Med Sqn from Robeck (to 3rd Battle Sqn, Grand Fleet).	**N Sea** — French-supplied pigeons help rescue downed RNAS seaplane (& 24).	**France** — Anglo-French tank developers first meet when British Mk I is demonstrated to Estienne at Morly.	

JUNE 1916	WESTERN FRONT 1	EASTERN FRONT 2	SOUTHERN FRONTS 3	TURKISH FRONTS 4
Tue 20 contd			400,000-500,000 enemies were at Salonika and not opposite Verdun.	
Wed 21	**Verdun** — Limited German gains on Mort Homme & W & S of Ft Vaux, but repulsed NW of Thiaumont works.			
Thu 22	**Flanders** — Narrow German penetration of British trenches at Givenchy. **Verdun** — **Germans introduce new phosgene** (Green Cross) **gas** nr Fleury. French gains at Fumin Chenois woods. Unsuccessful German attack on Hill 329.			
Fri 23	**Champagne** — German trench raids. **Verdun** — FINAL CRISIS: 30,000 Germans attack at 0600, capture Hills 320 & 321, Thiaumont & Fleury (stormed by Bavarians, French 129th Div destroyed), enter Froideterrés Work's ditches, but *Alpenkorps* & 103rd Divs fought to a standstill & French 407th Regt covers vital Ft Souville (*see* 26). Nivelle Order of the Day *'On ne passe pas* ' ('They shall not pass'), Pétain telephones *GQG* at 1200 & 1500 that E bank evacuation may be necessary (3 days req'd to save c400 guns), but Joffre gives him 4 more divs.	**Bukovina** — Keller's III Cav Corps retakes Kimpolung with 2060 PoWs & 7 MGs after 67$\frac{1}{2}$-mile advance S. All Bukovina in Lechitski's hands by 25.		
Sat 24	**British Somme barrage opens**, 2029 guns fire 1,732,873 shells, but c1/3 dud, although 109 German guns destroyed or damaged. BEF makes 70 trench raids & 40 gas attacks (-30). PM Briand visits Haig & urges attack without fail. **Verdun** — French counter-attacks at Fleury (-25) gain little (*see* 27).	Brusilov given Third Army in S Pripet, orders Eleventh Army to hold while flank armies continue.		
Sun 25	**Flanders** — BEF shell Lens. **Verdun** — French thwart attempted German advance W of Ft Thiaumont. French gains in Fumin-Chenois Woods. War Minister Gen Roques visits.		**Trentino** — Italians retake Asiago, Posina & Arsiero regained (27), as Austrians begin silent & orderly general retreat from salient (night 25) to prepared line holding $\frac{2}{3}$ of gains since 15 May (-26). **Salonika** — Sarrail told he may have to attack soon with French & Serbs alone (*see* 15 July).	**Armenia** — Turks after surprise crossing of Pontic Alps overwhelm 19th Turkistanski Regt. By 30 within 15 miles of coast road but held at 'Serpent Rock Hill'. **Secret War: Arabia** — Cairo intercepts Djemal radio message to Fakhri Pasha in Medina allowing £5000 spending in English gold.
Mon 26	**Verdun** — French gains nr Ft Thiaumont but 2-bde attack fails at Fleury. German attacks W of Hill 304 & nr Fleury. French 407th Regt's 1200 survivors withdrawn (2800 on 21).			**Persia** — Turks driven from L Urmia.

AFRICAN OPERATIONS 5	SEA WAR 6	AIR WAR 7	INTERNATIONAL EVENTS 8	HOME FRONTS 9
(-30), still 12,684 French in area (*see* 10 July).				
c240 British land on Ulenge I (Tanga Bay) & wade to mainland (*see* 5 July).	**Britain** — First of 3 Kipling articles in *The Times* (23 & 28) paying tribute to RN Submarine Service 'The Trade'.		**Neutrals: Mexico** — 400 Mexican regulars (38k) capture US 10th Cavalry troop (40 cas, incl 22 PoWs) at Carrizal, US demands PoW release (25, done 28, *see* 4 July). **Greece** — **Allies demand demobilization & Govt change:** PM Skouloudis resigns, Zaimis succeeds (*see* 27). **Spain** — *U35* (see SEA WAR 6) delivers Kaiser letter to King at Cartagena.	**Turkey** — Germans at Islahie railhead treat 39 British Kut PoWs too ill to continue as rest march into Taurus Mts (22), reach Adana by train (24) then sent back for railway labour. **Germany** — War profits taxation law.
		Germany — **French bombers attack Karlsruhe** (266 civ cas). **Public outcry for protection across Germany. W Front** — RFC observers engage 198 targets (16 on 23); 22 Anglo-German air combats.	**Secret War** — French agent David Bloch parachuted into Alsace in uniform, arrested (28, shot nr Mulhouse 1 Aug).	
	Adriatic — In Straits of Otranto Austrian *U15* sinks French destroyer *Fourche* & Italian AMC *Città di Messina*. Daytime cruiser protection for Otranto Barrage withdrawn. **N Sea** — SS *Brussels* (Fryatt) bound from Holland to Tilbury stopped by German torpedo boats. **Capt Fryatt** taken to Zeebrugge & thence to Ruhleben internment camp; court-martialled at Bruges for his ramming exploit of 28 Mar 1915, **shot** as *franc-tireur* (27 July). **Atlantic** — **World's first mercantile submarine** *Deutschland* (König) (*see* 9 July) makes 17-day transatlantic crossing Kiel-Baltimore with dyes, chemicals, precious stones & mail. Returns to Bremen (2-24 Aug) carrying assorted non-ferrous metals, rubber, nickel & tin (her max range 25,000 miles).	**Verdun** — Victor E Chapman first American volunteer fighter pilot with *Escadrille Americaine* k by Fokker.	**Secret War** — Many MI1c reports captured in SS *Brussels* (see SEA WAR). Collapse of 40+ train-watching posts in Occupied France & Belgium (*see* 27 July).	
Action of Lukigura: British & armoured cars defeat Capt Doering's 500 men, take 53 PoWs, 1 gun & 2 MGs. Lettow withdrawing from Kondoa Irangi under bombing. Belgian N Bde occupies Beharamulo, reaches L Victoria (30).				
Cyrenaica — Sayyid Idris meets Allied Mission for talks (-Sept). Anglo-Italian Agreement not to sign separate deal with Senussi (31, France adheres Mar 1917).	**Britain** — Admiralty post-Jutland inquest with Jellicoe & Beatty agrees to improve armour protection.	**W Front** — RFC spots 154 targets (5 German btys silenced), fights 16 air combats & shoots down 6 German kite-balloons.		**Britain** — Casement treason trial opens, death sentence (29, *see* 3 Aug).
		W Front — RFC observers engage 161 targets. 5 FE2bs (1 lost) of No 25 Sqn incl Capt A W Tedder (future MRAF) shoot down 2 Fokkers; 3 German kite-balloons brought down in flames.	Serb PM Pasic visits Paris. **Neutrals: Switzerland** — Germany threatens coal supply if cotton purchases not delivered. **Rumania** — 9 killed in Galati workers anti-war demo.	**Britain** — 7000 Vickers Barrow engineers lose strike v partial call-up (-3 July).

JUNE 1916	WESTERN FRONT 1	EASTERN FRONT 2	SOUTHERN FRONTS 3	TURKISH FRONTS 4
Tue 27	British recce raids from La Bassée canal to Somme line.		**Trentino** — Italians resume pursuit too slowly. **Carnia** — Italian XII Corps 'rectification ops' (-29) cost 3662 cas.	**Arabia** — Fakhri Pasha sorties from Medina, massacres Arab suburb: Feisal blockades at distance.
Wed 28	**Verdun** — French grenade attacks nr Hill 329 & Thiaumont Works. German counter-attacks fail. **Somme** — Zero day for Allied offensive postponed until 1 July (rain).	**Galicia** — Battle of Kolomea (24 June to 6 July): Lechitski shatters Austrian Seventh Army on 25-mile front E of Kolomea, taking 10,421 PoWs & 4 guns; enters Kolomea (29), reaches 12 miles S (30).	**Trentino** — Italian cav reach Pedescala NE of Arsiero. **Isonzo** — **First major gas attack on Italian Front** (-29): with help of hydrocyanide gas shell Austrians inflict 6600 cas on sleeping Italian 21st & 22nd Divs between Mt Cosich & sea in night raid before *Regina* Bde & 10th Regt regain trenches, but Austrians lose 1988 (416 PoWs) incl gas fatalities from blowback.	**Arabia** — 3 British ships land 8 Egyptian mtn guns, 4 MGs & 3000 rifles at Jeddah (*see* 16 July). **Persia** — Baratov's 8500 men & 14 guns hold Turk 2nd Div at Karind until night retreat on Kermanshah (evacuated 30).
Thu 29		**Vienna Crown Council attacks Conrad for 1st time**, Emperor orders him to give more info.		
Fri 30	**Verdun** — **French recapture Ft Thiaumont**. 65 French divs have engaged v 47 German. June losses: French 67,000, German 51,567 (incl 4 divs losing 71-90% of their inf).	**Galicia** — 2 Austrian divs from Italian Front begin arriving at Nadworna and Delatyn.		
Sat 1 July 1916	**Somme** — ANGLO-FRENCH OFFENSIVE, BATTLES OF THE SOMME (-18 Nov) BEGIN. First phase: **Battle of Albert** (-13): After 224,221 shells in 65 mins & explosion of 10 mines (0728) Allied attack begins at 0730. Combined Franco-British attack (19 divs) on 25-mile front N & S of Somme. 66,000 (later 100,000) British capture Montauban (early creeping barrage) & Mametz. French XX & I Colonial Corps strike for Péronne reach Hardecourt & Curlu outskirts taking c80 guns & 3000 PoWs. NW of Albert-Bapaume road British make little progress v strong German defences; small gain at Leipzig Redoubt S of Thiepval. British attacks at Gommecourt, Serre, Beaumont Hamel, Thiepval & La Boiselle all fail. At 1900 Rawlinson's cas est 16,000, but in fact British cas total 57,470 (incl 19,240k & 2152 missing (585 PoWs) largely to c100 MG teams) HEAVIEST LOSS EVER SUFFERED BY THE BRITISH ARMY IN ONE DAY 32 bns lose 500 cas. German cas est 8000 (*see* HOME FRONTS 6). **Verdun** — 132nd day of battle. (July) Germans form 2nd Storm Bn, 14 in all by 31 Dec. German combatant strength in W 2,260,000. French Army 1,447,000 inf; 93,500 cav; 495,000 arty; 125,000	German combatant strength only 590,000. **Pripet** — Austro-Germans regain 3 miles SW of Lutsk (-2). **Carpathians** — Lechitski advances NW of Kolomea, cuts railway at Mikoli-chin (4), despite Austro-German counter-attacks (2-3).	Italian losses 524,760 since 1 Jan incl 275,190 sick, but 800,000 called to colours in same period. **Isonzo** — Italian VII Corps launches diversion at Selz (Carso, S of Gorizia), some gains & PoWs (-3).	**Persia** — c16,000 Turks (Ali Ihsan Pasha) reoccupy Kermanshah, defeat Russians to N (19, *see* 3 Aug). **Yemen** — Idrisi's tribe captures Qunfidah on coast.

AFRICAN OPERATIONS 5	SEA WAR 6	AIR WAR 7	INTERNATIONAL EVENTS 8	HOME FRONTS 9
British Lake Force (2000, Crewe GOC from 17) advances S from R Kagera & via L Victoria. Maj Gen Gill & part of 3000-strong Portuguese Expeditionary Force land (-6 Sept) at Lourenço Marques (*see* 5 Jul).		**W Front** — 157 active German btys reported by RFC.	Austrian Berlin Ambassador letter says Monarchy can no longer survive the war. **Neutrals: Greece** — King signs demobilization decree (*see* 3 July). **Secret War** — German Hentig enters Chinese Turkestan, escapes Russian cordon (*see* 17 Oct).	
L Victoria — 320 British land & occupy Bukoba.		**W Front** — Heavy rains and low cloud (-30) restricts ops. 111 RFC personnel cas since 1, 17,000 hrs flown.	Britain & France completely abandon London Declaration (*see* 7 July).	**Russia** — Alexeiev suggests to Tsar a military dictator for supply. **Germany** — Liebknecht given 2 yrs hard labour (increased to 4 yrs 23 Aug) & dismissed from Army; 55,000 workers hold 3-day protest strikes. **Britain** — 400 German firms reported still trading.
		Mesopotamia — RNAS det withdrawn but 4 RNAS kite-balloons arrive.	British Foreign Office send Casement diary homosexual extracts to US, Grey rules v further copying (30).	
	Chancellor Bethmann again informs Adm Scheer of his opposition to unrestricted U-boat ops (*see* 4 & 12 July). **Med** — (June) German U-boats sink 43 merchant ships or 67,125t out of total (all seas) 87,293. (June) French Marine Ministry rebukes Bizerta *Préfet Maritime* for suggesting convoy answer to U-boats. **N Sea** — First German 15 in-gun battleship *Bayern* joins Fleet (sister *Baden* likewise Feb 1917).	**W Front** — 6 RE7s of No 21 Sqn RFC bomb Lille St Saveur stn engine sheds (repeated & successfully with 336lb bomb, 1st use from 7000-8000 ft, 1 July). Escort (both raids) 2 Martinsydes, 2 Moranes.	**Neutrals: USA** — Krupp rep Capt Tauscher acquitted of conspiracy charges. US Commissioner of Navigation reports 125,000t of shipping building for foreign owners (mainly British, *see* 7 Sept).	**France** — Alcohol duties increased. **Britain** — Army Council takes over 1916 hay & straw crops. D H Lawrence rejected for military service at Bodmin.
	Adriatic — Austrian raid on Straits of Otranto (*see* 9). **Med** — (July) **U-boat ace Arnauld** de la Perière (*see* 20 Aug) **perfects technique of destroying ships by long-range** (8000 yds) **gunfire** with new 4.1-in deck gun (replaces 3.5 in or 88 mm), saving torpedoes & lessening risks to U-boats, who also through signals intelligence & captured documents learn which Allied routes are patrolled, sink 33 ships (86,432t) in July. **Baltic** — (July) Russian submarines & destroyers sink or capture 4 German steamers (*see* AIR WAR 18).	**Somme** — **Anglo-French supremacy continues**. 185 British (out of 421 RFC with 14 balloons) & 201 French v 129 German aircraft. Verdun commitments elsewhere (& Immelmann's death) mean Germans have only 19 fighters v up to 66 British (Nos 24, 29, 32 & 60 Sqns) & c72 French Nieuports; DH2s & FE2s play havoc with recon planes & balloons and brush aside German fighters. BE2s & RE7s hit railways, trains, roads, HQs, dumps; RFC drop 39t bombs (1-16), Farmans & Caudrons often at night; RFC recon & arty obs units fly virtually unhindered while German aircraft are forced to defend within their own lines or over their own bases. But, from mid-July German reinforcements reach the Somme. **Salonika** — (July) 6 RNAS aircraft & French flight on Thasos I drop incendiary bombs on ripening crops in S Bulgaria (*see* 7). **W Front** — Maj Rees CO No 32 Sqn RFC single-handedly disperses 10 2-seaters nr Festubert & forces down 2 (Rees w, wins VC). 7 RFC aircraft missing (14 aircrew cas) incl 4 who cause 170 cas to 22nd Res Div at St Quentin stn. **Egypt** — RFC Middle East Bde (total 8 sqns) formed under Brig-Gen W Salmond to administer Salonika, Mesopotamia & E Africa units as well (*see* 17).	**Neutrals** — US Marines defeat Santo Domingo rebels (*see* 29 Nov)	**Britain** — RFP 61%, now 766,000 women in industry & commerce. Record low union unemployment of 0.4%. Somme barrage heard on Hampstead Heath. **France** — (July) *Le Canard enchaîne* satirical journal first published. Heavier excess profit taxes. **Germany** — (July) Radical anti-war art weekly *Kampf* founded at Duisberg.

JULY 1916	WESTERN FRONT 1	EASTERN FRONT 2	SOUTHERN FRONTS 3	TURKISH FRONTS 4
Sat 1 contd	engineers: 24,000 air service in 4,677,000 mobilized strength.			
Sun 2	**Verdun** — Falkenhayn issues **'The unequivocal order for the complete cessation of the attack'**, begins to transfer 60 heavy guns to the Somme, 2 divs from Verdun plus a div from every other army on W Front. **Somme** — Anglo-French repulse German 12th Res Div night attempt to retake Montauban. British 17th Div captures Fricourt, 19th Div (2400 cas) fights for La Boisselle (2-4). French capture Herbecourt S of Somme.		**Trentino** — Last Austrian attack on Mt Pasubio repulsed by *Volturno* & *Verona* Bdes.	**Armenia** — Battles of Bayburt & Dumalidag (-28): Yudenich attacks Turk Third Army. By 8 Russians 10 miles due N of Bayburt & 2 Turk corps in retreat.
Mon 3	**Somme** — British capture Ovillers-La Boisselle, 9th Scottish Div captures Bernafay Wood (E of Montauban). Falkenhayn visits F Below at St Quentin, replaces his CoS for allowing withdrawal S of Somme; Below obediently orders counter-attacks 'I forbid the voluntary evacuation of trenches'. **Verdun** — Germans take & lose Damloup work, their attacks on Avocourt & Hill 304 fail (5).		Italian Second Army reformed (HQ Cividale) for Isonzo offensive.	
Tue 4	**Somme** — British attack La Boisselle (-6). Gough's Res Army i/c of 8 divs on British I flank, La Boisselle-Hebuterne (8 miles). On cold wet day French capture 2 villages S of Somme (US war poet Alan Seeger k at Belloy-en-Santerre, aged 28, with Foreign Legion), now have 4000 PoWs & 6 miles of German 2nd line. Thunderstorm.	**W Russia** — Battle of Baronovichi (-14): Ragoza's Fourth Army (1000 guns, 21 inf & 5 cav divs) takes Austrian front line after shelling since 2 (*see* 14). **Pripet** — **2nd Great Russian advance**: Lesch's Third Army crosses R Styr at Kolki & Rafalovka, drives Linsingen W to R Stokhod.	**Rumanian terms for entry into war incl Salonika offensive v Bulgars** (*see* 17). **Trentino** — Italian advance continues (-7, *see* 9).	
Wed 5	**Somme** — British storm Horseshoe Trench. Germans massing in Mametz Wood. Germans recapture Estrées S of Somme. Legion (869 cas) relieved after sending back 730 PoWs & 4 MGs and repulsing 2 night counter-attacks (*see* 8).		**Occupied Serbia & Montenegro** — Guerrilla risings begin v weakened Austrian garrisons, continue for duration (*see* Mar 1917).	
Thu 6	**Somme** — British attack on Trônes Wood delayed for 24 hrs.	**Pripet** — Disorderly German retreat in Chartorysk salient between Styr & Stokhod rivers; 30,000 PoWs & 30 guns lost since 4.		British War Ctee discuss Arab Revolt: Sherif gets £125,000 pm by 27 for duration (*see* 1 Sept): Murray to prepare to occupy El Arish and Aqaba. CIGS cables him suggesting helping Arabs sabotage Hejaz Railway.
Fri 7	**Somme** — British 38th Div (nearly 4000 cas -12) repulsed at Mametz Wood; they capture Leipzig Redoubt (& night 8/9), Contalmaison (lost in evening). 2 div GOCs replaced for failure (9).	Hindenburg cables Falkenhayn urging one E Front command (*see* 30). **Galicia** — Austrian generals sabre back fleeing German troops v Lechitski.		
Sat 8	**Somme** — First British 30th Div attacks secure most of Trônes Wood; German shelling & counter-attack compels withdrawal. Legion has 433 cas failing to storm 'Chancellor`s Trench' (-9), not captured till 1 Aug.	**Pripet** — Lesch breaks through N of Lutsk, crossing R Stokhod and Arsenovich & Ugli, 25 miles advanced in 4 days on 40-mile front. Kaledin's cav blocked 25 miles from Kovel. **Carpathians** — Lechitski captures Delatyn rail jctn, under 32 miles from Hungarian border.		

AFRICAN OPERATIONS 5	SEA WAR 6	AIR WAR 7	INTERNATIONAL EVENTS 8	HOME FRONTS 9
540 British land & meet Belgians at Nyamirembe, latter disperse 300-strong German rearguard at Kato (3).		**W Front** — 6 RE7s of 21 Sqn set fire to munition dumps at Bapaume with 336lb shrapnel bombs (as on 1). 2/Lt Ball in Nieuport 17 of No 11 Sqn scores his 1st confirmed victory (Roland nr Arras).	Russian Col Tatarinov arrives at Bucharest to conclude a military convention (see 4 & 17).	**Russia** — Duma Bill gives peasants equal rights, but Duma suspended (3) till 14 Nov. **France** — Serb Soldiers' Flag Day.
	N Sea — 2 lines of U-boats patrol Heligoland Bight (-4 Aug, see 14).	**Bulgaria** — French air raid on Sofia from Salonika. **W Front** — 30 Anglo-German air combats. RFC (7 aircraft missing) bomb Cambrai, & Comines stns, shoot down 3 German aircraft. **Haig & Rawlinson thank RFC for its work.**	Russo-Japanese Far East mutual consultation treaty, Russia cedes 60 miles of Chinese E Railway. **Neutrals** — Allies lift Greek blockade. US militia can be absorbed into Army.	**Britain** — Irish Rebellion Commission Report published makes Chief Secretary 'primarily responsible' (see 31). Stock Exchange minimum prices finally removed, first wartime free market. **Germany** — Settlement Law for military pensions farm purchase, esp in Baltic area.
NRFF resumes advance through 6000-ft Ukinga Mts.	**N Sea** — Scheer's Jutland report to Kaiser stresses 'A victorious end...can only be achieved by using the U-boats against British trade'. Beatty's Battlecruiser Fleet Gunnery Ctee reports on Jutland. **Black Sea** — Goeben & Breslau shell Tuapse & Lazarevskoye, sinking steamer Kniaz Obolensky (see 22). **E Med** — Col Kress requests U-boat support for imminent Turk Suez Canal offensive, but only 1 sent, too late.	**W Front** — Low clouds inhibit flying (-6).	**Neutrals** — Conciliatory (Mexican) Carranza answer to US June notes; joint commission proposed 12, US accepts 28. Rumanian PM Bratianu puts 3 intervention conditions to French Ambassador (see 17).	**Germany** — Colonial & Interior Ministers visit Hindenburg's HQ (-6). Müller diary: Kaiser 'suffers so from loneliness'.
British 1st Div (Hoskins) advances 8 miles to R Msiha N of Nguru Mts, halt after 250-mile advance since 22 May (-1 Aug, see 5 Aug).	U-boat campaign against N Sea fishing vessels begins (36 sunk) (see 11). **E Med** — U39 sails, lands Lt Todenwarth & 7 men with munitions for Senussi, N Africa (fetched back 13 Oct).	**Somme** — RFC twice strafes German inf cols from 1200-2000 ft (-6).		
Gold Coast Regt (1428 men, 2 guns and 12 MGs) sails for E Africa (see 4 Sept).		**W Front** — 6 RFC FE2bs of No 23 Sqn attack Douai fighter base (15/27 20lb bombs hit).		**Britain** — Hospital ships land 10,112 Somme w at Southampton & Dover. MI5 circular warns Chief Constables that Germans seeking to recruit circus and stage performers as spies. **France** — Central Food Supply C'tee formed.
RN & 500 Indian inf (landed 5) occupy Tanga, Usambara railway terminus (see 20).	**N Sea** — Minelayer UC7 depth-charged off Lowestoft by HM motor boat Salmon. RN strengthens cruiser patrol N of Shetlands. Minelayer U77 sunk by RN escorts.	**Salonika** — No 17 Sqn RFC arrives from Egypt.	Britain & France rescind 25 Feb 1909 London Declaration (see 29 Oct & 6 Nov 1914).	**Britain** — **Lloyd George succeeds Kitchener as War Minister** (see 11 Dec). Lord Derby Under-Secretary for War. Southampton receives record 6174 w.
Belgian S Bde resumes advance from Kitega (E of L Tanganyika), 30 miles S by 16.		**Occupied Belgium** — c7 RNAS aircraft & a balloon direct Anglo-French heavy gun shelling of Tirpitz Bty at Ostend (-9); photorecon plane hit by AA at 13,000 ft (better photos taken from 14,000 ft 29)		**Russia** — Edict calls up non-Russians for reserve work with Army (see 30). **Britain** — Montagu Munitions Minister.

JULY 1916	WESTERN FRONT 1	EASTERN FRONT 2	SOUTHERN FRONTS 3	TURKISH FRONTS 4
Sun 9	**Somme** — Trônes Wood fighting continues (-14). French advance along Bray-Péronne road, taking Biaches & Hill 97 with La Maisonette Farm (10); repulse counter-attacks there (15 & 17).		Cadorna orders Trentino advance to slow down, forces to transfer to Isonzo from c21. Italian ops in Cadore & Costena valleys (-11), Travenanzes ops (-31).	**Palestine** — Up to 16,000 Turks (3rd Div under Kress) with German technical units march (mainly at night) from Shellah, NW of Beersheba (*see* 19).
Mon 10	**Somme** — Very hot weather, no wind: British 38th Div attacks Mametz Wood; most of wood secured 11 & finally occupied am of 12 (c2400 Germans evacuated 11/12) by British 62nd Bde of 21st Div. Green Howards of 23rd Div capture Contalmaison village (remains) taking 188 PoWs. German cas now 40,187 excl lightly w (*see* 31).	Russians claim 300,000 PoWs since 4 June. **Pripet** — Germans stiffen resistance (reinforced 11) on Stokhod W bank.	**Trentino** — *Alpini* bn fails to take Corno di Vallarsa, 2 Trentino volunteers with it captured, court-martialled & shot by Austrians at Trent (*see* HOME FRONTS 15).	**Armenia** — Russians retake Mamahatun.
Tue 11	**Verdun** — 5 German divs attack, 30 Germans reach outskirts of Ft Souville (all k), but overall gains 436 yds deep by 872 yds (-12) S of Fleury, all lost to counter-attacks (*see* 20). **Somme** — British repel counter-attacks on Contalmaison. BEF now has 7500 PoWs & 26 guns.		War Office agrees to pack (mule) transport for British Salonika Army, 15,000 mules supplied from Egypt, Britain & USA by mid-Aug incl 2000 for Serbs from Cyprus. 120,000 sun-helmets arrive from Egypt (12, *see* 27).	**Mesopotamia — Maude takes over British Tigris Corps** from Gorringe (*see* 28 Aug).
Wed 12	**Somme** — British repulse further counter-attacks at Contalmaison.			
Thu 13	**Somme** — Battle of Albert ends. **Champagne** — French trench raid success.	**Galicia** — Heavy fighting in *Südarmee* centre NW of Buczacz on R Styrpa; Russian Seventh Army takes 12,000 PoWs.		
Fri 14	**Somme — Battle of Bazentin Ridge**: 4 BEF divs (22,000) break into German 2nd position on 3½-mile front after dawn 0325 surprise attack & 5-min bombardment, capture Longueval & Bazentin le Petit with 2000 PoWs. 2nd Cav Div (102 cas) rides on High Wood, has one charge causing 48 cas (withdrawn at nightfall); 18th Div secures Trônes Wood. Haig & Foch visit Rawlinson to congratulate him on success. Germans hurry 3 divs up to plug gap.	**W Russia** — Battle of Baronovichi ends: Russian losses 80,000, mainly to shellfire. STAVKA decided to abandon it (9), German losses 16,000.		
Sat 15	**Somme — Battle of Delville Wood** (-20): 3153-strong SA Bde, ordered to capture & hold wood at all costs, secures most of it. For 5 nights & 6 days S Africans hold out v 3 divs' counter-attacks & shelling by 180 guns (*see* 19 & 20). British cav fail to break through at	**Pripet** — Sakharov's Eleventh Army (night 15/16) pre-empts Marwitz attack on S Lutsk salient thanks to agent network's warning, reaches R Lipa, takes Mikhailovka and 13,000 PoWs (*see* 20).		**Mesopotamia** — c96,000 British-Indian troops, 202 guns with over 32,000 Indian followers, av daily temp over 120° F; 12,000+ invalided out July (993 deaths from disease). **Armenia** — Yudenich occupies evacuated Bayburt.

AFRICAN OPERATIONS 5	SEA WAR 6	AIR WAR 7	INTERNATIONAL EVENTS 8	HOME FRONTS 9
2 *Königsberg* guns begin shelling British Msiha Camp (c570 shells cause c60 cas, -9 Aug).	RN light forces deploy (-14) to prevent German commerce raider breaking out into Atlantic (false alarm). Blockade-runner *Deutschland U155* arrives at Norfolk (Va). **Adriatic** — Austrian cruiser *Novara* (Horthy) sinks 2 RN Otranto barrage drifters; damages 2 more & takes 9 British PoWs, line later moved S (37 drifters in 5 gps, 13, but 75 really needed). **Constantinople** — *Goeben* only slightly damaged by 3 RNAS bombs dropped on Stenia Creek by Handley-Page bomber flown from Hendon, N of London (22 May) via France, Italy, Salonika & Mudros (8 June).	**Britain** — Hit-&-run single floatplane raid on Dover (night 9/10). **W Front** — 24 Anglo-German air combats (RFC lose 3 aircraft, Germans 2); RFC makes 7 bombing raids incl Cambrai & Bapaume stns.		
Tunisia — 1st French planes land, used with MG-armed lorries v Senussi (*see* 15 Sept).	**Adriatic** — Austrian *U17* sinks Italian destroyer *Impetuoso* in Straits of Otranto. **N Sea** — British freighter *Calypso* torpedoed.			
	N Sea — 3 HM armed trawlers *Era, Nellie Nutten* & *Onward* sunk by gunfire by *U46, U49, U52* & *U69* (*see* Aug). *U69* shells Seaham (Durham), 1 woman k.	**Somme** — Lt-Col Dowding CO of RFC 9th Wing (Battle of Britain victor 1940) w by German fighters leading 17-aircraft bombing of Bois d'Havrincourt.	**Neutrals : USA** — Film *America Preparing* exhorts 'quality we possess — we must have quantity'.	
Belgian Govt agrees to further limited advance.	RN begin cruiser/destroyer sweeps along Norwegian coast (-27). Bethmann concedes to Adm Holtzendorff right of *submerged* U-boats in Med to attack when *submerged* transports between Malta & Aegean, but COs responsible for any mistakes (15).	**W Front** — French ace-to-be Xavier de Sevin scores his 1st victory over Chamouille (Champagne). RFC 18 Sqn night bombs 8 targets (night 11/12) incl La Bassée.		
100 Sind inf repel 170 Germans attacking Korogwe Bridge (Smuts' supply line).			Allied munition & finance conferences (14-15) in London. **Neutrals: Greece** — Tatoi Forest fire nearly consumes royal summer palace and King.	
L Victoria — Lake Force takes Mwanza (began landing to E 11) but 500-man garrison escapes S (-16 *see 16*). Deventer's 2nd Div takes Mpondi on Central Railway, resumes advance S (19). German rearguard mauls 2 Belgian bns at Djobahika.	**N Sea** — *U51* torpedoed by HM submarine *H5* in Ems estuary. **Adriatic** — Damaged Italian submarine *Balilla* scuttles off Cape Planka, NW of Lissa I, to escape surrender to 2 Austrian torpedo boats.			**France** — 49 anti-war delegates at only Teachers Unions Congress held (-15).
568 British take German Segera Hill post & 1 gun.	**Adriatic** — RN submarine *H3* mined & sunk off Cattaro.	**Somme** — RFC bombs 13 targets & claims 6 German aircraft for no loss.		**Austria** — Ex-*Reichsrath* Trentino deputy Cesare Battisti (Italian PoW) executed. **Germany** — War Ministry reminds military region commanders to use unions, after arresting strike leaders.

JULY 1916	WESTERN FRONT 1	EASTERN FRONT 2	SOUTHERN FRONTS 3	TURKISH FRONTS 4
Sat 15 contd	High Wood, withdraw (16). **Verdun** — French recapture & then lose Bty C & CP 119 nr Fleury (-16).			
Sun 16	**Somme** — British 62nd Bde relieved at Mametz Wood (night 15/16). Since 12, heavy German guns have inflicted 950 cas.	**Baltic Provinces** — Slight Siberian (Russian Twelfth Army) advance SE of Riga peters out v Below's Eighth Army (-21).	**Trentino** — Asiago Plateau fighting peters out.	**Arabia** — Egyptian 4-gun mtn bty shells Taif (Turk stronghold) (*see* 22 Sept).
Mon 17	**Somme** — British capture Waterlot Farm E of Longueval; Ovillers cleared of Germans by 48th Div.		**Macedonia** — Serbs begin to move to take over 60 miles of front W of R Vardar. Sarrail told to be ready to attack on 1 Aug in combination with Russo-Rumanian thrust S of Danube.	
Tue 18	**Somme** — Strong German counter-attacks at Longueval & Delville Wood.			**Mesopotamia — War Office given full control of ops** by War Cabinet; C-in-C India responsible to Army Council. **Armenia** — Russians occupy Gumusane, capture 800 Turks 15 miles SW of Bayburt. **Arabia** — HMG ratifies treaty with Ibn Saud, Emir of Nejd (*see* 26 Dec 1915).
Wed 19	**Somme** — Germans outflank left flank of S African Delville Wood garrison & compress pocket. German attacks on Longueval, Waterlot Farm & Trônes Wood. German Second Army N of Somme becomes new First Army (Gen F Below), from the Somme to R Cologne (NW St Quentin) Second Army (Gen Gallwitz, latter also Army Gp Cdr). RND becomes 63rd (Naval) Div. **Flanders** — British First Army diversionary but inept daylight attack at Fromelles (-20) fails bloodily, new 5th Aust Div has 5500 cas. **Verdun** — Gen von François replaces Gallwitz (to Somme) i/c W of the Meuse.	Conrad vainly protests v being put 'under German guardian-ship'.		**Sinai — 2nd Turk Offensive v the Suez Canal begins** (*see* 24) from Oghratina. Stotzingen ordered from Damascus to Beersheba (20). **E Persia** — Action of Gusht Defile (-21): Dyer defeats Sarhad tribes-men.
Thu 20	**Somme** — 778 surviving S Africans relieved at Delville Wood. 4 British divs begin attacks on High Wood (-30). Maj W Congreve VC (posthu-mous), DSO, MC, Legion of Honour k, aged 25. **Verdun** — Mangin's French attack in Souville-Thiaumont sector gains ground (& 24, 28).	Heir apparent Austrian Archduke Charles i/c *Südarmee*, Seventh and Third Armies. **Pripet** — Sakharov captures Berestechko on R Styr, Galician border, crosses river taking 14,000 PoWs (21).	Greek Army demobilization nearly completed.	**Armenia** — V Caucasus Corps occupies Ardasa. **Mesopota-mia** — *Shamal* NW wind begins 6 weeks late. **Persia** — Niedermayer arrives in Tehran from Afghanistan via Russian Turkestan (invalided home from Baghdad Feb 1917).
Fri 21	Falkenhayn laments that no more German troops from quiet sectors can feed Somme battle until relieved by 'fought out' divs. He requires 7 such divs to replace those already transferred to Somme (*see* 24).	**Pripet** — Bezobrazov's Guard Army (11 divs, 134,000 men and 396 guns) formed (*see* 28). **Galicia** — Austrians retreat & begin to evacuate Brody (*see* 25). Heavy rain (23-28) delays Brusilov's Seventh and Ninth Armies' resumed offensive.		
Sat 22	**Somme** — Heavy fighting from Pozières to Guillemont. French repel counter-attacks S of Amiens-Péronne high road.	**Galicia** — Sakharov advances	**Trentino** — *Alpini* bn & 154th Regt night attack and gain footing N of Mt Cimone summit (23) dominating Arsiero to S (Austrian counter-attacks repelled 31), but attack on Bocchetta di Portule (6395 ft) fails. **Dolomites** — Italian I & XVIII Corps take Rolle Pass & 2 peaks, occupy Paneveggio village (31) in Val Travignolo.	
Sun 23	**Somme — Battle of Pozières Ridge** (2nd phase of Somme battle) begins (-3 Sept). Anzac			

AFRICAN OPERATIONS 5	SEA WAR 6	AIR WAR 7	INTERNATIONAL EVENTS 8	HOME FRONTS 9
L Victoria — 250 British capture 3 scuttled German steamers at head of Mwanza Gulf (*see* 25).				**Britain** — **War Savings Week** (-22). **Germany** — War Ministry reverses policy & increases inferior 'Thomas process' steel orders, but without fixing priorities.
	N Sea — British battlefleet exercises off Shetlands (-20).		Draft Russo-Rumanian treaty sent to Bucharest, envisages 7 Aug war entry (*see* 23).	**Britain** — Munitionette pay rates fixed, 41/2 d per hr at 18+.
Smuts reports steady clearance of Usambara area; Germans driven down R Pangani.		**Baltic** — German floatplanes bomb Reval naval base.	*London Gazette* blacklists c80 US firms trading with enemy (US protests 28).	**Britain** — Employers & unions agree to postpone holidays during war.
	Aegean — First of RN-led Greek refugee irregular raids on Turk Asia Minor (20, 24); booty incl 3200 cattle (mainly sheep), continue into autumn as do Italian raids from Dodecanese. Turks complain to US (30) re use of irregulars; Admiralty defends ops (15 Oct) but due to other needs ceases cattle rustling (26 Oct).	**Somme** — 30-40 German aircraft seen over BEF Fourth Army front (12 combats). **Sinai** — RFC discover 8000 Turks preparing for offensive (Brig-Gen E Chaytor GOC NZ Mtd Rifle Bde w as observer on this recon) (*see* TURK FRONTS).	Sweden orders ships to fire at submarines infringing 29 Nov 1915 conditions.	**Britain** — PM again refuses union demand to control food prices.
British main body meets troops from Tanga. Anglo-Belgian Entebbe Conference (-23). **L Tanganyika** — Maj Gen Wahle evacuates Kigoma (*see* 28).		**Somme** — 4 DH2s of No 24 Sqn defeat 11 German aircraft over Flers (1 Fokker & 2 Rolands lost); similar action v 7 Fokkers (3 Aug).	Greece agrees new £800,000 Anglo-French loan (*see* 8 Nov 1915).	**Britain** — Mesopotamia Debate in Parliament. Building work over £500 value with steel forbidden except under licence. Federation of British Industries formed.
		W Front — 4 German *Fl Abt 40* bombers attack Andruicq munitions dump on Calais-St Omer railway: 23 sheds & 8000t ammunition, 1 mile of track destroyed (night 21/ 22).		**Belgium** — All Belgians of 18-40 called up.
	Black Sea — *Breslau* escapes new Russian dreadnought *Imperatritsa Maria* with stern splinter damage (*see* Sept).	**W Front** — Weather poor for flying (-28).	**Russian Foreign Minister Sazanov** (since 1910) **resigns**, PM Stürmer takes over (*see* I Feb & 24 Nov). **Neutrals: USA** — Bomb kills 9 & wounds 40 in San Francisco (War) Prepared-ness Parade; 2 radical Labour leaders given life (released 1939). Senate votes naval building programme.	**Britain** — Silver badge granted for war disabled. **Germany** — Kaiser's staff discuss 'the necessity to raise the Emperor's participation'. (One suggests holiday.)
RN Force occupies Pangani on coast & Mkwaja (27). **Botha visits Msiha Camp.**	**N Sea** — Harwich Force (3 cruisers & 12 destroyers) covering new 80-mile 'Beef		**Russo-Rumanian military** (Rudeanu) **convention signed** at Chantilly, but Rumanian	**Turkey** — Food Board created.

JULY 1916	WESTERN FRONT 1	EASTERN FRONT 2	SOUTHERN FRONTS 3	TURKISH FRONTS 4
Sun 23 contd	Corps captures Pozières village. XIII Corps recaptures most of Delville Wood.			
Mon 24	**Somme** — German counter-attacks at High Wood & Guillemont. BEF has advanced 3¼ miles on 6-mile front, taken 11,119 PoWs & 56 guns & engaged 16 German divs (8 drawn into res); 2090 British guns have fired 4.5m shells.		Cadorna approves Italian contingent for Salonika (*see* 11 Aug).	**Sinai** — 16,000 Turks advance to within 10 miles of Romani & entrench.
Tue 25	**Somme** — **All Germans cleared from Pozières village.** Haig, Foch & Fayolle agree joint attack for 30. Rawlinson diary on *Battle of the Somme* film 'Some of it very good but I cut out many of the horrors in dead and wounded'.	**Galicia** — Sakharov advances on Brody (within 5 miles, 27), defeats Linsingen on R Slonuvka despite Austrian 106th *Landsturm* Div from Italian Front.		**Armenia** — **Yudenich occupies evacuated Erzincan, farthest point W,** splitting & routing Turk Third Army, 34,000 cas (17,000 PoWs) by 28.
Wed 26		Falkenhayn visits Conrad at Teschen.		
Thu 27	**Somme** — British advance in Delville Wood, fighting continues nr Pozières & at Longueval. **Aisne & Champagne** — German diversionary attacks.		**Salonika** — One British div suffering 150 sick pd from malaria. **Italian Front** — General Italian movement towards Isonzo begins, 232 medium guns & c220 trench mortars by 30.	**Arabia** — Yenbo (Medina's port, incl Stotzingen mission to Yemen) surrenders to Emir Abdulla. **Persia** — Sykes' 500 men leave Kerman for Yezd.
Fri 28	**Somme** — British 2nd Div captures Delville Wood & Longueval while Anzacs advance nr Pozières.	Brusilov Offensive resumes. **Pripet** — 250,000 Russians (gas shell barrage on part of sector) v 115,000 Austro-Germans: Lesch & Kaledin partly cross Upper Stokhod; Guard Army takes 3 villages, 46 guns, 65 MGs & 11,000 PoWs. **Galicia — Sakharov enters Brody** (40,000 PoWs, 49 guns & 100 MGs since 15). Brusilov's Seventh & Ninth Armies attack astride Dniester, former crosses R Koropyets to N (31), having taken c8000 PoWs & 33 guns.		
Sat 29	**Somme** — 2 failed German attempts to retake Delville Wood. Hand-to-hand fighting N of Pozières; Germans repulse Australian attack on the Windmill. CIGS letter to Haig, 'The Powers that be are beginning to get a little uneasy...the casualties are mounting up'.	**Falkenhayn, Conrad & Col Gancev (Bulgaria) sign convention for action v Rumania;** Mackensen given Danube Army for it (*see* 3 Sept).		**Mesopotamia** — Gen Lake reports to CIGS no advance until troops & transport refitted; CIGS agrees (31). **Arabia** — Britain re-affirms Holy Places' Muslim independence. **Armenia** — First Battle of Ognot (-1 Aug): Yudenich's IV Caucasus Corps attacks Turk Second Army.
Sun 30	**Somme** — Very hot, clear day. Joint Franco-British attack N of Somme improves situation on Allied right flank, Guillemont entered (fighting continues 31), Maurepas reached.	**Hindenburg & Ludendorff take over Front down to Lemberg** with 3 Army groups (-31); Brusilov's Intelligence Section cas estimates since 4 June: SW Front 450,000; Austrian 600,000, 330 guns (only 5000 German PoWs); **Galicia** — Lechitski pursues Austrian Seventh Army S of Dniester towards Stanislau.		**Sinai** — Advance guard actions (*see* 4 Aug).

AFRICAN OPERATIONS 5	SEA WAR 6	AIR WAR 7	INTERNATIONAL EVENTS 8	HOME FRONTS 9
	Trip' Holland-Thames route, clashes twice with 6 German destroyers from Zeebrugge before latter retire. Soon after 4-9 ship convoys (E & W-bound) organized with 5 close & 5 distant escorts (*see* 21 Sept).		counter-proposal (25).	
NRFF (1200) defeats Capt Braunschweig's S Detachment at Malangali, drives it towards Iringa. Belgian bn takes Kasulu.				**Britain** — Record credit (£450m) voted in Commons. Total for 1916-17 £1.05bn. Irish Home Rule debates (-31).
Lake Force takes Ilola, 62 miles S of Mwanza.			US Ambassador *Times* protest v Ruhleben Camp inhumanity (*see* 6 June).	**Britain** — Enlisted Men's Civil Liabilities scheme in force, help with rent, school fees & national insurance. **Russia** — †Lenin's mother in Petrograd, sister Anna arrested by 19 Sept.
W Desert — British-Italian armoured car raid from Sollum. **E Africa** — Gold Coast Regt lands at Mombasa (2nd WI Regt arrives 27).				**Britain** — **Commissions of Enquiry into Dardanelles** (Cromer) **and Mesopotamia** (Hamilton). Lloyd George vilifies conscientious objectors. Central Tribunal (27) finds 4378 genuine cases (692 refuse to appear); 250 sent to Dyce nr Aberdeen stone quarries late Aug for 8d pd, 1 dies early Sept (*see* 19 Oct).
		Italy — Austrian seaplane bombing raids on Bari & Otranto. **Black Sea** — German Army airship *SL10* FTR from planned raid on Sevastopol & Batumi.	**Occupied Belgium** — **Capt Fryatt** of GER liner *Brussels* **shot at Bruges by order of German court martial** for trying to ram U-boat (*see* 8 July 1919).	**Britain** — Wool manufacture declared munitions work.
S A Motorcycle Corps (Deventer's 2nd Div) occupies Dodoma on Central Railway, 100 miles of it in British hands. **L Tanganyika** — Belgian S Bde occupy Kigoma rail terminus, scuttled gunboat & 1 *Königsberg* gun found.		**Britain** — 6 German Navy airships drop 69 bombs over Norfolk & Lincs (night 28/29, no civ cas). **Somme** — Guynemer's Nieuport survives 86 hits & an LVG is his 11th victory. **W Front** — 4 Martinsyde Scouts of 27 Sqn successfully bomb (2 x 112lb, 3 x 20lb) Mons stn; 14 Anglo-German air combats.		**Britain** — Radio installation compulsory for all ships. Bank holiday postponement. RAMC request another 150 doctors (180 found by 18 Sept).
		W Front — 20 RFC aircraft bomb Douai & Hervilly airfields. RFC helps range 110 targets.	German note to US Berlin Ambassador refuses British offer to allow US food shipments into Poland from USA. **Canada** — Duke of Devonshire made Gov-Gen.	
Belgians reach Ruchugi on Central Railway, 50 miles E of Kigoma.	**Secret War** — RN Q-ship crews to wear War Service Badges (+ certificates later) to prevent any captured being shot as pirates.	**Germany** — 6 French & 3 RNAS aircraft raid benzine stores at Mulheim (*see* 12 Oct).	**Neutrals : USA** — Sabotage suspected in $40m munitions explosion at Black Tom Island nr Jersey City NJ (42 cas).	**Russia** — **Martial law in Turkestan** following Muslim rising v reserve work conscription, 3309 Govt cas before order restored.

JULY 1916	WESTERN FRONT 1	EASTERN FRONT 2	SOUTHERN FRONTS 3	TURKISH FRONTS 4
Mon 31	**5 German divs sent from W Front to E Front during July**. Joffre summons Foch to get him to persuade (vainly) Haig to launch broad-front attacks (*see* 11 Aug). **Somme** — German cas since 1 July 160,000 incl in at least 67 counter-attacks; **BEF 196,081** (158,786 on Somme) **worst month of war** (*see* Mar 1918); French cas 49,859. **Verdun** — (July) French cas 31,000; German 25,969.			
Tue 1 August 1916	**Somme** — German attack N of Bazentin-le-Petit fails. Repeated British assaults on Thiepval Salient (1-5); S side driven in c1000 yds by 5.		**Macedonia** — Allies spread over 170-mile front but not yet ready due to heat, poor roads & supply difficulties. **Russian Bde** of 5000 **lands at Salonika** (*see* 11). Offensive postponed to 4, then till Rumania signs agreement with Allies (not until 17, *see* 9 & 11).	**Armenia** — Russian 66th Div captures Ognot. (Aug) Turk Gov of Sivas estimates 30,000 deserters in his area.
Wed 2	**Somme** — Very hot day (88°F). German attack on Delville Wood repelled. **Verdun** — French capture 2550 PoWs & Fleury (-3), lose it and regain it (4,*see* 6).	**Hindenburg appointed to command whole front** (he & Ludendorff visit Kovel & Lemberg (3) but Austrians then withdraw consent). **W Russia** — German gas attack in Smorgoni area fails (& 22).		**Armenia** — **Turk Offensive** (-15): Kemal's XVI Corps attacks 9000 Russians at Mus & Bitlis (*see* 5).
Thu 3	**Somme** — British advance W of Pozières.	Brusilov meets Kaledin & Bezobrazov at Lutsk, decides to renew drive for Kovel (*see* 8). **Pripet** — I Turkestan Corps captures village 4 miles W of R Stokhod but Austro-German/ Polish Legion counter-attack forces it E (-4). **Carpathians** — Austrian counter-offensive makes few gains (-14). German 1st Inf Div arrives at Kirlibaba Pass (10).		**Persia** — Ali Ihsan resumes advance, fights Baratov (5-7,*see* 10). **Arabia** — Fakhri Pasha sorties from Medina & drives Ali 20 miles S (-4). **Sinai** — Turks begin night advance v Romani position.
Fri 4	**Somme** — British & Austra- lians capture German 2nd line trench system on 2000-yd front N of Pozières with 1750 PoWs, advance continues (5).	**Galicia** — Sakharov renews offensive S of Brody, takes 8581 PoWs & 7 villages (-6); only 4 miles NE of Lemberg-Tarnopol railway (10).	**Italian Front** — SIXTH BATTLE OF THE ISONZO (-17): begins after elaborate preparation incl air photo-graphs with feint in Monfalcone coastal sector by 14th & 16th Divs (29 bns & 199 guns) (-10). Duke of Aosta's Third Army has 16 divs & 1251 guns (533 heavy or medium) + 774 mortars (138 heavy 10-in mortars) for cutting wire entanglements v Austrian Fifth Army (Borcovic) 9 divs and 540 guns (147 heavy).	**Sinai** — **Battle of Romani** (-5): Turks (Kress), 30 guns & 38 MGs drive back 2 ALH Bdes & reach Wellington Ridge, but NZ & 5th Mtd Bdes retake it forcing Turk retreat (5) minus 5000 cas & 4 guns. British loss 1140 & 9 MGs (-9) out of 25,000. **Armenia** — Grand Duke Nicholas inspects RN Armoured Car Unit at Sarikamish; in action by 27 (*see* 4 Sept).
Sat 5	**Somme** — Rawlinson's Fourth Army 'Appreciation' stresses manpower economy, victory now only feasible in 1917.	**Galicia** — Hindenburg visits Zborov behind *Südarmee* which fights Battle of Zalozce (7-10).	**Macedonia** — Bulgars cross Greek frontier to S of Monastir & occupy 2 villages (-7, *see* 9).	**Armenia** — Kemal reoccupies Bitlis & Mus (6), taking 2 guns & 2 MGs.
Sun 6	**Somme** — Slight British advance E of Pozières. Res		**Isonzo** — Main Italian assault at 1600 after 9 hr intensest arty	**Sinai** — British reoccupy Katia (see 8), Turk rearguard actions

AFRICAN OPERATIONS 5	SEA WAR 6	AIR WAR 7	INTERNATIONAL EVENTS 8	HOME FRONTS 9
S Africans take Saranda & Kilmatinde on Central Railway. By July sick ratio to battle cas 31.4:1; Smuts 200 doctors short.	**Pacific** — Adm William B Caperton made C-in-C US Pacific Fleet (-Apr 1919, incl S Atlantic patrols off Brazil during hostilities).	**Britain** — 8 airships are dispersed by unpredicted winds, 103 bombs scattered over 6 counties (no cas), Kent-Notts (night 31 July/1 Aug). **W Front** — 11 Anglo-German air combats.	British-Italian Corporation founded to encourage trade.	**Ireland** — H E Duke becomes Chief Secretary. **Britain** — Consolidated lists of enemy businesses to be wound up.
RN & 150 troops occupy Sadani opposite Zanzibar (*see* 15). 8th SA Bn takes Ft Mgari (Great Rift Valley).	**Channel** — (Aug) Flanders UB boats sink 18 ships (6747t). **Adriatic** — Italian submarine *Pullino* goes aground on Galiola reef, captured but sinks in tow. **N Sea** — (Aug) RN deploys simulated fishing fleet in attempt to trap marauding U-boats. **Baltic** — RN submarines made a separate flotilla under Cdr Cromie DSO.	**Adriatic** — 10 Italian Capronis drop 4t bombs on Austrian Whitehead torpedo factory, Fiume; extensive fire & damage (*see* 13 Sept). **Britain** — (Aug) 1st flight of DH4 day bomber. Constantinesco MG/airscrew synchronizer gear flight-tested in BE2. **W Front** — Mannock transfers to RFC from RE despite eye defect, pilot's certificate 28 Nov. **Germany** — (Aug) Development of Gatling-type engine-driven 'motor guns' begun.	**Neutrals : USA** — French $100m loan opens. New British £50m loan terms announced (16).	**Britain** — 1st RFP fall, 1%. **Petrol rationing for commercial & private users. NZ** — Conscription for duration (*see* 7). **Bulgaria** — (Aug) New ctee to supply people & Army. **Germany** — (Aug) Scientist W Wein complains physicists not being best employed.
	Med — **Austrian saboteurs blow up & capsize Italian battleship *Leonardo da Vinci*** in Taranto (248 dead). Italy makes no public announcement but 1917 raid in Zurich on Austrian consulate proves sabotage. **Adriatic** — 4 Franco-Italian destroyers pursue 2 Austrian to within 15 miles of Cattaro & survive *U4* ambush on return.	**Britain** — 6 Zeppelins raid E Anglia (night 2/3, 1 civ cas) despite *Vindex* Bristol Scout attack (first carrier home defence op). **Somme** — RFC helps range 19 btys & finds 6 MG emplacements. **Occupied Belgium** — 6 BEs & 3 Moranes (1 lost) in 5-hr long-range attack on Brussels Zeppelin sheds (4 nr misses); 16 RNAS aircraft strike St Denis Westrem airfield (SW of Ghent) & RFC bomb Coutrai & Bapaume stns.		**Italy** — Agriculture Minister given food control powers (*see* 16 Jan 1917). **Britain** — Lloyd George sees *Battle of the Somme* film.
L Tanganyika — Belgian S Bde occupies Ujiji, begins Central Railway advance on Tabora (10).	First of 17 accident-prone, fast steam-powered K-class large submarines comes into RN service (*see* 29 Jan 1917). **N Sea** — 4 RN C-class submarines sail from Lerwick (Shetland) under tow on epic 3500-mile voyage to Baltic via Archangel (21), rivers & canals by barge, reach Petrograd 9 Sept, but hampered by unusable electric batteries so manage only 2 patrols before winter.	**E Front** — German heavy bomber unit *Rfa 501* (Krupp) formed at Vilna-Porubanok. **W Front** — RFC ranges 127 targets; 5 Martinsydes (1 lost) bomb Zeppelin sheds at Cognelée & Ronet sidings, Namur.	Anglo-French official papers on German barbarity published. British War Propaganda Bureau claim: 'We swept the German news out of the American papers'.	**Britain** — **Casement hanged at Pentonville Prison**. Balfour 2nd anniversary naval statement. Union 'Triple Alliance' discuss demobilization with PM (*see* 11 Sept). **Austria** — 4 Czech deputies in touch with Masaryk imprisoned.
250 Germans repel KAR coy on NRFF E flank nr Lupembe (NRFF occupy 18), but retreat before reinforcements (*see* 29).	**Aegean** — British escorts sink *UB44*.	**Sinai** — Up to 17 RFC aircraft (1 lost to AA fire) active backing Battle of Romani (-9), shoot down 1 German aircraft & direct monitor fire.		**Canada** — Dominions bond issue settles debts to Britain. **Britain** — 27,000 soldiers released for harvest.
Smuts resumes main advance through Nguru Mts on Morogoro (C Railway): 7000 men & 36 guns v c2000 Germans.		.	Britain arranges to buy Norwegian fishing catch. Anglo-Dutch fish agreements (12 & 26). Poincaré letter to Tsar insists on Rumanian intervention's urgency.	
	Italian Navy begins transporting & supplying troops for	**W Front** — French ace Fonck forces undamaged Rumpler 2-	**Occupied Poland** — Pilsudski founds Faithful Service Order,	

AUGUST 1916	WESTERN FRONT 1	EASTERN FRONT 2	SOUTHERN FRONTS 3	TURKISH FRONTS 4
Sun 6 contd	Army begins struggle for Mouquet Farm (-3 Sept,*see* 26). **Verdun** — German counter-attack defeated, but regains Thiaumont work twice (8-9).		barrage yet v Austrian 58th Div (Gen Zeidler on leave), 42 guns, 65 MGs involves Capello's VI Corps' 6 divs, 603 guns & 390 mortars. They storm Mt Sabatino (1998ft) in 45mins & part of Podgora, taking 8000 PoWs, 11 guns & 100 MGs. Former success much aided by Col Badoglio's exhaustive recces & planning as CoS VI Corps & his leading of 6 bns of 45th Div to assault (*see* 27). *Abruzzi* Bde storms Oslavia & Hill 165 to S, *Cuneo* Bde takes Grafenberg on Podgora; *Pavia* Bde storms Mt Calvario (603 ft). Italian XI Corps (87 bns & 217 guns) captures all 4 humps of Mt Michele (Carso) & enters village taking 1000 PoWs from Austrian VII Corps then gains whole of N Carso (-9, *see* 10).	v mtd troops (-7).
Mon 7	**Somme** — German attacks N & NE of Pozières. British attack outskirts of Guillemont.	**Galicia** — Lechitski resumes offensive with gas shell preparation, advances 12 miles to Stanislau, takes it & 10,581 (3500 German) PoWs (10), identifies German *Karpat-enkorps* from Verdun (8).	**Isonzo** — *Lambro* & *Etna* Bdes storm Hill 188 & Peurna heights. Some *Cuneo* patrols reach Isonzo in night. Austrians blow up rail bridge & counter-attack at Grafenberg.	Anglo-Russian Agreement with Persia to raise 22,000 military police.
Tue 8	**Somme** — British gain 400 yds at Guillemont — Germans still hold S end of village, repulse Allied attacks (9). British 2nd Div attacks Waterlot Farm to NW (-9).	**Pripet** — Russian Guard & Third Armies attack towards Kovel, make no gains (-9). Guard losses 55,292 since 25 July (9).	**Isonzo** — **Italians** clear W bank of middle Isonzo, secure all Podgora; 4 bns cross road bridge to **enter Gorizia** on E side, Lt Baruzzi (28th Regt, 12th Div) first in, raises Italian flag on station, winning gold medal.	**Sinai** — Turks abandon Oghratina but repulse Anzac Mtd Div pursuit (322 cas) at Bir-el-Abd (9), but evacuate it (11).
Wed 9	**Somme** — German 18th Res Div 8288 cas (ie over 50%) since 24 July.		**Salonika** — Local Allied offensive: Allies shell Bulgar line S of L Doiran, French 17th Colonial Div (15,000) occupies abandoned stn & Hill 227 (-10, *see* 16).	
Thu 10	**Somme** — **K George visits the front** (-15), tells Rawlinson of a 'cabal' (incl Lord French, Churchill & F E Smith) which plans to oust Haig & curtail Somme offensive.		**Serbia** — Gen Winckler replaces Gen Gallwitz i/c German Eleventh Army, 2 German divs (1 from Vosges, W Front) reinforce Bulgars. **Isonzo** — On Carso Austrian Doberdo-Monfalcone line collapses into full retreat for the Vallone, but Italian 23rd Div forces them out. Austrians establish new line NE of Gorizia with 3 divs & 4 bdes of reinforcements (incl 2 divs from E Front) that block Italian VI & VIII Corps.	**Persia** — Turks occupy Hamadan, Daulabad & Bijar (*see* 20).
Fri 11	**Somme** — Joffre dissatisfied with offensive developing into innumerable minor actions, demands return to Allied attacks on broad front and writes to Haig proposing capture of line Thiepval/ HighWood/Ginchy/Combles/ Somme by 3 ops beginning 22. Then (c 1 Sept) attack to be against Grandcourt/ Courcel-ette/Martinpuich/Flers/Morval/ Rancourt/ Bouchavesnes.		**Salonika** — Italian 35th Div (11,000) & 32 guns **lands** (-25), relieves French 57th Div by 27. Gen Cordonnier now i/c French Army of the Orient.	
Sat 12	Joffre (with Foch) & Haig confer at Beauquesne. Haig proposes prelim combined attack from the Somme to High Wood on 18 (*see* 16). K George & Pres Poincaré also meet at	Brusilov now claims 378,408 PoWs, 405 guns, 1326 MGs, 367 mortars, 100 searchlights & 15,000 sq miles of territory at cost of 550,000 cas. **Galicia** — *Südarmee* finally yields Strypa	**Isonzo** — *Lombardia* Bde storms Nad Logern & San Grado di Morna, while *Regina* Bde occupies Oppachiasella ruins, 1565 PoWs in all.	**Armenia** — Turk III Corps engages 5th Caucasus Rifle Div in Boran area but is blocked (-13,*see* 15).

AFRICAN OPERATIONS 5	SEA WAR 6	AIR WAR 7	INTERNATIONAL EVENTS 8	HOME FRONTS 9
	Macedonia (1 div initially, later 46,000 effectives).	seater to land & alights nearby to take PoWs. RFC Sopwiths break up German 10-bomber formation E of Bapaume.	given sword of honour having resigned as Legions' 1st Bde CO (*see* 26 Dec). **Montenegro** — PM Radovic proposes union to Serbia, no reply (*see* 11 Jan 1917).	
Sahara — 200 Senussi, 1 gun & 1 MG arrive at Ghat as French prematurely evacuate Tibesti Mts (-17, *see* 7 Dec).	Admiralty deny German press allegations that British hospital ships being used as transports. RN transfers 4 'W'-class (& 23) small submarines to Italian Navy.	Aerial observation engages 166 targets, mainly on Somme, 170 (8), 177 (9).		**NZ** — Excess profits tax and loan authorized. **Britain** — August Bank Holiday generally postponed (*see* 18).
		W Front — 3 FE2bs of No 25 Sqn defeat 6 Roland biplanes over Bethune, forcing them to jettison bombs over own lines. **Britain** — 9 Zeppelins scatter 173 bombs over E England & Scotland (night 8/9, 21 of 26 cas in Hull). Admiralty now has 114 warships with AA guns able to engage Zeppelins.	**Portugal decides to extend military help to Europe** (*see* 3 Jan 1917). Allies agree on terms for Rumania.	
	Adriatic — RN submarine *B10* destroyed by Austrian air raid on Venice dockyard, 3 sister boats recalled (Oct) after 4 W-class boats, sold to Italy, arrive.	**Occupied Belgium** — 2 RNAS Sopwith 1½ Strutters bomb & hit Zeppelin sheds nr Brussels & Namur (repeated 25).		**Britain** — Duke of Sutherland offers 12,000 acres for ex-servicemen re-settlement.
Kraut checks British pursuit at Matamondo for day after evacuating Ruhungu position (8-9). Deventer's 2nd Div begins 60-mile Central Railway advance to Kilosa (-22) v 5 rearguard stands (*see* 25).		**W Front** — Weather restricts flying (-19).	Anglo-Italian Pallanza Economic Conference (-14).	**Turkey** — Decree removes Armenian churches from Etchmiadzin to Jerusalem Catholicate. **Britain** — Chancellor estimates £3.44bn war debt by 31 Mar 1917. Distilling fixed at 70% of previous output.
			Bethmann in Vienna (-12), Austro-German friction over Poland (*see* 16). Lloyd George in Paris.	

AUGUST 1916	WESTERN FRONT 1	EASTERN FRONT 2	SOUTHERN FRONTS 3	TURKISH FRONTS 4
Sat 12 contd	Beauquesne (5 miles SSE of Doullens). **Somme** — British advance on a mile front NW of Pozières. German High Wood counter-attack (& 17-19). French gain German 3rd line trenches N of river.	winter line & retreats by night 10 miles to R Zlota Lipa. Lechitski occupies Nadworna.		
Sun 13	**Somme** — British 15th Div captures Munster Alley. Arty duels N & S of the river (14).	**Transylvania** — Austrian First Army (Arz) formed v Rumania.	**Isonzo** — *Catanzaro* Bde takes Hill 246, 3 other positions with 900 PoWs gained at heavy cost.	
Mon 14		Hoffmann diary: 'Continual friction with the Austrians and almost more with *OHL*'. Russian Third & Guard (now Special) Armies returned to W Front command.	**Isonzo** — General Italian attack all along line (-17) without appreciable gains but heavy losses.	**S Persia** — Sykes' 460 men & 2 guns reach Yezd, leave for Isfahan (28, *see* 11 Sept).
Tue 15		Brusilov has received 26 extra divs since 12 June (but Austro-Germans 33$\frac{1}{2}$ incl 23 German). **Galicia** — Lechitski reaches Solotwina W of Stanislau, gains heights S of Jablonitsa Pass (22).		**Armenia** — Fighting starts S of Kigi between Turk IV Corps & new 6th Caucasus Rifle Div which drives former S of Ognot (18-25).
Wed 16	**Somme** — Foch visits Haig, latter then replies to Joffre's letter of 11; certain local ops are inevitable, Haig has arranged with Foch a combined attack for 18; another to follow (22). But Haig can make no promises of subsequent ops dates, insufficient forces for early large-scale attack on Thiepval front, British advance W & SW of Guillemont. French capture trenches along 12-mile sector astride river with 1300 PoWs, repel German attacks N of Maurepas (18).		**Salonika** — French 17th Colonial Div captures La Tortue at 2nd attempt but twice forced out Doljeli (2-17), 1100 cas since 9. British bn captures Horseshoe Hill in support to W (17).	
Thu 17	**Somme** — British capture trench NW of Bazentin. German counter-attack held NW of Pozières. **Verdun** — French Moroccan Colonial Regt secure Fleury & Thiaumont (-18) for good, repel German attacks (19, 27-28).		**Italian Front** — At 1800 **Cadorna suspends most successful Isonzo offensive yet** after 3-4 mile gains on 15-mile front , 51,232 cas (12,128 missing) for 49,035 Austrian (20,000 PoWs) & 30 guns. **Macedonia** — **Pre-emptive Bulgar offensive into Greece** (-28): 2 Bulgar cols attack Serb Danube Div nr Florina & capture stn, deploy 18,000 men (-19) to drive back Serb Third Army at W end of Allied line while Bulgar Second Army at E end begins advance to Struma.	
Fri 18	**Somme** — British 33rd Div attack at High Wood fails (German counter-attack, also 23 & 24), British advances towards Ginchy & Guillemont.	**Falkenhayn, Conrad & Enver sign convention for action v Rumania.**	**Macedonia** — Bulgars take Florina.	
Sat 19	**Somme** — German counter-attack (20). British advance to Thiepval Ridge.			

AFRICAN OPERATIONS 5	SEA WAR 6	AIR WAR 7	INTERNATIONAL EVENTS 8	HOME FRONTS 9
	N Sea — Dutch convoy escort destroyer *HMS Lassoo* mined & sunk.	W Front — RFC bombs Douai airfield 3 times (86 bombs). Mesopotamia — RFC No 30 Sqn (13 serviceable BE2cs + 14 arriving or being overhauled, 1) scores 1st victory, Fokker over Shumran airfield (bombed at night 14, *see* 23 Sept).	Sino-Japanese troop clash in Manchuria; Japan gets apology & indemnity (23 Jan 1917).	Britain — **1st 6 tanks leave for France** (*see* W FRONT 15 Sept). Russia — Union of Towns has spent 125m roubles on wounded & relief care (only 8m from donations).
RN sqn lands 314 troops to capture Bagamoyo 35 miles N of Dar-es-Salaam (*see* SEA WAR 21).	Britain — (c) First 12 CMBs (ordered Jan) delivered. N Sea — RN submarines *E41* & *E4* collide & sink on exercise (15 survivors); both boats salvaged & *E41* reused. Red Sea — Cruiser *D'Estrées* embarks French Arab Revolt mission chief Col Bremond for Jeddah.	E Front — (c) Boelcke on visit to Kovel invites Richthofen to join his new unit (*see* 23).		Britain — Munitions Minister says annual 1914-15 18pdr shell output now made in 3 wks.
		Somme — 2/Lt Ball in Nieuport Scout attacks 5 Rolands, forcing 2 down, destroys 2 more (22) in 11 Sqn action with about 15 German aircraft (4 lost); makes another kill (with 60 Sqn, 28) from 4 aircraft attacked; 2 more kills (31).	Bethmann to Kaiser after Austria visit: 'The authority of the Army High Command (Conrad) is completely buried, with the Emperor ... the Field Army & the population'. **Secret War** — BEF Intelligence 2i/c deplores spying emphasis on Switzerland rather than Holland (*see* 6 Dec).	Britain — 2nd Industrial Fatigue report argues v Sunday work or continuous overtime (*see* 8 Oct).
Action on R Wami (Dakawa): 2nd SA Mtd Bde outflanks but fails to trap *Abteilung Schulz*, river bridged 20.			**Rumania agrees to join Allies**, signs military convention to enter war by 28. **Neutrals: USA** — JP Morgan Bank announces $250m 2-yr loan to Russia. **Greece** — German & Bulgar notes (-18) to justify seizing Greek territory.	Germany — Meat ration fixed. Britain — Lloyd George at National Eisteddford.
	N Sea — **Whole High Seas Fleet puts to sea (-19) for penultimate time** until Apr 1918 with aim of shelling Sunderland &/or drawing British warships onto 5 lines of U-boats (24 in all); 8 Zeppelins scout. RN submarine *E23* (one of 25 on patrol) puts 2 torpedoes into battleship *Westfalen* (one of 18 & 2 battlecruisers) forcing her back to port, but Scheer persists & a Room 40-aided Jellicoe has sailed to meet him at 1700, 5 hrs before Scheer sorties.			Britain — Army hutting costs so far £24.5m. Commons Public Accounts Ctee condemns extravagant war contracts. Labour MP Arthur Henderson made Govt Labour Adviser, appeals to munition workers not to take holidays (24).
	N Sea — British Grand Fleet cruisers *Nottingham* & *Falmouth* (3 hits each) sunk in actions between 0557 & noon	W Front — Since 19 Mar *Esc 3* of French *Cigognes* (Stork) Group (Brocard) has scored 39 confirmed victories & 26		Germany — Ruhr coalminers strike v food shortages & inflation (-c28).

AUGUST 1916	WESTERN FRONT 1	EASTERN FRONT 2	SOUTHERN FRONTS 3	TURKISH FRONTS 4
Sat 19 contd				
Sun 20		Hindenburg-Ludendorff letter to Kaiser after Ludendorff's resignation threat (evasive reply 23). Brusilov re-distributes right-wing corps between his 4 armies (-21).	**Secret War** — Austrians crack new Italian cipher system in 38 hrs. **Salonika** — Sarrail & his 5 Allied cdrs agree to postpone offensive but launch counter-offensive as Bulgar 7th Div causes 380 cas to retreating French. Serb Gen Jurisic-Stürm replaced i/c Third Army by Gen Vassic.	**Armenia** — IV Caucasus Corps retakes Mus bridge & 500 PoWs. **Persia** — Baratov halts on Sultanbulak Pass 50 miles N of Hamadan, has 7000 fit troops & 22 guns v 17,000 exhausted Turks.
Mon 21	**Somme** — Fresh German counter-attack nr Thiepval (2 more to S fail 22). Fighting S of Thiepval ends in slight British gain (23). British advance on 1/2- mile front NW of Pozières.		**Salonika** — British raiders (4 cas) blow up 5 bridges E of Struma (& 23).	
Tue 22	**Somme** — Haig chides Rawlinson for failing to take Guillemont. German counter-attacks at Guillemont repulsed. (23)	**Galicia** — **Turk 19th** (arr 13) **& 20th Divs** (Gallipoli veterans) **take over 12-mile sector** between *Südarmee* German divs (*see* 7 Sept).	Italian successes in Dolomites (& 24). **Macedonia** — Bulgar First Army storms Serb ridge W of L Ostrovo 5 times only to be thrown off; take only 1 position (23, *see* 26). British lorries bring up Serb reinforcements.	
Wed 23			**Carnic Alps** — Italian XVIII Corps begins advance to drive Austrians from Fassa Alp, captures Mt Cauriol (27, *see* 23 Sept).	**Mesopotamia/Persia** — Battle of Rayat: Russians defeat Turks who lose 2300 PoWs.
Thu 24	**Somme** — British GHQ letter to Gen Rawlinson (Fourth Army) emphasizes it is vital to secure Ginchy, Guillemont & Falfemont Farm without delay. Foch's co-operation secured (25); attack to be launched on 29 but thunderstorms postpone it repeatedly to 3 Sept. German attacks W of Ginchy. British advance towards Thiepval & Delville Wood. French bn Frère (2nd Bn, 1st Regt, 1st Div) captures all of Maurepas (-25) from Bavarians.		**Salonika** — Greek IV Corps hands over forts N of Kavalla to Bulgars (*see* 12 Sept). RN monitor *Picton* shells them in 2 villages on coast.	
Fri 25	**Somme** — British secure Delville Wood & repulse attacks S of Thiepval. **Champagne** — German attack W of Tahure repulsed. **Ypres** — New 4th Cdn Div arrives (*see* 3 Sept).	**Dobruja** — **Russian Dobruja Detachment** (50,000, 3 divs) **crosses Danube into Rumania**, invades Bulgaria (27).	Bulgars occupy Seres in NE Greece.	
Sat 26	**Somme** — German counter-attack nr Thiepval. Australians capture heavily fortified Mouquet Farm.		**Macedonia** — Serbs hold firm, arty duels (-30).	
Sun 27	**Somme** — British 3rd Bde attacks Grevillers.	RUMANIA INVADES HUNGARIAN TRANSYLVANIA	**Italian Front** — Col Badoglio promoted Maj Gen, aged 44.	

AFRICAN OPERATIONS 5	SEA WAR 6	AIR WAR 7	INTERNATIONAL EVENTS 8	HOME FRONTS 9
	(20) by *U52*, *U63* & *U66*, forcing Jellicoe (29 battleships) northward during fleet moves that bring Beatty (6 battlecruisers) 42 miles N of Scheer before latter turns for home. Harwich Force (5 cruisers & 20 destroyers) shadows but not able to make night torpedo attack as Jellicoe wanted (*see* 13 Sept).	probables in 338 air combats over Verdun & Somme.		
	Med — *U35* (Arnauld) returns to Cattaro after record-breaking 25-day cruise (since 26 July) sinkings with 900 shells & 4 torpedoes: 54 ships (32 Italian carrying 50,000t coal), totalling 91,000t mainly in W Med (French patrol areas,*see* 4 Oct).		Austro-Montenegrin talks broken off.	**France** — Law for the taxing of war profits.
	N Sea — RN submarine *E54* torpedoes & sinks *UC10* at Schouwen Bank.		Peru declares neutrality.	**Britain** — Almost all exports to Sweden prohibited. Directorate of Graves Registration & Enquiries formed.
				Britain — Commons food prices debates (-23).
Smuts' main advance resumes from Dakawa, but 2nd SA Mtd Bde checked at Mlali (24-26) though 2 German naval guns abandoned.		**Britain** — Army Zeppelin *LZ97* scatters 34 bombs over Suffolk (night 23/24, no cas). **W. Front — Germans form first regular fighter squadron** *Jasta 1* (Capt Martin Zander), Bolcke's *Jasta 2* (30, *see* 17 Sept), both and two more units assigned to Somme.		**Britain** — War Charities Registration compulsory.
	N Sea — Battleships *Valiant* & *Warspite* (only just out of Jutland repairs) collide, repairs (-28 Sept).	**Britain** — 6 of 12 Zeppelins (*L13* damaged by cruiser *Conquest*) cross E Coast, *L31* drops 44 bombs on E London (first since 14 Oct 1915), causing 49 civ cas (night 24/25), 2 of 15 defending aircraft crash on landing (thunderstorms thwart 8-Zeppelin raid 29).	Anglo-French Calais Financial Conference agrees exchange rate.	
1st SA Horse engages Kraut's rearguard 18 miles S of Kilosa, advances 28 miles by 2 Sept.	**N Sea** — U-boat sinks armed boarding steamer *HMS Duke of Albany*.	**W Front** — RFC helps engage 53 German gun positions (31 direct hits). **Palestine** — 3 RN seaplane carriers off Haifa send 10 seaplanes to bomb Turk dump & railway at Afule, then ships separate to attack Gulf of Adalia factory (27), Adana rail stn (29) & targets N of Jaffa.		
Rhodesians & Baluchis occupy Morogoro on Central Railway (Smuts enters 27), 115 miles E of Dar-es-Salaam; 28,000 British oxen lost since 25 May. Lake Force begins advance S on Tabora, awaits news from Belgians 50 miles to W (*see* 5 Sept).	**Adriatic** — Austrian air raid sinks an RN Otranto drifter (96 on strength 10 Sept spending 10 days at sea, 3½ in port).	**Rumania** — 2 French pilots arrive at Bucharest from Verdun via London, Oslo & Archangel; request 50 pilots & 55 aircraft from Paris (29, *see* 31 Dec).		
British 1st and 2nd Divs link on Railway 12 miles E of Kilosa.			RUMANIA MOBILIZES & DECLARES WAR ON	**Rumania** — Bucharest: Crown Council at Cotroceni Palace,

AUGUST 1916	WESTERN FRONT 1	EASTERN FRONT 2	SOUTHERN FRONTS 3	TURKISH FRONTS 4
Sun 27 contd		via 8 major passes, a month earlier than Falkenhayn expected; Kaiser's reaction 'The war is lost'. **Carpathians** — Lechitski (17 divs) attacks on 75-mile front between Nadworna and Dorna Watra, takes Mt Pantyr (29)		
Mon 28	**Somme — Army Gp Crown Prince Rupprecht created** for duration. Gen Gallwitz i/c German Second Army records that since 26 June 1068 field guns of 1208 in his 2 armies, & 379 of his 820 heavy guns have been captured, destroyed or become unserviceable.	**Prince Leopold of Bavaria replaces Hindenburg as C-in-C East** (Hoffmann his CoS real chief). Austrian monitors shell Danube towns.		**Mesopotamia — Maude succeeds Lake as C-in-C** thanks to CIGS, Maj-Gen Cobbe VC takes over Tigris Corps which now has 64 river steamers supplying 460t pd but 560t needed, 3 railways being built. 11,000 troops invalided out (Aug).
Tue 29	FALKENHAYN (German CoS) DISMISSED BY KAISER, REPLACED BY FM HINDENBURG WITH GEN LUDENDORFF (1st QMG) AS HIS ASSISTANT. **Somme** — Since 1 July British have taken 15,469 PoWs, 86 guns & 160 MGs.	HINDENBURG CHIEF OF STAFF, LUDENDORFF FIRST QMG (GHQ Pless to Feb 1917). **Transylvania** — Rumanians occupy evacuated Kronstadt, Petrosani & Kezdiasarhely.	**Salonika** — British relieve French up to Vardar valley.	
Wed 30	Col Estienne promoted Brig Gen and crd of French Assault Arty (tanks).		**Albania** — Italians occupy Tepeleni.	
Thu 31	**Somme** — 4 German counter-attacks fail at Delville Wood; British XV Corps suffers heavy cas. Fierce German counter-attacks between Ginchy & High Wood. By this time BEF has consulting psychiatrist & neurologist for 'shell shock' cases. **Artois/Flanders** — British gas attacks at Arras & Armentières. **Verdun** — French defensive Battle of Verdun ends.	Austrian losses since 4 June 614,000, German 150,000 incl 15,000 today.		
Fri 1 September 1916	**Somme** — 4 German counter-attacks fail at High Wood (& 3, 8 & 15) but they recapture E side of Delville Wood.	Turk VI Corps placed under Mackensen. **Galicia** — Shcherbachev takes 19,000 PoWs on R Zlota Lipa (-4).		**Armenia** — Turk IV Corps attacks S of Kigi but Russian reinforcements stabilize front by 10 (see 15). French Arab Mission reaches Alexandria.
Sat 2	**Somme** — Rawlinson inspects British tank force & is dissatisfied with readiness (see 10 & 15).			**Egypt** — GOC & McMahon confer on Arab Revolt at Ismailia (see 12, 13 & 27). **Arabia** — Turk Berne Legation press release denigrates Sherif's revolt, most Arabs fighting for Sultan.

AFRICAN OPERATIONS 5	SEA WAR 6	AIR WAR 7	INTERNATIONAL EVENTS 8	HOME FRONTS 9
			AUSTRIA. **Neutrals: Greece** — Venizelos addresses Athens protest meeting v King's policy (Metaxas dismissed 26).	K Ferdinand rebuffs opposition to split with Berlin 'Then I have conquered the Hohenzollern who was in me, I fear no one'.
	Aegean — British warships shell Bulgar Kavalla forts.	**Rumania** — First Army Zeppelin raid on Bucharest (night 28/29, 4 more in Sept).	GERMANY DECLARES WAR ON RUMANIA (TURKEY 30). ITALY DECLARES WAR ON GERMANY.	
NRFF occupies Iringa (760 Germans evacuate 27) in S Highlands, 250 miles marched since 25 May. Hannyngton's 2nd EA Bde (1st Div) crosses R Msumbisi in heavy rain.		**W Front** — Storm wrecks 5 No 21 Sqn aircraft in hangar.	**Neutrals: USA** — Army & Navy Appropriation Acts authorize $580m spending & create Council of National Defense. Marine Corps Reserve created and USMC increased to 15,578.	**Turkey** — Petrol prices rise 80% (Rumania's entry). **Britain** — Local Authorities urged to keep postwar work registers. Mobile labour squad to finish munition factories building.
Lettow retreats over R Ruvu. 1st Div pursues across (31-1 Sept).	3 postponements of final decision on unrestricted U-boat warfare (30 Aug - 3 Sept). German Supreme Command to play Solomon.	**W Front** — No 24 Sqn encounters first 3 Albatros DI Scouts (*Jasta 1*). **Macedonia** — Allied air raid on Buk bridges NE of Drama.	**Neutrals: Greece** — Venizelists seize Salonika barracks & proclaim provisional republic.	
Smuts' advance split by Uluguru Mts; 600 SA mtd troops go round W side, 1900 British march on Dar-es-Salaam (*see* 4 Sept). **W Desert** — British armoured cars capture Senussi convoy NW of Jaghbub (*see* 10 Oct). **W Africa** — Slavery abolished in Nigeria.	Allied shipping losses 205,000t (British 23 ships worth 43,354t with 8 lives lost). Total incl 77 ships (129,368t) to U-boats in Med. 2 U-boats lost. **At Pless Hindenburg & Ludendorff press for unrestricted U-boat war without delay**, Bethmann's opposition now confined to timing & fear of breach with Scandinavia. Fronts must be stabilized lest Holland & Denmark declare war while Germany has no reserves (*see* 3 Sept).	**Somme** — German aircraft losses in combat since 1 July — 51. RFC W Front k & missing 66.	US *Deutschland* note to Allies says international law observed (see SEA WAR 23 June).	**Germany** — **Hindenburg letter to War Minister demands doubled munitions**, trebled artillery/MG production by May 1917 (*see* 9 Sept). **Britain** — Musical *Chu Chin Chow* opens in London for duration & beyond (2238 perfs).
Belgian bn (135 cas & 4 MGs lost) beaten at Mabama, another ambushed S of Katunde (2) but a third holds Usoke railway stn as advance on Tabora begins, repulsing German attack (93k) from there (7).	**Channel** — (early Sept) 3 Flanders UB-type boats sink over 30 ships in a wk without encountering one warship (570 ASW vessels available); 1949 British merchantmen now armed with guns. **Black Sea** — New Russian dreadnought *Imperatritsa Maria* fires at & pursues *Goeben* (rescues Turk seaplane) to within 60 miles of Bosphorus (*see* 20 Oct). **Aegean** — 23 Allied warships & 4 transports (from Salonika) anchor 4 miles off Piraeus nr Greek Fleet at Salamis (*see* INT'L EVENTS).	**Somme** — RFC observers help destroy or damage at least 28 German guns (66 btys engaged). **Egypt** — 25 bombs dropped on Port Said (46 cas incl 26 Europeans), 1 damages RN carrier *Raven II*. RFC bomb El Arish airfield (6 & night 15/16) & 6 BE2cs (2 lost) raid camps & camel lines at Mazar (2, *see* 17).	BULGARIA DECLARES WAR ON RUMANIA. Britain & Russia sign Sykes-Picot Agreement. (Sept) Anglo-Russian Bureau (propaganda) opens in Petrograd. **Neutrals: Greece** — Allied fleet seizes 13 interned Austro-German ships.	**Britain** — RFP 65% (up 5%). Munition factories total 4212 (with 435 canteens for 640,000 workers). Civilian war prisoners to be supplied to private firms. (Sept) War Propaganda Bureau starts monthly *War Pictorial* magazine (circ 750,000 by Nov 1917).
	Channel — Dover Patrol begins laying illuminated mined indicator nets 30-84ft deep across Dover Straits (-Feb 1917) but bad weather leaves only 25% working. Only 8 U-boats in 190 passages forced to dive (23 Dec 1916 to 6 June 1917).	**Britain** — Combined raid on London by 12 Navy & 4 Army Zeppelins thwarted by adverse weather, navigational & technical problems; c16t bombs scattered across 11 counties & N London suburbs (only 16 cas). At 0223 2/Lt Leefe Robinson (awarded VC, first in Britain) in BE2 of No 39 Sqn RFC shoots down Army *SL 11* (Schramm) at Cuffley, Herts (all 16 crew k). **Occupied Belgium** — 17 RNAS aircraft drop 82 bombs on Ghistelles airfield SE of Ostend (repeated 9 & 23), St Denis Westrem attacked by 18 (7), Zeppelin sheds nr Brussels	**Neutrals: Greece** — Allies demand control of posts & telegraphs, Greece accepts (3). **Switzerland** — Germany to release 253,000t coal & steel for food. **USA** — Wilson nomination acceptance speech.	

SEPTEMBER 1916	WESTERN FRONT 1	EASTERN FRONT 2	SOUTHERN FRONTS 3	TURKISH FRONTS 4
Sat 2 contd				
Sun 3	**Somme — Fourth major joint Allied push** (to aid Rumania): At 1200 French Sixth Army attacks N of Somme, captures most of Cléry & German defences along road N to Le Forest & Le Forest village, but at jctn with BEF (on extreme left) little help possible & Germans launch strong counter-attacks (4). **Battle of Guillemont** (-6): large-scale British attack, 20th Div captures Guillemont & part of Mouquet Farm. Battle of Pozières Ridge ends. Continuous fighting nr Falfemont Farm. British attacks on Schwaben Redoubt & High Wood fail. **Verdun** — German attack fails on Vaux-Chapitre defences. French gradual if costly advances (-13). **Ypres** — Cdn Corps hands sector to I Anzac Corps & is switched to Somme (*see* 15 & 20).	**Carpathians** — Lechitski success nr Dorna Watra, takes 4500 PoWs SE of Halicz (5, see 7). **Dobruja** — Mackensen's tri-national Danube Army invades.		
Mon 4	**Somme** — Vain British attack on Falfemont Farm, Haig congratulates Rawlinson for finally capturing Guillemont. French VII Corps improves newly won positions round Cléry. S sector: French Tenth Army (Micheler) attacks S of river on new 5-mile sector from Chilly to Barleux, but gains little in heavy fighting (-6) except for Soyecourt (*see* 9).	**W Russia** — German gas attacks fail nr Baronovichi.	**Italian Front** — Cadorna issues orders for next Isonzo attack (*see* 14).	**Armenia** — RNAS armoured cars engage Kurds W of L Van.
Tue 5	**Somme** — British capture Falfemont Farm & link with French I Corps across Combles ravine (its attack to SE fails 6). French take Ferme de L'Hôpital (½-mile E of Le Forest). French VII Corps clears Cléry & links with XXXIII Corps (Sixth Army right wing) which has captured Ommiecourt (S bank of Somme). **Allies secure whole of German 2nd line**. They advance 1500 yds E of Guillemont & capture most of Leuze Wood. **Verdun** — Tavannes tunnel blows up killing 1000 French (news kept secret, *see* 13).	**Hungary** — Rumanian 1st Div occupies Orsova on Danube. **Dobruja** — Mackensen attacks Tutracaia fortress (its 15 forts taken 6) on S bank of Danube, with 25,000 PoWs (Rumanian 17th Div) & 115 guns for 7902 cas.	**Dolomites** — Italians have cleared Val Cismonfree.	
Wed 6	**Somme** — British capture Leuze Wood & advance to Ginchy. Asquith inspects Fricourt ruins; French guns smash 10 German counter-attacks SW of Barleux & S of Belloy.	**Transylvania** — Falkenhayn's Ninth Army formed (*see* 16). Rumanians occupy capital Hermannstadt.		
Thu 7		**Galicia** — Lechitski takes burning Halicz on Dniester. Turk XV Corps loses 1500 cas (-8, *see* 16) but stands firm after 10-mile retreat.		**Mesopotamia** — Col Grey made Director of Inland Water Transport. Tigris supplies 726t pd (18).
Fri 8	**Hindenburg & Ludendorff in first visit to W Front**, hold meeting at Cambrai (*see* 16) to develop new tactical doctrine of defence - in-depth; *OHL* publishes key lessons (25, *see* 1 Dec). **Somme** — Glos Regt suffers heavy cas in attack nr W end of High Wood. German			

AFRICAN OPERATIONS 5	SEA WAR 6	AIR WAR 7	INTERNATIONAL EVENTS 8	HOME FRONTS 9
		(27).		
Smuts to his wife 'We are having a terribly hard time'. German rearguard delays 2nd Div S of Kilosa. NRFF marches SE from Iringa, occupies Muhanga (11) and Hange (14, *see* 28).	**Unrestricted U-boat warfare to be postponed until peace initiative** (Pless council, Chancellor, Adm Holtzendorff, Hindenburg & Ludendorff present,*see* 25).	**Rumania** — Constanza bombed, Bulgars bomb Bucharest (5). **W Front** — RFC bombs 2 airfields & 4 other targets; helps engage 77 German btys. Lt Bowman (No 29 Sqn DH2) survives Fokker collision to score 32 victories in all. **E Front** — *Rfa 501* flies 1st mission: SSW R6 'Giant' with 2 escorts bombs Holodezne rail stn. R6 & similar R5 (delivered 4 Sept) are Brobdingnagian biplanes of ingenious design. Joined in spring 1917 by SSW R4 & R7, *Rfa 501* flies at least 17 raids (records incomplete) on rail stns, troop camps & supply dumps in adverse weather (-13).		
Fall of Dar-es-Salaam to RN who find 450 unarmed Germans & 4 wrecked steamers. GHQ there (12), British supplies by 4 Oct. Gold Coast Regt first in action (-6) taking Mt Kikarungu.			**Neutrals: Greece** — Compton Mackenzie interviews German Ambassador Baron Schenck (deported 7) & takes surrender of German Piraeus head agent (Capt Hoffmann). **USA** — Joint US-Mexican Commission begins work in New York (-15 Jan 1917).	**Britain** — TUC at Birmingham (-9) demands full rights back postwar, protests v military control of labour & cost of living. Balfour appeals to Glasgow shipyard unions (5).
Lake Force resumes advance S (-9), again marches 16 & reaches Ndala (25, *see* 28).				
		W Front — Flt Sgt McCudden (DH2 pilot in 29 Sqn) scores first of 57 victories in I Anzac Corps Ypres sector. RFC 5th Bde (2 lost) bomb 2 German airfields E of Bapaume, destroy 1 aircraft on ground.		**Germany** — Kaiserin doing her best to stop Kaiser getting bad news on blockade & harvest.
Actions nr Kisaki (-8): c2600 Germans & 22 MGs beat 1700 S Africans, forcing retreat & halt (-13). On coast British land & occupy both Kilwas 140 miles S of Dar-es-Salaam (1100 land & occupy Mikindani 120 miles S of Kilwa, 13).		**W Front** — RFC bombs 12 German airfields (6 twice).	**Neutrals: USA** — US Shipping Board created to form Govt-owned merchant fleet (*see* 22 Dec). Congress authorizes Wilson to retaliate v Britain, signs legislation (8). Emergency Revenue Act doubles normal income tax (8).	**France** — Lloyd George at Verdun, praises defence. Pres Poincaré visits 13, MC conferred on town.
	N Sea — Dover Patrol monitors shell Flanders coast between Middlekerke & Westende (-15) as diversion for Somme offensive.	**Flanders** — 3-4 German aircraft bomb 3 Allied airfields nr Dunkirk.		

SEPTEMBER 1916	WESTERN FRONT 1	EASTERN FRONT 2	SOUTHERN FRONTS 3	TURKISH FRONTS 4
Fri 8 contd	counter-attacks on Mouquet Farm (-12).			
Sat 9	German GHQ transferred from Charleville to Pless. **Somme — Battle of Ginchy**: British 16th (Irish) Div (Irish nationalist & poet Lt Tom Kettle k, aged 36) capture Ginchy, 7 miles E of Albert & trenches W & E of Leuze Wood. S sector: Germans begin counter-attacks v French Tenth Army round Berny & recover some ground (-12). Col Lossberg, CoS German First Army, awarded *Pour le Mérite* for outstanding W Front service.	**Pripet** — Kaiser visits Kovel, awards Hoffmann *Pour le Mérite*. **Transylvania** — Battle of Selimbar: Rumanians advance SW of Hermannstadt. **Dobruja** — Mackensen (Bulgar 1st Inf Div's cav) takes Silistria on Danube S bank.		
Sun 10	**Somme** — German counter-attack fails at Ginchy, British advance E of Guillemont, Rawlinson discusses tanks' role in forthcoming attack (*see* 15).	**Carpathians** — Pflanzer-Baltin sacked from Austrian Seventh Army, Kirchbach replaces. Austrians retreat W of the Gyergyo & Czik valley.	**Salonika** — 6 British dets demonstrate (161 cas) along R Struma, further cross-river raids (15 & 23).	
Mon 11	**Somme** — British guns detonate German munition dump nr Grandcourt. Rawlinson issues orders for 3rd great British assault (*see* 15).	**Gen Averyanov to STAVKA. '… we are close to complete exhaustion of the manpower reserve'. Carpathians** — Lechitski takes Mt Capel Kapul (5000 ft) & links with Rumanian Fourth Army (12). **Rumania** — Averescu given Third Army.	**Salonika** — Turk 50th Div (11,979 men, 16 guns & 12 MGs) begins taking over Drama seaward sector of Bulgar line.	**Mesopotamia** — Brooking's 1900 British (196 cas) & 14 guns beat c5000 Arabs (est 1200 cas) at As Sahilan NE of Nasiriya (Euphrates). **S Persia** — Sykes reaches Isfahan (*see* 11 Nov).
Tue 12	**Somme** — After 6-day delay (bad weather & muddy ground) French Sixth Army resumes offensive after Allied bombardment opens at 0600: 'Good progress' reported with Bois d'Anderu and Bouchavesnes captured on Bapaume-St Quentin road.		**Macedonia — Allied offensive begins** on W flank at 0600. Serb First Army captures foothills of Mt Kajmakcalan ('butter-churn') (8284 ft) 25 miles ESE of Monastir. Bulgars occupy Kavalla port. French 156th Div attacks W to Florina, 6 miles E by 17.	**Arabia** — Col Parker interviews sheikhs aboard HIMS *Dufferin* (-16) after seeing Feisal & 4000 riflemen nr Rabegh (9), see SEA WAR 13).
Wed 13	HINDENBURG ACHIEVES DE FACTO COMMAND OF CENTRAL POWERS' ARMIES (*see* INT'L EVENTS; 15). *OHL* (German Supreme Forces Cmnd) for the purpose becomes *OKL* (Supreme War Cmnd). **Somme** — French I Corps advance SE of Combles; VII Corps repulses heavy counter-attacks at Bouchavesnes. **Verdun** — At citadel Pres Poincaré confers Legion of Honour on the fortress 'against whose walls the highest ambitions of Imperial Germany have broken'; Pétain, Joffre, Nivelle & Mangin all present.		**Salonika** — British 65th Bde (22nd Div) storms German 59th Regt's Machukovo village salient, taking c70 PoWs & 9 MGs for 586 cas but loses it (-14).	**Mesopotamia** — Tigris Corps completes Sheikh Saad-Sinn rear lt railway (begun June). Maude opposes CIGS Tigris retreat to Amara idea (14).
Thu 14	**Somme** — British storm trenches SE of Thiepval & 11th Div the 'Wonderwork'. Haig & Rawlinson confer, Haig urges determined assault on Martinpuich. French I Corps captures Le Priez Farm; French XXIII & VII Corps both stalemated; 78 German counter-attacks since 1 (*see* 30).	**Transylvania** — Battle of Merisor-Petrosani (-22) N of Vulcan Pass: Rumanian First Army attacks towards Hatszeg. Austrian codebreakers get warning of Rumanian counter-attack.	**Italian Front — Seventh Battle of Isonzo** (-17): After lengthy arty preparation incl gas shells Italian Third Army (14 divs, 966 guns, 584 mortars) attacks at 0900 on 6-mile front, captures Nova Vas Hills 144, 265 & 208 (Carso) with 1800 PoWs, later regained by Austrians (Fifth Army, 101 bns & 409 guns). **Macedonia** — Italians & French make diversionary attacks in Doiran-Vardar sector. Serbs break through at Gornichevo on Florina road & capture 32 Bulgar guns.	
Fri 15	**Somme — Battle of Fiers-Courcelette** (-22): From 0620, after 40-min shelling, 14 divs (2	Rumanian Crown Council decides to transfer half Transylvanian Armies to face	**Dolomites** — Monte Rosa *Alpini* Bn captures Mt Cauriol (7605 ft) at 4th assault, then Mt	**Armenia** — Front stabilizes S of Ognot (*see* 26).

AFRICAN OPERATIONS 5	SEA WAR 6	AIR WAR 7	INTERNATIONAL EVENTS 8	HOME FRONTS 9
Main British (1st Div) advance reaches Tulo but Lettow's 2200 men & 24 MGs check it at R Dutumi (-12).		**Somme** — 25 German aircraft (2 lost) in air combat.	Pooling of Allied gold reserves announced. **Neutrals: Greece** — 'Greek reservists' shoot at French Athens legation, Govt apologises (11, for what is really a secret French ploy).	**Germany** — Hindenburg & Ludendorff meet industrialists Gustav Krupp & Carl Duisberg (IG Farben) to discuss workforce shortage & Hindenburg programme. **Austria** — Common Ministers Council discuss food crisis, War Minister mentions malnutrition signs in Army (*see* 10 Jan 1917).
British 2nd Div occupies Kidodi & halts with 1946/6696 men unfit. Belgian S Bde fights at Lulanguru (-12) in railway advance on Tabora.	Adm Haus & German U-boat chief Lt Kophamel at Pola agree to split German U-boats retroactively between own & Austrian flag for prize court legal purposes (Francis Joseph approves 1 Oct).	**W Front** — Unfavourable weather (-13).		
	Black Sea — 2 Bulgar torpedo boats hit Russian mines off Varna (1 sunk).		**Neutrals: Greece** — PM Zaimis resigns; Kalogeroulos succeeds (16).	British War Office sets up Demobilisation Dept.
Wahle's c2000 men retreat from Tabora (nights -18/19).	**Baltic** — Unsuccessful German torpedo plane attack on Russian battleship *Slava*.	**USA** — Curtiss tests **first radio-guided flying bomb**, a 40hp Hewitt-Sperry biplane (308lb bomb load).		
	N Sea — Admiralty reluctantly approves Jellicoe's strategy of retaining Grand Fleet N of Lat 55° 3' (Farne Is) to avoid losses to U-boats (*see* 18 Oct).	**Adriatic** — 22 Capronis with Italian-built Nieuport fighter escort bomb Trieste.	**Kaiser, Hindenburg, Bethmann, Enver & Tsar Ferdinand confer at Pless** (*see* 16).	**Germany** — *OHL* presents Chancellor & War Minister with demands for compulsory civil mobilisation (incl women) & military age increase to 50. Chancellor rejects (30, *see* 14 Oct).
British 3rd Div occupies Kisaki & rejoins 1st Div. Belgian N Bde loses 2 guns to Capt Wintgens NW of Tabora.				
7th SA Horse ford malarial R Mgeta, 5 miles E of Kisaki (*see* 19).	Due to Med losses Admiralty decides Salonika & EEF troops must travel overland via	**Adriatic** — FIRST SUBMA-RINE SUNK BY AIR ATTACK: 2 Austrian Lohner flying-boats		

SEPTEMBER 1916	WESTERN FRONT 1	EASTERN FRONT 2	SOUTHERN FRONTS 3	TURKISH FRONTS 4
Fri 15 contd	Cdn & 1 NZ) & 32 of 49 FIRST TANKS IN ACTION (5 ditched, 9 break down, 10 hit) advance 2000-3000 yds behind creeping barrage on 6-mile front capturing Flers, Martinpuich, Courcelette & High Wood by 1100 in German 3rd line. British Gds Div advance (Raymond Asquith, PM's son, k) towards Les Boeufs held up by 'Quadrilateral' (between Ginchy & Bouleux Wood). French I Corps inf advance at 1500 & make slight progress N of Priez Farm. Arty & MG fire halt French movement nr Rancourt. S sector: French Tenth Army renews its attacks S of Somme on Santerre Plateau, captures 3 villages (-17) & repulses frequent counter-attacks. Micheler regrets lack of reserves prevents follow-up ops. **Somme** — (Germans) 146 extra heavy guns sent to First & Second Armies & 144 worn-out guns replaced (-8 Oct). Hindenburg issues his 1st formal op order: 'The main task of the Armies is now to hold fast all positions on the Western, Eastern, Italian and Macedonian fronts and to employ all other available forces against Rumania'	Bulgaria. **Pripet/Galicia** — (c) Gen Kaledin & Eighth Army HQ transferred S to command, troops between Lechitski & Sakharov, Gourko's Special Army takes over Brusilov's N flank.	Gardinal (7723 ft) to NE (23), beats off Austrian attacks (-28).	
Sat 16	**Somme** — British repulse counter-attack nr Courcelette, but 5 German relief divs now oppose exploitation. Allies capture Dunibe Trench. NZ Div advances N & W of Flers. **Hindenburg** arrives at Cambrai, **orders construction of semi-permanent defence line (5-30 miles) to the rear** (Hindenburg Line, see 23).	**Galicia** — Second Battle of the Narajowka and Zlota Lipa (-17): 4 Russian divs with gas attack Turk XV Corps which holds despite c5000 cas (see 30). **Transylvania** — Rumanian Second Army occupies Baraoltu dominating Kronstadt-Földvar railway 30 miles from frontier. **Falkenhayn takes command of Ninth Army**. **Dobruja** — Mackensen attacks Rasova-Tuzla line (-20), but retires to re-stock with heavy shell. Turk 25th Div repulses Rumanian counter-attacks (22).	**Isonzo** — Italians capture San Grado di Merna, Hill 208S, & all Hill 144, but fail to take Hill 123 & Veliki Kribach farther E. **Macedonia** — Serbs v Bulgars in forest fighting on Mt Kajmakcalan foothills (-18). **Italy** — Lt Col Douhet, CoS Italian 5th Div & air power advocate, arrested for writing strong criticisms of *Comando Supremo* to War Minister; court-martial imprisons him for a year from 15 Oct (see AIR WAR 1 Jan 1918).	
Sun 17	**Somme** — British 15th Div consolidate gains at Martin-puich.		Italian offensive suspended due to bad weather after 17,000 cas & 4500 Austrian PoWs. Breaches in wire not wide enough for rapid inf assault (see 9 Oct). **Macedonia** — **Russian** Bde & **French** 57th Div **recapture Florina**; Bulgars retreat slightly N to R Brod by 20.	*Sinai* — Anzac Mtd Div attacks Mazar 45 miles E of Romani; 2200 Turks evacuate 18 miles to El Arish (19).
Mon 18	**Somme** — British Gds Div captures the 'Quadrilateral' (to depth of 1000 yds). French I Corps executes 2 successful local (evening) surprise attacks & gain ground S & SE of Combles.			*Sinai* — British raid Bir-el-Tawal 30 miles S of Kubri.
Tue 19	**Haig submits request to War Office for 1000 tanks. Somme** — French repulse counter-attacks E of Cléry (night 19/20).	**Galicia** — Shcherbachev's Seventh Army has taken 25,000 PoWs (8000 Germans) & 22 guns since 31 Aug. **Transylvania** — **Falkenhayn's Ninth Army attacks Rumanian First** in Merisor	**Macedonia** — Serb Drina Div takes Mt Kajmakcalan's 7769-ft E peak but evicted by Bulgars (26, see 30).	

AFRICAN OPERATIONS 5	SEA WAR 6	AIR WAR 7	INTERNATIONAL EVENTS 8	HOME FRONTS 9
	Marseilles, India units & Anzacs for Britain to go via Cape, system begins c20 Oct. More categories of trade switched, from 11 Dec. **Adriatic** — *see* AIR WAR. **Red Sea** — Cruiser HMS *Fox* shells & seaplanes strafe Wejh, Arabia, but Turks defiant.	bomb & sink French submarine *Foucault* , then land & save crew. **W Front** — RFC helps engage 85 German btys (29 silenced) & drops 8t bombs on 15 targets; claims 15 German aircraft, loses 14 aircrew & 6 aircraft. 2/Lt Ball destroys or forces down 10 German aircraft (-28, *see* 4 Oct). **S Tunisia** — 4 French Farmans bomb Senussi base, but 1 crashes.		
		Germany — Navy airships *L6* & *L9* destroyed in accidental fire on ground. **W Front** — RFC aircraft & balloon collide with fatal results.	**A German-led Central Powers Supreme War Council agreed** but Emperor Charles revokes Austrian signature after 21 Nov.	**Germany** — 39 industrialists tell War Ministry workers cannot exceed 9 hrs pd, Army to release skilled workers & 'open up the great Belgian labour basin' (*see* INT'L EVENTS 3 Oct). **Britain** — Churchill to Fisher 'My poor "land battleships" have been let off prematurely & on a petty scale. In that idea resided one real victory'.
		W Front — Capt O Boelcke leads **first combat patrol** of 6 *Jasta 2* **brand-new Albatros DII fighters** to shoot down 5 No 12 Sqn BE2cs (1 to Boelcke) returning from Marcoing stn raid. **Rich-thofen's first victory** is an (11 Sqn) FE2b escort (*see* 23). **Sinai** — German Fokker thwarts RN bombardment of El Arish by shooting down 2 Sopwith Baby seaplanes (another lost to MG ground fire) & bombing the 4 warships. But German sqn later withdrawn to Beersheba.	Greece demands German return of IV Corps (*see* S FRONTS 12).	
Belgians occupy Tabora (largest inland town) after 400-mile march, take 2000 captives & release c195 interned civilians (*see* 27). 2700 Portugese invade across R Rovuma, occupy Menasi Bay			New Greek PM offers to join Allies & enter war on fixed date as soon as Greek forces helped to prepare.	

SEPTEMBER 1916	WESTERN FRONT 1	EASTERN FRONT 2	SOUTHERN FRONTS 3	TURKISH FRONTS 4
Tue 19 contd		defile, drives it S of Petrosani (20), but Rumanian 11th Div counter-attack re-enters town (25).		
Wed 20	**Somme** — Rawlinson delays next Fourth Army attack to 23, he & Haig agree that British cav should be withdrawn. Fierce German counter-attack almost retakes Bouchavesnes but driven out after desperate fighting. Cdn Corps pull out of line after 6000 cas but fighting again 26 (*see* 28).	**Rumania requests French Military Mission** (*see* 15 Oct), now 38 Central Powers divs facing her. **Pripet** — Germans repulsed nr Kovel-Rovno railway & along R Stokhod.	**Macedonia** — Allied advance hampered by fodder shortage, waiting for arty, & Bulgar fortified San Marco monastery 2 1/2 miles NW of Florina (*see* 2 Oct). Today Sarrail's target day for Monastir's fall (17 miles N).	
Thu 21	**Somme** — NZ troops take 'Cough Drop Alley' & a section of Flers line. British 1st Div captures Starfish Trench.			
Fri 22	**Somme** — Battle of Flers-Courcelette ends. British advance E of Courcelette on fine sunny day. Robertson & Rawlinson take tea; CIGS intimates that Lloyd George concerned about cas toll & Haig's direction of battle.			**Arabia** — Ghalib Pasha's 2000-Turk Taif garrison surrenders to Abdulla.
Sat 23	HINDENBURG LINE BEGUN (*see* AIR WAR 9 Nov). **Somme** — Rawlinson postpones today's ops to 25. British 23rd Div advances E of Martinpuich.		**Italian Front** — Italian XVIII Corps captures Mt Cardinal (*see* 2 Oct) in Cadore area but Austrian mine explosion regains Mt Cimone d'Arsiero (Astico valley, Trentino) lost 23 July.	
Sun 24	**Somme** — British repulse counter-attack W of Lesboeufs.			
Mon 25	**Somme** — **Battle of Morval** (-28): Allied attack at 1235. British with 2 tanks capture Lesboeufs & Morval & almost surround Combles. Slight French Sixth Army advance at Rancourt (captured), Les Priez Farm & Frégicourt (-26).			
Tue 26	**Somme** — Battle of Thiepval Ridge (-28): British with 13 tanks capture Thiepval (18th Div German soldier writes '... it was absolutely crushing'), Combles (56th Div with 2 tanks and 2 French regts) & Gird Trench; **first air-tank co-operation** with 21st Div at Guedecourt (400 PoWs) captures 500 yds of trench for 5 cas. Foch redirects main	**Transylvania** — Battle of Hermannstadt (-29): **Falken-hayn's Ninth Army attacks in fine weather towards Roten-turm Pass** (11,555 ft) which German *Alpenkorps* crosses, **Hermannstadt retaken** (29), 3000 Rumanian PoWs in First Army defeat.		**Armenia** — **First snow falls**. Turks evacuate Mus, their Second Army losses 30,000 (since 2 Aug) reducing it to 60,000. Russian losses 50,000 since June incl Persia. Early winter quarters for both sides.

AFRICAN OPERATIONS 5	SEA WAR 6	AIR WAR 7	INTERNATIONAL EVENTS 8	HOME FRONTS 9
(29). 1st Div KAR ford R Mgeta (bridged 25) but floods & strong defence restrict bridgehead till Dec.				
249 British from Wiedhaven on L Nyasa occupy Songea.	**Baltic** — Much abler Vice Adm A J Nepenin replaces Kanin as Russian Baltic Fleet C-in-C, but Supreme War Council forbids intensified submarine offensive.	**W Front** — Rain most of the day. **Salonika** — RFC No 47 Sqn & balloon section land.	Essad Pasha's Albanian Govt set up at Salonika. **Occupied Poland** — Polish Legions made Austrian Army formations and not recognized as Polish Army (*see* 5 Nov).	**Britain** — Railway workers given 5s pw extra after strike threat; women get war wage for 1st time (3s pw). **Germany** — 1st issue of *Spartakus* published.
	N Sea — German warships capture *SS Colchester* (Dutch convoy straggler) & take her into Zeebrugge.	(c) Kaiser opposes air raids on Italian cities, 2 Navy Zeppelins not transferred to Austria who lack spare suitable aircrew.		**Turkey** — Export Commission created to control trade. **Britain** — Manpower Distribution Board formed (*see* 19 Dec).
Advance GHQ War Diary: 'Very heavy [since 20] rains are reported from all quarters ... the best that can be hoped ... is to prevent them [troops] starving for the next week or 10 days'.		**Somme** — After another victory Guyenemer's Spad 7 hit by French 75mm AA fire, but only suffers bruised knee on landing. Richthofen scores 2nd victory, a Martinsyde of 27 Sqn (3 lost to *Jasta 2* for 1 Albatros collision). **Mesopotamia** — RFC bomb Shumran bend German airfield nr Kut, destroy 1 aircraft on ground (another hit 2 Nov). **Britain** — 9 of 12 Zeppelins reach E England (night 23/24), drop 371 bombs causing 170 civ cas (151 in London) but *L33* forced to crash-land after AA & fighter hits, *L32* shot down in Essex by 2/Lt F Sowsey in RFC BE2c (39 Sqn). For many subsequent nights Londoners take refuge in underground railway from 1730.		**Russia** — Tsar approves creation of Public Health Ministry. **France** — French & Chinese workers clash in Le Creusot works.
		W Front — 60 RFC fighters (3 lost) destroy 4+ German aircraft, in group attacks on Cambrai area airfields. **France** — Dunkirk has 17 cas to German bombs (1 raider shot down). **Germany** — 2 French aircraft drop 12 bombs on Krupp, Essen.		**Canada** — £20m war loan £16m over-subscribed.
Tripolitania — Sultan's Gov-Gen of N Africa Suleiman-el-Baruni lands at Misurata from U-boat, establishes 'Republic of Tripoli' (*see* 16 Jan 1917).	Bethmann informs Count Bernstorff, Ambassador to USA, that unrestricted U-boat warfare remains an option 'to relieve the Somme front and bring England to her knees'.	**Somme** — RFC 4th Bde helps silence 34 German btys. 1st Bde (17 aircraft) hits 2 troop trains, Libercourt stn (Douai-Lille main line) & 2nd Bde Lille stn (night 25/26). **Britain** — 6 of 9 Zeppelins drop 127 bombs on Lincs, Yorks & Lancs (74 cas night 24/25). *L31* (Mathy) scouts Portsmouth.	**Neutrals: Greece** — **Venizelos** & Adm **Koundouri-otis** sail for Crete (rebelled 24) escorted by French torpedo boat; **form provisional govt** (29).	**Britain** — British Army Council requisitions leather. **Ireland** — W B Yeats writes 'Easter 1916' poem.
		Somme — German inf surrender to RFC contact patrol aircraft; No 60 Sqn Nieuports destroy 2 German kite-balloons with Le Prieur rockets & 7 RFC crews strafe troops (6 on 27).		

SEPTEMBER 1916	WESTERN FRONT 1	EASTERN FRONT 2	SOUTHERN FRONTS 3	TURKISH FRONTS 4
Tue 26 contd	French attack due N on Sailly - Sallisel (V Corps covers their right flank) but launched at 1600 achieves little (vainly repeated 27). (c) Fayolle tries to resign due to this failure.			
Wed 27	**Somme** — British attack Stuff Redoubt & advance N of Flers. Thiepval (ruins) captured by British after hand-to-hand fighting. **Verdun** — French repulse attack at Thiaumont-Fleury.			CIGS vetoes British troops for Rabegh unless Arab Revolt collapses.
Thu 28	**Somme** — British capture most of Schwaben Redoubt & Cdn Corps advance 1000 yds N & NE of Courcelette (-30). French advance at Morval.			**S Persia** — Action at Saidabad: c250 British & 1 gun beat c300 tribesmen & take town SW of Kerman.
Fri 29	**Somme** — British capture strongly fortified Destremont Farm. Col H Elles, aged 36, appointed to cmnd British tank force. Haig orders offensive for 12 Oct.	**Transylvania** — Battle of Praid-Sovata (-3 Oct): **Second Army launches last Rumanian offensive.**	**Macedonia** — Gen Cordonnier comes under Bulgar fire on recce 5 miles N of Florina (horse w), gets Sarrail to postpone attack from 30 to 3 Oct (*see* 5 Oct).	
Sat 30	**Somme** — British now hold all Thiepval Ridge except part of Schwaben Redoubt, advance S of Eaucourt l'Abbaye. The 6 German divs from Le Transloy to the Ancre are replaced (-13 Oct) by 9 (4 from Verdun, 2 from Flanders, 3 from Belgium). German guns fired 7,027,440 shells in Sept, 126 counter-attacks made.	**Galicia** — Battle of Brzezany (-2 Oct): III Caucasus Corps attacks Turk XV Corps, which loses 5045 men but regains positions & takes 500 PoWs (*see* 6 Oct).	**Macedonia** — **Serb Drina Div** finally captures both Mt Kajmakcalani peaks (*see* 2 Oct) **just inside Serbia**. British 27th Div (364 cas) launches major attack across R Struma via 2 bridges (laid 29), capturing villages SW of Seres road & 250 PoWs with 3 MGs (*see* 1 Oct).	**Mesopotamia** — CIGS cables C-in-C India '... no fresh advance to Baghdad can at present be contemplated'. **India: NW Frontier** — Blockade of Mohmands begins.
Sun 1 October 1916	(Oct) German Army now has 205 divs (198 in Sept), 128 in W. **Somme** — **Battle of the Transloy Ridges** (-18): British Fourth Army advance with 5 tanks between Eaucourt & Le Sars (on Albert-Bapaume rd) on 3000-yd front. **Battle of the Ancre Heights** (-11 Nov) begun by Fifth Army with 4 tanks.	**Transylvania** — Battle of Petrosani (-3): Rumanians retreat to frontier. Falkenhayn put i/c Austrian first Army (Arz) as well.	**Trentino** — Italians take trenches in Val Transvenanzis, successes in Travignolo & Pellegrino valleys (4-5), Avisio region. **Salonika** — British repel Bulgar attacks on their Struma bridgehead (-2, *see* 3).	**Armenia** (Oct) — Turk Third Army (reformed into 6 divs of I & II Caucasian Corps) has 50,000 deserters till heavy snow forces many back for food. Kemal takes over Second Army which loses 2 divs to Mesopotamia & 3 more dissolved. Turks muster only c94,000 yet Russians estimate 344,000 so Yudenich overmans winter lines.
Mon 2	**Somme** — German counter-attack at Eaucourt. British lose Le Sars, weather breaks: 'rain fell in torrents , and the battle area became a sea of mud...	**Carpathians** — 2 regts of VII Siberian Corps twice refuse to attack (-3); 3 soldiers shot & 6 imprisoned; **1st of 12+ mutinies** (-13 Jan 1917).	*Alpini* seize crests of Mts Colbricon, Costabella (5), over 6000 ft. **Albania** — Italians occupy Santa Quaranta on coast (-4) & Premeti inland (9).	

AFRICAN OPERATIONS 5	SEA WAR 6	AIR WAR 7	INTERNATIONAL EVENTS 8	HOME FRONTS 9
Belgians occupy Sikonge & Ipole before retiring to Tabora. **Ethiopia** — Muslim 'Emperor' Lij Yasu, focus of Turco-German intrigue (supporters defeated by 2 Nov) deposed for Empress Judith; Ras Tafari (Haile Selassie) regent & heir to throne (*see* 11 Feb 1917). 450 Lake Force KAR reach Central Railway E of Tabora. NRFF repels 5 German coys at Mkapira but recrosses R Ruhuje.			Austrian Foreign Minister Burian submits peace offer proposals to Francis Joseph's 'most sympathetic attention' (*see* 18 Nov).	**Germany** — Hindenburg letter to Bethmann urges proper feeding of workers. **Austria** — German Ambassador describes economic climate as 'simply wretched'; Bethmann forwards to Kaiser (30). **Britain** — Asquith pledges not to recruit skilled workers. Board of Trade organizes overland delivery of Italian fruit & veg. Munitions holiday (-1 Oct) replaces postponed Whitsuntide & Aug holidays. Churchill appears before Dardanelles Commission (*see* 17 Oct). Tory *Morning Post* tells Lloyd George to stick to his desk in Whitehall.
		RFC losses 1195 aircraft since 12 June, 1725 gained. RFC personnel losses 415 (all causes) since 12 June.	German Hague Ambassador Kühlmann appointed to Constantinople.	
Smuts writes to Gov Schnee & Lettow suggesting honourable surrender & personal meeting; both refuse. **⅔rds of German colony now in British hands.**	Allied Sept shipping losses 315,000t (British 42 ships worth 104,572t with 20 lives lost) incl 45 ships worth 229,163t in Med to U-boats (*see* 31 Oct).	**W Front** — German Sept losses 27 aircraft to 123 Anglo-French, RFC attacks 3 airfields. Trenchard writes to War Office via Haig for more numerous efficient fighters. RFC has flown a record 22,500 hrs (Sept) & suffered record 147 cas. RFC takes 500 air photos of the Somme. (Sept) French Army retires its airships after c60 sorties, they are transferred to anti-U-boat patrol work.		**Britain** — Winding up of enemy banks worth £58.8m to date. **Germany** — War Ministry unifies 3 procurement agencies into Weapons & Munitions Procurement Office.
E Africa — British begin to evacuate 12,000-15,000 malaria cases (-31). Over 12,000 S Africans sent home. **W Africa** (Oct) — The King of Nikki rebels v French. In Cameroons French Holy Ghost Fathers replace German Pallotine Fathers. **Morocco** (Oct) — *U20* off R Dra just fails to land arms for tribesmen in S.	**Med** — Kaiser telegram congratulates U-boats on sinking over 1mt shipping (*see* 6). **Secret War: W Med** — *U35* fetches German agent Lt Canaris from sailing boat off Cartagena for return (*see* 4) to Germany from Spain; she sinks new British-built French sloop *Rigel* off Algiers (2). (Oct) 119 U-boats in service, 96 available for ops (*see* 6). Flanders new longer-ranged UBII-type boats sink 298 ships (104 neutral) worth 289,558t (-31 Jan 1917) esp British colliers supplying French industry (39% reduction, *see* 10 Jan 1917). UCII minelayers lay 128 new minefields (953 mines) that sink 60 (13 neutral) ships worth 82,379t between Flamborough Head (British E Coast) & Gironde estuary (SW France, *see* 6 & 29).	**Britain** — 7 of 11 Zeppelins drop 201 bombs (57 on London), 2 civ cas: 2/Lt WJ Tempest in BE2 of No 39 Sqn RFC shoots down Navy airship *L31* (Mathy) at Potters Bar, N of London, 19 dead, no survivors (night 1/2).		**Russia** — Protopopov made Interior Minister at Tsarina's urging. **Britain** — RFP up 3% to 68%. Churchill letter thanks Conan Doyle for praising his tank efforts. **Turkey** — Papers publish CUP Conference's defence of Armenian policy.
	Arctic — *U43, 46* & *48* carry out 8-day op against Allied shipping off N Cape & Murmansk coast; 14 ships sunk, 9 captured. (In summer	**W Front** — Rain & strong W winds reduce air ops (-7), low clouds 11 & 13.		

OCTOBER 1916	WESTERN FRONT 1	EASTERN FRONT 2	SOUTHERN FRONTS 3	TURKISH FRONTS 4
Mon 2 contd	men died from the effort of carrying verbal messages' (official historian Gen Edmonds). Preparations for another great British attack c12 are soon abandoned. **German First Army report recommends that Germany produce her own tanks.** Haig tells Pres Poincaré that Germans must not be given 'a moment's peace'.	**Transylvania** — Rumanian First Army breaks through Rotenturm Pass taking 3000 Bavarian PoWs & 13 guns. **Rumania** — Manoeuvre of Flamandra: Averescu crosses Danube v Mackensen's rear, takes 13 guns, but poor bridges, Austrian monitors, & sudden flood force withdrawal (-3).	**Salonika** — Bulgar poet Dimcho Debelyanov k, aged 29, in action with British between Dolno and Gorno villages.	
Tue 3	**Somme** — Successful British 47th Div counter-attack at Eaucourt l'Abbaye. **Verdun** — 800 French guns begin silencing German arty (-20).	**Pripet** — Russian Eighth Army gains some ground W of Lutsk (-5). **Transylvania** — Battle of Kronstadt & the Geisterwald (-9): Falkenhayn attacks Rumanian Second Army, forces it from Fogaras (6) & retakes Kronstadt (8), takes Törzburg and pass (8-9). Rumanian Fourth Army continues advance in N.	**Macedonia** — Bulgars retreat to R Crna line (night 2) after general Allied attack. British capture Yenikoi village E of Struma & hold v Bulgar attacks (-4), cas 1248 since 30 Sept, 1375 Bulgars k, 342 PoWs taken.	**Arabia** — Sherif Hussein shown HMG-Ibn Saud Treaty, furious (*see* 30).
Wed 4	**Somme** — Heavy rain & increasingly poor ground postpones Rawlinson's planned offensive ops for 48 hrs.			
Thu 5	**Somme** — British advance NW of Eaucourt; French advance E of Morval. **Verdun** — *OHL* letter to German Crown Prince decrees that 'every unnecessary saphead and length of trench must be evacuated' to spare troops for the Somme (*see* 20).		**Macedonia** — Gen Cordonnier scouts Bulgar defences from French plane (early instance of general making personal air reconnaisance).	**E Persia** — Tanner replaces Dyer as GOC Seistan force.
Fri 6	**Somme** — Haig informs Rawlinson that he will prolong battle until winter (weather permitting).	**Galicia** — Third Battle of the Narajowka and Zlota Lipa: Russian Seventh Army attacks Turk XV Corps (3015 cas).	**Trentino** — *Alpini* Bn repulse counter-attacks on Busa Alta (-10). **Macedonia** — Allied attack on Sarrail's orders, only Serbs gain shallow Crna bridgehead at Brod for heavy losses (-7, *see* 14) but Germans move 3 bns to sector from Vardar (-10 qv) after Bulgar bn opposite Serbs mutinies.	
Sat 7	**Somme** — Franco-British attack at 1345 on Albert-Bapaume road. British advance 1000 yds & 23rd Div recaptures Le Sars; 5 divs in attacks on Butte de Warlencourt (-5 Nov). French advance NE of Morval & threaten Sailly (gains there 8, fighting in village 16-17).			
Sun 8	**Somme** — British advance N & E of Courcelette; German counter-attack achieves slight success. Canadians capture, then lose, Regina Trench & the 'Quadrilateral'.	**Rumania** — Kaufmann's Germans occupy Danube I nr Ruschuk.	**Italian Front** — Arty active on whole front.	
Mon 9	**Somme** — British advance E of Le Sars towards Butte de Warlencourt, 25th Div captures Stuff Redoubt (*see* 20).	German Twelfth Army disbanded. **Galicia** — *Südarmee* counter-attacks E of Brzezany.	**Eighth Battle of the Isonzo** (-12): Italian Second & Third Armies' 225 bns, 26 dismtd sqns, 1305 guns & 883 mortars v Austrian Fifth Army 107 bns & 538 guns. Bombardment begins. **Trentino** — Italians regain N slope of Mt Pasubio, more progress in Vallarsa valley (11 15, 17), repel counter-attacks (19); 372	

AFRICAN OPERATIONS 5	SEA WAR 6	AIR WAR 7	INTERNATIONAL EVENTS 8	HOME FRONTS 9
	600 steamers - mainly British - have delivered 1mt of coal & 1½ mt supplies to Russia.) In response, 3 RN submarines operate from Archangel (*see* 2 Nov).			
	Irish Sea — U-boat lays mines off the Clyde (also Isle of Man, Nov).		Kaiser thinks unlimited U-boat war would be 'suicide'. **Occupied Belgium** — Gov-Gen Bissing decrees **forced labour in Germany for Belgian unemployed**, 15,000 deported by 24, 50,000 by 19 Nov (*see* 9 Nov). **Neutrals: Greece** — Kalogeropoulos resigns, more officers leave to join Venizelos in Crete (2). **Spain** — RN Intelligence agent AEW Mason worries about promising British decorations to Spaniards.	
	E Med — *U35* (Arnauld) sinks French auxiliary cruiser *Gallia* (14,900t) off Cape Matapan, carrying 2000 French & Serb troops. Panic ensues, 600 dead. *UB47* (Steinbauer) sinks empty British (ex-Cunard) troopship *Franconia* (18,150t) 195 miles SE of Malta, 12 lost.	**W Front** — 2/Lt Ball posted back to England with 9 victories since May incl possible (1).		**Austria** — Richard Strauss' opera *Ariadne auf Naxos* opens in Vienna. **Britain** — Women offered free munitions work training.

France — 2nd War Loan (-29) earns Fr 10bn. |
| **E Africa** — Deventer's patrols reach Malongwe & Lake Force, **whole Central Railway in Allied hands.** First trolley vehicle reaches Dodoma. | **High Seas Fleet U-boats ordered to resume merchant shipping targeting**, but no torpedoeing without warning (-31 Jan 1917) also to send 4 more U-boats to Med (after 22 Aug request for 3, *see* 25). | | | **Germany** — Centre Party clears Chancellor in advance for liability for unlimited U-boat war. **France** — Uncultivated land, buildings & farm animals requisitioned. **Britain** — Substitution scheme for unfit soldiers to go into agriculture.

Turkey — Provisional Law of Agricultural Service promulgated. |
| **E Africa** — 2/2nd KAR from Kilwa occupy Njinjo (42 miles away) & win skirmish (9).

E Africa — British proclamation on justice. **Ethiopia** — Govt troops occupy Harar after Pretender Yasu flees. | FIRST U-BOAT SINKING OFF US COAST: 5 merchant ships (3 British, 1 Dutch, 1 Norwegian) worth 20,388t captured & sunk off Newport (Rhode I) by *U53* (Rose) after refuelling there (left base 17 Sept, returns 20 Oct, *see* 18 Nov). | **Germany** — AIR FORCE (*LUFTSTREITKRAFTE*) ESTABLISHED: Imperial Order in Council to amalgamate 'all means of air combat and air defence with the Army, in the field and in the home areas, into one unit' (*see* 15 Nov). | Archduke Charles summoned to meet Kaiser at OHL (Pless), imminent Central Powers peace offer discussed, *see* 14 & 18)

Neutrals: Greece — **Venizelos arrives in Salonika, forms provisional govt** (10, Allies recognise 16); Lambros heads new official govt (8). | **Britain** — **Prohibition on Sunday munitions work in force.** |

OCTOBER 1916	WESTERN FRONT 1	EASTERN FRONT 2	SOUTHERN FRONTS 3	TURKISH FRONTS 4
Mon 9 contd			PoWs & 8 guns taken.	
Tue 10	**Somme** — (S) French Sixth Army resumes offensive (-21); woods captured NW of Chaulnes & ground gained toward 3 villages with 1400 PoWs on 3½-mile frontage; repulses counter-attacks at Bois de Chaulnes taking 1702 PoWs (11).	**Tsar's order officially ends Brusilov Offensive** (but *see* 16). **Transylvania** — Averescu takes over Second Army which halts in Predeal Pass (3415 ft).	Gen Otto von **Below made Army Group cdr for Macedonia** (-22 Apr 1917, HQ Uskub = Skopje) to stiffen Bulgars, requests reinforcements (20); 6 bns (3 *Jäger*) & 48 guns sent from W & E Fronts, formed into Div Hippel by mid-Nov. Another 6 bns follow from W Front (*see* 18). **Isonzo** — Italians attack at 1450 in pouring rain, capturing in Austrian 1st line 5034 PoWs, Hills 86 & 95, Mt Sober (E of Gorizia), Nova Vas village & Hill 144 (Carso). Futurist architect Antonio Sant' Elia k, aged 28.	**Mesopotamia** — **New C-in-C India Monro** (appointed 1) at Basra, visits Tigris Front, cables CIGS (19) that forward positions easy to maintain. **Arabia** — Feisal's 7000 Arabs retreat SW from Bir Abbas to Hamra before Turk advance from Medina (actually 80 camel-men).
Wed 11		**Transylvania** — First Battle of Oituz (-27): Rumanian Fourth Army (Prézan) eventually halts Arz's Austro-Germans on border (22).	**Isonzo** — Thick fog prevents fighting.	
Thu 12	**Somme** — British attack on 4-mile front Eaucourt-Bapaume, gain 500-1000 yds. French have taken 40,125 PoWs since 1 July (announced 19).		**Isonzo** — Italians push Austrians E of R Vallano. Ops suspended in evening after total of 8200 PoWs taken in 2-mile advance for 24,000 cas (*see* 31). **Salonika** — British War Office Ctee 'We have had to deal with a specially virulent...malarial infection in a body of troops unseasoned to tropical conditions' (304 1916 deaths to 11 Nov, *see* 5 Nov).	
Fri 13		**Transylvania** — Rumanian Second Army checks pursuers in Predeal (town falls) & Bodza Passes, but **Falkenhayn** advances through Törzburg Pass to Rucar **6 miles inside Rumania. Rumanians forced from Transylvania except in NE**. Germans also enter gap between Rumanian Fourth Army & Lechitski. **Hungary** — Archduke Charles opens HQ at Grosswardein.		
Sat 14	**Somme** — French gains S of river on 1¼-mile front. British 39th Div finally captures Schwaben Redoubt.		**Macedonia** — Allied frontal assault fails to take a single Bulgar trench despite gas shell use; French 1490 cas, Russian 600. Sarrail has final row with Cordonnier, cables Joffre (16) who agrees to recall him (19); Gen Leblois takes over (20).	
Sun 15	**Somme** — German gains nr Schwaben Redoubt & Thiepval. Rawlinson inspects Longueval, Delville Wood & High Wood & discerns stiffening German resistance. (S) Gen Micheler (French Tenth Army) complains of being starved of reserves & 'reduced to the role of a watchdog for Fayolle' (Sixth Army).	Alexeiev reports to Tsar only 1.4m reserves after 1 Nov, ie under 5 months supply. **Galicia** — *Südarmee's* Battle of Lower Narajowka (-22). **Rumania** — Gen Berthelot arrives at Bucharest (French Military Mission left Paris 1, eventually 1200 strong); (*see* AIR WAR), having seen Alexeiev (11) at Mogilev who urges Rumanians to hold R Sereth not the Carpathians I (*see* 20 Jan 1917).		**Sinai** — 2300 British & 2 guns raid Magharah in S.

AFRICAN OPERATIONS 5	SEA WAR 6	AIR WAR 7	INTERNATIONAL EVENTS 8	HOME FRONTS 9
W Desert — Senussi leader Sheikh Ahmed leaves Baharia Oasis for Siwa (*see* 17).		**W Front** — BEF rifle fire brings down German aircraft nr Souchez, 500 RFC photos taken of 4 stns attacked (c100k at Douai), 2 more at night (11/12).	**Neutrals: Greece** — **Allied ultimatum for Greek Fleet's surrender** by noon (11, *see SEA WAR*) plus all but 3 coast batteries & Piraeus-Larissa railway, **accepted** (11).	**France** — Insurance law for soldiers. **Britain** — Royal Commission on Wheat & Flour Control appointed, appeals for as much wheat sowing as possible (14). Commons votes £300m war credit.
E Africa — 1/2nd KAR defeat c76 Germans in Kilwa push to Ft Kibata (seized 14).	**Greek Fleet disarmed**: 2 battleships & armoured cruiser *Averoff* stripped of shells & breech blocks, crews reduced to 1/3. Allies tow cruiser *Helle*, 19 destroyers & torpedo boats, 2 submarines & 12 auxiliaries to Keratsini. French hoist tricolour on them & occupy Salamis Arsenal (7 Nov). **N Sea** — **Norway prohibits belligerent submarines from using her territorial waters.** (Ban extended to all foreign submarines 1 Feb 1917).		Asquith's speech on 'No patched-up peace'. **Neutrals: USA** — Council of National Defense formed.	
		Germany — No 3 Wing RNAS, **1st British strategic bombing unit**, flies 1st major op from Luxeuil (Vosges) with 21 aircraft (3 lost) v Mauser Oberndorf small-arms factory (*see* 23); 34 French aircraft (6 lost) participate. German fighters attack there & back (*see* 23). **W Front** — Canadian RNAS Collishaw scores 1st of 60 victories.	**Neutrals: Greece** — Adm Fournet demands Allied control of police, no Greek citizens to carry arms, no war material to Thessaly, but wheat exports can be resumed (*see* 16).	**Britain** — Lloyd George in Commons says too many call-up exemptions being granted. (c) **Army Reserve Munitions Workers Scheme begun to release unskilled workers under 30.**
			Neutrals: Norway — Belligerent submarines prohibited from territorial waters (*see* 4 Nov).	**Russia** — **Worst month for strikes**, 189 (177 political) involve 189,776 strikers. **Germany** — 30,101 British PoWs. **Britain** — 39,020 German PoWs.
	Black Sea — Russian submarine captures Turk armed transport *Rodosto*. **Med** — RN SNO Malta Rear-Adm Ballard proposes 3 convoys pw system to Admiralty who study it but French C-in-C opposes (*see* 11 Jan 1917).		Conrad memo to Francis Joseph's military cabinet chief on Ludendorff 'He is attributed with the statement "Germany's victory prize...must be Austria"', warns of 'Bismarckian ruthlessness'.	**Turkey** — Maximum bread prices fixed, but removed due to black market (21).
Morocco — Sultan opens great fair at Fez, Lyautey gains many notables' loyalty (*see* 1 Nov).		**W Front** — Lt N Prince (5 victories), American creator of *Esc Lafayette*, dies of wounds. **Somme** — 333 German aircraft support First Army v 293 RFC (W Front totals RFC 563, German c885 of which 451 v French).		

OCTOBER 1916	WESTERN FRONT 1	EASTERN FRONT 2	SOUTHERN FRONTS 3	TURKISH FRONTS 4
Mon 16	**Somme** — Frosty nights (16/17 to 20/21). No Allied ops.	**Pripet** — **Last blow of Brusilov Offensive**: Gourko's Special Army attacks on 12-mile front towards Vladimir-Volinski (-17) but German artillery too powerful. **Carpathians** — Austrian Seventh Army attacks Russo-Rumanian junction, Germans take Gyimen Pass (2364ft). Austro-German mtn troops fail to breakout across Rotenturm Pass (-18).		**Arabia** — **Capt T E Lawrence of Arab Bureau lands at Jeddah** from HMS *Lama* ; meets Abdulla & Ali (17, *see* 24). So far Arabs have received 3260 rifles, 32 MGs, 16 guns & 3344t food.
Tue 17		**Rumania** — Austrian VI Corps reaches Agas 8 miles inside frontier, but Austrians beaten in Uzul Valley (& 27).		
Wed 18	**Somme** — Battle of the Transloy Ridges ends: British advance from 0340 N of Guedecourt & French take Sailly. French XXXIII Corps (Sixth Army) attacks S of Somme to broaden French salient at La Maisonnette (SE of Biaches), but Germans push it back (21). Joffre urges a continued powerful BEF offensive (Haig & Rawlinson met 17 & had intended to suspend ops 20).	Successful Rumanian 1st Div attack in R Aluta (Orsova) area; no Austrian attack till 28.	**Serbia** — Serbs capture Veljeselo 1½ miles N of Brod, repel German counter-attack (350+ cas, 20 & 22).	**Egypt** — GHQ moves to Cairo from Ismailia where Lt-Gen Dobell's new Eastern Force HQ opens.
Thu 19	**Somme** — Prolonged heavy rain turns parts of battlefield into quagmires. Planned British Reserve Army attack postponed 48 hrs.	**Dobruja** — Battle of Topraisar-Cobadinu (-21): **Mackensen breaks through causing Rumanian retreat** astride Russians & takes Tuzla on coast (20).		
Fri 20	**Somme** — **Coldest day of battle so far**. British repulse heavy counter-attacks on Schwaben & Stuff Redoubts. **Verdun** — Nivelle commits 603 guns (incl 2 15.7-in rail guns v forts) & 15,000t of shells to shelling 3½-mile front; they silence all but 100 of c450 German guns (-24) using 530,000 75mm & 100,000 155mm shells.			**Arabia** — McMahon gives Wingate political control of revolt (*see* 6 Dec).
Sat 21	**Somme** — British advance taking 5000 yds of trenches (1018 PoWs) between Schwaben Redoubt & Le Sars & 39th Div captures Stuff Trench.	**Transylvania** — Falkenhayn drives Rumanian Second Army 12 miles across frontier at Törzburg Pass, Austrians 7 miles inside via Bodza Pass.	**Macedonia** — Rains & fogs turn Kenali & Crna sectors into a Greek Flanders, postponing ops till Nov (*see* 10 Nov).	
Sun 22	Joffre sees Haig, brief row soon ends, as former wants pressure kept up during winter, however done. **Somme** — In bitter cold, French capture slight ridge W of Sailly.	**Galicia** — Stiff fighting N of Halicz (-23). **Dobruja** — CONSTANZA FALLS to Mackensen with much grain & oil.	**Macedonia** — Italian *Cagliari* Bde begins move from E of L Doiran to Florina sector by lorry over appalling roads (*see* 18 Nov).	
Mon 23	**Somme** — British capture 1000yds of trenches towards Transloy. **Verdun** — Germans evacuate battered Ft Douaumont as untenable (night 23/24).	**Rumania** — Battle of Tirgu Jiu (-29) S of Vulcan Pass which Falkenhayn storms (24) despite snow.	**Salonika** — 300 British (34 cas) trench raid German Porsale position (52 cas), thrice-wounded Pte H W Lewis wins theatre's first VC (*see* 31).	
Tue 24	**Verdun** — **First Offensive Battle of Verdun** (-18 Dec): Nivelle & Mangin send 3 picked & compass-guided divs (29 bns) to assault 7 tired & depleted German divs (16 bns in front line) through mist, **reoccupy Ft Douaumont** & capture 6000 PoWs (*see* 26). May positions regained.	**Rumania** — Falkenhayn S of Törzburg Pass & fighting nr Kimpulung. **Dobruja** — Mackensen reaches Mejidia on Danube-Black Sea railway, occupies Cernavoda on Danube after Rumanians blow bridge (25).	**Macedonia** — French (SW of L Prespa) contact Italian cav at Koritsa, Allied line now loosely across Balkans (*see* 12 Feb 1917).	**Arabia** — **Lawrence first meets Feisal** at Hamra, decides he is the potential leader. HIMS *Hardinge* arrives at Rabegh with Egyptian mtn guns from Jeddah.

AFRICAN OPERATIONS 5	SEA WAR 6	AIR WAR 7	INTERNATIONAL EVENTS 8	HOME FRONTS 9
		Somme — 5 Anglo-French aircraft destroy 2 German aircraft, extensive RFC night bombing.	**Neutrals: Greece** — Allies land reinforcements to keep order after anti-Allied Athens demos (15) & seize 3 more Greek warships. **USA — 1st birth control clinic outside Holland opens in New York.**	**Ireland** — 130,241 enlistments to date, 161,239 men still available from 557,827 of military age.
W Desert — British seize Dakhla (-22) & Baharia Oases (19).	**Adriatic** — Italian SS *Bermuda* rams & sinks Austrian *U16* after latter sinks Italian destroyer *Nembo* off Albania.		**Neutrals: China** — German envoy Hentig enters, returns home (9 June 1917) via US.	**Britain** — Commons food price debate, Board of Trade Pres strongly v rationing.
	N Sea — HM submarine *E38* torpedoes small German cruiser *München* during **brief High Seas Fleet sortie**, last till 23 Apr 1918, peters out before Dogger Bank in rough seas & Scheer's knowing British aware of it.	**W Front** — Unfavourable flying weather (-19), rain & sleet.	Baron Burian suggests peace initiative to Bethmann at Pless, Kaiser approves (25). Both ministers also agree to proclaim Polish independence as soon as possible. Dr Benes achieves agreement with French to separate Czech PoWs from other Austrian ones.	**Egypt** — New gold pound coinage removes Sultan of Turkey's image. **Britain** — Men of 41 called up.
E Africa — Last German post N of Central Railway cleared. Deventer contacts Northey. German attacks in Iringa & R Ruhuje districts (*see* 22).	**Adriatic** — Austria's most successful U-boat, *U27* (first of class of 8 coastal boats), launched at Pola, commissioned 14 Feb 1917.		Anglo-French Boulogne Conference recognizes Venizelos' Prov Govt.	
	Black Sea — Battleship *Imperatritsa Maria* capsizes after internal explosion at Sevastopol.		Germany protests to China over French hiring of 30,000 Chinese labourers. **Neutrals: Greece** — Govt agrees to withdraw half troops at Larissa, puts Army almost on peace footing by 25.	
Italian Somaliland — 200 dervishes dispersed & 500 stock recovered (*see* 11 Feb 1918). **E Africa** — Wahle's col breaks through small SA force (night 21/22).		**W Front** — RFC helps engage 184 targets & bombs extensively. Germans bomb Querrieu, Corbie & Amiens (night 20/21).		**Germany** — Chancellor & *OHL* agree on War Minister's removal & establishment of War Munitions Office.
E Africa — Portuguese now 8 miles N of R Rovuma (*see* 12 Nov). Maj Kraut storms NRFF Hill at Mkapira & invests position (-30) until beaten over R Ruhuje minus 124 cas, 1 gun & 3 MGs.		**Britain** — 2 German aircraft (1 lost to Dunkirk RNAS) drop 4 bombs on Sheerness (no cas); 1 aircraft's 3 bombs on Margate wounds 2 (23). **W Front** — 48 Anglo-German air combats, RFC lose 2 aircraft, claim 7.		
E Africa — Maj Gen Wahle ambushes British force, breaks through to Lettow between Northey & Iringa in next 3 wks; captures 50 British & 2 guns at Ngominji SW of Iringa (29).		**Germany** — 13 Sopwith 11/2 Strutters of No 3 Wing RNAS damage 3 Thyssen blast furnaces at Hagendingen, N of Metz (*see* 10 Nov). **W Front** — Fog & rain restricts flying (-25 & 27).		
				Britain — Munitions Ministry to pay 75% cost of temporary crèches for children of married women workers.

OCTOBER 1916	WESTERN FRONT 1	EASTERN FRONT 2	SOUTHERN FRONTS 3	TURKISH FRONTS 4
Wed 25	**Somme** — Many supply trucks stuck in deep mud around Montauban, ammo shortages hamper Allied guns. **Verdun** — Lt Louis Franchet d'Esperey (son of general) of 401st Inf Regt k before Vaux, aged 18.		British give in to French & agree to send one more div to Salonika. **Isonzo** — Italian arty bombardment (-28, *see* 1 Nov).	
Thu 26	**Somme** — Rawlinson postpones planned offensive to 30 (prohibitive weather). **Verdun** — 4 German counter-attacks & another (27, *see* 28) repulsed.	**Rumania** — Tirgu Jiu: Rumanian First Army routs lone 11th Bav Div (2000 PoWs & 4 guns), pursues (-2 Nov).		
Fri 27	**Somme** — Rawlinson, on short break at Versailles, confides to his diary that weather is so bad it will be a physical impossibility for British inf to advance; even a short advance will wear the troops out. He despairs privately of further Allied advance (31).	**W Russia** — Russians forced to R Shchara E bank.		
Sat 28	**Somme** — Very wet & cold day, British make slight progress NE of Lesboeufs. **Verdun** — French shell Ft Vaux (*see* 2 Nov).			**Persia** — Baratov captures 2 villages nr Hamadan.
Sun 29	**Somme** — Allies capture Dewdrop & Hazy trenches.			
Mon 30	**Somme** — **British Reserve Army redesignated Fifth Army** & reinforced with guns from Third Army & all available 52 tanks for limited ops astride Ancre Valley.			**Arabia** — **Sherif Hussein proclaims himself 'King of the Arab Lands'** (*see* 4 Nov); Anglo-French protests.
Tue 31		Russian Sixth Army censor reports soldiers saying 'after	**Salonika** — NE of Struma British 28th Div captures	**Mesopotamia** — Maude visits Nasiriya (-2 Nov) on Euphrates,

AFRICAN OPERATIONS 5	SEA WAR 6	AIR WAR 7	INTERNATIONAL EVENTS 8	HOME FRONTS 9
E Africa — 4th SA Horse inflict 57 cas on Germans 12 miles N of Iringa.	**Med** — 26 U-boats assigned (incl 4 in Black Sea & 8 en route or preparing to leave).	**Somme** — Boelcke's *Jasta 2* shoots down 3 RFC arty aircraft. **Balkans** — 5 RNAS aircraft leave Imbros to fly to help Rumania, 4 reach Bucharest; 4 more aircraft sent 21 Nov (*see* 31 Dec).		
	Channel — 11 **German destroyers** (Capt Michelsen) from Zeebrugge **raid in Dover Straits** (night 26/27). 24 German ships transferred from High Seas Fleet (23) to aid U-boat passage of the Straits. 7 net barrage drifters & 2 destroyers sunk for no loss despite Dover Patrol's 18 alerted destroyers (6 'Tribals' from Dover briefly engage). British destroyer *Zulu* mined, sister ship *Nubian* torpedoed (*Nubian* undamaged bow section & *Zulu* stern section salvaged & mated to create unique HMS *Zubian*; she sinks *UC50* (4 Feb 1918), *see* 23 Nov. Bethmann informs German High Cmnd question of unrestricted U-boat warfare exclusively Kaiser's concern as C-in-C.	**Somme** — 5 DH2s (24 Sqn) beat off c20 German aircraft.	**Neutrals: USA** — Wilson tells Cincinnati Chamber of Commerce 'I believe that the business of neutrality is over. The nature of modern war leaves no state untouched'.	**Germany** — Bethmann visits Pless & opposes military age extension to 60; Gröner promoted Lt Gen to head **new War Munitions Office** (created 1 Nov). **Britain** — £60m New York loan announced. Rumania Flag Day.
Ethiopia — Battle of Chembebit (Sagalle, or Shano): Ras Tafari's (Haile Selassie) 95,000 royal troops defeat Lij Yasu's father Negus Ras Mikael of Wollo; he is led in chains to Addis (*see* 11 Feb 1917) but Lij Yasu escapes till Jan 1921.				**Australia** — 3 Cabinet Ministers resign v conscription, referendum (28) defeats it by 72,476 votes.
	Irish Sea — British Donaldson liner *Marina* (18 lost, incl 6 Americans) sunk without warning by U-boat off Fastnet.	**Somme** — Capt O **Boelcke** (40 victories), **first great air combat tactician k**, aged 25, in Albatros mid-air collision over Pozières with *Jasta 2* wingman Lt Erwin Boehme during dog-fight in which 8 German fighters down 3 RFC arty aircraft & a Nieuport. One of 12 German aircraft losses in Oct.	Anglo-German Agreement to exchange interned civilians over 45. U-boat sinks US SS *Lanao* off Portugal.	**Germany** — Gröner drafts compulsory 'Patriotic Auxiliary Service Bill' for males 15-60. Socialist *Reichstag* Deputy's speech v 'preventive arrest' gains 3 parties' support.
	Aegean — U-boat torpedoes Greek volunteer transport *Angeliki*. **N Sea** — 2 RNAS seaplanes recce Schillig Roads from carrier *Vindex* but fail to find boom; no CMB attack carried out. Jellicoe warns of '...serious danger that our losses in merchant ships ... may by the early summer of 1917 have such a serious effect ... as to force us into accepting peace terms'.			
	RN has 47 Q-ships, from drifters to medium-size steamers. **Adriatic** — Allied Taranto conference on Otranto Barrage ducks single cdr question but Italians will transfer 22 trawlers from Tyrrhenian, plus add 18 small torpedo boats & 38 aircraft (30 French at Corfu).			**France** — Butter, cheese & oilcake become state commodities. **Germany** — Lt-Gen Stein succeeds Hohenborn (dismissed 28) as War Minister. **Britain** — Scheme to supply coal to Italian & French Mediterranean ports. Shops early closing in force (8pm Mon-Fri, 9 pm Sat). Haig's private sec Philip Sassoon to Lord Northcliffe 'Now that almost everyone has lost someone, it is very easy to arouse criticism'.
E Africa — British reorganized into Hoskins' 1st Div around	(Oct) 353,600t Allied & neutral shipping (49 British worth	**W Front** — Allied Oct loss 88 aircraft + over 99 RFC		

OCTOBER 1916	WESTERN FRONT 1	EASTERN FRONT 2	SOUTHERN FRONTS 3	TURKISH FRONTS 4
Thu 31 contd		the war we'll have to settle accounts with the internal enemy'. Russian losses 4,670,000 k & w, 2,078,000 PoWs, 1m+ missing. **Rumania** — German Ninth Army losses since 11 Sept : 9072.	Bairakli Jum'a with 320 Bulgars & 2 MGs for 231 cas.	travels first 90 miles by rail.
Wed 1 November 1916	**Joffre letter to Haig specifies broad lines of combined action in 1917** (Haig agrees by letter 6, *see* 15). **Somme** — French repulse counter-attack at Sailly-Saillisel & advance NE of Lesboeufs. Allies announce 72,901 PoWs; 303 guns; 215 mortars & 981 MGs captured since 1 July.	**Transylvania** — Falkenhayn advances beyond Törzburg, Predeal & Rotenturm Passes (-5). **Dobruja** - Sakharov replaces Zayonchkovski i/c Danube Army (now 8 divs) & orders end to 'shameful flight'. By 5, 27 Russian divs in Rumania (Fourth, Eighth & Danube Armies).	**Italian Front — Ninth Battle of the Isonzo** (-4): Italian Second & Third Armies attack at 1110 E of Gorizia & on Carso. In former some ground gained on San Marco slopes despite waist-deep mud, in latter *Toscana* Bde (D'Annunzio a vol) seizes Velike Kribach (1125 ft), 5 other objectives taken & held or regained after Austrian attacks (night 1/2).	Lawrence crosses Red Sea from Jeddah to Port Sudan in cruiser HMS *Euryalus* , goes on to Khartoum for talks. **Armenia** — (Nov) Turk getting only ⅓ rations despite German motor cols & efforts. Second Army Kharput hospital has 900 deaths pm. Third Army losses 60,000 men to cold, plague, lice and typhus (July 1916 to spring 1917).
Thu 2	**Somme** — British capture trench E of Gueudecourt. **Verdun** — Germans evacuate Ft Vaux (night 2/3).			**Mesopotamia** — Maude leaves Basra for front (*see* 15 & 25).
Fri 3	**Verdun** — 2 French patrols reoccupy Ft Vaux.		**Isonzo** — 4 Italian bdes take Volkovniak, Dosso Faiti, Hills 123 & 126. **Salonika** — French War Minister Gen Roques visits (-12) & largely clears Sarrail from Allied complaints.	**Arabia** — British treaty with Sheikh El-Katr.
Sat 4	**Somme** — Haig & Foch confer with Rawlinson who supports Cavan ('... conditions are far worse than in the First Battle of Ypres ...') after joint recon of ground and gets 33rd Div attack v Le Transloy cancelled, instead Ancre ops.		**Isonzo** — After turning move on Salone fails, Cadorna halts offensive due to bad weather & heavy losses (28,000 cas), 9000 Austrian PoWs taken. Italian losses in Seventh to Ninth Isonzo battles (since 14 Sept) 75,500; 21,500 Austrian PoWs taken in their c63,000 loss.	**Arabia — Sherif Hussein crowned 'King of the Arabs' at Mecca.** Allies recognize him as de facto King of Hejaz (6,*see* 22) but do not attend coronation.
Sun 5	**Verdun** — French 9th Div reoccupies whole of Vaux. **Somme** — British in see-saw action nr Butte de Warlencourt. French capture most of Saillisel (*see* 8) & attack St Pierre Vaust Wood (advance continues 6). Anzacs capture, then lose Bayonet Trench.		**Salonika** — British 1916 evacuations of sick (esp malaria cases) to Malta total 20,278 incl 4789 invalided home.	
Mon 6		**Bukovina** — Lechitski success in 2 passes S of Dorna Watra v Austrians, but Central Power reinforcements stall the advance.		
Tue 7	**Somme** — British gain ground E of Butte de Warlencourt & repulse night counter-attack at Beaumont Hamel. French capture Ablaincourt & Pressoir S of Somme, repulse German counter-attacks (12, 14 & 15).	**Transylvania** — Falkenhayn repulsed in Tolgyes Pass (N) sector but drives beyond Vulcan & Predeal Passes. His Group Krafft captures Sardoui 16 miles S of Rotenturm Pass (8).		Wingate cables London that regular bde + guns needed to secure Rabegh (War Cabinet decide to send one (9 & 16, *see* AIR WAR 7).
Wed 8	**Somme** — German counter-attack at Saillisel (slight gains 6), but French capture whole village (11-12).			
Thu 9		**W Russia** — Germans take 3400 PoWs at Skrobova.		

AFRICAN OPERATIONS 5	SEA WAR 6	AIR WAR 7	INTERNATIONAL EVENTS 8	HOME FRONTS 9
Kilwa (*see* 15 Nov) & Deventer's 2nd Div on Central Railway.	176,248t with 197 lives, a record so far (*see* Dec) incl 44 ships or 125,152t to Med U-boats.	personnel. RFC help engage 169 German btys.		
Sudan — Acting Gov-Gen & Sirdar Col Stack succeeds Sir R Wingate.	**Secret War** — **Grand Fleet receives daily Room 40 summaries of all German naval movements & changes**. (Early Nov) Italian Navy discover French reading their codes, but this continues into 1918. Mercantile U-boat *Deutschland* reaches New London on 2nd transatlantic voyage (*see* 10 Dec). **Adriatic** — Italian torpedo boats raid Pola. **France** —12 Japanese-built *Arabe*-class destroyers ordered (completed Sept-Oct 1917).	**Britain** — (Nov) Air Board orders 8000 Hispano-Suiza engines. **Rumania** — *LZ97* raids Bucharest (German 1st Sqn raids 14, 20, 22 & 12-15). **W Front** — High winds & poor weather hampers ops (-8 & 12-15).	Turkey declares of Paris (1856) & Berlin (1878) treaties null & void. **Neutrals: USA** — (Nov) Film *Somewhere in France* released.	**Britain** — RFP 78%, up 10%. Loaf of bread up ¹/₂ d to 9d. (Nov) Patriotic mob breaks up Cardiff Peace Conference. **Germany** — Gen Gröner made Deputy War Minister & given economic authority over military regions.
	Arctic — *U56* sunk by Russian patrol craft gunfire off Lapland. **Black Sea** — Russian Fleet shells Constanza (& 4). **N Sea** — British destroyers rescue Dutch *SS Oldambt*, routing 5 German destroyers.		**Secret War** — Asst Chief Commissioner Thomson meets Jewish master spy Alex Aaronsohn by St James's Park; Aaronsohn arrives Cairo 12 Dec.	**Russia** — Petrograd Central War Industrial Ctee appeals to working classes to disregard alarming rumours.
Sudan — Maj Huddleston occupies Kulme (Darfur).	**E Med** — French warships shell Adalia, S Turkey.	**W Front** — RFC help range 120 targets but lose 5 aircraft.		
		W Front — RFC drop 74 bombs on Douai stn & HQ farm S of Houthulst Forest.	**Neutrals: Greece** — Venizelists attack loyal troops at Ekaterini. **Norway** — Forbids coasts to U-boats (*see* 30 Jan 1917). **Austria** — Emperor's letter to PM states plan to give Galicia self-rule within new Poland.	**Britain** — Army appoints Director of Savings. **Germany** — *Reichstag* adjourns.
	N Sea — High Seas Fleet destroyers with *Moltke* & 3rd Battle Sqn rescue *U30* & *U20* (abandoned) gone aground in fog off Borsbjerg, Denmark, but RN submarine *JI* (Laurence) torpedoes battleships *Grosser Kurfurst* & *Kronprinz* forcing them back to harbour.		**Germany & Austria proclaim 'Independent State of Poland'.** Polish recruiting for German Army announced (16) gains only 370 volunteers from 22.	**France** — Serb Soldiers' Flag Day. **Britain** — No Guy Fawkes' Night celebrations allowed.
Sudan — Huddleston's 150 troops defeat & kill Sultan Ali Dinar (2500) at Giuba nr French Equatorial frontier.	**Black Sea** — *UB45* mined off Varna, *UC15* also lost to unknown cause (Nov). *UB46* mined off Bosphorus (7 Dec). **E Med** — *UB43* (Mellenthin) torpedoes & sinks P & O armed liner *Arabic* (11 crew lost) off Cape Matapan.			
E Africa — Ft Kibata repels 400 Germans (-8). British occupy Mpotora, 70 miles SW of Kilwa.	**Baltic** — 2 Russian destroyers mined & later laid up.	**Arabia** — Maj Ross' RFC flight drives Turk planes from Emir Zaid's camp.	Bethmann tells Burian German war aims, latter calls them impossible (15). **Neutrals: USA** — WILSON RE-ELECTED PRES (*see* 19). Jeanette Rankin (Montana) 1st Congresswoman. **Neutrals: Greece** — Adm Fournet seizes Salamis naval arsenal, sees King (9).	
E Africa — Wahle attacks British Malangali post (-12) which is relieved by Murray's 400 British.	**E Atlantic** — US SS *Columbian* sunk by U-boat nr Cape Finisterre (NW Spain).	**Somme** — German aircraft strafe Australians N of Guedecourt.		**Britain** — Govt wins Commons confidence vote but 76 MPs oppose & 35 abstain.
		Occupied Belgium — 6 RNAS Short seaplanes (1 FTR) bomb	Bethmann *Reichstag* speech replies to Grey on causes of	**Britain** — Post Office's shortage of boys impairing

NOVEMBER 1916	WESTERN FRONT 1	EASTERN FRONT 2	SOUTHERN FRONTS 3	TURKISH FRONTS 4
Thu 9 contd		**Dobruja** - Sakharov occupies Hirsova (also Topalu 12 miles SE, 11) & Dunarea on Danube E bank, fighting for Cernavoda Bridge (-12) ends in retreat to Dunarea.		
Fri 10	**Somme** — British capture E section of Regina Trench N of Thiepval. French capture some trenches NE of Lesboeufs.	**Transylvania** — Second Battle of Oituz (-15).	**Serbia** — Serb-French attack in Crna bend, nets 1000 PoWs & 10 guns (-11) incl many newly arrived Germans (*see* 14). **Salonika** — 3 Greek (Venizelist) bns come under British command (*see* 18).	
Sat 11	**Somme** — Battle of the Ancre Heights ends: British arty preparation begins, British inf capture Farmers Rd nr Regina Trench.	**Transylvania** — Second Battle of Tirgu Jiu (-18): in Group Kühn's attack Lt Rommel's Württemberg Mtn Coy captures Mt Lescului (3937 ft) & descends to plain (12).		**Arabia** — Lt-Col Joyce arrives at Rabegh with 250 Egyptians & Sudanese.
Sun 12		**Transylvania** — Rumanian First Army retreats in Jiu & Aluta Valleys.		**S Persia** — Sykes occupies Shiraz, organises 3700 S Persia Rifles & 6 guns by 1 Dec.
Mon 13	**Somme** — **Battle of the Ancre begins** (-18): with 10 divs, 5 tanks & 282 heavy guns in wet fog at 0545: Fifth Army (Gough) storms Beaumont Hamel (1200 PoWs) also St Pierre Division & Beaucourt in mile-deep advance. 30,000lb ammonal **mine detonated at Hawthorn Crater;** c360 men of 3rd Bn German 62nd Regt buried alive. Op (-14) directed by Lt-Col Freyberg, RND (thrice w & wins VC). Australian-born writer & RND Coy Cdr F S Kelly k at Beaucourt.	**Transylvania** — Falkenhayn takes Kimpulung S of Törzburg & retakes railhead S of Vulcan Pass.	**Serbia** — After fog lifts Serbs reach ridges E of Crna & Monastir taking 600 German PoWs, forcing Gen Winckler to evacuate Kenali valley position (held since early Oct) night 14/15.	
Tue 14	**Somme** — British 190th Bde (63rd RN Div) & 2 tanks capture Beaucourt (Ancre) with 400 PoWs, driving major salient into German Ancre defences. Author L/Sgt H H Munro ('Saki') k, aged 46, by sniper at Beaumont-Hamel.			
Wed 15	CHANTILLY CONFERENCE: Allies discuss (Joffre presiding) 1917 offensives on W, E & S fronts to be timed from first fortnight of Feb 1917 to cause maximum dispersal of German	Brusilov says 'Rumania is a difficult ally'. His SW Front has only 412 heavy guns (over 122mm). **Transylvania** — **Falkenhayn** brings heavy guns through Törzburg Pass &	**Serbia** — Franco-Serb advance continues to 4 miles S of Monastir despite rain, and a blizzard (night temp 1°F, *see* 17).	Baghdad Railway tunnel dug through Mt Amanus. **Mesopotamia** — Maude reorganizes MEF into I & III Indian Corps plus Cav Div. **India : NW Frontier** — 4th Action of Hafiz

AFRICAN OPERATIONS 5	SEA WAR 6	AIR WAR 7	INTERNATIONAL EVENTS 8	HOME FRONTS 9
		Ostend docks & Zeebrugge (repeated 15 & 17), 19 RNAS bombers raid Ostend (10, 10 bombers repeat 12). Zeebrugge again bombed (22 & 28); little damage but German torpedo boats lie up at Bruges. **Somme** — **RFC** helps fire on 203 targets (40 direct hits) & **discovers Hindenburg Line works**. RNAS No 8 Sqn (from Dunkirk units) joins Somme fighting, destroys 24 aircraft for loss of 2 pilots (-31 Dec). **Largest air battle yet**: c30 German fighters intercept 12 British bombers & 14 escorts destroying 5 (BE2c to Richthofen) & damaging 3; 26 other air combats.	war. Asquith Guildhall speech assures Venizelos & Armenians of British sympathy; no separate peace possible.	telegram deliveries.
	Baltic — During attempted raid (night 10/11) on Russian patrol lines in Gulf of Finland, nr Reval, 7 wartime-built German destroyers (*V75, S57, V72, G90, S58, S59* & *V76*) out of 11 (10th Flotilla) sink in unsuspected minefields (400 survivors), **largest single action destroyer loss**; Adm Langemarck relieved of cmnd. **N Sea** — RNAS seaplanes attack Ostend & Zeebrugge (& 15). **Britain** — The King informed that Asquith wants Beatty to succeed Jellicoe i/c Grand Fleet, the monarch approves heartily (22, *see* 29).	**Germany** — 9 RNAS bombers raid Volklingen steel works (14 repeat 11); St Ingbert blast furnaces bombed (12, *see* 24). **W Front** — RFC directs fire on 150 targets. Lt Shirtcliffe of No 25 Sqn destroys a German aircraft from Douai with a phosphorus bomb from 11,000 ft. No 27 Sqn drops 44 bombs on Valenciennes airfield; 4 German airfields & 4 stns bombed (night 9/10, contd night 10/11).	Germany warns Greece that war material transfer to Allies a neutrality breach.	
		Egypt/Palestine — 6 RFC aircraft apiece raid Maghdaba (100 miles E of Ismailia) & Beersheba. German aircraft bombs Cairo (13, 39 cas) & Suez (17) but little damage.	Anglo-French-Italian London Munitions Conference.	**Austria** — Archduke Charles recalled to Vienna by Emperor's illness. **Canada** — Militia & Defence Minister, Gen Hughes, resigns. Sir E Kemp succeeds (23).
E Africa — Portuguese occupy Lulindi.			Count Bernstorff to German Mexico City Minister 'The Imperial Govt would see with the greatest of pleasure the Mexican Govt's consent to... a [U-boat] base in its territory' (*see* 17 Jan 1917).	
E Africa — Capt Wintgens attacks 250 British at Lupembe (-15) 3 times to cover Wahle's main retreat to E.		**Germany** — Hallenstein, CO 'Giant' bomber unit *Rfa 500*, k flying experimental Dornier V1 fighter.	Lansdowne British Cabinet memo suggests negotiated peace. **Occupied Belgium** — Cardinal Mercier appeals v deportations, Belgian Govt likewise to neutrals (22), also Pope (29).	**Britain** — Asst Chief Commissioner Thomson interrogates Mata Hari at Scotland Yard; she is sent back to Spain (*see* 13 Dec). **Austria** — Food Control Office established to replace 3 ministries involved (*see* 5 Jan 1917).
E Africa — German attack on Songea repulsed night 14/15.	**Aegean** — *U73* mine (12 laid 28 Oct) in Zea Channel sinks 12,009t French armed liner *Burdigala* (*see* 21).	**Somme** — RFC ranges 157 German btys, No 15 Sqn observers direct gunfire that annihilates c1350 German inf.		**Russia** — **Duma attacks on PM & by implication Tsarina**, 'Is this folly, or is this treason?' (Miliukov), (*see* INT'L EVENTS 24).
E Africa — Maj-Gen Hoskins takes command at Kilwa, rest 1st Div arrive by sea (-29). Smuts has lost 33,500 animals since mid-Sept. Nigerian Bde sails from Lagos for Dar-es-		**Germany** — Lt-Gen EW von Hoeppner appointed C-in-C Air Force: *Kommandierenden General der Luftstreitkrafte* (Kogenluft). CoS is Col Thomsen, previously *Feld-*	Allied Paris Conference (-16) on Greece & Poland (protest 18). †Count Tschirschky, Austria's Berlin Ambassador.	**Russia** — Grand Duke Nicholas warns Tsar of Tsarina & Rasputin's harmful influence. **Germany** — (c) 1918 conscript class, all under 19, begins to join for training;

NOVEMBER 1916	WESTERN FRONT 1	EASTERN FRONT 2	SOUTHERN FRONTS 3	TURKISH FRONTS 4
Wed 15 contd	forces. Somme — German counter-attack N of Chaulnes.	captures Tirgu Jiu, **20-25 miles inside Rumania.**		Kor: 1st Indian Div with 12 aircraft & armoured cars defeats 6000 Mohmands in Peshawar Valley.
Thu 16	Each BEF army forms AA gp under one cdr with 36-64 guns each (-27). **Somme** — British advance E of Beaucourt but lose some ground E of Butte de Warlencourt.	First of 11 German armoured car MG platoons formed, mainly for E Front.	**Salonika** — British temporarily capture 2 villages E of Sturma as diversion but fail at Tumbitza Farm (18) due to too short a bridge.	
Fri 17	**Somme** — **First snow falls,** night 17/18.		**Serbia** — Weather clears, 2nd *Zouaves* get onto Hill 1212.	**Sinai** — British 12 in water pipe (made in US) reaches Romani, 600,000 gal pd. **S Persia** — Successful British show of force in Arabistan from Ahwaz (-7 Dec).
Sat 18	**Somme** — Battle of the Ancre ends with 8 tanks participating. Existing tank coys expanded into bns (*see* 1 Feb 1917). BATTLES OF THE SOMME END: In final attack, reluctantly allowed by Haig, 4th Cdn Div & part of 18th Div gain 1000-yd deep bulge on front of 3 miles, but Grandcourt not reached by 32nd Div (GOC relieved & 2 bde cdrs). German losses 45,000 since 1 (BEF Nov total 46,238). **Verdun** — Joffre agrees to one more Nivelle attack (*see* 11 Dec); preparations incl 16 miles of roads & 6 miles of lt railway.		**Serbia** — Despite deep snow Serb Danube Div captures Hill 1378, Italians storm Ostretz Hill & 2 other features (-19), French ford R Viro and Russians capture 3 villages S of Monastir. Germans & Bulgar burn & evacuate it (night 18/19) & retreat 4 miles. **Macedonia** — 5144 trained Greek troops now available with 5184 animals.	
Sun 19	**Somme** — British cease ops.	**Rumania** — Falkenhayn's Group Kühne reaches Filiasi road net 40 miles SE of Tirgu Jiu; Capt Picht's motorized bn diverted W from Filiasi to open Iron Gates and railway from behind (20, *see* 22).	**Serbia** — **Fall of Monastir to Allies**: Serb & French cav ride in 4 yrs to the day since Serbs captured town from Turks in First Balkan War, 1912 (*see* 5 Dec 1915). Sarrail thanks all nations & claims first French victory since the Marne. Fighting to N of Monastir (22).	
Mon 20		Tsar summons Gourko from Special Army to act as CoS (Alexeiev ill - Mar 1917), he arrives at STAVKA (23).		
Tue 21		**Rumania** — Falkenhayn's Cav Corps (Schmettow) occupies Craiova (capital of W Wallachia), road to Bucharest open. Gen Janin at STAVKA finally gets Alexeiev to send 2 divs to aid Rumanians.	**Serbia** — Italian 63rd Regt captures Bratindol. German 42nd Regt has had 2665 cas since last wk of Oct, only 146 come out of line.	
Wed 22	Robertson chairs meeting at War Office, attended by Haig &	Austro-Germans retake Orsova on Danube. Capt Picht seizes		**Arabia** — King Hussein forms first govt.

AFRICAN OPERATIONS 5	SEA WAR 6	AIR WAR 7	INTERNATIONAL EVENTS 8	HOME FRONTS 9
Salaam (-27, *see* 10 Dec). **S Algeria** — 6 French garrisons & 2 mobile groups (1750 troops) v Senussi; Ft Polignac attacked & supply convoy destroyed (25- 28, fort evacuated 17 Dec).		*flugchef* .		**malnutrition a problem.**
		Britain — Haig asks for an extra 20 fighter sqns for 1917. RFC capture first Albatros D1 Scout, forced down by BE2. **Somme** — RFC helps knock out at least 10 German guns (65 btys engaged), destroys 3 German aircraft; 6 Martinsydes bomb Hirson stn (Belgium). German night raid destroys 21 French aircraft at Cachy, 90 miles away. **Arabia** — 6 No 14 Sqn RFC aircraft land at Rabegh to support Arabs; airfield built (*see* 24).	**Neutrals: Greece** — Allies demand dismissal of Central Powers Ministers & surrender of war material (*see* 24).	**Britain** — Food Control Regulations empower Board of Trade which orders potato stocks return (20). 12,000 Sheffield engineers strike (-18) obtains colleague's release from HM Forces.
		Germany — French bomber pilot Capt Beauchamp in 1¹/2 Strutter 'Ariel' flies epic 812-mile **first ever 'shuttle' raid**: Luxeuil (Vosges)-Munich (rail stn bombed)-San Donadi Piave (nr Venice). Beauchamp kia over Verdun (Dec). **W Front** — RFC ranges 141 targets, 16 aircraft in air combat (3 lost, 3 damaged), destroy 3 German in day & night bombing.	Russian PM Stürmer furious at pretended Russo-German peace talks. **Occupied Belgium** — Germans arrest Brussels Council.	**Russia** — Poltava Gendarme chief reports on Kremenchug soldiers' camp 2-day riot. **Australia** — PM Hughes forms new Cabinet after walking out of Labour Party anti-conscription meeting.
	Asst Navy Sec Franklin Roosevelt letter to London embassy denies neutral US Navy actions on 8 Oct (qv).		Francis Joseph receives Burian report on Berlin peace plan talks 'and expressed his keen satisfaction at ... peace being discussed at all'.	**Britain** — Lloyd George tells Hankey Somme offensive 'a bloody & disastrous failure'; not willing to stay in office if 1917 repeat.
E Africa — Gold Coast Regt lands at Kilwa.	**Baltic** — Russian cruiser *Rurik* mined badly in bows, but operational again early 1917.		Wilson peace note to combatants.	**Germany** — Hindenburg cables Bethmann 'the solution of the labour question becomes more pressing every day' (*see* 21). Scheer visits *OHL* at Pless to press for unrestricted U-boat war.
	Aegean — Largest ship victim of war: British hospital ship (but without wounded aboard) 48,158t White Star liner *Britannic* (78 cas), sister ship of the *Titantic*, sunk in Zea Channel by *U73* mine, hospital ship *Braemar Castle* mined (22).		†EMPEROR FRANCIS JOSEPH OF AUSTRIA peacefully, aged 86, having told PM 'if that is the case [domestic discontent] we must make peace without taking any ally into consideration at all'. **Great nephew Archduke Charles succeeds,** aged 29. **Diplomacy** — Zimmermann (Germany, replacing Jagow) & Viscount Motono (Japan) become Foreign Ministers.	**Germany** — *Bundesrat* accepts Auxiliary Service Bill (*see* 29).
	N Sea — Only sailing raider of the World Wars: German	**W Front** — RFC destroy 2 German aircraft.		

NOVEMBER 1916	WESTERN FRONT 1	EASTERN FRONT 2	SOUTHERN FRONTS 3	TURKISH FRONTS 4
Wed 22 contd	Adms Jackson & Bacon. It decides to press Joffre to include British offensive into 'Belgian Corridor' for 1917. Haig & Robertson adamant that a comparatively limited advance will deny Germans use of key Roulers-Thourout rail line; advance of 20 miles will cut Ghent-Bruges line & compel Germans to evacuate Zeebrugge, Ostend & entire Belgian coast (*see* 8 Dec).	& just holds Turnu Severin v Rumanian 1st Div (-24) until relieved by Austrian cyclist bde.		
Thu 23		**Mackensen crosses Danube** at 0400 in thick mist on 32-mile front between Islatz & Zimnitza with 40 bns + 188 guns v 18 bns + 48 guns. Austrians build pontoon bridge by 1800 (25). (c) Prézan replaces Iliescu as Rumanian CoS & effective C-in-C.	**Serbia** — French & Serbs take 3 villages N of Monastir, capture Hill 1050 7 miles NE (26,*see* INT'L EVENTS).	
Fri 24			**Salonika** — Turk 46th Div begins to arrive E of Struma, takes over 20-mile sector S of Seres (1-10 Dec,*see* 4 & 6 Dec).	
Sat 25		**Rumania** — Falkenhayn's Group Kraftt occupies Rimnik S of Rotenturm Pass (Falkenhayn's Germans foiled at Slatina 25-26). Mackensen turns Aluta position by advancing towards Alexandria & Rosiori. Rumanian authorities begin leaving Bucharest for Jassy as general retreat ordered.		**Mesopotamia** — Maude telegram to CIGS omits date of forthcoming offensive (*see* 13 Dec).
Sun 26	*OHL* issues equivocal instruction on role of forthcoming *Siegfried Stellung* (Hindenburg Line): 'Just as in times of peace, we build fortresses, so we are now building rearward defences. Just as we have kept clear of our fortresses, so we shall keep at a distance from these rearward defences'.	Mackensen reaches Alexandria, 50 miles from Bucharest, & contacts Falkenhayn.		**Sinai** — British railway reaches Mazar, 20 miles from El Arish (*see* 20 Dec).
Mon 27		**Rumania** — Falkenhayn's *Alpenkorps* captures Curtea de Arges & 41st Div Slatina on R Aluta. Bulgars (Mackensen) take Giurgevo on Danube.	**Macedonia** — Allies finally repair Ekshisa rail bridge (line to Monastir).	
Tue 28		**Carpathians** — Lechitski captures heights E of Jablonitsa & Kirlibaba Passes in relief offensive to aid Rumania (-13 Dec) (*see* 1 Dec). **Rumania** — Mackensen fighting at Calugarino, 17 miles S of Bucharest, forces R Niaslova (30).		**Mesopotamia** — British complete Qurna-Amara railway along Tigris.
Wed 29		BATTLE OF BUCHAREST (-3 Dec). Falkenhayn captures Pitesti. Rumanian First and		

AFRICAN OPERATIONS 5	SEA WAR 6	AIR WAR 7	INTERNATIONAL EVENTS 8	HOME FRONTS 9
	square-rigged *Seeadler* leaves Germany for S Seas disguised as Norwegian timber ship (had been British-built 1878 & US-owned until *U36* captured her 24 July 1915). Crew hide among cargo as ship passes through British Northern Patrol.			
	Channel—13 German destroyers from Zeebrugge damage 1 Dover barrage drifter, but make off when challenged.	**W Front** — **Richthofen kills Maj Lanoe Hawker** VC (9 victories), RFC after epic 35-min duel nr Bapaume; the 'Red Baron's' 11th victory. RFC ranges 163 targets. No 25 Sqn FE2bs incl Capt Tedder (future MRAF) repulse 20 German fighters (2 crashed), 4 other German aircraft shot down (3 damaged).	**Greek provisional Govt at Salonika declares war on Germany & Bulgaria.**	**Austria — New Emperor Charles' proclamation to peoples, announces imminent coronation as K of Hungary. NZ** — 1st conscription ballot.
E Africa — 1st British Morogoro-Dar-es-Salaam train run on Central Railway.		**Germany** — 9 RNAS bombers raid Dillingen air works & shoot down a German fighter nr Trier (& 27 Dec). **Arabia** — **First bombing of Hejaz Railway**: 2 RFC Martinsydes from Sinai cause only slight damage to targets N of Maan.	**Russian PM & Foreign Minister Stürmer resigns. Trepov succeeds. Neutrals: Greece** — Adm Fournet demands 10 mtn btys by 1 Dec, sees King (26).	**Britain** — †Sir Hiram Maxim, 1889 inventor of modern machine gun, aged 76, London.
	E Atlantic — Unescorted French battleship *Suffren* (making only 9 kts) sunk with all hands by *U52* off Lisbon.			**France** — Law on war labour disabled. Industrial Reconstruction Ministry formed 26.
L Nyasa — Wahle's 303-strong rearguard, 1 gun & 3 MGs surrender at Ilembule to Murray's 450 motorized troops.	**N Sea** — German destroyers raid Lowestoft (RN armed trawler *Narval* sunk) as diversion while disguised raider *Möwe* leaves Kiel on 2nd cruise (returns to Kiel 22 Mar 1917).			
		Britain — 7 of 10 Zeppelins raid N England, drop 206 bombs (41 civ cas), but 2 lost to 40 defence sorties (record so far). 2/Lt I V Pyott of No 36 Sqn RFC in BE2 shoots down *L34* (Dietrich) off Hartlepool with 71 rnds mixed incendiary/ball ammunition from his Lewis gun, 20 crew all k (night 27/28). RNAS Flt Sub-Lts E Cadbury & E Pulling shoot down *L21* (Frankenberg) after chase to 8 miles off Lowestoft.	**Neutrals: USA** — Federal Reserve Bank cautions member banks v further buying of belligerents' war bonds. **Diplomacy** — **Anglo-French-Italian wheat Ex**ecutive formed in London (see 3 Dec)	**Russia** — Petrograd Military Censorship Commission reports 'Dissatisfaction begins to show itself more' in letters *from* Army as well as to it.
	Aegean — RNAS seaplanes bomb Bulgar coast (-2 Dec).	**Britain** — **First daylight aircraft raid on London**: at 1150 LVG cIV (Ilges & Brandt) drops 6 22lb bombs between Brompton Rd & Victoria Stn (10 civs w). LVG later force-lands nr Boulogne (crew taken PoW). **W Front** — Fog almost eliminates flying (-3 Dec).	Kaiser arrives in Vienna to attend Hofburg Chapel lying-in-state. **Neutrals: Dominican Republic** — US military govt proclaimed.	**France** — Secret Chamber session (-7 Dec).
	N Sea — **Beatty appointed C-in-C Grand Fleet**, aged 45 (*see* 4 Dec); Adm Sir C			**Britain** — Board of Trade empowered to take over S Wales coalfield. **Germany** —

NOVEMBER 1916	WESTERN FRONT 1	EASTERN FRONT 2	SOUTHERN FRONTS 3	TURKISH FRONTS 4
Wed 29 contd		Second Armies retreat behind R Arges W of capital (night 29/ 20).		
Thu 30	**Verdun** — Crown Prince Wilhelm temporarily relin- quishes Army Group command. **Somme** — (end Nov) Foch writes, 'The general employment of the tank can obtain this result [a rapid advance] and allow the infantry, after taking the first positions, to continue and extend its action. Heavy tractor-drawn artillery can contribute to give the attack its necessary speed. The armoured vehicle will be tomorrow's cavalry and become the arm of exploitation ... it is their production that will regulate the march of the offensive, in fact the war itself'.	**Galicia** — Russians repulsed on R Zlota Lipa. **Dobruja** - Russian & RNAS armoured cars (left Odessa 13, arr Hirsova on Danube 27), (7 damaged) lead attack (-I Dec) at Topalul aiding IV Siberian Corps (9000+ cas) to take 2 Bulgar-held hills.	**Italian Front** — Gen arty action.	**Mesopotamia** — MEF ration strength 221,150 men & 74,420 animals. Each inf bde has 16 MGs, each inf bn 8 Lewis MGs. Army has 60 mortars.
Fri 1 December 1916	*OHL* issues first manual on de- fensive warfare, stipulates elastic defence-in-depth. During Battle of the Somme, depth of positions has grown & German casualties extraordi- narily high (*see* 6).	**Carpathians** — Lechitski driven off Rakida & Kirlibaba heights but pushes up Trotus Valley (3), takes peak com- manding Jablonitsa Pass (4). **Rumania** — **Govt leaves Bucharest for Jassy. Battle of the Arges** (-5): Rumanian 3- div counter-stroke takes 3000 PoWs & 20 guns from Mackensen, but **Falkenhayn joins up** to save 217th Div (2) & Russian 40th Div remains inactive till vain attacks (4 & 5).	**Italian Front** — Italian Sixth Army formed.	
Sat 2				
Sun 3		Falkenhayn signs 3-day armistice allowing Bucharest's evacuation (arsenal & forts blown up 4).	**Serbia** — Serb Drina Div captures Gruniste E of Crna, then Staravina (4).	
Mon 4	Fayolle diary 'Paris rumours...Foch will be replaced by Nivelle, and Joffre by X ...' (*see* 9).	**Galicia** — Fighting W of Stanislau & Tarnopol.	**Salonika** — Turk XX Corps HQ arrives E of Struma, rest of formation by 11 Jan 1917 (*see* 31).	**Arabia** — Parker Pasha leaves Hejaz, hands gold to Maj Joyce (*see* 19).
Tue 5		**Rumania** — Col Norton- Griffiths MP sabotages Ploesti oilfields (827,000t petrol) as Falkenhayn's Group Morgen approaches & occupies (6).		**Arabia** — Turks retake Qunfideh on coast S of Mecca & drive Feisal back to Yanbo where Lawrence soon arrives.
Wed 6	Berlin Casualty Office ceases to publish regular casualty lists (*Verlustliste*), giving names, regts & other particulars. Henceforward alphabetical lists of individuals appear with no indication of unit or even the front concerned. **Verdun** —	**Pripet** — Fighting W of Lutsk. **Rumania** — FALL OF BUCHAREST: Mackensen rides in on a white charger, on 67th birthday. Kaiser celebrates with champagne. 8000 Rumanian 1st Div survivors & 26 guns surrender on R Aluta	**Salonika** — British again suspend op to capture Tumbitza Farm (-7), but capture 2 Turk PoWs from 46th Div; British front now 90 miles.	**Mesopotamia** — First rain since Kut's fall (*see* 26). **Egypt** — High Commissioner McMahon dismissed, Wingate succeeds (29).

AFRICAN OPERATIONS 5	SEA WAR 6	AIR WAR 7	INTERNATIONAL EVENTS 8	HOME FRONTS 9
	Madden, Jellicoe's CoS, becomes 2 i/c replacing Adm Sir C Burney. Vice-Adm Sir W Pakenham takes over battle cruisers. **Black Sea** — Russians commission 2 seaplane carriers (max 18 aircraft) and they soon sink German coaster *Irmingard*; 4 Rumanian-owned liners also converted.			*Reichstag* debates Auxiliary Service Bill (-2 Dec).
W Africa — Col Haywood sent on recruiting mission.	**N Sea** — German raider (ex-liner) *Wolf* (Nerger, 458 mines, & small seaplane) breaks out for worldwide 15-month cruise (-24 Mar 1918; *see* 18 Jan 1917) that sinks 15 ships or 38,391t. **Channel** — Q-ship *Penshurst* sinks *UB19* (left Zeebrugge 22) (*see* 14 Jan 1917). *U49* on maiden voyage (Nov) sinks 40,000t shipping in Channel & Biscay. (Nov) British shipping losses 49 ships (7 to mines) worth 168,809t in total to U-boats of 325,218t (164,130t or 40 ships in Med).		Francis Joseph's funeral: Kaiser; Tsar Ferdinand; Kings of Bavaria & Saxony; Crown Princes of Germany, Sweden & Turkey attend. **Neutrals: Greece** — Reserve officers called up. Govt refuses Allied demands & their troops land at Piraeus (*see* 1 Dec).	**Britain** — 15,000 Manchester engineers strike v low wage award (-6 Dec). Asquith War Ctee accepts in principle national male service for all up to 55.
Sudan — Ali Dinar's sons reported surrender ends Darfur Revolt.	(Dec) U-boats sink 167 ships (39 British worth 109,936t, 58 Allied, 70 neutral) worth 276,400t. **Adriatic** — (Dec) Monitor *Earl of Peterborough* arrives at Venice to support Italian Army. **Greece** — French C-in-C Adm Dartigue involved in Athens fighting (*see* 12). Battleship *Mirabeau* fires 4 shells nr Royal Palace forcing Constantine & family into cellar (*see* INT'L EVENTS).	**Verdun** — (Dec) Plan to expand RFC to 106 regular & 95 res sqns. **Britain** — First flight of Royal Aircraft Factory SE5 single-seat fighter (prototype crashes Jan 1917). **Italy** — Austrians bomb Vicenza. **W Front** — (Dec) RFC loses 27 aircraft in action, 17 within BEF lines.	**Neutrals: Greece** — **King's troops** (40+k) fight **3000 Allied sailors & marines** (227 cas) for 3½ hrs in Athens outskirts until armistice leads to Allied withdrawal (-2).	**Britain** — RFP up 6% to 84%. New PoW food scheme to prevent surplus reaching enemy. (Dec) **Women's Army Auxiliary Corps formed** (*see* 31 Mar 1917). **France** — 1918 conscript class call-up authorized (happens spring 1917).
E Africa — British Kilwa Force occupies Ngarambi, 30 miles NW of Ft Kibata.		**W Front** — *Esc Americaine* redesignated *Esc Lafayette*.	**Neutrals: Greece** — Allies declare blockade & embargo all Greek vessels. Venizelists fight Royalists, Athens (former massacred 6).	**Austria** — Emperor Charles takes command of Armed Forces. **Russia** — Duma attack on 'dark forces' behind throne (*see* 31).
	E Atlantic — *U38* shells Funchal, Madeira, sinking 3 ships (*U156* repeats 12 Dec 1917) & French sloop *Surprise* off port.		Anglo-French Clementel Agreement to run Allied & chartered neutral shipping (*see* 5 Jan 1917).	
	Jellicoe succeeds Adm Sir H Jackson as **First Sea Lord** (post offered 22 Nov). He forms an Admiralty Anti-submarine Div under Rear-Adm Duff.	**W Front** — RFC loses 2 aircraft in air combat, claims 9 Germans shot or forced down.		**Britain** — Lloyd George resigns, after Asquith changes mind over smaller war ctee demand.
E Africa — Portugese invested at Newala, Marumba & Majembi but escape over R Rovuma to Nangedi which Germans occupy (8-20).		**W Front** — Weather prevents flying (-9 & 17-19) or very little (12-15).	Emperor Charles informs Foreign Minister that Germany now 'a pure military dictator-ship'.	**Germany** — **Hindenburg Auxiliary Service law,** all males 17-60 liable. **Britain** — Asquith resigns. King asks Bonar Law to form govt but Asquith twice refuses to serve under him so Lloyd George becomes PM (*see* 7). Barnbow National Shell Filling factory (nr Leeds) explosion kills 35 munitionettes.
E Africa — Action at Ft Kibata (-9): Lettow attacks 800 British with 3 (German) guns & seizes Picquet Hill, causing 127 cas (*see* 15).	**E Atlantic** — Destroyer HMS *Ariel* sinks *UC19* with modified explosive sweep (high speed paravane,*see* 13).		**Neutrals: Greece** — Compton Mackenzie & 100+ Allied agents land on Syra I to control E Med cables; all Cyclades in British hands by Feb 1917.	**Italy** — Socialist peace resolution defeated 293-47.

DECEMBER 1916	WESTERN FRONT 1	EASTERN FRONT 2	SOUTHERN FRONTS 3	TURKISH FRONTS 4
Wed 6 contd	Germans capture trenches at Hill 304, French recapture (7).	after 125-mile retreat E.		
Thu 7				**Sinai** — Chetwode GOC new Desert Column (*see* 21). **Aden** — British bde retakes Jabir & Haturn (150+ Turk cas).
Fri 8	Joffre agrees with proposed British offensive to Belgian coast, urges 5 divs be landed. British GHQ & Admiralty rule out landing more than 2 divs.	**Rumania** — Battle of R Cricov (-12) as Rumanians retreat NE on Rimnicu Sarat. Germans claim 70,000 PoWs, 184 guns, 115 MGs (1-9) & 20 miles E of Ploesti by (11). Hungarian 51st Honved Ing Div occupies Sinaia S of Predeal Pass.	**Salonika** — British 60th (London) Div begins to land (from W Front), its 179th Bde sailed to Katerini (11-Feb 1917), Thessaly as check with French & Italian 35th Div on Greek Royalist troops.	
Sat 9	Terrier letter from Paris to Lyautey 'The name that is in every mouth is...General Nivelle'.			
Sun 10			**Serbia** — Russo-Serb attacks v Hill 1050 fail (-11) v German *Guard-Schützen* Bn.	**Mesopotamia** — Maude issues operation orders. **Arabia** — K Hussein meets Anglo-French Missions at Jeddah, requests then declines 6 bns for Rabegh (-11,*see* 2 Jan 1917).
Mon 11	**Somme** — Violent Allied arty bombardment. **Verdun** — Preparatory French bombard-ment by 760 guns (350 heavy).		**Serbia/Salonika** — In last major order Joffre orders Sarrail 'to suspend all operations for the time being'; **Allies go onto winter defensive**. Monastir under shellfire throughout. **Albania** — Italian XVI Corps cdr Gen Bandini drowned in *Regina Margherita* sinking (see SEA WAR), Gen Ferrero replaces him.	
Tue 12	GERMANY MAKES PEACE PROPOSALS. **Foch removed by Joffre from command of N Army Gp** (d'Esperey succeeds 27); **JOFFRE SUCCEEDED BY HIS CHOICE, NIVELLE** (announced 16, assumes duties 17) as C-in-C of the Armies of the N and NE (W Front), who cancels long-planned French blow S of Somme.	**Rumania** — Russians help Rumanians rally on R Jalomitsa & SW of Buzeu, but forced back (13-14).		**Sinai** — CIGS to Murray 'The PM wishes you to make the maximum possible effort during the winter' but no reinforce-ments (*see* 21).
Wed 13				**Mesopotamia** — **Maude begins Tigris offensive** (-14) with 48,500 men, 174 guns & 24 planes v 20,600 Turks & 70 guns: Sannaiyat shelled & Shatt-el-Hai Canal bridged (6 pontoon bridges by 18), (*see* AIR WAR 14).
Thu 14	Both sides make heavy raids nr Ypres.	**Rumania** — Falkenhayn enters Buzeu in push for Braila & Galatz (Danube towns); all Wallachia in German hands, military govt established at Bucharest.	**Macedonia** — Fighting nr Monastir & arty fire in L Doiran sector, also local fighting in Crna bend (20).	

AFRICAN OPERATIONS 5	SEA WAR 6	AIR WAR 7	INTERNATIONAL EVENTS 8	HOME FRONTS 9
Algeria : Sahara — 1200 Senussi besiege Agades (-3 Mar 1917), wipe out 54 camelry (28). Senegalese bn sails from Marseilles to Dakar (4 Jan 1917) & crosses Nigeria (*see* 8 Feb 1917).				**France** — Govt wins confidence vote 344-160. **Britain** — LLOYD GEORGE BECOMES PM. Call up of non-skilled munition workers agreed. **Turkey** — Interior Ministry reports to Grand Vizier 702,900 Armenians relocated by 31 Oct.
			Allies blockade Greece. Their citizens leave Athens but Ambassadors see King (9).	**Russia** — **Murmansk-Petrograd Railway open.**
				Britain — New War Cabinet first meets. **Germany** — Hindenburg given (1st) 1914 Grand Cross of the Iron Cross. Raw Materials Office merger/ closure agreement on non-essential industries to save transport. **Russia** — Tsar at Tsarskoe Selo (-19).
Morocco — Lyautey returns to Rabat & accepts War Ministry, leaving by submarine. Gouraud becomes Resident-General (12, *see* 29 May 1917). **E Africa - Cunliffe's Nigerian Bde** (3448) **lands at Dar-es-Salaam** (-19), 400 sick by 31 when it reaches R Mgeta.	**N Sea** — Merchant U-boat *Deutschland* returns to R Weser.	**Arabia** — RNAS seaplanes from carrier *Raven II* bomb & strafe Turks nearing Yanbo (-11) helping check their advance.	Allies demand Greek demobilization & intercept King's radio messages to Berlin.	**Britain** — Lord Davenport appointed Food Controller.
	Adriatic — Italian battleship *Regina Margherita* (many cas incl Capt) sunk by 2 *UC14* mines off Valona, Albania, returning to Taranto for refit (Italy only announces on 20 Jan 1917). **Baltic** — Vice Adm Nepenin's Fleet order v non-saluting becomes unpopular with officers & men.	**W Front** — RFC helps spot for 33 targets, 3 German aircraft destroyed but 2 RFC aircraft damaged or destroyed. Allied air raids on Zeebrugge.	**Grey resigns as British Foreign Secretary** after exactly 11 yrs in office. **Balfour succeeds. Neutrals: Greece** — Adm Fournet relieved of com for 1 Dec action.	**Britain** — Lord Derby succeeds Lloyd George as War Minister. Labour Ministry formed.
	Carson succeeds Balfour as First Lord of the Admiralty. E Med — Adm Dartigue relieved of cmnd for Athens débâcle, Vice Adm Gauchet takes over as French & titular Allied C-in-C (outside Adriatic & Aegean) (16), for duration.		GERMAN 'PEACE NOTE' TO ALLIES: Bethmann in *Reichstag* says Central Powers willing to negotiate in neutral country but does not detail 'propositions' (*see* 30). **Neutrals: Greece** — King regrets Athens incidents via Paris Ambassador.	**France** — Briand creates 5-man war cabinet incl new Armaments Minister (Thomas). **Germany** — Kaiser's warlike speech to troops at Mulhouse, Alsace. Gen Gröner addresses unique TU Congress at Berlin, orders War Office bureaux to recognize unions (13). **Britain** — Munitions Ministry Trench Mortar Ctee formed.
	Black Sea — Russian warships shell Bulgar grain mills at Balchik N of Varna. **E Atlantic** — Destroyer HMS *Landrail* depth charges & sinks *UB29* in SW Approaches.	**Mesopotamia** — RFC drive off sole German recon sortie & spot for arty & U-boats.	French PM Briand sums up German peace note as 'Heads I win, tails you lose'. **Neutrals: Spain** — German Madrid Military Attaché radios Berlin about Mata Hari perhaps knowing Allies can read code.	**Portugal** — Military coups (-14) fail. **France** — Prototype Renault light tank ordered (conceived by Col Estienne & Renault July), limited production approved (30).
		Turkey — RNAS bomb Kuleli-Burgas rail bridge 20 miles S of Adrianople (& Razlovci, Occupied Serbia, 15). **Mesopotamia** — RFC BE2c scatters Turk Shumran pontoon bridge, leaving only Tigris Ferry till 17. 2 RFC BE2cs shoot down Albatros nr Kut (20). 2-10 aircraft attack Turk depots E of Kut (21-22, *see* 24).	**Allied 24-hr ultimatum to Greece (accepted 15).**	**Austria** — PM Dr Körber resigns v Emperor's talks with Hungary. Count Clam-Martinitz succeeds (20). **Britain** — Commons votes £400m war credit (total 1916/17 £1.75bn: war costs £5.5m pd).

DECEMBER 1916	WESTERN FRONT 1	EASTERN FRONT 2	SOUTHERN FRONTS 3	TURKISH FRONTS 4
Fri 15	**Verdun** — GREAT FRENCH ATTACK (N of Ft Douaumont): 2-mile penetration at 1000 recaptures Vacherauville, Hill 342 (Poivre Hill), Louvemont & Les Chambrettes with 3500 PoWs. Mangin employs 4 divs (with 4 in res) against 9 German divs. Within 4 days French front E of Meuse is re-established almost as on 20 Feb. French take 11,387 PoWs; 115 guns; 44 mortars; 107 MGs. Nivelle leaves Verdun for *GQG* that evening with farewell words 'The experiment has been conclusive... I can assure you that victory is certain'. Guillaumat takes over French Second Army.			
Sat 16	**Verdun** — French 133rd Div (Passaga) recaptures Bezon-vaux & Hardaumont. German counter-attack regains Les Chambrettes Farm (17).	**Pripet** — Russian positions between Kovel & Lutsk captured (restored 18). **Dobruja** — Sakharov retreats N on Braila (-20, *see* 21).	Greek Army begins evacuation of Thessaly under Allied supervision, (Anglo-French control officers, *see* 18 Jan 1917).	**Mesopotamia** — 7 Gurkhas & Punjabis swim Tigris on empty oilcans; 4 return to report Turk patrols still there (awarded Indian DSM).
Sun 17	**Artois** — Marwitz takes over German Second Army from Gallwitz (-22 Sept 1918) who goes to Fifth Army (Verdun).	**Dobruja** — Bulgars break through, causing chaos; 1st Cossack Div's radio stn & cipher captured, new code (21) no more secret.		
Mon 18	**Verdun** — **First offensive Battle of Verdun ends**: 4th (French 126th Div) Zouaves recapture Les Chambrettes Farm. Mangin thanks his XI Corps 'We have the method and we have the leader [Nivelle] it gives us the certainty of success'.	**Rumania** — Allied retreat towards R Sereth line, mud slowing German pursuit; Falkenhayn checked 30 miles W of Braila. **Dobruja** — RNAS armoured car unit leaves Tulcea by barge for transfer to Braila (8 cars arrive there 21).		**Mesopotamia** — RHA bombard new Turk Shumran bridge.
Tue 19				**Arabia** — British in Cairo meet French request for £40,000 in gold to give Arabs.
Wed 20	Haig and Nivelle first meet.	**Galicia** — Severe fighting W of Brody. **Rumania** — Russian 12th Cav Div reaches Odobesti 15 miles NW of Focsani (after 450-mile ride without losing a horse).	Maj Wetzell memo urges Austro-German spring 1917 offensive from Isonzo & Trentino as the only operations, which if successful, would immediately benefit the Western Front, but Ludendorff rejects (*see* 23 Jan 1917).	**Mesopotamia** — Cav Div (54 cas) fails to bridge Tigris 4 miles W of Shumran (*see* AIR WAR 20).
Thu 21	Joffre's powers as C-in-C French Armies are further limited (*see* 26). Letter from Nivelle to Haig: 'If our grand [spring 1917] offensive succeeds, it is certain that the Belgian coast will fall into our hands as a result of the retreat of the German Army and without a direct attack'. Nivelle urges Allies should attempt to destroy main German armies on W Front. To form a French strategic res of 27 divs, BEF to relieve French 20-mile sector	**W Russia** — Fighting S of Dvinsk. **Dobruja** — Sakharov drives Bulgars into L Babadagh S of Tulcea.		**Sinai** — **Anzac Mtd Div occupies El Arish** (1600 Turks evacuated to Magdhaba 20, *see* 23). RN arrive 22.

AFRICAN OPERATIONS 5	SEA WAR 6	AIR WAR 7	INTERNATIONAL EVENTS 8	HOME FRONTS 9
E Africa : Ft Kibata — Baluchis retake Picquet Hill in night attack with 1st theatre use of Mills grenades; Gold Coast Regt takes hill to W.	**Aegean** — British warships shell Bulgar Gulf of Orfano (SW of Kavalla) 15 & 22.			**France** — Barbusse publishes realistic war novel *Le Feu*, earns title 'Zola of the Trenches' (200,000 copies sold by July 1918). **Britain** — Liquor Control Board (powers extended 26) says excessive drinking still hampering war effort. **Germany** — Minority Socialist manifesto demands statement of peace terms.
		W Front — 15 indecisive Anglo-German air combats. No 57 (FE2d) Sqn arrives.		**Rumania** — Bratianu forms Coalition Govt, Ionescu joins (25).
			Neutrals: Greece — Royalist Govt issues warrant for Venizelos' arrest for high treason & Athens Archbishop anathematizes him (26). **USA** — Ends her extra-territoriality agreements with Turkey due to her treatment of Armenians & Syrians.	
			Wilson's peace conference circular note asks national objectives (*see* 26).	**Britain** — Food Restriction Orders limit meal courses, fixed prices for soldiers in London.
			Lloyd George's first speech as PM rejects peace talks without definite proposals '... we shall put our trust rather in an unbroken army than in broken faith'. British safe conduct for Austrian Ambassador from US.	**Britain** — National Service Dept announced under Neville Chamberlain (appt 10 Nov).
E Africa — 5th SA Inf from Songea take Njambenjo with food & cattle.	Chancellor Bethmann comes under sustained pressure from German Army & Navy for unlimited U-boat warfare without delay (20-26).	**E Front** — German Navy airships *L35* (Ehrlich) & *L38* (Dietrich) arrive at Wainoden for Op *Eiserne Kreuz* (Iron Cross), a raid on Petrograd advocated since early 1915 by Grand Adm Prince Heinrich, C-in-C Baltic Fleet (*see* 28). **W Front** — 5 *Jasta 2* fighters (led by Richthofen) shoot or force down 5 DH2s. RFC observers engage 85 targets incl destroying 3-gun AA bty, takes 741 photos.	Ludendorff urges immediate unrestricted U-boat war in view of Lloyd George reply.	
	N Sea — RN destroyer *Negro* sunk by collision with flotilla leader *Hoste*.		**Neutrals: Greece** — Allied note demands control of communications & Venizelists' release. Similar conditions demanded 31 before blockade lifted (*see* 10 Jan 1917).	

DECEMBER 1916	WESTERN FRONT 1	EASTERN FRONT 2	SOUTHERN FRONTS 3	TURKISH FRONTS 4
Thu 21 contd	(Bouchavesnes to Amiens-Roye road) by 15 Jan 1917, starts (25).			
Fri 22	**Mangin i/c French Sixth Army, Micheler to head Res Army Gp for 1917** spring offensive, Duchêne takes over latter's Tenth Army.	**Rumania** — Battle of Casin (-16 Jan 1917): Allies eventually check Archduke Joseph's 4-div advance along 3 Carpathian valleys.		**Mesopotamia** — Maude begins trenching ops v Turk Khadairi Bend S bank position (-7 Jan 1917).
Sat 23	**Champagne** — German trench raids. French repulse 2 attacks (31).	**Rumania** — Battle of Rimnicu Sarat (-27): Falkenhayn's 10 divs take town (27), 10,000 PoWs, 2 guns & 58 MGs.	**Salonika** — 2 British night trench raids in L Doiran sector (another 26). **Italian Front** — Bad weather since 10 Dec.	**Sinai** — Action at Magdhaba: Chauvel's Anzac Mtd Div & Camel Corps(146 cas) storm 5 redoubts, taking 1282 PoWs & 4 guns see 27).
Sun 24		**Dobruja** — Bulgars attack Sakharov Macin bridgehead E of Braila, fails again (31).		**Mesopotamia** — British cav blow up Arab Ft Gusab 18 miles SE of Kut, (see AIR WAR).
Mon 25	Christmas: Maj Wetzel and *OHL* estimate that US expeditionary force on W Front not possible before spring 1918.	Tsar's Order to Army and Navy stresses no thought of Peace till 'final victory' (see INT'L EVENTS).		**Armenia** — Fighting round L Van, Turks driven S (28). **S Persia** — Action of Dasht-i-Arjan: c400 British & Persians forced back to Shiraz (-28).
Tue 26	JOFFRE RESIGNS as C-in-C French Armies, is CREATED MARSHAL OF FRANCE, first since 1870.	**Rumania** — Russian 124th Div holds Vizural v Bulgars (-28) mainly due to 8 RNAS cars before retreating. Austrian First Army begins Trotus valley offensive (-7 Jan 1917).		**Mesopotamia** — Heavy rains (-6 Jan 1917) prevent major ops.
Wed 27	**Foch** moves to new assignment at Senlis as '**Military Adviser to French Govt**' (*see* 12 Jan 1917).			**Sinai** — Murray & Chetwode decide on advance to Rafa.
Thu 28	**Verdun** — Fierce German counter-attack at Mort Homme.		**Secret War: Salonika** — Serb Col Dimitrievic (codename Apis) of Black Hand secret society arrested at Serb Third Army HQ on charges of planning a mutiny & murder of Crown Prince (*see* 30 Mar & 2 Apr 1917).	
Fri 29	**Somme** — Haig's Battle of the Somme Dispatch published, covers BEF ops 15 May to 18 Nov 1916. He divides battle into 4 phases, lists capture of 38,000 PoWs &125 guns. **Haig stresses that fully half German Army engaged and defeated** and that British troops (many only partially trained) surpassed all expectations.	STAVKA conference (-31) includes Tsar and all 3 Front C-in-Cs, Brusilov decides, in principle, to launch 1917 offensive.		
Sat 30				

274

AFRICAN OPERATIONS 5	SEA WAR 6	AIR WAR 7	INTERNATIONAL EVENTS 8	HOME FRONTS 9
E Africa — Deventer's 3 cols (2000+) fail to trap Capt Lincke's 500 SE of Iringa (-29) despite fight at Muhanga (25-28) 70 miles NW of Mahenge.	**Holtzendorff memo urges unrestricted U-boat war**, can force England to peace table in 5 months ie before 1 Aug 1917 & harvest if begun 1 Feb. **Adriatic** — 4 Austrian destroyers raid Otranto Barrage (night 22/23): only 1 drifter damaged but 2 French destroyers hit, 2 & 1 Italian damaged in collisions (*see* 15 May 1917). **Britain** — New Shipping Ministry orders 5 types of standard merchant ship (3000-8000t) — Apr 1917.	Sinai — 13 BE2cs of No 67 (Australian) & No 14 Sqns attack Turk Magdhaba camps with 126 bombs (*see* TURK FRONTS 23).	**Count Czernin succeeds Baron Burian as Austrian Foreign Minister.**	**Britain — Food, Pensions & Shipping Ministries formed.** Air Board reformed as Air Ministry for aircraft supply. **France** — Rome Naval Attaché letter charges Caillaux with defeatist Italian Govt interview.
E Africa — NRFF (1900 + 6 guns) advances from Lupembe v Capt Langenn to Mkapira (-16 Jan 1917) without trapping foe.				
		Mesopotamia — First British aircraft over Baghdad since Nov 1915, Hereward de Havilland's BE2c.	Bethmann maintains that unrestricted U-boat war a foreign policy matter.	
E Africa — 48 hrs heavy rain postpones Smut's renewed ops on R Mgeta (*see* 1 Jan 1917).		**W Front** — First RFC Sopwith Pup Sqn (No 54) arrives in France, now 38 active sqns with 700 aircraft v 33 *Jagdstaffeln* (estab 14 each). No day flying possible.	Tsar's order to troops rejects German peace note. British colony PMs & Indian reps invited to Imperial Conference. **USA** — Cecil B De Mille's film *Joan the Woman* glorifies France and wins acclaim.	**France** — Lyautey begins as War Minister after Briand persuades him to stay even though military supply now under civil control.
	RNAS raid on Galata camps (Dardanelles) & Zeebrugge.		Central Powers (excl Bulgaria) reply to Wilson's note suggesting immediate meeting of delegates. Anglo-French London Conference discusses peace proposals (-28).	**Britain** — Heavier shipping loading announced to add 250,000t capacity.
Togo — Anglo-French agreement on temporary administration.	**E Med** — RNAS seaplanes damage Baghdad Railway's Chikaldir Bridge on Gulf of Alexandretta. **Aegean** — Escorted French battleship *Gaulois* sunk by *UB47* (Steinbauer) 30 miles E of Cerigo between Crete & Peloponnese.	**E Med** — RN seaplane carriers *Ben-my-Chree* & *Raven II* launch 9 aircraft which hit (4 bombs) & damage strategic Chikaldir bridge (Baghdad railway), nr Gulf of Alexandretta; Turk heavy guns for Baghdad delayed.		**Russia** — Economic conference at STAVKA
		E Front — Poor weather rules out *Op Eiserne Kreuz* primary target; nor can alternatives (Reval, Helsinki, Oesel, Dago) be reached due to severe icing. *L35* force-lands in pine forest at Seemuppen; damaged beyond repair (28/19). **W Front** — RFC aid British arty to get 25 direct hits on trench points & gun pits.	**Neutrals: Switzerland** — Lenin applies for Zurich residence 1-year extension.	
		W Front — Bad weather hampers flying (-30).		
			ALLIES REJECT GERMAN PEACE NOTE as 'empty & insincere'. Anglo-Chinese labour agreement for W Front.	**Germany** — War Ministry dismounts 16 cav regts. **Hungary — Emperor Charles crowned King Charles IV at Budapest. Russia** — Tsar tells British Ambassador 'In the

DECEMBER 1916	WESTERN FRONT 1	EASTERN FRONT 2	SOUTHERN FRONTS 3	TURKISH FRONTS 4
Sat 30 contd				
Sun 31	Haig promoted to Field Marshal. 106 French, 56 British, 6 Belgian & 1 Russian divs oppose 127 German divs (44 new divs formed in 1916). German Army has 16,000 MGs, each div has 48 mortars. In 1916 it has raised 1050 btys (4200 guns). French Army has 40,000 motor vehicles.	**Rumania** — Falkenhayn gains ground W & S of Focsani despite snow.	**Serbia** — (c) Turk 177th Inf Regt (3598, 4 guns & 6 MGs) reinforces German Eleventh Army (-5 May 1918). **Salonika** — (Dec) French 16th Colonial & 76th Divs have arrived.	

AFRICAN OPERATIONS 5	SEA WAR 6	AIR WAR 7	INTERNATIONAL EVENTS 8	HOME FRONTS 9
E Africa — Only 62,334 fit British native carriers from 150,000 recruited.	In last qtr of 1916 only 959,000t neutral shipping (723,000t Norwegian) enters British ports compared with 3,442,000 Jan-Mar. Grand Fleet now mostly equipped with Poulsen-arc jam-resistant radios. **Channel** — Dover Patrol has 5 cruisers & 35 destroyers & many smaller craft with 10 French destroyers (Adm Ronarc'h).	**Rumania** — 60 French aircraft delivered since mid-Oct.	**Neutrals : USA** — 14 journals publish Dutchman Raemakers' brutal anti-German cartoons (John Buchan initiative).	event of revolution; only a small part of the Army can be counted on to defend the dynasty'. **Russia — Rasputin murdered** (night 30/31 *see* 3 Jan 1917). By now 14,648,000 men mobilized incl 47.4% of male peasants. **Austria** — Nearly 5m men mobilized (800,000k, 1m badly wounded/sick) but 20 new divs formed.

FOCUS ON THE FRONTS

1914

The final prewar crisis was caused by the fatal shooting of Archduke Francis Ferdinand, heir to the Austrian throne, at Sarajevo (Bosnia) on 28 June 1914. The assassin, Gavrilo Princip, was a Bosnian *not* a Serb — although he *had* attended Belgrade University. His accomplice, Cabrinovic, was undeniably Serbian. Both were arrested and sentenced to 20 years' penal servitude. The repercussions of their crime would cost the lives of at least 9,700,000 combatants and perhaps 10 million civilians (including deaths from genocide, starvation and influenza).

Austria declared war on Serbia on 28 July 1914. When Russia mobilized, as a demonstration of solidarity with fellow Slavs, Germany declared war on Russia and France. German armies invaded neutral Belgium to outflank France's border fortresses. This flouting of a solemn treaty (Treaty of London 1839) and international law obliged Britain to declare war on Germany (4 August 1914). She made preparations to dispatch a small (two corps), but highly professional, expeditionary force to France.

France was determined to pursue her long-cherished war of revenge against Germany and her army was wedded to a philosophy of *l'offensive à l'outrance* (all-out offensive). C-in-C Joffre's 'Plan XVII' envisaged an invasion of Alsace-Lorraine followed by an advance to the Rhine. It almost entirely neglected to take prudent steps to meet any other contingency than a sweeping French victory. The result was that, when the German Chief of Staff, Moltke, implemented the so-called 'Schlieffen Plan' (that of his 1891-1905 predecessor) for a vast scything advance through Belgium and northern France, designed to trap the French armies, it came close to success. Only the mistakes and moral inadequacy of Moltke (a sick man) paralleled by the iron nerve, adaptability and organizational genius of Joffre and the Paris garrison commandant, Galliéni, saved France and the Allied cause in the First Battle of the Marne (September 1914). The Belgian Army, belatedly joined by British reinforcements, made a defiant stand at Antwerp. In early October, the Belgians retreated down the Channel coast. By 15 October 1914, the continuous entrenched Western Front had been established from the sea to Switzerland. Furious German attempts to break through at Arras and Ypres were conspicuously unsuccessful.

Two big Russian armies — gallantly but very ineptly led and poorly equipped — immediately lurched into East Prussia. Although ultimately disastrous, their misguided onslaught did serve to force the Germans to withdraw forces from the West at a critical time. Hindenburg crushed the Russians at Tannenberg (late August 1914). A Russian invasion of Galicia (Austrian-ruled Poland) proved less easy to contain, being blocked a few miles east of Cracow.

Despite the massive potential threat posed to Britain's traditional naval supremacy by the German Navy, the latter remained in harbour. Commerce raiders, U-boats and minelayers made some mischief but the formidable German Pacific Squadron (von Spee) was bloodily annihilated off the Falklands by British battlecruisers in early December 1914. Shortly afterwards came that strange interlude, the 'Christmas Truce' on the Western Front, when spontaneous outbreaks of fraternization took place between British and German (particularly Bavarian) troops. For a 'brief shining moment' (to use one later and borrowed phrase but perhaps apposite here), a hell-bent, war-crazed continent teetered on the edge of the sulphurous abyss.

1915

Both sides made attempts to break through the Western Front but to little effect despite huge casualties. Not even the German chlorine and phosgene poison gas-cloud attacks (April and December) achieved any decisive result. British operations continued to be gravely hampered by lack of high-explosive shells and heavy guns. During the first winter of trench warfare (1914-15) BEF C-in-C Sir John French had repeatedly asked for more shells and vast increases in high-explosive output. He was told that he must economize. In spring 1915, the British guns were, with few exceptions, rationed to **four** shells per gun per day ('not to be used unless necessary'!). Hand grenades were improvised from discarded bully beef and jam cans. War Minister Kitchener, when pressed by Prime Minister Asquith, denied that there was a shell shortage. But Colonel Charles Repington, military correspondent of *The Times*, after returning from the front, revealed that the British attacks at Festubert (April) had failed almost entirely because of lack of HE projectiles to dislodge the Germans from their strongpoints.

On 21 May 1915, a headline in the *Daily Mail* screamed 'The Tragedy of the Shells'. The paper asserted that Kitchener 'had starved the army in France of high explosive shells'. Kitchener claimed (perhaps with some justice) that his comments had been misinterpreted by Asquith. Be that as it may, drastic action was obviously called for. On 26 May, the British Government announced the creation of a Ministry of Munitions with wide powers, to be headed by David Lloyd George. The Ministry began to function on 2 July 1915 and quickly achieved dramatic results. Four months later an inter-allied munitions organization was established by Lloyd George and his equally dynamic French counterpart, Albert Thomas. In spring 1916, Kitchener attempted to persuade a brilliant engineer, Herbert Hoover (later US President) to renounce his American citizenship and join the Ministry of Munitions as Lloyd George's eventual successor. Nothing had been settled when Kitchener was drowned and Lloyd George took over the War Office (June 1916).

Kitchener had seen, with unusual clarity, that the war would last for at least three years and that Germany 'will only give in when she is beaten to the ground'. He laid detailed plans for a 'New Army' of 70 divisions (1.2 million men) by 1917; all would-be volunteers unconnected with the Territorial system. As a young volunteer in the Franco-Prussian War, Kitchener had noted with disgust how the French Territorials had decamped en masse from the hastily improvised Prussian Army of the Loire.

French left the BEF in December 1915 and was succeeded by Haig. A bitter argument over Allied grand strategy was now in full swing. Haig and the new Chief of Imperial General Staff, Robertson, belonged to the so-called 'Westerner' faction, which advocated total concentration of all fighting men and guns in France. The opposing 'Easterners' (including Lloyd George and Churchill) advocated decisive action against the weaker brethren among the Central Powers; Austria, Italy (the latter entered the war on the Allied side in May 1915) and Ottoman Turkey. She had entered the war in November 1914 but by early February 1915 had been defeated both in the Russian Caucasus and near the Suez Canal. The British had invaded and taken the Gulf end of Turkish-ruled Mesopotamia (modern Iraq), initially to protect their oil fields in SW Persia. A powerful Anglo-French fleet attacked the Dardanelles in February-March 1915, and an Australian, New Zealand, British and French force began landing on the Gallipoli Peninsula south-west of Constantinople in April. If this operation had been launched sooner, Turkey might have been knocked out of the war, permitting unhindered communication with Russia through the Black Sea. But Allied procrastination and mismanagement merely reproduced all the features and senseless slaughter of the Western Front. And an over-optimistic British autumn dash up the Tigris for Baghdad, to offset the Gallipoli failure, ended down river in another entrenched stalemate at Kut.

Denied large-scale supplies of Allied munitions, the Russians had to endure from April successive crushing German offensives in the south (Mackensen) and in the west (Hindenburg) supported by overwhelming concentrations of heavy artillery. All Russian Poland, including Warsaw (4 Aug), was overrun by the Germans. The Eastern Front did not stabilize until late September 300 miles to the east by which time the Tsar's armies had sustained over 2 million casualties, half of them prisoners, with the loss of nearly 3000 guns. The Tsar himself had felt impelled to replace his uncle Grand Duke Nicholas as C-in-C (5 September) thus further divorcing himself from the vital events on the home front. No wonder Falkenhayn, the German Chief of Staff, felt he had achieved his spring aim of 'the indefinite crippling of Russia's offensive strength'. He withdrew victorious divisions across the Central Powers' superb railway network to strike down Serbia which had ferociously resisted her Austrian attackers for over a year. In a little over six weeks (October-November), Mackensen's veterans, aided by Bulgaria's stab-in-the-back intervention, had overrun Serbia leaving her armies to make a memorable winter retreat to Albania and the sea. Franco-British landings at Salonika (N Greece) were too little and too late to affect the outcome.

The four Central Powers now formed an unimpeded bloc. Furthermore, Austria's initial two-front burden had been decisively eased and she was standing up well to Italy's opportunistic attacks on the Isonzo and in the Alps (June onwards). The one foe that really united her polyglot army was the traditional Italian one it had humbled before in 1848-49 and 1866. Falkenhayn felt he was now free to pursue his most cherished strategic aim to wear down the already sorely-tried French Army so that *'breaking point would be reached and England's best sword knocked out of her hand'* (Dec). The Entente should collapse before the new Kitchener armies could exert their million-strong pressure on the Western Front.

Only in remote African theatres did the Allies score clear-cut 1915 military successes. Anglo-French colonial forces completed the hard-won conquest of the Cameroons (October 1915-February 1916) after Botha's South Africans had triumphantly overrun German South-West Africa (February-July 1915) in a model campaign of desert logistics and Boer-mounted commando advances. Imperial forces were now available to invade German East Africa after a year on the defensive.

1916

The overrunning of Serbia by Central Powers forces (including Bulgarians), the evacuation of Gallipoli and the siege of Kut in Mesopotamia blighted many of the pet schemes of the 'Easterners'. Once again, Allied plans for 'decisive offensives' on the Western Front received top priority. Massive Anglo-French combined operations were scheduled for spring 1916. But Falkenhayn struck first at Verdun on a quiet sector of the front. The war's longest battle began on 21 February and lasted until December. The German preliminary bombardment was the heaviest yet seen in war. The most sanguinary fighting took place for possession of Forts Douaumont (February) and Vaux (June); at Hill 30; and on a hill called Le Mort Homme ('Dead Man's Hill'). Douaumont was levelled to the ground and the very earth around it reduced to the consistency of fine talcum powder. The defenders were led by General (later Marshal) Philippe Pétain, under the watchwords *Ils ne passeront pas!* (They shall not pass!). And they did not pass! A round-the-clock, week-in week-out shuttle service of motor trucks kept the garrison constantly supplied. The prolongation and ferocity of the fighting soon bore little or no relation to the intrinsic importance of the German objective; 66 French and 42 German divisions were decimated. The German Chief of Staff, Falkenhayn, intended to 'bleed the French Army white'. If the successful French counterattacks of August-September 1917 are included, casualties at Verdun totalled a round *million* (550,000 French, 450,000 German).

The Allied reply to the Verdun onslaught came in the Somme valley during July-November. But Haig's unimaginative frontal attacks and the lamentable performance of the British artillery (despite adequate supplies of shells) brought no decisive result for the toll of 420,000 British and 195,000 French casualties. The battlefield debut of the tank (15 September) was on too small a scale to affect it. Disagreements over the Western Front stalemate and the fall of Rumania helped bring down the Asquith Government; David Lloyd George was appointed Prime Minister by King George V in December 1916. On the Eastern Front the now better-equipped and trained Russians under Brusilov had already launched a surprise offensive that, in June, made spectacular gains between the Pripet marshes and the Carpathians.

Between 4 June and 15 August 1916, the Austro-Germans suffered 700,000 casualties (including 360,000 PoWs); Russian losses stood at 550,000. In near-desperation, the Central Powers were forced to transfer no fewer than 44 divisions from all fronts to meet Brusilov's deadly threat. But Rumania's entry into the war at the end of August, and the disasters which soon befell the cocksure Rumanians 'really brought his [Brusilov's] offensive to an end, by radically changing his mission, from the destruction of the Austro-Hungarian armies to the preservation of Rumania, about a quarter of the Russian army had been drawn into the task of preventing a total Rumanian collapse. It was an ignominious end to an undertaking that had promised so well   By the end of the offensive, Brusilov's armies had lost 1,412 000 men. Brusilov's offensive was the last flourish of Imperial Russia...'. ['The Brusilov Offensive: From Victory to Failure' by Geoffrey Jukes (*Purnell's History of the First World War*, Vol 4, No 9, London, 1970.)].

The British force besieged at Kut in Mesopotamia, had to surrender to the Turks in April 1916 (the largest such capitulation since Kabul in 1842). But this was the Ottomans' only success. Late in the previous winter (February 1916), the Russians under Yudenich had captured the strongly fortified city of Erzerum in Turkish Armenia. A second Turkish attack on the Suez Canal failed in August, while the Arab Sherif of Mecca proclaimed a revolt and received the assistance of a British mission, which included the extraordinary Captain T E Lawrence. Lawrence helped organize the Arab army and, during 1916-18, gave invaluable assistance to the British forces in Palestine by forming and securing their right flank.

In East Africa, a prolonged British and Belgian offensive directed by Smuts overran most of Germany's last colony but at heavy cost from disease and without ever decisively defeating Lettow-Vorbeck's resilient defenders.

Germany had begun unrestricted submarine warfare in February 1915, but repeated American protests since the sinking of the liner *Lusitania* and other atrocities forced Berlin to suspend the campaign in April 1916. When Scheer, new commander of the German High Seas Fleet , attempted to repeat the bombardment of English coastal towns earlier carried out by his predecessor, he provoked the one and only general fleet action of the war — Jutland, or Skaggerak as the Germans called it. British losses were heavier but the German fleet never ventured out again with serious intent. In an attempt to force the British to their knees, the all-out U-boat campaign was resumed in February 1917.

The venerable Austrian emperor, Francis Joseph II, died on 21 November 1916, aged 86. He was succeeded by his grand-nephew, the Archduke Charles. Although not previously suspected of having any interest in or aptitude for anything beyond soldiering and devotion to his glamorous wife Zita and infant son, Charles was soon making earnest endeavours to save his gravely threatened inheritance and conclude peace. Renewing his efforts the following spring, he employed his brother-in-law, Prince Sixtus of Bourbon-Parma, to act as intermediary between the Austrian and French governments. However, neither this initiative nor a 'peace note' from Pope Benedict XV (August 1917) bore fruit. Other (less august) 'peacemakers' were the British peer, Lord Lansdowne, the German Baron von der Lancken and millionaire American industrialist Henry Ford.

TABLES

	Population	Peacetime Strength 1 July	Mobilized	Corps	Inf Divs	Cav Divs	Other Units	Guns	MGs
Austria	49.8m	480,000	2,000,000	17	49	11	2 divs 16 bdes	c3000	c1464+
Germany	65.0m	880,000	4,500,000	41	82	11	6 divs 32 bdes	c7400	4500
Belgium	7.5m	48,000	217,000	-	6	1	fortress troops	324	108 +fortress
Britain	46.4m	255,000	713,514	3	6	1	-	1859	c200
France	39.6m	823,251	3,781,000	21	72	10	12 divs	5108	5100
Russia	167.0m	1,400,000	4,500,000	37	114	29	-	c5672 (estab)	2432 (est)
Serbia	5.0m	30,000	459,500	-	12	1	1bde c45 bns	c458	n/a

Army Mobilization August 1914

1914 WESTERN FRONT TABLES

French Troops Aug 1914

Armies & Fortresses	2,689,000
Interior	935,000
N Africa	157,000
Total	3,781,000

Battles of the Frontiers Forces Aug 1914

German Field Army (Moltke) 1,485,000 men, 5580 guns (480 heavy), c2118 MGs, 500 lorries in 78 inf (28 res) +10 cav divs, 14 *Landwehr* bdes

First Army (Kluck) 320,000, 84,000 horses, c910 guns, 396 MGs, 81 lorries in 14 inf +3 cav divs + 3 *Landwehr* bdes
Second Army (Bülow) 260,000 men, c796 guns, 324 MGs, 81 lorries in 12 inf divs + 2 *Landwehr* bdes
Third Army (Hausen) 180,000 men, c574 guns, 216 MGs, 81 lorries in 8 inf divs +1 *Landwehr* bde
Fourth Army (Württemberg) 180,000 men, c630 guns; 216 MGs 45 lorries in 10 inf divs + 1 *Landwehr* bde
Fifth Army (Crown Prince) 200,000 men, c714 guns, 324 MGs, 45 lorries in 13 inf +2 cav divs +5 *Landwehr* bdes
Sixth Army (Rupprecht) 220,000 men, c946 guns, 288 MGs in 14 inf + 3 cav divs+ 1 *Landwehr* bde
Seventh Army (Heeringen) 125,000 men, 530 guns; 162 MGs in 9 inf divs + 1 *Landwehr* bde.

Belgian Field Army (K Albert) 117,000 men, 324 guns, 108 MGs, 12 aircraft in 6 inf + 1 cav div
French Army (Joffre) 1,071,000-2,669,000 men, c3156 guns, 1668+ MGs, 220 motor vehicles, 138 aircraft in 72 inf (25 res & Territorial) +10 cav divs (52,500); 8 res & Territorial divs reinforced 821,400 fortress troops

First Army (Dubail) 256,000 men, c760 guns, c348 MGs in 14 inf + 2 cav divs
Second Army (Castelnau) 200,000 men, c760 guns, c348 MGs in 14 inf + 2 cav divs +1 mixed col bde
Third Army (Ruffey) 168,000 men, c472 guns, 246 MGs in 10 inf + 1 cav div
Fourth Army (Langle) 193,000 men, c716 guns, c318 MGs in 13 inf + 1 cav div
Fifth Army (Lanrezac) 254,000 men, 110,000 horses, 800 guns, c312 MGs in 12 inf +4 cav divs

BEF (French) 103,691+ men, 40,000 horses, 410 guns (20 heavy), 152 MGs in 5 inf + 1 cav div + 1 inf bde.

Battles of the Frontiers Losses Aug 1914

Belgian	12,330+
British	14,409; 38 guns
French	210,993 (excl Territorial & garrison units)
German	c220,000(?); 24+ guns

Marne Forces 5 Sept 1914

Allied Armies (Joffre) 1,082,000
French Sixth Army (Maunoury) 60,000 in 9½ inf + 2 cav divs
BEF (French) c100,000, 362 guns in 5 ⅓ inf + 1 cav div (5 bdes)
French Fifth Army (d'Esperey) 13 inf + 2 cav divs
French Ninth Army (Foch) 8 inf + 1 cav div
French Fourth Army (Langle) 9 divs
French Third Army (Sarrail) 8 inf + 1 cav div
German Army (Moltke) 900,000
First Army (Kluck) 10 inf + 3 cav divs
Second Army (Bulow) 8 inf + 2 cav divs
Third Army (Hansen) 6 divs + 1 *Landwehr* bde
Fourth Army (Württemberg) 8 divs + 1 *Landwehr* bde
Fifth Army (Crown Prince) 6 divs facing French Third

Marne Losses 5-10 Sept 1914

French	c80,000
British (6-10 Sept)	1701
German	(c15,217 PoWs); 36 guns; c112 MGs; 3 flags

Siege of Antwerp Losses 27 Sept-10 Oct 1914

Belgian	18,000 + 33,000 interned in Holland
British	2746 (936 PoWs)
German	

First Ypres and Yser Forces 18-20 Oct 1914

Belgian Army (Albert) 48,000 rifles, 350 guns, 6 inf + 2 cav divs
French Marine Bde (Ronarc'h) 6000
British 7th Div (Capper) 17,948, 63 guns
British 3rd Cav Div (Byng) 3994, 6 guns
French 87th & 89th Territorial Divs
French Cav Corps (de Mitry) 4 divs
British I Corps (Haig) 2 divs
British III Corps (Pulteney) 2 divs
British II Corps (Smith-Dorrien) 2 divs
Cav Corps (Allenby) 9000 in 2 divs, 30 guns
German Fourth Army (Württemberg) 13 divs, 400+ guns
German Sixth Army (Rupprecht) 14 inf + 8 cav divs, up to 700 guns

First Ypres and Yser Losses 14 Oct-30 Nov 1914

Belgian (18-30 Oct)	18,522
French	50,000
British (14 Oct - 30 Nov)	58,155 (incl 5951 Indian Corps from 23 Oct)
German (13/15 Oct-24 Nov)	134,315+ (31,265 missing & PoWs).

1914 W Front Losses

Belgian	c50,000; c170 guns (excl fortresses)
French	995,000
British	95,654; 80 guns; 84 aircraft
German	677,440+ ; 200+ guns (19 lost to BEF); c112+ MGs

1914 French dead by arm

Infantry	283,320
Cavalry	3790
Artillery	8560
Engineers	2880
Air service	32

1914 EASTERN FRONT TABLES

E Prussia Forces Aug 1914

German Eighth Army (Prittwitz) c200,000 (7000 cav), 774 guns, 50 aircraft, 2 Zeppelins in 9 inf +1 cav div +6 *Landwehr* & *Landsturm* bdes
Russian NW Front (Jilinski) up to 400,000 (20,000 cav), 1660 guns, 12 aircraft in 23½ inf + 8 cav divs
First Army (Rennenkampf) c160,000, 492 guns in 12 inf +5 cav divs +2 rifle bdes
Second Army (Samsonov) c240,000, 1160 guns in 1½ inf +3 cav divs +1 rifle bde

Poland & Galicia Forces Aug 1914

Austrian 800,000, 2000 guns, 42 aircraft in 4 armies & 2 army dets with 37 inf (by 30 Aug) +10 cav divs
Russian SW Front (Ivanov) 1,250,000, 3000 guns in 4 armies with 53½ inf (by 30 Aug) +9 cav divs

Lemberg Losses 5 Aug-11 Sept 1914

Austrian	300,000 k & w; 100,000 PoWs; 300 guns; 9 flags
Russian	210,000 k & w; 45,016 PoWs; 182 guns

Tannenberg Losses 25-31 Aug 1914

German 10,000-15,000
Russian 30,000 k & w; 92,000 +PoWs (60 trainloads) incl 13 generals; c500 guns

Masurian Lakes Forces 5 Sept 1914

German Eighth Army (Hindenburg) c250,000, 1074 guns in 13 inf +2 cav divs +6 other bdes
Russian First Army (Rennenkampf) c200,000, 924 guns in 14 inf +5 cav divs +2 rifle bdes

Masurian Lakes Losses 5-15 Sept 1914

German	c70,000
Russian	c100,000 k & w; 45,000 PoWs; 200 guns

Lodz Forces 11 Nov 1914

German Ninth Army (Mackensen) c250,000 in 11 inf +4 cav divs & *Landwehr*
Russian First, Second & Fifth Armies 500,000-600,000 in 10 corps +3 cav divs

Lodz Losses 11-25 Nov 1914

German	c35,000 k & w
Russian	c70,000 k & w; 25,000 PoWs; 79 +guns

1914 Eastern Front Losses

German	c275,000 (3000 PoWs); 13 +guns; 1 Zeppelin
Austrian	up to 1m (129,000 PoWs); c700 guns
Russian	1,800,000 (486,000 PoWs) incl 85,000 evacuated sick; 900 guns

1914 SOUTHERN FRONTS TABLES

Serbia Forces Aug 1914

Serb Army (Crown Prince Alexander, CoS Putnik) c215,000 front line incl c7800 cav (459,500 mobilized, but 50,000 without rifles), c458 guns (132½ btys) in 12 inf divs + 1 cav div + 1 bde + c45 bns (frontier troops) = c213 bns, 40 sqns.

First Army (Boyovic) c55,000, 104 guns (26 btys) in 4 inf divs (52 bns) + 7 sqns

Second Army (Stepanovic) c71,000, 132 guns (33 btys) in 4 inf divs (64 bns) + 10 sqns

Third Army (Jurisic-Stürm) c32,000, 64 guns (16 btys) in 2 inf divs (28 bns) + 5 sqns

Uzice Army (Boganovic) c26,000, 44 guns (11 btys) in 1 inf div, 1 inf bde (24 bns) + Indep Cav Div c3000 (16 sqns), 4 guns

Belgrade Group c9 bns, 2 sqns, 40 guns (10 btys)

Obrenovac Group c11 bns, 22 guns (5½ btys)

Other frontier troops c25 bns, 52 guns (13 btys)

Montenegrin Army (Vesovic) c50,000 militia in 4 divs, a few guns

Austrian Balkan Army (Potiorek) c200,000, 810 guns (135 btys), 348 MGs in 13 inf divs + 1 cav div + 14 bdes (12 mtn) + 3 *Landsturm* bdes + 2+ reinforcement bdes = 284+ bns, 62 sqns

Second Army (Böhm-Ermolli) 7 inf divs (131 bns) + 1 cav div (42 sqns), + 336 guns (56 btys) (soon transferred to E Front)

Fifth Army (Frank) 4 inf divs (79 bns) + 3 bdes (I mtn) + 15 sqns + 234 guns (39 btys)

Sixth Army (Potiorek) 2 inf divs + 11 mtn bdes (74 bns) + 5 sqns + 240 guns (40 btys)

Danube Flotilla (Capt Grund) 6 river monitors

Serbia Forces Nov 1914

Serb Army (Putnik) c226,000 (c7000 cav), 452 guns in 11 inf div + 1 cav div + 1 inf bde + 35 bns.

First Army (Boyovic) 3 inf divs (44 bns) + Ljubovija Det + 9 sqns, 98 guns (24½ btys)

Second Army (Stepanovic) 4 inf divs (63 bns) + 27 sqns (incl cav div) + 136 guns (34 btys)

Third Army (Jurisic-Stürm) 3 inf divs (40 bns) + 6 sqns + 72 guns (18 btys)

Uzice Army (Boyanovic) 1 inf div, 1 inf bde, Lim dets (34 bns), 2 sqns, 48 guns (12 btys)

Belgrade Det (Zhivkovic) 17 bns + 1 sqn, 36+ guns (9 btys)

Obrenovac Det 16 bns, 12 guns (3 btys)

Branicevo & Kraina Gps 12 bns + 16 guns (4 btys)

Austrian Balkan Army (Potiorek) 284, 810 rifles, 600 guns

Sava River sector 55 bns (mainly *Landsturm*)

Fifth Army (Frank) 97,000 rifles in 4 divs + 3 bdes = 127½ bns, 20 sqns, 53½ btys

Sixth Army (Potiorek) 144, 000 rifles in 5 divs + 11 bdes = 110 bns, 12 sqns, 84 btys

1914 Serbia Losses

Serbs c170,000 (c15,000 PoWs); 42 guns

Montenegrin unknown

French 24 sailors; 2 guns (with Montenegrins)

Austrian 227,088 (45,000 + PoWs); 179 guns; 36+ MGs; 1 river monitor

1914 TURKISH FRONTS TABLES

Armenia Forces Nov 1914

Turk Third Army (Hasan Izzet Pasha) 189,562 men, 60,877 horses, 160 guns in 7 inf +5 cav divs +1 mobile gendarmerie div +22 frontier guard bns
Russian Caucasus Army (Vorontsov) 100,000 (15,000 cav), 256 guns in 3 inf +3 cav divs + 1 coastguard (Batumi) fortress div +9 inf & 2 cav bdes +13 inf bns

1914 Armenia Losses

Turk	c38,000; 2 guns
Russian	c15,000; 6 guns

1914 Egypt Losses

British	35
Turk	unknown

1914 Mesopotamia Losses

British (incl RN)	892 (18 PoWs & missing)
Turk	2200 (1423 PoWs); 21 guns; 2 MGs

1914 Tsingtao Losses

Japanese	5655; 1 cruiser; 1 destroyer; 1 torpedo boat
British	75
German	4743 (4043 PoWs); 130 guns; 100 MGs; 40 cars; 5 gunboats; 1 torpedo boat; 1 aircraft
Austrian	1 cruiser

1914 AFRICAN OPERATIONS TABLES

Togoland Forces Aug 1914

German 8 Army & Police officers, 560 African *Polizeitruppe* increased to 300 Europeans & 1200 soldiers, 3 MGs
British 1073 & 3 guns
French 665 & 2 guns

Cameroons Forces Aug 1914

German (Col Zimmermann) 243 Germans(raised to 700 Europeans), 2805 African askaris & police, c12 guns, 36 MGs
British WAFF (Dobell) 360 officers & NCOs, 7733 African askaris, 15 guns, c40 MGs
French (Chad, Congo, Gabon, Ubangi) 7595, 3 guns, 2 MGs

1914 W Africa Losses

British	600+ (incl 33 RN); 2 guns; 7 MGs
French	318+
German	338 k & w; c2273 PoWs (incl civilians); 4 guns; 3 MGs; 2 aircraft; 1 armed vessel

SW Africa Forces Aug 1914

German 3140 men (all white) incl 500-strong camel corps + 7000 male settlers, 37 guns, 22 MGs, 2 aircraft
S African Mounted Riflemen 5 regts and 18 guns in permanent force plus 44,193 white citizens in first year (1913) of Active Citizen Force

1914 S & SW Africa Losses

British	1077 (409k in rebellion); 2 guns
Boer rebels	540k +6000 PoWs
German	60+
Portuguese	182 (37 PoWs)

E Africa Forces Aug 1914

German (Lettow-Vorbeck) 305 German officers & NCOs (Army & Police), 4626 askaris, 67 MGs, 3 gunboats on L Tanganyika, 1 gunboat on L Nyasa, 1 steamer, 1 tug & 2 steam pinnaces on L Victoria
British 62 officers, 2319 KAR, 17 MGs, 6 steamers & 3 tugs on L Victoria, 5 steamers on L Nyasa
Belgian 15,000 (26 coys)

1914 E Africa Losses

British	987 (16 deaths from disease, 103 PoWs & missing); 10 MGs
German	401+; 1 gun

1914 SEA WAR TABLES

Fleets on Mobilization 1914

	Allied Powers				Central Powers		
	Britain	France	Russia	Japan	Germany	Austria	Turkey
Tonnage	2,224,000	793,000	405,000	579,000	l,054,000	195,000	70,415
Men	113,145	65,450	58,100	51,200	76,850	38,609	31,000?
Dreadnoughts	22	4	7 (1)	4 (2)	13 (3)	3 (4)	-
Battlecruisers	10	-	- (5)	2 (6)	4	-	1
Predreadnoughts	41	20	13	5	22 (8)	12	2
Cruisers	114	37	15	27	52	9	2
Destroyers	221	83	98	50	142	25	9
Torpedo boats	-	69	20	50	116	42	10
Gunboats (incl river) & sloops	59 (9)	11	17	4	9	10 (10)	24
Submarines	73	57	49	13	28	-	-
Minelayers	7	4	4	2	1	1	9
Seaplane carriers	1	1	-	1	-	-	-

Notes (1) Russia: 7 completing
(2) Japan: +2 laid down
(3) Germany: +4 building
(4) Austria: +1 building
(5) Russia: 4 laid down
(6) Japan: +2 launched
(8) Germany: +8 coast defence ships
(9) Britain: (Includes 13 minesweepers)
(10) Austria: 10 river monitors

Allied Warships Completed 1914-18

	Britain	France	Italy (1)	Japan	Russia	USA (1)
Dreadnoughts	13	3	3	4	7	6
Battlecruisers	5	-	-	2	-	-
Cruisers	-	-	2	-	-	-
Light cruisers	54	-	-	-	-	-
Monitors	39	-	10	-	-	-
Aircraft carriers	16	4	1	-	7	-
Destroyers	329	7	28	38(2)	36	77
Torpedo boats	-	-	32	-	-	-
Gunboats	-	11	1	-	14	4
Sloops	134	46	-	-	-	-
Patrol vessels	88	99	-	-	-	1
Minelayers	-	-	-	11	11	-
Minesweepers	156	52	37	-	8	42
Trawlers	397	-	-	-	-	-
CMBs/MTBs	124	18	299	-	-	50 for Italy &
		France				
River gunboats	24	12	2	-	13 small	-
Landing craft	360	-	-	-	53	-
Motor launches	580	-	-	-	24	36+ for Russia
Submarines	98	26	46	2	40	55
Submarine-chaser	-	-	-	-	-	448
Naval Tonnage						
11 Nov 1918	2,714,000	600,000	415,000	694,000	590,000	1,282,000
Naval Personnel						
11 Nov 1918	408,316	150,000	40,000+	63,225+	120,000	80,000

(1) Italy/USA: includes ships completed in her netural period
(2) Japan: 12 destroyers for France
(3) Russia: ships completed up to the Bolshevik Revolution.

Central Powers Warships Completed 1914-18

	Austria	Germany	
Dreadnoughts	1	6	
Battlecruisers	-	5	
Light cruisers	3	14	
Destroyers	5	107	
Torpedo boats	21	92	
Minesweepers	-	148	
Coastal minesweepers	-		141
Motor gunboats	-	4	
Motor torpedo boats	3	16	
Motor launches	-	51	
River patrol craft	1	-	
U-boats	17	318	
Naval tonnage 11 Nov 1918	232,000		1,400,000
Naval personnel 11 Nov 1918	200,000+		

1914 Royal Navy Losses

20 warships comprising 2 battleships; 9 cruisers; 2 torpedo gunboats; 1 destroyer; 4 submarines; 1 aircraft carrier; 1 AMC. Total 124,172t
19 auxiliaries comprising 1 hospital ship; 2 colliers; 16 trawlers & drifters. Total 19,165t
Total naval cas: 6109 or 2.97% of av 205,500 strength

1914 Allied & Neutral Merchant Shipping Losses

100 ships (64 British with 69 lives) worth 303,000t (241,201t British) of which 55 ships lost to surface ships, 3 to U-boats, 42 to mines (ie 1 for every 24 mines laid). 27 British merchant ships attacked or damaged (3 lives lost), all but 4 by German surface ships. Britain loses 45 fishing vessels (95 lives lost), all to mines or warships. In addition 82 British steamers (182,335t); 3 sailing vessels (1710t); 11 French steamers (5285t); 6 Russian steamers and 13 sailing vessels detained in German and Turk ports.

1914 U-boat Losses & Gains

5 lost, but 11 commissioned making total strength of 34, with 169 building or on order

1914 AIR WAR TABLES

1914 Air Strengths

	Aircraft	Seaplanes	Airships	Balloons	Personnel
Belgium	24				
Britain	218 (39 RNAS)	52	8		2073
France	126	15 (5 usable)			
Russia	190				75 pilots
Germany	232	35 (20 usable)	11	39+	
Austria	75	22	1	10	

1914 Air Raids

Paris 10 : 60 cas
Britain 2 : No cas; £40 damage; 8 defence sorties
Germany 8 :

1914 INTERNATIONAL EVENTS TABLES

1914 Exchange Rates (to the £)

Argentina	5	Pesos
Austria	24	Kronen (crowns)
Brazil	8.8	Milrei
Bulgaria	25.2	Lev
Chile	13.3	Pesos
China	6-8	Taels
Denmark	17.7	Kronen (crowns)
France	25.2	Francs
Germany	20.8	Marks
Italy	25.2	Lira
Japan	9.7	Yen
Mexico	9.7	Dollars
Netherlands	12.3	Florins or guilden
Norway	17.7	Kronen (crowns)
Russia	9.9	Roubles
Spain	25.2	Pesetas
Sweden	17.7	Kronen (crowns)
Turkey	c106	Piastres
USA	4	Dollars 89 cents
Uruguay	c4.8	Pesos

1915 WESTERN FRONT TABLES

Second Ypres Losses 22 Apr-25 May 1915

British (-31 May) 59,275 (6341 Canadians); 4 guns
French c10,000; 47 guns
Belgians 1530
German (excl Marine & XXII Res Corps dets) 34,933

Second Artois Losses 9 May-18 June 1915

French 102,533 (2463 PoWs)
British 28,267
German 49,446 (7436 PoWs to French)

Second Champagne Forces 25 Sept 1915

French Centre Army Group (Castelnau) 35 divs, 900 heavy guns, 200 aircraft
French Fourth Army (Langle) 16 divs + 3 cav divs
French Second Army (Petain) 14 divs
German Third Army (Einem) 8 divs ⎤
                                    ⎬ 60 aircraft
German Fifth Army (Crown Prince) ⎦

Third Artois and Loos Forces 25 Sept 1915

French Tenth Army (D'Urbal) 18 divs, 1000 guns (400 heavy)
BEF First Army (Haig) 13 divs, 951 guns (300 heavy), 161 aircraft, 4 kite balloons
German Sixth Army (Rupprecht) 7 divs, 376 guns (64 heavy)

Second Champagne Losses 25 Sept-7 Oct 1915

French (-7 Oct) 143,567
German 85,000 (19,293 PoWs); 150 guns

Third Artois and Loos Losses 25 Sept-16 Oct 1915

French 48,230
British (-16 Oct, Loos +) 61,693 (incl 2 generals & 28 bn COs k)
German c56,000 (c26,000 at Loos) incl 3153 PoWs to BEF + 2150 PoWs to French;
    18 guns (at Loos); 32 MGs (at Loos)
Germans took 3748 Allied PoWs in Artois.

1915 W Front Losses

French 966,687; 2750 guns (incl 1914)
British 296,583 (4820 OR PoWs); 4 guns
German (excl Jan 1915 but incl Jan 1916) 652,270 of which 110,250 v BEF (incl
    6372 PoWs) & 28,500+ PoWs to French; 168+ guns (1200 guns lost, all causes
    and fronts, by 31 May 1915)

1915 French dead by arm

Infantry	323,160 (worst full year)
Cavalry	3260
Artillery	11,100
Engineers	6960
Air service	260

1915 EASTERN FRONT TABLES

Winter Battle of Masuria Forces 7 Feb 1915

German Eighth (Below) & Tenth (Eichhorn) Armies c250,000, 1199 guns in 15 inf +2
    cav divs
Russian Tenth Army (Sievers) 250,000, 396 guns in 11 inf +2½ cav divs

Winter Battle of Masuria Losses 7-22 Feb 1915

German c7500+ many more sick; 14 guns
Russian 56,000; 185 guns; 200 MGs

Gorlice-Tarnow Forces 1 May 1915

German Eleventh Army (Mackensen) 126,000, 624 guns in 10 inf + 1 cav div
Austrian Fourth Army (Archduke Joseph Ferdinand) 90,000, 253 guns in 8 inf +1 cav
    div
Russian Third Army (Radko-Dmitriev) 219,000, 679 guns (only 4 heavy) in 18½ inf
    +5½ cav divs

Gorlice-Tarnow Losses 1 May-22 June 1915

German Eleventh Army 87,000
Russian up to 1m; 224 guns; 600 MGs

1915 Eastern Front Losses

German 246,264+ (15,784 PoWs); 26 + guns
Austrian 714,367+ (364,281 PoWs); 810 guns; 352 +MGs
Russian 2,452,000 (1,042,200 PoWs); 3000 guns; 1211 MGs

1915 SOUTHERN FRONTS TABLES

Serbia Forces Oct 1915

Serb Army (Putnik) c220,000, c700 guns: 227+ MGs in 12 inf divs + 1 cav div

First Army (Misic 3 divs ⎤
Third Army (Jurisic-Stürm) 2 divs ⎬ 120 bns & 330 guns
Timok Army (Gojkovic) 2 divs ⎦

Second Army (Stepanovic) 2 divs + 1 cav div

Macedonian Group (Boyovic) 2 divs + 3 3rd Ban formations

French (Sarrail) c40,000 in 3 divs

British (Mahon) c5000, 48 guns from 10th Div (Salonika)

Central Powers (Mackensen) c300,000, c1500 guns in 21 inf divs

Austrian Third Army (Kövess) 7 divs

German Eleventh Army (Gallwitz) 7 divs with 74 bns, 504 guns

Bulgar First Army (Boyadiev) 4 divs

Bulgar Second Army (Todorov) 3 divs

1915 Serbia Losses

Serb c200,000 (c174,000 PoWs of which c70,000 w); c597 guns; 48 MGs; 12
mortars; 208 ammo wagons

Montenegrin unknown

French 4965; 6 guns

British 1189; 8 guns; 24 MGs; 3 mortars

Austrian 7000 (for Belgrade alone)

German 8000+

Bulgar 6277 v Anglo-French alone

1915 Italian Front Losses

Italian 278,500 (22,500 PoWs)

Austrian 165,000 (30,000 PoWs)

Italian Front Forces May/June 1915

Italian (Cadorna) 875,256 men, 2121 guns (132 heavy, 320 mtn), 613 MGs, 3950
motor vehicles in 35 inf, 1 *Bersaglieri* and 4 cav divs + 2 *Alpini* gps with 415 bns, 116
sqns, 326 btys, 58 aircraft, 5 airships

Isonzo: Third Army (Duke of Aosta) 6 inf + 2 cav divs
           Second Army (Frugoni) 8 divs + 2 *Alpini* gps

Carnia: *Alpini* gp of 19 bns, 1 cav sqn, 32 guns

Trentino: Fourth Army (Nava) 5 divs
           First Army (Brusati) 6 divs

Comando Supremo Reserves 10 inf + 2 cav divs

Austrian SW Front (Archduke Eugene) 100,000 men in 14+ divs, 21 sqns with 162
becoming 234 bns, 87 becoming 155 btys, 136 aircraft, 1 airship

Izonzo: Fifth Army (Boroevic) 7 divs

Carnia: 14½ bns

Trentino: First Army (Dankl) 2 divs

1915 TURKISH FRONTS TABLES

Sarikamish Losses 21 Dec 1914-15 Jan 1915

Turk   c 75,000 (10,800 + PoWs, 15,000 frostbite) 53+ guns;
Russian   28,000 (12,000 frostbite); 6 guns

Armenia Losses 15 Jan 1915-31 Dec 1915

Turk   Unknown
Russian   6000-7000

Gallipoli Forces 25 Apr 1915

MEF (Hamilton) 75,056 men, 140 guns
  ANZAC (Birdwood) 30,638 men, 7618 horses
  British 29th Div (Hunter-Weston) 17,649 men, 3962 horses
  RND (Paris) 10,007 men, 1390 horses
  1st French Div (Amade) 16,762 men, 3511 horses

Turk Fifth Army (Liman) 84,000 (62,000 combatants in 6 divs)
  III Corps (Essad Pasha) 5th, 7th & 9th Divs
  XV Corps (Col Weber) 3rd & 11th Divs (Asiatic shore)
  Army Reserve 19th Div (Kemal) + cav bde

Gallipoli Losses 25 Apr 1915-9 Jan 1916

British (incl Indian) c171,433 (incl 48,683 evacuated sick and 308+ PoWs) out of
  410,000 incl Anzacs and 4950 Indians
Australian 26,094 (70 PoWs)
New Zealand 7473 (incl 25 PoWs, 206 deaths from disease & those wounded more
  than once) out of 8556
French 47,746 (incl 20,873 evacuated sick) out of 79,000
Allied total 252,000; 28+ guns
Turk 251,309 (official figure, other estimates even higher) incl 21,000 deaths from
  disease; 1687+ PoWs; 64,000 evacuated sick

Suvla Bay Forces 6 Aug 1915

MEF (Hamilton) 126,700, 334 guns
  Helles: VIII Corps (Douglas) 26,000, 114 guns in 4 divs
  Anzac: ANZAC (Birdwood) 37,000, 44 guns in 3 divs + 3 bdes
  Suvla: IX Corps (Stopford) 20,700 (initially), 56 guns in 6 divs
  French: CEO (Bailloud) 13,000, c120 guns in 2 divs
Turk Fifth Army (Liman) c76,000 effectives, 189 + guns in 16 divs +3 bns +1 cav bde
  N Group (Essad Pasha) c20,000, 76 guns in 3 divs +1 regt
  S Group (Wehib Pasha) c40,000, 94 guns in 6 divs
  Anafarta Det (Maj Willmer) 2000, 19 guns in 4 bns, 1 coy, 1 sqn (covering Suvla
  Bay)
  XVI Corps (Feizi Bey) at Bulair c14,000 in 3 divs

Suvla/Anzac Losses 6-29 Aug 1915

Anzacs 5800 + 1200 at Hill 60
British & Indian 20,800 + 1200 at Hill 60
Turk 7832+ (figure excludes 6-8, 14 & 17-20 Aug)

1915 Mesopotamia Losses

British (excl RN) 12,681 (406 PoWs); 1 gun; 3 gunboats; 3+ aircraft
Turk (incl Arabs) 23,922 (5056+ PoWs); 36 guns; 5 MGs; 1 gunboat & 1 steamer

1915 Egypt Losses

British 524
Turk 1702 + (716 PoWs); 3 MGs

1915 Aden Losses

British 80+ ; 2 guns
Turk 40 PoWs

1915 India Losses

British 225

1915 AFRICAN OPERATIONS TABLES

1915 E Africa Losses

British 1069 (297 PoWs & missing, 234 died of disease); 3 MGs
German 501+ ; 1 gun; 1 MG; 2 gunboats on lakes

S W Africa Losses to 9 July 1915

S African 432
German 523 k&w; 4000 PoWs; 37 guns; 22 MGs; 2 aircraft.

1915 SEA WAR TABLES

German Shipping Losses (-31 Jan 1915)

287 steamers worth 795,365t sunk, captured, seized or detained
64 sailing vessels worth 71,168t sunk, captured, seized or detained

Austrian Shipping Losses (-31 Jan 1915)

32 steamers worth 111,619t sunk, captured, seized or detained

1914 German & Austrian Shipping Blockaded or Interned Abroad (-31 Jan 1915)

724 steamers worth 2,878,533t & 100 sailing vessels worth 198,630t

Allied Dardanelles Submarine Successes 13 Dec 1914 - 2 Jan 1916

2 old Turk battleships; 1 destroyer; 12 sloops & small craft (incl 5 gunboats); 7, 9 or
  11 transports; 44 steamers (incl 36 over 1000t); 147/8 or 188 sailing vessels
Germans concede only 25 steamers & 10 damaged (c53,000t) + c3000t of small
  craft
4 RN & 3 French submarines lost in 32 passages

Italian & Austrian Naval Strength May 1915

	Italy	Austria
Battleships	23	20
Cruisers	9	7
Destroyers & torpedo boats	93	87
Submarines	21	7
Aircraft	20 ·	60
Airships	3	
Mines	2999	n/a
Torpedoes	1924	
Sailors (all ranks)	42,000	38,609+
Coal stocks	493,000t (initial consumption 60,000t+ pm)	n/a
Oil fuel	137,520t	n/a
Hospital ships	4	1
	233 warships all types	
	12 armoured trains for coast defence	

1915 German Baltic Shipping Losses Oct-Dec 1915

c20 steamers sunk or damaged worth c45,000t

1915 Royal Navy Losses

40 warships including 6 battleships; 2 cruisers; 2 river gunboats; 8 destroyers; 10
  submarines. Total 119,890t
127 auxiliaries incl 41 colliers & oilers, 65 trawlers & drifters. Total 155,222t
Total naval cas 5590 or 2.2% of av 254,200 strength, lowest annual loss of war

1915 Allied & Neutral Shipping Losses

468 ships (286 British with 2471 lives) worth 1,176,829t (845,621t British), of which
  396 to U-boats
U-boat official figure 636 ships worth 1,191,704t
766 British merchantmen now armed with guns

1915 U-boat Losses & Gains

17 lost (1 in Baltic, 4 in Med & Black Sea, 10 in N Sea) but 52
commissioned making total strength of 64
Most successful 1915 U-boat: *U33* (in Med) 40 ships worth 121,246t

1915 AIR WAR TABLE

1915 Air Raids

Paris	3:	13w
Britain	27:	(1 Zeppelin lost, 2 damaged); 1525 Zeppelin bombs; 747 cas; 150 defence sorties (17 aircraft damaged); 3 aircrew deaths
London	4:	278 bombs; 329 cas; 97 buildings hit; 91 fires caused
Germany	51:	940 bombs

1916 WESTERN FRONT TABLES

Verdun Forces 21 Feb 1916

German Fifth Army (Crown Prince/Knobelsdorf) 140,000 men initially from 10 of 19 divs, 1220 guns (654 heavy)
Verdun Fortress area (Herr) 150,000 men in 6 divs & 60 forts with 270 guns.

Verdun Forces 1 June 1916

German Fifth Army (Crown Prince/Knobelsdorf) 20 divs, 2200 guns (1730 heavy)
French Second Army (Nivelle) 20 divs, 1200 guns (570 heavy)

Somme Forces 1 July 1916

BEF (Haig) c500,000 men, 100,000 horses incl 5 cav divs & 1637 guns (427 heavy), 410 aircraft (27 sqns), 14 balloons
Fourth Army (Rawlinson) 16 divs (4 in res)
Third Army (Allenby) 2 divs
French Sixth Army (Fayolle) 13 divs (8 in res) & 1089 guns
German Second Army (F Below) 11 divs (5 in res)

Somme Losses 1 July-18 Nov 1916

British (55 divs engaged) 419,654 (35,939 Australian 26,574 Canadian, 9956 NZ): 16 tanks; 972 aircraft (190 missing & incl accidents)
French (20 divs engaged) 195,000
German (95 divs engaged) 419,989 (72,901 + PoWs); 1447+ guns (303 captured); 215 mortars; 981 MGs; 164 aircraft destroyed + 205 driven down damaged (RFC figs); and 6+ balloons

Verdun Losses 21 Feb-18 Dec 1916

French (66 divs engaged) 362,000
German (42 divs engaged) 336,831 (17,387 PoWs); c46 + guns; 44+ mortars; 107 MGs; c80+ aircraft; 6+ balloons

1916 W Front Losses

French 876,000; 3500 field guns (1500 worn out, 800 destroyed or captured)
British 643,246; 16 tanks; c1500 aircraft (?)
Belgian 16,000
German 962,488 (incl temporarily missing & excl Jan); c1912+ guns; 259+ mortars; 1088+ MGs; c500 aircraft (?)

French dead by arm 1916

Infantry	221,920
Cavalry	2830
Artillery	16,800 (highest year)
Engineers	5475
Air arm	620

1916 EASTERN FRONT TABLES

Lake Naroch Forces 18 Mar 1916

Russian Second Army (Ragoza) 350,000+ , 1271 guns in 20 divs
German Tenth Army (Eichhorn) 75,000, 300 guns in 7 divs

Lake Naroch Losses 18 Mar-14 Apr 1916

Russian 122,000 (12,000 frostbite deaths)
German 20,000

Brusilov Offensive Forces 4 June 1916

Russian SW Front (Brusilov) 600,000+ , 1938 guns (168 heavy) in 40 inf & 15 cav divs
    Eighth Army (Kaledin) 200,000, 716 guns in 11 inf & 4 cav div
    Eleventh Army (Sakharov) c125,000, 200 guns in 8 inf & 1 cav div
    Seventh Army (Scherbachev) c125,000 in 7 inf & 3 cav divs
    Ninth Army (Lechitski) 150,000, 495 guns (47 heavy) in 10 inf & 4 cav divs
Austrian Army Group (Archduke Frederick) c500,000, 1846 guns (545 heavy) in 38½ inf (2 German) & 11 cav divs
    Fourth Army (Archduke Joseph Ferdinand) 150,000, 549 guns (174 heavy) in 12 inf & 4 cav divs
    First Army (Duhallo) 3 inf & 1 cav div
    Second Army (Böhm-Ermolli) 5 inf & 1 cav div
    Südarmee (Bothmer) 6 inf divs (German 48th Res Div)
    Seventh Army (Pflanzer-Baltin) 107,000, 150 medium & heavy guns in 12 inf & 5 cav divs

Rumanian Forces 27 Aug 1916

620,000 (440,000 effectives) under CoS Dimitri Iliescu , 1300 guns (768 modern), 574 MGs, 14 aircraft (35/60 pilots untrained) in 4 armies with 23 inf divs (13 newly formed, 5 without MGs) & 2 cav divs
First Army (Culcer) c4½ divs, 3 cav bdes
Second Army (Grainiceanu) c4 divs, 4 cav bdes
Third Army (Averescu) c4 divs, 1 cav bde
Fourth Army (Prezan) c4 divs, 1 cav bde
Gen Res 2-3 divs
1 cruiser guardship; 4 auxiliary cruisers; 3 torpedo boats; 11 small gunboats & guardships; 4 river monitors; 8 river torpedo boats; c10 patrol boats

Central Powers Forces v Rumania 27 Aug/Sept 1916

Austro-German Ninth Army formed 16 Sept (under Falkenhayn) 228 guns in 5 inf & 2 cav divs + *Alpenkorps* (1 div)
Austrian First Army (Arz) 3 inf divs, 3 *Jäger* bdes, 30 assorted bns, c5000 frontier police, 36 guns (soon 100)
Danube Army (Mackensen)
German 101st Div; Bulgar Third Army (Toshev) with 3 inf & 1 cav div; Bulgar 12th Div opposite Iron Gates; Austrian Danube Flotilla; Turk VI Corps (15th & 25th Divs)

Brusilov Offensive Losses 4 June-18 Oct 1916

German 150,000 (-31 Aug)
Austrian 750,000 (380,000 PoWs) ⎤ 405 guns; 1326 MGs; 367 mortars (by 12 Aug)
Turk 17,792+
Russian 1,412,000 (212,000 PoWs)

1916 Eastern Front Losses

German 350,000 (35,000 PoWs) of which 60,000 (c8000 PoWs) and c50 guns in Rumania
Austrian 1m (470,000 PoWs); c700 guns+
Turk 17,792+
Bulgar not available
Russian 2,404,000 (344,000 PoWs)
Rumanian 350,000 (150,000 PoWs); 359 guns; 346 MGs

1916 SOUTHERN FRONTS TABLES

Trentino Offensive Forces May 1916

Austrian *Strafexpedition* (Archduke Eugene nominally, Conrad directing, HQ Trento) 157,234 inf, 1056 guns (262 heavy incl 46 superheavy of 305mm+) in 14 divs

    Eleventh Army (Dankl) 85,238 inf (103 bns) + 811 guns in 7 divs

    Third Army (Kövess) 71,966 inf (89 bns) + 245 guns in 7 divs

Italian Army (Cadorna)

    First Army (Pecori-Giraldi) 8 divs + 2 bdes with 176 bns (15 *Alpini* & 4 *Bersaglieri*) + 851 guns (36 heavy)

Reserves 90 bns (4 divs)

Trentino Offensive Losses 15 May-17 June 1916

Italian 52,000 (40,000 PoWs); 400+ guns (120 medium & heavy)

Austrian 44,000 (2000 PoWs & 14,000 sick)

Macedonia Forces Aug 1916

Allied Armies of the Orient (Sarrail) c375,000 (3300 cav), 1032 guns, 1300+ MGs in 16½ divs (201 bns)

    British Salonika Army (Milne) 119,176 (incl 36,000 inf), 370 guns in 5 divs (60 bns)

    French Army of the Orient (Cordonnier) 115,396 (2844 cav), 346 guns in 5 divs (52 bns) with 47,894 horses & mules, 6801 wagons, 1169 cars

    Serb Army (Crown Prince Alexander, Gen Boyovic) 122,549, 284 guns in 6 divs

    Italians (Petitti) 11,000, 32 guns in 1 div (12 bns)

    Russians (Dietrichs) 5000 in 1 bde (6 bns)

Bulgar Army (Prince Boris, Gen Gekov) c200,000, 900 guns in 9 divs (172 bns)

    Bulgar First Army (Gesov) 3 divs

    German Eleventh Army (Winckler) 3 divs (1 German)

    Bulgar Second Army (Todorov) 3 divs

1916 Macedonia Losses

Serb (Aug-Dec) 27,551 (exc deaths in hospital)

French 13,786 battle cas

Russian (exc 16 Oct-15 Dec) 1701

Italian 342

British 5048 + 29,594 malaria hospital admissions (21,902 evacuated)

Greek (to 15 Jan 1917) 78

Bulgar est 52,000 (c6500 PoWs); 42+ guns; 5+ MGs

German (Oct-Dec) 8000+ (c1500 PoWs)

1916 Italian Front Losses

Italian 440,780 (40,000+ PoWs); 400+ guns

Austrian 110,562+ (44,116+ PoWs)

1916 TURKISH FRONTS TABLES

Armenia Forces 10 Jan 1916

Turk Third Army (Mahmud Kamil Pasha on leave, Abdul Kamil Pasha deputising) 70,000-75,000 inf, 130 guns in 11 divs + 15-20 gendarme/ frontier guard bns + 2nd Cav Div
Russian Caucasus Army (Yudenich) 80,000 inf, c10,000 cav, 230 guns in 5 divs + 3 inf regts + 20 Cossack regts + 20 aircraft

1916 Armenia Losses

Turk 118,100+ (30,800 PoWs); 429 guns+ (incl 300 in Erzerum fortress)
Russian (incl Persia) 72,300+; 4 guns; 2 MGs

1916 Egypt Losses

British 3504 (304 PoWs); 136,110 sick admissions
Turk (incl Arabs) 6708+ (5249+ PoWs); 8 guns; 9 MGs

1916 Arabia Losses

Turk c4400 (mainly PoWs); 26 guns
Arabs unknown

1916 Mesopotamia Losses

British 42,105 (10,911 PoWs); 50 guns; 45+ MGs
Turk (incl Arabs) 11,500 (830+ PoWs) + many more sick; 2+ guns; 8+ MGs

---

1916 AFRICAN OPERATIONS TABLES

1916 E Africa Losses

British 3876 (96 PoWs & missing, 1103 died of disease); 4 guns; 1+ MG
Belgian 1276; 2 guns; 4 MGs
Portuguese 845+ European sick
German 2086+ (1000+ PoWs); 17 guns; 19 MGs; 1 gunboat

Cameroons Losses 1914-16

British 1469 + 858 invalided out + 574 carriers k, w or died of disease (8219 invalided out)
French 2708 + 1231 invalided out
German 6575; c4 guns; c20 MGs interned in Spanish Muni
    1605+ (1003+ PoWs); 8 guns; 16 MGs; 2 aircraft

1916 SEA WAR TABLES

Jutland Forces 31 May 1916

	Grand Fleet	High Seas Fleet
Dreadnoughts	28	16
Batttlecruisers	9	5
Predreadnoughts	-	6
Armoured cruisers	8	-
Light cruisers	26	11
Destroyers	77	61
Seaplane carriers	1	
Minelayer	1	

Total tonnage 1,250,000
Total crews 60,000 45,000

1916 Royal Navy Losses

52 warships including 3 battlecruisers; 2 battleships; 7 cruisers; 1 monitor; 16 destroyers; 4 sloops; & 12 submarines. Total 190,378t
170 auxiliaries incl 44 colliers & oilers & 100 trawlers & drifters.
Total 180,440t Total naval cas 12,050 out of av strength 316,100 or 3.81% of av strength 316,100, highest annual loss of war.

1916 Allied & Neutral Losses

1157 ships (396 British) worth 2,348,000t (1,237,634t British) of which 964 to U-boats, 161 to mines, 32 to surface ships
U-boat official figure 2,208,709t (1,045,058t in Med)

1916 U-boat Losses & Gains

22 U-boats lost (4 in Black Sea) but 108 commissioned making total strength 149
Most successful 1916 U-boat: U35 (in Med) 122 ships worth 266,643t

1916 U-boat Narrow Seas Minelaying

Flanders U-boats lay 472 mines sinking 2 destroyers, 5 minesweeper trawlers & 20 steamers. In all 195 mine groups laid mainly off British E coast.

1916 AIR WAR TABLES

1916 Air Raids

Paris	1:	54 cas
Britain	52:	(8 Zeppelins lost); 3458 Zeppelin bombs; 1063 cas; 369 defence sorties (51 aircraft damaged, 5 aircrew deaths)
London	3:	113 bombs; 158 cas; 111 buildings hit; 36 fires caused
Germany	96:	917 bombs
Constantinople	2	
Venice	1	
Bucharest	c13	

RFC Strength 29 Sept 1916

1035 aircraft abroad
1677 aircraft at home
30 aircraft under test
1195 aircraft struck off since 12 June
1725 aircraft taken into service since 12 June
64 service + 33 res sqns
28 sqn stns
22 training stns (+12 building)
47,649 personnel (1392 under training)
952 new pilots since 18 June
5071 motor vehicles
37 firms making aircraft
87 firms making spare parts

1916 INTERNATIONAL EVENTS TABLES

Portuguese Forces 9 Mar 1916

12,000+ regular troops (4300 incl 2800 African in Mozambique)
1 coast defence ship; 3 old cruisers (1 off E Africa); 5 destroyers; 1 sloop; 4 torpedo boats; 13 gunboats (2+ off E Africa); 7 river gunboats; 2 minelayers; 1 submarine; 2 patrol vessels; 1 fishery protection vessel

1916 HOME FRONTS TABLES

1916 Russian Munitions Production

1,321,000 rifles; 11,072 MGs; 1482m SAA; 8208 field guns; 33m shells

1916 British Munitions Production

1,168,899 rifles, 33,200 MGs; 295.5m SAA; 150 tanks; 4947 guns; 5554 mortars; 128m shells.

MAPS

Western Front: 1914-18

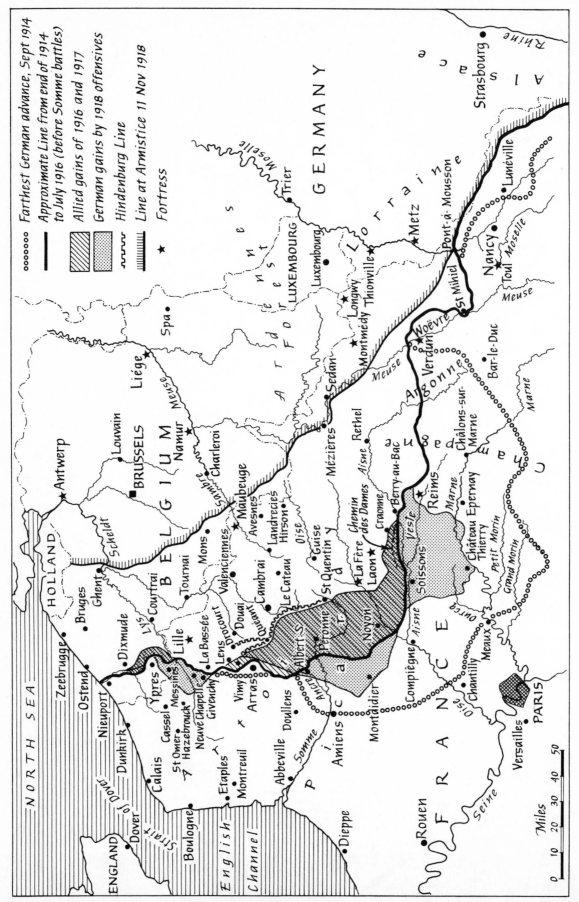

Western Front: Ypres Salient 1914-18

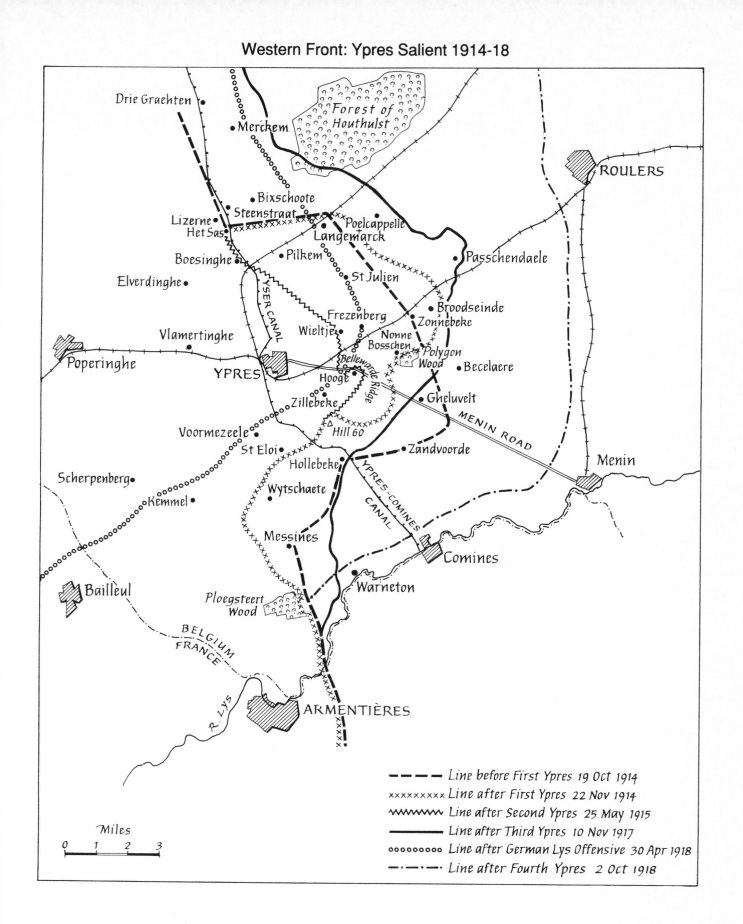

Drie Graehten
Merckem
Forest of Houthulst
ROULERS
Bixschoote
Steenstraat
Lizerne
Het Sas
Poelcappelle
Langemarck
Boesinghe
Pilkem
St Julien
Passchendaele
Elverdinghe
YSER CANAL
Broodseinde
Frezenberg
Zonnebeke
Vlamertinghe
Wieltje
Nonne
Bosschen
Polygon
Wood
Poperinghe
YPRES
Bellewarde Ridge
Hooge
Becelaere
Zillebeke
Gheluvelt
Voormezeele
Hill 60
MENIN ROAD
St Eloi
Zandvoorde
Menin
Hollebeke
Scherpenberg
Kemmel
Wytschaete
YPRES-COMINES CANAL
Messines
Comines
Bailleul
Warneton
Ploegsteert
Wood
BELGIUM
FRANCE
R. LYS
ARMENTIÈRES

Miles
0   1   2   3

- - - - -   Line before First Ypres 19 Oct 1914
xxxxxxxxx   Line after First Ypres 22 Nov 1914
wwwwwww   Line after Second Ypres 25 May 1915
─────   Line after Third Ypres 10 Nov 1917
ooooooooo   Line after German Lys Offensive 30 Apr 1918
─·─·─·─   Line after Fourth Ypres 2 Oct 1918

Western Front: Verdun 1916-17

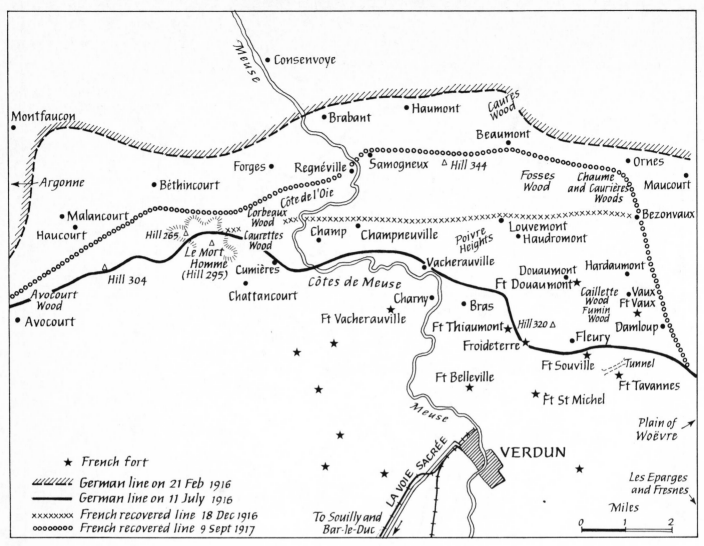

French fort

//////// German line on 21 Feb 1916

———— German line on 11 July 1916

xxxxxxx French recovered line 18 Dec 1916

ooooooo French recovered line 9 Sept 1917

Meuse

• Consenvoye

Montfaucon

• Brabant • Haumont Caures Wood

Beaumont

• Forges Regnéville • Samogneux △ Hill 344 • Ornes

← Argonne

• Béthincourt Côte de l'Oie Fosses Wood Chaume and Caurières Woods Maucourt

• Malancourt Corbeaux Wood xxx • Bezonvaux

Haucourt Hill 265 △ Caurettes Wood Champ • Champneuville Louvemont Hardaumont

Le Mort Homme (Hill 295) Poivre Heights • Haudromont

△ Hill 304 Cumières • Vacherauville • Douaumont • Vaux

Avocourt Wood Chattancourt Côtes de Meuse Ft Douaumont ★ Caillette Wood Ft Vaux

• Avocourt Charny • • Bras Fumin Wood Damloup

Ft Vacherauville Ft Thiaumont ★ Hill 320 △ • Fleury

Froideterre ★ Ft Souville ★ Tunnel

Ft Belleville ★ Ft Tavannes ★

★ Ft St Michel Plain of Woëvre ↗

Meuse

VERDUN Les Eparges and Fresnes →

LA VOIE SACRÉE Miles

To Souilly and Bar-le-Duc ← 0   1   2

Western Front: Somme 1916-18

BEF THIRD ARMY
Hébuterne
Gommecourt • Bucquoy
Puisieux
Serre
Miraumont
Irles
Beaumont Hamel
Grandcourt Pys
Beaucourt
St Pierre Divion
Grévillers • Bapaume → Cambrai
Warlencourt Ligny-Thilloys
Le Sars △ Butte de Warlencourt
Destremont Farm
Schwaben Redoubt
Stuff Redoubt Courcelette
Eaucourt
Gueudecourt
Le Transloy
Thiepval □ Mouquet Farm
Leipzig Redoubt
Martinpuich
Flers
High Wood
Lesboeufs
Bazentin
Delville Wood Morval
Poziéres
Longeuval
Ginchy
Sailly-Saillisel
Ovillers
Waterlot Farm
Leuze Wood
St Pierre Vaast Wood
Contalmaison
Mametz Wood
Guillemont
Frégicourt
Albert
La Boisselle
Trônes Wood
Combles
Rancourt
BEF FOURTH ARMY
Fricourt Mametz
Montauban
Falfemont Farm
Le Priez Farm
Maurepas
Le Forest
Maricourt
Bouchavesnes
Ville
Curlu
Cléry
Morlancourt
Somme
Omiecourt
Mt St Quentin
Bray
Péronne
Herbécourt
Biaches
FRENCH SIXTH ARMY
Somme Chipilly
Chuignes
Dompierre
Proyart
Belloy-en-Santerre
Barleux
Amiens
Estrées
Framerville
Berny
Soyécourt
Somme
Ablaincourt
Pressoir
Chilly 2 miles • Chaulnes

ooooooo Allied front line 1 July 1916
——— German front line 1 July
– – – German front line by 31 July
– · – German front line 1 Sept
— — German front line 1 Oct
•—•—• German front line 20 Nov

Miles
0   1   2   3

Fortress

Limit of Russian advances 1914-15

Limit of Austro-German advances 1915-16

Regained by Brusilov, June-Aug 1916

German gains in Sept-Oct 1917

German penetration into Russia by 3 Mar 1918 (Treaty of Brest-Litovsk)

After 3 March 1918

Miles
0   50 100 150 200

German landings 1917-18

FINLAND

Lake Ladoga

Viipuri

Lovisa

Helsinki

Bjorko

Kronstadt

Hangö

Reval

ST PETERSBURG (Petrograd)

Tsarskoe Selo

Gulf of Finland

Narva

Yamburg

Gatchina

Dagö

Estonia

Moon I.

Pernau

Osel

Dorpat

Gulf of Riga

Pskov

Baltic Sea

Windau

Moscow

Riga

Libau

Courland

Latvia

Mitau

Jakobstadt

Shavli

Dvinsk

Memel

Lithuania

Dvina

Königsberg

Kovno

Smolensk

Tula (main state arsenal)

Danzig

L. Naroch

Gumbinnen

E. Prussia

Vilna

Mogilev (Stavka 1915-17)

Orel

Tannenberg

Masuria

Osovyets

Grodno

Minsk

Berezina

Dnieper

Thorn

Narew

Don

Novo Georgievsk

Prasnysz

Baranovichi

R U S S I A

Warsaw

Bug

Brest-Litovsk

Pinsk

Priper

Kursk

Voronezh

Kalish

Poland

Vistula

Lodz

Pripet Marshes

Desna

Radom

Pilitsa

Lublin

Lutsk

Rovno

Zhitomir

Belgorod

Silesia

Vistula

Ivangorod

San

Brody

Berdichev

Kiev

Kharkov

Vorskha

DON COSSACKS

G E R M A N Y

Cracow

Jaroslav

Lemberg

Tarnopol

Ukraine

Poltava

Donetz

G a l i c i a

Przemysl

Stanislau

Dnieper

Donbas Coalfields

Carpathian Mountains

Dniester

Ekaterinoslav

Rostov

A U S T R I A

Czernowitz

Bug

Taganrog

Budapest

Bukovina

Nikolayev

H U N G A R Y

Prutn

Kishinev

Bessarabia

Sea of Azov

Danube

Tisza

Transylvania

Moldavia

Odessa

Kherson

Crimea

Kuban

R U M A N I A

Dobruja

Sevastopol

Belgrade

SERBIA

Black   Sea

Eastern Front (Southern Sector): Galicia, Bukovina and the Carpathians 1914-17

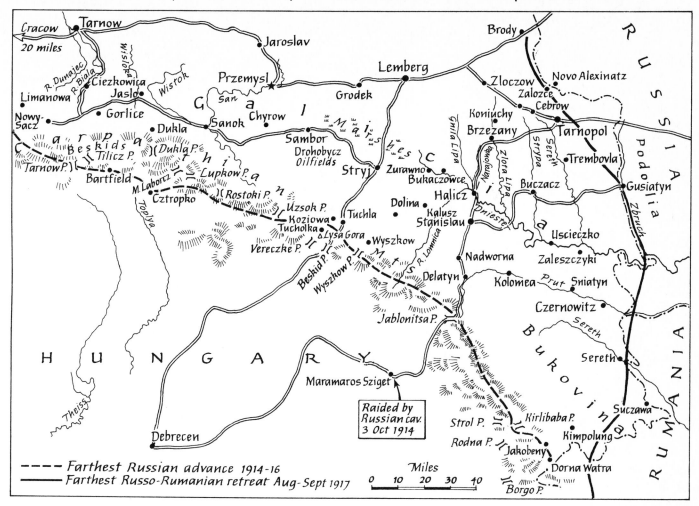

Raided by
Russian cav.
3 Oct 1914

- - - - Farthest Russian advance 1914-16
———— Farthest Russo-Rumanian retreat Aug-Sept 1917

Miles
0   10   20   30   40

Eastern Front: Rumanian Campaign 1916-17

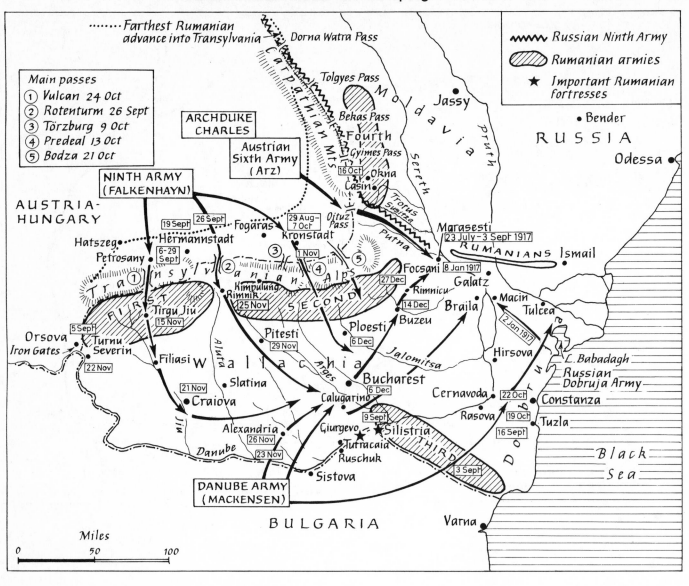

...... Farthest Rumanian advance into Transylvania

Dorna Watra Pass

Main passes
1. Vulcan 24 Oct
2. Rotenturm 26 Sept
3. Törzburg 9 Oct
4. Predeal 13 Oct
5. Bodza 21 Oct

wwww Russian Ninth Army

Rumanian armies

★ Important Rumanian fortresses

Tolgyes Pass

Jassy

• Bender

RUSSIA

Odessa •

ARCHDUKE CHARLES

Austrian Sixth Army (Arz)

Bekas Pass

Fourth

Gyimes Pass

16 Oct

Okna

Casin

M o l d a v i a

Sereth

Pruth

NINTH ARMY (FALKENHAYN)

AUSTRIA-HUNGARY

19 Sept 26 Sept

Fogáras

29 Aug-7 Oct

Oituz Pass

Putna

Marasesti
23 July - 3 Sept 1917

RUMANIANS Ismail

Hatszeg •••• Hermannstadt

Kronstadt

③

1 Nov

⑤

Focsani

8 Jan 1917

Galatz

Petrosany

6-29 Sept

② ④

27 Dec

Rimnicu •

14 Dec

• Macin

Tulcea

2 Jan 1917

T r a n s y l v a n i a n A l p s

Kimpulung

Rimnik

25 Nov

S E C O N D

Braila

Hirsova

Orsova

5 Sept

F I R S T

Tirgu Jiu

15 Nov

Ploesti

6 Dec

Buzeu

Iron Gates

Turnu Severin

Filiasi

Pitesti

29 Nov

Jalomitsa

L. Babadagh

Russian Dobruja Army

22 Nov

W a l l a c h i a

Alutu

Arges

Bucharest

6 Dec

Cernavoda •

22 Oct

Constanza

21 Nov

Slatina

Calugarino

Rasova

19 Oct

Tuzla

• Craiova

Jiu

9 Sept

Silistria

T H I R D

16 Sept

Alexandria

26 Nov

Danube

Giurgevo

Tutracaia

Ruschuk

Sistova

3 Sept

D o b r u j a

Black Sea

23 Nov

DANUBE ARMY (MACKENSEN)

B U L G A R I A

Varna •

Miles

0   50   100

Southern Fronts: Serbia and Salonika 1914-18

AUSTRIA - HUNGARY

RUMANIA

Belgrade

Bucharest

Sabac

Orsova

Ram

Loznitsa

Semendria

Jadar

Valjevo

Negotin

Bosnia

Ruschuk

Kragujevac

Zajecar

Sarajevo

Uzice

Vidin

W. Morava

Danube

Drina

Kraljevo

Lom-Palanka

Herze-
govina

Sistovo

SERBIA

Niš

Morava

Novibazar

Pirot

MONTENEGRO

Mitrovica

Leskovac

Tsaribrod

Kosovo

Pristina

Sofia

BULGARIA

Cattaro

Podgoritsa

Prizren

Vranje

Cetinje

Kustendil

Kumanovo

Maritsa

Scutari

Gostivar

Uskub (Skoplje)

Struma

San Giovanni
di Medua

Veles

Istip

Vardar

Prilep

Kuleli Burgas

Durazzo

Crna

Ft Rupel

Tirana

L. Ochrid

L. Doiran

Drama

ALBANIA

Ochrida

TURKEY

Elbasan

Monastir

Kavalla

Dedeagach

Adriatic
Sea

Pogradec

Berat

Florina

Macedonia

Koritsa

Thasos

Valona

Salonika

EPIRUS

Strait of
Otranto

GREECE

Allied Entrenched Camp
Dec 1915 – Apr 1916

Corfu

Thessaly

Aegean Sea

——— Front Dec 1916 – Sept 1918

Miles

0   50   100

Southern Fronts: Italian Front 1915-18

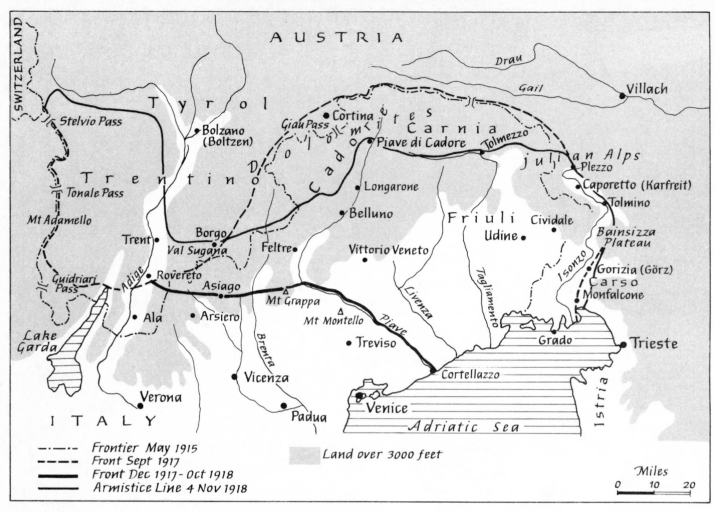

SWITZERLAND

AUSTRIA

Drau

Gail

• Villach

Tyrol

Stelvio Pass

Giau Pass

• Cortina

D o l o m i t e s

Carnia

j u l i a n   A l p s

• Bolzano
(Boltzen)

Piave di Cadore

Tolmezzo

• Plezzo

T r e n t i n o

C a d o r e

• Caporetto (Karfreit)

Tonale Pass

• Longarone

• Tolmino

Mt Adamello

Trent •

Borgo

• Belluno

F r i u l i

• Cividale

Bainsizza
Plateau

Val Sugana

Feltre •

Vittorio Veneto

Udine •

Guidriari
Pass

Adige

Rovereto

Asiago

△ Mt Grappa

Piave

Tagliamento

Isonzo

Gorizia (Görz)

Carso

Monfalcone

• Ala

• Arsiero

△ Mt Montello

Brenta

Livenza

Lake
Garda

• Treviso

Grado

Istria

• Trieste

• Vicenza

Cortellazzo

• Verona

• Padua

Venice

Adriatic Sea

I T A L Y

—·—·— Frontier May 1915
— — — Front Sept 1917
————— Front Dec 1917 - Oct 1918
————— Armistice Line 4 Nov 1918

Land over 3000 feet

Miles
0   10   20

Turkish Fronts: Armenia and the Caucasus 1914-18

Astrakhan

RUSSIA

Azov Sea

Timashevskaya

Kerch
Taman

Kuban R.

Volga Delta

Novorossisk

Ekaterinodar

Stavropol

Tuapse

N Caucasus

Vladikavkaz

Petrovsk

Black Sea

Caucasus Mountains

Georgia

Derbent

Poti

Tiflis

Batumi

Farthest Russian
advance July 1916

Atina
Vice
Mapavri
Rize

Arhavi

Azerbaijan

Samsun

Lazistan

Aleksandropol

Karakilise

Mastagi

Trebizond
Pontic Alps

Oltu

Delijan

Ganja
(Elizavetpol)

Gök-cay

Aksu

Baku

Ardasa

Gümüsane

Bardiz

Kars

Erevan

Kurdamir

Alyat

Zara

Bayburt

Ilica

Sarikamish

Etchmiadzin
Igdir

Sivas

Erzincan

Erzerum

Köprüköy

Mt Ararat (17,112 ft)

Hasankale

Karakilise

TURKEY

Mamahatun

Dyadin

Bayazit

Aras

Kigi

Ognot

Malazgirt

Murat-su (Euphrates)

Muş

Murat-su

L. Van

Van

Dilman

Safian

Bitlis

Tabriz

S
e
a

Aleppo

Diyarbekir

Siirt

L. Urmia

PERSIA

Enzeli

Miles

0   50   100

299

Turkish Fronts: Mesopotamia and West Persia 1914-18

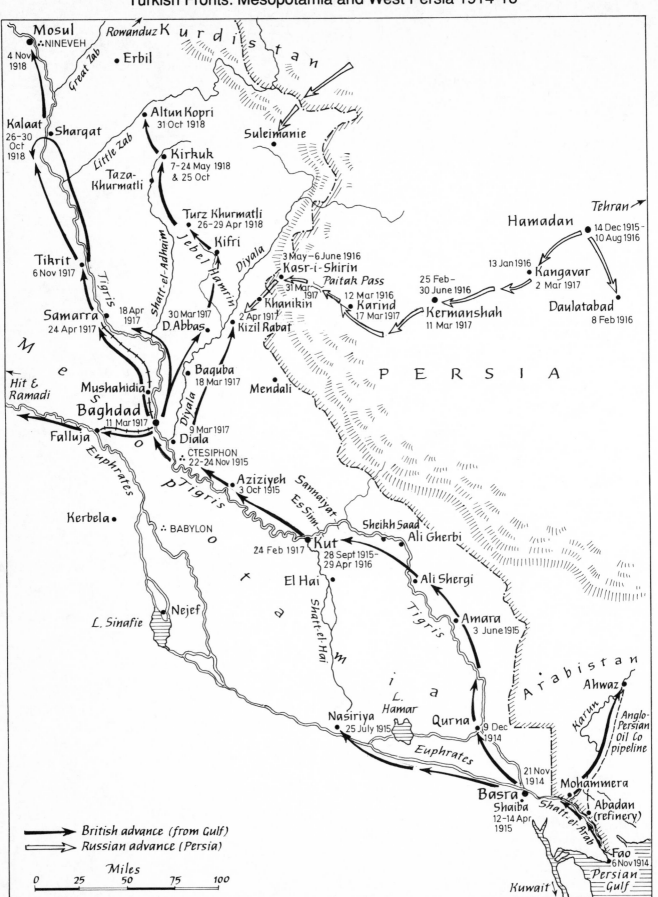

Mosul
∴NINEVEH
Rowanduz
Kurdistan
4 Nov 1918
Great Zab
• Erbil
Kalaat
26-30 Oct 1918
• Sharqat
Altun Kopri
31 Oct 1918
Suleimanie
Little Zab
Kirkuk
7-24 May 1918
& 25 Oct
Taza-Khurmatli
Tehran
Hamadan
14 Dec 1915 - 10 Aug 1916
Turz Khurmatli
26-29 Apr 1918
13 Jan 1916
Kangavar
2 Mar 1917
Tikrit
6 Nov 1917
Kifri
Jebel Hamrin
Diyala
3 May - 6 June 1916
Kasr-i-Shirin
25 Feb - 30 June 1916
Daulatabad
8 Feb 1916
Samarra
24 Apr 1917
18 Apr 1917
Shatt-el-Adhaim
30 Mar 1917
D. Abbas
31 Mar 1917
Paitak Pass
Khanikin
2 Apr 1917
12 Mar 1916
Karind
17 Mar 1917
Kermanshah
11 Mar 1917
P E R S I A
Kizil Rabat
M e
Baquba
18 Mar 1917
Mendali
Hit & Ramadi
Mushahidia
Baghdad
11 Mar 1917
Diyala
Falluja
9 Mar 1917
Diala
∴CTESIPHON
22-24 Nov 1915
Euphrates
s
Aziziyeh
3 Oct 1915
Sannaiyat
Es Sinn
Kerbela •
∴BABYLON
o
Sheikh Saad
Ali Gherbi
Kut
24 Feb 1917
28 Sept 1915 - 29 Apr 1916
p
El Hai
Ali Shergi
L. Sinafie
Nejef
t
Shatt-el-Hai
Tigris
Amara
3 June 1915
a
Arabistan
Ahwaz
m
L. Hamar
Anglo-Persian Oil Co pipeline
Nasiriya
25 July 1915
Qurna
9 Dec 1914
Karun
i
Euphrates
21 Nov 1914
Mohammera
Basra
Shaiba
12-14 Apr 1915
Shatt-el-Arab
Abadan (refinery)

British advance (from Gulf)
Russian advance (Persia)

Miles
0   25   50   75   100

Fao
6 Nov 1914
Persian Gulf
Kuwait

Turkish Fronts: The Dardanelles and Gallipoli 1915-16

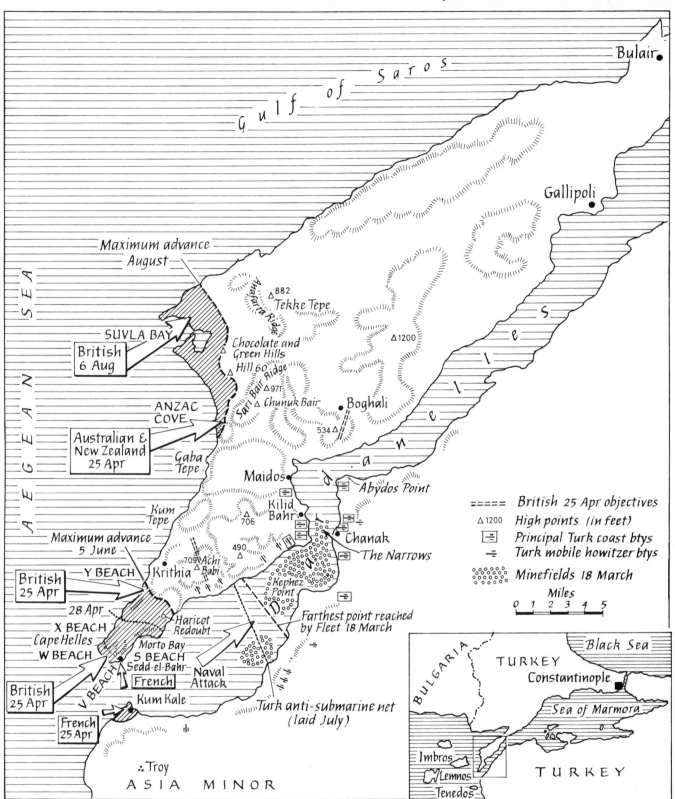

Bulair

Gulf of Saros

Gallipoli

Maximum advance
August

△ 882
Tekke Tepe
△ 1200

Chocolate and
Green Hills
SUVLA BAY
British
6 Aug
Hill 60
△ 971
Sari Bair Ridge
△ Chunuk Bair
Boghali

ANZAC
COVE
534 △

Australian &
New Zealand
25 Apr

Gaba
Tepe

Maidos
Abydos Point

Kum
Tepe
Kilid
Bahr
△ 706

Maximum advance
5 June
490 △
Chanak
The Narrows

709 △ Achi
△ Babi
British
25 Apr
Y BEACH
Krithia

Kephez
Point

28 Apr
Haricot
Redoubt
Farthest point reached
by Fleet 18 March

X BEACH
Cape Helles
W BEACH
Morto Bay
S BEACH
Sedd-el-Bahr
French
Naval
Attack

British
25 Apr

Kum Kale

French
25 Apr

Turk anti-submarine net
(laid July)

Troy
ASIA MINOR

AEGEAN SEA

D a r d a n e l l e s

===== British 25 Apr objectives
△ 1200 High points (in feet)
Principal Turk coast btys
Turk mobile howitzer btys
Minefields 18 March

Miles
0 1 2 3 4 5

Black Sea
BULGARIA
TURKEY
Constantinople
Sea of Marmora
Imbros
Lemnos
TURKEY
Tenedos

Turkish Fronts: Sinai, Western Desert and Palestine 1914-18

TURKEY (ASIA MINOR)

Adalia

Gulf of Adalia

Kastelorizo I.

Adana

BAGHDAD RAILWAY

Gulf of Alexandretta

Alexandretta

R. Euphrates

Aleppo

M e d i t e r r a n e a n S e a

CYPRUS

Latakia

Hama

Homs

Ruad I.

Tripoli

Beirut

Rayak

Damascus

S y r i a

Sidon

L e b a n o n

Tyre

Acre

Nazareth

L. Galilee

Deraa

Sollum

Mersa Matruh

Sidi Barrani

W. Desert

Cairo

Haifa

Megiddo

Afuleh

Jordan

Amman

Azrak

Siwa Oasis

Baharia Oasis

Senussi operations 1915-17

LIBYA

Farafra Oasis

Dakhala Oasis

Kharga Oasis

Nile

Nablus

EsSalt

Fronts
Dec 1917-Sept 1918
Mar-Oct 1917

Jericho

Jerusalem

Dead Sea

Mountains of Moab

Miles
0   100   200

British railway
19 May 1916 Apr-Aug 1 Dec 1 Mar
1917

Jaffa

Gaza

Rafa

Hebron

Beersheba

Kerak

Palestine

Alexandria

Port Said

Romani

Bir-el-Abd

El Arish

Tafila

Suez Canal

Katia

Magdhaba

Kossaima

Abu-el-Lissal

Maan

Kantara

Ismailia

Turks 23 Feb 1915

Cairo

River Nile

Bitter Lake

British 1916
Canal defence

Suez

Nekhl

W. Desert

S i n a i
(E. Desert)

Aqaba

Mudauwara

E G Y P T

Gulf of Suez

HEJAZ RAILWAY

Tor

R e d   S e a

H e j a z

Miles
0   50   100

Wejh

Medina

African Operations: Africa's European Colonies 1914

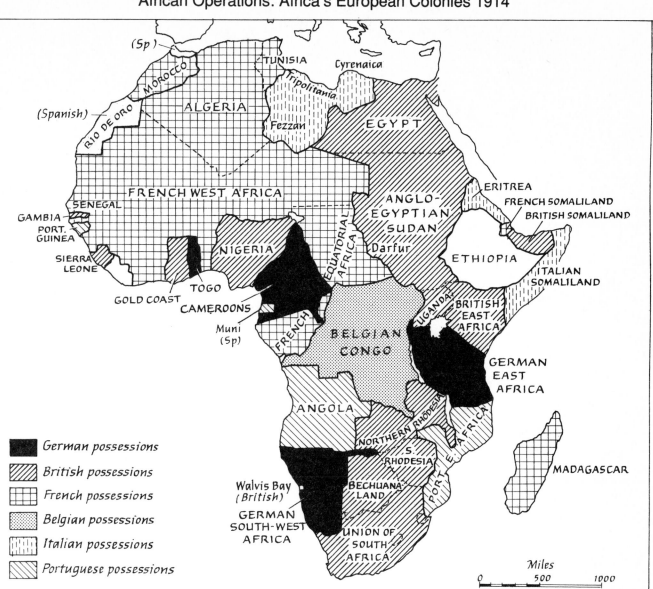

(Sp)

(Spanish)

RIO DE ORO

MOROCCO

ALGERIA

TUNISIA

Cyrenaica

Tripolitania

Fezzan

EGYPT

ERITREA

FRENCH SOMALILAND

BRITISH SOMALILAND

GAMBIA

SENEGAL

PORT. GUINEA

SIERRA LEONE

FRENCH WEST AFRICA

NIGERIA

ANGLO-EGYPTIAN SUDAN

Darfur

ETHIOPIA

ITALIAN SOMALILAND

GOLD COAST

TOGO

CAMEROONS

Muni (Sp)

FRENCH EQUATORIAL AFRICA

BELGIAN CONGO

UGANDA

BRITISH EAST AFRICA

GERMAN EAST AFRICA

ANGOLA

NORTHERN RHODESIA

S. RHODESIA

PORT. E. AFRICA

MADAGASCAR

Walvis Bay (British)

GERMAN SOUTH-WEST AFRICA

BECHUANA-LAND

UNION OF SOUTH AFRICA

German possessions

British possessions

French possessions

Belgian possessions

Italian possessions

Portuguese possessions

Miles

0   500   1000

African Operations: Togo and Cameroons 1914-16

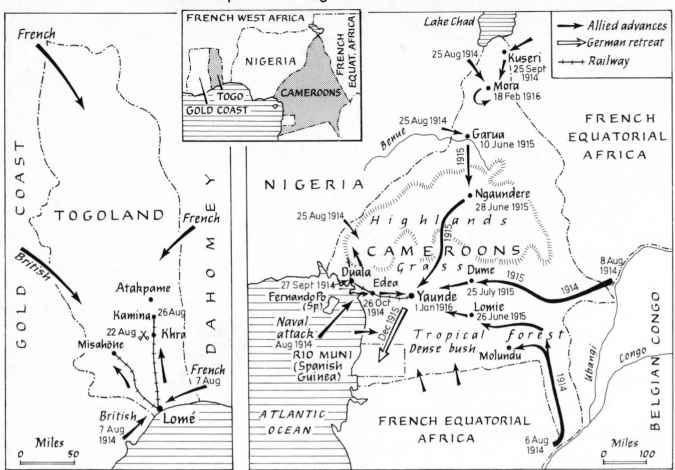

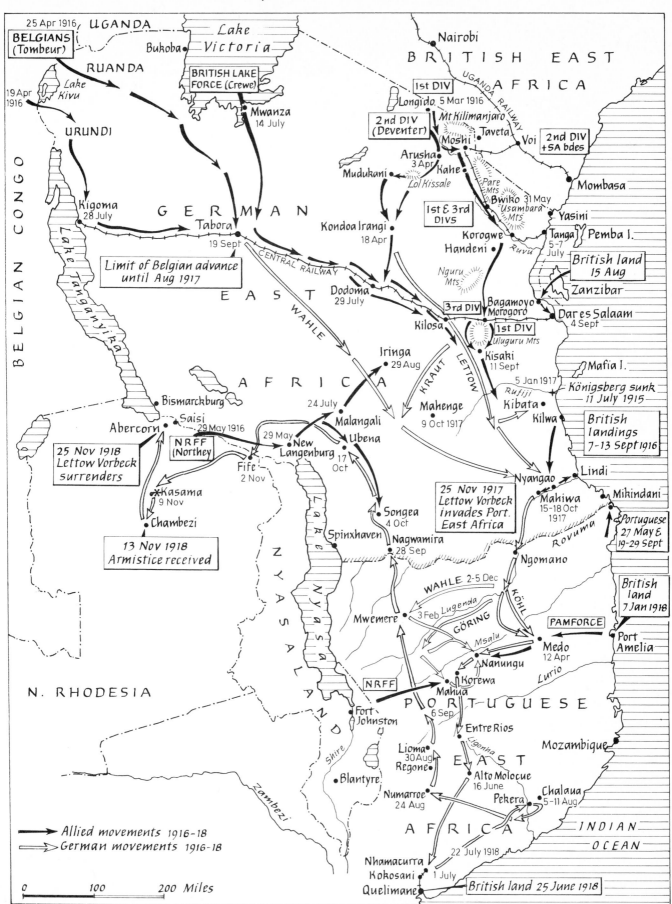

African Operations: South-west Africa 1914-15

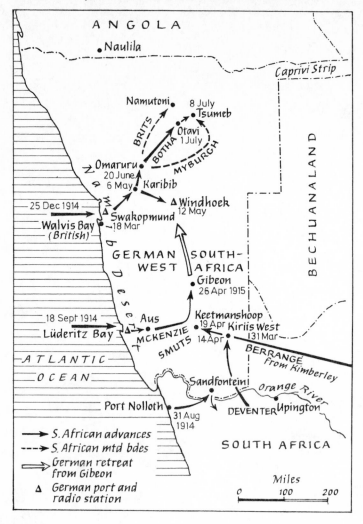

ANGOLA

•Naulila

Caprivi Strip

Namutoni• 8 July
•Tsumeb

BRITS

Otavi
1 July

BOTHA

MYBURGH

Omaruru•
20 June
6 May • Karibib

△Windhoek
12 May

25 Dec 1914

△ Swakopmund
18 Mar

Walvis Bay
(British)

GERMAN SOUTH-
WEST AFRICA

•Gibeon
26 Apr 1915

18 Sept 1914

Aus•

Keetmanshoop
19 Apr Kiriis West
14 Apr 31 Mar

Lüderitz Bay

MCKENZIE

SMUTS

BERRANGE
from Kimberley

BECHUANALAND

ATLANTIC

OCEAN

Sandfontein•
Orange River

Port Nolloth
31 Aug
1914

DEVENTER Upington

SOUTH AFRICA

→ S. African advances
----→ S. African mtd bdes
⇒ German retreat
from Gibeon
△ German port and
radio station

Miles

0   100   200

Sea War: North Sea and British Home Waters 1914-18

Shetland Is.

N o r t h e r n   B a r r a g e

xxxxxxxxxxxxxxxxxxxxxxxxxxxx xxxx

Pentland Firth KIRKWALL xxxxxxxxxxxxxxxxxxxxxxxxxxx
Anglo-American mine-barrage
laid May-Nov 1918   Stavangar
SCAPA FLOW xxxx
+
17 Oct 1917
Convoy destroyed

NORWAY   SWEDEN

L. Ewe Moray Firth
CROMARTY

Skaggerak

Kattegat The Sound

GRAND FLEET

ROSYTH Firth of Firth
Glasgow Leith

JUTLAND ✕
31 May – 1 June 1916

N O R T H   S E A

DENMARK

Horns Reef

Newcastle
Tyne
Hartlepool
Whitby 16 Dec 1914
Scarborough

DOGGER
BANK
24 Jan 1915

German Bight

Amrum Bank Tondern

Heligoland

Belfast

N. Channel

Barrow-in
Furness
(Vickers)

Hull

Liverpool
Manchester
Humber
Grimsby

HELIGOLAND
28 Aug 1914 BIGHT ✕ Jade Bay
CUXHAVEN
HAMBURG

Canal

KIEL

IRISH
SEA

Terschelling Frisian Is.
Texel

Borkum
EMDEN
WILHELMSHAVEN
BREMEN

HIGH SEAS FLEET

3 Nov 1914
Yarmouth
Lowestoft
24 Apr 1916

3 R N
cruisers
+
22 Sept
1914

HOLLAND

HARWICH

The Hague
Rotterdam

St George's
Channel

PEMBROKE
Cardiff
Swansea Bristol

London
Thames Estuary

CHATHAM
THE DOWNS
Dover
Barrage
Zeebrugge
Ostende

PORTSMOUTH
Southampton
Folkestone
Calais
Boulogne

DOVER

PLYMOUTH
Newhaven
B E F
supply routes

PORTLAND
Falmouth
+ Formidable
1 Jan 1915

Dieppe

CHERBOURG
Le Havre

BREST

Neutrals

KIRKWALL British Contraband
Control· Bases

Whitby British towns bombarded
by German Navy

◻ Naval bases

xxxxxx Mine barriers

Miles
0   50   100   150   200

307

International Events: Europe 1914

SOURCES

OTHER CHRONOLOGIES

Bowman, John S (exec ed) *The Twentieth Century: An Almanac* (Harrap, London 1986)

Carruth, Gorton & Associates (ed) *The Encyclopedia of American Facts and Dates* 6th ed (Crowell Co, New York 1972)

Freeman-Grenville, G S P *Chronology of African History* (OUP 1973)

Irving S and Kull, Nell M *A Short Chronology of American History*, (Rutgers UP, New Brunswick NJ 1952)

Keller, Helen Rex *The Dictionary of Dates* 2 vols (Macmillan, New York 1934)

Matei, Horia C et al *Chronological History of Romania* 2nd ed (Editura Enciclopedica Romana, Bucharest 1974)

Moody, T W, Martin, F X, and Byrne, F J A *A Chronology of Irish History to 1976: A New History of Ireland Vol VIII* (Clarendon Press, Oxford 1982)

Trager, James (ed) *The People's Chronology: A Year-by-Year Record of Human Events from Prehistory to the Present* (Heinemann, London 1980)

Williams, Neville *Chronology of the Modern World* (Barrie and Rockliff, London 1966)

CHRONOLOGIES 1914-18

Committee of Imperial Defence *Principal Events* (Official History of the War) (HMSO, London 1922 reprinted by London Stamp Exchange 1987)

Daily Telegraph History of World War I Wall Chart, Keith Simpson (1981)

Dearle, N B, *An Economic Chronicle of the Great War for Great Britain & Ireland 1914-1919* (Economic and Social History of the World War, Carnegie Endowment for World Peace, Humphry Milford/OUP, London 1929) [Supplement on 1920-1922]

Debyser, Felix *Chronologie de la Guerre Mondiale de Serajevo à Versailles (28 Juin 1914-28 Juin 1919)* (Payot, Paris 1938)

Gleichen, Maj-Gen Edward, Lord (ed) *Chronology of the War* Vol 1 1914-1915, Vol 2 1916-1917, Vol 3 1918-1919 plus small atlas vol (Ministry of Information/Constable, London 1918-1920); reprinted without atlas by Greenhill Books, London as one vol *Chronology of the Great War* (1988)

Mudd, Thomas B R *The Yanks were there: A Chronological and Documentary Review of World War I* (Vantage Press, New York 1958)

Official History of the Canadian Forces in the Great War 1914-1919 Gen Series Vol I Chronology, Appendices and Maps (Patenaude, Ottawa 1938)

Rowe, R P P *A Concise Chronicle of Events of the Great War* [to 10 Jan 1920] (Philip Allan, London 1920)

The Times Diary and Index of the War 1914-1918 [to 10 Aug 1920] (Hodder, London 1921, reprinted by Hayward 1985)

OTHER REFERENCE AND GENERAL HISTORIES

Banks, Arthur *Military Atlas of the First World War* (Heinemann, London 1975 reprinted 1989 by Leo Cooper)

Bayliss, Gwyn M *Bibliographic Guide to the two World Wars: An annotated survey of English language reference materials.* (Bowker, London & New York 1977)

Bell, A C *The Blockade of the Central Powers 1914-1918** (1937, HMSO, London 1961)

Bruce, Anthony *An Illustrated Companion to the First World War* * (Michael Joseph, London 1989)

Dupuy, R Ernest & Dupuy, Trevor N *The Encyclopedia of Military History from 3500BC to the Present** (Book Club ed 1970)

Edmonds, Brig-Gen Sir James E *A Short History of World War 1* (OUP, London 1959)

Encyclopedia Britannica, especially 12th edition (1922)

Encyclopaedia of Islam

Enser, A G S , *A Subject Bibliography of the First World War 1914-1978* (Deutsch, London 1979)

Esposito, Vincent J (ed) *A Concise History of World War 1* (Pall Mall Press, London 1964)

Falls, Cyril *The First World War* (Longman, London 1960)

Gilbert, Martin *First World War Atlas* (Weidenfeld, London 1970 reprinted 1985)

Gliddon, Gerald (ed) *First World War: List of 700 Books in Print* (Gliddon Books, Norwich 1990)

Hammerton, John *The War Illustrated* 9 vols (Amalgamated Press, London 1914-19)

Hammerton, J & Wilson, H W *The Great War* 13 vols (Amalgamated Press, London 1914-19)

Heinl Jr , Col Robert Debs *Dictionary of Military and Naval Quotations* (US Naval Institute, Annapolis, Maryland 1966)

Herwig, Holger H, & Heyman, Neil M *Biographical Dictionary of World War I**(Greenwood Press, London 1982)

Mitchell B R *European Historical Statistics 1750-1975* 2nd rev ed (Macmillan, London 1981)

Morris, B (ed) *Encyclopedia of American History* 6th ed (Harper & Row, New York 1982)

Mourre, Michel *Dictionnaire des Personnages Historiques de Tous Les Temps* (Bordas, Paris, Brussels & Montreal 1972)

Nash, D B *Imperial German Army Handbook 1914-1918* (Ian Allan, London 1980)

Palmer, A W *A Dictionary of Modern History 1789-1945* (Penguin ed 1964)

Purnell's History of the First World War 6 vols (BPC, London 1969-71) updated as *Marshall Cavendish Illustrated Encyclopedia of World War 1** 13 vols (USA 1984-86)

*Statistics of the Military Effort of the British Empire during the Great War** (War Office, HMSO, London 1922)

Terraine, John *The Great War: A Pictorial History* (Hutchinson, London 1965)

Terraine, John *White Heat: The New Warfare 1914-1918** (Sidgwick, London 1982)

The Great War 1914-18 Bertram Rota Book Catalogue 245 (London 1988)

The Illustrated War Record 5th ed (Headley Bros, London nd but 1919)*

The Times History of the War 22 vols (London 1914-19)

Thoumin, Richard *The First World War* [eyewitness anthology] (Secker ed, London 1963)

Tuchman, Barbara W *The Guns of August —August 1914* (Four Square paperback edition 1964)

Valluy, Gen J E (with Pierre Dufourcq) *La Première Guerre Mondiale* 2 vols (Larousse, Paris 1968)

Vansittart, Peter *Voices from the Great War* (Cape, London 1981)

Webster's Biographical Dictionary (G & C Merriam Co, Springfield, USA 1969)

Wilson, Trevor *The Myriad Faces of War: Britain and the Great War 1914-1918* (Polity Press, Cambridge 1986)

Winter, J M, *The Great War and the British People* (Macmillan, London 1985)

Woodward, David R & Maddox, Robert Franken *America and World War 1: A Selected Annotated Bibliography of English-Language Sources** Wars of the United States vol 6 (Garland, New York & London 1985)

* = contains chronology

SARAJEVO TO OUTBREAK

Cassels, Lavender, *The Archduke and the Assassin* (Frederick Muller, London 1984)

Thomson, George Malcolm *The Twelve Days 24 July - 4 August 1914* (History Book Club, London 1964)

WESTERN FRONT

See also Chronologies & Other Reference and General Histories

Edmonds, Brig-Gen Sir James *Military Operations: France and Belgium* 13 vols (HMSO, London 1922-1948) and *The Occupation of the Rhineland 1918-1929* (IWM/HMSO, London 1987)

General

Lupfer, Timothy T 'The Dynamics of Doctrine: The Changes in German Tactical Doctrine During the First World War' Leavensworth Papers No 4 (US Army, July 1981)

Overstraeten, Gen R Van (ed) *The War Diaries of Albert I, King of the Belgians* (Kimber, London 1954)

1914

Owen, Edward *1914 Glory Departing* (Buchan & Enright, London 1986)

Spears, Brig-Gen E L *Liaison, 1914: A Narrative of the Great Retreat* (Heinemann, London 1930)

Terraine, John *Mons: The Retreat to Victory* (Pan Books ed, London 1972)

Van Creveld, Martin *Supplying War: Logistics from Wallenstein to Patton* (CUP 1977)

1915

Clark, Alan *The Donkeys* (Mayflower-Dell paperback ed, London 1967)

1916

Blond, Georges *Verdun* (Mayflower-Dell, London 1976)

Farrar-Hockley, A H *The Somme* (Pan Books ed, London 1966)

Horne, Alistair *The Price of Glory: Verdun 1916* (Macmillan, London 1962)

1917

Spears, Brig-Gen E L *Prelude to Victory* (Cape, London 1939)

1918

Barnett, Correlli 'A Successful Counter-Stroke: 18 July 1918' from *Old Battles and New Defences: Can We Learn from Military History?* (Brassey's London/Oxford 1986)

Middlebrook, Martin *The Kaiser's Battle 21 March 1918: The First Day of the German Spring Offensive* (Allen Lane, London 1978)

Moore, William *See How They Ran: The British Retreat of 1918* (Sphere Books paperback ed, London 1975)

Rudin, Harry R *Armistice 1918* (Yale UP, New Haven 1944)

Terraine, John *To Win a War 1918 The Year of Victory* (Sidgwick & Jackson, London 1978 and Macmillan paperback 1986)

Armies, Formations and Units

American Battle Monuments Commission *American Armies and Battles in Europe : A History, Guide & Reference Book* (US Govt Printing Office, Washington 1938)

Becke, Maj A F *Order of Battle Part 4 (GHQs, Armies and Corps) 1914-1918* (HMSO, London 1945)

Bergot, Erwan *The French Foreign Legion* (Tatoo paperback, Wyndham, London 1976)

Merewether, Lt-Col J W B, and Smith, Sir F *The Indian Corps in France* 2nd ed (Murray, London 1919)

Stallings, Laurence *The Doughboys: The Story of the AEF, 1917-1918* (Harper & Row, New York 1963)

Turnbull, Patrick *The Foreign Legion* (Mayflower paperback ed, London 1966)

US War Department *Order of Battle of the United States Land Forces in the World War: AEF* (US Govt Printing Office, Washington, 1937)

Tanks

Cooper, Bryan *Tank Battles of World War I* (Ian Allan, 1973)

Liddell Hart, Capt B H *The Tanks: The History of the Royal Tank Regiment* Vol I (Cassell, London 1959)

Royal Tank Regiment, 50th Anniversary Souvenir 1917-1967 (London 1967)

Biographies

Barnett, Correlli *The Swordbearers: Studies in Supreme Command in the First World War* (Eyre & Spottiswoode, London 1963/Penguin 1966 & 1986)

Blumenson, Martin *The Patton Papers 1885-1940* Vol I (Houghton Mifflin, Boston 1972)

Falls, Cyril *Marshal Foch* (Blackie & Son, London/Glasgow 1939)

Farago, Ladislas *Patton: Ordeal and Triumph* (Arthur Barker, London 1966)

Griffiths, Richard *Marshal Pétain* (Constable, London 1970)

Hart, Capt Basil Liddell *Foch: Man of Orleans* (London 1931)

Holmes, Richard *The Little Field-Marshal, Sir John French* (Cape, London 1981)

Manchester, William *American Caesar: Douglas MacArthur 1880-1964* (Arrow paperback ed, London 1979)

Salisbury-Jones, Maj-Gen Sir Guy *So Full a Glory: A Life of Marshal de Lattre de Tassigny* (Weidenfeld, London 1954)

Vandiver, Frank E *Black Jack: The Life and Times of John J Pershing* 2 vols (Texas A & M UP 1977)

Weaponry

Hogg, Ian V *The Guns 1914-18* (Pan/Ballantine ed, London 1973)

EASTERN FRONT

Brusilov, Gen A A *A Soldier's Note Book 1914-1918* (Macmillan, London 1930)

Churchill, Winston S *The World Crisis: The Eastern Front* (Butterworth, London 1931)

Gourko, Gen Basil *Memories & Impressions of War and Revolution 1914-1917* (Murray, London 1918)

Hoffmann, Maj Gen Max *War Diaries and other Papers* Vol I (Secker, London 1929)

Jukes, Geoffrey *Carpathian Disaster: Death of an Army* (Ballantine, London 1971)

Kettle, Michael *Russia and the Allies 1917-1920: Vol I The Allies and the Russian Collapse March 1917-March 1918* (Deutsch, London 1981)

Knox, Maj-Gen Sir Alfred *With the Russian Army 1914-1917* 2 vols (Hutchinson, London 1921)

Littawer, Vladimir S *Russian Hussar* (J A Allen, London 1965)

Perrett, Bryan & Lord, Anthony *The Czar's British Squadron* (Kimber, London 1981)

Stone, Norman *The Eastern Front 1914-1917* (Hodder, London 1975)

Wildman, A *The End of the Russian Imperial Army* 2 vols (Princeton UP, 1980 & 1987)

Wrangel, Alexis *The End of Chivalry: The Last Great Cavalry Battles 1914-1918* (Hippocrene Books, New York 1982)

Russian Revolution and Civil War

Bradley, J F N *Civil War in Russia 1917-1920* (Batsford, London 1975)

Bunyan, James & Fisher, H H *The Bolshevik Revolution 1917-1918: Documents and Materials** (Hoover War Library Publications No 3, (Stanford UP, Stanford, California 1965)

Bunyan, James *Intervention, Civil War, and Communism in Russia April-December 1918* (John Hopkins University, Baltimore 1936)

Footman, David *Civil War in Russia* *(Faber, London 1961)

Jackson, Robert *At War with the Bolsheviks: The Allied Intervention into Russia 1917-1920* (Stacey, London 1972)

Luckett, Richard *The White Generals: The White Movement and the Russian Civil War* (Longman, Harlow 1971 & 1988)

McCauley, Martin *Octobrists to Bolsheviks: Imperial Russia 1905-1917** (Documents of Modern History, Edward Arnold, London 1984)

Mawdsley, Evan *The Russian Civil War* (Allen & Unwin, Boston 1987)

Seaton, Albert *Stalin as Warlord* (Batsford, London 1976)

Shukman, Harold (ed) *The Blackwell Encyclopedia of the Russian Revolution* (Oxford 1988)

Trotsky, Leon *How the Revolution Armed: The Military Writings and Speeches* Vol 1 *The Year 1918** (1923: New Park Publ, Britain 1979)

Weber, Gerda & Hermann *Lenin Life and Works* (Macmillan Chronology Series, London 1980)

Zeman, Z A B (ed) *Germany and the Revolution in Russia 1915-1918* (Documents: OUP, London 1958)

Finland

Hannula, Lt-Col J O *Finland's War of Independence* (Faber, London 1939)

Jagerskiold, Stig *Mannerheim Marshal of Finland* (C Hurst, London 1986)

Upton, Anthony F *The Finnish Revolution 1917-1918* (Univ of Minnesota Press, Minneapolis, 1980)

Mannerheim, KG, *The Memoirs of Marshal Mannerheim* (Cassell, London 1953)

*   = chronology included

SOUTHERN FRONTS

Italian Front Bertoldi, Silvio *Badoglio* (Rizzoli, Milan 1982)

Bovio, Col Oreste 'The Italian Army in World War I' *Revue Internationale d'Histoire Militaire* No 39 (Rome 1978)

Falls, Cyril *Caporetto 1917* (Weidenfeld, London 1966)

Gooch, John *Army, State and Society in Italy 1870-1915* (Macmillan, Basingstoke & London 1989)

McClure, William 'Italian Campaigns', 'Caporetto' & 'Asiago' from *Encyclopedia Britannica* 12th ed (1922)

Prichard-Agnetti, Mary (trans) *The Battle of the Piave June 15-23, 1918* issued by the Supreme Command of the Royal Italian Army (Hodder, London 1921)

Rothenberg, Gunther E *The Army of Francis Joseph* (Purdue UP, W Lafayette, Indiana 1976)

Villari, Luigi *The War on the Italian Front* (Cobden-Sanderson, London 1932)

Serbia & Salonika

Anon "Salonika Campaigns' from *Encyclopedia Britannica* 12th ed (1922)

Atkinson, Maj Charles 'Serbian Campaigns' from *Encyclopedia Britannica* 12th ed (1922)

Falls, Capt Cyril *Military Operations: Macedonia* 2 vols (HMSO, London 1933 & 1935)

Fryer, Charles 'The Watch on the Danube: The British Naval Mission in Serbia 1914-1916' from *The Mariner's Mirror* vol 73 No 3 (Greenwich 1987)

Ministère de la Guerre *Les Armées Françaises dans la Grande Guerre* Tome VIII (Paris 1925-34)

Nicol, Graham *Uncle George: Field-Marshal Lord Milne of Salonika and Rubislaw* (Reedminster Publications, London 1976)

Palmer, Alan *The Gardeners of Salonika: The Macedonian Campaign 1915-1918* (André Deutsch, London 1965)

Villari, Luigi *The Macedonian Campaign* (Fisher Unwin, London 1922)

TURKISH FRONTS

General

Celiker, Brig Gen F (Retd) 'Turkey in the First World War' from *Revue Internationale d'Histoire Militaire* No 46 (Ankara 1980)

Emin, Ahmed *Turkey in the World War* (Yale UP, New Haven 1930)

Larcheur, Commandant M *La guerre turque dans la guerre mondiale* (Chiron, Berger-Levrault, Paris 1926)

Trumpener, Ulrich 'Suez, Baku, Gallipoli: The Military Dimensions of the German-Ottoman Coalition 1914-18' from Neilson, Keith & Prete, Roy A *Coalition Warfare: An Uneasy Accord* (Wilfred Laurier UP, Waterloo, Canada 1983)

Winstone, H V F *The Illicit Adventure: The Story of Political and Military Intelligence in the Middle East from 1898 to 1926* (Cape, London 1982)

Arabia

Liddell Hart, B H ' *T.E.Lawrence' In Arabia and After* (Cape, London 1935)

Macro, Eric *Yemen and the Western World* (C Hurst, London 1968)

Tabachnick, Stephen E & Matheson, Christopher *Images of Lawrence* (Cape, London 1988)

Yardley, Michael *Backing into the Limelight: A Biography of T.E. Lawrence* (Harrap, London 1985)

Armenia

Allen, W E D & Muratoff, Paul *Caucasian Battlefields: A History of the Wars on the Turco-Caucasian Border 1828-1921* (CUP 1953)

Egypt and Palestine

Falls, Capt Cyril *Military Operations: Egypt and Palestine Part II from June 1917 to the End of the War* (HMSO, London 1930)

Falls, Cyril *Armageddon 1918* (Weidenfeld, London 1964)

Macmunn, Lt-Gen Sir George, & Falls, Capt Cyril *Military Operations: Egypt and Palestine to June 1917** (HMSO, London 1928)

Wavell, Col A P *The Palestine Campaigns* * 3rd ed (Constable, London 1932)

Gallipoli

Aspinall-Oglander, Brig-Gen C F *Military Operations Gallipoli* Vol II (Heinemann, London 1932)

Denham, H M *Dardanelles: A Midshipman's Diary* (Murray, London 1981)

James, Robert Rhodes *Gallipoli* (Batsford, London 1965)

Pugsley, Christopher *Gallipoli: The New Zealand Story** (Hodder, Auckland 1984)

Kemal Ataturk

Kinross, Lord *Ataturk: The Rebirth of a Nation* (Weidenfeld, London 1964).

Revue Internationale d'Histoire Militaire No 50 (1981) on Ataturk by Turkish Commission of Military History

Volkan, Vamik D & Itzhowitz, Norman *The Immortal Ataturk: A Psychobiography* (Univ of Chicago Press, 1984)

Mesopotamia and Persia

Barker, A J *The Neglected War: Mesopotamia 1914-1918* (Faber, London 1967)

Barker, A J *Townshend of Kut* (Cassell, London 1967)

Braddon, Russell *The Siege* [Kut] (Cape, London 1969)

Burne, A H *Mesopotamia: The Last Phase* (Gale & Polden, London 1936)

Goodman, Susan *Gertrude Bell* (Berg, Leamington Spa/Dover 1985)

Moberly, Brig-Gen F J *The Campaign in Mesopotamia* * 4 vols (HMSO, London 1923-27)

Moberly, Brig-Gen F J *Military Operations in Persia 1914-1919* (1929; repr HMSO/IWM 1987)

AFRICAN OPERATIONS

Farwell, Byron *The Great War in Africa* (Viking, London 1987)

Lucas, Sir Charles *The Empire at War Vol IV Africa* (OUP 1924)

West Africa

Haywood, Col A & Clarke, Brig F A S *The History of the Royal West African Frontier Force* (Gale & Polden, Aldershot 1964)

Moberly, Brig-Gen F J *Military Operations Togoland and the Cameroons* * (HMSO, London 1931)

South and South West Africa

Buxton, Earl *General Botha* (Murray, London 1924)

Meinjtes, Johannes *General Louis Botha: A Biography* (Cassell, London 1970)

Wheeler, Douglas L & Pelissier, René *Angola* (Pall Mall Press, London 1971)

East Africa

Clifford, Sir Hugh *The Gold Coast Regiment in the East African Campaign* (Murray, London 1920)

Crowe, Brig-Gen J H V *General Smuts' Campaign in East Africa* (Murray, London 1918)

Downes, Capt W D *With the Nigerians in East Africa* (Methuen, London 1919)

Hodges, Geoffrey *The Carrier Corps: Military Labor in the East Africa Campaign 1914-1918* (Greenwood Press, Westport, Connecticut 1986)

Hordern, Lt-Col Charles & Stacke, Maj H *Military Operations:East Africa* (HMSO, London 1941)

Lettow-Vorbeck, Paul von *My Reminiscences of East Africa* (Hurst & Blackett, London 1920)

Mackenzie, John 'The Naval Campaigns on Lakes Victoria and Nyasa 1914-18' from *The Mariner's Mirror* Vol 71 No 2 (Greenwich, 1985)

Miller, Charles *Battle for the Bundu: The First World War in East Africa* (Macdonald & Jane's, London 1974)

Moyse-Bartlett, Lt-Col H *The King's African Rifles: A Study in the Military History of East and Central Africa 1890-1945* (Gale & Polden Aldershot 1956)

Shankland, Peter *The Phantom Flotilla: The Story of the Naval Africa Expedition 1915-16* (Mayflower Books ed, St Albans 1969)

Sibley, Maj J R *Tanganyikan guerrilla: East African campaign 1914-1918* (Pan Ballantine ed, London 1973)

French Africa

Howe, Sonia E *Lyautey of Morocco* (Hodder, London 1931)

Service historique de l'armée (Lt-Cols Weithas & Remy) *Les Armées Françaises pendant la Grande Guerre* Tome IX vol 2 (Paris 1930)

Usborne, Vice-Adm C V *The Conquest of Morocco* (Stanley Paul, London 1936)

Senussi Revolt and Italian Africa
Evans-Pritchard E E *The Senussi of Cyrenaica* (Clarendon Press, Oxford 1949)
Gaibi, Maj A *Manuale di Storia Politico-Militare delle Colonie Italiane* (War Ministry Official History, Rome 1928)

SEA WAR

General
British Vessels Lost at Sea 1914-18 (Patrick Stephens, Cambridge 1977 repr of 1919 Admiralty publication)
Conway's All the World's Fighting Ships 1906-1921 (Conway Maritime Press, London 1985)
Encyclopedia Britannica 12th ed (1922)
Frere Cook, Gervis and Macksey, Kenneth *The Guinness History of Sea Warfare* (Guinness, Enfield 1975)
Marder, Arthur J *From the Dreadnought to Scapa Flow* 5 vols (OUP 1961-70)
Pemsel, Helmut *Atlas of Naval Warfare* (Arms & Armour Press, 1977)
Winton, John *The Victoria Cross at Sea* (Michael Joseph, London 1978)

Arctic, Baltic and Black Seas
Greger, René *The Russian Fleet 1914-1917* * (Ian Allan, Shepperton 1972)
Mawdsley, Evan *The Russian Revolution and the Baltic Fleet:War and Politics February 1917-April 1918* (Macmillan, London 1978)
Wilson, Michael *Baltic Assignment: British Submarines in Russia 1914-1919* (Leo Cooper, London 1985)

Mediterranean
Denham, HM *Dardanelles: A Midshipman's Diary 1915-16* (John Murray, London 1981)
Elliott, Peter *The Cross and the Ensign: A naval history of Malta 1798-1979* (Patrick Stephens, 1979)
Halpern, Paul G *Naval War in the Mediterranean* (Allen & Unwin, London 1987)
The Italian Navy in the World War 1915-1918 Facts & Figures (Rome, 1927)

North Sea and Grand Fleet
Roskill, Stephen *Admiral of the Fleet Earl Beatty* (Collins, London 1980)
Temple Paterson, A *Tyrwhitt of the Harwich Force* (Macdonald, London, 1973)

Naval Intelligence
Beesly, Patrick *Room 40: British Naval Intelligence 1914-1918* (Hamish Hamilton, London 1982)

Cruiser Warfare
Bennett, Geoffrey *Coronel and the Falklands* (Pan ed, London 1967)
Fayle, C Ernest *Seaborne Trade* Vol 1 *The Cruiser Period* (John Murray, London 1920)

U-boat War
Ritchie, Carson *Q-Ships* (Terence Dalton, Lavenham, Suffolk 1985)
Tarrant, VE *The U-boat Offensive 1914-1945* (Arms & Armour Press, London 1989)

German Navy
Herwig, Holger H *Luxury Fleet: The Imperial German Navy 1888-1918* (Ashfield Press paperback ed, London 1987)

Pacific
Howarth, Stephen *Morning Glory: A History of the Imperial Japanese Navy* (Hamish Hamilton, London 1984)

AIR WAR

Books
Bickers, Richard Townshend *The First Great Air War* (Hodder, London 1988)
Bowen, Ezra (& Editors of Time-Life Books) *Knights of the Air* (Time-Life Books, Alexandria, Va 1980)

Brown, D, Shores, C and Macksey, K *The Guinness History of Air Warfare* (Guinness Superlatives, Enfield 1976)
Bruce, JM *British Aeroplanes 1914-1918* (Putnam, London 1957)
Cole, Christopher and Cheeseman, EF *The Air Defence of Britain 1914-1918* (Putnam, London 1984)
Cole, Christopher (ed) *Royal Flying Corps 1915-1916 [Communiqués]* (Kimber, London 1969; repr 1990)
Cole, Christopher (ed) *Royal Air Force 1918* [Communiqués] (Kimber, London 1968; repr 1990)
Dollfuss, Charles and Bouché, Henri *Histoire de l'Aéronautique* (L'Illustration, Paris 1937)
Finne, R *Sikorsky: The Early Years* (Airlife, Shrewsbury 1987)
Fitzsimons, Bernard (ed) *Warplanes and Air Battles of World War I* (BPC, London 1973)
Fredette, Raymond H *The First Battle of Britain 1917/18* (Cassell, London 1966)
Gibbons, Floyd *The Red Knight of Germany* (Cassell, London 1933)
Gray, Peter L and Thetford, Owen *German Aircraft of the First World War* 2nd edition (Putnam, London 1970)
Grey, CG (ed) *Jane's All the World's Aircraft* (Sampson Low, Marston, London 1919)
Imrie, Alex *German Fighter Units June 1917-1918* (Osprey, London 1978)
Imrie, Alex *Pictorial History of the German Army Air Service* (Ian Allan, London 1971)
Jones, HA *War in the Air* Vols 2-6 & Appendices (Clarendon Press, Oxford 1928-37; repr Hutchinson 1969)
Mason, Francis K and Windrow, Martin *Battle Over Britain* (McWhirter, London 1969)
Middleton, Edgar *The Great War in the Air* 4 vols (Waverley Book Co, London 1920)
Morrow, John H Jr *German Air Power in World War I* (U of Nebraska P, Lincoln 1982)
Penrose, Harold *British Aviation: The Great War and Armistice, 1915-1919* (Putnam, London 1969)
Raleigh, Sir Walter *War in the Air* Vol 1 (Clarendon Press, Oxford 1922)
Rimmell, Raymond Laurence *Zeppelin! A Battle for Air Supremacy in World War I* (Conway Maritime Press, London 1984)
Robertson, Bruce (ed) *Air Aces of the 1914-1918 War* (Harleyford, Letchworth 1959)
Robinson, Douglas H *The Zeppelin in Combat* (Foulis, London 1961) and *Giants in the Sky* (Foulis, London 1973)
Sikorsky, Igor *The Winged S* (Hale, London 1939)
Supf, Peter *Das Buch der Deutschen Fluggeschichte* 2 vols (Drei Brunnen Verlag, Stüttgart 1956-58)
Taylor, John W R et al (ed) *The Guinness Book of Air Facts and Feats* 3rd ed (Guinness, Enfield 1977)
Weyl, AR *Fokker: The Creative Years* (Putnam, London 1972)
Whitehouse, Arch *The Zeppelin Fighters* (NEL ed, London 1972)
Woodhouse, Jack and Embleton, G A *The War in the Air 1914-1918* (Almark, London 1974)

Aircraft Profiles
(All published Profile Publications, Leatherhead/Windsor 1965/67)
No 9 Gray, Peter L *The Albatros DV*
No 17 Andrews, CF *The SPAD XIII C.1*
No 25 Gray, Peter L *The Fokker D. VII*
No 26 Bruce, JM *The de Havilland D.H. 4*
No 31 Bruce, JM *The Sopwith Camel*
No 37 Bowers, Peter N *The Curtiss JN-4*
No 38 Bruce, JM *The Fokker Monoplanes*
No 43 Gray, Peter L *The Pfalz D. III*
No 49 Andrews, CF *The Nieuport 17*
No 61 Cattaneo, Gianni *The S.V.A. Ansaldo Scouts*
No 62 Bruce, JM *The de Havilland, D.H. 9*
No 68 Strnad, Frank *The Thomas-Morse Scout*
No 73 Bruce, JM *The Sopwith Triplane*
No 74 Bruce, JM *The Short 184*
No 79 Bowers, Peter M *The Nieuport N.28C-1*
No 85 Bruce, JM *The R.E. 8*
No 86 Gray, Peter L *The Siemens-Schuckert D III & IV*
No 103 Bruce, JM *The S.E. 5*
No 109 Bruce, JM *The Hanriot D.D. I*
No 115 Grosz, Peter M *The Gotha GI-V*
No 121 Bruce, JM *The Sopwith 1^{1}/2-Strutter*

No 127 Gray, Peter L *The Albatros DI-DIII*
No 145 Bruce, JM *The de Havilland D. 10*
No 151 Haddow, George *The O. Aviatik (Berg) DI*
No 157 Bruce, JM and Noël, Jean *The Breguet 14*
No 163 Grosz, Peter M *The Roland CII*
No 169 Bruce, JM *The Sopwith Dolphin*
No 175 Haddow, George *The Phönix Scouts*
No 181 Bruce, JM *The de Havilland D.H. 5*
No 187 Cowin, Hugh *The Junkers Monoplanes*
No 193 Bruce, JM *The Bristol M.1*
No 199 Grosz, Peter M *The Pfalz D XII*
No 200 Bruce, JM *The Martinsyde Elephant*

INTERNATIONAL EVENTS

Luebke, Frederick C *Bonds of Loyalty: German-Americans and World War I* (N Illinois UP, 1974)
Luebke, Frederick C *Germans in Brazil: A comparative history of cultural conflict during World War I* (Louisiana UP, Baton Rouge 1987)Ritter, Gerhard *The Sword and the Sceptre: The Problem of Militarism in Germany* Vols 3 & 4 (Allen Lane, London 1973)
Shanafelt, Gary W *The Secret Enemy: Austria-Hungary and the German Alliance* 1914-1918 (Columbia UP, NY 1985)

Espionage and Intelligence
Andrew, Christopher *Secret Service: The Making of the British Intelligence Community* (Heinemann, London 1985)
Busch, Tristan *Secret Service Unmasked* (Hutchinson, London 1950)
Haswell, Jock *British Military Intelligence* (Weidenfeld, London 1973)
Kahn, David *The Codebreakers: The Story of Secret Writing* (Weidenfeld, London 1968)
Kahn, David *Hitler's Spies* (Arrow Books ed, London 1980)
Keay, Julia *The Spy who Never Was: The Life and Loves of Mata Hari* (Michael Joseph, London 1987)
Seth, Ronald *Encyclopedia of Espionage* (New English Library, 1972)

Prisoners of War
Garrett, Richard *P.O.W.* (David & Charles, Newton Abbot/London 1981)
Moynihan, Michael (ed) *Black Bread and Barbed Wire: Prisoners in the First World War* (Leo Cooper, London 1978)
Reid, Maj Pat & Michael, Maurice *Prisoner of War* (Hamlyn, London 1984)

HOME FRONTS

Rickards, Maurice & Moody, Michael *The First World War: ephemera , mementoes, documents* (Jupiter Books, London 1975)

Propaganda and Films
Haste, Cate *Keep the Home Fires Burning: Propaganda in the First World War* (Allen Lane, London 1977)
Isenberg, Michael T *War on Film: The American Cinema and World War I 1914-1941* (Fairleigh Assoc Dickinson UPs, Rutherford NJ 1981)
Reeves, Nicholas *Official British Film Propaganda During the First World War* (Croom Helm, London 1986)
Sanders, Michael L & Taylor, Philip M *British Propaganda during the First World War 1914-18* (Macmillan, London 1982)

Austria
Brook-Shepherd, Gordon *The Last Habsburg* (Weidenfeld, London 1968)
McGarvie, Michael Francis *Joseph I: A Study in Monarchy* (Monarchist Press Assoc, London 1966)
Redlich, Joseph *Austrian War Government* (Yale UP, New Haven 1929)

Britain
Gilbert, Martin *Winston S Churchill Vols 3 & 4 1914-1922* (Heinemann, London 1971-72)
Hamilton, J A B *Britain's Railways in World War I* (Allen & Unwin, London 1967)
Lloyd George, David *War Memoirs* 2 vols (Oldhams, London 1938)

Bulgaria
Constant, Stephen *Foxy Ferdinand 1861-1948 Tsar of Bulgaria*

(Sidgwick, London 1979)

France
Becker, Jean-Jacques *The Great War and the French People* (Berg, Leamington Spa 1985)
Fontaine, Arthur *French Industry During the War* (Yale UP, New Haven, 1926)
Saint Loup *Renault* (Bodley Head, London 1957)

Germany
Feldmann, Gerald D *Army, Industry and Labor in Germany 1914-1918* (Princeton 1966)
Hull, Isabel V *The Entourage of Kaiser William II 1888-1918* (CUP, London 1982)
Manchester, William *The Arms of Krupp 1587-1968* (Bantam Books ed, New York 1970)
Palmer, Alan *The Last Kaiser: Warlord of the Second Reich* (Weidenfeld, London 1978)
Whittle, Tyler *The Last Kaiser: A biography of William II German Emperor and King of Prussia* (Heinemann, London 1977)
Williamson, Gordon *The Iron Cross: A history 1813-1957* (Blandford, Poole 1984)
Wrisberg, Maj-Gen Ernest von *Wehr und Waffen 1914-1918* (Koehler, Leipzig 1922)

Portugal
Wheeler, Douglas L *Republican Portugal: A Political History 1910-1926* (Univ of Wisconsin Press 1978)

Rumania
Seicaru, Pamfil *La Roumanie dans la Grande Guerre* (Minard, Paris 1968)

Science and Technology
Crow, Duncan (ed) *Armoured Fighting Vehicles of World War One* (Profile Publications, Windsor 1970)
Haber, L F *The Poisonous Cloud: Chemical Warfare in the First World War* (Clarendon Press, Oxford 1986)
Hartcup, Guy *The War of Invention: Scientific Developments 1914-18* (Brassey's, London 1988)

Turkey and the Armenian Massacres
Gurun, Kamaran *The Armenian File: The Myth of Innocence Exposed* (Rustem/Weidenfeld, London/Istanbul 1984)
Lang, David Marshall *The Armenians: A People in Exile* (Allen & Unwin, London 1981)
Nassibian, Akaby *Britain and the Armenian Question 1915-1923* (Croom Helm, London 1984)
Walker, Christopher J *Armenia: The Survival of a Nation* (Croom Helm, London 1980)

Women
Ewing , Elizabeth *Women in Uniform through the centuries* (Batsford, London 1975).
Marwick, Arthur *Women at War 1914-1918* (London 1977)

Peace Movement
Moorehead, Caroline *Troublesome People: Enemies of War 1916-1986* (Hamish Hamilton, London 1987)

Poets
Bridgwater, Patrick *The German Poets of the First World War* (Croom Helm, London & Sydney 1985)
Cross, Tim *The Lost Voices of World War 1* (Bloomsbury, London 1988)
Reilly, Catherine W *English Poetry of the First World War: A Bibliography* (George Prior, London 1978)
Stallworthy, Jon (ed) *The Oxford Book of War Poetry* (OUP 1984)
Symons, Julian *An Anthology of War Poetry* (Penguin, 1942)

Periodical & Newspapers
Stand To! The Journal of the Western Front Association 1980-
The Times (London) Aug 1914-Dec 1918
War Monthly 1974-82 (as Military History 1982-84)
Warship Journal 1983-85

GLOSSARY

Note: This alphabetical list includes not only abbreviations and terms used in the Chronicle, but also ones that readers might encounter in First World War literature. Usually it is restricted to terminology originating in the war itself. For a fuller and fascinating treatment of language used but often long pre-dating 1914-18, such as most regimental nicknames, see *Soldier and Sailor Words and Phrases* by Edward Fraser & John Gibbons (Routledge, London 1925), and *The Long Trail, What the British Soldier Sang and Said in the War of 1914-18* by Eric Partridge with John Brophy (Revised edition 1969, Sphere).

A

AA	Anti-aircraft guns or gunfire
Abdul	British slang for Turk
About turn	BEF slang for Hébuterne, France
Ace	Airman who has shot down at least 5 aircraft, originally a French 1915 definition
AChD	Army Chaplains' Dept (British), made Royal 22 Feb 1919 for war work. Grew from 117 to 3416 (Aug 1918)
ACM	Air Chief Marshal
Ack-Ack	(from Signallers code for 'A') anti-aircraft guns or fire
ADC	Aide-de-camp, officer on monarch's, general's or governor's staff
AD Corps	Army Dental Corps (British)
Adj	Adjutant
Adm	Admiral
admin	administration
AEC	Army Educational Corps (British)
AEF	American Expeditionary Forces (in France). Cynics said it stood for 'After England Failed'. Irreverent members called it 'Arse End First'.
AFSR	Armed Forces of South Russia, united White Volunteer Army and southern Cossacks 1919-20
Ah wee	British rendition of French *Ah oui*
AIF	Australian Imperial Force (Australian troops overseas)
Air pill	Bomb dropped by aircraft
'Alf a mo, Kaiser!'	British expression from a popular 1914 recruiting poster

ALH	Australian Light Horse (mounted infantry)
Alleyman	A German from French *Allemand*, gave way to Jerry
All Highest	Prussian title of the Kaiser's, from the German *Aller Hochst*
Alpini	Italian mountain troops (founded 1876), the 52 bns (8 regts) of 1915 expanded to 78 bns in 1916.
am [of 12]	morning [of the 12th]
AMC	Armed Merchant Cruiser
Antwerp Expresses	German Army term for large HE shells from their success on that city
ANZAC	Australia New Zealand Army Corps
Anzac	Australia/New Zealand beach and sector at Gallipoli. Originally suggested as simpler telegraphic code by British Lt A T White at ANZAC HQ, Cairo
AOC	Army Ordnance Corps (British), awarded title Royal for war work Nov 1918
APM	Assistant Provost Marshal (British Military Police), unofficially 'A Permanent Malingerer'
appt	appointed
approx	approximately
Apres la gare	Never, from the French *Après la guerre*
Archie	Anti-aircraft gun or its shell after music hall performer or song
Arditi	Italian picked assault troops formed 1917. Each corps (26 maximum) had a battalion-strength group of these specially trained young men with a higher issue of automatic weapons & grenades, & some flame-throwers *see Stosstruppen*
Arminteers	British slang for the French border town of Armentières and its famous mademoiselle
Armstrong hut	British small collapsible wood & canvas building
Army	Formation of several corps (qv) & their component divs
Army Council	Five military members, civil and finance members administering British Army since 1904

Arty	Artillery		(several could be jointed together) for destroying barbed wire and mines invented by Maj RL McClintock RE (1908-14) in India, hence name
ASC	Army Service Corps (British), also known as 'Ally Slopers' Cavalry' or unfairly 'Army Safety Corps'. Grew from 14,491 men with 246 motor vehicles to 327,603 (Sept 1918) with 125,149 motor vehicles (1 Mar 1919). Awarded title Royal Nov 1918.	Bankers' Battalion	British 26th Royal Fusiliers
		Bantam	British soldier under minimum Army height of 5ft 3in (35th Div once all Bantam)
Ash can	US Navy term for depth charge	BAR	Browning Automatic Rifle, US light machine-gun first produced Feb 1918, 52,000 by Armistice
Asiatic Annie	Turk heavy gun at the Dardanelles		
Askari	African native soldier	Barbette	Fixed armoured shelter in a warship behind which a gun revolves on a turntable (part of a turret from French *barbe* for beard)
Asquiths	British term for French matches, user had to 'wait and see' if they lighted		
Assoc	Association	Barishnya	British N Russia troops' term for unmarried Russian girl
Asst	Assistant		
A/S	Anti-submarine	Baron	An Army commander (British slang)
ASW	Anti-Submarine warfare	Barrage	Continuous artillery fire along a selected sector, and derived from the French (*see* creeping barrage). Also a large sea minefield
Ataman	Chief of Cossack host		
Attaboy	American baseball slang, became popular in England 1917-18		
		Bat boat	Sopwith flying boat
Aus	Australian	Batman	An officer's servant
av	average	Battalion	Basic unit of infantry formed of several companies (usually 4). Several battalions (usually 3) formed a regiment (all armies except British). 1914 full establishment strengths seldom thereafter ever achieved: Austrian 1064 all ranks; Belgian 1000+; British 30 officers & 992 other ranks; French 22 officers & 1030 ranks (750, 1918); German 26 officers & 1050 other ranks (reduced to 980 men then 880 on 1 July 1918); Russian 18 officers & 958 ranks; Italian 1000 (1915); American (1917) 27 officers & 1026 enlisted men
AVC	Army Veterinary Corps (British), jestingly rendered as 'All Very Cushy'. Grew from 519 men to 29,452. Awarded title Royal 1920 for war work (*see* RAVC).		
Avec	Spirits, as in *Café avec* (request for liquor)		

B

b	born		
BA	*Brieftauben-Abteilung* ('carrier pigeon unit', ie bomber unit)	Battery	Basic unit of artillery (4-8 guns). All powers except Britain, Germany, Austria & Russia began with 4-gun field batteries. Germany (from 6) and Russia (from 8) reduced to 4.
Baa lamb	Battleship HMS *Barham*		
BAB	Telephone code most commonly used in British trenches from 1916	Battle-bag	Naval airship (British slang)
		Battle bowler	Early name for British steel helmet
Baby Killers	Churchill's insult to the German Navy for bombarding Scarborough 16 Dec 1914. Soon applied to Zeppelins	Battlecruiser	Fast but lighter armoured (than battle-ship) capital ship since 1908 in British, Japanese and German navies (*Goeben* in Turkish)
Baby Monitors	British Dover Patrol term for M-class monitors		
Bags, the	Sandbags on trench parapet	Battle surplus	British personnel left out of an attack in order to rebuild the unit, also called the Lifeboat Party
Balb, to	Airman's jargon for getting an opponent in a bad position, of American origin		
		Battling Third	British destroyer flotilla (qv) with Harwich Force
Ballo, Ballyhooly	BEF nicknames for French border town of Bailleul, a haven till 1918		
		Bav	Bavarian
Bangalore torpedo	A 6ft -long pipe-like explosive device		

Bde, bde	Brigade		(German), especially in Alsace.
BE	Biplane Experimental (British). The BE8 was nick-named the Boater.	Bn, bns [5] bn	Battalion(s) [5] billion
Beachy Bill	Large Turk gun at Gallipoli opposite Anzac	Boloism	Treason in high places, from French traitor Bolo Pasha executed 1918
Beaucoup	French word that became Allied term for 'plenty of'	Bombers	Grenade-throwing troops or bombing aircraft
Beetle off	British airmen slang for 'to fly straight'	Boob, the	A guardroom or military prison, of American origin
BEF	British Expeditionary Force (in France)	Bond Street ribbon	Medal or decoration given for British Home Service
Behemoths, the	Grand Fleet's 3rd Battle Squadron (8 *King Edward VII* class battleships)	Box barrage	Protective artillery fire put down on 3 sides of troops
Belgeek	British slang for Belgium or a Belgian	Box-respirator	British-made gas helmet of 1916
Belly band	British flannel cholera belt	Brass hat	A staff officer or senior officer from the gold lace on their cap. In Navy a Commander & higher
Belly flopping	British term for crouching rushes by attacking troops		
Bersaglieri	Elite Italian riflemen (founded 1836, *bersaglio* means target), 12 regts (68 bns incl 10 of cyclists) in 1915 became 21 by war's end	Brigade	Infantry, cavalry or artillery unit of 2-6 battalions, regiments or batteries; 2-4 brigades made a division. An American infantry brigade (1917) had 6 infantry battalions plus 1 MG battalion with 8469 all ranks, almost as big as many Allied and German divisions by then.
Bert	BEF slang for Albert, town N of the Somme		
Big Bertha	German gunners' nickname (after the Krupp owner) *'die dicke Bertha'* 'the fat Bertha' for the 2 Krupp-made 42cm (16.5-in) siege howitzers that smashed the Liége forts in 1914. Allies erroneously applied it to the 1918 Paris Gun (*see* Long Max).	Brig-Gen	Brigadier-General, most junior general officer (1-star general in Second World War parlance). British Army abolished rank 1920, replaced by one of Colonel-Commandant until rank of Brigadier introduced 1928
Big noise, a	American slang for VIP	Brigade-major	Principal staff officer of a British Brig-Gen, usually a captain
Birdcage	PoW barbed wire enclosure at the Front, also final Allied entrenched area N of Salonika	British warm	Short coat worn by British officers, not officially uniform till 1918
Black Maria	British slang for large German shell, emitting black smoke. German term was *Schwarz Maria*	Brownies, the	British Women's Land Army or Government girl messengers, from their uniform
Blighty	British slang for British Isles (from the prewar Army in India), hence Blighty one, a wound to ensure going home	BSA	British South Africa Police.
		Buck	A dapper private (US Army); too full of talk (British)
Blimp	A small non-rigid airship (Allied)	Bully beef	Corned beef in a tin
Blue Cross	A 1917 German poison gas (from shell's colour coding)	*Bundesrat*	Upper House of German Parliament. Set up 1871 to represent princes of the German States
Blue Cross, the	Auxiliary Veterinary Service (British civilian), first animal hospital in France before 16 Dec 1914 at Sequeux, 30 miles from Dieppe	Burglars	Bulgarians (British slang)
		Butterfly boat	Cross-Channel leave ferries, especially Le Havre-Southampton
Blue Devils	French *Chasseurs Alpins*	Butt-notcher	A sniper
BMA	British Medical Association	Byng Boys	Canadian troops (from their GOC 1916-17)
Boche	French term of abuse for Germans with many derivatives. Origin disputed, not used till after 1870-1 but may be contraction of *Alboche*, slang for *Allemand*		

C

c	circa, approximately
C3	Men unfit for active service overseas (British Military Service Act 1916)
Cafard, le	French Army term for nervous debility after long duty in the trenches
Cagnas	French Army word for barracks, used by some Canadian units
Caimani di Piave	Italian Army unit of volunteer swimmers in that river 1917-18.
Calm-laylas, the	British nickname for Egyptian Labour Corps, from its chants to camels
Camouflage	Deception of the enemy by artifical scenery and dummy guns, etc or dazzle paint schemes at sea, from the French *camoufler* to bind or veil. Adopted into English 1914-15
Canteen eggs	Gas attack (British)
Capital ship	Battleship or battlecruiser, yardstick of naval strength
Capt	Captain
'Carl the Caretaker's in charge!'	Anglo-American W Front phrase for finding a quiet German sector opposite
cas	casualties
Catsood	Drunk, from the initial French price (*quatre sous*) of a drink at an *estaminet* or village café
Catwalk	Brick pathway across sodden fields, usually 1 brick (9 in) wide
Cav, cav	Cavalry
CB	confined to barracks - a punishment
Cdn	Canadian
Cdr, cdrs	Commander, rank and position
Cdt	Commandant
CEC	Central Executive Committee of Bolshevik (Communist) Party
CEF	Canadian Expeditionary Force (overseas)
Central Powers	Germany and Austria-Hungary due to their central position in Europe between France and Russia. Bulgaria and Turkey added 1914-15
CEP	*Corpo Expecicionario Portugues* (W Front)
CFS	Central Flying School (Britain)
CGT	*Comité Général du Travail* (French trade union founded 1895)
Chauchat	French 1915 LMG. Despite its legendary

	faults US Army accepted 37,000 as its main weapon until the Browning.
Challenge ships	American term for the ships *Orleans* & *Rochester* sent to France (May 1916) to test the U-boat blockade
Char d'assaut	A tank (French)
Cheka	Soviet political police, original KGB
Cherry Nobs	British Military Police, from their cap colour
Chicken, the	US Army slang for the national eagle badge
Chinese attack	A trick or feint
Chinese Rolls-Royce	A Ford van (RASC)
Chink, a	Chinese Labour Corps member in France
Chm	Chairman
Chit	Army official form or anything written
C-in-C	Commander-in-Chief
CID	Committee of Imperial Defence (British, founded 1906)
CIGS	Chief of the Imperial General Staff (British)
circ	circulation (of publications)
Civvies	Plain clothes as opposed to uniform
Click	To get what you want; especially to get home
CMAR	'Can't manage a rifle', RAMC spelt backwards
CMB	Coastal Motor Boat (British), *see* Scooter
Cmdre	Commodore
CMH	Congressional Medal of Honor (US)
Cmndt	Commandant
CNS	Chief of Naval Staff
CO	Commanding Officer
Co	Company (business)
Coffee cooler, a	A shirker (US Army)
Coal-box	British slang for a heavy German shell. German word was *Kohlenkasten*. French phrase was *Gros Noir*.
Col	Colonel
col	column
Colco-Pari	Salonika Front term for how much, from the Bulgarian and used of illicit bargaining

Comb-out	to clear out men of military age from civilian work	Creeping barrage	A barrage lifted at regular intervals (usually 50 yds every 90 seconds) ahead of advancing troops
Comic cuts	BEF term for intelligence summaries at brigade level & above	Cricket ball, a	Type of British hand grenade
Commo	Communication trench	crimed	Entered on British Army 'crime sheet' as an offender
Compo	Pay	Crown, the	British slang for Sergeant-Major, from the sleeve badge
'Comrades of the Mist'	US Navy phrase for the Grand Fleet	Crucifix corner	Calvary cross on a French roadside or crossroads
Conchy	conscientious objector	Crucifixion	*See* FP1
Cons-Gen	Consul-General (diplomatic official)	Crump	Sound of the explosion of a large shell
contd	continued	Crystal Palace Army	Nickname for RND (qv) from their S London depot, hence glasshouse sailors. Also site of Imperial War Museum 1920-4, visited by 3m people. Crystal Palace also christened twin-tall pithead structures at Loos, France (1915).
Contour chasing	Low flying		
Cordite	smokeless explosive introduced in 1889, so-called from its cord-like appearance		
Cook's tour, a	British term for a new unit's look at the trenches or a VIP visit to them		
Cookhouse official	Any baseless rumour (British)	CSM	Company Sergeant-Major (British)
Cooshu, a	A sleep, from the French *coucher*	Ctee	Committee
Corned dog	Canned beef	CUP	Committee of Union and Progress, Young Turks' political party 1908-18
Corp	Corporation	Cup and wad	British slang for tea and a bun in the canteen or YMCA hut
Corps, Army	In full *corps d'armée* from the French all-arms formations first developed in 1800 to be miniature armies. Comprised 2-3 divisions with supporting units. (1914: German c44,000 men & 160 guns; French c38,000 & 120 guns; Russian c35,000 & 144 guns; British c36,000 & 152 guns) Italian (1915) 40,250 men & c104 guns.	Curtain fire	A continuous wall of artillery fire to seal off an area
		Cushy	Comfortable, also La Cauchie, nr Arras, France
		Cuthbert	British term for one who avoided military service as being indispensable elsewhere. First coined by *Evening News* cartoonist 'Poy' who drew frightened looking rabbits.
Corpse ticket	Identity disc. In the British Army a green one was buried with the owner and a red one retained for record purposes.		
CoS	Chief of Staff, either to a commander or as head of an armed force.	**D**	
Coy, coy	Company, sub-unit of a battalion. Infantry ones all had 4. 1914 establishments: German 5 officers & 259 other ranks; Austrian 4 officers & 260 other ranks; Russian 4 officers & 240 other ranks; British 6 officers & 232 other ranks; American 1917 6 officers & 250 enlisted men.	d	died
		[3]d	[three] pence
		DADOS	Deputy Assistant Director of Ordnance Services (British). One for each division, supervised issue of over 20,000 items from guns to toothpaste. Hence Dado nickname for cholera belt.
Cp	Corporal		
CP	Command Post	Dandy	Fine, excellent. American term adopted by British from Canadian & US troops.
CPI	Committee on Public Information (US)		
CRA	Commander Royal Artillery (for a British div or higher)	Darts	(French *flechettes*, German *Stahlpfeil* .) Early air-dropped anti-personnel weapon used in clusters
Crab grenade	British name for a type of German grenade	Dazzle	Striped naval camouflage (Allied) invented 1917 by the marine artist Cdr Norman Wilkinson RNVR
Crappo, a	French trench mortar, from *crapaud*		

DBR	Damaged beyond repair		armies. German 17,500 men, 4000 horses, 72 guns & 24 MGs (1914) became 12,300 men, 3000 horses, 48 guns, 120 mortars, 222 MGs, 6-12 lorries (1918). Austrian (1914) c15,000 men, 42 guns, 28 MGS. British 18,073 men, 5592 horses, 76 guns, 24 MGs became 13,035 men, 3673 horses, 48 guns, 36 mortars, 208 MGs, 14 cars & lorries (1918). French c15,000 men, 36 guns, 24 MGs (1914) became 11,400 men, 48 guns, 18 mortars, 324 MGs (1918). Russian 14,140 men, 48 guns, 32 MGs (1914). Belgian c22,000 men, 72 guns (1914). Serb (1914) 13,000-16,000 men, 26-44 guns. Bulgar (1915) 24,000 men, 44-66 guns. Italian (1915) 16,393 men, 2693 horses, 32 guns, 24 MGs. American (1917) 28,061 men, 72 guns, 260 MGs.
DCM	Distinguished Conduct Medal (British, 1862) for Army NCOs and men for gallantry in field (24,620 with 481 bars awarded with 4957 and 1 bar to Allied armies 1914-20)		
DCNS	Deputy Chief of Naval Staff		
De-bus, to	Official British Army term coined for troops getting off motor transport		
Decoy ships	*See* Q-ships		
Depot ship	Mobile supply base for warships, especially submarines and destroyers		
Dept	Department	Division	Cavalry. (1914 establishments) German 5278 men, 5590 horses, 12 guns, 6 MGs (1914). British (BEF 1914) 9269 men, 9815 horses, 24 guns, 24 MGs. Belgian + French (+12 MGs) 5000/5250 men, 12 guns. Austrian c4500 men, 12 guns, 16 MGs. Russian 3466 men, 12 guns, 8 MGs.
Derby, a	British volunteer enlisted under the Derby scheme of October 1915		
Der Tag	The Day, specifically the belief that it was a German Navy toast to victory over the British Fleet		
Desert, to swing it across the	British EEF phrase for contriving one's way to hospital	Dixie	A camp cauldron
Destroyer	In full torpedo boat destroyer (TBD), small gun & torpedo-armed warship for screening battlefleets against other destroyers and submarines	DH	De Havilland, British aircraft make
		DMC	Desert Mounted Corps (British)
		DMI	Director of Military Intelligence
Det	Detachment	DMO	Director of Military Operations
Devil's Wood	Delville Wood on the Somme, originally 160 acres dense woodland & under-growth	DNC	Director of Naval Construction (British)
		DNI	Director of Naval Intelligence
D/F	Direction-finding	Do an alley	To go off, from the French *aller*
DFC	Distinguished Flying Cross	Dock	A military hospital (British slang)
DFM	Distinguished Flying Medal	docs	documents
DG	Director-General	Doing it	BEF slang for Doingt, nr Péronne (Somme)
DH	De Havilland, British aircraft make		
		DORA	Defence of the Realm Act (British)
Digger	An Australian or New Zealand soldier. Originally used of goldminers from the mid-1850s & revived by New Zealand troops in France 1916. Australian troops adopted it 1917 (Official History).	Doughboy	American soldier nickname, particularly infantrymen, dating from the Mexican or Civil Wars and derived from adobe huts or large buttons respectively. Much pre-ferred to 'Sammies' (qv) or 'Teddies' (after Roosevelt), the original British nicknames & apparently chosen when US 1st Div CO asked for alternatives.
Dimback	A louse		
Dingbat	Australian slang for batman		
Dinky	Mule	Dough nuts	Royal Navy term for the 8-man Carley float (life-saving raft)
Dir	Director		
Dirigible	Balloon or airship directed by steering gear	Dover Patrol	Royal Navy force in the Channel to protect crossings & attack the occupied Belgian coast
dismtd	dismounted	dow	died of wounds
Div, div(s)	Division(s)	Dreadnought	Battleship built since 1906
Division	Infantry. Basic formation of combatant	DSC	Distinguished Service Cross, British

naval decoration (1914) for officers below rank of Lt-Cdr. Also stood for 'Decent Suit of Civvies' to those awaiting demobilisation.

DRLS — Dispatch Rider Letter Service (British)

Drowning Flotilla — Dover Patrol nickname for the German Flanders U-boat flotilla due to its heavy losses

DSM — Distinguished Service Medal, British naval decoration (1914) for all non-commissioned ranks

DSO — Distinguished Service Order, British decoration (1886) for officers (9003 with 787 bars, 1916-on, conferred plus 1491 and 9 bars to 12 Allied armies 1914-20)

Duay — My own, wartime slang apparently from the British Royal motto *Dieu et Mon Droit*

Duckboard — Slatted timber path or walk in trenches & camps, so-named from the sloping boards for duckhouses. Hence duckboard glide for stealthy night movement & duckboard harrier for a messenger.

Dug-out — Underground shelter in the trenches, British slang for retired officer recalled to service

Dullmajor — Interpreter for British PoW camps in Germany, from German *Dolmetsher* (interpreter)

Dumdum bullet — From Dumdum arsenal nr Calcutta in India. A soft-nosed bullet which expands & lacerates on impact. Both sides accused the other of using such illegal ammunition.

Duncars — Armoured cars attached to British Dunsterforce in NW Persia and Baku 1918

Dun Cow — SS *River Clyde* at Gallipoli

Dunsterforce — Special British force equivalent to a reinforced brigade for operations in N Persia & at Baku, 1918

E

E — East/Eastern

Earthed — An aircraft brought down (British term)

Eatables — BEF slang for Étaples, Pas-de-Calais town

EEF — Egyptian Expeditionary Force (British, 1916-19)

EFC — Expeditionary Force Canteens, British supply organization on all fronts

Egg shells — Cruiser HMS *Achilles*

Elephant, the — British Martinsyde aircraft

Emden, sank the — Sarcastic British phrase for units getting too much publicity after HMAS *Sydney*'s lauded victory

Emma — British signaller's code letter 'M'

Empire Battalion — 17th Royal Fusiliers, wealthy unit raised in 10 days of August 1914

EMSIB — Acronym for E Mediterranean Special Service Intelligence Bureau, a British Cairo-based counter-espionage body

Entente — Name for Allied nations, from the Anglo-French *Entente Cordiale* of 1904

eqpt — equipment

eqvt — equivalent

Erfs — Eggs, British rendering of *oeufs*

Ersatz — German official word for reserve troops, soon applied to reliefs & substitutes of all kinds

Esc — *Escadrille*, French air squadron

ESMA — Listen! Arabic used by British EEF

est — estimated

estab — established

excl — excluding

F

FA — Field Artillery

Fairy light — Very pistol flare (BEF)

Fan Tan — Name of British tank paid for (£6000) by En Tong Sen of the Malay States

FANY — First Aid Nursing Yeomanry Corps, British female Territorial unit founded 1909. Worked for Belgian Army from Oct 1914. Allowed to drive British ambulances in France from 1 Jan 1916. Staffed 3 French ambulance units from 1917.

Fashy — Angry, from the French *fâché*

Fernleaves, the — New Zealander troops, from their badge

FIDAC — *Fédération Inter-Alliée Des Anciens Combattants*, Allied veterans organization; 1st London Congress 1924

Field officers — Colonels, Lieutenant-Colonels, Majors (ie not company or general officers)

Field rats — Prussian Guard scorn for ordinary line troops

Finee — No more, all gone! From the French *fini*

Fivepence halfpenny — Derisive British Army term for something not there ie the supplementary Government daily rations allowance

	never seen by the soldier
Flaming onions	British slang for a German AA shell, apparently suggested by its similarity to Bretons selling street onions
Flapper's delight	British subaltern on leave in female company
Flight	Aircraft unit of 5-6 aircraft (RFC/RAF)
Floating Ls, (or ELLS)	Royal Navy Harwich Force destroyer flotilla with L names, also known as Battling Ls
Florrie Ford	Motor car or lorry, linked to Florrie Ford the actress
Flotilla	Naval unit of destroyers etc or on inland waters
Flt [Lt]	Flight [Lieutenant]
Fly boys	Contemptuous Dublin term for English evading conscription by crossing to Ireland
FM	Field-Marshal
FP1	Field Punishment No 1 (British offender lashed to gunwheel for given period)
Franc-tireur	French, literally 'free shooter' from the Franco-Prussian War of 1870-1. The spectre (largely) of these irregular guerilla marksmen haunted the Germans in 1914.
Fred Karno's Army	British New Army song-line after the period's popular comedian
Fred Karno's Navy	Dover Patrol, due to its variety of vessels (24 types)
Ft	Fort
[360] ft	[360] feet
[10]-ft	[10]-foot (cliff, etc)
Freikorps	German irregular volunteer armed units of varying status that existed from the Armistice until 1922. About 120 of these 'free corps' formed, totalling 250,000 men. Most were of brigade or battalion strength with their equally-paid right wing veterans (especially officers) fore-shadowing the Nazis.
Frightfulness	German war policy (*Shrecklichkeit*) of inspiring terror by wanton ruthlessness. Allied press term that became a Services joke.
Frigo	Frozen or chilled meat
Fritz	A German, particularly in 1914-15. Also Royal Navy word for U-boat
Front	Russian and Soviet term for army group (several armies)

Frontiersmen, Legion of	25th (Service) Battalion, Royal Fusiliers, served E Africa. Derived from an Empire body founded 1906.
FTR	Failed to return (aircraft or airships on operation)
Fuller phone	British Army tap-proof field telephone, replaced the Buzzer model from 1916
Funk-hole	Colloquial term for small shelter or dugout, any safe refuge or job. Current in BEF by 29 Nov 1914.
Funky Villas	BEF term for Fonquevillers village nr Hébuterne, France
Furphy	Australian for rumour, originated at Melbourne on speculation as to their destination

G

G	Gulf
Galloping Lockharts	British term for mobile field kitchens
gals	gallons
Gas bag	Airship
Gas guard	Night sentry duty to detect gas & strike a warning gong
Gas patrols	British RAMC parties sent to detect mustard gas concentrations & warn passing troops
Gaspirator	British slang for gas mask
Gassed at Mons	Whereabouts unknown. British joke reply perhaps precisely because no gas was used at Mons 1914.
Gat	Revolver (Canadian)
GCR	Gold Coast Regiment (British West African troops)
Gd(s)	Guard(s)
Geddesburg	BEF name for Montreuil, site of GHQ, after Sir E Geddes became DG of Transportation there. Probably suggested by Gettysburg.
Gentle Annie	Turk gun at the Dardanelles
George	British term for airman, equivalent to Jack and Tommy for the two older Services
GER	Great Eastern Railway (British)
GHQ	General Headquarters
Gin Palace	Battleship HMS *Agincourt*, perhaps because originally built for Turkey
Glory hole	Any small billet or dugout, also German

	position nr Festubert captured at heavy cost
GOC	General Officer Commanding (British)
GOC-in-C	General Officer Commanding-in-Chief (British)
Gold stripe	British sleeve marking denoting a man wounded badly enough for removal to base hospital or home
Go one better	Motto of British 42nd (E Lancs) Territorial Div
Gong	Medal (old British Army term)
Gooseberry	Small ball of barbed wire
Gorgeous wrecks	Unflattering name for British Volunteer Defence Corps from their GR brassards. 'Govt rejects' was alternative usage
Gotha	Name used for almost all German heavy bombers, from the type's town of manufacture
Got me?	Do you understand? Phrase from a wartime American film in which the hero interrogates with a revolver.
Gott Strafe England !	God punish England. German slogan spoken, published & inscribed everywhere.
Gov-Gen	Governor-General
Govt	Government
GQG	*Grand Quartier Général* (French GHQ)
Grabenkameradschaft	German for comradeship of the trenches, a feeling that separated 1914-18 front-line soldiers from all other participants
Grand Fleet	Main British force of capital ships & their escorts based at Scapa Flow & Rosyth. So dubbed by its commander Jellicoe; did not officially replace Home Fleet till May 1916.
Granny	Any large howitzer, originally the first British 15-in weapon of April 1915
Grasshopper	Military Policeman (British)
Green Cross Shell	German type of poison gas shell
Green Cross Society	Women's Reserve Ambulance Society (British) formed 1916 for hospital & nursing work, so-called from their badge
Green envelope	Ordinary British Army envelope for writing home and sent unsealed
Greyback	British Army flannel shirt (from its colour)
Ground Hog Day	US Army slang for Armistice Day, ie everyone came out of cover
Ground stunt	British air term for ground attack

GSO	General Staff Officer
Guardian Angel	Parachute for escaping from a burning balloon
Gumboots	Trench waders, introduced to BEF from 1915
Gwennie	Royal Navy equivalent of Archie (qv)

H

Hairbrush grenade	Early British trench weapon
Hairy, a	Large British draught horse for medium or heavy artillery
Half Crown Battalion	Any 2/6th Bn, from the official designation
Hammer blows	German term first used to describe Verdun Offensive
Handcart Cavalry	Nickname for British Stokes mortar units
Hans Wurst	German term for an infantryman
Hard tack	Biscuit
Hard tails	Mule
Harkers	Men sent out on listening patrol
Harry Tate's Cavalry	Nickname for British Yeomanry, after the well-known comedian
Harry Tate's Navy	RNVR (qv)
Harwich Force	British cruisers & destroyers based at that E Coast port
Hate	Artillery bombardment (British slang) from Ernst Lissauer's Sept 1914 'Hymn of Hate'
Hazy Brook	BEF slang for Hazebrouck, French Flanders
HE	High explosive
Heine (Hiney)	A German, in US & Canadian Army parlance, from Heinz
Hellfire Corner	Lethal spot nr Menin Gate, Ypres & many other dangerous W Front places
Herbaceous borders	Royal Navy's 'Flower class' sloops of 1915 on. (Names chosen by Admiralty's Acting Librarian).
Heroine of Loos	Mlle Emilienne Moreau, a 17-yr-old French girl who won the MC protecting British wounded by killing 3 Germans at that battle
HMG	His Majesty's Government (British)
HMIMS	His Majesty's Indian Marine Ship (British)
HMS	His Majesty's Ship (British warship)

HMY	His Majesty's Yacht (British)	i/c	in command or in charge
hols	holidays	Iddy Umpties, the	Nickname for British signallers & the 17th Div, from its dot-dash sign
Hommes forty	W Front term for a French railway van, from their capacity	IEF	Indian Expeditionary Force: 'A' for France, 'B' for E Africa, 'C' for Egypt and 'D' for Mesopotamia
Honved	Royal Hungarian *Landwehr* (qv) part of Austria's 5-part Army as renamed spring 1917. Organized in 32 infantry regts (96 bns) or 8 divs (increased by 17 regts to 12 divs), 10 hussar regts (2 cav divs) & 140 guns (9 regts or 35 btys became 24 regts).	Iggry	'Hurry up', British EEF term from the Arabic word
		IJN	Imperial Japanese Navy
		ILP	Independent Labour Party (British)
Hop out	BEF pronunciation of Hopoutre, suburb of Poperinghe, nr Ypres	Imperials, the	Dominion & Colonial troops' term for comrades from the Mother Country
Hop over	An attack, going over the top	[12-] in	[12-] inch
Horse of Troy	Nickname for SS *River Clyde* from her copying of the famous strategem enacted so near Gallipoli	incl	included/including
		indep	independent
Hostility Men	Royal Navy term for volunteers for the duration	Inf, inf	Infantry
		info	information
Howitzer	A short stubby gun firing heavy shells at low velocity & high angle. A dominant weapon in calibres from 75mm up to Big Bertha (qv).	Insp-Gen	Inspector-General
		int'l	international
HQ	headquarters	IRB	Irish Republican Brotherhood
Hun	Abusive term for a German, apparently derived from the Kaiser advising German troops sent to China in July 1900 to act like the Huns under Attila	Iron Cross	German gallantry award founded in 1813. Revived 1870 & 1914. Anything from 80,000 to c250,000 awarded.
Hunland	British airmen's term for any territory with German troops	Iron Division	Newspaper-coined compliment to British 13th Division (Gallipoli & Mesopotamia). Also Kaiser's prewar term for his 3rd Brandenburg Division. Also earned by the French XX Corps (11th & 39th Divs), French 20th & Russian 4th Divisions, Belgian 3rd (Liège) Div.
Hurrah Kanaille	Prussian cavalry's derogatory term for infantry, equivalent to 'cannon fodder'		
Hush Hush Army	Dunsterforce (qv)		
Hush Hush Crowd	British Tank Corps	Iron ration	Soldier's emergency ration not supposed to be eaten except by officer's permission but not uncommonly 'destroyed by shellfire' & replaced by fresh issue. Hence 'Jerry's iron ration' humorous British term for shells fired at Germans.
Hush Hush Operation	Projected British 1917 landing on Flanders coast		
Hush Hush Ships	Royal Navy expression for various unusual warship classes		
		ISP	Independent Socialist Party (German)
Hypo-helmet	Flannel bag with eye-pieces soaked in anti-gas solution, British equipment first made 10 May 1915	'It'	British nickname for phone-tapping apparatus used in trenches & No Man's Land
I		Ivan	A Russian soldier
		Ivory Cross	British dental organization giving free or low-cost treatment especially to demobilized soldiers
I	British abbreviation for Intelligence. Gen Staff Dept I(a) for enemy orders of battle; I(b) to prevent such information reaching the enemy & to examine civilians in newly-captured areas; I(c) counterespionage, maps & topography; I(d) the press and I(e) radio intercepts.		
		IWW	International Workers of the World (American Communist Party)
IB(s)	Incendiary bomb(s)		

J

Jackies	US Navy term for seamen
Jack Johnson	Anglo-Saxon slang (from negro heavy-weight boxer) for large low-velocity German shell first used by Lt-Col Swinton official eyewitness or war correspondent Sept 1914
Jacko, a	British EEF term for a Turk
Jam tin grenade	Home-made BEF weapon first used Nov 1914
'Japan'	From the French *du pain* , BEF word for bread
Jctn	Junction (railway)
Jericho Jane	Australian name for long-range Turk gun in Jordan Valley, eventually destroyed by RAF July 1918
Jerry	A German soldier
Jerry, to	To understand, hence Jerry over for 'Lights out!' when aircraft crossed British lines at night
Jewel of Asia	Nickname for Turk gun on that side of the Dardanelles
Jigger, up the	In the trenches
Johnny	A Turk, dating from Crimean War
Josephine	French Army nickname for its 75mm field gun
Joy Bag	British souvenir bag, usually a sandbag, from the trenches
Joy Spot	BEF officers' term for a good hotel or restaurant behind the line
Joy Waggon	Practice aircraft at a British flying school

K

K(1)	Popular press shorthand for Kitchener's first Hundred Thousand volunteers of Aug 1914
K	King
KG5	Battleship HMS *King George V*
k	killed
Kadet	Constitutional Democrat (liberal Russian party)
Kai	New Zealand troops' Maori word for food
Kamerad	German for comrade and used as a word of surrender, hence British 'to Kamerad'
'Kaiser's Own'	British derisive nickname for King's

Royal Rifle Corps due to their Iron-cross resembling Maltese cross cap badge

Kapai	New Zealand troops' Maori word for very good, capital
Kaput	German for *kaputt*, finished
KAR	King's African Rifles (British East African native troops)
KCB	Knight Commander of the Bath
KG	Knight of the Garter
Khakis, the	German name for British troops
kia	killed in action
King's certificate	British 'Served with honour' discharge, designed by Bernard Partridge of *Punch* , etc
Kitch	Kitchener 'New Army' recruit
Kite balloon	Artillery observation balloon
Kiwi	New Zealand soldier, also British airmen's slang for ground crew (flight-less bird)
Kiel whale	British PoW term for nauseous fish-meal
Knife rest	Spiked iron bar laid in barbed wire or wooden frame surrounded in barbed wire as quickly movable obstruction for roads etc
Knuts, the	British Dover Patrol term for VIPs on passage to France
Komuch	Ctee of Members of the Constituent Assembly, Russian SR anti-Bolshevik govt on the Volga 1918
Kosh	Trench raid club, from the London roughs' weapon
Kr	Kroner
kts	knots
Kultur	German education and Allied term of abuse for it.
KuK	*Kaiser und König* , appellation 'Imperial and Royal' for the Austrian armed forces (and other services) from Emperor Francis Joseph also being King of Hungary

L

L	Lake
LAMB	Light Armoured Motor Battery (British armoured car unit)
Land Girls	British female wartime farmworkers
Landowner, a	British description of a dead man on the W Front

Landship	Tank	LMG	Light Machine-gun, a British platoon weapon from Feb 1917 (2 Lewis guns by Mar 1918). Each German company had 3 belt-fed slightly lighter Bergmann from Mar 1917 (afterwards doubled).
Landsturm	German (men aged 20-45; untrained 9 yrs service) and Austrian 3rd line troops (extended to ages 18-55). Latter began as 210 bns with 10 Hussar half-regts. Expanded to 286 bns of 800 men or less (no artillery). Serbia also had a *Landsturm* of about 50,000 men	London Declaration	1909 international law (71 articles) on contraband and blockade. Not ratified by Britain.
Landwehr	German (men aged $27^1/_2$-$38^1/_2$; 11 yrs service) and Austrian 2nd line troops (*see Honved* for Hungarian *Landwehr*). Former mobilised 314 bns in 47 bdes as fortress and frontier guards, subsequently helped form 26 divs. Latter mustered 8 inf divs (120 bns), 5 mtn regts (16 bns), 9th Cav Div, 64 field howitzers (16 btys) doubled to 128 guns & howitzers (24 btys).	Lone Howitzer, the	British 4.5in howitzer in a Loos chalk-pit till knocked out Aug 1917. Barrel at the Imperial War Museum.
		Lone Pine	Turk position at Gallipoli captured by the Australians and so-named because of its original landmark
Lazy Eliza, a	Trench expression for long-range large shell	Lone Star	A 'one-pip' subaltern from his single badge
lb(s)	pound(s)	Lonely Officers' Dances	British EEF phrase for Lady Allenby's Cairo dances for officers on leave
L/Cp	Lance-Corporal nicknamed Lance-Jack. Lowest NCO appointment		
Ldg Mech	Leading Mechanic	Long Bertha	A big Krupp gun
LEA	Local Education Authority (British)	Long Horn	Early type of Maurice Farman biplane (MF7).
League of Remembrance	Princess Beatrice's organization for helping widows & daughters of dead British officers	Long Jump, the	British airman's phrase for transferring from Home to overseas service
Leaning Virgin	Damaged (Nov 1914) statue of the Virgin Mary on the spire of the Church of Notre Dame des Berbières at Albert, France. Its fall on 16 Apr 1918 was supposed to symbolize the war's imminent end.	'Long Max'	German gunners' nickname for the 15-in naval gun that shelled Dunkirk from Luegenboom
		Lord's Own, the	Battleship HMS *Vengeance*
Leap-frogging	Trench warfare term for successive waves of troops leap-frogging through each other to capture objectives	Lorry hopping/ jumping	Catching a lift at the Front
		Lousy Wood	BEF pronunciation of Leuze Wood on the Somme
Lebel Mam'selle	French Army nickname for its rifle	Lt	Lieutenant
Lewis gun	Gas-operated, air-cooled machine gun (perfected by US Col Isaac N Lewis 1911) with 47-round circular drum magazine for ground use. 133,104 made in Britain (9434 sent to 7 Allies). Used in British, French & US aircraft (97-round ammunition pan) from Sept 1914 and by Belgian (known as 'Belgian Rattlesnake' to Germans) and British infantry (from Sept 1915).	lt	light
		Lt-Cdr	Lieutenant-Commander (naval)
		Lt-Col	Lieutenant-Colonel, usually a battalion CO
		Lt-Gen	Lieutenant-General, usually a corps commander
		Luger	German Army (1908) and Navy (1905) automatic 9mm pistol, officially called Parabellum Pistole '08
Lid	Helmet		
Limpets	British newspaper term for civilians clinging to stay-at-home jobs	Lyddite	British high-explosive named after Lydd in Kent where it was first made
'Liveliness, a certain'	Churchill's expression in a 19 Aug 1914 Admiralty communiqué that became a popular catch-phrase	**M**	
		[1.5]m	[1.5] million
Lizzie	Big shell or gun from HMS *Queen Elizabeth* at the Dardanelles Mar-May 1915	Maconochie	British tinned meat and vegetable ration, from the firm suppling it. Applied in jest to MC and MM, the stomach and the telephone

Madelon	French soldiers' tune, song and dance especially at Verdun		intelligence service, established 1909 (19 staff grew to 844 1914-18)
Mafeesh	Arabic for dead, used by British on Turk fronts as much as Napoo (qv) on W Front	Middx	Middlesex
Maggie	Nickname of battleship HMS *Magnificent*	Mine-bumping, the	Grand Fleet 3rd Battle Sqn, sent ahead on a N Sea sweep (*see* Wobbly Eight)
Mainga	Zulu word for water used by S African troops	Minnie	Nickname for *minnenwerfer*, a large German trench mortar & its shell
Maj-Gen	Major-General, usually commanded a division	mins	minute(s)
Maleesh	Arabic for never mind, used on Turk fronts	ML	Motor launch
Mangle	To machine gun, especially British airmen's term	MM	Military Medal, British Army decoration from 1916 for all other ranks (115,577 awarded with 5989 bars 1916-20 plus 7389 with 6 bars to 11 Allied armies)
MAS	*Motobarca armata silurante* (torpedo-armed motor launch), Italian	MMS	Military Message Service, British women's medical organization numbering 2000 by the Armistice
Maternity jacket	RFC double-breasted tunic		
Mauser	German small arms manufacturer of standard pistols, rifles & automatic weapons	MO	Medical Officer/Orderly
		Mob store	Mobilization store
maximum	maximum	Mobile, to do a	British EEF terminology for a desert route march
Maxim	Machine gun, from its 1884 inventor Sir Hiram Maxim	Moo-Cow Farm	Mouquet Farm nr Thiepval on the Somme
MC	Military Cross, British Army decoration (1915) for Captains, Lieutenants & Warrant Officers (37,081 awarded with 3157 bars plus 3609 with 9 bars to 13 Allied armies)	Mopping up	Trench warfare term for troops following the initial waves, method first used by BEF at Arras Apr 1917. French called it *nettoyage*.
		Morgenroth	German forlorn home death song 'Morning bright'
M & D	'Medicine and Duty', cure for British Army malingerers	Mossy Face	British air term for Bois d'Havrincourt (SW of Cambrai)
MD	Military District (Russian)		
MEBU	Pillbox from the German *Machinengewehr-Eisenbeton-Unterstand* ('machine gun iron concrete emplacement')	Mother	Not only one of the first tanks but also the first British 9.2-in howitzer (Oct 1914-July 1916) & many subsequent weapons
MEF	Mediterranean or Mesopotamian Expeditionary Force (British)	Mournful Maria	Dunkirk air/sea raid siren
Mermaid's visiting card	US Army identity disc, a wry allusion to an, in fact, unfounded danger of U-boat attack	Mouth organ	Stokes mortar bomb
		Movies, the	Searchlights hence movie man for their operators
Mesop/Mespot	Mesopotamia	MP	Military Police, Member of Parliament (British)
Mesopolonica	Composite of above & Salonika to convey British troops' unresolved destination	MRAF	Marshal of the Royal Air Force
		[1¹/₂]mt	[1¹/₂] million tons
Methusilier	Austrian Remount Unit member, from his advanced years	Mt(s)	mount or mountains
MG(s)	Machine gun(s)	Mtd	Mounted
Micks	Irish Guards or any Irish troops	mths	months
MI1c	Literally Military Intelligence Section 1c, British Secret Service 1916-21	Mtn	Mountain, esp troops and artillery
MI5	British internal security and counter-	MTV	Motor Transport Volunteers

Muckle Flugga Hussars	British 10th Cruiser Sqn on blockade duty between the Orkneys and Greenland	NRFF	Nyasaland-Rhodesia Field Force
		NSW	New South Wales
Munitionette	British woman war worker	NUR	National Union of Railwaymen (British)
Mustard gas	Poison gas named after its pungent smell, otherwise Yellow Cross from its shell markings	NY	New York
		NZ	New Zealand
Mystery port	Richborough, Kent. Base of Channel Barge Service & train ferry, much enlarged Mar 1916 - Mar 1917	NZEF	New Zealand Expeditionary Force.

N

N	North/Northern
NACB	Navy and Army Canteen Board (British) founded Apr 1916
'Nails in the Coffin of the Kaiser'	US minelayers' description of the 1918 Northern Mine Barrage
Napoo	There is no more, from French *il n'y en a plus*, hence napooed 'killed'
Narky	HM Sloop *Narcissus*
National Guard	US State troops and also British City of London Volunteer Corps of 2 bns
NCO	Non-Commissioned Officer
Newton pippin	A type of British rifle-grenade
Niet Dobra	Russian for no good used by British troops in N Russia
Niffy Jane	Cruiser HMS *Iphigenia*
Nissen hut	British corrugated iron roofed semi-cylindrical wooden building designed 1916 by Canadian mining engineer Lt-Col PN Nissen, DSO, RE, 47,000 soon ordered
nm	nautical mile
Noah's doves	Australian description of reinforcements or comrades at sea on Armistice Day
No Man's Land	Ground between opposing trenches, belonging to neither side. Used in medieval land tenure 1328 and militarily by Engels 1870, but for Great War apparently first printed in a British official narrative of 15 Sept 1914.
Nonstop	Trench expression for a long-range shell passing overhead
Norperforce	Unofficial acronym for British force in N Persia and Baku Nov 1918-1921
Not Forgotten Association	British organisation to support disabled veterans (30,000+ at end of 1923)
nr	near

O

Oblt	*Oberleutnant*, German senior lieutenant
obs	observation
OC	Officer Commanding, more usually written than spoken *see* CO
OCAC	Officer Commanding Administration Centre (British New Army and Territorial depots from 1915)
Office, the	Airmen's term for cockpit
Old Contemptible	Original regular BEF soldier from Kaiser's presumed 19 Aug 1914 sneer at 'General [*sic*] French's contemptible little army'
OHL	*Oberst Heeresleitung*, German Supreme Command
Oil Can	German 250mm (10-in) trench mortar shell
Old Bill, an	Old soldier, veteran (British) from Capt Bruce Bairnsfather's 1914 cartoon character. Nickname given to a London bus on W Front throughout
Old one eye	Repair ship HMS *Cyclops*
Olive branch	British post-Armistice reinforcement
'Omms and Chevoos'	BEF vernacular for French railway truck capacity
On the tapes	Ready to start, from the white tapes used to mark the 'lie out' positions for attacking infantry
Oofs	British slang for eggs (French *oeufs*)
OP	Observation Post, often called 'O Pip'
Ops	Operations (military)
ORs	Other ranks ie not officers
Out there	W Front
Outfit, an	Aircraft squadron
Over there	France (US) from the 1917 marching song
Over the top or the lid	To leave a trench for an attack

Overseas men	British subjects abroad who came home to enlist		Armentières
Owl, the	Equivalent of Second World War's 'Careless talk costs lives'. Verses about the wise old silent owl were displayed at French railway stations & in Britain.	PM	Prime Minister
		10 pm	10 per month
		10pm	10 o'clock
Ox & Bucks	Oxfordshire & Buckinghamshire (Light Infantry)	*Poilu*	French soldier, from the French 'hairy' for his unshaven appearance, apparently first applied to elderly reservists. Word traceable back to Balzac's *Le Médecin de Campagne* (1833)

P

pa	per annum	Policeman's truncheon	Early British hand grenade with streamers attached
Parasol	Type of high-wing monoplane	Pop	BEF shortening of Poperinghe, 7 miles from Ypres
Parlt	Parliament		
PBI	Poor bloody infantry	pop	population
pd	per day	Pork and beans	British nickname for Portuguese troops on W Front from tinned rations they were fond of
[7] pdr	7-pounder (gun)		
Penguins, the	Nickname for the WRAF derived from the bird's inability to fly	Potato-masher	German hand grenade (from shape)
		PoW	Prisoner(s)-of-War
perf(s)	performance(s)	PP's	Princess Patricia of Connaught's Light Infantry (Canadian)
Petrol Hussars, the	Duke of Westminster's armoured cars sent to Egypt 1916		
		PR, the	Battlecruiser HMS *Princess Royal*
PG	Battleship HMS *Prince George*	Pre-dreadnought	Battleship built before 1906, slow and usually bearing only 4 main guns
PH helmet	Early British gas helmet (late 1915, replaced Hypo-helmet), replaced by box-respirator (qv)		
		prelim	preliminary
		Princess Mary's gift box	Brass box of cigarettes or tobacco & pipe sent to every British soldier or sailor on active service after Oct 1914 appeal realised £131,000
Pharaoh's Foot	Nickname for Volunteer companies of Europeans raised in Egypt 1915		
Pill-box	Small concrete blockhouse used by Germans from 1917		
		prod	production
Pimple	British slang for a hill. Noteworthy pimples were at Vimy, Gallipoli & Salonika.	Pronto	Spanish for 'hurry up', adopted from US troops who gained it in the Mexican War
		Prov	Province or Provisional
Pineapple	German 4lb grenade and a type of gas	Provost-Sergeant	NCO policing a camp
Pink	Secret, from the colour for HMG secret telegrams	Pte	Private
		Pudding basin	British steel helmet
Piou-piou	French soldier, prewar word soon replaced by *Poilu*	Pulpit, a	Artillery observation ladder (British)
		Pup tent	US Army 2-man infantry tent
Pip-Emma	British signaller's code for pm	Pusher	Aircraft with rear-mounted engine
Pip-squeak	Small German HE trench shell. Term officially banned in BEF	PV	Paravane anti-sea mine device
Pirates, the	German U-boats	pw	per week
Platoon	Small sub-unit of infantry (58 estab, 50 av in British Army 1914, 31 by 1918) or other troops, 3-4 formed a company (2 sections in US Army (59 men, 1917) each of 3 squads, sections in British Army)	PZ	British Fleet tactical exercise battle from signal flags that announced it
Plug Street	BEF rendering of Ploegsteert village nr		

Q

Q	Queen
QAIMNS	Queen Alexandra's Imperial Military Nursing Service (British). Founded 1902, grew from 463 members (1914) to 10,304 (1918); 112 died on service. Known as Red Capes from their uniform.
QARNNS	for Royal Navy branch
QE	Battleship HMS *Queen Elizabeth*
QF	Quick-firing
QM(G)	Quartermaster (General)
QMAAC	Queen Mary's Army Auxiliary Corps (British), title of WAAC (qv) from 9 Apr 1918
Q-ships	Allied anti-U-boat armed ship decoys, disguised as ordinary merchantmen. Royal Navy used 235 (39 lost from all causes). They sank up to 13 U-boats in over 70 duels. French, Italian & US Navies also operated some. The Germans fitted out 8 decoy vessels from Dec 1915, for the Baltic.
Quakers	Colloquial name for conscientious objectors, also old word for dummy gun
Quash	From Arabic *khwush* for good, used by British on Turk Fronts
Queenstown Navy	US destroyer flotilla based at Queenstown, Ireland 1917-18
Quick Dick	British gun on W Front
Quirk, a	Pilot learning to fly, or any unusual aircraft
qv	*Quod vide*, which see

R

R	River
RA	Royal Artillery. Grew from 132,920 all ranks & 1859 guns (1 Aug 1914) to 548,780 (1 Aug 1918) & 11,437 guns (11 Nov 1918). Lost 48,949 dead. *See* RFA, RGA, RHA.
RACD	Royal Army Clothing Dept
Race card, the	Morning Sick Report (British)
RAF	Royal Air Force
Raffish	RAF slang for any non-uniformed RAF or Royal Aircraft Factory personnel
Rag-Pickers	Field Salvage Corps (US Army)
Rainbow Division	US Army 42nd Div drawn from 27 states & all colours, hence also called All America Div
RAMC	Royal Army Medical Corps. Grew from 18,728 all ranks (Aug 1914) to 144,152 (Aug 1918)
RAN	Royal Australian Navy
Rapatrie	French term for those repatriated from German-occupied areas, adopted by British
'Rat Catcher Churchill'	German press abuse for Churchill after his 21 Sept 1914 speech
RAVC	Royal Army Veterinary Corps. Grew from 519 all ranks (4 Aug 1914) to 29,452 (Aug 1918) treating a maximum of 90,000 animals at any one time.
RC	Roman Catholic
RCAF	Royal Canadian Air Force
rd	road
RE	Royal Engineers. Grew from 11,689 all ranks (1 Aug 1914) to max 239,386 (1 Aug 1917). Also stands for Reconnaissance Experimental, British aircraft types.
Rear-Adm	Rear-Admiral
recce(s)	reconnaissance, reconnoitre(s)
recon	reconnaissance, reconnoitre(s) [in Air War]
Red Cap or Red Hat	Military Police (British)
Red Coats	British Women Inspectors of the Anti-Poison Gas Dept, from their uniform
Red Hussar	British Govt wartime brand of cigarette (*see also* Ruby Queen)
Red Lamp	British term for a French *Maison tolérée* (official brothel). Red Lamp Corner was a dangerous spot with a warning red light nr Festubert.
Red Triangle Man	British nickname for a YMCA member, from his badge
Regt	Regiment. Permanent unit of any arm under a colonel. Inf regts had 3 bns (Austrian 1914 estab 4356, Russian 1914 3535, US regt 1917 3832) and 2 regts made a bde in all armies except British. Cav regts (German 676+, Austrian 926+ & 4 MGs, Russian c866, French 683, British 551 & 2 MGs). Arty regts (German 36 field guns, 16 or 32 heavy guns, French 12 field guns & 554 men).
rep	representative
req'd	required
Res	Reserve
Rest Camp	British term for place of recuperation & light duties behind front, also port waiting point for going on leave

Ret	retired	Rooty	Old British Army word for bread
RFA	Royal Field Artillery. Grew from 51,228 all ranks (Aug 1914) to max 350,096 (Apr 1917)	Rouen, a client for	BEF VD hospital at Rouen
		rpd	rounds per day
RFC	Royal Flying Corps (formed 13 May 1912). Grew from 1200 (Aug 1914) to 144,078 (Mar 1918)	rpg	rounds per gun
		RSFSR	Russian Socialist Federative Soviet Republic, Soviet Russia's official title
RFP	Retail Food Price (British). 100 in July 1914, the working class cost of living was always at least 10% less	RSM	Regimental Sergeant-Major
		RTO	Railway Transport Officer (British)
RGA	Royal Garrison Artillery (British), responsible for siege, heavy, coast & mountain guns. Grew from 33,834 (1 Aug 1914) to max 210,554 (Aug 1918)	Ruby Queen	British Govt brand of ration-issue cigarettes. Occasional nickname for young nurse or Sister of fresh complexion
RHA	Royal Horse Artillery (British). Grew from 7538 all ranks (1 Aug 1914) to max 18,009 (May 1917)	Ruhleben Song	British PoW camp concert of May 1915, over 4000 British civilians were interned there
RIC	Royal Irish Constabulary	Rum jar	Type of German trench mortar shell
RIMS	Royal Indian Marine Ship	Rupert	British nickname for an observation balloon
RM	Royal Marines (British). Grew from 18,000 to 55,000, suffered 11,921 cas (-5 Apr 1919).		

S

RM [5 bn] [5 billion] *Reichsmark*	(German currency)	[10] s	[10] shillings
RMLE	*Régiment de Marche de la Légion Étrangère* (1915-18 9 citations)	S	South
		SA	South African
RMLI	Royal Marine Light Infantry	SAA	Small-arms ammunition (for rifles, pistols & MGs)
RN	Royal Navy	Saida	Arabic for Good day! Used on Turk fronts
RNAS	Royal Naval Air Service (formed 23 June 1914). Jokingly rendered Really Not A Sailor.	Salient, the	The Ypres Salient
RND	Royal Navy Division. Became 63rd (Royal Naval) Div 19 July 1916 on W Front but kept naval terminology	Sally Booze	BEF vernacular for village of Sailly la Bourse
		Salvo	Salvation Army Rest & Recreation hut
rnds	rounds	Sam Browne	Officer's field service belt, named after its Indian Army designer
RNR	Royal Naval Reserve		
RNVR	Royal Naval Volunteer Reserve	Sammies	Unpopular British nickname for US Army troops suggested by *Punch* 13 June 1917. Soon replaced by Doughboys (qv).
'Road of Remembrance'	Embarkation route to Folkestone harbour, England for troops going to & from France		
		San Fairy Ann	No matter, British pet version of *Ça ne fait rien*
Roger	British code term for poison gas cylinder June 1916, changed later	Sandstorm medals	Egyptian Army decorations
Roody Boy	BEF rendering of Rue du Bois nr Neuve Chapelle, Flanders	Sang bon	Very good indeed (*cinq bon*)
		Sankey, a	French five-franc note
Rosalie	French nickname for the bayonet from M Theodore Botrel's war song published in *Bulletin des Armées* , autumn 1914	Sappers	Engineers
		Sausage	Observation balloon
Room 40	Royal Navy's decrypting unit, part of Naval Intelligence and named after its first office in the Admiralty	Sausage hill, to go to	To be taken prisoner by Germans

Scarlet runners	British bn dispatch carriers from their red arm brassard	SMS	*Seiner Majestät Schiff*, prefix to Imperial German warships
Scene shifter	Effective British heavy gun in 1917 Arras sector	SNO	Senior Naval Officer (British)
Scooters	Nickname for CMB (qv)	*Soixante-quinze*	75mm French QF field gun, from its calibre
Scrap of paper	A broken pledge from Chancellor Bethmann's 1914 remark to the British Ambassador	SOS course	BEF Sniping, Observation and Scouting Course, started 1916, one per Army
SDP	*Sozial-Demokratische Partei*	SOS signal	Rocket sent up to start British arty barrage v German attack; distress call from ship
Sec, sec	Secretary		
Section	Smallest military body or fire unit, 4 of about 12 men each led by NCO (7 men & NCO 1918) formed a British inf platoon or a cav troop; 2 guns in a battery. Squad in US Army (25 men). *Gruppe* of 8 men in German Army	Souvenir	A trophy from the front, hence to souvenir, to steal
		Sovnarkom	Council of People's Commissars, Soviet 'cabinet'
		Spad	French single-seater biplane (*Société Pour Aviation et Ses Dérivés*)
Senussi	North African Arab Islamic Sufi mystic brotherwood (estab 1837) opposed to European colonialism, especially strong in Cyrenaica	Sparks	Radio operator
		Sparks, to get the	To range an MG on the enemy barbed wire after dark
sgt	sergeant	Spartacus League	German revolutionary socialist party founded 27 Jan 1916 & led by Karl Liebknecht & Rosa Luxembourg. Named after the Thracian gladiator who led the third slave revolt against Rome (73-71BC).
Shell shock	Popular & official 1916 term for a neurosis contributed to by shellfire, one of 1914-18's medical discoveries. Later officially abolished & renamed Psycho-neurosis. Combat fatigue in modern US Army jargon.		
		Spit ball	Hand grenade (US Army)
Shock absorber	Air observer	Sports Ship, the	British SS *Borodino*, chartered Oct 1914 as officers' supply ship to Grand Fleet, Scapa Flow
Shocks	French town of Choques nr Bethune (BEF)		
Shooting Gallery, the	The front line	Sportsman's Battalion	British 23rd & 24th Bns of the Royal Fusiliers (France & E Africa). Composed of men up to 45 incl many ranchers, planters & farmers
Short horn, the	Type of Maurice Farman biplane		
Silent Deaths, the	Night patrol party on ambush in No Man's Land		
		Springboks, the	S African troops
Silent Susan	Type of German high-velocity shell	*Spurlos Versenkt*	Gone entirely. Catchphrase from Count Luxemburg's infamous 1917 message 'Sunk without trace'.
Sim's Circus	US Navy nickname for its first destroyer flotilla in European waters, after the commanding admiral		
		Sq	Square
Sister Susie, a	British woman doing Army work, especially Red Cross	sq [miles]	square [miles]
Skindles	Restaurant at Poperinghe named after the fashionable Maidenhead establishment	Squarehead	German, originally a seafarer's term but reinforced by German Army haircuts
		Sqn, sqn(s)	Squadron (warships or cavalry). 1914 cav strengths: German 169; French & Austrian 150; Russian c145; British 160
Skolka, to	To sell, from the Russian how much or many. Used by British N Russia troops for illicit trafficking in Army food		
		SR	Socialist Revolutionary (Russian peasant party)
Slacker, a	British press term for any man reluctant to enlist		
		SS	Steamship
SM	Sergeant-Major	St	Saint , Street
SMLE	Small-magazine Lee Enfield	Staff crawl	General's trench inspection tour (British)

Stand-to, the	Dawn to daylight alert for an attack (British) ended by Stand-down	TB	Tuberculosis
STAVKA	Tsarist and Red Army Supreme HQ	TBs	Torpedo boats
Stealth raid	Trench raid (British), generally without artillery support	TBD	Torpedo-boat destroyer
		Teddy bear	Name for shaggy goatskin or fur coats issued to BEF, winter 1915
Stink bomb	Mustard gas shell	temp	temperature
Stinks OC	Gas officer or instructor (British)	Terrier	British Territorial Army volunteer (since 1909 foundation)
Stn, stn(s)	Station(s)		
Stockbrokers' Battalion	British 10th Royal Fusiliers	TF	Territorial Force
		Theatre ship, the	Grand Fleet name for SS *Gourko* which also gave cinema showings
Stokes mortar	Light British trench mortar, 3-in & 4-in models, 12,363 made	Ticket	Discharge from the British Army. Pilot's certificate (British)
Stool pigeon	Informer, especially among PoWs	Ticklers	Jam, from the British manufacturers since 1903. Plum & apple rather than straw-berry always seemed to reach the ranks.
Stosstruppen	German picked shock troops formed from 1916		
Strafe	Punish, attack (German) as in *'Gott strafe England'*	Tiddly Chat	Cruiser HMS *Chatham*, tiddly meant smart
Strombos horn	Compressed air horn to give warning of German gas attack	Ti-ib	Very good, all right. From the Arabic *Tay-ib*, used on Turk fronts
Strs	Straits	Timbertown, HMS	RND name for Groningen Internment Camp, Holland
Subaltern	Second Lieutenant, most junior commis-sioned officer	'Tin, they've opened another'	Unflattering British reference to new arrival
Suicide Club	British term for any unit having risky duties	Tin hat	Steel anti-shrapnel helmet of early 1916
Suicide Corner	Lethal spot in Ypres Salient or elsewhere	Tin pirate	German U-boat
Sundenabwehrkanone	Anti-sin-gun, German Army slang for a padre	Tip and run raids	German naval coastal bombardments of Britain
		'Tipperary'	British popular song actually published a year before the war and written by Henry Williams of Birmingham. Became an international craze after the BEF sang it landing at Boulogne.
T			
T [2m]	[2 million] Turkish pounds		
Tabloid, a	Small Sopwith biplane	*Tirailleur*	French for sharpshooter, 4 regiments (Algerians, Tunisians, Moroccans, or Senegalese) won 6 citations each
Tails up	In good spirits, keen fighting. Nickname of Sir John Salmond who used it to the Air Council.		
		Tir de barrage	French for 'barring fire', same as curtain fire
Tape, to	To get the artillery range of a target. To mark out the ground for a night assem-bly by troops before an attack, or the line for a new trench.	Tirps	Royal Navy name for Admiral Tirpitz
		Tit-Bits	RFC weekly communiqué (began with 25-27 July 1915)
Taps	'Last Post' bugle call (US Army)		
Tattenham Corner	Grand Fleet term for narrow Firth of Forth entrance between May Island & Inchkeith where U-boats lurked	TM	Trench mortar
		TNT	trinitrotoluene explosive
		Toad, a	Type of German hand grenade
Taube	German monoplane (from the German for pigeon), used till 1916 (500 built)	Toby	A steel helmet
Tavarish	Comrade (Russian). Also used by British N Russia EF troops	Toc-Emma	Signaller's code for trench mortar

Toc H	War name for Talbot House, a rest & social centre at Poperinghe nr Ypres opened 15 Dec 1915 by Rev P H Clayton	US	United States
Toffee-apple	British 2in trench-mortar stick bomb	USMC	US Marine Corps. Grew from 13,725 (6 Apr 1917) to 78,841 (authorized strength 1 July 1918, 31,824 served overseas during war, 11,500 cas in France, 12,371 total).
Tommy	British soldier, from Tommy Atkins (Thomas Atkins, the archetypal private on Army forms since the early 19th century). Thomasina Atkins or Tommy Waacks applied to the WAAC.	USN	US Navy. Grew to 599,051 (8106 cas)
		USNA	US Naval Academy (Annapolis, Maryland)
Tony, a	A Portuguese	UXB	unexploded bomb
Toto	French Army word for vermin or lice		

U

V

Tractor	Aircraft with front-mounted engine	v	versus, against
Trade, the	Royal Navy's term for its submarine service	Va	Virginia
Trap ships	German Navy name for Q-ships	V & A	Victoria and Albert
Trench fever	Infectious disease transmitted by vermin, prevalent from 1915	VAD	Voluntary Aid Detachment. Territorial Women's nursing service founded 1909. Provided 122,766 male & female nurses of whom first 19 landed at Boulogne 21 Oct 1914 (142 died on service).
Trench foot	Blood circulation illness resembling frostbite, caused by wet & cold, often ending in gangrene		
Trench ring, a	Finger ring made from any scrap of war material such as a German aluminium shell nose	Van blanc Anglais	Whisky
		VC	Victoria Cross, highest British award for valour (579 awarded with 2 bars, 173 posthumous 1914-20)
Tripe	Sopwith biplane (British)		
Troop	Cavalry sub-unit (British 1914 troop, 33 all ranks) 4 formed a squadron	VD	venereal diseases
		Verst	Russian measurement of distance = 0.7 mile or 1.06 km
TU	Trade union		
TUC	Trade Union Congress (British)	Vice-Adm	Vice-Admiral
Tutoring	British war term for attaching new battalions to ones with trench experience	Vickers	British armaments company. Delivered 4 battleships; 6 cruisers; 62 lighter war-ships; 53 submarines; 100,000+ MGs; 5500 aircraft.

U

		Vickers MG	British standard heavy machine gun for air & ground use, 71,355 made (10,336 sent to 6 Allies)
U-boat	A German submarine from German *Unterseeboot*		
UB	Coastal U-boat, 155 built	Victory Medal	Awarded after March 1919 to all Allied forces. Bronze, with reverse inscription 'The Great War for Civilisation'. Over 5m issued.
UC	Minelayer U-boat, 104 built		
Umpty poo	Just a little more (French *un petit peu*) especially exhortation to labour gangs	Vlam	BEF colloquial for Vlamertinghe, Flanders
Undertaker's Squad	Stretcher bearers	vols	volunteers
Univ	University	Vrille	A spinning nose-dive, RFC from the French
UPS	Universities and Public Schools Battalions (British), ie 18th-21st Royal Fusiliers enrolled in 11 days Aug/Sept 1914. All but 20th (served to Apr 1918) disbanded Apr 1916, the men going to cadet schools or other Fusilier units.	VTC	Volunteer Training Corps (British). Title given Nov 1914 to *ad hoc* local home defence volunteers unfit for Army or not sparable. War Office took over as Volunteer Force May 1916. Men exempt from conscription were required to join. Peak recorded strength of the First World
Unstick, to	Leaving the ground (airmen's jargon)		

War's Home Guard equivalent was 299,973 (May 1917) in 328 bns & units of which 46,559 under (min 17) & over (55+) military age. Tasks included trench digging, transport & ambulance driving, coast and AA defence

W

W	West
w	wounded
WAAC	Women's Army Auxiliary Corps (British), recruited 56,000 women for the duration from 13 Mar 1917. (Of over 9500 in France, 500 clerks served with AEF at Bourges & Tours). Transferred 7000 women to WRAF.
WAF	Women's Auxiliary Force (British) founded 1915 for part-time volunteer workers. Became Victory Corps 1920
WAFF	West African Field Force (British)
War baby	Any young officer or soldier, or a child born during hostilities
War bird, a	Any elderly man keen to enlist
Wavy Navy	RNVR because collar & sleeve markings were wavy not straight
W/Cdr	Wing Commander
WDRC	Women's Defence Relief Corps (British) formed Sept 1914 to free men for war service
Weary Willie, a	Long-range shell high overhead
WEC	Women's Emergency Corps (British), launched 6 Aug 1914 by suffragette Mrs Decima Moore & 5 peeresses (-Nov 1918) especially for food collection & relief, interpreters for Belgian refugees. Started canteens at Compiègne & Paris.
Wet Triangle, the	Royal Navy term for Heligoland Bight
WFC	Women's Forage Corps (British) formed Mar 1917. 4200 women served for a year or duration in khaki as part of RASC.
WFF	Western Frontier Force (British), Egypt
Whippet	Light tank (British), 14 tons, top speed 8mph, crew 3, with 4 Hotchkiss or Lewis MGs. First used 26 Mar 1918
Whistling Percy	A German naval gun captured at Cambrai, Nov 1917
White Sheet	BEF vernacular for Wytschaete, Flanders
Whizz-bang	German field-gun shell
WI	West Indian

wia	wounded in action
'Wilhelm's Gun'	German dubbing of the Paris Gun in the Kaiser's honour
Willie	(Big and Little) Kaiser and Crown Prince after *Daily Mirror* cartoons
Wind fight	False alarm
Windy Corner	Hazardous due to enemy fire, especially nr Menin Gate of Ypres
Winkle	To capture individual prisoners by stealth
'Winning the war, anyway it's'	Sarcastic comment for seemingly unnecessary task
Wipers	BEF name for Ypres, also called 'Eaps
Wipers' Express	German 420mm shell during Second Battle of Ypres
wk	week
WL	Women's Legion (British), founded July 1915 by Marchioness of Londonderry. Paid and wore khaki, over 40,000 enrolled including over 4000 full-time canteen workers.
WNLS	Women's National Land Service (British), founded early 1916, recruited 9022 farmworkers for Women's Land Army (qv)
Wobbly Eight	Grand Fleet's 3rd Battle Squadron of 8 *King Edward VII* -class battleships
Women's Forestry Service	Formed 1917 for timber felling & cutting, c3000 employed
Women's Land Army	Founded 26 March 1917 and employed 29,000 women at farmwork (- 30 Dec 1919). Popular uniform of overall, breeches & leggings. Scotland had 1816 women in its own organization.
Woodbine, a	Dominion & Colonial troops' name for a British soldier due to his partiality for that cigarette
Woodbines, The packet of	Five-funnelled Russian cruiser *Askold* at the Dardanelles 1915
Woolly-bear	Large German shrapnel shell releasing brownish-black smoke
Wound-stripe	Small strip of gold braid on left forearm (British Army), first sanctioned 1916
Wozzer, the	Australian for Haret el Wazza, Cairo's 1915 brothel street
WRAF	Women's Royal Air Force formed 1 Apr 1918. 32,230 served at home, in France & Germany (from Mar 1919) until 31 Mar 1920 demobilization.
WRAS	Women's Reserve Ambulance Service (Green Cross Corps) (British), formed June 1915 mainly for London area

	especially between main rail stations
Wrens	*See WRNS*
Write off	Air service expression for total aircraft crash
WRNS	Women's Royal Naval Service, hence Wrens, founded 29 Nov 1917. Organized in 12 divs incl Mediterranean. Transferred 2033 ratings to WRAF. Max strength 6392 (21 Nov 1918). HQ Crystal Palace, London.
WSPU	Women's Social and Political Union (suffragette movement formed 1903)
WVR	Women's Volunteer Reserve (British), branch of Women's Emergency Corps formed by Viscountess Castlereagh Mar 1915 especially for farming & gardening. Over 10,000 at Armistice in 40 County coys in Britain and 4 bns in Canada.

X

X-ships	Twin-engined landing ships (6 knots) of shallow draft built for Fisher's projected invasion of N Germany, but used at Gallipoli
Xaroshie	Very good, quite right. British N Russia troops' term from the Russian

Y

Yallah	Go on, get on with it. Arabic used on Turk fronts
Yanks, the	Preferred British Army name for US troops on W Front
yds	yards

Yeo	Yeomanry, British volunteer cavalry
Y gun	Twin depth charge thrower aboard Allied anti-submarine vessels
Yilderim	Turk Army Group in Palestine 1917-18, literally 'Lightning' from the sobriquet of the conquering Ottoman Sultan Bayazid I (c1354-1403)
Yimkin	Arab for perhaps, used on Turk fronts
Ypres Day	31 Oct, Anniversary Day observed by British Ypres League (founded by FMs French & Plumer 1920)
yr(s)	year(s)

Z

Z-day	Zero day, date fixed for major operation
Zemstvo	Provincial or district council in Tsarist Russia, indirectly elected by electoral colleges for nobility, townsmen & peasantry. Functioned in 34 provinces from 1865-6 but did not apply to greater cities or non-Russian inhabited frontier provinces.
Zeppelin	German airship
Zeppelin in a cloud	Sausage & mash (mashed potato)
Zero (Hour)	Time of an attack, made known to troops employed at latest possible moment
Zig-zag	Steering an erratic course to evade U-boat attack
Zouaves	French white North African troops in khaki service dress, 5 regiments each won 6 wartime citations

INDEX TO MAIN EVENTS

A comprehensive index would occupy as much space as the Chronicle itself. The present index concentrates on major events, particularly battles, actions and sieges strictly so called in official national battle nomenclature. Major references to leading generals, heads of state, important government ministers and significant developments in technology are also covered. In general the index excludes references to individual ships and military units, and to place names other than major battles, actions etc.

In keeping with the nature of a chronology, references to the main Chronicle are by date rather than by page, and sub-entries are arranged in date order, not alphabetical order.

Date references are followed by a number in brackets to identify the column in which the reference will be found, ranging from '0' for the 'Sarajevo to Outbreak' column, to '9' for the 'Home Fronts' column. Thus '12 Mar '15 (1)' refers the reader to the Chronicle at 12 March 1915 in column 1 (Western Front).

Cross-references to other index entries are printed in roman type. For example 'see also Gallipoli' refers the reader to the index entry for Gallipoli. Cross-references to other parts of the book, such as areas of the Chronicle itself, or to Maps or Tables, are printed in italics. For example 'see also E Front from 3 Jan '15' refers the reader to further references in the main Chronicle's Eastern Front column starting at 3 January 1915. A cross-reference such as 'see also Tables for W Front 1914' refers the reader to the tabulated matter which supplements the main Chronicle.

A

Aden, 10 Nov '14 (4), 13 Jun '15 (4), 21 Jul '15 (4)
    losses 1915, *see Tables for Turk Fronts 1915*
Adriatic *see Air War from 30 May '15; Sea War from 7 Aug '14*
Aegean,
    air war, 4 Apr '15 (7)
    see also Sea War from 8 Aug '14
Afghanistan, German Missions to, 16 Oct '14 (4), 5 Dec '14 (4), 14 Apr '15 (4)
Africa, South *see* South Africa
Africa, South West *see* South West Africa
Africa, West *see* West Africa
Agagiya, Action at, 26 Feb '16 (5)
Air aces, deaths of,
    Pégoud, 31 Aug '15 (7)
    Count Holck, 30 Apr '16 (7)
    Immelmann, 18 Jun '16 (7)
    Prince, 15 Oct '16 (7)
    Boelcke, 28 Oct '16 (7)
    Hawker, 23 Nov '16 (7)
Air bombing,
    C-in-C Home Forces i/c London's defence, 10 Feb '16 (7)
    air raids 1914 1915 & 1916, *see also Tables for Air War 1914, 1915, 1916*
    Zeppelins, *see* Zeppelins
    early bombing raids, 6 Aug '14 (7), 14 Aug '14 (7), 26 Aug '14 (7), 29 Aug '14 (7), 30 Aug '14 (7)
    Paris is first capital bombed, 30 Aug '14 (7)
    first British air raid on Germany, 22 Sep '14 (7)
    German long-range sqn formed, 1 Nov '14 (7)
    Tirpitz advocates fire bomb raids on London, 1 Nov '14 (7)
    first British long-range raid, 21 Nov '14 (7)
    French form 1st Bombing Group, 23 Nov '14 (7)
    Warsaw bombed, 9 Dec '14 (7)
    Russians form world's first heavy bomber unit, 10 Dec '14 (7)
    first German raid on Britain, 21 Dec '14 (7)
    French Dorand bombsight, 1 Feb '15 (7)
    German policy, 12 Feb '15 (7)
    French Lafay bombsight, 1 Apr '15 (7)
    first major French raid on Germany, 27 May '15 (7)
    RFC suspends raids for lack of bombsight, 24 Jul '15 (7)
    Allied attack on Lille rail triangle, 23 Sep '15 (7)
    first Italian long-distance raid, 18 Feb '16 (7)
    first major British raid on Germany, 12 Oct '16 (7)
    first ever 'shuttle raid', 17 Nov '16 (7)
    first daylight air raid on London, 28 Nov '16 (7)

Air war,
    artillery spotting by aircraft, *see* Artillery
    bombing, *see* Air bombing
    strengths in 1914, *see* 28 Jul '14 (7) and *Tables for Air War 1914*
    early recon flights, 8 Aug '14 (7), 12 Aug '14 (7), 26 Aug '14 (7), 31 Aug '14 (7)
    first French casualty, 8 Aug '14 (7)
    first British airmen die on active service, 12 Aug '14 (7)
    first German pilot killed on active service, 12 Aug '14 (7)
    first RFC visual recon mission over German lines, 19 Aug '14 (7)
    first RFC aircraft shot down, 22 Aug '14 (7)
    first Austrian air casualties, 26 Aug '14 (7)
    early use of radios, 5 Sep '14 (7), 1 Dec '14 (7), 8 Dec '14 (7)
    first attack on warship by sea-based aircraft, 16 Sep '14 (7)
    world's first specialized fighter unit, 1 Mar '15 (7)
    new British recon camera, 2 Mar '15 (7)
    British adopt photo-mosaic mapping, 10 Mar '15 (7)
    RFC adopts five innovations, 10 Mar '15 (7)
    first direction of naval gunfire by radio from aircraft out of sight, 7 Apr '15 (7)
    first use of recon seaplanes with battlefleet at sea, 11 Jun '15 (7)
    first Fokker E1 victory, 1 Jul '15 (7)
    'Fokker scourge' begins, 1 Aug '15 (7)
    Fokkers inhibit French bombing, 1 Sep '15 (7)
    Fokkers temporarily grounded, 1 Sep '15 (7)
    first merchant ship sunk by air attack, 1 Feb '16 (6)
    first RFC single-seater fighter sqn in France, 7 Feb '16 (7)
    British defence responsibilities reallocated, 10 Feb '16 (7)
    first German 'barrage patrols' over Verdun, 21 Feb '16 (7)
    first Fokker forced landing behind BEF lines, 8 Apr '16 (7)
    British Air Board established, 17 May '16 (7)
    French leaflet raid on Berlin, 19 Jun '16 (7)
    Anglo-French supremacy over Somme, 1 Jul '16 (7)
    Germans form first regular fighter sqn, 23 Aug '16 (7)
    first submarine sunk from air, 15 Sep '16 (7)
    first Albatross DII combat patrol, 17 Sep '16 (7)
    first air-tank co-operation, 26 Sep '16 (1)
    largest air battle yet, 9 Nov '16 (7)
    RFC discovers Hindenburg line, 9 Nov '16 (7)
    Haig requests extra fighters for 1917, 16 Nov '16 (7)
    see also Air bombing; Air weapons;

Royal Flying Corps; Royal Naval Air Service; Zeppelins
Air weapons,
    RNAS drop first practice torpedo, 28 Jul '14 (7)
    first Lewis gun mounting, 22 Aug '14 (7)
    British fixed rifles, 30 Sep '14 (7)
    first victory by Allied MG-armed plane, 5 Oct '14 (7)
    Lewis gun jury rig, 22 Nov '14 (7)
    French test MG firing through airscrew, 1 Dec '14 (7)
    flechettes or aerodarts, 6 Dec '14 (7), 17 Dec '14 (7)
    MG on Vickers Gunbus, 25 Dec '14 (7)
    Russians test synchronized MG, 1 Jan '15 (7)
    French bullet deflector captured by Germans, 19 Apr '15 (7)
    Germans develop interrupter gear, 19 Apr '15 (7)
    Germans order Fokker E1 fighters, 19 Apr '15 (7)
    incendiary bullets, 17 May '15 (7) Fokker E1s with interrupter gear on W Front, 20 May '15 (7)
    RFC suspends bombing for lack of bombsight, 24 Jul '15 (7)
    Lewis gun on improvized mount, 25 Jul '15 (7)
    first ship torpedoed from air, 12 Aug '15 (7)
    first steam catapult launch of aircraft from ship, 5 Nov '15 (7)
    Russian interrupter gear, 1 Dec '15 (7)
    first British fighter with MG interrupter gear in France, 25 Mar '16 (7)
    Ranken darts, 31 Mar '16 (7)
    British salvage Fokker interrupter gear, 8 Apr '16 (7)
    first flight of French Spad S 7, 1 May '16 (7)
    first interrupter-gear in British sqn service, May '16 (7)
    French rockets v balloons, 22 May '16 (7)
    Allied incendiary bombs, 1 Jul '16 (7)
    British test Constantinesco synchronizer gear, 1 Aug '16 (7)
    Germans develop 'motor guns', 1 Aug '16 (7)
    US tests radio-guided bomb, 12 Sep '16 (7)
    British phosphorus bomb, 10 Nov '16 (7)
    see also Air bombing
Aircraft carriers,
    British in Dardanelles, 17 Feb '15 (7)
    US catapult launch from barge, 16 Apr '15 (7)
    Jellicoe demands, 1 Aug '15 (7)
    first ship torpedoed from air, 12 Aug '15 (7)
    British plane makes first take-off from, 1 Sep '15 (6)
    British steamer converted, 1 Sep '15 (6)
    British trial sortie, 4 Dec '15 (6)
    see also Seaplane carriers
Airships,

French shoot own down, 24 Aug '14 (7)
RNAS patrols over London, 22 Sep '14 (7)
British develop for A/S duties, 28 Feb '15 (7)
French adopt for A/S duties and minesweeping, 1 Mar '15 (7)
first British stn for A/S patrols, 8 May '15 (7)
French Army's, transferred to anti-U-boat patrols, 30 Sep '16 (7)
see also Zeppelins
Aisne,
    allied pursuit to the, 11 Sep '14 (1)
    front becomes static, 26 Jan '15 (1)
    see also W Front from 13 Sep '14
Aisne, First Battle of the,
    begins, 12 Sep '14 (1)
    Germans close to disaster, 13 Sep '14 (1)
    allied advance stalls, 18 Sep '14 (1)
Albania,
    rebels capture 3 towns, 9 Jul '14 (0)
    citizens ask for govt by international commission, 19 Jul '14 (0)
    Prince Burham-ed-Din head of Government, 27 Sep '14 (3)
    Serbs retreat into, 23 Nov '15 (3)
    Essad Pasha declares for Allies, 6 Dec '15 (3)
    Putnik resigns, 7 Dec '15 (3)
    Essad Pasha's provisional govt leaves Albania, 24 Feb '16 (8)
    Austrians occupy Durazzo, 27 Feb '16 (3)
    Essad Pasha sets up Govt at Salonika, 20 Sep '16 (8)
    see also S Fronts from 4 Sep '14
Albert, Battles of,
    begin, 25 Sep '14 (1), 1 Jul '16 (1)
    end, 13 Jul '16 (1)
Albert, King of Belgium,
    appeals to Kaiser as kinsman, 1 Aug '14 (8)
    rejects retreat from Yser line, 26 Oct '14 (1)
    decorated by King George V, 4 Dec '14 (1)
    vetoes BEF-Belgian Army amalgamation, 2 Jan '15 (1)
    receives Japanese sword of honour, 30 Jan '15 (8)
    visits British front, 8 Feb '15 (1)
    explores renunciation of neutrality, 5 Jan '16 (8)
Alexander, Crown Prince of Serbia,
    cables Tsar for help, 24 Jul '14 (0)
    signs mobilization order, 25 Jul '14 (0)
Algeria, 12 Apr '16 (5)
Allenby,
    commands cav in France & Flanders, 24 Aug '14 (1), 9 Oct '14 (1), 14 Oct '14 (1)
    GOC British Third Army, 23 Oct '15 (1)
Allies,
    and Greece, *see* Greece
    shipping losses 1914, 1915, 1916, *see Tables for Sea War 1914, 1915, 1916*

Aug '14 (1)
resigns as German COS, 14 Sep '14 (1)
Mombasa, British Indian force occupies, 31 Oct '14 (5)
Monitors see Naval technology
Monro,
new C-in-C MEF, 15 Oct '15 (4), 25 Nov '15 (4)
assumes command in Gallipoli, 28 Oct '15 (4)
succeeded by Murray as C-in-C MEF, 9 Jan '16 (4)
Mons,
Battle of, 23 Aug '14 (1)
retreat from, begins, 24 Aug '14 (1)
retreat from, ends, 5 Sep '14 (1)
Montenegro,
orders mobilization, 26 Jul '14 (0)
declares war on Austria, 5 Aug '14 (3), (8)
breaks relations with Germany, 8 Aug '14 (8)
Austria declares war on, 9 Aug '14 (8)
French naval guns in action, 19 Oct '14 (3)
Austrians invade, 9 Oct '15 (3)
declares war on Bulgaria, 15 Oct '15 (8)
King appeals for help, 30 Nov '15 (8)
Austrian offensive, 8 Jan '16 (3)
armistice with Austria, 12 Jan '16 (3)
surrenders, 17 Jan '16 (3)
Allied evacuation, 22 Jan '16 (6)
King denounces son's acceptance of Austrian terms, 23 Jan '16 (8)
PM accuses King of treason and resigns, 20 May '16 (9)
guerilla rising, 5 Jul '16 (3)
proposed union with Serbia, 6 Aug '16 (8)
Morhange, Battle of, 14 Aug '14 (1)
Morocco,
breaks with Germany, 19 Aug '14 (8)
worst French defeat, 13 Nov '14 (5)
Britain recognizes French Protectorate, 24 Dec '14 (8)
Battle of Oued Khellal, 29 May '16 (5)
see also African Ops from 31 Jul '14
Mortagne, Battle of the, 24 Aug '14 (1), 3 Sep '14 (1)
Mortars,
Indian Corps improvises, 19 Nov '14 (1)
British Trench Mortar Service formed, 26 Nov '14 (1)
first German trench mortar unit formed, 18 Dec '14 (1)
Stokes begins to design, 1 Jan '15 (9)
French 58mm trench mortar first used, 28 Jan '15 (1)
first French trench mortar used, 1 Apr '15 (1)
Stokes trial successful, 14 Apr '15 (9)
Dumézil designs, 1 Jun '15 (1)
Stokes demonstration, 28 Jun '15 (9)
Stokes ordered, 12 Aug '15 (9)
French first use 9.45-in heavy mortar, 25 Sep '15 (1)
Stokes production, 25 Sep '15 (9)
Austro-German superheavy in Serbia, 5 Oct '15 (3)
praise for Stokes 3-in, 28 Mar '16 (1)
Morval, Battles of, 25 Sep '16 (1)
Motor transport,
'Taxis of the Marne', 7 Sep '14 (1)
Austrians use in retreat in Galicia, 11 Sep '14 (2)
French use Paris buses, 9 Oct '14 (1)
BEF receives London buses, 31 Oct '14 (1)
in Verdun lifeline, 22 Feb '15 (1), 27 Feb '15 (1)
first lorries in E Africa, 29 Mar '15 (5)
Mount Sorrel, Battle of, 2 Jun '16 (1)
Munitions,
British & Russian output 1916, see Tables for Home Fronts 1916
Krupp-Vickers shell fuse agreement, 16 Jul '14 (0)
German War Ministry Raw Materials Section, 9 Aug '14 (9)
Anglo-French Commission created, 13 Aug '14 (8)

Vickers MG production, 22 Sep '14 (9)
Joffre orders shell economies, 24 Sep '14 (1)
British explosives shortage, 30 Oct '14 (9)
Russia orders US & British shells, 1 Jan '15 (9)
British TNT production, 17 Jan '15 (9)
Austrian scrap metal, 1 Feb '15 (9)
British Cabinet Munitions Production Ctee formed, 21 Feb '15 (9)
British ctee formed, 21 Feb '15 (9)
Lloyd George speeches, 28 Feb '15 (9), 9 Mar '15 (9)
British Shells & Fuses Agreement, 4 Mar '15 (9)
British Amatol production, 8 Mar '15 (9)
extension of British govt powers, 16 Mar '15 (9)
French Citroën shell factory, 17 Mar '15 (9)
British press campaign on shortages, 27 Mar '15 (9)
British Armaments Output Ctee, 31 Mar '15 (9)
British census, 7 Apr '15 (9)
Lloyd George chairs new ctee, 13 Apr '15 (9)
Asquith denies shell shortage, 20 Apr '15 (9)
British National Shell Factory, 13 May '15 (9)
British shell shortage, 14 May '15 (9)
Lloyd George British Munitions Minister, 25 May '15 (9), 16 Jun '15 (9)
first women in British private factory, 1 Jun '15 (9)
France diverts conscripts to factories, 1 Jun '15 (9)
British Ministry of Munitions Act passed, 9 Jun '15 (9)
British War Munition Volunteer Scheme, 24 Jun '15 (9)
US exports to Britain, 30 Jun '15 (8), 12 Aug '15 (8)
British Munitions of War Act pased, 2 Jul '15 (9)
Fisher made chairman of British Inventions Board, 5 Jul '15 (9)
British measures and plans, 28 Jul '15 (9)
Russian shells and rifles, 31 Jul '15 (9)
British Munitions Inventions Dept, 20 Aug '15 (9)
British National Shell Factories, 1 Sep '15 (9)
British profit limitation rules, 15 Sep '15 (9)
British measures, 1 Oct '15 (9)
Anglo-French agreement, 8 Oct '15 (8)
permanent Allied organization, 24 Nov '15 (8)
British Ministry controls research, 25 Nov '15 (9)
British Union Negotiating Ctee, 30 Nov '15 (9)
2026 British factories, 6 Dec '15 (9)
Russian delegation at Paris, 8 Dec '15 (8)
Belgian ammo factory blows up, 11 Dec '15 (1)
Lloyd George's 'too late' speech, 20 Dec '15 (9)
France, 850,000 employed, 25 Dec '15 (9)
Lloyd George speech shouted down, 25 Dec '15 (9)
Anglo-French conference, 29 Jan '16 (8)
Glasgow shop stewards prosecuted, 7 Feb '16 (9)
British munitions intelligence dept, 19 Feb '16 (9)
3078 British factories, 18 Mar '16 (9)
Britain and France exchange liaison officers, 1 Apr '16 (8)
British factory explosion, 2 Apr '16 (9)
British boys' welfare supervisors in factories, 19 May '16 (9)
Montagu succeeds Lloyd George as Munitions Minister, 8 Jul '16 (9)
Allied conference in London, 13 Jul '16

(8)
British munitionette pay rates, 17 Jul '16 (9)
improved British shell output, 15 Aug '16 (9)
British Industrial Fatigue report, 16 Aug '16 (9)
Hindenburg demands double, 31 Aug '16 (9)
4212 British factories, 1 Sep '16 (9)
Hindenburg & Ludendorff meet industrialists, 9 Sep '16 (9)
British Manpower Distribution Board, 21 Sep '16 (9)
Germany unifies 3 procurement agencies, 30 Sep '16 (9)
British women offered free training, 4 Oct '16 (9)
British ban on Sunday work, 8 Oct '16 (9)
British Army Reserve Munition Workers Scheme, 12 Oct '16 (9)
British creches, 24 Oct '16 (9)
new German War Munitions Office, 26 Oct '16 (9)
Anglo-French-Italian London Conference, 11 Nov '16 (8)
Munster, Second battle of, 26 Jul '15 (1)
Murray, succeeds Monro as C-in-C MEF, 9 Jan '16 (4)
Muslim world,
Kaiser orders inflammatory policy, 30 Jul '14 (8)
Kaiser's pledge on Muslim PoWs, 9 Sep '14 (5), (8)
Allies declare immunity for Holy Places, 2 Nov '14 (4)
Holy War declared by Sultan, 11 Nov '14 (4)
Holy War declared in Tripolitania, 8 Dec '14 (5)
British bureau for 'Muslim propaganda' urged, 28 Oct '15 (4)
Mwanza, Lake force takes, 14 Jul '16 (5)
Möwe, German raider sails, 26 Dec '15 (6)

N

Namur, Siege of,
begins, 19 Aug '14 (1)
ends, 25 Aug '14 (1)
Nancy see Grande Couronne, Battle of the
Narajowka, Battle of Lower, 15 Oct '16 (2)
Narajowka-Zlota Lipa,
Second Battle of the, 16 Sep '16 (2)
Third Battle of the, 6 Oct '16 (2)
Naval technology,
RNAS drop first practice torpedo, 28 Jul '14 (7)
British advocate anti-torpedo bulges, 21 Oct '14 (6)
balloons for fire direction, 24 Oct '14 (6), 19 Apr '15 (7)
first director control long-range gunnery, 8 Dec '14 (6)
Fisher proposes fast battlecruisers, 19 Dec '14 (6)
German small torpedo boats for Flanders coast, 1 Jan '15 (6)
British build monitors, 28 Feb '15 (6)
French echo-ranging research, 1 Mar '15 (6)
Admiralty orders Z Whaler patrol craft, 15 Mar '15 (6)
British bulge-protected warships on trial, 1 Apr '15 (6)
Duddell aerials in Grand Fleet, 1 Apr '15 (6)
first British motor launches ordered, 1 Apr '15 (6)
British monitors launched, 1 May '15 (6)
British tracking of U-boats, 1 May '15 (6)
first monitors arrive at Dardanelles, 8 Jun '15 (6), 12 Jul '15 (6)
first use of recon seaplanes with battlefleet at sea, 11 Jun '15 (7)
British stabilizing gun director, 1 Jul '15 (6)
British trials of depth charges, 1 Jul '15 (6)

British minesweeping paravane, 1 Oct '15 (6)
British work on sound receivers, 1 Nov '15 (6)
Russians order landing craft, 2 Dec '15 (6)
motor lighters or 'beetles', 19 Dec '15 (6)
British introduce depth charges, 1 Jan '16 (6)
first depth charge submarine kill, 22 Mar '16 (6)
first U-boat located by hydrophone, 1 Apr '16 (6)
Italian monitors commissioned, 28 Apr '16 (6)
first Italian MAS motor-launches, 1 May '16 (6)
German AII coastal craft, 3 May '16 (6)
effective RN depth charge appears, 1 Jun '16 (6)
British introduce paravanes, 15 Jun '16 (6)
first RN shore-controlled minefields, 15 Jun '16 (6)
RN K-class submarines introduced, 3 Aug '16 (6)
illuminated indicator nets, 2 Sep '16 (6)
only sailing raider, 21 Dec '16 (6)
Grand Fleet's jam-resistant radios, 31 Dec '16 (6)
see also Aircraft carriers; Q-ships; Seaplane Carriers; U-boats
Nek, The, Anzac attacks on, 7 Aug '15 (4)
Néry, Action at, 1 Sep '14 (1)
Neutrals see Int'l Events from 5 Aug '14
Neuve Chapelle, Battle of,
begins, 10 Mar '15 (1)
ends, 13 Mar '15 (1)
New Guinea,
Australian troops land, 11 Sep '14 (4)
German troops surrender, 21 Sep '14 (4)
New Zealand,
asked by Britain to seize German radio stns, 6 Aug '14 (4)
occupies German Samoa Is, 30 Aug '14 (4)
National Registration Bill, 24 Sep '15 (9)
Discharged Soldiers' Settlement Act, 15 Oct '15 (9)
National Registration, 15 Oct '15 (9)
Compulsory Service Bill passed, 10 Jun '16 (9)
conscription for duration, 1 Aug '16 (9)
profits tax and loan, 7 Aug '16 (9)
1st conscription ballot, 23 Nov '16 (9)
see also Anzacs; New Zealand forces
New Zealand forces,
arrangements for NZEF, 30 Jul '14 (8)
Samoa force sails, 15 Aug '14 (4)
NZEF sails from Wellington, 16 Oct '14 (9)
Anzac convoy leaves Aden, 26 Nov '14 (4)
NZEF lands in Egypt, 1 Dec '14 (4)
NZ & Australian Div formed, 18 Jan '15 (4)
3rd Reinforcement sails, 14 Feb '15 (9)
4th Reinforcement sails, 17 Apr '15 (9)
Wellington Bn captures Chunuk Bair, 8 Aug '15 (4)
6th Reinforcement sails, 14 Aug '15 (9)
Canterbury Mtd Rifles, 14 Sep '15 (4)
in Sinai, 16 May '16 (4)
at Battle of Romani, 4 Aug '16 (4)
in Battle of Flers-Courcelette, 15 Sep '16 (1)
NZ Div advances near Flers, 16 Sep '16 (1)
take 'Cough Drop Alley' & other trenches, 21 Sep '16 (1)
Nicaragua,
US troops land, 14 Aug '14 (8)
neutral, 5 Dec '14 (8)
Nicholas II, Tsar of Russia,
refuses German peace overtures, 3 Aug '15 (8)
takes supreme command, 5 Sep '15 (2)
issues stern order on discipline, 22 Sep '15 (2)
ends Brusilov offensive, 10 Oct '16 (2)
Nicholas, Grand Duke,

346

seems imminent, 31 Oct '14 (1)
First Battle of, Phase 2 (Gheluvelt)
begins, 31 Oct '14 (1)
First Battle of, Phase 3 (Nonne
Boschen), begins, 11 Nov '14 (1)
Salient becomes French responsibility,
15 Nov '14 (1)
Canadians take over north of Salient
from French, 7 Apr '15 (1)
Second Battle of, begins, 22 Apr '15 (1)
Second Battle of, ends, 25 May '15 (1)
Battle of Mt Sorrel, 2 Jun '16 (1)
see also Maps for W Front; W Front
from 24 Oct '14
Yser,
Battle of, forces & losses, *see* Tables for
W Front 1914

Battle of, begins, 16 Oct '14 (1)
Battle of, Germans retreat, 30 Oct '14 (1)
Battle of, ends, 10 Nov '14 (1)
see also W Front from 30 Oct '14
Yudenich,
replaces Bergmann, 6 Jan '15 (4)
winter offensive, 10 Jan '16 (4)
attacks Erzerum, 11 Feb '16 (4)
captures Erzerum, 16 Feb '16 (4)
occupies Erzincan, 25 Jul '16 (4)

Zalozce, Battle of, 5 Aug '16 (2)
Zamosc-Komarow, Battle of, 26 Aug '14 (2)

Zanzibar,
declares war on Germany, 5 Aug '14 (8)
declares war on Turkey, 5 Nov '14 (8)
Zeebrugge,
Allies evacuate, 12 Oct '14 (1)
occupied by Germans, 15 Oct '14 (1)
Zemstvos, union formed, 30 Jul '14 (9)
Zeppelins,
abortive raid on Liège, 6 Aug '14 (7)
French bomb sheds in Germany, 14 Aug
'14 (7), 8 Oct '14 (7), 26 Dec '14 (7)
French shoot down, 16 Aug '14 (7)
Behnke advocates raids on Britain, 20
Aug '14 (7)
Germans shoot down in error, 23 Aug '14
(7)
Russians shoot down, 5 Sep '14 (7)

British bomb sheds in Germany, 22 Sep
'14 (7), 21 Nov '14 (7)
fly recon for German naval force, 15 Dec
'14 (7)
first raid on Britain, 19 Jan '15 (7)
in Dogger Bank battle, 24 Jan '15 (7)
German targetting on Britain, 12 Feb '15
(7)
first detected by searchlight, 16 May '15
(7)
severest raid on Britain, 13 Oct '15 (7)
first raid in Salonika, 30 Dec '15 (3)
SL11 shot down at Cuffley, 2 Sep '16 (7)
see also Air bombing